The Rolling Stone
INTERVIEWS

The Rolling Stone INTERVIEWS

THE 1980s

by THE EDITORS of
ROLLING STONE

INTRODUCTION by
KURT LODER

EDITED by SID HOLT

ST. MARTIN'S PRESS/ROLLING STONE PRESS, *New York*

Design by Robert Bull Design

Library of Congress Cataloging-in-Publication Data

The Rolling stone interviews : the 1980s / the editors of Rolling
    stone : introduction by Kurt Loder.
        p.   cm.
        ISBN 0–312–02973–X—ISBN 0–312–02974–8 (pbk.)
        1. Entertainers—Interviews.   2. Rock musicians—Interviews.
    I. Rolling stone.
    PN1583.R65   1989
    790.2′092′—dc19   89–30096

First Edition
10 9 8 7 6 5 4 3 2 1

Contents

Introduction

THERE IS, of course, an element of glamor attached to the interview game. I myself have sipped tea in London with Paul McCartney and *café con leché* with Sean Connery on a parrot-infested terrace in the south of Spain. I've trudged the sweltering bush of the Australian outback with David Bowie, traded coy party banter in Paris with Prince, contemplated the stars above Jerusalem with Bob Dylan and hoisted toasts with Tina Turner on a balcony high above Budapest. I once got drunk with Keith Richards, too—or at least became severely disabled myself while attempting to equal his intake (a disastrous strategy, please be forewarned). And that's nothing. Other writers, several of them represented in this book, could recount even more colorful stories—of trailing after Sting through the streets of Rio, or discoursing with Madonna in the corridors of some ultra-luxe Tokyo hotel. It *does* all sound sort of fabulous: celebrity interaction, exotic locales, the possibility of unbridled dissipation—who could ask for anything more?

In actual fact, though, the serious interviewer—one who's done all the requisite homework, who knows whereof he or she speaks and who has questions of import to ask—is inevitably a wretched figure. Cursed from the outset with an impossible deadline, bleary from long nights of boning up on the subject's bio (and tracking down ancillary arcana) and more often than not rendered half-mad by the tortures of the international air-travel system, the hapless scribe arrives at last in some alien clime, inappropriately attired and buckle-backed with bags full of books, tapes, batteries, pens, pads and wads of widely disjointed notes, only to collide with that wall of caution and coiled loathing that so often characterizes the scene surrounding whatever celeb has deigned to sit for debriefing.

For the writer of magazine features—narrative accounts interlarded with the subject's most quotable mots—all of this is grist for the zippy account that will ultimately adorn four or five pages, with pics, of the assigning periodical. Even the most listless string of celebrity banalities can often be huffed into publishable shape with massive gusts of "color" and inventive lashings of "tone."

For the writer charged with bringing back a straight Q&A interview, however—a transcript of questions as asked and answers as given, to be edited and structured, to some extent, but eventually printed without narrative embroidery—all of the preliminary torments attendant upon any interview are but stations of the cross to be endured, with no hope of subsequent utility, along the way to that moment of truth when one finally sits down with the subject, alone, and turns on the tape recorder. It is at this point that the real work begins.

When ROLLING STONE began publishing its extended interviews back in the late Sixties, the idea of talking to pop musicians as if they actually had something to say was a definite novelty. Rock & roll, after all, had not been born of intellectual ferment. No one back in the Fifties had thought to ask Little Richard or Elvis Presley about the state of the world, or even the place of their music in it. Who among the readers of the fuddy-dud media of that period would have cared to know? The artists who pioneered rock & roll were scorned as bumpkin luck-outs, soon-to-be nobodies, the inconsequential flotsam of a fad-addled teen nether scene. Or so it was hoped.

By the mid-Sixties, of course, far from waning, rock & roll had become the musica franca of a new generation. By 1967, when ROLLING STONE appeared in San Francisco, rock had taken on a historical shape, one that could be savored, studied and assessed. ROLLING STONE attracted writers who had at least a transient acquaintance with higher education (often much more) and who had been soaking up rock & roll since its birth. Among the new breed of rock performers who were by then crowding the pop landscape—many of them erstwhile art students themselves—these writers found kindred spirits. They were all fans first, but with a common analytic inclination. They could converse with one another as peers, fellow initiates in the

True Knowledge. The interviews that resulted were refreshingly direct and open, beginning in a shared love of rock's liberating power and going on to contemplate the implications of that power for the unhip culture at large. This in-group approach could, it was true, also result in the most vapid fatuities. (To reread today Donovan's announcement that he had come to America to lead the flower-power revolution is to rediscover, after twenty years, one's original, overwhelming urge to smack him in the head.) But at their best, the ROLLING STONE Interviews often testified more vividly to the broad pull of rock's cultural undertow, as well as to "the state of youth," than any quickie news-mag field dig or four-color photo splash could ever hope to do.

By the time I arrived at ROLLING STONE, in the spring of 1979, many things had changed. Mainstream pop music had ballooned into a $4 billion-a-year business, hugely fueled by the disco dance hits of the period and the deracinated "corporate rock" of such monomial mediocrities as Journey, Boston, Styx and Kansas. The real rock action had for several years been taking place in New York City, to which ROLLING STONE had wisely relocated in 1977. The irresistible delirium, centered in such downtown boho dives as CBGB and Max's Kansas City, that surrounded the Ramones, Blondie and Talking Heads constituted the most electrically exhilarating rock scene since Swinging London in the mid-Sixties. In fact, the repercussions of this music—punk—had reached across the Atlantic to England, out of which bands like the Damned, the Sex Pistols and the Clash had proceeded to pour forth. It was an uproarious period. *Everybody* went out at night —to Bowery punk holes, to uptown "rock discos" like Hurrah, to any place where noise and drink and drugs could work their frazzling magic. This nonstop, indiscriminate nightlife fostered some interesting musical mutations. The interpenetration of punk and disco—two styles initially assumed to be antipathetic—begot electro-pop, the big-drum, dance-beat rock style that would rule much of the coming decade. African music began to be heard, and from Britain came punks, like the Police, who played reggae. At the same time, rap music—punk's black analogue—erupted in reaction to the glossy excesses of mainstream black pop. The Seventies, a widely reviled decade, came to an end on a number of very happening notes.

Then the Eighties got underway—and almost immediately, the bottom fell out of the record business. The music-buying public had suddenly grown bored with disco, and an increasing number of people had just about had it as well with the stale, aging superstars and faceless cookie-cutter corporate bands with which so many major-label rosters were overstocked. Rock radio—the music's major artery back in the Fifties and Sixties, when it had been a medium for exciting new sounds—had, by the mid-Seventies, rolled over and died in the bloodless hands of professional formatters and market-research weasels. It was a confusing time. In 1980, Studio 54, the New York disco mecca, closed its doors; Led Zeppelin disbanded; John Lennon was murdered. Nobody—not at most of the major labels, anyway, and certainly not in commercial radio—seemed to know exactly what was going on.

By 1981, the situation had grown dire. Grandmaster Fash and the Furious Five put out an astonishing rap album, *Adventures on the Wheels of Steel*, but white rock radio—which had zero interest in any music that wasn't generically rocklike or . . . well, white—didn't want to know. The biggest-selling "rock" record of the year was *Hi-Infidelity*, by REO Speedwagon, a slick journeyman group that exemplified the style of music that critic Deborah Frost later dubbed "power schlock." Another major mover was a greatest-hits album by the Doors—a group whose lead singer, Jim Morrison, had been dead for exactly a decade. Certain records were still selling, but nobody seemed very excited about them. And overall, industry sales figures were reaching new lows. Fortunately—at least from the music-biz point of view—1981 was also the year in which MTV, the world's first twenty-four-hour rock and pop cable-television channel, was born. After MTV, nothing would ever be quite the same again.

Music videos offered the music industry an intense new medium through which to stimulate sales, particularly among young, TV-conditioned consumers. But as a national video channel, MTV also focused, inevitably, on lowest-common-denominator acts. Cuteness became a major consideration, and in its first year, MTV was also widely criticized for its lack of black programming (a situation that, in large part, simply reflected a similarly dismal state of affairs in album-oriented rock radio). MTV changed as the Eighties wore on, adding black videos and more "underground" bands (or at least those underground bands that could afford to make videos) and even starting a small Spanish-language service. But rock music—which had once seemed the most important thing in the world to many of its fans—would never quite recover from the saturation exposure given it by MTV and the many video programs that followed in its wake. In the Fifties, the music had been borne aloft by the sheer novelty of its passion within the context of white-bread pop. In the Sixties, it thrived as the music of youth. But in the Eighties, an endless stream of rock was available to anybody at the flick of a remote control. The music was in many ways bigger than ever and, in some cases, maybe even more adventurous. (The work of such people as David Byrne, Peter Gabriel and Sting reflected the great infatuation among Eighties musicians with the ethnic exotica of Africa, South America and the Caribbean.) But it was no longer quite so special. And maybe never would be again.

Good music was still being made, of course—good music is *always* being made by somebody, somewhere. If the Rolling Stones were having trouble sustaining their career, for instance, impassioned young hard-rock bands such as Guns n' Roses were there to pick up the torch. And for those unimpressed by the current rock product, there was an unprecedented wave of reissues in the Eighties. Prompted by the maniacal archivists of England, Germany and Japan, American record companies began plundering their vaults and back catalogs in search of classic rock, blues, soul, country and R&B sides, thus keeping the music's roots alive for a new generation. If rock had become more of a business than ever before by the end of the Eighties, there was also cause for renewed hope that its rough, unvarnished spirit, at least, might never die.

From a journalistic point of view, however, there was another problem by the time the Eighties arrived. The traditional rock-star interview was no longer a novelty, having been largely subsumed in the wave of celebrity gush churned out by such newly successful magazines as *People*. By then, as well, the biggest of the traditional rock stars—Mick Jagger, Paul McCartney, Pete Townshend—had been *giving* interviews for fifteen years or more. The standard peer-group queries of the Sixties—all that drugs-and-revolution stuff—had long since lost their zing. What was there left to say beyond a rote recitation of warmed-over anecdotes or the flourishing of dog-eared career data?

The thought that occurred to me, and surely to others, was that age had become an issue in rock. We were all growing older and changing as surely as the music itself was, and this subject—a touchy one with some musicians entering the dreaded decade of their thirties—could in fact prove to be a most promising avenue of exploration for anyone interested in saying something new and human about the rock & roll era. Rock had started out as the music of indomitable youth; by the Eighties, however, many of its foremost practitioners were no longer young. They found themselves adrift, in many cases, on a shifting and often inhospitable scene. What did they have to say about it?

The interviews that follow—with actors, directors, promoters and producers as well as musicians—are all linked in some way to the Sixties. ROLLING STONE was a product of that period, and while the magazine has prospered and grown throughout the Eighties, it has continued to address the interests of its own generation. Many of the artists interviewed here—Bob Dylan, Neil Young, Paul McCartney, Mick Jagger—were stars in the Sixties, a part of the texture of those times. Others, such as Bruce Springsteen and David Bowie, stars of the Seventies, were deeply affected by the music and the ideals of the preceding decade. Steve Martin, Bill Murray and Robin Williams all bear the off-kilter imprint of Sixties kids; and while Woody Allen and Clint Eastwood may be Fifties guys, both launched their film careers (and their classic personas) in the Sixties. The Everly Brothers' pure-Fifties harmony hits were devotedly echoed by the Beatles, among other British Invasion groups. And without Sam Phillips—or at least without Elvis, whom he discovered—the Sixties would have been, at the very least, a much different and perhaps less-fabulous decade.

Interviews are by nature artificial situations, and yet to be successful, they must take place in an atmosphere of at least feigned intimacy. The simplest way for an interviewer to induce such an ambience is by demonstrating a detailed familiarity not only with the subject's history but with his or her areas of obsession. One really wouldn't want to sit down for a talk with Keith Richards or David Bowie, for instance, without being versed in the history of rhythm & blues. A conversation with Pete Townshend will be considerably less baffling if one knows that a "leaper" is a pill, not a plummeting suicide, and that London mods in the mid-Sixties liked to gulp down handfuls of them before tearing off on their Lambrettas. And if you're unaware of Jackie Brenston or Billy Lee Riley, or the connection between Johnny Ray and the Prisonaires, chances are you're not ready to exchange any but the most superficial pleasantries with Sam Phillips.

A good interviewer must have extensive expertise —he or she must be a historian, in fact. For this reason, the best interviewers, I think, tend to be specialists as obsessive in their field as are the objects of their interrogation. Robert Palmer's interview with Eric Clapton, included here, is definitive not only because Palmer obviously knows and admires Clapton's work but also because he is a deeply knowledgeable blues and jazz scholar and—anything but incidentally—a musician himself. Rarely have interviewer and interviewee been so sympathetically matched.

Some assignments, on the other hand, seem unpromising at best. When Jann Wenner, ROLLING STONE's publisher, suggested to me that it might be interesting to interview Joan Baez, and that in fact he was thinking of putting her on the cover of an upcoming issue, I was startled by the perversity of such a notion. *Joan Baez?* But I did the interview, and I learned that she was a very witty woman, that she had once been to bed with John Lennon and that one must never forget the central tenet of the interviewer's craft: Everybody has some sort of story to tell. And celebrities, no matter how towering their renown, are everybodies like the rest of us.

ROLLING STONE is now embarked upon its third decade; rock & roll upon its fourth. If you're reading this, chances are that you, like me and like most of those who took part in the discussions that follow, were at some point in your life ineluctably marked by this music, and by the times it defined, and by the great voices it has called forth. That ROLLING STONE continues to investigate the sources of rock & roll's extraordinary power in dialogues with the people who make it, or who have been shaped in some way by the cultural imperatives of the rock & roll era, is a tribute to the magazine's abiding documentary bent. That the music itself remains worthy of continued investigation after all this time and talk is a tribute to its artistic depths, and to the performers, of whatever age, who continue to plumb them.

—Kurt Loder
New York City
December 1988

The Rolling Stone
INTERVIEWS

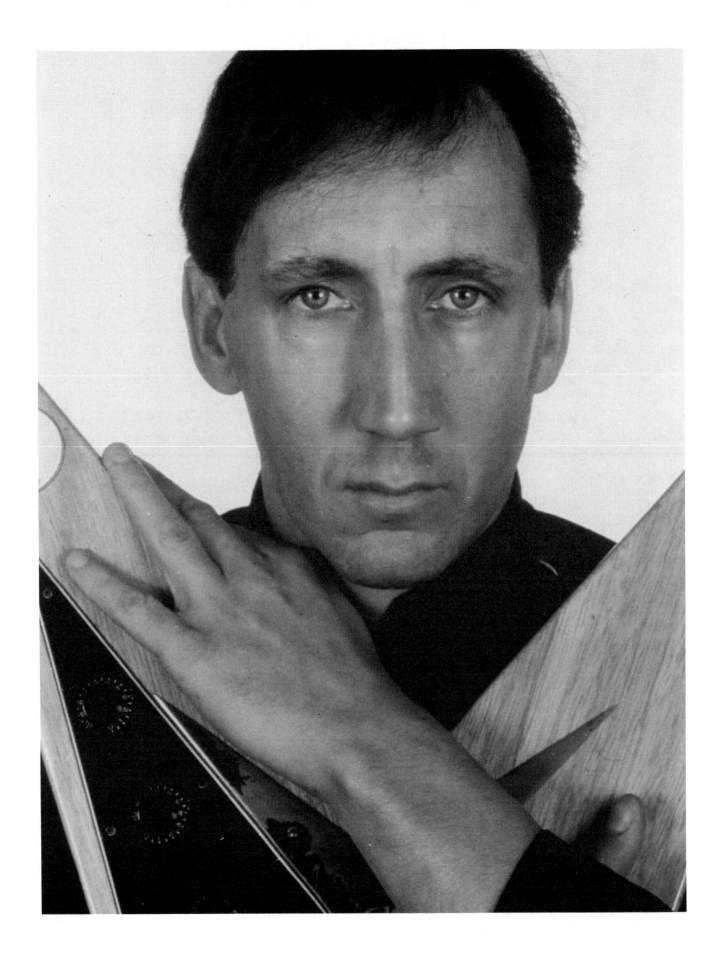

1

Pete Townshend

INTERVIEWED BY KURT LODER (1982)

Pete Townshend's party days were over by the time I caught up with him in the spring of 1982—a fact that put a considerable crimp in my usual interview strategy, which is to induce the subject to share as many drinks as possible along the trail to journalistic enlightenment. But Townshend had given up drinking and drugs, convinced that they were killing him. Fortunately, he hadn't given up talking.

As the leader of the Who from the group's inception in London in 1964, Townshend had become one of rock's great intellectualizers (and, on a bad day, its reigning windbag). His self-absorption could be wearying, but anyone who ever saw the Who onstage during its halcyon days is aware of Townshend's pervasive influence throughout the Seventies and Eighties as a hard-rock architect, a purveyor of cleansing frenzy and a rhythm-guitar innovator on an approximate par with Jimmy Page. This is a man who can back up his gab.

Townshend may never again attain the sort of ensemble peaks he hit with the Who. (The group officially disbanded seven months after this interview but had been effectively eviscerated by the death of drummer Keith Moon four years earlier.) His solo records, however, continue to merit interest, and when he chooses to step out from his self-imposed role of rock elder statesman, his playing can still strike evocative sparks.

—K. L.

PETE TOWNSHEND has met the enemy—and recognized the bleary eyes staring back at him across the chasm of the last two decades as his own. Townshend and his band, the Who, were the subject of a story in the first issue of ROLLING STONE, and over the last fifteen years, the magazine has published at least a half dozen substantial interviews with the guitarist (as well as such self-penned pieces as "The Punk Meets the Godmother," RS 252). This is Pete's third full-fledged ROLLING STONE interview; in the two years since his last one, he has suffered something very much like a middle-age breakdown. With the Who typically adrift in the wake of their awkward 1981 album, *Face Dances*, Townshend moved out on his family (wife Karen and daughters Emma, 13, and Minta, 11) and plunged into London's heady new nightlife. He made the scene with the New Romantic kids at a Club for Heroes. He raved all night at the venerable Venue. And he found himself gravitating—naturally?—toward the society types at the Embassy Club. The nights became a blur of booze and cocaine and pills, until one sobering day he realized he had become an alcoholic and a drug addict. He nearly died.

Townshend says he survived his two-year binge with some help from his family and friends, and that he has now started a new life. The Who may not be a major part of it: the group will probably continue to record, but Townshend will increasingly occupy himself with outside projects (such as "Ball and Chain," the track he worked on for Elton John's new *Jump Up* album, and the duet version of "That's Why the Lady Is a Tramp" he recently produced for New Romantic avatar Steve Strange and a frog-voiced French female singer named Ronny. He hopes to complete a book of short stories, and he'll continue turning out solo albums. His third, *All the Best Cowboys Have Chinese Eyes,* is his most explosively kinetic—and personally revealing—to date and features some of his strongest, most assured singing. Its visceral power would seem to confirm Townshend's contention that he's over whatever private horrors precipitated his extended bout of dissipation. But traces of pain and even confusion are apparent in the album's lyrics, and in the interview that follows.

It was conducted a few weeks before Townshend's thirty-seventh birthday and four days before he and the other members of the Who—Roger Daltrey, John Entwistle, Kenney Jones and perhaps a second guitarist, Andy Fairweather Low—were to begin work on the band's next album, due out later this year. We met in a softly carpeted art-deco suite in the St. James's Club, a discreet sanctuary tucked into the cul-de-sac of Park Place, a few minutes' stroll from St. James's Palace, but very far indeed from the rock & roll streets of Townshend's youth. Pete sat on a pale-blue velour sofa looking very English-eccentric in hound's-tooth bow tie, brown-and-beige saddle shoes and baggy checked trousers with a long, looping key chain. An Oriental waiter brought a luncheon trolley topped with a single, perfect, pale pink rose. Townshend ate a small grilled beefsteak. Wine was poured, but Pete drank milk.

The title of your new solo album, 'All the Best Cowboys Have Chinese Eyes'—what's that mean?

Basically, it's about the fact that you can't hide what you're really like. I just had this image of the average American hero—somebody like a Clint Eastwood or a John Wayne. Somebody with eyes like slits, who was basically capable of anything—you know, any kind of murderous act or whatever to get what was required—to get, let's say, his people to safety. And yet, to those people he's saving, he's a great hero, a knight in shining armor—forget the fact that he cut off fifty people's heads to get them home safely. Then I thought about the Russians and the Chinese and the Arab communities and the South Americans; you've got these different ethnic groups, and each has this central image of every other political or national faction as being, in some way, the evil ones. And I've taken this a little bit further—because I spent so much of my time in society, high society, last year—to comment on stardom and power and drug use and decadence, and how there's a strange parallel, in a way, between the misuse of power and responsibility by inept politicians and the misuse of power and responsibility by people who are heroes. If you're really a good person, you can't hide it by acting bad; and if you're a bad person, you can't hide it by acting good. Also—more to the point, really—that there's no outward, identifiable evil, you know? People spend most of their time looking for evil and identifying evil outside themselves. But the potential for evil is inside you.

I think the album is fairly cathartic in some ways. The writing ranged over the last two years, which have been very, very peculiar for me, 'cause I've been through a lot of really weird things. I went through the normal, continuing heart searchin' over the Who, and I lived away from my family for quite a long time as well; we have a house in the country, and I was living there, mainly. I made a lot of deliberate pleasure trips to New York and L.A. I spent some time in Paris, a lot of time in the country working on a book of short stories and other times just knockin' about with some of the London club-scene people.

I enjoy a lot of that life, in a way. But all the time, behind the scenes, I was writing songs and recording in fairly long spurts. Then, late last year, I had to abandon recording the solo album because I couldn't work. I was quite capable of spending all night doing nothing, but as soon as I actually tried to apply myself to something, I seemed to get physically exhausted. And very much unlike me, I had sort of drifted into the drug scene, because it's so much part and parcel of the club life, you know—taking cocaine to keep going all day, things like that.

That really drains you.

Yeah, and I hadn't realized quite how much. Because what happened was that I decided that it was a drinking problem, that I was an alcoholic. And I went to several doctors who confirmed that. So I stopped drinking, and I spent five days in a clinic, initially. A lot of hypnotherapy, individual therapy with various people. But I carried on with the drug thing a little bit. And then I realized that both things were really affecting me, that in order to assist me gettin' off alcohol, I had used a lot of tranquilizers. One in particular: a drug called Ativan, which is of the Librium-Valium variety. And I became addicted to it. So in January, I went to Meg Patterson in California; she'd helped Eric Clapton get off heroin. And she said that Ativan is more addictive than heroin.

Anyway, once I stopped taking everything—not just drinking, but doing *anything* at all—and started to be careful about my diet and got into a routine of regular exercise, the transformation was instant. Now I feel superhuman. Also, I had managed, with a lot of assistance from my wife, to reestablish myself in the family, and that's great for me. I mean, it's something I desperately missed.

Had drugs and drinking been the central causes of your family problems?

No, no, no. I've always had a drinking problem. Like every writer, in a way. But the family thing mainly had to do with work pressure—with my *inability* to stop working. Filling in time, when I had spare time, instead of working on relationships with my close friends and building up a solid, day-to-day empathy with my wife and family. After a long tour, say, I would tend to immediately immerse myself in something else, you know? I was always avoiding the main issue. And I think a lot of that comes out in the material on this album. Unfortunately, a lot of unhappiness comes

through. But there's also a great feeling that I seem determined to win somehow. You can feel it in a lot of the songs, that there's a determination to overcome. And I managed to do it.

Were you able to explain to your daughters what you were going through?

To some extent. I mean, it's early for me yet. You know, it's interesting you should say that—that's the kind of thing that never occurred to me, to ever even sit down and talk to my kids about the kinds of things I go through in my work. I'll sit down and talk to Paul Bonnick, my driver, about everything from my latest case of VD to the way I feel about the isolation of me kids. But I'd never sit down and talk to them directly. To a great extent, I suppose a lot of things that they know about me, they've read in newspapers. So I do have to start to deal with that.

During this period, did you also feel removed from the members of the Who? Did you see them a lot?

No, I didn't. The English tour last year was just too much to take. We weren't playing well enough. And a lot of that was because I was pretty peculiar most of the time. I think we all were, though. And Roger was really having serious doubts about whether or not we should go on.

How did you feel about that?

I suppose under normal circumstances I would have felt, hey, this is my opportunity to get out of the band and all the responsibilities it entails. But I didn't. I did the reverse—I really lammed into Roger, and I said, You know, we should really think seriously before we make any rash moves. I raised some of the points he'd raised to me in the past, when I'd felt the band had gone past its prime. I also told him I didn't feel that I could write for the band if it was just gonna go into a recording studio. I felt that we *had* to perform *live*. I need that live feedback as a writer. There were also rumors about Roger's being unhappy with Kenney, and Kenney's being unhappy with the fact he couldn't communicate with Roger. And there *was* a bit of communication breakdown. I think Roger felt very strongly that we really were missing Keith more than we knew. And . . . that I accepted. But he also felt that some of the changes we'd made—like bringing in Rabbit Bundrick on keyboards—had kind of disguised what was really wrong, which was that the *heart* of the band wasn't the same. And I have to agree with him—the heart of the band *isn't* the same. But that's not to say we still can't achieve a lot, in a different area, and continue to celebrate the magic that was there, but not get preoccupied with it. Anyway, everything's fine now. Roger got everyone at it, as usual, and it was all for the good.

How did the band feel about the last album, 'Face Dances,' for which you brought in the Eagles' producer, Bill Szymczyk?

Kind of mixed. It's not improvin' with age, either [*laughs*]. I think the chemistry was wrong, and it wasn't just Bill Szymczyk. I don't think we were really quite working together. Roger says that you could feel on *Face Dances* that the band wasn't a *band*. And what I'd like to see happen on the next album is for the Who to *feel* like a band, and *work* as a band.

Do you see the Who doing extended works in the future—not like 'Tommy,' necessarily, but other large-scale projects?

Well, first, I don't see the Who going on for very much longer. I think that with this next album, and with the next protracted period of work we do, we're really gonna throw ourselves into it 100 percent. And then we're gonna stop. I'm pretty sure of that. It's not because we want to, but because we've come to the point where we don't really want to go through all these periods when the public and our fans and the record company and even we don't know what the fuck's gonna happen next. The tension is just too much. And this period when we work on the band, I'm gonna really think about very little else. I'm worried about it, because I've become accustomed to doing lots of other things. And I like the richness of what I do in other areas. That's become almost as important to me as being in a band. And I think when you get to that point, you have to think very seriously about what it is you're doing it for. Because it's always been too important for us to do just because we enjoy one another's company. And I think basically one of the reasons we're working together at the moment is that we enjoy one another's company. It's as simple as that.

If the Who did break up, wouldn't there be something missing in all of your lives?

Yeah, I would say about a million dollars a year.

Nothing else? Are you all beyond that?

I think that, far from there being something missing, the very fact of not being involved in it anymore would allow us to take a different stance on what we've done—to enjoy it, to luxuriate in it, to celebrate it, to cherish it and to draw the best from it. Rather than always see the past as something that threatens our future—which is something that seems to be an irreversible feature of the band today. I don't know: I

think the Who will break up—not break up, but stop working—before the Stones do.

What's the difference between the two groups that would allow that to be so?

The Stones have got fuck-all else except rock & roll. And there is absolutely nothing wrong with that. But that's all they've got. And we have got a lot more. Nothing as important as what we've achieved, but we've got a lot more. Enough to allow us, I think, to even consider a last waltz, as it were. As far as our recording career, I don't know how many more records we'll do together or whether I'll continue to work with Roger the rest of me life. I don't really know.

Will the Who still tour to support the next album?

Yeah, I don't see any reason why we shouldn't do a certain amount of work. But after that, I really think we've had enough. At least for now, we seem to have to know that we're making one last big effort. We have to feel that there is an *end* to it; otherwise, I don't think we could really go in with the right mood.

Would you personally approach touring with a new attitude this time, trying not to get wiped out on the road?

Yeah, I would have to, because I'm never gonna drink again. In a way, I'm quite looking forward to it as a test. I'm happy to have sorted out my family problems once and for all. I always felt and hoped that it was possible. I didn't want to be a rock casualty in any sense, because I've always felt that one more rock casualty is just another headline for a couple of weeks, and then everybody gets really . . . not only bored, but everybody feels *betrayed*. Because although rock casualties make good copy in the *NME* Book of the Dead, they don't make good copy in the lives of rock fans, who have a slightly higher emotional involvement in the musical form than its just being, you know, like a circus, full of Berlinesque, decadent assholes who don't know how to spend their money, et cetera.

Your wife must be a remarkable woman, bearing up under all this public trauma.

Well, she doesn't like me to talk too much about us, but we met at art school in 1963, started going out together in 1965, when the group was established, got married in 1968, had our first child in 1969—and really, apart from a few ups and downs, we never suffered any major problems until the last couple of years. And we both feel that one of the problems was that I did overcommit when I took on a solo career. It was a great strain. And living in the same house and everything, we literally became estranged—we were like strangers. And it was only when I actually became so ill that I couldn't work that we had the time to sit down and talk. And then we stopped being strangers and we became friends and lovers again, and life is back to the way it was. Our marriage was made in heaven, there's no question about it. But you've got to work at marriage, and it's a different kind of work from what you do normally, and it's got a different end product. I'm sure this stuff is familiar as hell to everybody else, but it's all new to me.

You spent some time at Steve Strange's Club for Heroes, which was a mecca for London's New Romantics. What did you make of that scene?

I loved it. The only thing was, I nearly *died* there one night. The first night I went, I was with a couple of friends, and I ended up goin' blue—my heart practically stopped. I thought at the time that I'd probably gotten so drunk I didn't know what I was taking, and that I took some terrible drug. But I think I actually drank so much brandy I gave myself alcohol poisoning. I just went black. And that was my hero's entrance to a Club for Heroes: A seven-foot bouncer carried me out like a sack of potatoes.

But I did get to know Steve Strange quite well as a result of that, 'cause I went back later to apologize. And he turned out to be an absolute sweetheart. Very, very egoless, in a real sense. Superficially, totally preoccupied with image and everything, but underneath, not like that at all. And just stupidly vain like—for Christ's sake—*every woman* on the planet, every Western woman, is stupidly vain. We let *them* get away with it, you know: "Listen, the bomb's gonna drop in five minutes, but I can't go into the fallout shelter until I've done my makeup." That's okay from a woman, but for some reason, if Steve Strange says it, he's criticized.

I think people sometimes see you as one of the last of the great loons. With Keith Moon gone, and Kit Lambert, your former manager, having died last year, have you felt this image bearing down on you—a sort of compulsion to go out raving all night?

No. I actually feel torn in a number of directions. The thing I feel most conscious of is the responsibility to stay alive. Take Mick Jagger, for example. Mick is just bein' great at the moment. I think it's incredible to see him facin' up to who he is: workin', stayin' fit, living the kind of life he wants to live and still being involved in rock & roll. And never compromising on one single issue. And *stayin' alive*.

I don't think people really care if you loon or not, but they wanna see that you're enjoyin' life. It's no good staying alive if you're gonna be suicidal. But I

have been taught the intricate techniques of looning, and most of them I didn't get from Kit or Keith; I got them from my mother. Weaned by a loony!

Your mother, a musician herself, must know about the looning life.

She was actually the person who made me think about starting to treat myself as an alcoholic. I had gotten to the point where I was taking a drink in the morning just to feel *normal*. That lasted for about a month, and I was very worried about that. Then a guy in our road crew, who's a member of Alcoholics Anonymous, showed me a book written by an amazing guy named Max Glatt, who ran an enormous clinic here and did a lot of work with alcoholics. And I read immediately that I was alcoholic. There was absolutely no question about it. And when I was in Paris working with Elton John, I got to the point where that glass of brandy in the morning was *not* makin' me feel normal anymore, it was makin' me feel *ill*. So there was no way I could get my fix. And in a brief period of panic, I tried just about everything else in the world to try to feel normal again. And *none* of them worked. *Nothing.*

But then my mother suddenly decided to go into a clinic to stop drinking. She decided she'd had enough, and she *stopped*. And I knew, this time, that she'd stopped for life. They said it probably would be a good idea if she didn't go home straightaway, so she came to live with *me*. And two things happened: first, I was really inspired by her, and I wanted to show solidarity by stopping myself, once and for all. But also, a lot of my excuses were taken away. There's absolutely no question of it being genetic, anyway; I couldn't really say, "Oh, it's because everybody in my family is a drunk, that's why I'm a drunk."

One of my main excuses for getting drunk all the time was that I really do feel shy and uncomfortable in large gatherings and on social occasions, and I'd need it to relax. But the problem was that that first drink never really relaxed me. Neither did that second drink, and neither did that third drink. Tranquilizers weren't doin' it. Nothing was really doin' it. And then I suddenly realized, Why do you have to be relaxed? What's so great about being relaxed? You know—why not feel tense, and just get used to it? Some people have to live with much worse situations than just feeling *tense*. So this time, I just know I'm not gonna drink again.

You spent quite a bit of time hanging out with the aristocracy, didn't you? Are they good company?

People are very quick to say, "Oh, that crowd of shits." I don't think I met one shit, not one single real shit—and yet in *my* business, I could introduce you to a thousand. I was comfortable at the Embassy Club, because those people all knew exactly what I was going through. They were all very sympathetic. They fucking kept me *alive*.

It was a meander, a groping. But you *know* the answer to your problems. It's an inability to commit to things that you sometimes find you're embarrassed to commit to. Like when I think of myself as a rock & roll star, perhaps I feel a bit embarrassed about committing to take my kid to school every day. Because I don't want to be recognized, or I don't want my *kid* to be ostracized for coming to school in a big car. But I'm *sorry*—the daughter is the daughter of the father. And the father has a big car. And she's gotta live with it, and I've gotta live with it, and so do all her friends. That's unpleasant to have to deal with sometimes.

I suppose the irony of mingling with titled people—who would sympathize with this sort of problem—is that in a way you've transcended the British class system. Maybe it's changing . . .

I don't think Britain is *ever* gonna change. I'm afraid it's part of our tradition, and always will be. There's a lot of things that could change, and there's a lot of things that need to change, but I don't think that the aristocracy needs to change. You know—Why? What harm are they doing? They're a minority in this country. They've not got the power they used to have. They might have a few misappropriated possessions, but nothing I'd want. My house in the country is too bloody big anyway, and it's about a quarter of the size of most of these mansions.

Keith Moon has been dead nearly four years now. Do you think he'd be the same if he were still alive?

I don't know. It would have been a shame to have seen his obvious unhappiness increase. I think that's really what got to us, that he was never really happy. And with him, it wasn't a matter of doing what I've done—doing a U-turn and picking up the pieces—because I don't think he ever *knew* happiness. He was one of the most difficult people to return love to. Because he was such an expansive guy, and you had to act in such a sensational, larger-than-life manner, you know? I mean, you didn't say hello to Keith: It didn't matter if he'd only been out of the studio for five minutes, when he came back in, he insisted on kissing everybody on the lips.

Have you ever felt that you must be unhappy in order to create?

I've read that's Roger's impression. He once said, "God forbid the day that Townshend hasn't got any problems, because he won't write." I think if you're miserable, you write about things that are close to you. And if you're okay, you look a bit wider afield for subject matter. There's always plenty to get miserable about temporally.

So just because you're happy, it doesn't mean you become John Denver.

No. I mean, if you're unlucky enough to be born John Denver, there's not much you can *do*, really. But there are moments when I've listened to John Denver and he has actually gotten across to me the joy he feels from standing in the Colorado mountains. It's just that he does it in *every song*, and I get a bit bored with hearing about the mountains and the spring flowers and the trees and everything. I think they're going to look just as black as New York City when the bomb drops.

I gather you actually like New York quite a bit.

I love it. I've got a lot of friends there, like David Bowie. But there's something weird about it. I mean, I'll go to New York and ring Mick up, and I'll go and see David Bowie. But they're both over here now, and I wouldn't even *dream* of ringing 'em up. It's peculiar; it's a different kind of life for me. I like New York, but I don't see a hell of a lot happening. You know, the AM/PM club is just full of the same old musicians who've come from the same old gig, doing the same old thing. David Byrne has got the weight of the whole thing on his shoulders, as far as I can see, and the last time I saw him, he *looked* it, you know?

I read the piece you wrote about the Jam in 'Time Out' magazine. I know they're loved in Britain, but I've never been able to accept them as the heirs to the Who—I just don't think they deliver the sonic punch that the Who did. They're not that strong a group.

Well, I politely said that toward the end of the article. That there's not much music I don't like, but I don't like theirs. I like the image they're trying to put across, and I like their commitment. But somewhere, it's falling short. I think they're starting to realize that now, and maybe their new album gives an indication that they might be trying to improve. . . . I think I'd go further and say one thing I didn't say in that article, which is something my publicist said: "The Jam lacks a sense of humor." That's the thing.

Julian Lennon, John's son, is another young London

rocker of whom we may have a pretty jumbled image in the States. Is he okay?

I saw him last night, and he was *extremely* morose and arrogant, which is very unlike him. I think maybe he feels he's been used a lot. And I think, to some extent, he has. Particularly by all the flighty young girls on the make. I think that must be very strange for him. I mean, I was very flattered by it, when I had gotten onto the club scene, to suddenly be surrounded by beautiful blondes of seventeen. Then you suddenly realize that, basically, they're just standing next to you in the hope that there's going to be a photograph, or that you might give them a million pounds or something *stupid*. And five weeks later they look like they're *dying*. There's something very tragic about it, and I think Julian is too intelligent to go through that and not become a bit scarred by it.

Have you heard any of Julian's music?

No, I haven't. But Zak, who's Ringo's son, seems to think he's all right. And Zak's a very, very harsh critic.

Were you close to John Lennon during his five years of seclusion? Or did you grow close to his music?

No, I didn't, really. I liked the *Rock 'n' Roll* album a lot, and the *Imagine* album. But I didn't particularly enjoy his solo stuff. One of my favorite records of all time is "Strawberry Fields Forever." But I've always had very strange feelings about the Beatles, because for me they were too remote, as stars, and possibly always will be. I know the remaining members very, very well. I have a good relationship with Paul and Ringo, and I see George occasionally; he's a bit of a recluse, but I see him and I feel perfectly relaxed with him. We've got a lot in common, particularly the interest in mysticism, and gardening, and we live close to each other in the country. But John, never. . . . I spoke to him once on the phone. I was staying at the Pierre in New York—he had a suite there—and he came on the phone and we had a quick chat. I said, "Do you fancy a drink?" Not meaning, "Let's go get drunk." And he just said, "No, no, no. I'm just not into any kind of scene like that at all." And I said, "Well, what kind of scene?" You know? I wasn't suggesting a *scene,* I was suggesting getting together for a drink. And I thought then, you know [*croons*]: "Goodbye, John . . ." Perhaps I, like many others, was never meant to know him. And I wonder whether his chosen form of remoteness wasn't actually slightly instrumental in his eventual tragic death. In other words, can you really be Greta Garbo? You know? I mean, what

an idiot that woman was. She becomes a great big star and then says, "I want to be alone." Why didn't she just stay where she was in the first place? I know my unique status causes me a lot of problems, but nothing that I want to run away from. I know things can get out of control. . . . But I feel Lennon belonged to the people. And the irony, of course—the tragic irony—was that he seemed to be coming to terms with that and starting to work again.

How different is Lennon's sort of seclusion from that of someone like Eric Clapton? He seems pretty inaccessible, too.

I don't know what Eric really wants out of life anymore. I know that some of the things Eric finds very important, I don't give a damn about. You know, he was very hurt when he stopped being voted number-one guitar player in various guitar magazines. And I thought, "Well, how shallow." But that was important to him. I think he thinks of himself far more as a musician then as a "star." He's self-conscious of his image, I think, and, to a degree, his responsibility. But he's much more complex than appears on the outside.

Clapton duets with Jeff Beck on the 'Secret Policeman's Other Ball' album, and although neither of them seems to be trying too hard, Beck seems to walk all over Clapton. I think Eric's admirers wish he would step out and play a lot more.

Yeah, I do think Eric's made some fundamental mistakes that he can't reverse. You can't change the past, unfortunately. He was a heroin addict for two years. He lost two years of his life and career. And, unfortunately, a lot of the effects of heroin are irreversible, as you can see by reading William Burroughs. You know: Page one, crap. Page two, more crap. Page three, more crap. And the more the disciples gather round and read the crap, the more of that crap comes out of the man.

I really do love Eric a lot, otherwise I wouldn't have involved my life with him so much. And I don't see him doing anything wrong at all. I really enjoy what he does. I don't think it's necessarily the maximum of his potential, but then I don't see why he *should* work at the maximum of his potential, because that's not what he's pursuing. He's pursuing a kind of music that has more to do with finding a groove or expressing an emotion. Jeff, I think, is a much more troubled individual, much more torn, because he's capable of expressing *anything,* practically. Without doubt, the finest expressive rock player we've got—and yet, he seems to have nothing to *express* [*laughs*].

Robert Fripp once told me he admired Jimi Hendrix

because Hendrix had it all inside and his struggle was to get it out, whereas Fripp has all the technique to get it out but has a problem finding it inside.

What a wonderful thing to say, because it would hurt me to say it about somebody as nice as Robert Fripp, but, I mean, it's true. And I don't think I've ever really gotten to the bottom of what happens when I play the guitar.

More and more bands, particularly English ones, are dispensing with guitars in favor of synthesizers.

Yes. I think the guitar will be gone within ten years, myself. Microchips.

I've been listening to 'Tug of War,' Paul McCartney's new album. It may be the best thing he's done in a while—it sounds real nice. But it seems to have virtually nothing to do with rock & roll.

Do you think he ever really had anything to do with rock & roll?

Well . . .

No, he never did. You know, I could sit down and have a conversation with Paul about rock & roll, and we'd be talking about two different things. He's got a couple of years on me, but it could be *ten* years, we're so different. If he talks about rock & roll, I think he is talking about Little Richard. Whereas I don't think Little Richard *mattered,* you know?

But one of the reasons I'm excited about Paul's latest project is because it's him and George Martin working together again; because he's making a conscious effort to really get into serious record making, rather than pissin' about in home studios—which I, for one, think he's terrible at. When "Ebony and Ivory" came out, everybody was saying, "Christ, have you heard it? It's terrible." Well, I heard it, and I thought it was fuckin' *amazing!* I thought, "That's it, that's McCartney!" He's actually taken black and white, put a bit of tinsel around it, managed by hook or by crook to get Stevie Wonder to sing it, sit on black and white piano keys on a video . . . It's wonderful! It's gauche! It's Paul McCartney!

I've always said that I've never been a big fan of the Beatles: to me, rock was the Stones, and before that Chuck Berry, and before that maybe a few people who lived in fields in Louisiana. But I can't really include the Beatles in that. The Beatles were over with Herman's Hermits. That's not rock & roll. I was always very confused about the American attitude of thinking that the Beatles *were* rock & roll. Because they were such a big pop phenomenon. I've always enjoyed some of their stuff as light music, with occasional masterpieces thrown in. But with a lot of their things, you

can't dig very *deep.* Either you come up against Lennon's deliberately evading what it is that he's trying to say, so it's inscrutable, or Paul McCartney's self-imposed shallowness, because he sees music as being . . . I mean, he's a great believer in pop music, I think. But I wonder whether McCartney, perhaps, rests a little bit on the laurels of the Beatles.

Even an ostensibly glitzy group like Abba seems to me much more tied to rock & roll.

Absolutely. I remember hearing "S.O.S." on the radio in the States and realizing that it was Abba. But it was too late, because I was already transported by it. I just thought it was such a great sound, you know—great bass drum and the whole thing. They make great records. Also, what's quite interesting is that Abba was one of the first big, international bands to actually deal with sort of middle-aged problems in their songwriting. And it was quite obviously what was going on among them—that song, "Knowing Me, Knowing You."

Are you familiar with any of the Oi! bands, the post-punk skinhead groups? Some of them have apparently been co-opted by the neofascist National Front, and Oi! fans played a part in last summer's youth riots in Brixton.

Possibly, but who would you call an Oi! band?

Cocksparrer, Infa-Riot, any of those bands on 'Strength Through Oi!'

Yeah, see, I probably just haven't heard any of that. I mean, if somebody gave me an Oi! record to play, I probably just wouldn't play it. Because I object a little bit to . . . I know that there are a lot of little kids with their hair shaved off who wouldn't know who Hitler was if you put him to bed with them.

Yeah, that's what's so insidious about it: the music grabs you viscerally, but the message—not always, but sometimes—is horrifying.

This is the thing. There's a lot of people who are unfortunately putting into practice what Jerry Rubin and John Sinclair and Abbie Hoffman were talking about back in the late Sixties. Which was, "We're gonna use music for the revolution." And they believed that they were right and that rock music should be used for what they thought needed to be done. But rock can be used for *anything.* It's a very, very powerful and potent force, and it can also be used for fairly distasteful purposes. I remember being horrified seeing Alice Cooper beheading live chickens on stage. And it didn't really redeem him that I had smashed guitars, you know? Somewhere there was a line. I don't know whether it was just because it was live or because it was real blood. But the fact that he later went on to make some great records didn't redeem him, either. He's sick, tragic, pathetic—and will always be that way. I'll say hello to him in the street, but I'll never tip my hat to him.

The pathetic thing about Oi! music is that if it's supposed to be helping their cause, then I'm afraid it isn't working, folks. Because there you go, I won't even play their records. If I see an interview in the paper, I flip past it. So they're not gonna get to me with their bullshit, because I just don't even *read* it.

Simon Napier-Bell, who managed the original Yardbirds and also John's Children—Marc Bolan's first band —has been shopping a book around New York recently about the British music business in the Sixties. It's sort of strange—Bell's thesis is that many of the managers in those days were actually homosexuals who were in it for the unending supply of young boys.

I think there's an element of truth in that. I've always liked Simon Napier-Bell, but his gay side is probably the least wholesome part of him. As it was with Kit Lambert. And just for the record, if Kit Lambert was gettin' into rock music 'cause he was looking for boys, there was certainly no approach made to any individual in the Who—*ever*, under any circumstances. Maybe we weren't his type. And I only know of one boy who was seduced by him, in the very early part of our career, and that was a boy from Shepherd's Bush who was gay anyway. I mean, Simon Napier-Bell, mind you, is a different story—a *very* different story. Because I think Marc Bolan had a very suspicious history. A lot of the early mods—which Marc claimed he was—used to stand outside the Scene, used to be homosexual prostitutes to raise money to buy leapers [amphetamines]. And if Marc was there at the time he said he was, then it's unfortunately inevitable that he was one of those prostitutes.

I thought John's Children were a bit shallow. But Simon Napier-Bell is probably one of the few people who really did understand what Kit was going through, and the fact that Kit, as a homosexual in a very macho area of rock & roll, couldn't really display his homosexuality, couldn't find that very, very important person, that opposite, to fall in love with. Which, more recently, Elton John has publicly professed has been one of his problems.

In the fiction that you're writing, do you hope to reflect your time at all, your period?

Yeah, very much. I feel that I've woken up from a bit of a dream, with all my faculties operatin' and my sixth sense operatin', and I do know that there's something very *wrong* going on. And it has to be talked about and dealt with, and I think, as always, writers are the first people to start to express that.

Do you think it's a political or a spiritual malaise?

It's a combination of things. I really feel a disconcerting feeling that, suddenly, the responsibility for the planet is in *my hands*. Not mine exclusively—mine and yours and everybody's.

Your generation's.

Yeah. It's like it's not somebody else's problem. Suddenly, it's mine. I realize that I can't work in a capsule anymore. I've got to be conscious of what's happening in the world, I think it's never too late— and never too *soon*—to start something like that. I'm not just talking about the need for a global, intuitive reaction against nuclear weapons or the need for a kind of global stance on ecology. They're important issues. But it's something else, in a sense. I feel something else happening. I feel like there's an opportunity out there at the moment that mustn't be missed. I don't know quite what it is—it's just something I feel in me bones.

What about the European antinuclear movement, which argues that the presence of American missiles here could turn Europe into a battleground between two remote superpowers—that the battle itself might have little to do with Europe. Why not just forbid America to put any more missiles in Europe?

Now, how can you do that? America is our ally. How can we *forget* what happened in the last two wars? Can we suddenly turn around and say, "Sorry, we don't need you anymore"? You know, people came all the way over from America on ships and got shot in the hundreds of thousands to *save Europe*. People have got too short a memory. A lot of the people who are out doin' these disarmament parades and things are two generations away from that. They don't realize— particularly the German nuclear campaigners—that Europe is only *there* by the grace of God and America. I don't want to be *too* passionate and patriotic about it, but I think so much *shit* is spoken about America and American politics. America is responsible for the *free world* and continues to be. I mean, however socialist I take myself to be, I also enjoy my life as it is, you know? I *enjoy* living in the West. I was born here, and I like it the way it is. I don't mind if it changes *slowly*, and I'm not averse to the idea of creeping socialism or creeping communism—but slow, slow, slow. Let life, and let the world, evolve. Eventually, of *course*, everybody will have to be living at the lowest common denominator—I think communism is absolutely inevitable.

But it's time to start really working on this buildup of global consciousness. This is not gettin' cosmic, or hippie spaced-out, man. Everybody's *got* to start thinkin', I mean, start with prayer and work downward, you know? Because there's not very much else that's in our hands. I just say that I do not like what I see. It's not to say that I can put it right. Not only do I not know how to put it right, but I'm impotent—completely impotent. Really, what our generation has suddenly woken up and realized, I think, is that we are the generation with no balls. And I'm gonna keep repeatin' that until somebody shows me differently.

How could that be demonstrated?

Well, I don't know. I suppose by everybody acting as one for once. Perhaps Europe's preoccupation with its own security is drawing people together in a way that should be taken advantage of. To end with a nice epigram: This song on my album, "The Sea Refuses No River," has not got anything to do with my preoccupation with oceans. It's the Townshend family motto. My daughters, Emma and Minta, and I went to see a friend called Mark McCauley, who's a London so-cialite, runs the Embassy Club. Minta was fascinated with his posh accent and all that, and asked him whether he had family portraits on the wall and whether he had a family crest. And he said, "Why, of course I do. *Everybody* has a family crest, don't they, Pete?" I said, "Yeah, yeah, of course." And she said, "Where're our family portraits, and where's our family crest?" So I said, "Well, our family portraits are in the desk cupboard, third drawer down—you know, the Kodak Instamatics. And the family motto is in the *Book of Proverbs*. All you have to do is look it up." So Emma looked in the *Book of Proverbs* and, with Karen's help, came up with "The sea refuses no river." Which I *loved*. I thought it was great. It's just what this family's all about. And I got very involved in the idea, the true expression of the proverb and turned it into a song.

Later on, I had forgotten where it came from, and Emma went back and found it for me—in the *Oxford Book of Proverbs,* I think. And this bloody book opens up with "Wise men make the proverbs, fools repeat them." Which is a suitable epigram for the whole thing, really.

2

Bruce Springsteen

INTERVIEWED BY KURT LODER (1984)

I waited around for a week to talk to Bruce Springsteen, trudging down the West Coast from Tacoma to Oakland to Los Angeles with his 'Born in the U.S.A.' tour, and when we finally sat down together, it was a disaster. Springsteen was dispatched to my hotel room late one night following one of the four-hour concerts for which he was by then already renowned. He slumped into a chair and proceeded to turn into every interviewer's nightmare—a completely monosyllabic subject. It was clear that Springsteen distrusted the artificiality of the press interview (and who among those of us familiar with its tactics could blame him?). But he also seemed plain beat, so after an hour and a half of unenlightening grunts and mumbles, I suggested he bunk out for a while, and that we try again later.

By the time he turned up in my next hotel room, at the Sunset Marquis in L.A., a few days later, he seemed extraordinarily refreshed. (I subsequently gathered that it was around this time that he began keeping company with Julianne Phillips, the model he would later marry, but there was no whisper of this on the tour.) He sat down, popped open a Heineken and proceeded to ramble.

Springsteen has gotten a lot better at this sort of press ritual over the years—by now, he can turn a pithy phrase with the best of them. But at the time of this interview, he was still, to a fascinating extent, thinking out loud. At some points, adrift in seemingly endless digression, he appeared to meander. On playback of the tapes, however, his extraordinary monologue clearly cohered around a rhetorical structure of search and resolution—qualities central to the songs on 'Born in the U.S.A.' Here was a guy who was working things out—not insignificant things, either—in public. It made for great listening.

—K. L.

SEATTLE WAS the market, but Tacoma was Bruce Springsteen's kind of town. He and the E Street Band had flown in from Vancouver, British Columbia, on the second leg of their *Born in the U.S.A.* tour, and immediately everybody got sick. Something in the air. "The Tacoma aroma," locals call it, a lung-raking stench of noxious lumber-milling fumes and other foul industrial emissions that imparted a green-gilled tinge to most members of the Springsteen tour party and made Bruce himself sick to his stomach. Nevertheless, his first, sold-out show at the 25,000-seat Tacoma Dome went on as scheduled. Bruce is nothing if not a trouper.

He could have played the Kingdome, in Seattle, thirty miles away, where the air is clear and the ambience more upscale. But the smaller Tacoma Dome has better acoustics, and anyway, Springsteen—although he's something of an upscale guy himself these days—maintains a well-known interest in the embattled world of the working class. Tacoma, in its bilious way, was perfect.

He really was sick, though—white as a sheet when he took the stage and wiped out for sure when he left it four hours later. But he never let it show. He kicked off with a booming, boot-stomping "Born in the U.S.A." and then descended into several songs from his starkly brilliant *Nebraska* album, keeping the audience with him all the way. He's got his raps down on this tour, talking about "powerlessness" at one point and, at another, "blind faith—whether it's in your girlfriend or the government." "This is 1984," he tells the howling crowds, "and people seem to be searchin' for something." In Tacoma, before counting off the haunting "My Hometown," he delivered an extended plug for a community-action group called Washington Fair Share, which recently helped force the cleanup of an illegal landfill and is working to overturn Governor John Spellman's veto of a "right to know" law that would require local industries to inform employees of all toxic chemicals they're being exposed to on the job. "They think that people should come before profit, and the community before the corporation," Bruce announced. And then added, pointedly, "This is *your* hometown."

This is world-class rock & roll, all right, but something more besides. And in 1984, Bruce Springsteen has become something decidedly more than just another rock star with an album to flog. He is a national presence, his charisma co-opted by as unlikely an adherent as Ronald Reagan—even as Springsteen himself pokes relentlessly through the withered and waterless cultural underbrush of the president's new American Eden. In pursuit of what can only be called his dream, Springsteen has been tenacious: dropping out of Ocean County College in his native New Jersey in 1968 to take his unlikely chances as a songwriting rock & roller and stubbornly waiting out a devastating, yearlong legal dispute with his then manager, Mike Appel, that prevented him from recording for nearly a year in the mid-Seventies. After selling 2 million copies of his 1980 double album, *The River,* he followed it up with *Nebraska,* a striking, guitar-and-voice meditation on various kinds of pain and craziness in the American hinterlands, and then followed *that* up with *Born in the U.S.A.,* which treats some of the same themes within a full-bore band context and has suddenly become his biggest album to date.

As the tour progressed, Springsteen sat down for interviews in Oakland, California —where he plugged the Berkeley Emergency Food Project—and in Los Angeles, where he maintains a house in the Hollywood Hills. Asked how he keeps his tightly structured stage show fresh down to the last mock-rambling anecdote, he said, "It's a matter of, Are you *there* at the moment? Are you *living* it?" It's a test he appears to pass both on and off the stage.

Born in the U.S.A.," *the title track of your current album, is one of those rare records: a rousing rock & roll song that also gives voice to the pain of forgotten people— in this case, America's Vietnam veterans. How long have you been aware of the Vietnam vets' experience?*

I don't know if anybody could imagine what their particular experience is like. I don't think *I* could, you know? I think you had to live through it. But when you think about all the young men and women that died in Vietnam, and how many died since they've been back—surviving the war and coming *back* and not surviving—you have to think that, at the time, the country took advantage of their selflessness. There was a moment when they were just really generous with their lives.

What was your own experience of Vietnam?

I didn't really have one.

There wasn't any kind of political consciousness down in Freehold [New Jersey, where Springsteen grew up] in the late Sixties. It was a small town, and the war just seemed very distant. I mean, I was aware of it through some friends that went. The drummer in my first band was killed in Vietnam. He kind of signed up and joined the Marines. Bart Hanes was his name. He was one of those guys that was jokin' all the time, always playin' the clown. He came over one day and said, "Well, I enlisted. I'm goin' to Vietnam." I remember he said he didn't know where it *was*. And that was it. He left and he didn't come back. And the guys that did come back were not the same.

How did you manage to escape the draft?

I got a 4-F. I had a brain concussion from a motorcycle accident when I was seventeen. Plus, I did the basic Sixties rag, you know: fillin' out the forms all crazy, not takin' the tests. When I was nineteen, I wasn't ready to be that generous with my life. I was called for induction, and when I got on the bus to go take my physical, I thought one thing: *"I ain't goin'."* I had tried to go to college, and I didn't really fit in. I went to a real narrow-minded school where people gave me a lot of trouble and I was hounded off the campus—I just looked different and acted different, so I left school. And I remember bein' on that bus, me and a couple of guys in my band, and the rest of the bus was probably sixty, seventy percent black guys from Asbury Park. And I remember thinkin', like, what makes my life, or my friends' lives, more expendable than that of somebody who's goin' to school? It didn't seem right. And it was funny, because my father, he was in World War II, and he was the type that was

always sayin', "Wait till the Army gets you. Man, they're gonna get that hair off of you. I can't wait. They gonna make a *man* outta you." We were really goin' at each other in those days. And I remember I was gone for three days, and when I came back, I went in the kitchen, and my folks were there, and they said, "Where you been?" And I said, "Well, I had to go take my physical." And they said, "What happened?" And I said, "Well, they didn't take me." And my father sat there, and he didn't look at me, he just looked straight ahead. And he said, "That's good." It was, uh . . . I'll never forget that. I'll *never* forget that.

Ironic, then, that today you're the toast of the political right, with conservative columnist George Will lauding your recent Washington, D.C., concert and President Reagan invoking your name while campaigning in your home state.

I think what's happening now is people want to forget. There was Vietnam, there was Watergate, there was Iran—we were beaten, we were hustled, and then we were humiliated. And I think people got a need to feel good about the country they live in. But what's happening, I think, is that that need—which is a good thing—is gettin' manipulated and exploited. And you see the Reagan reelection ads on TV—you know: "It's morning in America." And you say, well, it's not morning in Pittsburgh. It's not morning above 125th Street in New York. It's midnight, and, like, there's a bad moon risin'. And that's why when Reagan mentioned my name in New Jersey, I felt it was another manipulation, and I had to disassociate myself from the president's kind words.

But didn't you play into the hands of professional patriots by releasing an election-year album called 'Born in the U.S.A.,' with the American flag bannered across the front?

Well, we had the flag on the cover because the first song was called "Born in the U.S.A.," and the theme of the record kind of follows from the themes I've been writing about for at least the last six or seven years. But the flag is a powerful image, and when you set that stuff loose, you don't know what's gonna be done with it.

Actually, I know one fan who infers from the rump shot on the album cover that you're actually pissing on the flag. Is there a message there?

No, no. That was unintentional. We took a lot of different types of pictures, and in the end the picture of my *ass* looked better than the picture of my *face*, so that's what went on the cover. I didn't have any secret message. I don't do that very much.

Well, what is your political stance? Election Day is two weeks away: Are you registered to vote?

I'm registered, yeah. I'm not registered as one party or another. I don't generally think along those lines. I find it very difficult to relate to the whole electoral system as it stands. I don't really . . . I suppose if there was somebody who I felt strong enough about at some point, someday, you know . . .

You don't think Mondale would be any better than Reagan?

I don't know. I think there are significant differences, but I don't know *how* significant. And it's very difficult to tell by pre-election rhetoric. It seems to always change when they all of a sudden get in. That's why I don't feel a real connection to electoral politics right now—it can't be the best way to find the best man to do the hardest job. I want to try and just work more directly with people—try to find some way that my band can tie into the communities that we come into. I guess that's a political action, a way to just bypass that whole electoral thing. Human politics. I think that people on their own can do a lot. I guess that's what I'm tryin' to figure out now: Where do the aesthetic issues that you write about intersect with some sort of concrete action, some direct involvement, in the communities that your audience comes from? It seems to be an inevitable progression of what our band has been doin', of the idea that we got into this for. We wanted to play because we wanted to meet girls, we wanted to make a ton of dough and we wanted to change the world a little bit, you know?

Have you ever voted?

I think I voted for McGovern in 1972.

What do you really think of Ronald Reagan?

Well, I don't *know* him. But I think he presents a very mythic, very seductive image, and it's an image that people want to believe in. I think there's always been a nostalgia for a mythical America, for some period in the past when everything was just right. And I think the president is the embodiment of that for a lot of people. He has a very mythical presidency. I don't know if he's a bad man. But I think there's a large group of people in this country whose dreams don't mean that much to him, that just get indiscriminately swept aside. I guess my view of America is of a real bighearted country, real compassionate. But the difficult thing out there right now is that the social consciousness that was a part of the Sixties has become, like, old-fashioned or something. You go out, you get your job, and you try to make as much money as you can and have a good time on the weekend. And that's considered okay.

The state of the nation has weighed heavily, if sometimes subtly, on the characters depicted in your songs over the years. Do you see your albums as being connected by an evolving sociopolitical point of view?

I guess what I was always interested in was doing a *body* of work—albums that would relate to and play off of each other. And I was always concerned with doin' *albums,* instead of, like, collections of songs. I guess I started with *The Wild, the Innocent and the E Street Shuffle* in a funny way—particularly the second side, which kind of syncs together. I was very concerned about gettin' a group of characters and followin' them through their lives a little bit. And so, on *Born to Run, Darkness on the Edge of Town* and *The River,* I tried to hook things up. I guess in *Born to Run* there's that searchin' thing; that record to me is, like, religiously based, in a funny kind of way. Not like orthodox religion, but it's about basic things, you know? That searchin', and faith, and the idea of hope. And then on *Darkness,* it was kind of like a collision that happens between this guy and the real world. He ends up very alone and real stripped down. Then, on *The River,* there was always that thing of the guy attemptin' to come back, to find some sort of community. It had more songs about relationships—"Stolen Car," "The River," "I Wanna Marry You," "Drive All Night," even "Wreck on the Highway"—people tryin' to find some sort of consolation, some sort of comfort in each other. Before *The River,* there's almost no songs *about* relationships. Very few. Then, on *Nebraska* . . . I don't know *what* happened on that one. That kinda came out of the blue.

Wasn't the central inspiration Terrence Malick's 'Badlands,' the film about mass murderer Charles Starkweather and his girlfriend, Caril Fugate?

Well, I had already written "Mansion on the Hill" during the last tour. Then I went home—I was living in a place called Colts Neck, New Jersey—and I remember I saw *Badlands,* and I read this book about them, *Caril,* and it just seemed to be a mood that I was in at the time. I was renting a house on this reservoir, and I didn't go out much, and for some reason I just started to write. I wrote *Nebraska,* all those songs, in a couple of months. I was interested in writing kind of *smaller* than I had been, writing with just detail—which I kind of began to do on *The River.* I guess my influences at the time were the movie and these stories I was reading by Flannery O'Connor—she's just incredible.

Was there something about Starkweather that struck you as emblematic of the American condition?

I think you can get to a point where nihilism, if that's the right word, is overwhelming, and the basic laws that society has set up—either religious or social laws—become meaningless. Things just get really dark. You lose those constraints, and then anything goes. The forces that set that in motion, I don't know exactly what they'd be. I think just a lot of frustration, lack of findin' somethin' that you can hold on to, lack of contact with *people,* you know? That's one of the most dangerous things, I think—isolation. *Nebraska* was about that American isolation: what happens to people when they're alienated from their friends and their community and their government and their job. Because those are the things that keep you sane, that give meaning to life in some fashion. And if they slip away, and you start to exist in some void where the basic constraints of society are a joke, then life becomes kind of a joke. And anything can happen.

Did the stark acoustic format you eventually chose for 'Nebraska' just seem the most appropriate setting for such dark material?

Well, initially, I was just doing songs for the next rock album, and I decided that what always took me so long in the studio was the writing. I would get in there, and I just wouldn't have the material *written,* or it wasn't written well enough, and so I'd record for a month, get a couple of things, go home, write some more, record for another month—it wasn't very efficient. So this time, I got a little Teac four-track cassette machine and I said, I'm gonna record these songs, and if they sound good with just me doin' 'em, then I'll teach 'em to the band. I could sing and play the guitar, and then I had two tracks to do somethin' else, like overdub a guitar or add a harmony. It was just gonna be a demo. Then I had a little Echoplex that I mixed through, and that was it. And that was the tape that became the record. It's amazing that it *got* there, 'cause I was carryin' that cassette around with me in my pocket without a case for a couple of weeks, just draggin' it around. Finally, we realized, "Uh-oh, that's the album." Technically, it was difficult to get it on a disc. The stuff was recorded so strangely, the needle would read a lot of distortion and wouldn't track in the wax. We almost had to release it as a cassette.

I understand "Born in the U.S.A." was actually written around the time of 'Nebraska'; do any other songs on the new album date from that period?

Actually, half of the *Born in the U.S.A.* album was recorded at the time of *Nebraska.* When we initially went in the studio to try to record *Nebraska* with the band, we recorded the first side of *Born in the U.S.A.,* and the rest of the time I spent tryin' to come up with the second side—"Bobby Jean," "My Hometown," almost all those songs. So if you look at the material, particularly on the first side, it's actually written very much like *Nebraska*—the characters and the stories, the style of writing—except it's just in the rock-band setting.

You seem to have taken a more spontaneous, less labored approach to recording this album. Max Weinberg, your drummer, says that the title track of 'Born in the U.S.A.' is a second take—and that he didn't even know the band was going to kick back in at the end until you signaled him in the studio.

Oh, yeah. That entire track is live. Most of the songs on *Born in the U.S.A.* are under five takes, and "Darlington County" is live, "Working on the Highway" is live, "Downbound Train," "I'm on Fire," "Bobby Jean," "My Hometown," "Glory Days"—almost the whole album is done live. Our basic style of recording now is not real tedious. The band is playing really well together, and in five or six takes of a song, they're gonna get it. *Born to Run* was the only album I really did extensive overdubbing on; it's also the only album where I wrote only one more song than we recorded. For *Born in the U.S.A.,* we recorded maybe fifty songs. The recording is not what took the time; it was the writing—and waiting till I felt, "Well, there's an album here; there's some story being told." We record a lot of material, but we just don't release it all.

Bootleg buyers contend that some of your unreleased material is among your best. Does the brisk bootleg trade in your unreleased material annoy you?

I guess nobody likes the feeling that they wrote a song and in some way the song is bein' stolen from them or presented in a fashion they don't feel they'd want to present it in—the quality isn't good, and they're so expensive. I don't have any bootlegs myself. I always tell myself that some day I'm gonna put an album out with all this stuff on it that didn't fit in. I think there's good material there that should come out. Maybe at some point, I'll do that.

You've turned two of your current hits, "Dancing in the Dark" and "Cover Me," over to producer Arthur Baker to convert into dance-mix singles—with what some of your fans see as bizarre results. What made you want to do that?

I heard this dance mix of Cyndi Lauper's "Girls Just Want to Have Fun" on the radio, and it was incredible. It sounded like fun, so I hooked up with Arthur. He's a character, a great guy. He had another fellow with him, and they were really pretty wild. They'd get on that mixing board and just crank them knobs, you know? The meters were goin' wild.

Did you have input into this?

Not much. The entire thing is Arthur Baker. He's really an artist. It was fun to just give him a song and see what his interpretation of it would be. I was always so protective of my music that I was hesitant to do much with it at all. Now I feel my stuff isn't as fragile as I thought.

You've also started doing videos recently. What do you make of the medium?

Video is a powerful thing, and I wanted to be involved in it in some fashion. But it presents a variety of problems. I didn't want to infringe on my audience's imagination by presenting some concrete image that was a replica of an image in the song, and I didn't want to create *another* story, because I was already tellin' the story I wanted to tell.

For "Dancing in the Dark," you brought in film director Brian De Palma and made a lip-synced concert video. Why?

Brian was great, because I had no time—we were getting ready for our first show—and he came in on real short notice and really took the burden off my shoulders. We did that video in about three or four hours. Lip-syncing is one of those things—it's easy to do, but you wonder about the *worth* of doing it. That video was great, though, because I noticed that most of the people that would come up and mention it to me were people who hadn't heard my other stuff. Very often they were real little kids. I was on the beach and this kid came up to me—I think his name was Mike, he was like seven or eight—and he says, "I saw you on MTV." And then he says, "I got your moves down." So I say, "Well, let me check 'em out." And he starts doin', like, "Dancing in the Dark." And he was *pretty good,* you know?

You've certainly achieved mass-market success this year. The 'Born in the U.S.A.' tour is selling out arenas across the country, and the album has sold over 5 million copies worldwide. Has becoming a rich man changed you at all?

Yeah, there's a change. It doesn't make living easier, but it does make certain aspects of your life easier. You don't have to worry about rent, you can buy things for your folks and help out your friends, and you can have a *good time,* you know? There were moments where it was very confusing, because I realized that I was a rich man, but I felt like a poor man inside.

In what way?

Just my outlook on things in general, because I guess it was formed when I was young. I mean, basically, you know, because of the lawsuit and a bunch of other things—and because of how long it would take me to make records—I didn't get to a situation where I had any dough in the bank till around the *River* tour. And this tour, we've been doin' great so far. But I don't know if money changes you. I guess I don't really think it *does* change you. It's an inanimate thing, a tool, a convenience. If you've got to have a problem, it's a good problem to have.

Obviously, you don't spend your money on clothes. What do you do with it?

I'm just figuring that out right now. One of the things I can do is play benefits and help people out that need help, people that are strugglin', you know, tryin' to get somethin' goin' on their own. Money was kind of part of the dream when I started. I don't think . . . I never felt like I ever played a note for the money. I think if I did, people would know and they'd throw you out of the joint. And you'd deserve to go. But at the same time, it was a part of the dream. Part of like . . .

The pink Cadillac?

Yeah, the pink Cadillac. Me and Steve [Van Zandt, the former E Street Band guitarist] used to sit around and say, "Yeah, when we make it, we're gonna do this and that. . . ."

What did you plan to do?

Mainly, we planned to be just like the Rolling Stones. They were the band we liked the best at the time. But you grow up, and when you finally put that suit of clothes on, sometimes they don't fit, or they fit differently, and you're a different person, and what you're gonna do is different, I guess. But in general, I do enjoy the success we've had, and the fact that we have an audience, and I've enjoyed the financial success that I've had. It's helped me do some things that I've wanted to do.

Would it be an exaggeration to say that you're a millionaire?

No, no. I definitely got that much.

What's your house in Rumson, New Jersey, like?

It's the mansion on the hill! [*Laughs*] It's the kind of place I told myself I'd never live in. But before this tour, I was lookin' for a big house, 'cause I was living in a real small house that I rented. I'd always rented, ever since I was a kid, and I realized I'd been playin' for twelve years, and I didn't have any sort of . . . nothin' that was like any kind of *home*. I had a bunch of old cars that I'd collected over the years, old bombs:

pickup trucks that I picked up for like $500, a '69 Chevy, an Impala that Gary Bonds gave me and a 1960 Corvette that was one of the few things I got out of *Born to Run.* And all these old cars were stashed away in different people's garages all across New Jersey. So I said, "Wow, I think I'm gonna get a big house." But what I really wanted to get was a farm with a big barn, where I can build a studio so I don't have to travel to New York to record all the time. Which is what I'm gonna get when I go back after this tour.

So the Rumson house is just a sort of way station?

All my houses seem to have been way stations. That's the kind of person I have been, you know? I don't like feelin' too rooted for some reason. Which is funny, because the things that I admire and the things that mean a lot to me all have to do with roots and home, and myself, personally, I'm the opposite. I'm very rootless in that sense. I never attach myself to any place that I am. I always felt most at home when I was, like, in the car or on the road, which is, I guess, why I always wrote about it. I was very distant from my family for quite a while in my early twenties. Not with any animosity; I just had to feel loose. Independence always meant a lot to me. I had to feel I could go anywhere, any time, in order to get my particular job done. And that's basically the way I've always lived. Lately, I've . . . I'm still not . . . I don't know if I'm a big family man. My family's been my band. I've always been that way. I think when I was young, I did it intentionally, because I knew I only had sixty dollars that month, and I had to live on that sixty dollars, and I couldn't get married or I couldn't get involved at the time. And then it just became my way of life, you know? It really became my way of life.

You were never on the verge of getting married?

No. I lived with a girl once. I'd never lived with a girl before. I was in my early twenties, and I'd never even lived with anybody.

How come?

I don't know. I'm not exactly sure. I guess I just wanted to be free to move, a roadrunner. It's silly, I guess. It sounds silly to me now when I say it. Particularly because I don't really value those ideals. I guess I see fulfillment, ultimately, in family life. That just hasn't been *my* life, you know?

But you're writing all these songs about relationships. What does your mother think about this situation?

I got an Italian *grand*mother, and that's all she asks me. She speaks half Italian and half English, and every time I go over it's "Where's you girlfriend? When are you gonna get married?"

Is it possible for you to have normal romantic attachments?

I guess so. I've had steady girlfriends in the past. I went out with a girl I met at Clarence's [E Street band saxophonist Clarence Clemons's] club. I'm just not really lookin' to get married at this point. I've made a commitment to doin' my job right now, and that's basically what I do. *Someday,* I'd like to have the whole nine yards—the wife, the kids.

And until then? I'm trying to picture Bruce Springsteen just asking a normal girl for a casual date.

You just do it. You're out in a bar or somethin', and you meet somebody, you can't worry. You gotta go ahead and live your life in as normal a fashion as possible. When I'm out, I don't really think that much about the other part of my life, about how people are looking at me. It's not *relevant,* almost. Somebody may go out with you once or twice because of who you are, but if you're a jerk, they're not gonna want to, because it's not gonna be any fun, you know? That kind of thing wears off pretty quick.

So you've never allowed yourself to become isolated, to slip into the Elvis Presley syndrome?

One of the things that was always on my mind to do was to maintain connections with the people I'd grown up with, and the sense of the community where I came from. That's why I stayed in New Jersey. The danger of fame is in *forgetting,* or being distracted. You see it happen to so many people. Elvis's case must have been tremendously difficult. Because, I mean, I feel the difference between selling a million records and selling 3 million records—I can feel a difference out on the street. The type of fame that Elvis had, and that I think Michael Jackson has, the pressure of it, and the isolation that it seems to require, has gotta be really painful. I wasn't gonna let that happen to me. I wasn't gonna get to a place where I said, "I can't go in here. I can't go to this bar. I can't go outside." For the most part, I do basically what I've always done. I'll walk into a club, and people will just say hi, and that's it. And I'll get up and play.

I believe that the life of a rock & roll band will last as long as you look down into the audience and can see yourself, and your audience looks up at you and can see themselves—and as long as those reflections are human, realistic ones. The biggest gift that your fans can give you is just treatin' you like a human being, because anything else dehumanizes you. And that's one of the things that has shortened the life spans, both physically and creatively, of some of the best rock & roll musicians—that cruel isolation. If the price of fame is that you have to be isolated from the people you write for, then that's too fuckin' high a price to pay.

You once tried to meet Elvis Presley by jumping over the wall at his Graceland mansion. The attempt failed, but have you met most of your other idols in the music business?

Well, I'm real ambivalent about meetin' people I admire. You know the old saying: Trust the art, not the artist. I think that's true. I think somebody can do real good work and be a fool in a variety of ways. I think my music is probably better than I am. I mean, like, your music is your ideals a lot of times, and you don't live up to those ideals all the time. You try, but you fall short and you disappoint yourself. With my idols, I just like their music. If the occasion comes up, I like to meet them, but I never really seek it out very much, because it's their music that I like in general. People always say they were disappointed by Elvis, they were let down. I'm not sure that's the right way to look at it. I don't think anybody was disappointed by his great records, you know? I think, personally, it's a hard way to go for everybody out there, and that he gave the best that he had, the best that he could get a hold of.

You, at least, seem unlikely ever to emulate Elvis' drug problems. Is it true that after nearly twenty years in the rock & roll world, you've truly never so much as smoked a joint?

I never did any drugs. When I was at that age when it was popular, I wasn't really in a social scene a whole lot. I was practicing in my room with my guitar. So I didn't have the type of pressure that kids might have today. Plus, I was very concerned with being in control at the time. I drink a little bit now. There's nights when I'll go out and do it up. But not too much when we're touring, because the show is so physically demanding, and you gotta be so prepared.

There's also a notable lack—in your songs, your stage show, your videos—of any sort of exploitative sexual imagery of the kind that routinely spices, say, MTV. Nor do you appear to encourage a groupie scene backstage at your shows. This is unusual for rock, and I wonder if it has anything to do with your growing up with a strong, working mother and two sisters.

I don't know. I think if you just try to have a basic respect for people's humanness, you just generally don't want to do those things. I think it's *difficult*, because we were all brought up with sexist attitudes and racist attitudes. But hopefully, as you grow older, you get some sort of insight into that and—I know it's corny—try to treat other people the way you would want them to treat you.

It's like my younger sister. When I was thirteen, my mother got pregnant again, and she really took me through the whole thing. We used to sit on the couch and watch TV, and she'd say "Feel this," and I'd put my hand on her stomach and I'd feel my little sister in there. And from the very beginning, I had a deep connection with her.

One of the best times I can ever remember was when she was born, because it changed the atmosphere of the whole house for quite a while—the old "*Shh,* there's a baby in the house." And I'd watch her all the time, and if she started cryin', I'd run down to see what was the matter. I remember one day I was watchin' her, and she was on the couch and she rolled off and fell on her head—she was about one, still a little baby—and I felt like, "Oh, that's it. Brain damage! My life is over, I've had it!" [*Laughs*] My family moved to California when she was like five or six, and we didn't see each other for quite a while. But every time we did, it was like automatic—like we'd never been apart.

I think that what happens is, when you're young, you feel powerless. If you're a child and you're lookin' up at the world, the world is frightening. Your house, no matter how small it is, it seems so big. Your parents seem huge. I don't believe this feeling ever quite leaves you. And I think what happens is, when you get around fifteen or sixteen, a lot of your fantasies are power fantasies. And I think that's one of the things that gets exploited by some of the more demeaning types of music. If you're a kid, you feel powerless, but you don't know how to channel that powerlessness—how to channel it into either a social concern or creating something for yourself. I was lucky; I was able to deal with it with the guitar. I said, "Well, I feel weak, but when I do this, when I feel this, when I hold it, I feel a little stronger. I feel like I've got some line on my life. I feel I have some control." That feelin' of weakness, of powerlessness, is there. And I think it gets exploited and misdirected.

One of the problems in the United States is that "united in our prejudices we stand," you know? What unites people, very often, is their fear. What unites white people in some places is their fear of black people. What unites guys is maybe a denigrating attitude toward women—or sometimes maybe women have an attitude toward men. And these things are then in turn exploited by politicians, which turns into fear—knee-jerk fear of the Russians or of whatever *ism* is out there. Or in a very subtle kind of indirect way—like some of our economic policies are a real indirect kind of racism, in which the people that get affected most are black people who are at the lower end of the economic spectrum. And I think somewhere inside, people *know* this—I *really do*. They don't fess up to it, but somewhere inside there's a real meanness in using things this way.

I think it's changing *some*what, but how many times in this election campaign did you hear that the major complaint against Mondale was that he was "wimpish"? It's still a very, very big part of the whole American culture. It's all wrapped up in a variety of different ways in my own music—dealin' with it, fakin' it, tryin' to get *over* fakin' it, tryin' to break *through* it. It's just . . . there's just so much . . . it seems to be . . .

Overwhelming?

Yeah.

What keeps you going at age thirty-five?

I was lucky. During the lawsuit, I understood that it's the music that keeps me alive, and my relationships with my friends, and my attachment to the people and the places I've known. That's my lifeblood. And to give that up for, like, the TV, the cars, the houses—that's not the American dream. That's the booby prize, in the end. Those are the booby prizes. And if you fall for them—if, when you achieve them, you believe that this is the end in and of itself—then you've been suckered in. Because those are the consolation prizes, if you're not careful, for selling yourself out or lettin' the best of yourself slip away. So you gotta be vigilant. You gotta carry the idea you began with further. And you gotta hope that you're headed for higher ground.

3

Keith Richards

INTERVIEWED BY KURT LODER (1981)

Keith Richards is an interviewer's dream. No utterance is off the record, no subject out of bounds, no tale too salacious to relate. In short, dish city.

Despite his mythic dissipation, Richards is a man of limber intellect. He can knock back a fifth of Rebel Yell—the cult bourbon he currently favors—during the course of a long conversation yet remain bafflingly cogent. He is a man of disarming charm, and a compulsive musician. After wrapping up the interview recorded here, he wandered off to an upright piano and began noodling around in a rolling, bluesy mode that seemed to fall somewhere between the style of Memphis Slim and Keith's own favorite, Johnnie Johnson. Richards' playing had a buoyant stride to it, transportingly supple—the music of a man tapped into the source.

When we talked, early in the fall of 1981, the Rolling Stones were rehearsing for a tour that would turn out to be their last for years to come. Although their latest album at the time, 'Tattoo You,' contained some of the group's finest mature work (including the tenderly fraternal "Waiting on a Friend"), the abiding impersonal tensions between Richards and Mick Jagger—two very different men—would sunder the band within five years (and, despite a reunion announced for 1989, appear to imperil its future). On that crisp September night, however, Richards was happy just to have the lads back—from France, from the England he'd long ago forsaken, from wherever—and at work once again on becoming the Rolling Stones.

—K. L.

I'VE JUST been closeted with Napoleon," Keith Richards said, tilting his wine glass in mock salute. "Mick's been sick. Got the flu, I think." It was exactly one week before the start of the Rolling Stones' first U.S. tour in three years, but Richards seemed unfazed by the loss of a much-needed all-night rehearsal. Looking very teenage-wasteland in a black bomber jacket, black T-shirt and black jeans, with blue-suede boots scrunched down around his ankles and a dark green scarf knotted at his waist, he nevertheless appeared healthy and in high spirits.

We were standing in the big country kitchen at Long View Farm, a remote but luxurious recording compound in rural Massachusetts where the Stones had been whipping their act into shape for the past month. It was 9:00 P.M., and the kitchen buffet was groaning with roasted meats, steaming lobsters and crocks full of fresh, buttered vegetables. Over in the dining alcove, Charlie Watts was panning his portable video camera across a large corner table where Bill Wyman and the two auxiliary keyboardists, Ian Stewart and Ian McLagan, sat lingering at their plates. I noticed that the famous heads are going gray now, the faces beginning to sag like trail-weathered saddlebags. "Look at your face, baby," Mick Jagger sings on the Stones' new album. "Look at you and look at me." For a moment, I caught myself looking into that mirror, too.

The upcoming Stones tour would be the most testing of their nineteen-year career. A law unto themselves in the past, they were now old beyond argument, and so found themselves in the position of having to go out once more and prove, in public, that they could still do it. That they still had the creative goods was not in question: *Tattoo You*, their new LP, showed all of the old power still surging, and the lyrics were informed by a rich new emotional complexity. It was the act that needed spiffing up.

Keith Richards was determined that all would be okay. At thirty-seven, ravaged by all the wild years of drug busts and screaming court headlines, he had begun to perceive an emerging order in his life. His longtime relationship with Anita Pallenberg, the mother of his two children, Marlon and Dandelion, had fallen apart in an ugly, public way, but his ongoing romance with Patti Hansen, a young model, offered hope of renewal. And even in middle age, he found, rock & roll still made a kind of perfect, powerful sense. So, once again, he gathered the Stones around him.

Out in the barn, a gleaming polished-pine stage had been constructed high up across the 100-foot width of the loft. A dozen or so feet below was a small living area that contained a fireplace, an expensive stereo system and a sideboard filled with good wines and spirits. Keith strolled in and slipped a cassette into the stereo. He announced it as "the best album of the year." It was the Neville Brothers' *Fiyo on the Bayou,* an exhilarating feast of rolling, New Orleans–style R&B. Keith poured himself a tumbler of Jack Daniel's, I grabbed a bottle of wine, and we settled at a table to soak in Aaron Neville's breathtaking rendition of the ancient doo-wop classic "The Ten Commandments of Love." Still suckers after all these years. Can the Stones cut it in 1981? All you had to do, said Keith, was start 'em up.

*W*hat's it like rounding up the Rolling Stones after three years and trying to play together again?

Um, surprisingly easy. Getting them over the idea of workin' on the road, that's the hard bit. You know, they're going, "*Ohhh, I don't* wanna go on the *road*." And I'm tryin' to hustle them, because I know that it's the only way to keep 'em together. They always feel good about it once they *do* it; maybe I kind of crystallize that feeling or focus it or whatever, because everybody feels the same way as me, but not at the same time. But if the band wants to stay together, then we do have to go on the road and we do have to work. And once we get up there and start rehearsing, it's great. And it only gets better and better, you know? The problem is—this has been one of my favorite gripes for years—that because of the way we work, doing a blockbuster tour every three years, we find ourselves on this cycle of working our way up to a certain point where we can say, "*now* we're breaking, *now* we're taking off into somewhere else." And then, because the tour stops—*boom*—we're never able to get *past* that point, to push it when it's still getting better. And three years later, we have to start again from scratch, going over the same ground to find out what we already know. That's the one thing that bugs me. I've always wanted to find out what would happen if we just kept *going*.

Judging by 'Tattoo You,' it seems like the band could keep going, creatively at least, for another twenty years. Hope so, anyway.

So do I, because nobody else has done it, you know? It's kind of interesting to find out how rock & roll can grow up. I mean, there are other examples, obviously, but on the sort of scale the Rolling Stones are on, and have been on for so long, it still seems that if we do *our* best, they respond to it immediately—the audience, the kids, whatever you want to call it. Some of them are not so young anymore. Nor are we.

The punks were fond of pointing that out during their moment in the spotlight.

That's like punks. They always come and go.

Did you find anything worthwhile in punk rock?

Yeah, there was a certain spirit there. But I don't think there was anything new musically, or even from the PR point of view, image-wise. There was too much image, and none of the bands were given enough chance to put their music together, if they had any. It seemed to be the least important thing. It was more important if you puked over somebody, you know? But that's a legacy from us also. After all, we're still the only rock & roll band arrested for peeing on a wall.

Apparently, the punks weren't impressed. They really seemed to hate bands like the Stones.

That's what we used to say about everything that went before us. But you need a bit more than just putting down people to keep things together. There's always somebody better at puttin' you down. So don't put me down, just do what I did, you know? Do me something better. Turn me on.

When and where did you write the material on 'Tattoo You'?

A lot of it was done in Paris. One of the tracks, "Worried About You," was done for *Black and Blue*. The rest were done in Paris between 1977 and last year. I mean, we cut over forty tracks for *Emotional Rescue*, but at that time it was a matter of picking out the tracks that were the nearest to completion, because we had a deadline that didn't allow us much time. On this album, we took longer. We started to think about this one soon after the last one came out, and we chose the songs a lot more carefully.

Will we be seeing more songs from those sessions in the future?

Oh, yeah, there's still loads. I mean, we could get another album out of that bunch. But that's an advantage you don't think about, really, with a band that goes on for a long time. One way or another, you end up with a backlog of really good stuff that, for one reason or another, you didn't get the chance to finish or put out because it was the wrong tempo or too long—purely technical reasons, you know? Sometimes we write our songs in installments—just get the melody and the music, and we'll cut the tracks and write

the words later. That way, the actual tracks have matured, just like wine—you just leave it in the cellar for a bit, and it comes out a little better a few years later. It's stupid to *leave* all that great stuff just for want of finishin' it off and gettin' it together.

Think of all the potential hits that might be lying around.

Yeah, and we probably don't even recognize half of them. I mean, you just don't know after a while. I'm the guy who said "Satisfaction" wasn't a single. That's what I know.

I gather you don't take the music business very seriously.

There's nothing *to* be taken seriously. No way. If you look at the music business over a long period of time, it's always put out mostly shit.

Is that why people aren't buying as much music as they used to? Is it a combination of shitty music and a bad economy?

Music is a luxury, as far as people are concerned. I'm not sayin' *I* believe that, but to people who haven't got work, and haven't got money, music will seem a luxury. In actual *fact*, music is a necessity, because it's the one thing that will maybe bring you up and give you just that little bit extra to keep on going or . . . Who *knows* what music does?

Apparently, you and Mick are still writing about whatever's happening to you at the moment. "Hang Fire," for instance, is explicitly about England, right?

Yeah: "Where I come from, nobody ever works, nothing ever gets done." They're going through their little traumas over there. It serves them right for kickin' us out.

What's happening to England?

It's coming to terms with a whole lot of problems that have been brewing for years, and the only thing it needed for these problems to come to a head was for the money to get tight. Everybody tolerates everything while they're doin' all right, Jack; but when they're not, it's "What the *fuck* . . . ?" Now they gotta deal with that.

How do you feel about the situation there politically? Are you at all political?

No. I watch it, you know. It's the height of cynicism for me to watch that whole power play go down. Just to see such hams get away with such a bad act over and over again, you know? I mean, it's an ongoing soap opera of the worst kind, but people still watch it.

Do you care? Do you think there may be some sort of ideal remedy?

No, there's no ideal thing. People are people, and they're pressured into one corner or another. What is politics? Politics goes down in everything. It's *always* ugly. Politics is an ugly word these days, and the only people who make politics an ugly word are politicians, because they're ugly *people*. Not necessarily ugly to start with—I'm givin' them the benefit of the doubt—but even if they aren't, they will be after a couple of years in Washington or Moscow or London, in that circle they move in. I always look upon it as, "Yeah, these are the guys who couldn't play Biloxi."

Do you get back to England very often?

Fairly regularly. This year I haven't, but for the past couple of years I've gone back around August for two months or so. After about a week in London, I tend to drift out to the country, where things never change. I go to a little village where there are only about three people who have ever *been* to London, you know—and it's only seventy miles away. "Oh, London? No, never been there. Too many people." It's kind of timeless there. It's a real great anchor for me. It still sticks in my throat a little that I can't, you know . . . what do you *mean* I make too much money to live here? You mean I can't *afford* to live in England? It's just kind of vindictive. I mean, I can't consider us part of the brain drain or anything like that, but they certainly flushed us down their john, you know? "In the bathroom of your heart, I've been flushed, dear."

"Neighbours" seems to be another slice of life—yours, I gather. Weren't you and Patti evicted from your Manhattan apartment earlier this year for playing music too loud?

Oh, a *couple* of them. Yeah, Patti and I are homeless at the moment. Mick wrote the lyrics to that—and he *never* has trouble with neighbors.

Just a quiet guy, right?

No, he's *not*. He's just *smart*. He got himself into a good old building with very thick walls and nobody particular around. I have a knack of finding a whole building of very cool people, you know, but there'll be one uncool couple—they're always a couple. And my apartment will always be either just above them or next door to them or just below. And they're the kind of people who'll knock you up at six in the morning, while you've just sort of got a little bit of music going. You're trying to be cool, 'cause you're aware of it, you know? By *now*, I'm aware that I can't blast the sounds. So I'm trying to be cool about it. And these people come up to our door saying, "We can't even hear Bugs Bunny on our TV, your music's so loud! Turn the kettledrums down!" So, I mean, I'm *plagued* by that kind of thing. I swear they're the same couple everywhere I go. They just follow me around: "Let's bug him; he's an asshole, he deserves it."

"Neighbours" is the first song I think Mick's ever really written for me. It's one I wish I'd written, that.

You and Mick appear to have one of the great friendships of our era. Is it really as solid as it seems?

Yeah. It's a true friendship when you can bash somebody over the head and not be told, "You're not my friend anymore." That's a true friendship. You put up with each other's bitching. People will think we're having these huge arguments and say, "Oh, will they split up?" But it's our way of working, you know? He's my wife. And he'll say the same thing about me: "Yeah, he's my wife."

I think the popular perception is that Mick is probably the better businessman of the two. Have you handled your money well?

I make it and I spend it, but it's set up in a way. Mick *is* pretty good at business. He's not as good as people think. He's probably not as good as *he* thinks. And he's probably not as bad as *I* think. Mick wants to know about every angle of everything, you know? Which is admirable—I certainly don't have the time or the inclination to find out those things. But we pool our information.

Do you ever feel you've become too rich to relate to your audience?

I just feel there's an audience out there, and as long as they want to hear it, I guess we'll go on making it.

How do rich people have the blues?

I don't know. I've never met a rich person yet who's *felt* rich. Because from my own experience, the bigger things get and the more money you make, the more it takes to run the whole show. Especially tax attorneys. And therefore, the more you have to go out and make more money to pay them to give you . . . it's a diminishing return, you know? I've never felt rich. I've never really thought about it. All I'm worried about is having enough to keep the show on the road, you know. As long as that's there, then it's all right. The rest of it—what am I gonna do with it anyway? I spend half my life in the studio, and when I'm not there, I'm hustling to get on the road again. So, I mean, I can spend it, but I don't know where it goes.

Do the Rolling Stones ever socialize with each other anymore?

Yeah, we're always in touch. Charlie bounces into New York or wherever once every couple of months. As far as I'm concerned, I'd just say that I'm continually thankful—and more so as we go along—that we have Charlie Watts sittin' there, you know? *He's* the guy who doesn't believe it, because he's like that. I mean, he doesn't think that his contribution is as—

Really?

Yeah. There's nothing forced about Charlie, least of all his modesty. It's *totally* real. He cannot understand what people see in his drumming.

That's amazing.

I think so.

What about Ron Wood? He's been part of the act for about six years now, but I think some people still tend to dismiss him as a kind of Keith Richards clone.

I was the one who was most apprehensive about taking Ronnie into this. He's a very good friend of mine, and I've worked on his solo albums. But he doesn't play like me. To me, Ronnie's keeping together that idea of the Stones sound that Brian [Jones] and I had. That's how I feel about Ronnie. He has an instinctive feel for what Brian and I originally worked out as far as guitars and the music go. Siamese twins—they both play. Look at it like this: There's one guy, he's just got four arms. That's the way I like to feel about it. Because when it comes out, it doesn't matter how many people are playing and who's doing what. When that sound comes out, does it hit you between the eyes and does it *grab* you?

Brian's been dead for twelve years now. Do you still think about him?

Yeah, I think about him every time we play "Time Is on My Side," or when I'm playing his guitar licks on "Mona." Brian, in many ways, was a right cunt. He was a bastard. Mean, generous, anything. You want to say one thing, give it the opposite, too. But more so than most people, you know. Up to a point, you could put up with it. When you were put under the pressures of the road, either you took it seriously or you took it as a joke. Which meant that eventually— it was a very slow process, and it shifted and changed, and it is so impossible to describe—but in the last year or so, when Brian was almost totally incapacitated all of the time, he became a joke to the band. It was the only way we could deal with it without gettin' mad at him. So then it became that very cruel, piss-taking thing behind his back all the time. It all came to a head when . . . he was with Anita at the time, and he started beating her up and kickin' her around. And I said, "Come on, darlin', you don't need this. Let's go. I'll just take you away." I didn't give a shit. I wasn't involved in it at the time. Just, "Let's go. I'll take you out of *this,* at least, then you can do what you want." So we split. It was very romantic—Marrakesh, tramping through the desert and all that crap. I mean, Brian was so ludicrous in some ways and such a nice guy in some ways. It was like they used to say about Stan

Getz: "He's a nice buncha guys." You just never knew which one you were gonna meet.

The Brian-Anita-Keith triangle is a centerpiece of 'Up and Down with the Rolling Stones,' by Tony Sanchez, which came out in 1979. Sanchez described himself as, among other things, your drug procurer, and his description of your lifestyle in those years—late Sixties, early Seventies—is one of almost total dissipation and addiction. Is any or all of this true?

Spanish Tony's book? Let's put it like this: I couldn't plow through it all because my eyes were watering from laughter. But the basic laying out of the story— "He did this, he did that"—is true. Tony didn't really write it. He had some hack from Fleet Street write it; obviously, Tony can hardly write his own name, you know? He was a great guy. I always considered him a friend of mine. I mean, not *anymore.* But I understand his position: He got into dope, his girlfriend OD'd, he went on the skids and . . . it's all this shit, you know? As far as that book's concerned, as far as, like, a particular episode, just the *bare facts*—yeah, they all happened. But by the time you got to the end, it was like *Grimm's Fairy Tales*—with emphasis on the *grim.* It's really all old stuff. You know, there are certain showbiz clichés that always seem to hold true. One is that there's no such thing as bad publicity, and the other is that the show must go on, right?

Have you seen Sanchez since the book came out?

Yeah, a couple of years ago.

Did you punch his lights out, or what?

No. I showed him a new shooter I'd gotten. I haven't seen him since.

What's become of Anita? Is she all right?

Yeah, she's fine, man. She's *fine.* I don't consider myself separated from Anita or anything. She's still the mother of my kids. Anita is a great, great woman. She's a fantastic person. I love her. I can't *live* with her, you know? I don't know if I really see that much less of Anita now than I ever have. She's in New York.

Doesn't it drive you nuts to live your personal life out in public?

Usually, it's not from within—not from Anita or Patti or myself. It's other people saying, "Oh, we should play this down." Which I'm not interested in doin', because the only way I've ever been able to survive any of this crap is by saying, "Anything you put on your front page, I can top it." Because I'll give you the real lowdown, which is far more interesting. The last thing I want is to seem that I'm hiding anything, or playing a *role.* Sure, you don't want to call up the *Daily News* and say, "Well, last night I screwed . . ."

27

But at the same time, I don't want anybody to think it's worth snooping around in my backyard thinking they're gonna pick up anything that they wouldn't learn by asking me.

As far as my relationships go, with Anita or anybody—I don't understand the meaning of separation. It's a legal phrase, that. And since I've never done anything *legally,* or never considered *whether* it's legal or not . . . I mean, I do what I do. The only areas of illegality that I've been involved in are ones that are questionable. Like, the question of victimless crimes. You can say that being a junkie is not really being a criminal, because it's just a law. But then again, junkies are the ones who buy the stuff from the dealers, the dealers make the money off the junkies, and dealers are the ones who go and corrupt the other kids, *da, da, da.* So where does the responsibility begin and end? I don't know. I don't really *care,* because it's a fact of life. I mean, all those questions are talked about by people who know *nothing* about it, as you well know. They're the ones who decide to put every patient they get on Methadone—to force them into the belief that if you've taken dope at all, you'd better get on Methadone right away, because you're always gonna need it. But they don't mention that for every patient those clinics get, they get bread from the Feds.

You've tried Methadone?

Only when I couldn't get nothin' else. What a *dopey* drug, you know—dopey in the sense of nondope. What a dopey nondope.

Did heroin affect your music, for better or worse?

Thinking about it, I would probably say, Yeah, I'd probably have been better, played better, off of it. I mean, sometimes people think they play better on dope, but it's . . . in actual fact, when I was onstage playing, or recording, and I was doped up, you know, and I listen to it now—I mean, sometimes I still have to play what I played then. "Right, I've gotta play this goddamn *junkie* music? Me? Now? I've *been* through it." And I still gotta play my junk licks. But I can't imagine what else I would have played, no matter whether I was drunk, on dope or on Preparation H —they sniff it, you know?

The thing about smack is that you don't have any say in it. It's not your decision anymore. You need the dope, that's the only thing. "Why? I like it." It takes the decision off your shoulders. You'll go through all those incredible hassles to get it and think nothing of it. Because that is the number-one priority: first the dope, then you can get home and do anything else that needs doing, like living. If you can.

Did you realize that you were addicted?

Oh, totally, yeah. I accepted that. It took me about two years to get addicted. The first two years, I played around with it. It's the greatest seduction in the world. The usual thing, snort it up. Then: "What do you mean I'm hooked? I've taken it for two days and I feel all right. I haven't had any for . . . *all day.*" And then you think that's cool. And it draws you in, you know?

How do you get off junk?

You just have to want to reach that point. I mean, I kicked it *loads* of times. The problem is not how to get off of it, it's how to *stay* off of it. Yep, that's the one.

Do you still feel drawn toward it?

I always, um . . . never say never. But no, no.

Obviously, some of the Stones' greatest music was made on dope.

Yeah, *Exile on Main Street* was heavily into it. So was *Sticky Fingers.* . . .

Was it difficult for you to record those albums?

No, I mean, especially with the Stones, just because they've been at this sort of point for so long, where they're considered, you know, "the greatest rock & roll band in the world. . . ." [*Laughs.*] God, my God —you gotta be joking. Maybe one or two nights, yeah, you could stick them with that. My opinion is that on any given night, it's a different band that's the greatest rock & roll band in the world, you know? Because consistency is fatal for a rock & roll band. It's *gotta* go up and down. Otherwise, you wouldn't know the difference. It would be just a bland, straight line, like lookin' at a heart machine. And when that straight line happens, baby, you're *dead,* you know?

Rock has an awfully high death rate, it seems. Among your contemporaries, John Lennon, Keith Moon, John Bonham—when you see them go, does it worry you?

There are risks in doing anything. In this business, people tend to think it'll never happen to them. But what a way to make a living, you know? Looking at the record over the last twenty-odd years, it goes without saying, I should think, that there is a very high fatality rate in the rock & roll music business. Look at the list, man, look at who's been scythed down: Hank Williams, Buddy Holly, Elvis, Gene Vincent, Eddie Cochran. The list is endless. And the *greats,* a lot of the greats have gone down. *Otis,* man. I mean, that one killed soul music.

I've always felt that Jimi Hendrix was the greatest loss. Did you know him?

Fairly well. By the period of his demise—to put it politely—he was at the point of totally putting down and negating everything that had made him what he was. I mean all the psychedelic stuff. He felt like he'd been forced to do it over and over again so many times, just because that's what he was known for. When I first heard him, he was playing straight-ahead R&B.

When was that?

I first heard him on the road with Curtis Knight, and then I used to see him play at a club called Ondine's in New York.

What did you think when you first heard him?

I thought I was watching someone just about to break. But as far as his being a guitar player, I mean, I was disappointed when the records started comin' out. Although, given the time and that period, and given the fact that he was forced into an "English psychedelic bag" and then had to live with it because that's what made him . . . one of the reasons that he was so down at the period when he died was because he couldn't find a way out of that. He wanted to just go back and start playing some funky music, and when he did, nobody wanted to know.

It was a weird period.

Yeah. Everybody got sort of carried on this tidal wave of success for doing outlandish things, until what they were really known for was the outlandishness of what they were doing and not *really* what they were doing. I mean, even with *Satanic Majesties,* I was never *hot* on psychedelic music.

Everybody's always put 'Their Satanic Majesties Request' down, but I've been listening to a clean copy of it recently, and there's some good stuff on there, despite the ridiculous mix.

The only thing I can say, from the Stones' point of view, is that it was the first album we ever made off the road. Because we stopped touring; we just burned up by 1966. We finished *Between the Buttons,* you know, "Let's Spend the Night Together," and *boom,* we stopped working for like a year and a half. And in that year and a half, we had to make another album. And that was insane—on acid, busted, right? It was like such a fractured business, a total alien way of working to us at the time. So it kind of reflects. It's a fractured album. There are some good bits, and it's weird, and there's some real crap on it as well.

Has having kids changed you at all? Your son, Marlon, is almost a teenager now, right?

Just about, yeah. He's beatin' the shit out of me. It's gotten to the point now, in the last few months, where I've noticed he's coming up and *reprimanding* me, you know? *"Dad!* Get up! There's a rehearsal. They're *waitin'!"* And I'm takin' it—I'm *takin'* it! "Yeah, okay, I'm ready. Give me my jeans." And he says, "Oh, *yeah*—you *look* like you're ready. You got one eye closed!" I don't really have to worry about Marlon, he's so together. I mean, he's been on the road since he was about a year old, so to him this is all totally normal. He used to crash out to "Midnight Rambler" every night behind my amp, you know?

It's nice not to have to be a disciplinarian.

Yeah. Or only if something's really grating on my hangover. But I've been lucky. I've never been forced into that position of saying, "Now look here, son, you can't do that." I'm still half waiting for my own old man to start knocking me about—"Bloody rock & roll! You fool!" *Bash!*

Your dad's still alive?

Yeah. I have not seen him. Occasionally, I write him a letter: "I really want to get together with you again," you know? And I get a really nice letter back. He's a great guy, but very hard to get to know. He was born in 1914, and I didn't have anything to say to him when I was eighteen. It was a total standoff, you know? And so I left home and got the band together with Mick and Brian.

Has your father ever seen Marlon?

No, no. I know what I should do, man, I know. I'm workin' on it now. In fact, I'm glad you asked me that. You reminded me, 'cause I sent him a letter about a month ago, saying, "If you wanna come over . . ." Either that or send him a ticket and say the plane's leaving, get your passport and get your ass over here. He's only been out of England once, and that was to France to get his leg blown up. The Anglo-American tour of Normandy, they called it.

Judging by some of the songs on 'Tattoo You,' your and Mick's attitudes toward women seem to have changed somewhat. With the exception of "Little T&A," that is . . .

Well, that song's just about every good time I've had with somebody I'd met for a night or two and never seen again. And also about the shit that sometimes goes down when you just sort of bump into people unknowingly, and not knowing the scene you're walking in on, you know? You pick up a chick and end up spending the night in the *tank,* you know?

On the other hand, "Black Limousine," for instance, seems more generous in its appraisal of a past relationship. Quite vulnerable, really.

Yeah, because time marches on, et cetera. And also, I guess, because the women in our lives at the moment have made a change in our attitudes toward it. I guess because everything that comes out from the Stones is just as it comes out. I mean, you just turn on the tap and it *pours* out. That's how we used to feel about it, and that's how we feel about it now. This is purely a guess, because I haven't really thought about it, but it seems logical that the people you're with are the ones who are gonna influence you most, whether you intend it or not. Mick might intend to sit down and write a real Stones song—you know: "*Blechhh!* You cruddy piece of shit, you dirty old scrub box!" But obviously, that's not the way he's feeling now. It's not the way I'm feeling now.

Would it be fair to say that you're both in love?

Oh, yeah. But I've *always* been in love.

It seems like you and Patti, though . . .

It's a big one, it's a big one. Yeah. It doesn't matter, I'll tell ya—yeah, I'm in love. Those are the things that, when you're at the other end of the scale, you know, and you think, "Oh, god*damn,* you can only be in love when you're eighteen or twenty-three or . . . But then you get older and suddenly—*bang!* One again! And you realize that was all a load of crap. And those are the things that turn you on, you know? Those are the things that make you look forward, keep you going. You say, well, if it *can* happen, keep on going. I mean, it's the greatest feeling in the world, right?

Love is good!

Love wears a white Stetson.

4

Bill Murray

INTERVIEWED BY
TIMOTHY CROUSE (1984)

Bill Murray stepped into the vacuum briefly created by Chevy Chase's departure from the original cast of 'Saturday Night Live,' and has gone on to become the most artistically interesting survivor of the early lineups. One wouldn't call Murray a comedian in the traditional sense of the stand-up performer. Instead, his trademark is a comic persona that seems to have been forged in some extraterrestrial dimension. It's all irony and attitude, and one that blossoms in improvisation. Murray has made some, shall we say, routine movies ('Meatballs,' 'Stripes'), but he, personally, has been great in them. He gave the only really uproarious performance in 'Ghostbusters,' one of the biggest summer-comedy megahits of the decade. And he also turned up, uncredited, as Dustin Hoffman's pal in 'Tootsie,' another smash, essaying a cameo part that had no relation to the picture's plot, but one in which Murray was terrific. He is a filmmaker's dream: an actor who can crack up an audience just by walking into a scene.

Like the painters who founded the surrealist movement, Murray—the most surrealistic comic actor now working in mainstream films—is the product of a staunch Catholic background. Which means, inevitably, that he also has a Serious Side—one that he unveiled in his only real non-hit to date, 'The Razor's Edge.' ROLLING STONE sent interview vet Timothy Crouse to probe this somber aspect of the Murray persona in 1984, but he, too, returned laughing.

—K. L.

THE HIT MOVIE *Ghostbusters* had just opened when I did the first of several interview sessions with Bill Murray in early June. The week before, entertainment reporters from all over the country had been flown into New York, and Murray had done his conscientious bit to publicize the picture, giving at least seventy-five interviews in two days. He was exhausted.

He was also very happy. The film had opened to generally enthusiastic reviews, grossing over $13 million in its first weekend. The critics had consistently singled out his performance as the film's strongest asset. He had starred before in summertime comedy hits—*Meat-*

balls and *Stripes*—but this was something else. Overnight, a consensus seemed to have formed, not just in the movie business, but in the public's mind as well, that Murray had joined the ranks of those stars whose presence in a film makes all the difference.

This special status, only just acquired, will soon be tested. Before making *Ghostbusters,* Murray had spent about five months in England, France and India playing the part of Larry Darrell, a seeker after truth, in a remake of the classic 1946 film version of Somerset Maugham's 1944 novel *The Razor's Edge.* (The title comes from the Katha-Upanishad: "The sharp edge of a razor is difficult to pass over; thus the wise say the path to Salvation is hard.") At the time of the interviews, the film was still being edited. It opens in October. Murray says that his performance emphasizes Larry Darrell's sense of humor, but the part is unalterably dramatic, and it remains to be seen whether the public will accept such a radical departure from the comic roles for which Murray has become known.

The first of our sessions took place on an oppressively humid day at the house Murray rents at Sneden's Landing, on the Hudson River, a short drive from Manhattan. The house is a renovated green barn, with additions. A white gallery running across part of the second story gives it a Russian look.

When I arrived, Murray was off attending a birthday party with his two-year-old son, Homer. I walked over to the party with Murray's wife, Mickey, who used to work as a talent coordinator for *The Dick Cavett Show* and is now a full-time mother. Mickey took charge of Homer, and Murray and I got into his Wagoneer and drove to a roadhouse he likes on the Hudson. He bought me lunch. When I tried to pay my own way, he checked me with a favorite dictum of Dan Aykroyd's: "You don't pull coin in my town."

After lunch, we dropped in at a local garage to see how repairs on Murray's old Rambler were coming along, and then stopped by the post office and the library. As the afternoon progressed, Murray occasionally lapsed into brooding silences. This somber side of his personality was a revelation, and it has since occurred to me that it may provide a bass line against which his comic improvisations seem all the more spontaneous and abandoned.

Back at the house, Murray took a shower and emerged with slicked-back hair, suavely smoking a pink cigarette with a gold filter. He jumped on the powerfully built Homer and pretended to eat him. Homer squealed, "Enough! Enough!" We went outside and sat down under some walnut trees to begin the interview. Homer came out and aimed a squirting garden hose at some bed sheets hanging on a clothesline. The Jamaican housekeeper, Eda, yelled at him to stop, but it didn't really matter—it had started to rain. We then retired to the second-story gallery. No sooner was the tape recorder turned on than the sky exploded with a resounding peal. The interview was shouted over a thunderstorm out of the Catskills that would have awakened Rip van Winkle.

The other two sessions were conducted on the terrace of Murray's sunny, sparsely furnished penthouse on the Upper East Side of Manhattan. During the first session, when the sun grew hot, Murray bunched up his aloha shirt and put it on his head like a hat. Before the second, he fortified himself with his favorite sandwich: peanut butter, lettuce and mayonnaise on pumpernickel.

At the time of these interviews, I had just finished reading *Wired,* Bob Woodward's book about John Belushi, and I couldn't help being struck by the contrast between Belushi's life and Murray's. Both actors grew up in suburbs of Chicago, began their careers with the Second City improvisational company and went on to make their names on *Saturday Night Live.* But—at least according to *Wired*—success unnerved Belushi, drove him to drugs in search of the confidence he never possessed and brought out the boor and the bully in him.

Murray seems not to suffer from these afflictions. Whether or not he takes the occasional drug, I couldn't say, but drugs obviously form no important part of his life. Boorishness is not his style. His manners—perhaps a vestige of his Catholic upbringing—are often elegant. (He's the only man my age who has ever held my coat for me.) His attention is focused largely on others: his wife, son, brothers, sisters. He's interested in spiritual disciplines, and they seem to have had a salutary effect on him.

One senses that he's achieved at least the beginnings of an inner balance and is not easily thrown by outside events (though he still does get upset when the housekeeper shrinks his good socks). Seeing him deal with fans in the street (who accost him about once every five yards), one gets the impression that Murray has learned the ancient trick of watching himself with amused detachment. He now possesses the only magic that can protect a pilgrim passing through the flames of Hollywood—a genuine sense of humor.

I know that you come from Chicago, but I'd be interested to know your social background.

That's tough to call. My father was a lumber-company salesman, and he got promoted to vice-president about six months before he died. He was just about to start making the dough.

When did he die?

He died December 1969, when I was seventeen. I was a junior in high school. He never made a lot of money, and we had nine kids in the family, so even a lot of money wouldn't have made much difference. I grew up in a suburb called Wilmette, and people had money there, but we weren't among them.

Did everyone work to help support the family?

Well, it wasn't like that. My father did it, really. We paid our way through high school, 'cause we all went to a Catholic school—except for two of my brothers, who were heathens and went to public school. My brothers and I, we would caddy in the summer, and my sisters would baby-sit.

Where do you fit into the family constellation?

Fifth. I like to say that they peaked with me, and it was all downhill after that. I was sort of in an odd spot, but I guess everybody thought they were in an odd spot in our family. I had the misfortune of reaching adolescence at a time when the world turned upside down, and I somehow had to represent the changing society to my parents—with limited success. I was speaking for the entire culture, everyone from Tim Leary to the Airplane.

Were you a problem in school?

Well, the schools are still standing. But I was an underachiever and a screw-off. I remember I took the National Merit Scholarship Test, and I scored high enough to win, but when I got the score back, there was an asterisk next to my name, meaning I had qualified for the National Merit Scholarship but wouldn't get one because I wasn't in the top half of my class. Which was devastating, really bad news, 'cause my father would have loved to have heard that somebody was going to come up with the money for college.

What was the matter with you in school?

This is the same conversation I had with my teachers then. "What's wrong, Bill? Something bothering you? Something wrong at home?" I don't know, I just didn't care for school much. Studying was boring. I was lazy. I'm still lazy. And I had no interest in getting good grades. In grade school, I was basically causing trouble all the time. But not very serious trouble. When I got to high school, I started to meet a more sophisticated kind of troublemaker. I mean, these guys were really smart—with 148 IQs—and really nuts, the first guys that got kicked out of our school for grass. They just traveled on a different plane than the general Jesuit "all right you'll study tonight, you'll crack them, you'll come in and you'll shut up" sort of attitude. I mean, you couldn't have long hair in our school, so these guys would let their hair grow really long and grease it down so it looked like it was short, and you'd see them on the weekends, and you couldn't believe how much hair they had, 'cause they'd washed it. They put up with all the grief that the preppie crowd gave them for being greasers, and they didn't care. Because come the weekend, they were doing a completely different thing than the guys from Wilmette who were trying to drink beer and get high. They didn't have any interest in being part of the social scene at this preppie Catholic school. They were downtown, stoned, listening to blues.

So where were you? Were you downtown at the blues joints?

Well, no, I was not. I was basically in the middle. It was all right, because I got to look at both sides. I didn't know from downtown and the blues joints, but at the same time, I didn't have enough money to really have a lot of fun. I didn't have a car; I didn't have a driver's license until God knows when. So I basically relied on friends; they were my wheels. Or I'd take a bus or hitchhike. And in the suburbs, that's really low-balling it. Everybody else's parents drove them, or they had their own car. My parents just looked at me: "Your brother hitchhiked to school, and *you'll* hitchhike to school."

Were you close to the people in your family?

I was pretty close to my sister Peggy. She was the one close to me in age.

What has she become?

She's become a parody of herself. No, she lives in the suburbs, and she's got three kids. She's an activist. She's about as active as anybody can get. She drops out of bed rolling. Gets a lot done. She always was that way. So when I went into my bad phase, in college, she had no time for me. At that point, the only decent relationship I had in the house was with the dog.

What was the dog like?

The dog was the greatest dog in the world. Cairn terrier, one of those little dogs. My mother's dog. He was one of these dogs that will play fetch forever. And he just loved to go for walks. I would take him for walks to Evanston, about a fifteen-mile walk. His feet would be sore, but he would love it. This was my bad period. Everybody had left the house. My oldest brother was in the Air Force, my second oldest brother was living downtown, one sister was in the convent, another sister had moved away somewhere.

My day would basically begin around twelve or one. I'd wake up, and I'd eat like about eight fried eggs and about half a loaf of toast, and then I'd drink about half a gallon of milk, and then I'd hang around, I'd read, I'd listen to the radio, I'd make a few phone calls. And then, at about 5:30 or six, when my mother was going to come home, I'd split. And I'd come back around four or five in the morning. I'd be lying there in bed, and my mother would scream at me, "I want you here when I get back."

I'd have been downtown, hanging out with my brother Brian Doyle-Murray. Also, I had friends who went to Northwestern. I'd walk the streets of Evanston all night long. Walk home or ride home on the subway in the middle of the night. It was so cold in the winter, I would just jump in front of cars to get them to give me a ride. And they were so scared, so glad I didn't have a gun, they'd give me a ride home.

When was the first time that you figured out that you might want to be an actor?

Well, I was in *The Caine Mutiny* at school. I played Keefer, a sleaze guy who rats on everybody. It wasn't much of a part. The only great thing about it was that you got to get out of class for a few hours, and that was like getting a three-day leave in the Army, because class was hell.

Then they had another show, *The Music Man.* I auditioned for the part of the Music Man because I could sing. I auditioned for the part with two other guys, but someone else got it. Then we three auditioned for the barbershop quartet, and we got those parts. One day after school, I walked by the school theater, and there were girls in there, and I just walked in. It was an all-boys school, you know, so it was like, *girls*—you wanted to take your clothes off. They were attractive girls, too, and they were wearing almost no clothes, 'cause it was a dance audition. A woman turned around and said, "Now, who's going to audition to be a dancer?" I just jumped up and said, "I'm a dancer." And people were like, "Huh? What? Come on." So I went up onstage. I just wanted to sort of stand behind these girls, really, get as close as I could. I did my little audition, just clowning around, really. The woman said, "Okay, you, you, you and you," and she pointed to me, and I was in. So I told my friends, "Hey, I'm not going to be in the barbershop quartet—I'm a dancer now." They said, "What? *Why?*" I said, "I don't know, man, I don't know. It's just an instinct."

It turned out to be a good move, because the dancers rehearsed at night. The dancers rehearsed at 7:30, 'cause the dance instructor was a real dancing teacher, and her only time was between 7:30 and ten at night. So it meant that I would go home, eat dinner and say, "Mom, I gotta go out." And I would leave the house, which was even better than leaving school. I would get to go out for three hours, and it turned out that the dancers were like the kind of people I was telling you about who were misfits in that school. They were slightly nuts and had different tastes in all areas. We had just incredible times. Sometimes the dance teacher would say, "I have to leave early," and we'd go, "Oh, that's too bad; that means we just have another hour to drink gin out of Coke bottles and jive down with these girls; that's just too damn bad." And I'd come home half-snookered on gin and Coke, and my mom would say, "How was it?" and I'd say, "Uh, I hurt my foot." She was thinking I was Baryshnikov or something, since I was so dedicated. I had the greatest time of my high-school career doing that show, so I got hooked on show business.

What was your next step?

Well, I took one acting class in college, 'cause I

thought it'd be a piece of cake and there were a lot of girls in it. I knew I could act as good as these girls could, just by seeing them around the coffee shop. And I figured if you were a man and went into a course that was mostly women, you couldn't get a worse grade than your co-star. And all these girls were getting good grades, because the teacher was kind of working the ropes. He was running "the artist one" by them —you know, "Oh, yes, I am an artist." But when class was over, he was lonely and so on. So as long as you never looked funny at him while he was staring at a girl, you got a good grade. But I only hung in there for one semester. That was that.

So, still there was no star that you were following.

Still no star I was following. And it really only happened because my brother Brian started acting, and I went and started seeing him. Brian is five years older than I am. After high school—when I was still a grade-school punk—he vanished. He went to school out in California for a while and then quit and became a railroad switchman. He put a couple cars into San Francisco Bay once, but I guess all railroad men do something like that. He did a lot of weird things.

When my father died, Brian came back and was supposed to support the family. He got a good job, and if he'd stayed in it, he'd have ended up a very wealthy man. But after six months, he quit the job and went to work at Second City. He had started by taking workshops there, and then he went to work there full time. That drove my mother completely around the bend. She couldn't believe it.

Brian lived in Old Town, where all the hippies were, and I started hanging out at his place. That's where I met Harold Ramis and John Belushi and Joe Flaherty and Del Close, who directed the show, and Bernie Sahlins, who ran Second City. They thought I was a riot—weekend hippie, you know, going back to my straight life in the 'burbs every night.

I had good friends at Northwestern, and I would drag them down there, and we would all weasel our way into the show for free and watch. After you'd seen the show a hundred times, they couldn't really expect you to pay.

Were you and Brian the family cutups?

No, everybody was a cutup. Everybody was funny.

Was your father funny?

He was real funny, and he was a very tough laugh. He was very tough to make laugh. He was very dry, very dry. He sure as hell wasn't going to laugh unless it was really funny.

My father's father was the real nut. He was crazy till the day he died. He lived to be ninety. He was the kind of guy who had the light-up bow tie. But you'd really have to beat on him to get that bow tie out there. He would do it only at the most tastefully tasteless occasions.

He was a real good man, my grandfather. He always had licorice in his pocket, and he always had a Budweiser and a Camel. He had false teeth. There was always a baby in our family, and he'd always say, "Come here, little baby." And then he'd pop out his teeth exactly like the ghost in *Ghostbusters* and just scare the hell out of the baby. My mother'd get really pissed at him. "Grandpa! How could you scare him like that?" He wouldn't say anything; he'd just drink his beer.

Is your mother funny?

Well, I didn't used to think she was funny, but now I realize she's like completely out of control, nuts. I just never noticed it. I sort of took it all seriously, you know, and acted like it was normal. Now I realize that she's funny to watch at least sixty percent of the time, like the way it's funny to watch a baby panda fall over stuff in the zoo. I finally started taping her phone calls when I worked on *Saturday Night Live*. I couldn't believe that someone could go on like that, and I realized that I'd been listening to that my whole life. I mean, you can really hear her mind work. I steal her stuff all the time.

Can you think of an example?

Well, not really. I mean, I steal so much that sometimes Brian will laugh, and he'll say, "Mother." If I'd started paying attention to my mother when I was twelve instead of trying to sneak out of the house and avoid her, not only could I have handled her a little better, but I could have gotten a much better education about women and about people. But it was a fear of the unknown, I guess. Now she's become a show-business mother. She's gone around the bend. I remember when she came out to Hollywood one time, and we took her to the Polo Lounge. Brian called Doug Kenney [co-founder of the *National Lampoon* and co-writer of *National Lampoon's Animal House*] and said, "Page my mother at the Polo Lounge." So this guy who looks like a Mexican general walks through saying, "Lucille Murray, Lucille Murray" at the top of his lungs, and the entire Polo Lounge is looking around for Lucille Murray, and she gets up to, like *visual applause* from the entire crowd. And all of a sudden, she just like snapped. She started talking like *Photoplay* magazine circa 1959, about Eddie Fisher and Liz Taylor and Richard Burton and all this stuff. For about six or seven weeks she was completely around the corner. She would call me up and say stuff like, "Well, they have to come to *you* now." I mean, we'd taken her into our dark little world, and now she was a show-business authority. It was insane. This was my mother, this was the woman who'd said to me, "Couldn't you be happy doing community theater?" And now she was cutting my deal for me.

When had she said that about community theater?

Just in the beginning, after Second City. Maybe she said it to Brian, actually. She didn't see any money in acting, even though Brian had gotten good reviews in Chicago and was really great in the show. Or it may have been in the period when he'd gone out to Hollywood and tried to get different kinds of work and was starving again. She said, "This is not working. Couldn't you try community theater?" She wanted him to do anything to make some dough. "Fine, you're having a ball, but I still have an eight-year-old to feed at home." I mean, how she managed to get all the rest of the family raised is amazing. How my father did it on the little money *he* made was amazing.

It must have been around the time we've been speaking of—say, 1971—that you first met John Belushi. As I'm sure you know, Bob Woodward's book 'Wired' portrays Belushi as very talented but also as one of the most obnoxious people of the age. Would you care to comment on that?

Well, I haven't read the book. I've gotten tired of defending Belushi. Of saying, "Well, the picture that's been drawn of him is not accurate." So let me try something new. Maybe he's going to become a historical figure like Captain Bligh, and they'll keep doing remakes of the story. Like there'll be another *Wired*, which will say his problem was that he was exercising too much. That these fitness regimes that he went on, karate classes and all that, really made him snap, and he was just an Albanian and they're not supposed to exercise, they're just supposed to eat and talk and make jokes. Which I think is just as viable an explanation for whatever happened, or will be in a hundred years, because by then it won't matter how he died, because obviously he would have been dead by then anyway. But whatever he did that made him important enough to last that long will make him interesting.

I don't remember the exact circumstances of how we met. But he was young, and he was funny, and he was really free on the stage. He didn't have the same sort of technique as anybody else. He would just make great choices.

What do you mean by "choices"?

Well, the way he would react in a scene, especially improvising. There'd be several people onstage thrash-

ing around, trying to figure out exactly what was happening. And rather than thrash in the conventional way, Belushi would be thinking, thinking very fast, and he would make an active choice, rather than a combative sort of word-game choice. He would polarize the scene one way or the other. He'd make a decision to do something, and as soon as he did it, it was such a strong move that the entire scene just shifted to that direction. It wasn't necessarily always stealing a scene—he'd make a choice, and all of a sudden all the other parts would fall right in. Sometimes he'd be the center of it, sometimes he'd make the others the center. It never looked like he was thinking furiously. It was almost like a martial art. To have a guy who could do that was like having one guy who could swim. He's your best friend.

When did you first work with Belushi?

I might have improvised with him once or twice at Second City. But I didn't work with him until I got to New York. It was on the *National Lampoon Radio Hour*. John was one of the producers. He dragged all these people out to New York—Flaherty and Harold and Brian—and got them on the radio. A lot of people stayed at his place. Then he put *The National Lampoon Show* together, and we went on tour—Philadelphia, Ontario, Toronto, Long Island. That was in 1975. Later we opened off-Broadway in a place called the New Palladium. I was Belushi's roommate on the road. We drank a lot of Rolling Rock in those days.

You mean you weren't doing coke all night long?

No, no, no. We didn't have any money to do coke. Coke wasn't a big deal anyway at that time.

Were you doing any drugs?

Oh, smoking grass. But basically we were juicers at that time. At most of these gigs, we got free drinks, so we drank. We were still starving actors, so we had to get whatever perks we could get. We drank Champa Tampas at the New Palladium, champagne and orange juice. It was a special there. And it's a great drink to work on, because it's got that sugar pump, and it's nice and cold. And the air conditioning was no good in that place, and we were just drenched with sweat. After three shows on a Saturday night, you'd literally have to wrap up your shirt in a paper bag and put it inside a plastic bag.

Everybody in the show was good: Belushi, Gilda Radner, my brother Brian, Harold Ramis, Joe Flaherty and later Richard Belzer. One night something happened and I came late, so I got to watch the scenes. And it was the funniest show I'd ever seen in my life. They were the funniest people in the world. I was laughing so hard. And I'd already done the show for three and a half months.

How did you get from the Lampoon show to 'Saturday Night Live'?

Well, while we were in the stage show, they started to cast *Saturday Night Live with Howard Cosell* and *Saturday Night Live* at the same time. People from both programs would come and watch our show. We all auditioned for Lorne Michaels of *Saturday Night Live*. Things dragged on and on, and Brian and I and Belushi were going to take the job on *Saturday Night Live with Howard Cosell,* 'cause it didn't look like Michaels was going to hire us. Then Belushi got hired for *Saturday Night Live,* and Brian and Chris Guest and I took a job on *Saturday Night Live with Howard Cosell.* Everybody else was on the other show. So we were on TV, and they were on TV. But they were the show, and we were on with the Chinese acrobats and elephants and all sorts of crazy acts, and we would get cut almost every other week. And then that show got canceled, and we got a job working on a documentary that TVTV was making about the Super Bowl. Michael Shamberg was doing it, and he wanted to have funny people doing funny things with the situation.

Then Shamberg asked me if I wanted to work for him on the next couple of documentaries, so I went out to California for nine months. During which time *Saturday Night Live* kept rolling, and Chevy [Chase] left the show, and they wanted somebody new, and they called me up. I'd worked with Gilda and Belushi in the Lampoon show; I'd met Danny [Aykroyd] when we were both in Second City. So they just figured I knew the styles. "We've worked with him. He's all right."

What was it like coming on as the new guy?

Well, it was tough. I had to spend about six months being the second cop, second FBI guy. The first week I was on, they gave me sort of a test. They gave me a lot of stuff to do, and I went crazy, I loved it. I roared. I was there on a look-see basis. I had a three-show deal. It was three shows, see if I can do it. After the first show, Lorne said, "Well, I guess you'll be moving here to New York." So that made me feel good, but then and for the next six months, I didn't have anything to do. They gave me a lot the first week, and then I realized how competitive it really was.

The hard part was, the writers made the show, and the writers didn't know me, so they'd write for who they knew. If you do a great scene one week, the next week the writers would write for you. If you blew a joke in somebody's sketch, you were history. You were invisible. I blew a joke in one of Anne Beatts' sketches, and she still hasn't forgiven me.

What was the joke, and how did you blow it?

We were four guys running clubs, and I was opening a new bar called the Not Just a Meat-Rack Bar. I blew the line. I had the office right next to hers, and she wouldn't even look at me for at least six weeks. It was like that. If you blew a joke, people didn't trust you. If you blew a joke, what you basically did was you failed to get this writer's joke to 20 million people that were watching the show. Twenty million people would have laughed if you'd said those words properly. It was very serious. And I blew one of Michael O'Donoghue's jokes. It was the Burger King sketch. The counterman said, "How do you want yours? We'll make it any way you want it." And I was supposed to say, "I want mine with the blood of a Colombian *cocoi* frog on it." What happened was I went out there and for the heck of it, I wore this brand-new yellow silk baseball jacket that someone had given me. It was the most beautiful thing I've ever seen in my life. I said, "I'll wear it in the sketch. I look so damn good in it." We'd rehearsed the sketch, done it in blocking, so on and so forth. For the real show they put stage blood into this Colombian-frog burger, and whoever it was sprayed blood all over this jacket. I just about went nuts. I guess I blew the line first, then they sprayed the blood all over me. This is my classic *Saturday Night* story. They sprayed the blood all over me, completely destroyed the jacket, I had blood all over my hands, and I had two minutes to get out of this clothing. Taking off the jacket, I got blood all over everything. I had two minutes to get on a wig, a mustache on my lips and a pillow in my stomach to look like Walter Cronkite. And all this stuff was being done while the band was playing "Contusion," by Stevie Wonder, at top volume. The makeup guys were fighting about how much gray to put in my hair. I'd blown O'Donoghue's joke, and I was now in danger of blowing myself completely out, because I had this huge pillow and it never fit; the zipper didn't close. There was blood still all over my hands and the wig and everything. The band screeched to a halt, and the guy said, "Five seconds." And I went absolutely crazy. I went absolutely hysterical. I shrieked like a banshee, and the audience started laughing. They said, "This guy's having a breakdown." But then I pulled it together, and I was funny in the sketch, and that was really when I realized that it could be fun because it was so ridiculous. That was when I finally relaxed. But I had to blow a big joke in order to do it.

Let's take a big jump over six comedy movies to the present. Now you're doing your first straight role in 'The Razor's Edge'—and not only is it a straight role, but it's the story of a man on a spiritual quest. How did you get into that kind of a project?

Well, I'd become friends with John Byrum, the director and writer [*Heart Beat* and *Inserts*]. We wanted to do something together because we got along. I liked the way he talked about Hollywood. He says terrible things about Hollywood and everything in it. And he used to make me laugh talking about that, so I figured that he knew what he was talking about when it came to movies. We grew up about a mile apart from each other, so we had a lot in common without ever talking about it. He had a couple of projects I didn't particularly want to do. Then he sent a book to my house, and it was *The Razor's Edge*. I'd never read it, and I read about fifty pages or so, and I said, "This is great, this is what I want to do." I called him up, and I called up a guy at Columbia, Shel Schrager, and said, "I'd like to do this." And he was encouraging. John said he'd been planning to do it for ten years. He said that he wanted me to work with him on the screenplay, and John had a reputation for not letting anybody change a word of anything he wrote. So we started talking about it, and I suggested that we should work under the most difficult conditions we could find— like bars and places where there was a lot of activity.

Why did you suggest that?

Well, I believe that good things come from difficult conditions, and I thought that no matter how badly we did, at least we'd have the experience of trying to concentrate on one thing while being distracted all the time. So we would work in bars where the jukebox would be on, and places where there were a lot of people. We were constantly being interrupted by people coming over and saying, "Hey, aren't you on *Saturday Night Live?*" and stuff.

We traveled around. We went to practically all the restaurants and bars in the tri-state area—Manhattan, New Jersey, upstate, southern New York—and we'd try to work. Then, after a while, it got so we couldn't work at home; it was too distracting. So we would take trips. We both had to get in shape. I weighed about 205 pounds. So we went to spas like Calistoga, above San Francisco, and we'd sit in the mud baths, and then we'd go in the mineral baths, and then we'd get a massage, and then we'd work. It got so we could work any time in the day or night. And the finish to it is that we finally ended up in India; we were in a *gompa*—a monastery—in Ladakh, at 17,000, 16,000

feet. And it was chaos, absolute chaos. There were all sorts of Englishmen running around screaming and monks saying, "You can't do this, you can't do that." There were Moslems. We were in the middle of almost a religious war. John and I just sat down on the bottom step of this place and talked like there was nothing going on at all. And I said, "You know, we're the only people here that are prepared for this." It was great. We ended up being not taken by all the distraction.

How many times did you read the book?

We kept using it as a reference. I probably read it . . . twice, three times maybe. I carried it around with me for a few months, and sometimes I'd just open it the way you open some sort of mystic book—just open at a page and read. I got the story right away, I think.

What was the story that you got?

Well, the story I got was of a guy who sees that there's more to life than just making a buck and having a romantic fling. I'd experienced that, and I knew what that was, so I had my own ideas about how it played. We wanted to update it, make it more modern in attitude, if nothing else, even though it is a period movie. There are things in it that came from our own lives or that were happening to us while we were doing the movie.

Like what?

Like, it was very easy for us to substitute [*laughing*] our wives in the role of Isabel, who's the girl who's driving Larry nuts.

Now, Isabel is a girl from a well-to-do Chicago family who has known Larry Darrell since childhood, and loves him, and wants to marry him. Larry comes back from the First World War, and he still loves Isabel, but he doesn't want to get married anymore. He wants to go off and "loaf," as he puts it—that is, to study and think. How do your wives fit the part of Isabel?

[*Laughing*] Well, I'm on dangerous ground here, but at moments they demand regular, socially acceptable behavior. Just at times. Those times really glare, especially when this is what you're thinking about all day. You're thinking about the story when someone says, "We have to go to Such-and-such's party because she invited me. . . ." And if you say, "Well, *you* don't like her; I don't like her—what are we going there for?" all of a sudden, that's why the lady is a tramp.

In the book, at least, Larry goes first to Paris, and then to the north of France, and works in a mine where a fellow worker introduces him to mystical books. He ends up going to the Far East, and finally, in India, he has a spiritual experience of a high order. Did you go to the same parts of India?

No. I don't know why we didn't want to go down to the lowlands, where Larry went. I think we just sort of saw the mountains all the way, you know?

All right, then, what was your Indian experience about?

Well, we went over there first on a reconnoiter to see what it would be like to shoot there. We went to Bombay, and we went to Delhi, and we went to Kashmir, to Srinagar—which was really interesting. The British lived in houseboats on the lake there, because they weren't allowed to own land. We didn't go to Ladakh, in the Himalayas, because we couldn't get in—the weather was bad.

John went back later, with the production manager and the producer and the set designer and the cinematographer. They got into Ladakh that time, and they said, "This is it; this is definitely the ticket. We don't need Bombay; we can double the same thing in Srinagar."

A few months later, we went back to shoot. We spent a week in Delhi and then got on a charter for Srinagar. It was my birthday. As we took off, I was sitting in the back, screaming, *"Yeaugh, yeaugh,"* just whipping this jet to go. I was so excited that we were actually going up to the mountains on my birthday. I've always, always, loved the mountains. I didn't see my first one until I was eighteen, and then I wanted to see them all. But the biggest mountain I'd ever been on was 14,000 feet, and when I read that a *base camp* in the Himalayas is at 14,000 feet, that's when I realized that this would be *the* mountain experience.

So what was Srinagar like?

It's a beautiful place, on a mountain lake. The architecture is straight out of *The Arabian Nights*. They sell rubies and silks on the street. They're strong people up there—Moslems—with blazing blue eyes.

The local production guys had gotten us cars to drive us to the locations. They were old things that looked sort of like Ramblers. There was one car that said "Director," another that said "Producer," and my car said "Hero." And all the kids would run after, going, "Hero! Hero! Hero!" And there would be women leaning out of windows from the third or fourth floor going, "Hero! Hero!" They also built me a trailer, which they were proud of, 'cause they knew movie stars sat in trailers. So they built one on the back of a flatbed truck, which was basically a plywood doghouse with no windows. There was no air in it. The one time I went in there, all the Indians were sleeping in it, 'cause they got used to me not being there, so I just stretched out on the floor.

You next went up to Ladakh.

That's a great flight. You realize just how big the mountains are: You're not flying *over* them, you're flying *between* them. Coming in to land, the plane goes between two mountains, and there is about forty feet of clearance on either side. When the wind comes up, the planes don't go there, because you can lose forty feet in half a second. You've never really lived until you've landed a plane in that shoe box there.

At the airport, we were met by a fleet of black jeeps driven by Tibetan Mongols, who drive like cowboys. A big chain of black jeeps set out and headed toward the monasteries, where we were going to shoot. In sixty miles of the Himalayas, I saw about all the spectacular things I ever saw in the Rockies. It was like a hall of fame of mountain majesty. There were stupas everywhere—these big reliquaries—and monks walking on the road. Then we came over a rise and saw the first *real* mountain. It wasn't Everest or anything, it was just one of the boys, and it was much bigger than the biggest mountain I'd ever seen.

Anyway, we kept driving up, and we started to go past abandoned, fortress-like monasteries. The first one I saw, I thought, "Nobody lives there now, but people did live there for 850 years." It looked kind of frightening. Then I thought, "If *that* one frightens me, what about the ones that have people in them?"

Well, we finally arrived at *our* monastery, the one we were going to stay at. All the equipment trucks were already there—big trucks with crazy paint jobs and horns and spangles and reflectors and lights all over them. It looked like the circus had come to town. You had to walk up a steep path, and you were exhausted, breathing like a dog when you got there, and there were all these monks staring at you. There's a big open courtyard surrounded by a wall painted with creatures from the Buddhist scriptures. They were all painted by the uncle of the man who owned the Yaktail Hotel, where we stayed, in the nearby town of Leh. There was a giant prayer wheel about five feet tall, and there were two sets of giant steps on opposite sides of the courtyard, one leading into the shrine of the giant Golden Buddha and the other leading to the prayer room where they would do the tea service.

It soon became clear that no one on our side was really talking to the monks. In fact, I had the impression that we'd come unannounced. Pretty soon, difficulties began to arise, and nobody seemed to know how to address them. The crew spoke Londonese or Cockney, we spoke American, the production manager from India spoke Hindi, his assistant director spoke some sort of curds and whey, and it was like the tower of Babel. Nobody on our side spoke Ladakhi, which is a language that's spelled exactly like Tibetan but pronounced differently. We were always looking around over our shoulder like, "They're gonna kill us," and sure enough, things got out of hand right away.

We had these young boys to play junior monks. We'd hired them in Srinagar. Typical movie stuff: "Can we have your son for two weeks, madam? We're gonna shave his head." So we put these kids in monk's robes, shaved their heads and gave them cute little prayer wheels, and we set up to shoot them walking across the courtyard of the monastery. The monks were watching from the upper window, checking us out. Whoever was in charge there had obviously picked out the number-one zealot and told him to keep an eye on the movie crew, because suddenly this insane Buddhist monk, who couldn't have been more than twenty-one, started screaming and yelling and coming down like a fighting cock on this completely stoned-out Indian assistant director. Our A.D.'s were basically stoned on hash the whole time, which was disconcerting. Then more of their guys got into it, and more of our guys, and pretty soon it was screaming, all-out war.

It turned out that our little monks were turning their prayer wheels the wrong way. It was a major thing to them, like, "Just a second, Jesus is supposed to be *right side up* on that crucifix, you know." The monks were going crazy. And then one of the guys, who could speak almost every language ever invented, said, "Well, what do you expect, these kids are *Moslems*." Which was like, "I'll throw a little gasoline on the barbecue." They went really crazy. That was when Byrum and I were just sitting on the steps like nothing was going on at all. It was our English A.D.—who eventually snapped and completely lost his mind—who found a way to settle this thing with the monks. "Do you have any young boys who would be interested in being in the movies?" he asked them. So we hired four Buddhist kids from the neighborhood, and they spun their wheels the right way.

We'd also needed an older man to play the high lama. They were reading actors for it in London, and I said, "Look, we're going to find the guy over there; don't worry about it. We're not going to hire Ben Kingsley to play this part; we're going to find a real guy to do this." Well, we found the guy—he was the uncle of the owner of the Yaktail Hotel, the same guy who did the paintings—but he didn't speak a word of English. So then we needed a Ladakhi who spoke English, to teach him his lines, but we couldn't find anyone. But the hotel owner had given me the address

of this monk who worked up at some school center and spoke English. He turned out to be younger than me, and his name was Chiptan Chostock, but we called him Tip. Tip spoke English, Hindi, Ladakhi, Tibetan, Kashmiri—you name it. He would huddle together with the old guy and repeat the line, "You are closer than you think," over and over. They did it for hours at a time. Once Tip arrived, we had no more problems with the monks. It was like, "Hey, he's one of our guys." It was like having an Indian scout. All of a sudden, we had somebody who spoke all of the languages, and the unspoken language, too.

Anyway, he became my partner. He was just so interested in everything. He loved riding in the jeep and looking through the camera. And we put him in the movie. Here's this incredibly spiritual guy who walks 200 miles back and forth between this monastery and the school where he teaches. And these A.D.'s are saying, "Can we get Tippy-Tip in here, please." "Does he need any makeup?" "No, he's very dark already, he'll be fine."

The last night I was there, he said, "I want you to come over to my place." I thought, okay, I'll see where he lives, meet his family; I'll probably have to sign a lot of autographs, have my picture taken with the sisters. So we drive to Tip's father's, which is on the outskirts of Leh, a big house with a garden. We go inside, and I'm thinking that we maybe should have asked the driver in. Tip said, "I did ask him in, but he wouldn't come in because he's a Shiite, and Shiites won't take anything from Buddhists." By this time, Tip's father had appeared, and he said, "But we Buddhists take everything from them." At which point I realized that Tip's father spoke English. Now Tip had gone to a school where he learned with a lot of English people—he learned English from me as well—but there was no explanation for his father's English, because he'd lived in this place for his whole life, and anyone who spoke English had only come but recently, and he didn't have any truck with anybody. He just sort of knew it, intuitively. Which was real spooky, 'cause you got it real clear that this guy spoke the language and wasn't trying.

We sat down and started making buttered tea, and Tip's mother came with various desserts made out of butter. So, after about a gallon and a half of buttered tea, all twelve courses of buttered desserts, they said, "Would you like to stay for dinner?" I thought that was pretty good, considering that these people all weighed about 105 pounds apiece. I said I really had to go back. So, they showed me the house, they took me to the kitchen. It was a dark room, and there were all these Asian faces, and the walls were full of these copper pots covered with carbon, and there was a hole in the ceiling where the smoke went out, and it looked right up to the stars. The stars were very bright, they lit up this room and everybody's faces and all the pots on the wall. And all of a sudden, all the children—there were twelve—sort of materialized out of the walls. The father looked like Fu Manchu—he was the only man I saw over there who was over six feet tall—and I was attacking him and tickling him, and hitting myself on the head with pots, and showing him my stomach, and stuff like that. We were all laughing, and all the sound was going right up through the skylight. There was a perfect exchange of something between the stars and what was happening in the room. I don't think I've ever felt comfortable like that. I felt like if I stayed there longer, something magical would happen, like they'd break down and say, "Okay, Bill, you passed the test; you're one of us." I really wanted to stay there. They were so free, so open. They made you feel that you could act like a fool and not feel bad about it, and they made you feel like there was more to it than that, and if you watched yourself, you'd know even more.

One of the things that makes Maugham's novel so interesting is the very convincing picture it gives of a man who's had some kind of spiritual experience.

Yeah, I'm just thinking you're going to ask me what kind of spiritual experience I've had. Well, I didn't go to Woodstock. I saw a poster for it. I don't know. I had more powerful spiritual experiences back a few years ago, when I had my first encounters with the mountains and the oceans. It was just a matter of being high and seeing a different order—as opposed to whatever the hell I knew when I was eighteen years old. School and lunch. And beer. Aside from those three, I didn't have much experience. And girls. So there was just something different happening. I saw there was something else to see. I can't describe it. It's just a better feeling than usual. And yet it's perfectly ordinary because it's intended to be perfectly ordinary. It's not like lightning bolts hitting you on the head. It's not flying. It's just different.

I heard that you had to agree to do 'Ghostbusters' in order to get the backing for 'The Razor's Edge.' Is that how it worked out?

What happened was, John Byrum and I had *The Razor's Edge* in a developmental stage at Columbia—they'd given us a little dough to write the screenplay, but nobody was getting in to work early to find out

how the rewrites were going. Then Dan Aykroyd called me up with this *Ghostbusters* idea, and I said, "Yeah, this is great." He sent me about seventy-five pages, and within an hour there was a deal. They had a producer, they had a caterer, they had a director, they had everything. But it wasn't at any particular studio yet; it was just a project floating in space. Then all of a sudden, all of the studios found out about it, and they all wanted it. So Dan said, "Well, we gotta get going on this." I said, "Well, you know, I'm really trying to get this other thing done. I'm trying to convince the studio to give us the go." And he said, "Well, tell 'em they can have *Ghostbusters* if they do *The Razor's Edge*." So, another forty-five minutes later, we had a caterer and a producer and a director for *The Razor's Edge*. We went out and shot it last summer. Columbia started getting impatient about *Ghostbusters*. All the time we were in Ladakh, we'd get these messages that were like three days old, saying, "Is Bill finished? He's supposed to be doing *Ghostbusters* on the twenty-fifth." I made the mistake of calling America from Agra, that white building—you know, the Taj Mahal. There's a phone booth at the Taj. They said, "You gotta get right back." I wanted to take ten days off. I was so tired that I couldn't even get out of the hotel room in Delhi for four or five days. I didn't really do anything except sleep. Then I found out that they were going to have the rough version of *The Razor's Edge* ready by the end of the week, so I decided to fly to London and see it. Flew to London, saw it. The next day I got on the Concorde, flew to New York and went from the airport to the set on Madison and Sixty-second Street. I weighed about 171 pounds, I think. I'd lost 35 pounds. So I started eating right away [*laughs*]. A production assistant said, "Do you want a cup of coffee?" And I said, "Yeah, and I want a couple of doughnuts, too."

For the first few weeks, I was getting beaten to go to work. It was like, "Where's Bill?" "Oh, he's asleep." Then they'd send three sets of people to knock on the door and say. "They really want you." I'd stumble out and do something and then go back to sleep. I kept thinking to myself, "Ten days ago I was up there working with the high lamas in a *gompa*, and here I am removing ghosts from drugstores and painting slime on my body." It was kind of tough to get into it for about a month. I thought, "What the hell am I doing here?" I mean, you'd look around on the set in Ladakh, and there were thirty-five monks looking at you, just looking at you. And you realized that they were looking for a reason. It was a reminder all the time. A reminder that you're a man and you're going to die, so you'd better not waste this time here. So, when I got to New York, I would be sitting there looking across the street, and there'd be the entire staff of Diana Ross Productions waving out of the window, then coming over to get autographs. That was the first day on the job. All of a sudden, it was like a whole different world. But after a while it became nice, working on the movie, and I sort of got into the rhythm of Hollywood again, as opposed to Ladakh. It was fun being with Dan and Harold Ramis. Acting-wise, they're fantastic. But also, they're very much aware of the situation, that you are just a guy, and then for thirty seconds or a minute and a half, you're a movie star, and then you're a guy again. And then you're a movie star again. They know the difference, and they see the hilarious things that are happening all around while you're supposedly being a movie star.

What sort of things happen to the movie star?

Well, I don't know, people coming up to me and saying, "Dan, I think you're the greatest; you're the best one on the show." [*Laughs.*] So I would sign Dan's name. Then people would ask him, and he'd sign my name. And all that goofiness. People screaming at you on the street. Like, we were walking down the street in our *Ghostbusters* outfits, and this black guy looks at us and says, "Hey the *wrong* stuff!"

Had you had time to think about your part in 'Ghostbusters' at all? I mean, there you were, wham, off the Concorde, onto the set.

Not a bit. I just did it. Harold and Dan wrote the script. Wherever there wasn't a line, they'd say, "Well, we gotta have a line here." We just made stuff up. When I saw the movie the other night, I realized more of it was improvised than I thought. Especially the action stuff.

I'd never worked on a movie where the script was good. *Stripes* and *Meatballs,* we rewrote the script every single day. I think most movie actors change their lines nowadays. I didn't used to think so. Then I worked

for Dustin Hoffman [in *Tootsie*]. Dustin changed all his lines a lot of the time. He gave a different performance every single take. He shot five different movies. Even if he didn't change the lines, he would change the meaning. How they cut that movie, I don't know. I think it's the only way to work. I don't believe that you can give the same performance every take. It's physically impossible, so why bother? If you don't do what is happening at that moment, then it's not real. Then you're holding something back.

Are you fed up with comedy?

I think all the comedies that we all do, they all get better. And even though they're not perfect or maybe silly to some people, we learn each time about how to do it. People don't expect master carpenters to get it right after they do six chairs, and we've only done six movies. You've got to do a lot of them, and it takes time, and there's just so much pressure, because the money is so big. There's only so many movies made a week. I mean, in the old days, I would have made fifty-five movies by now, and I'd have worked with a lot of people and learned a lot. As it is, I've worked with six directors, seven directors, eight directors, something like that. You know, that's peanuts compared with what the old guys did. And I'd like to work with a lot more actors, too, though it's the directors that really teach you something, and cinematographers. Those are the guys that know. There's like a pure knowledge there; there's no clowning around. They either know it or they don't. You can't lie about it.

Are you expecting to do more serious parts in the future? Does that depend on whether 'The Razor's Edge' is a success?

Well, to a certain extent, it does depend on whether *The Razor's Edge* is a success or failure, because if directors see it and they say, "That guy can act a little," then I'll get offered jobs from serious directors. As it is now, I'm in the phone book under *K* for *Komedy.*

5
Steve Martin

INTERVIEWED BY
BEN FONG-TORRES (1982)

The Eighties have been a strange decade for the cutting-edge comics of the Seventies. Richard Pryor nearly died while freebasing cocaine and hasn't been quite as convulsively funny since. John Belushi did die, and his old 'Saturday Night Live' cohorts, Dan Aykroyd and Chevy Chase, have gone on to mint millions appearing in the most unabashedly abysmal examples of Hollywood yok-fodder. Happily, Bill Murray and Lily Tomlin are another story, and so—as always—is Steve Martin.

In the Seventies, Martin utilized his middle-class WASPness as the ironic base for a wild-and-crazy stand-up act. His essential seriousness didn't become apparent until he made the move to films. Often teaming up with director Carl Reiner, a member of Sid Caesar's legendary TV comedy team in the Fifties, Martin has done memorable work on a relatively modest scale. His movies have not always been box-office smashes, but they have never been simple schlock, either—which, in Martin's case, is more to the point. 'Dead Men Don't Wear Plaid,' which inserted his bumbling gumshoe into a screen environment constructed largely of classic flatfoot-film footage, was a technical tour-de-force and a true film rarity—a comedy with a seamlessly conceived visual style. 'The Lonely Guy,' a surprisingly tender duet-for-schlubs that co-starred the estimable Charles Grodin, perfectly captured that unique sense of urban yearning that so distinguished the Bruce Jay Friedman book upon which it was based. And 'Roxanne'—Martin's gentle 1987 update of Rostand's 'Cyrano de Bergerac'—was a deservedly popular hit.

The dark and uncompromising 'Pennies From Heaven,' however, may still be Martin's most ambitious work to date. And the following interview that it occasioned—with Ben Fong-Torres, one of ROLLING STONE's *earliest contributors—remains among the most revealing that this somewhat remote performer has given.*

—K. L.

SO I WANTED everything to cease, and I wanted to throw the dice." Steve Martin, overdosed on success, threw his dice and what a number he rolled: the lead in *Pennies From Heaven*. In this MGM tragi-musical, which zigzags from doomed darkness to dreamy fantasies, Martin plays Arthur Parker, a song-sheet salesman, who lies and cheats, sings and dances—who does just about everything, in fact, but act funny. For a man who rose to stardom through comedy, Martin was clearly taking the biggest risk of his career.

It was a role Martin worked hard to get. He had to learn dramatic acting—from the director, Herbert Ross—and take tap-dancing lessons for months, well into the production of the film. He had to accept what amounted to a year's retirement from, to put it mildly, a wildly successful comedy career. And he even had to butt up against his own friend and manager, Bill McEuen. "I just think he shouldn't be doing a dramatic role at this point," McEuen said, a few weeks before the movie opened. "I would've been happier if he'd done a couple more comedies first, then tried something different."

But Steve would not be stopped. Martin had seen *Pennies* in its original form, as a six-part, nine-hour television series produced by BBC in 1976 and shown later in the United States on various PBS stations. "I couldn't believe it," Martin said. "I'd sit there and go, 'This is the greatest thing I've ever seen.' What the movie's about is so common to everything. Arthur's desire to be like what the songs told him. I saw this great parallel to when I was growing up in the Fifties. The rock & roll songs were so simple, everything was so simple. You loved her, you got her, you lost her. Pop music now, or in the Sixties, was complicated, but these songs were just, 'Here's what life is gonna be.' And that promise has been made to people of our generation as well as to people of Arthur's generation."

Ten days after *Pennies* opened, Martin's mood was a reflection of the film's business—a mixture of disappointment, optimism and caution. Backed by rave reviews, it did well in New York City, but elsewhere reviews were mixed and business was so-so. "I'm disappointed that it didn't open as a blockbuster," said Martin, "and I don't know what to blame, other than it's me and not a comedy." About the critics? "I must say that the people who get the movie, in general, have been wise and intelligent; the people who don't get it are ignorant scum."

When Martin got the role in *Pennies,* he was thirty-six years old and the hottest comedian in the country. His concerts competed with large rock shows, drawing audiences of 25,000 people. Two albums had sold more than a million copies each, and a third had the million-selling single "King Tut." He played Vegas and published a best-selling book, *Cruel Shoes*. All four of his NBC specials have given that beleaguered network something to smile about. And his first full-length feature film, *The Jerk,* grossed $100 million on an investment of some $4.5 million. In fact, it was on the strength of *The Jerk* that Martin was mentioned as a possible Arthur Parker when Herbert Ross began casting *Pennies*. Several other actors, among them Al Pacino and Richard Dreyfuss, were sent scripts. But Rick McCallum, executive producer of *Pennies,* says most of the actors were put off by the "unsympathetic" nature of the Parker character and by the work the part required.

When Martin met with Ross and writer Dennis Potter, at Martin's home in Beverly Hills, Potter recalls, "Steve started talking about Arthur, what he felt about the part. As he talked—he actually put on a hat and did a tentative dance—he instinctively understood Arthur, and from that moment on, I had no doubt." Ross, who got into film as a choreographer and has directed a few dancers (*The Turning Point* and *Nijinsky* being among his credits), calls Martin "literally the only actor in Hollywood who is equipped to do a musical. There is not one actor who has the skills that he does."

We are at Martin's house in Beverly Hills. From the outside, it looks like a forbidding fortress. But inside, it's sunlit, wide-open spaces, all white walls (or, more often, half walls or columns with rectangular cutouts) and gray carpeting, with careful, tasteful and clearly professional decorating. Furnishings are mostly contemporary, in greens, roses and maroons. Bookshelves are filled with a substantial library of histories and collections of American art (there are two dozen books on James McNeill Whistler alone), along with leather-bound scripts from Martin's films and TV specials. It is a house with no clutter, no magazines on the coffee table, no records strewn about (in a cabinet, though, one finds albums by Steely Dan, Kraftwerk, Devo, Mozart and tapes of Thirties music). On the walls hang artwork, both modern and nineteenth century, including a John Henry Twachtman. Martin has been a serious "looker" since college days and a collector since he could afford to be one.

Offstage, with friends or strangers, Steve is, simply, off. He's a cooperative interview, but he doesn't want to talk about fellow comedians, he says, "because all I'm gonna do is say nice things, and it's gonna be so boring." He wants to keep his relationship with Bernadette Peters (co-star of *Pennies*) private. And the same goes for his art collection. Agonizing over whether to even talk about it, he explains, "As a comedian, I'm willing to trade out my private thoughts about things that are personal to me for space in the magazine, and I'm willing to say dumb things that, six months later, I go, 'Why did I say that?' But when it comes to art, which is so personal—and I'm not trying to make it part of my personality—I'm not willing to say dumb things about it. I want the freedom to be stupid about it, to learn about it, to think about something I still don't understand. It's like why I'm a vegetarian. I don't know. I can't defend myself, and I don't have to de-

fend myself. It's like the artist doesn't have to explain or justify anything about it. And I think it's important for me to keep that position, for my own personal health."

But on occasion, Martin the comedian emerges. He notices my scribbling into a notebook. "What're you writing down?" he asks.

I tell him, "Striped dress shirt, black slacks . . ."

"Well," he volunteers, "my shoes are mauve. They're dress shoes, but I want to break them in, so I'm wearing them two hours a day." He chuckles.

And the socks?

"Oh, I'm breaking in these socks, too."

Why did you decide to take such a risk with your career?

I was asked about that before I went into the project, and there was no hesitation. When I first started doing my act, it was not . . . normal. It was not what was expected. That's why the public caught on to it. And I said, "If I start getting trapped by my own sameness, I'm not doing what they secretly want, which is for me to do what I want to do."

The last time I saw you, you said this movie would be the biggest challenge of your life. Did your expectations come true?

More than I thought, I was in such a state. I'd been on the road—about seventeen years. But three years really steady, and it was debilitating. You get physically tired, emotionally tired, and start wondering what you're doing.

It got to the point where when I'd do new material, it sounded like old material even to *me* [*puzzled laugh*]. And one thing I didn't understand that frustrated me was, I was doing comedy and the audience was doing an *event*. They were at an event, and I was going, "Wait a minute. This is my little joke. Why are you waving balloons at me during my joke?"

I needed a break. I wasn't looking for a dramatic role; I didn't know what I was looking for. Then this thing came along, and it was like seeing the perfect circle. You knew you had to enter it.

After the first weeks of shooting, did you feel confident about your acting, or was there fear?

[*Laughs*] I would not allow myself to be afraid. I

thought that would really hurt me. I felt I had been through so much. I'd faced 20,000 people in concert, and I refused to be intimidated. It was not easy.

What has it been like for you to see the film?

There's something about the movie that overwhelms me, and it's touching, and it's different, and I love what it's saying, even though I can't express it. When I was in college—one reason I was in show business is I'd read a poem and think, "God, that thing is beautiful." And I would get in my speech class and read the poem. I wanted to pass it along. The thrill for me is when a sympathetic person watches this film and gets the same feeling I had when I saw the BBC version.

Was your goal always to be in movies?

Yeah, stand-up comedy was really just an accident. I was figuring out a way to get onstage. I made up a magic act and, "Hey, I'm in show business," and that led to nightclubs. I felt like a comedian—that was my work. As I got into the movies, I was reminded, "Hey, this is really why I got into show business." I *do* like the movies. It's so condensed. You get to try and make it right.

But there's nothing more condensed than a one-liner to an audience that laughs right back.

But with movies you've got constantly new material, constant new challenges.

Wasn't it in college [Long Beach State, 1964] that you hit on your particular brand of comedy?

College totally changed my life. It changed what I believe and what I think about everything. I majored in philosophy. Something about non sequiturs appealed to me. In philosophy, I started studying logic, and they were talking about cause and effect, and you start to realize, "Hey, there *is* no cause and effect! There is no logic. There is no anything!" Then it gets real easy to write this stuff, because all you have to do is twist everything hard—you twist the punch line, you twist the non sequitur so hard away from the thing that set it up, that it's easy . . . and it's *thrilling.*

For a while there you thought about becoming a teacher.

But then I thought, "I can't give up show business." I'd studied philosophy and realized the only true value was accomplishment. So I changed my major, transferred [to UCLA] and went into theater.

You were already doing some comedy. Where did you first perform onstage?

At this club, the Prison of Socrates, on Balboa Island [near Newport Beach]. It was Hoot Night, and I got up and just threw everything in to try and get to fifteen minutes. So I had my magic, and I read

poetry and played the banjo, and I juggled. It's exactly what I'm doing now.

What kind of response did you get?

Gosh, I don't know. Part of the thing, when you're young and naive, is that you think you went over when you didn't, and that's what keeps you going. Your desire's so great to do it, you don't just quit.

How did you meet your manager, Bill McEuen?

Well, I used to go to high school with his brother, John, and we slowly communicated. We didn't get together, though, till I started writing for the Smothers Brothers. I was about twenty-two when we decided to sign a management thing, and neither of us, I swear to God, knew what we were doing. [*Dumbstruck voice*] "I got a manager now. . . ."

I can't believe the intensity of his devotion. He tape-recorded everything you did back in the early days.

Sure. He used to sit out there every night, watch every show and laugh. And I'd hear his laugh and it'd sort of keep me going. It was like him and me, kind of cheering each other up. I know I'm dying, he knows I'm dying, and we're laughing about it.

For a while you slipped into a hippie look. How much did it reflect your life?

Well, I was just going through a stage, like anybody. I was listening to rock music. I smoked some marijuana. That was when I was about twenty. Marijuana's so strange in that you can get a lot of different things from it. When you first start smoking it, you really get high, and then after a while you just get *tired.* When I started writing, I quit.

How did you get the job writing for the Smothers Brothers?

I had written a stack of things in college, in creative writing class. I had a girlfriend who was a dancer on the show, and she showed Mason Williams [the head writer for *The Smothers Brothers' Comedy Hour*] my stuff. Mason paid me out of his own pocket at first.

After your hippie phase, around 1971, you started wearing white suits. How contrived was that?

It seemed at the time like something really far out. It was planned, and then the white suit became gurulike when I started achieving success. But when I cut my hair, I didn't do it to think, "Well, this will help me in show business." I just wanted to forget about the past.

Even before the white suit, you were doing some strange things, not only in your act but especially after the shows, leading crowds out into the streets and going to McDonald's and ordering 300 hamburgers and one French fry.

That's what I had to learn in acting, that it was the

degree of your commitment to an idea that made it successful or not. The idea could be wrong, but you must be committed, and that's what I was to the act at that time. All the way.

I remember the first time I ever walked out of the hall at the end of the act, and the audience came with me and I had them all get in a swimming pool—which was empty—and then I swam over the top of them, and they all put their arms out, and I thought, "Gee, there's a breakthrough! I'm gonna do this every time now." It was that spirit, I think, that caught fire to the rest of my act. I stopped going outside because it got too dangerous. I realized if I go out and take three thousand people, someone's gonna get run over.

That's when the concerts became "events."

But even after that, there were great shows, shows that thrilled me. It was like playing an instrument. The audience was an instrument. I can do this and they'll do *this*. There was a period of, like, a year and a half where I felt so good; my body, my fingers, everything was working. When it got beyond that . . . I don't want sour grapes, like I was selling out 20,000-seat concerts and was unhappy. I wasn't, on one hand. It was the traveling, the circumstances—it just got me. I started doing things like collapsing onstage. It was a signal.

What about the time you had to go to the hospital?

It was a concert in Knoxville, Tennessee, with about seven thousand people in, like, a gymnasium. They were hanging from the rafters. It was about 100 degrees outside and humid, so it must've been 125 degrees onstage. The first five minutes I could feel sweat coming from my *hair* and running down my face. And the suit got soaked through. And I was about a half-hour into the act when I realized I couldn't go on. I had to leave. They called the medics and took me to the hospital. It was just exhaustion. I was a wreck.

How did it affect your performance? Did your act become rote?

No, that wasn't the problem. My act was always formulated. It's not like you get depressed and go out and do a lousy show. You could be exhausted, and something happens and you're on top of it. That's the enigma of performing. You can be very down and go out there and suddenly feel it. Or be very high and never connect with the audience. I started getting tired when I was getting into the nonconcert situations, like Atlantic City or Las Vegas. I felt something was missing.

When you began to get a lot of media attention, people tried to explain why you hit when you did. Did you agree with their assessments?

You know, in those articles I always looked for something larger. I always felt there was a deeper meaning to what I was doing than just being "wild and crazy," something more philosophical. I had a view that there was something funny about trying to be funny. I needed a theory behind it in order to justify it at the time, but now I don't. I see it for what it was. It was just fun, and it was stupid, and that's why it was successful.

But a lot of stupid comics have failed. Why did you succeed?

It was like everyone was ripe, and I was there and had the act I'd been doing for ten years, and boom, you know? I just think people wanted something new. I mean, I wanted something new, so I sort of became it.

You were one of the most popular guest hosts of 'Saturday Night Live.' Was there an instant chemistry?

It grew over the years. After a couple of times, it was a lot easier to write for me, and we had things to go to. I was not much of a contributor, except for my monologues.

When you were invited on to 'SNL,' did you already know the show?

Sure, I saw the very first show and I loved it. *Saturday Night Live* was a huge force. It made movie stars—John Belushi, Dan Aykroyd, Bill Murray. They and Richard Pryor and Lily Tomlin and myself were the comedy of the Seventies.

Do you have plans to work with 'SNL' cast members in movies?

Oh, I'd love to. We had a project at one point with me, Belushi and Aykroyd called *The Three Caballeros,* but it went the way of a lot of projects. Belushi and Aykroyd and Murray and Laraine [Newman] came on my special [November 25th, 1981, on NBC]. There's a nice camaraderie, but we're not the best of friends. Belushi was over here the other night with Don Novello [Father Guido Sarducci], and we sat around, talked and bullshitted. That was fun. You don't get a chance to get real close because . . . "I'm off!" or they're gone. You know, you really see each other only at rehearsals.

Do you plan to get back to the stage soon?

I want to stay in contact with live performing. Once you lose it, you've lost something real important. I want to go back with something really fresh. I need six months at the Comedy Store to get back into shape, and I look forward to going back. I'd like to start from the bottom again. Work up a whole other *feeling.* And to get that feeling again of *funny.* Who even wants the big halls again? That's been done.

Can a successful Steve Martin still play the jerk who thinks he's making it when he's actually making a fool of himself?

I'd still be that character. That's me. I can't walk out and be a somber Lenny Bruce or change the focus of my material. Onstage, when I say I've made it, it doesn't mean careerwise or celebritywise. It means [*smugly*], "I'm good." You can always think you're good when you're really not.

How are you coming up with new material now?

My act was ad-libbed, really, for over ten years, and the good ad-libs stayed, and that's how it evolved. I sat down and wrote some things, but pretty much everything was, "Hey, that'll work," laying at night in your bed and going, "Well, that's another good idea!" [*Laughs.*]

You met Bernadette Peters, the story goes, four years ago at a dinner in Las Vegas. What was it about her that attracted you?

I liked her because she was independent. I respected her for it, and I knew it wasn't going to be, you know, "Oh, Steve, what are we going to do now? Where're you going?" She was in show business, we could talk.

Offstage you're very serious and kind of distant.

That's what my close friends say, too, you know.

Why is it that you come off cold to people?

You know, I can't answer that. That's for a shrink to answer. I'm a lot better at it now than when I was touring. When you're touring and if you go to a party, there's automatically a celebrity-audience distance. It follows you around, especially when you're on the road in small towns. Any time there is awe, it gets very difficult to be normal, to be yourself. But I'm not saying that that's what made me the way I am. I've probably always been distant.

As a kid, too? In high school and college?

Well, I had one very close friend in high school and college, two different people. Otherwise, it was hard to get to know people. But I had real good rapport with these specific friends. We had this communication, generally through humor.

When you're at the Comedy Store working out bits, do you just do your spot and split? Do you hang out with the other comics?

[*Dryly*] No.

Do you appreciate a comic like Andy Kaufman, who seems more interested in arousing the audience than in getting laughs?

I've only seen Andy Kaufman be funny. I always felt like if what I was doing then hadn't broken through, I would eventually have gone on to something like that. I always felt like Andy Kaufman was the next step.

What about other comics? Do you keep tabs on them?

Not much. I can look at it almost objectively because I don't feel like one anymore. I feel like I've moved . . . changed somehow, and it's so far behind me in some spiritual way. I feel more inclined toward the movies now. I'm not looking for my next college date. I want to be a comedian-actor.

What about your next movie, 'Dead Men Don't Wear Plaid'? [Martin, through the magic of film archives, carefully contrived writing, meticulous set designs and film editing, plays scenes with Humphrey Bogart and Alan Ladd. The film is due out in May.]

Well, Carl Reiner and George Gipe and I were rewriting a script I had written called *Depression.* As we rewrote it, we realized we didn't like it, and we didn't know how to fix it. We were having lunch one day and somebody said, "What if we cut to a scene from an old movie and have our character placed into the movie, by matching sets and stuff?" So it started out as one scene. Then, "What if we did a whole picture like that?"

What is the story line?

It's set in the 1940s. I'm a detective, and Humphrey Bogart taught me everything I know, and I'm so good I've surpassed him. He starts to slip, and I have to let him have it and let him know that all the things he taught me, rules like "Never fall in love," that they're wrong. And he's got some really great looks. He really feels bad. There're like twenty or thirty stars in it, and it's brilliantly constructed. It's a mystery, and it all comes to a conclusion. Using other movies' dialogue, that's amazing. It's one of those movies that's just fun; it takes you away. I have a grudge with a lot of comedies, that they're so poorly made and they look crummy. This picture looks good; it's funny and it's got character.

I heard you met recently with Stanley Kubrick in London.

It's not the kind of stuff you want to put in the papers. That's the way deals are blown. But I met with him in London for about eight hours. He likes *The Jerk,* and we talked about doing something together. He's working on a script.

You're also the executive producer of a late-night show on NBC called 'Twilight Theater' [a pilot will air in February].

Well, that's strictly a title. I just go in and see how it's going. It's part of my television deal; we created a production company that feeds ideas to NBC, and late night really appealed to me. We're doing a prime-time situation comedy with Martin Mull—that's in development—and *Twilight Theater,* which is our version of those Alcoa anthology shows from the late Fifties. We've got Roddy McDowall as the host, and it looks like we present great drama. He sits by the fireside and pulls books off the shelves and introduces the next, you know, piece of art, and it's all sort of pompous. Then we do New Wave, with a punk-expressionist set.

Now that you're two films past it, what do you think of 'The Jerk'?

I saw it recently; it came on cable TV. I sat there and . . . "You know, this is pretty funny." I liked it. There are things I would've done different, but I recognized that was me then; that's the style of the film.

'The Jerk' got worked over by the critics, and that came around the time you were being slammed for the 'Cruel Shoes' book. Other writers said you were repeating too many bits and putting out too many albums. How did you respond to all this?

The thing that's wrong is that [the critics] try to make you ashamed of your work. And nobody has the right to do that. We do this out of—oh, I can't say why [*laughs*]. I was gonna say *love,* but that's not true. *Love* sounds like you're implying [*in a sincere voice*], "I want to go out there and make those people happy." And I've never thought that. I wanted to get onstage and exercise this craft. It's to please yourself.

Or to make the world a better place?

I'll tell you, I'm sure musicians don't feel they're going out there making people happy. They're happy with moving their fingers across the neck of that guitar, and that's the way I felt. It just happens in comedy that that's superficially what it looks like you're doing. I never thought I was making them happy. I always figured they *hated* me. I felt happy that the show went right, and if I had this elevating moment, I felt there was communication. That's why when the thing got out of control and certain individuals in the audience—you know, the rock-audience syndrome, with some guy throwing a beer bottle at you and the people running up onstage. That really got to me because it threw everything out of sync. I learned how to handle it, but I didn't want to *have* to handle it.

How have you handled the money that's come with success?

Well, I don't want to sound like I have $100 million. I did well. I have no complaints.

You have what? About $50 million?

That's about *$80* million [*laughs*]. I have no problems with money at all. I'm not depressed because of it. It's so relative. You can quibble over $100 but not over $100,000. But I hesitate to discuss money because it's—I don't care who you are, there's a real hatred of rich people, there's hostility—this real snide attitude toward the rich as though you didn't earn it and that it was easy or that there's a great difference between the rich and the not-rich. What's the difference? I mean, I didn't start it out as a business. There are two things—what you do and the business of what you do—and I don't feel like a businessman.

Bill McEuen told me that he wanted to do well more to have freedom than for the money. But he also said, "While we're hot, why not take it? If we don't, we'll hate ourselves in ten years."

I have to tell you something. Bill vacillates, and it depends on the mood he's in. Sometimes he'll say, "Fuck you, we're only doing this for the money, and if we don't get the money, we're not gonna do it." Other times he's the most artistic, dedicated, devoted-to-art person I've ever met. And I think all of us are like that. You're making so much on a concert tour, and it excites you a little and you go, "How *much?*" There's a certain thrill to it. It's detached. I don't care if I'm getting five cents for a show or $100,000, it's just as hard. The work is the same, and you're not gonna let it die. I mean, you're out there sweating, working for something else.

You know, talking about selling—that's a whole style. You're on the road, you're selling records, it's a period of your show-business life that maybe happens once, or two or three times. Everything's coming together. The road was meant to sell records, it was meant for you to be out there and be Number One; it was to do everything, to explode and ride that wave. But it only comes every once in a while, and now I'm happy. I intentionally beached to calm it down, to let it subside, because if you're on that wave, pretty soon it's gonna break, just by its own weight.

Is there that sense of having retired a champ? You didn't quit, but you stepped back by your own choice.

That's right. Pull it back and just say, "I'm gonna get sick of this, *they're* gonna get sick of it," and you just go . . . [*Martin leans back, allows himself one of his wide, eye-closing smiles, breathes out and sits up again*] "that was wonderful."

6

Elvis Costello

INTERVIEWED BY
GREIL MARCUS (1982)

Greil Marcus is surely music criticism's most professorial practitioner. His presence on the asking end of any interview inevitably makes the subject sound more cogent, focused and, all in all, thoughtful *than he or she is likely ever to have sounded before. In Elvis Costello, Marcus confronted one of the prickliest performers of the nascent Eighties—a post-punk with an affinity for Cole Porter—and won him over, in large part, with the sheer breadth of his erudition. Sounds like an egghead fiesta, perhaps, but the resulting interview is illuminated by the intensity of the two men's common concerns.*

Costello's career—established in the late Seventies with such powerful albums as 'This Year's Model' and 'Armed Forces'—has never quite recovered from the race-baiting 1979 bar brawl pondered below. Oblivious to pop trends, he has remained an acutely expressive songwriter and can still be a thrilling live act. But his initial acerbity—or something —has worked against him. Over the years, his audience has settled into a substantial —but not chart-shaking—core of admirers, and toward the dwindling end of the decade, his longtime label, CBS, quietly dropped him. It would be too facile to position Costello as the English Randy Newman . . . but that seems to be the drift.

—K.L.

I N 1977, ELVIS COSTELLO emerged in London as one of the unquestioned originals of modern pop music. Just twenty-two when he released his first album, *My Aim Is True,* he seemed master of every rock & roll move—on record and off. He combined the brains of Randy Newman and the implacability of Bob Dylan, the everyman pathos of Buddy Holly and the uniqueness of John Lennon. Everything was up for grabs in his music: love, money, status, hope, fear and, perhaps most of all, the very notion of control. No punk in terms of craft, he rode the punk wave because he communicated a more authentic bitterness than any punk; his demands on the world were more powerful, and thus his rejection of the world when it failed to deliver was more convincing.

In 1982, Elvis Costello remains known almost solely through his music—and the scandalous "Ray Charles" incident, which made the papers across the country and across the water. Aside from a 1981 appearance on Tom

Snyder's *Tomorrow* show, Costello had not sat down for a comprehensive interview with an American journalist until this summer—and no interview has appeared in a U.K. publication since 1977.

With the release of his eighth album, *Imperial Bedroom*, Costello and his band, the Attractions—Bruce Thomas, bass; Steve Nieve, keyboards; and Pete Thomas, drums —opened an American tour this July 14 at Santa Cruz, California, to a jabbering crowd of surfers and college students. There, he performed his songs, two hours' worth—plus Elvis Presley's "Little Sister," his first cover of his namesake. Three nights later, to a bigger, far more various and receptive crowd in Berkeley, Costello performed his view of the world—a show that ripped through the night.

The next day we met for a five-hour conversation. Wearing an unmistakable pair of red shoes, Costello was serious about the situation—his first real interview with a national publication—but also very much at ease. We talked about his aversion to journalists; Brecht and Weill; the presence of Hank Williams in *The Last Picture Show;* the theological dispute between Sam Phillips and Jerry Lee Lewis that preceded the recording of "Great Balls of Fire"; Costello's course of study in high-school English ("second-half-of-the-twentieth-century working-class British literature—*Saturday Night and Sunday Morning, The Loneliness of the Long-Distance Runner, Billy Liar*); Frank Sinatra's incandescent version of "I Can't Get Started (with You)," from the album *No One Cares*, especially the unique spoken introduction (" 'Each time I chanced to see Franklin D.,' " Costello reminded me, " 'he always said, "Hi, buddy," to me' "); Sonny Boy Williamson's "Little Village"; Billie Holiday; Mel Tormé; Charlie Rich; Peter Guralnick's *Lost Highway;* Kay Kendall; Isabelle Adjani; and—

And, we will need another interview, another time. As for what I have taken from that conversation—what seems, given how little Costello has spoken for print, most fun-

damental and necessary—I've compressed some passages, left myself out of the dialogue when I did no more than say, "And then . . . ," and stitched the result together with narrative. Five years after, one must begin at the beginning.

Declan McManus was born in London in 1955 and grew up there, attending Catholic schools. For his last two years of secondary school he moved to Liverpool to live with his mother, by that time divorced from his father, Ross McManus, a big-band singer and solo cabaret performer.

I graduated from secondary school in 1973. It was the first year of one million unemployed in England in recent times—in Liverpool, anywhere up north, it was worse. I was very lucky to get a job. I had no ambition to go into further education; I just went out and got the first job I could get. I went along to be a chart corrector, tea boy, clerk—because I wasn't really qualified for anything. I got a job as a computer operator, which happened to be comparatively well paid: about twenty pounds a week. I'd just put tapes on the machines and feed cards in, line up printing machines—all the manual work the computer itself doesn't have arms to do.

I had something of an ambition to be a professional musician. I was already playing guitar in high school —playing in folk clubs on my own. I was writing my own songs—dreadful songs, performing them more or less religiously. I didn't think the songs were worth recording—but the only way you get better is to play what you write. Then you have the humiliation of being *crushed*—if they're obviously insubstantial. If you don't put them over, you quickly learn from experience.

I stuck out the first computer job for about six months; at the same time, I got into a group in Liverpool, a sort of folk group—we'd do a few rock & roll tunes, and songs of our own, but we weren't getting anywhere. The Cavern was still there—and that's where I met Nick Lowe, just before I came to London, in '74. He was still with Brinsley Schwarz; it was the *autumn* of their career. We'd do a few of their numbers in our set; we had a show at a little club, they were playing at the Cavern, and we went along and met in the bar and started chatting. He was in a real proper group that recorded records! That was the first time I'd ever spoken to anybody that was in a group—and his attitude *even then* has been reflected in the way he's been since. When we've worked together, it's been, "I can't see what's so difficult about it, it's just four chords"—and he'd bang them out. He always had that attitude—it was quite a revelation to me.

What was the beginning of your life as a fan?

My father was with Joe Loss—the English Glenn Miller, I suppose. He was with him from about 1953 to 1968, and then he went solo; his instrument is trumpet, but he's a singer. After the years with Joe Loss, he went out as a cabaret artist; he does social clubs and nightclubs and cabaret, drives around himself.

The first records I ever owned were "Please Please Me"—and "The Folksinger," by John Leyton. I was at a little bit of an advantage because my father was still with Joe Loss then—he used to get quite a lot of records, because they would cover the hits of the day. He'd often have demonstration copies, even acetates; as late as 1966, Northern Songs would still send Beatles acetates out to the orchestras to garner covers for [live] radio play. I've got them at home. As my father was the most versatile of the three Joe Loss band singers, I was fortunate—he got the records and just passed them on to me.

I was just into singles, whatever was on the radio —the Kinks, the Who, Motown. It was exciting . . . I was in the Beatles fan club when I was eleven; I used to buy the magazines. The one kind of music that I *didn't* like was rock & roll—as a distinct form. The girl next door loved the Shadows and Cliff Richard —I thought that was really old hat. Someone who lived across the road from my grandmother liked Buddy Holly—I thought that was terribly old-fashioned, I couldn't understand why anybody liked it. It never occurred to me that someone as *archaic* as Chuck Berry could have written "Roll Over Beethoven"—because I was quite convinced that George Harrison had written it.

The only time it changed, the only time it went a bit peculiar, where it maybe went a bit *clandestine,* was when I went to live in Liverpool. I was never very taken with psychedelic music—but my dad went a bit psychedelic around the edges, about 1968. He grew his hair quite long; he used to give me Grateful Dead records, and *Surrealistic Pillow.* I'd keep them for a couple of weeks and then sell them at the record exchange and buy Marvin Gaye records. When I went to live in Liverpool, I discovered everyone was still into acid rock—and I used to *hide* my Otis Redding records when friends came around. I didn't want to

be out of step. To the age of sixteen, it's *really crucial* that you're *in*—and I tried hard to like the Grateful Dead or Spirit. I tried to find somebody of that sort that I could like that nobody else did—because everyone would adopt his group, and his group would be *it:* someone weird like Captain Beefheart. It's no different now—people trying to outdo each other in extremes. There are people who like X, and there are people who say X are wimps; they like Black Flag.

I actually "saw the light" when I was already playing—coming back to London, seeing a lot of groups, Nick Lowe and the Brinsleys, pub-rock groups. I think you get very earnest when you're about sixteen to eighteen, and everyone at school was listening either to the psychedelic groups or singer-songwriters: it was all very *earnest, pouring out your inner soul.* In London I discovered that all the music I liked secretly, that I'd been hiding from my friends—that was what was great fun in a bar: Lee Dorsey songs! Suddenly it was all right to *like it;* that was when I saw the light. There was nothing wrong with it.

In England, now, there's a prejudice against that era, the prepunk era; the bands tend to get ridden down: "Oh, that's just pub rock." I'd much rather any day go and see NRBQ playing in a bar than I would the most illustrious of our punk groups in England, because I don't think they have anything to do with anything. They're horrible—and *phony,* and *dishonest* as well.

Who are you talking about?

The Exploited—and the whole Oi! business.

Bands like the Anti-Nowhere League?

Now, the Anti-Nowhere League, I quite like them, because they're just *animals:* they drive around in a van that says, "We're the Anti-Nowhere League and You're Not!"—I mean, that's great.

The Damned were the best punk group, because there was no art behind them; they were just enjoying themselves. There was no art behind them that *I* could see. They were just—*nasty.* I loved them from the start. I liked the Pistols as well—but you could see the concern behind it. It's dishonest to say, "Oh, yes, we were just *wild*"; they weren't just wild. It was *considered* and *calculated.* Very art. The Clash as well.

While all that was going on, I had a little group in London. I'd moved from one computer job to another; it was a total bluff, really. I knew nothing about it, but I knew enough of the jargon. It was ideal: waiting for the machine to do the work, there's a lot of free time for writing and reading. In the evenings we'd try to play rock & roll, R&B numbers, some country songs—a real pub-rock mixture. There was no focus to it; it was aimless. We could get through the usual bar-band repertoire—but I remember Pete Thomas, now the Attractions' drummer and *then* a drummer in a quite successful pub-rock band, Chilli Willy, coming to see us—he was a *celebrity* to us—and he walked out after about thirty seconds. I think he came to see our worst-ever gig—but with no offense to the guys, we weren't very good.

It was the usual thing—trapped in mediocrity. So I went out on my own again, solo. That's very hard, because there's no real platform for solo singing unless you sing traditional music or *recognized blues,* doing re-creations—you know how *reverent* Europeans are.

It was difficult to develop an original style. I have no idea who it was I might have been imitating, whether consciously or unconsciously. I was playing on my own, trying to put my songs across. I suppose I should have had a band behind them—but playing alone did build up an *edge.* I did the odd show just to keep up, to keep trying to *improve* the ability to play. You'd soon know if a song was bad if you were *dying* in a club; you'd have to put more edge on it. Playing on your own, you'd have the tension—you could increase the tension at will, not relying on anybody to pick up the beat.

McManus made a guitar-and-vocal demo and hawked his songs to various record companies. The one that responded was Jake Riviera and Dave Robinson's new Stiff label, emerging in 1976 out of the pub-rock scene and bridging the gap to punk.

On the first demo tape that I sent to Stiff, that brought me the *gig,* as it were, there were only two or three songs that ended up on *My Aim Is True.* There were a lot of raw songs—and looking at them now, rather precious songs, with a lot of chords. Showing-off songs. I was very impressed by Randy Newman, and wrote a lot of songs with that ragtime feel. I was very impressed with those funny chord changes that he used to play and I was emulating that on guitar. They came out convoluted; they weren't poppy at all—they had pretensions to a sophistication they didn't have.

That exactly coincided with punk. But I was working—I didn't have the money to go down to the Roxy and see what the bands were doing: the Clash, the Pistols. I just read about them in *Melody Maker* and *NME* the same as anyone else. Joe Public. I was living in the suburbs of London—I couldn't afford to go to clubs uptown. They were open until two o'clock in the morning, I couldn't afford taxis—the tubes are closed just after midnight. All these bands were playing in the middle of the night. I don't know who went to the bloody gigs—I can only guess they were rich people with cars and lots of drugs.

I got up at seven in the morning, and so I couldn't go. I was married, with a son; I couldn't take the day off. I took enough time playing sick, taking sick time off of my job, just to make *My Aim Is True.*

Then I started listening to the records that were coming out, because I'd got this snobbish attitude: So *little* of any worth had come out for a few years. When the first few punk records came out, I suddenly started thinking: "Hang on—this is something a little bit different."

I mean, I spoke with someone the other day who said that when the first Clash album came out, he was *outraged.* I remember being outraged, and thinking, "If *this* is what music's going to be like"—I remember Joe Strummer describing their sound as a sea lion barking over a load of pneumatic drills, which *is* what their first album sounds like when you first hear it—I remember hearing it and saying, "If that's what it's going to be like, *that's it.* I'll quit before I've done anything."

Then I listened to that album on headphones—we lived in a block of flats and we couldn't really play music at night—and I listened right through the night. I thought, "Well, I want to see what this is about. And I'll listen to it until I decide it's rubbish, and I'll probably *quit,* if that's the way music's going to be, or else I'll see something in it." I listened to it for thirty-six hours straight—and I wrote "Watching the Detectives."

We were all living in this block of flats, and nobody had an awful lot of money—I don't want to sound like my-deprived-background, but nobody did. And there were all these people in 1977, when the Jubilee was on, *wasting their money* on a bloody street party for the queen. Perhaps it sounds small-minded now, but I used to really enjoy playing "God Save the Queen," *loud,* because all the little old ladies would be so outraged.

"God, did you see the Sex Pistols on the TV last night?" On the way to work, I'd be on the platform in the morning and all the commuters would be reading the papers when the Pistols made headlines—and said "fuck" on TV. It was as if it was the most awful thing that ever happened. It's a mistake to confuse that with a major event in history, but it was a great morning—just to hear people's blood pressure going up and down over it.

I wrote a lot of songs in the summer of 1977: "Welcome to the Working Week," "Red Shoes," "Miracle Man," "Alison," "Sneaky Feelings," "Waiting for the End of the World," "I'm Not Angry," all more or less in one go, in about two or three weeks.

Your first single was "Less than Zero." When did you write that?

Earlier in the year. I saw a program with Oswald Mosley, the leader of the British fascist movement of the Thirties. And there he was on TV, saying, "No, I'm not anti-Semitic, of course I'm not—doesn't matter even if I was!" His attitude was that *time* could make it all right! It was a very English way of accepting things that used to really irritate me, really annoy me. The complacency, the moral complacency there—that they would just *accept* this vicious old man: not string him up on the spot!

This was the time when the National Front and the British Movement were recruiting with great success—and they, of course, derived directly from Mosley's old British Union of Fascists.

They were the same old bastards, the same old weirdos that kept reappearing and denying they had any fascist overtones, and then there would be pictures taken of them dressing up in pervy Hitler Youth uniforms. They're really *sick* people. If there wasn't a danger that some people of limited intelligence would take them seriously, they'd be sad and you'd feel sorry for them. But you can't. There are people gullible enough and there are enough problems—the same way as you've got here. You can point fingers and say, "These are the people who are the source of all your problems: It's the black people." It's the same as saying, "It's the Jews. . . ." I'm English, but my ancestry is Irish, and they used to say the same about the Irish as well. My wife's Irish. Sooner or later, we'll probably have to leave England—because I'm sure the people of England will try and send the Irish back.

We cut the first singles without any impact. My immediate reaction was, "Well, maybe I haven't got it." If I'd been somebody like Johnny Cougar, signed to a major label—someone with a five-album deal for a million dollars—I suppose I would have felt, "Well, I'm secure now, I can write some songs," but I wasn't sure. Stiff was running from week to week—we were totally independent, we weren't licensed, we had no national distribution: it was mail-order. We finished the album in six-hour sessions; there were no days in the studio. Jake said, "Well, we're going to put it out"—but one moment it was going to be Wreckless Eric on one side, me on the other, as a way of presenting two new writers. There were a million ideas a

day floating around; it was all improvised and all governed by a very limited budget.

You had picked your name well before that?

I hadn't picked it at all. Jake picked it. It was just a marketing scheme. "How are we going to separate you from Johnny. This and Johnny That?" He said, "We'll call you Elvis." I thought he was completely out of his mind.

Riviera was right, perhaps because he knew Declan McManus could live up to his new name. With 'My Aim Is True,' recorded with the American country-rock band Clover and produced by Nick Lowe, Costello stepped out as a major figure in British new music; the American release of the LP on CBS later in the year, a brilliant appearance on 'Saturday Night Live' and his first tour with the newly recruited Attractions, brought, if anything, an even more fierce response in the U.S. Along with Lowe and Riviera, Costello left Stiff for the now-defunct Radar label (Costello now records for F-Beat in the U.K.), and he and the Attractions followed a remarkable first year with 'This Year's Model' ("A ghost version of 'Aftermath,' " Costello told me, noting that, having never been much of a Rolling Stones fan, he'd never heard the record until a few months before making 'This Year's Model.' He responded to my comments about the strength of the LP with the information that Nick Lowe's contribution was to "sweeten it"—that furious album was sweetened?) and a tour far more confident and hard-edged than the one that had preceded it.

In 1979, Costello offered perhaps his most ambitious record, 'Armed Forces'—originally and more appropriately titled 'Emotional Fascism.' It was a tricky, allusive set of words, voices and shifting instrumental textures, primarily influenced, Costello says, by the music he and the Attractions had been able to agree on as listening material while touring the U.S. in a station wagon; David Bowie's 'Low' and 'Heroes,' Iggy Pop's 'Lust for Life' and 'Idiot,' Kraftwerk's 'Autobahn' and, most of all, Abba's 'Arrival.' (" 'Oliver's Army' was most successful," Costello says of the LP's U.K. hit, a bright, poppy cut that would have been released as a single in the U.S. had Costello been willing to take out the line characterizing army recruits as "white niggers"—the whole point of the tune. "That was the aim," he says. "A grim heart in the middle of an Abba record.") As Jim Miller has written, on 'Armed Forces' "personal relations are perceived as a metaphor for relations in society at large. . . . [Costello's] stance may begin with private refusals, but it ends with public references."

In a bizarre manner, that truth was acted out, on its head, during Costello's 1979 tour of the States, when one night in a bar in Columbus, Ohio, at odds with Bonnie

Bramlett and other members of the Stephen Stills Band, Costello suddenly denounced Ray Charles as "a blind, ignorant nigger," said much the same about James Brown and attacked the stupidity of American black music in particular and America in general. Bramlett decked him; the incident quickly made the papers, then 'People' magazine, and the resulting scandal forced a New York press conference—Costello's first real face-to-face encounter with journalists since the fall of 1977—where he tried to explain himself and, according to both Costello and those who questioned him, failed. This from a man who had produced the first album by the Specials, the U.K.'s pioneers of interracial music? Who at some risk had taken on the National Front with "Night Rally" and appeared at Rock Against Racism concerts—and who, again to quote Jim Miller, was plainly "obsessed with the reality of domination wherever it occurs"? A man who had ended 'Armed Forces' with a blazing cover of Nick Lowe's "(What's So Funny 'bout) Peace, Love and Understanding?"—a song that, as Costello performed it, was, yes, ironic, especially given such nightmares as "Goon Squad," which preceded it, but was nevertheless not a joke? What happened?

It's become a terrible thing hanging over my head—it's horrible to work hard for a long time and find that what you're best known for is something as idiotic as . . . this.

Do you really think that this incident is what you're best known for?

Yes. The first thing that a lot of people heard about me was that incident. I think it outweighs my entire career—which is a pretty depressing prospect. I'm absolutely convinced.

Fred Schruers wrote a piece about it—a sort of "tenor of the tour" ["What'd I Say?" RS 291]. About the fact that we went around with "Camp Lejeune" on the front of our bus—Camp Lejeune, where they train the Marines. He said it was like an exercise in paranoia. To an extent, it was. The anti-journalist thing we were doing, the anti-photographer thing, had reached an almost excessive level by that point. Schruers said that the press were looking for something to crucify me with, and I fed myself to the lions. There were words to that effect. I remember them distinctly. And I couldn't help but agree, to a certain extent, looking—aside from the incident itself—dispassionately at the effect of what happened.

What actually happened was this: We were in the bar—Bruce Thomas and I were in the bar after the show in Columbus, Ohio. And we were *very* drunk. Well, we weren't drunk to begin with—we were reasonably drunk. And we started into what you'd prob-

ably call joshing. Gentle gibes between the two camps of the Stills Band and us. It developed as it got drunker and drunker into a nastier and nastier argument. And I suppose that in the drunkenness, my contempt for them was probably exaggerated beyond my *real* contempt for them. I don't think I had a real opinion. But they just seemed in some way to typify a lot of things that I thought were wrong with American music. And that's probably quite unfair. But at the exact moment—they did.

Things such as what?

Insincerity, dishonesty—musical dishonesty.

How so?

I just think they're . . . This is difficult, because this is getting right off the point. Because now I'm getting into mudslinging.

But now we're trying to talk about what it was really about.

What it was about was that I said the most outrageous thing I could possibly say to them—that I *knew*, in my drunken logic, would anger them more than anything else. That's why I don't want to get into *why* I felt so affronted by them, because *that's* not important. It's not important because . . . they don't mean *anything* to me. They don't even mean anything *now* —I don't feel any *malice* in the way I feel that they probably *exploited* the incident to get some free publicity.

My initial reaction—I can tell you now—to seeing Bonnie Bramlett get free publicity out of my name was that, "Well, she rode to fame on the back of one E.C., she's not gonna do it on the back of another." But that was before the consequences of what had happened had sunk in—that was a flip way of dismissing it.

Did you have any idea of how dangerous, or how exploitable, or how plainly offensive, what you said would be in a public context?

No, because it was never intended—if I hadn't been drunk, I would never have said those things. If it had been a considered argument, I probably would have either not pursued the argument to such extreme length, or I would have thought of something a little bit more coherent, another form of attack, rather than just *outrage*. Outrage is fairly easy. Not in terms of dealing with the consequences, but in terms of employing it as a tactic in an argument.

With the press conference in New York a few days later, the situation reminded me of nothing so much as the "We're more popular than Jesus" blowup with the Beatles.

It had approximately the same effect on our career. The minute the story was published nationally, records were taken off playlists. About 120 death threats—or threats of violence of some kind. I had armed bodyguards for the last part of that tour.

And not since?

For one tour since. Not armed, but . . .

But not now?

We take more care with security than we did before.

Were records taken out of stores?

I don't know—there may have been. Just like people won't sell South African goods. I mean—quite rightly so! Until there was an explanation.

The press conference was unsuccessful because I was *fried* on that tour. This is aside from the incident; now I'm talking from a personal point of view.

It was at that point that everything—whether it be my self-perpetrated *venom*—was about to engulf me. I was, I think, rapidly becoming not a very nice person. I was losing track of what I was doing, why I was doing it and my own control.

In your first interview, in 1977 with Nick Kent of 'NME,' you made a famous statement: words to the effect that all you knew of human emotions were revenge and guilt. Those words have been endlessly quoted—I've quoted them, they're irresistible. Now you're describing that as venom—as if your artistic venom, what you put into your music, had engulfed your own life.

I think it did. I think it started to take over. You see, I think that after a while—apart from anything else, looking from a purely artistic point of view—it started to become a problem for me to incorporate the wider, more compassionate point of view that I felt; I was trying to put that forward in some of the songs, and it was so much at odds with the pre*conception* of the image.

When we were playing, the frustration of that just ate me up. And with my lack of personal control of my life, and my supposed emotions, and drinking too much, and being on the road too much—

I'm not saying I wasn't responsible for my actions; that sounds like I'm trying to excuse myself. *But I was not very responsible.* There's a distinct difference. I was completely irresponsible, in fact. And far from carefree—care*less* with everything. With everything that I really care about. And I think that, inasmuch as it was said that we fed ourselves to the lions, you could say that *whatever* the incident was, it was symptomatic of the condition I was in, and that I deserved what happened regardless of the intentions of the remarks.

But it was only quite recently that I realized that it's not only the man on the street, as it were, who's never heard of me otherwise, who's only read *People* —that it's not only people like that who know only

this about me. When we were recording *Imperial Bedroom*, Bruce Thomas was in the next studio while I was doing a vocal. Paul McCartney was there, and Michael Jackson came in to do a vocal—everything was very nice. Everyone was getting along fine until somebody introduced Bruce as my bass player. And suddenly—there was a freeze-out. Michael Jackson was—"Oh, God, I don't dig that guy . . . I don't dig that guy."

He had heard about it thirdhand, from Quincy Jones. Two guys I have a tremendous amount of admiration for. It depressed me that I wouldn't be able to go up to him—I wouldn't be able to go up and shake his hand, because he wouldn't want to shake my hand. *Or* James Brown, for that matter. But what could I say? What could I say? How could you explain such a thing? But there is nothing I'd like more.

Costello and the Attractions returned to England, wondering if they could ever return to America, and made 'Get Happy!!': "Our version of a Motown album," Costello says. "I had the feeling people were reading my mind— but what could I do, hold up a sign that read, 'I Really Like Black People'? Like Tom Robinson or Joan Baez? Turn myself into Steve Marriott: 'My skin is white but my soul is black'?"

The band almost broke up; Steve Nieve quit, Costello finished up a European tour with Martin Belmont of the Rumour, and then Costello quit—briefly.

The band put itself back together and produced 'Trust,' a singer's showcase, and 'Almost Blue,' a less-than-convincing country music tribute recorded in Nashville and produced by Billy Sherrill. One sweltering night in 1981 in Los Angeles, Costello—with two of the Attractions and Nick Lowe—took part in the taping of a George Jones Home Box Office special; puffed up with the mumps and swaddled in heavy clothes, he proved himself more of a professional and more of an artist than the country superstars who clowned and fussed their way through their numbers. On record, he has again found all of his voice: 'Imperial Bedroom' is his most adventurous and successful recording since 'Armed Forces' or 'This Year's Model.' Costello's thoughts on quitting the game, his state of mind after 'Get Happy!!,' remain worth considering.

I didn't want to do anymore. I didn't see any point. It was a question of deciding whether we were going to be a *cult act.*

We were operating on such a low level. I was aware of the fact that there was no way that *Get Happy!!* was going to be a Number One record—or, in a different sense, any record at all. *That* record was called another

"Angry Young Man" record! We were a little, pigeoned cult—"Oh, yeah, they're the Angry Young Man act. We've got them numbered."

We weren't actually achieving any change if we weren't selling more records than REO Speedwagon. So long as we were only as commercially effective as Randy Newman—

Randy Newman doesn't really play for the people who should hear his songs. He plays to polite, amused—I sat sickened through the best concert I think he's done in London, at Drury Lane just after *Good Old Boys* came out; people were guffawing through "Davy, the Fat Boy." I couldn't watch him for the audience.

That was the way I felt: that we were comfortably contained within the business, instead of having some dramatic effect on the structure of the business. You'd just be another pawn. The people that formed United Artists—they had control over their own artistic destiny by forming the company. Barring being able to do that, you can actually change the structure of the scene that you're working within by being the biggest thing in it.

There's also the possibility of affecting the way people actually respond to the world.

Well, that's the initial intention of writing the songs to begin with, isn't it?

That's the view that you put into that *one song*—whether it be about something extremely large, or not at all. I wrote a song called "Hoover Factory"—about a lovely deco building that was going to be torn down. I said, "It's not a matter of life or death—but what is?"

There is a song on *Imperial Bedroom*, "The Loved Ones," that is the hardest song to get over. Considering it's got such a light pop tune, it's like saying, "Fuck posterity; it's better to live." It's the opposite of *Rust Never Sleeps*. It's about "Fuck being a junkie and dying in some phony romantic way like Brendan Behan or Dylan Thomas." Somebody in your family's got to bury you, you know?

That's a complicated idea to put in a pop song. I didn't want to write a story around it—I wanted to just throw all of those ideas into a song. Around a good pop hook.

And that, in a nice, simple statement, is a philosophy of pop: from a man whose work and career have shown that the pursuit of such a philosophy is anything but simple—and also worth the candle.

7

Neil Young

INTERVIEWED BY JAMES HENKE (1988)

Few things have proved so difficult for Sixties rock stars as maintaining their musical credibility into middle age. (Ask Mick Jagger.) That Neil Young has been one of the few to do so is a tribute to his openness, both as an artist and as a fan of the music. Virtually alone among the West Coast studio-rock elite that dominated American airwaves in the Seventies, Young found much to be admired in punk and, subsequently, the synth rock of such Eurogroups as Kraftwerk in the early Eighties. Since he first appeared on the scene in 1967 with Buffalo Springfield, Young has made records in an often exhilarating jumble of styles—folk, thrash, rockabilly, "blues." For some critics, this tendency has marked him as a feckless eccentric, too remote from the prevailing urgencies of Eighties rock to do relevant work, and too wealthy, by now, to really give a damn. Some listeners have also been put off by his primitivism, his what-the-hell productions, his wavering relationship to pitch.

For Young's admirers, these are nits hardly worth picking. To them, Young is a rock original, and his music a highly personalized enterprise conducted outside the orbit of transient fashion. They admire his unpretentiousness and his constancy. He has remained an exemplar of what might be called the hippie ideal, a graduate of that school of thought that rates music as something too meaningful to be pursued entirely for commercial gain. His 1988 video for the anti-ad-rock song "This Note's for You," directed by Julien Temple, drew a line that many of his peers and pals—including beer salesmen Eric Clapton and Steve Winwood—found themselves on the wrong side of. Talk about relevance.

Young places great value on spontaneity, both in his music and in the interviews he occasionally agrees to do. Unlike more cautious stars, he appears to have no desire to know what kinds of questions are going to be asked, or where they might lead. The result, at least in the following case, is an interview that actually goes somewhere.

—K.L.

YOU DON'T MIND doing this on the move, do you?" Neil Young asks as he slides behind the wheel of his 1950 Plymouth Special Deluxe, one of the roughly thirty-five cars in his ever-expanding collection.

Spring has barely arrived, but the temperature in the hills south of San Francisco has already hit the nineties, and Young is dressed accordingly—his shirt is open, and he's wearing a pair of frayed cutoffs, sneakers and blue shades. Bits of gray have streaked his familiar sideburns and shoulder-length hair, but Young still looks very much as he did seventeen years ago, when he moved up here to redwood country and bought what he now calls Broken Arrow Ranch.

The ranch was one of the rewards of Young's first burst of success. *After the Gold Rush,* the third solo album he recorded after leaving Buffalo Springfield, reached the Top Ten in 1970, and both *Déjà Vu* and *4 Way Street,* recorded with David Crosby, Stephen Stills and Graham Nash, hit number one. For a while, CSNY seemed like the American Beatles, and Young was their John Lennon, the passionate, slightly eccentric rocker who gave the group its edge.

But CSNY self-destructed, and after reaching number one in 1972 with *Harvest* and the single "Heart of Gold," Young moved away from the mainstream. "This song put me in the middle of the road," Young wrote about "Heart of Gold" in his liner notes to his three-album retrospective, *Decade.* "Travelling there soon became a bore so I headed for the ditch. A rougher ride but I saw more interesting people there."

By 1979, when Young last sat for an in-depth interview with ROLLING STONE, he had reached another peak, both critically and commercially, with the country-tinged *Comes a Time* and the punk-inspired *Rust Never Sleeps. The Village Voice* named him Artist of the Decade, and there was every reason to think

he'd continue to maintain a high level of success in the Eighties.

But Young signed to David Geffen's newly formed Geffen Records early in the decade, and the pairing proved to be a frustrating one for both sides. The five albums Young recorded for the label rank as the worst selling of his career. His intermittently brilliant but quirky stylistic experiments—techno-rock on *Trans* (1982), rockabilly on *Everybody's Rockin'* (1983) and country on *Old Ways* (1985)—caused even his staunchest supporters to lose their patience.

Young insists that the label is the real villain behind that slump, and he even claims that his best work during the period was never released. Geffen, for its part, refuses to respond to Young's allegations. "I don't want to get into a pissing match with him," says label president Ed Rosenblatt.

No matter who was at fault, Young is clearly delighted to be back on Reprise, the Warner Bros. subsidiary he was with in the Seventies. He is also determined to prove that Geffen —which at one point even sued him for deliberately making noncommercial records—was wrong. But in typical Neil Young style, his first album for Reprise—though his strongest, most consistent effort in years—is hardly a sure commercial bet. *This Note's for You* features Young and the Bluenotes, a horn-powered nine-piece band; they work up a sweat on ten blues tunes inspired by such early Young faves as Jimmy Reed and John Lee Hooker. And the album's title cut finds Young railing against rock & roll's increasing involvement with Madison Avenue.

"There's a line," Young says, "one of the first fucking lines that's ever been drawn where pop stars really have to show their stuff, show where they're really coming from. I mean, if you're going to sing for a product, then you're singing for money. Period. That's it. Money is what you want, and this is how you get it."

Over the course of the two sessions that made up this interview—the second one was also conducted on the move, in Young's 1954 Cadillac limousine—Young, who's now forty-two, was equally emphatic about his loyalty to the Bluenotes and even indicated that the gut-wrenching rock & roll he's played with Crazy Horse may be a thing of the past.

But Young has never been a one-band man, and he's already recording a new Crosby, Stills, Nash and Young album up at his ranch. That album is expected to be released this fall, and in the meantime Young and the Bluenotes will be hitting the road for an extended U.S. tour. As for the distant future, Young will no doubt keep everyone guessing—just as he has for the past two decades.

What prompted you to get back together with Crosby, Stills and Nash?

Well, there's a certain energy you get from singing with people you've known for twenty-five years. People who have been through all these changes with you. Gone up and down with you. Seen you do things that are wrong and seen you do things that are brilliant. Seen you fucked up to the max, you know? And you've seen them do all these things. And yet we're still here. Just to hear what it sounds like when we sing together after all these years—I was curious. I've wanted to do it for the last two or three years. And now it's possible.

I think that CSNY has a lot to say. Especially Crosby. His presence is very strong. Him being strong and surviving and writing great songs and being part of a winner is really a good role model for a lot of people in the same boat.

So he's really cleaned up?

He's doing fine. His emotions are slightly shattered, because he's just abused his emotions for so long by not letting them out. But now that he's pure and can let his emotions out, his highs are real high, and his lows are real low. Those are just the extremes of his personality. But he pulls out of his lows, and they don't turn him toward any problem areas or anything.

How about Stills?

He's definitely the rowdiest of the four of us, as far as abuses and things like that. But he's at a time in his life when things are real important. He's just been married, and his wife's pregnant. There are a lot of

new things happening. And he and I playing together is a nice resurgence.

He didn't seem so together when they profiled CSN on 'West 57th.'

The thing that surprised me was the fact that CSN actually did the show. I mean, what are they gonna do next, *Geraldo*? And they obviously weren't thinking clearly, because every tour that CSN has ever done, Stephen has gone out the window. He blows out before he goes on the road. He blows out heavily. So what do they do? They set up a TV guy to be there when it happens. What kind of stupid move is that?

You two have had a stormy relationship.

We're like brothers, you know? We love each other, and we hate each other. We resent each other, but we love playing together. I see and hear so much in Stephen that I'm frustrated when it isn't on record or something. There have been a lot of frustrations through our whole lives with each other, but there's also been a lot of great music. He continuously blows my mind with the ideas that he has for my songs. He's one of the greatest musicians I've ever met in my life. Great singer. Incredible songwriter.

But what's he like as a person? He came off like a jerk on that show.

He's a tormented artist. He's the definition of the tormented artist. And he's a great fucking bluesman. But he's got a lot of monkeys on his back, and they're not letting him do his thing. I just hope he makes it.

And what's Nash like?

Nash is a very straight, very sincere kind of organized guy, dedicated to quality and very reliable. And he's an extremely good singer. Amazing pitch. He likes to be on top of it. He takes a lot of pride in being totally able to accomplish whatever it is that has to be done. Without Nash, there would be no Crosby, Stills and Nash at all. It would have been over a long time ago.

Are there plans for a CSNY tour?

They wanted to book a tour, and I said no way. I don't want to have anything to do with a tour. When the record's finished and we know what we've got, that's the time to talk about a tour.

Also, everyone needs to really get in shape if we tour. There's no way getting around the fact that a CSNY tour would be a nostalgia tour to a great degree. CSNY is Woodstock—it's that era, that whole generation. So why go out there and not be at our physical best? If people are looking at us as their brothers who they went through all these changes with, do they want to see somebody who's not together? No, they want to see someone who's superstrong, who's endured, who's a survivor and is still creative and looks better than ever. So I think we have a responsibility, and I don't think we've lived up to it yet.

Crosby's recovered to a point. But he needs to recover his physical strength and endurance. His endurance is low because he's very big. And he moves very slowly. This is a problem that has to be solved. You can't go out there with all the spirit in the world. You have to have a physical body that can sustain the gruel of a world tour.

From time to time, there are also rumors of a Buffalo Springfield reunion. Is there any truth to them?

Well, there actually have been several Buffalo Springfield reunions in the last two years. At Stills's house. We just get together every couple of months and play. The original guys—Richie [Furay], Dewey [Martin], Bruce [Palmer], Stephen and I. We've done this three, maybe four times, and I'm sure we'll do it again.

Is there a chance you'll record with them?

It's crossed my mind, but I'm committed to CSNY, and there's no way I'm gonna do CSNY and Buffalo Springfield.

When you look back at that time—Buffalo Springfield, CSNY, the Sixties—how does it all seem now?

I had a great time. I think a lot of us had a great time back then. But I don't see myself as being stuck in the Sixties or anything like that—except that I still have long hair.

What about the idealism of the period? In "Hippie Dream," you sang, "The wooden ships are a hippie dream, capsized in excess."

I wrote that one for Crosby. But I guess it could have been for me, or for anybody. It's really about the excesses of our whole generation. From hippie to yuppie—I mean, it's been quite an evolution.

What do you think about drugs? A lot of people have an image of you as having been a big druggie.

That's a myth. I mean, how would I have kept this together for so long if I was on drugs? It'd be impossible. You could not do what I have done if you were into drugs. I mean, I used a few drugs. I smoked a lot of grass in the Sixties, continued to smoke grass into the Seventies and dabbled around in other drugs. But I never got hooked on . . . you know, never got out of hand with the harder drugs. I experimented, but I think I'm basically a survivor. I've never been an alcoholic. Never used heroin.

There must have been a lot of heroin around you. Two of your friends—Danny Whitten, a guitarist with Crazy Horse, and Bruce Berry, a roadie—died of overdoses. And of course there was Crosby.

There was never any heroin directly around me, 'cause people knew how I felt about it. Anything that killed people, I didn't want to have. Anything that you had to have, that was bigger than you, I'm not for that.

"The Needle and the Damage Done," from 'Harvest,' was one of the first antidrug songs.

I wrote that about Danny Whitten. He'd gotten so wasted, so strung out, that he OD'd and almost died.

He finally did OD and die shortly after 'Harvest' was released. Had he known the song was about him?

He must have. I never sat down with him and said, "Danny, listen to this." I don't believe that a song should be for one person. I just tried to make something that everyone could relate to.

What about cocaine? At the Last Waltz you came onstage with a lump of cocaine under your nose.

I was fried for the Last Waltz. I was on my way out, falling onstage, and someone said, "Here, have some of this." I'd been up for two days, so I had some. And I was gone, you know? I'm not proud of it; I don't think people should see that and think, "Wow, that's cool."

When they were editing the film, they asked me if I wanted to have that removed. And Robbie Robertson said, "The way you are is kinda like what the whole movie's about—if you keep on doin' this, you're just gonna die, so we're going to stop doing it." They just caught me at a bad time. I had been on the road for forty-five days, and I'd done two shows the night before in Atlanta, and I just got carried away, and we just blew it out the window. So I was still up.

But I don't do that anymore. I'm one of the lucky ones who was able to do that and able to stop. But it wasn't that easy to stop that lifestyle. I had to spend some time. The monster kept coming back every once in a while. I could stop for three or four weeks or a couple of months, then I'd get back into it, just for one or two nights, then I'd stop again. It took a long time. I don't even know if it's over now.

Do you still smoke grass?

I haven't smoked any since October 7. The main reason is that on October 7, Elliot Roberts, my manager, called and told me that it looked like I was going to get off Geffen Records. And I had just smoked this big bomber, and I almost had a heart attack. I was so happy, but I was too high to enjoy it. So I stopped. I just didn't have my senses, my faculties together enough to enjoy the moment.

You'd been trying to get off Geffen for a long time.

They had a very negative viewpoint of anything that I wanted to do, other than straight pop records that were exactly what they wanted to hear. They saw me as a product that was not living up to their expectations. They didn't see me as an artist.

Geffen actually sued you for not making commercial records around the time of 'Old Ways.'

There was a whole other record, the original *Old Ways,* which Geffen rejected. It was like *Harvest II.* It was a combination of the musicians from *Harvest* and *Comes a Time.* It was done in Nashville in only a few days, basically the same way *Harvest* was done, and it was co-produced by Elliot Mazer, who produced *Harvest.*

There's *Harvest, Comes a Time* and *Old Ways I,* which is more of a Neil Young record than *Old Ways II. Old Ways II* was more of a country record—which was a direct result of being sued for playing country music. The more they tried to stop me, the more I did it. Just to let them know that no one's gonna tell me what to do.

I would have thought that Geffen would have wanted another 'Comes a Time' or 'Harvest.'

That's what we thought. I was so stoked about that record. I sent them a tape of it that had eight songs on it. I called them up a week later, 'cause I hadn't heard anything, and they said, "Well, frankly, Neil, this record scares us a lot. We don't think this is the right direction for you to be going in."

The technopop thing was happening, and they had Peter Gabriel, and they were totally into that kind of trip. I guess they just saw me as some old hippie from the Sixties still trying to make acoustic music or something. They didn't look at me as an artist; they looked at me as a product, and this product didn't fit in with their marketing scheme.

When you look back at the five albums you made for Geffen, how do you think they stand up?

It's hard for me to disassociate the frustrations that I had during that period from the actual works I was able to create. I really tried to do my best during that period, but I felt that I was working under duress.

In all my time at Warner Bros., they never canceled a session. For any reason. And it happened several times at Geffen. It was blatant manipulation. It was just so different from anything I'd ever experienced.

They buried *Everybody's Rockin'.* They did less than nothing. They decided, "That record's not gonna get noticed. We're gonna press as few of those as possible and not do anything."

There was another record of mine, called *Island in the Sun,* which will probably never be heard. It was the first record I made for Geffen. The three acoustic songs on *Trans* are from it. But they advised me not to put it out. Because it was my first record for Geffen, I thought, "Well, this is a fresh, new thing. He's got some new ideas." It didn't really register to me that I was being manipulated. Until the second record. Then I realized this is the way it is all the time. Whatever I do, it's not what they want.

I'm gonna try and expose those things that I tried to do on *Decade II,* which should come out next year. Now that I'm back on Reprise, I can do whatever I want. So I can do *Decade II.* On Geffen, *Decade II* would have been impossible, 'cause it's a three-record set, and they would never do that. There's no way they could make the money they want to make out of it.

'Trans' surprised a lot of people. I don't think anyone expected you to make an album with synthesizers.

Trans resulted from a fascination with machines and computers taking over our lives. This image of elevators with digital numbers changing and people going up and down the floors—you know, people changing levels all under the control of a machine. And drum machines, the whole thing. And here I was, like an old hippie out in the woods, with all this electronic equipment. I mean, I was astonished.

I had a whole video thing in mind for that record. I had characters and images of beings that went with all the voices. There was one guy I called Tabulon, who sang on "Computer Age." He had a big speaker in his chest, and his face was a keypad, and he kept hitting his face. [*He demonstrates, with a quick blow to his face.*] But I could never get anybody to make the videos. I could never get anybody to believe that the fucking idea was any good.

What about 1986's 'Landing on Water'? That album holds up pretty well.

That album was like a rebirth, just me coming back to L.A. after having been secluded for so long. I was finding my rock & roll roots again. And my vibrancy as a musician. Something came alive; it was like a bear waking up.

What had you been doing during hibernation?

I had just been up here in the woods. And I'd been working on a program with my son Ben, who has cerebral palsy. It just kind of took me away for a while, made me think about other things. I never really lost interest in music, but there were other things in my life that were real important. My real soul was taken up with things I didn't want to sing about.

Although if you listen to *Trans,* if you listen to the words to "Transformer Man" and "Computer Age" and "We R in Control," you'll hear a lot of references to my son and to people trying to live a life by pressing buttons, trying to control the things around them, and talking with people who can't talk, using computer voices and things like that.

It's a subtle thing, but it's right there. But it has to do with a part of my life that practically no one can relate to. So my music, which is a reflection of my inner self, became something that nobody could relate to. And then I started hiding in styles, just putting little clues in there as to what was really on my mind. I just didn't want to openly share all this stuff in songs that said exactly what I wanted to say in a voice so loud everyone could hear it.

Both of your sons have cerebral palsy. How badly handicapped are they?

Well, Ben, who's nine, is a great little guy, a wonderful little human being. He's got a really beautiful little face, and he's got a great heart, and he's a lot of fun to play with. We've got a really great train set that we play with, a huge train set that he controls with buttons and stuff.

He's learning how to communicate and play games and solve problems using a computer. And he is handicapped inasmuch as he has severe cerebral palsy, and he is a quadriplegic, and he's a non-oral child. So he has a lot of handicaps. Cerebral palsy is a condition of life, not a disease. It's the way he is, the condition he's in. He was brought into the world in this form, and this is the way he is. A lot of the things that we take for granted, that we can do, he can't do. But his soul is there, and I'm sure that he has an outlook on the world that we don't have because of the disabilities.

My son Zeke has very mild cerebral palsy. He's a wonderful boy, and he's growing up to be a strong kid. He's going to be sixteen in September, and one of the things he really wants to do now is get his driver's license. He's a great guy, a great kid, and he's got a great heart.

What causes cerebral palsy?

No one knows. That's the thing. Just why they were born with cerebral palsy is a question that Pegi [Young's wife] and I ask, and Carrie [Snodgress, Zeke's mother] and I ask. There's no way to tell. My third child, Am-

ber, is just a little flower, growing like a little flower should. It took Pegi a lot of preparation to get ready to have another kid, because it was really hard for us to face the chance that things might not work out right. But so many doctors told us that it had nothing to do with anything. I went and got myself checked, because I was the father of both kids. And the doctors said, "It may be hard for you to believe this, but you had two kids, and there's no connection between them at all. It's a fluke that both have cerebral palsy."

Often in my life, I've felt that I was singled out for one reason or another for extreme things to happen. This was hard to deal with. We've been dealing with it, and we've learned to turn it around into a positive thing and to keep on going. It was something that brought Pegi and I really close together, just having the strength to have another child and having her be such a beautiful little girl and having everything work out. Just believing. Coming around to believing that it's okay for us to try again.

In 1986 you put on a concert to raise money for a school for the handicapped.

The Bridge School. We've got it going now. Ben goes there. Learning how to communicate, basically, is what the school is all about.

We spent two years in another program. It was an almost Nazi kind of program. They had us doing these things that didn't help our child, but they had us convinced that if we didn't do the program, we were not doing the right thing for the kid. And it kept us busy all the waking hours of the day, seven days a week, forever—until the kid was better.

We had no time to ourselves. Can you imagine what that's like? We couldn't leave the house. We had to be there doing this program, and it was an excruciatingly difficult thing for the kid to go through, because he was crying almost all day, it was so hard. We lasted a couple of years before we just couldn't do it anymore.

When we left that, we went to a simpler type of program, and we decided to stop concentrating on the physical side so much and start trying to get the kid to communicate. It's our life's work almost now.

It was the most difficult thing I think I've ever done. That's why when someone says they can't do something because it's too hard, it makes me mad. I get upset about that.

How much has your kids' condition affected your political outlook?

I think it's affected it quite a bit. I became much more involved in family, taking care of the family, making sure the family was secure. And I related to

Reagan's original concept of big government and federal programs fading away so that communities could handle their own programs, like day care. That was the crux of his domestic message, and I thought the idea was good. I thought it would bring people together. But it was a real idealistic thing, and people didn't really come together.

You got a lot of flak for coming out in support of Reagan in 1984. Were there other reasons he appealed to you?

I was very disillusioned with Jimmy Carter. On a political level, I don't think we ever should have given back the Panama Canal. I just have a gut feeling that that was a huge mistake made out of guilt, not out of reasoning. He was going to make up for all the other bad things we'd done in the world by giving back the Panama Canal. I also think it was wrong to have let the armed forces deteriorate to a point where our strength was less than it had been at a time when other superpowers were growing. I just don't think it was good ball playing. I'm not a hawk. I'm not one who wants to go to war and flex muscles and everything, but I just don't believe that you can talk from a weakness. I think it is as straightforward as that. Everybody in the world is playing hardball, and if we say we're not going to play hardball anymore, we're playing powder puff, we're going to start by putting down the hardball, I don't think it's going to work. People are going to confuse that as a weakness and take advantage of it.

Mondale, as far as I was concerned, was not going to do much different from what Carter had done. So I was for Reagan, and I thought it was an important issue. Now, to be for a president doesn't mean that you agree with everything that president does. But I thought that was an important issue, and I thought that was the right way to go, and I still stand behind it.

What do you think about the way things turned out?

Well, so many things have happened. I think he really did want to do the things that he said he wanted to do. I was disappointed in many of the things that happened during his administration. But I thought that the ideas that were behind a lot of the things he tried to do were things that I could relate to. I just couldn't back away from that.

Who do you support in the current presidential race?

Well, I would not like to see George Bush as president of the United States. I don't think the former leader of the CIA should be president. We need someone with compassion, someone who has a lot of feelings and a lot of savvy. That's why I don't see one

person at this point. I think that the one person I would like to see as president of the United States is Bill Bradley. But he's not going to be a candidate. Unfortunately, I don't think the Democrats have anyone who can beat Bush. I like Jackson, and I kind of like Dukakis. But I think Jackson's the best. He's the guy I would like to see just for interest's sake. I would like to see what would happen, because there would be a lot of change.

Musically, you seem to be obsessed with change. At Geffen you went through synth rock, country and rockabilly, and now your first album on Reprise is a blues record.

It's just the way I am. When I was in school, I would go for six months wearing the same kind of clothes. Then all of a sudden I'd wear all different clothes. It's change. It's always been like that.

You've taken a lot of heat for all the stylistic changes.

When people think that I'm just doing this on a whim, it discounts the music. Music is immediate to me. It's something that's happening right now, and it's a reflection of what's going on with the people who are making it. It has nothing to do with what they did or what they are going to do.

You know, I used to be pissed off at Bobby Darin because he changed styles so much. Now I look at him and I think he was a fucking genius. I mean, from "Queen of the Hop" to "Mack the Knife." Dig that. And it didn't mean that he didn't believe in "Queen of the Hop" when he turned around and did a Frank Sinatra thing.

Yet I come up against this because I experiment around and I play different kinds of music. In my eyes, it doesn't make what I'm doing any less valid. Right now, I love the Bluenotes, to a point where it feels so right to me. I'll do other things, but I think I'm gonna come back to this over and over again. I mean, playing with a horn section and playing with this band is just so great.

I think it's the best support I've had for the kind of music I was into. Everything has come together at the right time for this. There's a special thing that happens when the music is right. When it's not hard to do. When things aren't a problem. And you just play, and everybody likes it, and they start grooving. That makes me write a new song every morning when I wake up, instead of thinking, "Well, if I write this, are the guys gonna be able to play it, or have I got the right band, or do I know anybody who really understands who I am, who I can actually play music with?"

Yet you said something similar when you did the 'Old

Ways' record and toured with the International Harvesters—that you were happy and that country was what you'd be doing from then on.

At the time, I really did feel good doing it. And it was a lot of fun. And then one morning I woke up and all I could hear was this massive fucking beat. And my guitar was just rising out of it. I just heard rock & roll in my head, so fucking loud that I couldn't ignore it.

And so you went back to Crazy Horse—something you've done time and again throughout your career.

That's true, and I may come back to Crazy Horse again some day, but it seems more and more doubtful to me. The kind of music I played with Crazy Horse was a younger kind of music. And I'm not younger —I'm older. And the experience that I have of playing all the different kinds of music that I've played so intensely has a place to come to in the Bluenotes. I can incorporate everything I've done in my life into this band—blues, country, rock & roll. Nothing else that I had done in the past had the kind of passion that Crazy Horse had, but the Bluenotes do. So this is what makes me wonder what's gonna happen with Crazy Horse.

You've just finished a full-length video called 'Muddy Track,' which is about one of your last tours with Crazy Horse.

I had two little video-8 cameras, which I left running all the time. I would just come into rooms and put them down on the table. And the point of view is really from the camera. The camera takes on an identity—its name is Otto—and people start talking to the camera. And this camera saw a lot of things that really go down on a tour that are not cute or funsy-wunsy. It's not like the pop-band-on-the-road type of thing. There's a lot of guts in it, a lot of feeling.

The great thing about Crazy Horse is that they're not technically great players, but they have a lot of passion.

Well, that's what Crazy Horse is all about. And they bring out a part of me that's very primitive. We really put out a lot of emotion—which is easy for a kid to relate to. So it's very childlike. I've had some great times with Crazy Horse.

How do you feel about playing that kind of rock & roll when you're in your forties?

Muddy Track covers a lot of that. Covers that feeling, you know? There's some wild stuff in there where we do speed metal. A lot of the music is only the beginnings and ends of songs. The songs themselves aren't there. It's like the interviews are only the interviewer. And you hardly ever see me. You only hear questions. It's an interesting concept of your point of view. And it talks about what it's like to be forty-one, forty-two, and still be doing that kind of music.

And the question is, how long can you keep doing it? And really be doing it? Or do you become a reenactment of an earlier happening? That's a question I ask myself.

Do you think Crazy Horse started to become a reenactment?

Toward the end it was starting to. I could feel it starting to slip away. And I never wanted to be in front of people and have them pay to see me when I'm not 100 percent there. And if you feel that energy slipping away, then you've got to fold your deck, you know, get out.

So are you saying that rock & roll is really a younger person's medium?

I'm not really sure. There's no doubt that it is a younger person's medium. The question is whether it can also be an older person's medium. That's why I love the Bluenotes. They afford me the same kind of passion and expression as rock & roll, but in a more experienced and evolved way.

So that's why I feel real good about the music I'm playing now. It's something that I believe in and that I'm comfortable with. It's real; it's what's really happening to me now in my life.

8

Mick Jagger

INTERVIEWED BY
CHRISTOPHER CONNELLY (1985)

It is perhaps possible that there could exist, on some nether rack of the interviewer's artillery, a question with which Mick Jagger has not been potted at over the course of his quarter century on the top rungs of the rock & roll game. Possible—but I can't think what it would be, and (since we're being honest here) neither can you. Jagger's combination of shrewdly cultivated charisma, indigenous wit, great native charm and an almost amusing inclination to manipulate every interview situation to his benefit can be daunting. The only prescriptive is total preparation, and even that's not guaranteed— especially if he finds the interviewer to be simply tiresome. (Not as remote a possibility— if we may continue in this candid vein—as you might imagine.)

Despite all the Q&As he's endured over the twenty-six years since the Rolling Stones charted their first single in Britain, Jagger remains a fascinating character. Unlike his songwriting partner, Keith Richards (for whom the term devil-may-care *might have been coined), Jagger has always seemed inclined toward calculation and control (it's part of what makes him a great songwriter, not to mention singer). And inevitably, there have been* miscalculations. *The disco days of the late Seventies—which Jagger seemed to spend cavorting almost nonstop with his fellow moneyed swells—took a toll on his integrity, at least as publicly perceived. While Richards lived out the rock & roll life to its limit (occasionally behind bars), Jagger seemed in danger of disappearing into the meaningless roil of international tabloid celebrity. By the time the following* ROLLING STONE *interview was conducted, he was forty-one years old and about to release his first solo album, 'She's the Boss.' Although ineffectively produced and lacking the ensemble spark that makes the Stones a nonpareil instrumental unit, the album contained good songs and spawned two Top Forty hits. It didn't* sell *all that well, though; nor did 'Dirty Work,' the next album he did with the Stones. Jagger's second solo outing, the 1987 album 'Primitive Cool,' was an undeserved bomb (containing, as it did, several good songs and at least one great one: "Party Doll").*

By this point, the Rolling Stones' future was in serious doubt—a state of affairs caused (at least according to Richards) by the menopausal Jagger. Keith made the next move, finally releasing his first solo album in the fall of 1988. 'Talk Is Cheap' was a good, smoking Keith Richards record, but it lacked a certain something—call it calculation, call it control. Which was odd, because Jagger's solo opuses had both been . . . well, a little light in the devil-may-care department.

As the Eighties drew toward a close, Mick and Keith reunited onstage in New York City for the Stones' induction into the Rock & Roll Hall of Fame and announced that they were, indeed, still rolling. You can imagine the cheers.

—K.L.

MICK JAGGER, it seems, cannot sit still. Seated behind a console at the Power Station, in New York, Jagger is fidgeting with strips of paper that have the song titles for his new solo album written on them. Over and over, he rearranges them, in search of the ideal sequence. Then, once the master tapes are cued up and clicked on, he's out of his chair—tail shaking, lip-syncing, playing air guitar, even winking. For someone so notoriously blasé offstage, this guy seems pretty keyed up.

Why is Mick Jagger so excited? Mainly because his first solo LP, tentatively dubbed *She's the Boss,* is due out soon, and it's the forty-one-year-old singer's boldest attempt yet to establish an artistic identity for himself apart from the Rolling Stones. Jagger's previous attempts at acting and screenwriting have been flops, and his general lack of interest was all too noticeable during the promotion of the Stones' last studio LP, *Undercover,* which sold disappointingly. But with the active encouragement of the Stones' new label, Columbia, Mick says he finally started thinking about his solo debut.

"Atlantic would just say, 'Okay, we have another Stones album,' and then wait eighteen months," he explained. "Whereas CBS would say, 'Hey, Mick, you know, we want you to do two solo albums.' So I thought, 'Wow, they really want me to do it. Okay, I will.' "

Of course, it's not just his record that's

fueling his good mood these days: He's an involved father to his three daughters, Karis, 13 (by singer Marsha Hunt); Jade, 13 (by Bianca Jagger); and the infant Elizabeth Scarlett (by Jerry Hall). He and Jerry tend to the sprout, but the eldest two have been dispatched to British boarding schools. "New York is a terrible place to bring up kids," he mourns.

Right now, though, his album is foremost in his thoughts, and justifiably so: While its raucous, unhinged spirit is certainly reminiscent of the Stones' work, its sound is more aggressively contemporary, from the rhythm-section fury of "Just Another Night" and "Running Out of Luck" to the wild wit of "She's the Boss" and "Lucky in Love." The album is further proof that Jagger, unlike most forty-plus performers, can stake out contemporary musical territory without embarrassing himself.

Jagger is, of course, the most written-about living performer in the history of rock & roll, and he is quite adroit at deflecting overly pungent inquiries. He can be gracious (he shakes your hand when he meets you . . .) and brusque (. . . but not when he says good-bye). It is, after all, business—something Mick Jagger is *very* good at.

So I heard that Paul McCartney wanted to play on your record—on a track ["Hard Woman"] that already featured Pete Townshend.

Well, I was doing some overdubs with Peter in London, and Paul was working on *Broad Street*. Actually, it was this disco thing he was working on.

The disco version of "No More Lonely Nights"?

Yeah, which I haven't heard since.

You're a lucky man.

[*Laughs*] I've got to be careful you don't get me bitchy, because if I get bitchy, it's *all* going to come out. [*Pause*] Yeah, Paul kind of . . . but I'd done all the tracks by then.

He came in with a bottle of cognac or something?

It was my *birthday*, that's why! It was really nice. Paul has always been very polite and nice to me. He said, "I've never done a disco mix before," and I kind of very patronizingly said, "Oh, well, *wow*." [*Laughs*] I mean it's *true*, I was doing them in 1978: "Miss You," with Bob Clearmountain.

Of course, he was doing solo records in 1970. Why a solo record now? What made the timing right?

I had just finished doing the Stones album, and it hadn't come out; I'd just done a bunch of videos; and I just wrote a bunch of songs *very* quickly when I was in the Caribbean. So I did some demos, and the demos kind of worked well.

Traditionally, solo albums by people who are still in groups have been born of frustration.

It wasn't from any great frustration. I was, you know, feeling in the mood for it, and I thought, "Stop *talking* about the solo record you *might* do one day." I didn't think about it too much, to be honest. I just went ahead and did it.

When did you let the rest of the band know that you were planning to do it?

As soon as I was planning on doing it. They knew contractually that CBS had said, "We want you to do this," and I said, "Well, do you mind if I take this time out?" For instance, Bill [Wyman] has done like four solo albums, and Ronnie [Wood] has done a lot of solo projects. And Keith [Richards], he's done, maybe not very many records, but he did the [New Barbarians] tour with Ronnie.

I think that the Stones didn't want it to be a shit record: "Mick, don't make a shit record, because that's going to reflect on us." And I said, "No, if it's a shit record—if I think it's shit, and CBS thinks it's shit—it won't go out."

There were stories that they were furious.

I don't think they were furious about it, because we talked about it. I talked about it with Keith, and he said, "Hey, if you want to do it, go ahead. Don't forget you're taking a chance." I said, "Well, yeah."

You know, you've got to take chances in life. Nothing ventured, nothing gained.

Are you a chance-taking sort of guy?

Well, I think I've gotten a little bit *too* safe. I'm not saying the Rolling Stones are safe, but there was always Keith to fall back on, and there were a lot of safety nets.

Were you happy with the last record, 'Undercover'?

Yeah, I liked it. It didn't sell perhaps as much as I would have liked, though it sold over two million copies—I shouldn't really complain. There was plenty of stuff on it that was mine: "Undercover," "She Was Hot." Keith contributed to all that stuff. Some was completely his. But it wasn't like I was frustrated with it because it wasn't my material.

There will be speculation, I guess, that your solo record means the Stones are winding down.

I don't think so. I mean, we're going into the studio in January, and we're planning a tour for next year. Ronnie said so on MTV! [*Laughs*] Who am *I* to say there isn't going to be?

Just to press the point, say five or ten years down the road . . .

Well, forget it! [*Laughs*] I don't want to *think* about it!

I mean, there can't really be a Rolling Stones when you're all fifty.

No, I don't think so, either. So, maybe subconsciously, I'm thinking, "Hey, I better do it now." I don't want to wait until I'm that old to do it; it seems silly.

It must have been fun to work with new musicians for a change.

Yeah. I started off with Sly [Dunbar] and Robbie [Shakespeare] and all the people I knew, really. We had Jeff Beck, and we had Jan Hammer at the beginning, and then I had Chuck Leavell and Eddie Martinez—he's a guitar player. So that was sort of the beginning, and then later on we had Michael Shrieve on one track. And on the ballad ["Hard Woman"] we had Tony Thompson. Herbie Hancock did some overdubs. And Pete Townshend played acoustic guitar.

Nice to give the guy a little work now and then.

Yeah. [*Laughs*] Keep him away from his publishing business at Faber and Faber.

Did you write these songs the way you usually write material for the Stones? Don't you normally headbang with Keith a bit?

Usually, I hit them around with people, with Keith. Sometimes I write them all down and say, "Hey, this is it." Or sometimes I'll say, "Well, this really can use a bridge." This time I really tried to have them *done*. I got them much more ready than I would have with the Stones, because with the Stones—with any band —the great advantage is that they all kick the tunes around for you. You can't really expect guys that you've got in to do that. But even though I got the demos down, it didn't matter, because the guys that I worked with were very involved. They weren't going, [*bored*] "Oh, yeah, thanks." In that way, it wasn't really that different from working with the Stones.

How did you pull together the producers, Bill Laswell and Nile Rodgers?

Bill's a real kind of thinking guy. We sat around, talked about musicians, and the idea sort of fell into place. And then Nile was working with Jeff Beck on an album. So then, when he finished that, I said, "Maybe it's good to do some tracks with Nile." And I'd written a few different songs. I said to Bill, "I'm going to play them to him," and it went from there.

Did you want it to sound different from the Rolling Stones?

Well, you got to remember that a lot of this stuff is kind of subconscious with musicians. I knew it was never going to sound like the Rolling Stones, and the great thing about it was the mystery: I was throwing elements together, and I didn't know what was going to happen—nor did the musicians. And they were having fun. All of them were really up for it.

For you as a vocalist, what's the difference between singing with a guy like Beck and singing with Keith and Ronnie?

Not a tremendous amount of difference really. I mean, Jeff's very much a lead player; he doesn't like to play parts over and over, which Keith and Ronnie would do. That's a great difference. But I had Eddie to play the parts. And then the similarity is that very few guitar players will play the same solo twice, so you better get it. You know, there's a certain point where you've got to catch that heat, that flash.

Obviously, I know Keith and Woody much better than I know Jeff, though I've known Jeff for years. But I'm not quite as attuned to him or the other musicians when they're really on, whether this guy will play forever like this and get better and better, or whether he's just going to do it once and go, "Well, that's it, guy. You didn't get it. Good-bye."

How did Beck turn out to be?

Very patient. And very hard-working. I went home at like two in the morning, and he was still in there. That's not bad.

Have you thought about videos yet?

Yeah. While I was writing the songs, I was thinking of videos. I was thinking visually a little bit more than normal.

Some people think that's a dangerous trend.

I think it's good. Not all lend themselves to visual treatment, and I'm not saying I wrote or rewrote or changed or whatever. But when you start to get a cinematic approach—when you have something down, and you think about it—it does bring certain images. I mean, the creative thing works in a very odd way. How do you write a song? I don't know. It comes out, and it's a miracle really. It just comes out, and you have these visual images, and you think, "Well, let's carry them a little bit further and make them a little more cinematic or something."

You know, "Lucky in Love" and "Running Out of Luck"? Before, I would maybe have had to change it: "Oh, I can't have two songs with luck." I use that, so that becomes a kind of slightly thematic thing, if I want to use that for a video.

You almost have a Prince-type piano attack on "Just Another Night."

Oh, yeah, yeah, yeah. Bill [Laswell] did that. And I think we did it well before "When Doves Cry." It was almost contemporary. See, I'm a big Prince fan, I'm not gonna hide that. He was on our '81 tour— you know what happened to him?

He comes on for five minutes, they throw two cans at him, and he leaves.

I mean, he was supposed to do four or five more gigs. He was big then already. He wasn't any kind of thing I discovered under a bush.

That was a tough time for cross-pollination of audiences.

Well, I think it was just the clothes really. The underwear. [*Laughs*] The *underwear!* It wasn't the singing or the style or anything like that.

Didn't you think he was a prima donna for not hanging in there and taking the heat?

To be honest, I never saw what happened. I don't think it was really serious. I don't think he was hurt. I mean, hey, they throw a lot of cans anyway. I mean when I go on, they throw *everything* [*laughs*].

I went to see him in Detroit, and his audience is all fourteen-year-old girls clutching their Instamatic cameras and screaming their heads off. He ends with this tremendous version of "Purple Rain," but everybody is filing out. And the third night in Detroit he just started screaming at them.

You get these funny audiences. It's got to change the way you act and the show you do. I remember with the Stones, we used to play for a college crowd, and we were used to *mature* people. They were older. And to go from that to playing for the thirteen-year-olds with the Instamatics who are just screaming and not knowing any of the tunes, really, is kind of *weird,* you know? The Stones went through this whole phase where we got really bored playing, because all they wanted to hear were the hits, and they didn't want to know about the blues, and we were feeling very blues purist.

How do you decide what to play on tour these days?

The things that excite me to play are either newer songs we've never done or old ones but done slightly different than we've done before. When you play outdoors or even the big arenas, you tend to keep the shows exactly the same. You can't just throw in a number like you're in a club, because you have 90,000 people, the lights and the sound and all that, and it's just such a production. At the beginning of the tour, the set tends to be long, and you shorten it a little bit. You see what goes down well and what doesn't. If a number's bombing, even if you're enjoying it, you tend to leave it out.

What sort of stuff doesn't go over well?

They don't like ballads, for one thing. They don't want to hear them. Not from us. We play anything that's slow, they start to go for the hot dogs.

What recent shows did you like? Did you see Springsteen?

Yeah, I saw Springsteen in his long stint at the Meadowlands [in New Jersey].

Did you stay for the whole show?

[*Pause*] Oh, yeah. [*Laughs*] Sure, through the bear and everything. I liked it. I thought the band sounded wonderful; I thought he sounded wonderfully well. It was better than when I saw him the last time around. I thought the drums sounded fantastic. I took the kids also. To tell you the truth, the kids did not like it very much.

Did you and the kids catch the Jacksons' 'Victory' tour?

I wasn't around. I wasn't in the neighborhood. Some real hard-rock people—people that I wouldn't imagine liking it—said they liked it very much. They [the kids] didn't go, either. I don't think they wanted to. I think they're too old already.

What did you think of all the Jacksons' business problems?

I only know what I've read in the newspapers. I don't want to be an expert, but I think the ticket price was too high. I think Michael knew it. I think it was terribly disorganized at the beginning—it was a joke. I mean, everyone went through this in the *Sixties.* You don't put ticket prices—ticket prices are $17.50 or whatever it is—I mean you don't . . . twenty, thirty dollars . . . you don't *do* that. I don't think it's very

complex. You don't rate more than the regular ticket price. If you have a very expensive show, you might add a dollar.

When did you get involved in the real nuts-and-bolts side of touring?

I think when I *had* to, like 1969, I think. Especially post-Altamont . . . I was really into the tour before then. I kinda let that one go. I thought that was all San Francisco and Bill Graham and the Grateful Dead, and . . . I'm not making excuses. Of course, a lot of it was my fault, blah-blah-blah. But to that point in time, there wasn't really—I hate to use the word, but I think it's a good one—there was no *industry* really. It was all very amateur night: There were a few professional promoters, and fewer honest ones. So the artist had to become interested.

We had gone to Australia, and there was no roof, and it was 110 degrees. So I remember telling Rod Stewart, "Say, Rod, when you go down there, don't forget to take a roof, and put it in your contract. I mean these guys don't give you a roof!" [*Laughs*] So I got interested in that. You can't get yourself *too* involved, because you gotta play.

What were your impressions of Michael Jackson when you worked with him?

I thought he was really professional. You know, sings his ass off—he's real easy.

I thought "State of Shock" was great.

A lot of people didn't like it. I think it could have been much better produced, but you know, I enjoyed doing it. I like doing the duets occasionally—I did one with Peter Wolf, Carly Simon, Peter Tosh . . .

You and Willie and Julio, I'm sure . . .

[*Laughs*] Hey, yeah, we'll get it together . . . that was a hilarious one. [*Hysterically*] Willie and *Julio!*

Did you see Duran Duran when they came?

No: I saw them personally; I didn't go to their show. The kids went.

Did they like it?

Loved it. My children's boyfriends dress like Simon LeBon, wear the makeup, you know. It's hilarious.

Do you like their records?

Who?

Duran Duran.

[*Closes eyes, smiles, remains silent for fifteen seconds.*] Uh, right . . .

[*Laughs*] C'mon, Chris, gimme a *break!*

I know I've got another question here. . . . Here we go: Do you go back and listen to your old records?

Yeah, sometimes. Most artists might once in a while, when the band might get together. But I don't think many people do. There might be a time when it's probably good to hear them, like when we go on the road. Go and research all the stuff and say: "Hey, that's really a good song. We could do that this way," or "We never did that onstage."

You've mentioned "Shattered" as a song you're particularly proud of.

Yeah, I think that's really good, it's kinda unusual. There's quite a few songs on that album [*Some Girls*] I think are good. I still like things like "Miss You." I think that has a directness and feeling. The whole album has something in it.

At the time, you thought it was the best record you had done since 'Let It Bleed.'

Yeah, I think it probably is. I mean, *Tattoo You* was full of some good material—some of it was quite old, and some not old. I think "Start Me Up" was good.

That was just sitting around in a vault?

Well, it was from *Emotional Rescue*. It was just *sitting* there, and no one had taken any notice of it. There were like forty takes. What happened, I think, is we made it into a reggae song after, like, take twelve, and said, well, maybe another time. I used take two. And I found it, put it together . . . it was one of Keith's sort of tunes . . . I wrote the lyrics, put it on, and Keith said, "I can't believe it, it's just wild."

There are two new books about the band that have just been published: 'Symphony for the Devil,' by Philip Norman, and 'Dance with the Devil,' by Stanley Booth. Have you read either of them?

You know, I really haven't. First of all, I'm not really interested in reading books about myself; there are a lot of books out there I'd like to read rather than books about me or the Rolling Stones. The Stanley Booth one perhaps would be good to read. At least Stanley Booth did actually know the Rolling Stones, and I know Stanley Booth. Where Philip Norman doesn't know the Rolling Stones; I wouldn't know him if he walked in now. I read some extracts from it, with the sensationalist stuff in it. It looks pretty cruddy, what I read.

Both books do recount some of the seamier sides of the Stones' activities—sex, drugs, the works. Is it difficult for you as a parent to think about your kids reading some of that stuff?

I can't do anything about it.

How do you feel about it?

How do I feel about it? I don't know really—I haven't really thought about it. You're throwing the question at me kinda as a bit of a curve. Ummm, I really haven't thought about it. I guess they know most of it, and I think it's not particularly—I don't think it's very good for them. Ummm, I mean, that's one of the things I have to put up with. I mean, *they* have to put up with. It's a little unfair for them. But I suppose all kids have to put up with their parents.

Frequently, the allegation is made that a lot of people who meet up with the Rolling Stones wind up in trouble: fucked up, dead, with drug problems or something like that. And there's the implication that the band somehow is a malevolent force that destroys people's lives. What's your response to that?

Ummm, I think it's unfortunate if it happened. I would not like to think of myself as someone who would take somebody on purpose, or even not on purpose, and make them into something . . . you know, ruin their life. What's inevitable is that there are breakdowns in relationships, people have problems. . . . I mean, most [people] in the artistic community have severe kinds of problems with drugs and stress. It happens not only in the music community, and show business generally is a high-stress occupation. Yeah, there's no doubt that's happened. I don't want to pick on anybody, but what about the Pretenders, you know? I'm not pointing fingers. But it seems to be something that comes along in that way of life, and over a long period of time there are bound to be some casualties. It just happens. Maybe I'm being real cynical; I don't want to be.

I'm just thinking, who did I personally damage? Who did I actually do over?

Brian Jones?

Brian Jones? No way, José. I disclaim on that one. As a group, I'm sure there's many. But, me personally, I'm trying to think . . .

Marianne Faithfull?

Marianne, you know, she nearly killed *me*, forget it! I wasn't going to get out of there alive, Marianne Faithfull and Anita Pallenberg! I mean, *help!*

Do you ever see her?

Marianne, yeah, I see Marianne. I see her around, like you say. I haven't seen her properly for a little while. Since she broke up with her old man—I saw her then. She was really upset, and I talked to her a little.

And then Anita, I haven't seen her for a while. She's sort of gone straight, and she's in London. When I saw her last, I didn't recognize her. She looked pretty good.

Speaking of cleaning up, Ron Wood went into a drug detox center in England, right?

Yeah. Sounded horrible to me, the one he went to. This guy rang *me* up, screaming, 'cause Woody had given them my name. This guy yelled at me, 'cause Woody checked out. Like, "It's your fault he left." Hey, it was my idea to get him *in* there.

Was it?

Well, I'm sure I wasn't the only one.

There's a bunch of bands now that make a point about their being real clean.

Aaah, there was always the clean-living kid next door. That's how the Beatles were sold. That's how Frankie Avalon or Elvis was sold. Fact or fiction. But, honestly, I'm afraid journalism has a lot to answer for. Responsible journalism is a very good thing, but irresponsible journalism . . . we have a lot of it. More in the U.K. than here.

Now, Duran Duran can't get really upset about that. They think it's really bad if people write, "Duran Duran was all drunk." They were saying to me, "So we were all drunk, but we're such a teenybop group. We didn't really ask for that; that's what we got. And if they write about that, then people go out and they copy us, and we don't want that. We think it's irresponsible [journalism]." Well, it's not irresponsible to write about it in, like, [*sotto voce*] *your* magazine, but in a newspaper with sensationalist headlines . . .

Well, you're planning to set the record straight on your own life by writing an autobiography. Word has been that your first draft wasn't juicy enough for the publishers. What's the story?

I didn't really want to put out the book in the way that the first draft was. It was too flip. The publishers wanted to put it out. They wanted to pay me the money, and I just said, "No, not this time. Let me get some more stuff on it."

I didn't have any problem remembering . . . I mean, you can't remember every detail. What's more difficult to put into perspective is like the Seventies. Much easier to put the Sixties into perspective than the Seventies.

What is your perspective on the Sixties?

Wait to read the book! [*Laughs*] It's really complex, though, you know? Obviously, it's a personal one. But also one of the society I found myself in when I was growing up. I was kind of a late grower-up. People didn't grow up at fifteen then; they grew up when they were twenty. The way that they changed, and the way that America changed, and your own personal experiences, and how that worked, and also the overview you've got now: what society was like and all those millions of examples of things that makes the mosaic up for the real picture.

Sort of an edge . . .

Yeah, well, you got very aggressive and very frustrated, you know. With not being able to hold the reins and the obviously stupid things going on. The

ripoffs. And all the politics and the social upheaval that was happening all over the world. There's a lot of social stuff in there that's never *really* been looked at. And I talked to people who really want me to get that right. You know, professors and stuff, not bullshit artists.

What's hard about the Seventies?

Well, you know, it's just *closer,* and it was a time of retrenchment a little bit. It doesn't sort of fit quite so well. And I was getting older and what was happening? Was I just kind of going along in the groove of it or the momentum that was already there? I don't know. I just haven't got the keys to it yet.

Moving up to the Eighties, how do you view the rise of conservatism, both here and in the U.K.?

I think it's awful. I don't like all this religion stuff involved. Traditionally, in England, we really don't.

What about your family? Are any of your daughters following in your footsteps?

Well, I like to watch them move and see if they can play, you know? My oldest [Karis] plays the harp. It's kind of amusing to watch. Not an instrument of instant carryability. It's tough. Tough on the fingers and the back when you wanna move it. But she likes it. She plays piano also.

Now, the littlest one, I bought her a xylophone. Yeah, they love all that. It's one of those things that you hit it and it doesn't make a musical noise, but a ball goes jumping up in the air.

How old is she now?

Seven months.

It must be fun to have her.

Yeah, it's fun, you know? It is fun. And then my brother has six kids. They're not all his, but they're his family. So they come over and it's like insanity.

Do you counsel them at all like your typical daddy?

You have to counsel them a little bit all the way through, you know? It's good if they come and talk to you, but obviously kids don't like to really talk. . . . I really shouldn't talk about them too much, because when they read it, they'll become embarrassed.

Okay. One last thing: If the record does well, what will you do?

I don't know really. I'd be real happy if it does well. I'd be happy if people like it and they like the kind of direction—if they appreciate it and they just enjoy the record. I hope it sells, but you can't guarantee. I've been around long enough to know that.

Ah, but what if it's really successful?

Yeaaahhh! I'm going to move to the East Side! Is *that* your question? [*Laughs.*]

9

Joan Baez

INTERVIEWED BY KURT LODER (1983)

Just three years after Elvis Presley exploded onto the national pop scene with "Heartbreak Hotel," Joan Baez emerged as the bright new star of the 1959 Newport Folk Festival. Elvis was in the Army by then; Buddy Holly was dead; and Jerry Lee Lewis was in cradle-robbing disgrace. With some of rock's heaviest hitters out of action, and a lot of original fans now in college—where the soulless music of the white teen idols who sought to replace Presley seemed very out of place—the stage was set for a commercial flowering of the folk-roots movement that had been bubbling on the East Coast, at least, since the Forties. In 1959, and on into the Sixties, Joan Baez, the folkie Madonna from Boston University, was this phenomenon's fairest blossom.

Baez explicitly combined the qualities of folkie purism and social virtuousness. She was an inspiration to a generation of young women who grew their hair long and free and parted it in the middle. And of course, she was anathema to many hard-core rock & rollers. But without her patronage (among other things), Bob Dylan might have had a rather different route to public recognition of his songwriting gifts. The Beatles apparently liked her, too. And she once got to sing "You've Lost That Lovin' Feeling" backed by Phil Spector himself (although the less said about that, the better).

Joan Baez was a product of the same youth culture that helped create rock & roll, and whether you found her inspiriting or insufferable, you could never accuse her of having sold out her beliefs. In the end, when she had to choose between pursuing her political goals and maintaining a viable recording career, it was the beliefs that she stuck with. Now forty-eight, Baez records only occasionally, usually for foreign markets. She continues to be an activist for peace and human rights, particularly in Latin America. And she still sings the old songs—for those who ever found them to be so—beautifully.

—K. L.

I WAS a kid then, when she was the queen. That voice, the sad ballads, the thrum of nylon strings—major relevance among the girls at school who were into Ayn Rand and black leotards. I listened, too: her sail-away soprano was so hypnotic, so . . . *achingly pure*. She was as new then, as decidedly different, as, say, David Bowie would be a dozen years later. She changed my life a little. Who could forget: Joan Baez, she warmed up for the Sixties.

But I wasn't expecting that loopy moment at the end of the Grammy Awards telecast on February 23, when John Denver, the show's host, announced a windup medley of hits from that sacred decade, the Sixties. Denver intoned the Beatles' "A Day in the Life" with the gravity of a parson at graveside. And then, suddenly, a lone figure with an acoustic guitar scurried out across the Shrine Auditorium stage. It was Joanie! Without a word, she began picking the chords to "Blowin' in the Wind." Denver harmonized, and slowly the evening's award winners drifted back in to add their famous voices to the swaying refrain. Even the audience got sucked in. It was weird.

I wondered: Can Joan Baez still be at it? Miss Protest? Barefoot daughter of the moneyed middle class, Quaker-bred pop star, wisecracking pacifist, half-Mexican Madonna of the ancient English laments? The great straight lady of the hipster Sixties—still at it in 1983?

As it happened, we had been talking for some time. Long hours in Manhattan hotel rooms, phone calls from her home outside San Francisco and from France, where she recently toured to promote the true cause of pacifism. She's a riot, actually, with her legs crossed up under a royal-blue muumuu, and a helpless gossip. We talked about people she knew: Bob Dylan, the Beatles, the Grateful Dead, the great Phil Spector, Mario Savio (leader of Berkeley's free-speech movement), Martin Luther King. The odd randy film star. She is vibrant when she throws back her head

and laughs, often about herself. And yes, she says, she's still at it.

There's her career, of course, such as it is. Her last "hit" was "Diamonds and Rust," the celebrated ode to Bobby, in 1975. In 1979, she withdrew to devote three years to the establishment of her own pacifist group, Humanitas International. Joan sees this as her real life: calling convocations on Latin American fascism, raising modest sums for human-rights efforts. Doing good.

Still, one must live. Last summer she surfaced with a tape of seven self-penned songs she had recorded with members of the Grateful Dead. Record companies didn't want to know: Joan Baez? How quaint. Maybe if she adapted, got hip. But Joanie's not about to throw her life into this lousy business again. "It'll always be this way," she said one drizzly afternoon over tea. "I'm not interested in talking about music. If there's a choice between people picking and singing in one room and a group of mothers of disappeared Argentinians in another room, I'm gonna go and talk to the mothers."

She knows she can be prissy. She's afflicted with dignity. But she's no prude; she's been around, made some seminal scenes. Her father, Alberto Vinicio Baez—a now-retired physicist, UNESCO consultant and author of a standard textbook called *The Spiral Approach to Physics*—was a peripatetic scholar. His second daughter, born on Staten Island, New York, on January 9, 1941, started traveling early and has never really stopped: little Joanie in Paris and Bangkok; teenage Joanie, the queen of the late-Fifties Boston coffeehouse scene; Joanie at Newport with Dylan, in Selma with King, at Woodstock with child; Joanie in Hanoi, ducking U.S. bombs.

She was there at the beginning of big pop culture, and she's still at it. Alone now: her marriage to draft resister David Harris is history, of course, and her thirteen-year-old son, Gabriel, moved out a few months ago to live with some friends down the street. She sees her younger sister, Mimi (who runs the prisoner-outreach organization Bread and Roses), more than her older sister, Pauline, who lives way off in Carmel. Her parents are divorced. So Joan travels; she sings when she can, wherever she's wanted. They love her in Europe, where she's released records in a flurry of languages, but not in Russia and the less lovable Latin American states, where she's been forbidden to perform.

She is enormously likable. Knows how to relate. She can be jolly in jeans, dishing the civil-rights scene and the old folkie days, or she can be a proper young matron chatting up the VIPs at a wine-and-cheese freeze gathering, inhaling homilies from the likes of Teddy Kennedy even though she abhors all politicians on principle. Anything for the cause. And the career? She wants to start over again, maybe on a small label. She knows this will be an uphill enterprise for the woman still remembered, with a snicker, as the author of such deathless lines as "My life is a crystal teardrop." She's a total outsider now, but she can laugh about it. Al Capp, the late mad-dog cartoonist, defamed her in a vicious, transparent parody, as "Joanie Phoanie," the dilettante folk-commie. But today, at forty-two, Joan Baez is as committed as ever to the pacifist vision of peace and world unity. She dares to be quaint. She's still at it.

Why have your new songs received the cold shoulder from U.S. record companies?

I don't think my tape is salable as an album in this country. I have offers for it from Europe. But I think it needs to be a much better album. It needs other people's material on it. I never had to bother much thinking about my career before, but I do now if I want to have one in the States. Things aren't exactly popping here. I've been gone for three years.

You recorded this tape with Mickey Hart of the Grateful Dead. Do you go back a long way with them?

Not really. I met them through Mickey. He came out to my house one day banging on a drum, hopping around the front yard and yelling to me over the din about how rhythm is father, melody mother, and the sisters are harmony. So we got together and decided we would make an album. He spent about three months cleaning up rat remains and putting together chewed-up wires in his funky little studio. The musicians were all Mickey's friends, and then the Dead all played on different parts.

Do you think you'll record with them again in the future?

No, it didn't work, really. They were very polite to me, but basically I was an intrusion. The fact is, there's too much dope intake for me to break through. If I'm gonna say something, that's the last place in the world that they want to hear it. So one of the reasons I don't think we could ever really sort of get off together is that I don't do dope, and they all do. Lots of it. Their music takes you to another place, but basically, I've never been there.

I understand one of your new songs, "Children of the Eighties," was inspired by an odd concert you played in Europe—a rock & roll show in which you were billed between Genesis and Frank Zappa.

That was in Ulm, Germany. I didn't realize that they were making bets backstage that I would just get dumped off the stage. I was a little nervous, because there were 55,000 very happy, doped-out kids there—*whee,* rock & roll and drugs and sex. A sort of rerun of the Sixties, but not quite making it, so everyone had to drink a little bit more. I looked at this crowd and thought, "Oh, Jesus Christ." I worked for twenty minutes very, very hard trying to establish contact. And I did. Then I talked to them—about war and peace and human rights and Argentina—and I brought them down to earth, which is where people have to land if they're ever going to think. And this *thing* began to happen. By the end of forty minutes, they were calling for "Blowin' in the Wind," "We Shall Overcome." They were weeping, they were lighting candles. I meant something to them—I represented the Sixties, that was clear. I stood for John Lennon, Bob Dylan, people they needed as heroes. They are fresh out of heroes in the Eighties.

You and Dylan reunited onstage at a Peace Week concert in Los Angeles last June. What state of mind did he seem to be in?

I really have no idea. But I love singing with him. He isn't in tune, the phrasing is nuts, and he always wants to do a song I've never heard before. This time he read it off his arm, and he couldn't see. I begged him to do something we knew, but he wanted to do this Jimmy Buffett tune, "A Pirate Looks at Forty." He scribbled it all over his wrist, and then forgot to take his jacket off. It's always an interesting happening when Bob appears.

Did he mention the Clash? Apparently, he saw them not long ago and really liked them.

Yeah. He said, "These English groups have a lot to say." I said, "*Well,* I can't *wait* to hear about it." What's the Clash like, do you know?

Politically exuberant. Did Dylan say anything about his current religious posture?

He didn't bring it up, and I'm not interested in hearing about it.

Your relationship with Dylan has spanned a lot of interesting history. Where shall we start—1958? Your father moved the family back East so he could teach at MIT, and you entered Boston University—the theater school, wasn't it?

I don't know *why* I went in the theater school, because I hated every second of it. After a while, I just dropped out, flunked everything. My report card was quite something: It had on it every variety of how you can flunk, from F's to zeros to X's. There was one A, but it was a misprint of an F. So it was not my forte. But that whole time, what was happening to me was, out of my boredom and distaste for school, I was really drawn into the whole scene of coffee shops and singing and the early English folk songs. That was just really beginning to go very strong.

Where did you first hear this stuff?

Well, the very first things I ever heard—after Harry Belafonte, which up until then represented folk music—were by Odetta. She was my goddess, and I learned everything she sang. And Joe Mapes was somebody who sang back then. And in Harvard Square, there was an overabundance of . . . not just records—Big Bill Broonzy, you know, and Cynthia Gooding and John Jacob Niles—but everybody sitting in coffee shops *imitating* them.

Didn't your father take you on your first visit to one of the coffee shops?

To Tulla's Coffee Grinder. I think he regretted it about five minutes after we walked in. It was a family do: "Let's go see if what we heard about these coffee shops is true." Plus, Dad was worried about his daughter, you know? But I was lost right on the first visit. I mean, I was ready to join up and pick up the guitar, which I did. And after that, I just hung out in the coffee shops.

The Club 47 was the hub of that scene. What was it like when you arrived?

There were three people there [*laughs*]. It was a jazz club, and they had Tuesday nights off. The women who ran it had seen me perform somewhere, and they said they'd give me Tuesday nights for ten dollars. So I said sure, you know—I was grabbing at a little dough.

And so I went. I remember my mother was there, and my boyfriend showed up, and I blushed and lost the words in the middle of a song. There were about nine people, and they were all friends. Then the word started getting around, and the next week there were thirty or forty people, and the week after that . . .

It was pretty casual during most of the time I was there. I mean, people would blow in through the windows on motorcycles with guitars over their shoulders, and I'd say, "*Whee,* c'mon up and sing," you know? But also during that time, I had bought the idea that I was the Virgin Mary—that that was a pretty good deal. So I was beginning to play out a role that someone had given me. I mean, I was very *stuffy* about my music. And I think around the middle of that period Newport happened, 'cause I remember coming back and seeing lines around the block for Joanie's little concert. They upped me to $12.50, I think, at that point.

That was after the 1959 Newport Folk Festival, when Bob Gibson brought you up to sing?

Yeah. I had met him when he was headlining at the Gate of Horn, in Chicago, and I was the opening act. It had been my first big venture into nightclubs—the only one. But he was a sweetheart to me, and he invited me personally to Newport and said that he would invite me on the stage, 'cause I wasn't well known enough to have my own slot. We sang "Virgin Mary Had One Son" [*laughs*] and "Jordan River." I think that was all.

And the crowd went wild?

Well, yeah, they did. I was surprised.

Did you go out and celebrate afterward?

I didn't believe in that in those days. I probably went home and prayed.

Was Newport '60 more of an event for you?

The next year? Oh, yeah. I had my own set, and I was already crowned, um, whatever.

By that point, you had been signed by Vanguard Records. How was your first album recorded?

It took four nights. We were in some big, smelly ballroom at a hotel on Broadway, way up by the river. We couldn't record on Wednesday nights because they played bingo there. I would be down there on this dirty old rug with two microphones, one for the voice and one for the guitar. I just did my set; it was probably all I knew. Just put 'em down. I did "Mary Hamilton" once, that was it. [*Adopts a codgerlike wheeze.*] That's the way we made 'em in the old days. As long as a dog didn't run through the room or something, you had it. That album still sells.

How did you deal with success at such a tender age?

Just as badly as everybody else does. It was complicated by the image given to me: *Zap,* you're the Virgin Mary, the Madonna. I thought that was a terrific idea. In fact, I was sure I *was,* and I felt very benign and wonderful. Because up until then—I was eighteen—the only image I had of myself was of a dumb Mexican. I'd come from a place where Mexicans were called dumb peach-pickers. So I already had a big identity problem. I was just sorting things out, and all of a sudden somebody said, "*Bingo,* you're the Madonna with the achingly pure soprano." Well, who isn't gonna opt for that if those are your choices?

Was your success strictly musical at first, or did you immediately corner the market on youthful idealism?

No, I hadn't really emerged. I think I was probably known for some civil-rights work at that time, but it wasn't clear to anybody—and it wasn't clear to *me*—what I was doing. It was *so* unclear that one time, somewhere in the South, I stood up in front of an audience and said, "There's something I want to say, but I don't know what it is." [*Laughs*] It was just screaming in my head. It was my little socially conscious soul wanting to do something and not really knowing how or where to begin. And part of getting out of that was the combination of political action and Dylan's music. Because he clarified what I . . . I mean, he didn't *do* what he wrote about—*I* did what he wrote about, in a sense. I *was* politically active. But to have it in song was what was so miraculous to me, because I didn't write then. And I've never written that well anyway.

When did you first meet Dylan?

Oh, I was with my very, very jealous boyfriend at the time. It was at Gerde's Folk City, on Washington Square, where they had hootenannies and whatever. Everybody always went there. And somebody said, "Oh, you've gotta come down and hear this guy—he's terrific." And so I went down with my very, very jealous boyfriend, and we saw this scruffy little pale-faced dirty human being get up in front of the crowd and start singing his "Song to Woody." I, of course, internally went completely to shreds, 'cause it was so beautiful. But I couldn't say anything, 'cause I was next to my very, very jealous boyfriend, who was watching me out of the corner of his eye and trying to mentally slaughter Dylan, I think. And then Bob came over and said, "Uhhh, hi"—one of those eloquent greetings—and I just thought he was brilliant and superb and so on. And I think shortly after that, he wrote "Blowin' in the Wind."

And you dropped the jealous boyfriend?

No, I was an idiot. I stayed with him for a long time.

You and Dylan eventually did become romantically involved, though. How long did it last?

You mean what period of three months was it? Um, Bob and I spent some time together. I honestly don't know what the year was.

You did accompany him on that celebrated 1965 English tour—not an altogether happy trip, I gather.

I just sort of trotted around, wondering why Bob wouldn't invite me onstage, feeling very sorry for myself, getting very neurotic and not having the brains to leave and go home. That would be the best way to describe that tour [*laughs*]. It was sort of just wasted time.

You had been at Newport in 1965 when Dylan "went electric" with the Paul Butterfield Blues Band and was booed by the folk purists. Did you realize then the significance of what he did?

No, I didn't. I just thought he was very brave to do it, even though I didn't like the sound of it. But I *learned* to like it, because he was still writing wonderful stuff. I don't know how he stood it, though. I could never have done that—not that I ever *wanted* to, but I don't think I could've done it.

You've never wanted to be a rock & roll singer?

No, never, I'm happy to say. I don't think I could handle what it supposedly stands for, or doesn't stand for, not with my particular makeup. I mean, I'd have a *job* right now, but the hell with that.

A real Sixties question: Where were you when Kennedy was assassinated?

I was in a vegetable store [*laughs*]. I really don't care that much, you know? People have this *thing* about it, and it's sort of unfortunate that a president who was basically a myth, like most presidents, has to be everybody's last memory of the most terrific thing that ever happened to them.

One year after Kennedy's death you sang at the first student uprising of the Sixties—the clash at Berkeley between school administrators and the campus free-speech movement. What was it like?

I was very involved with that. Because I was helping run the Institute for the Study of Nonviolence at the time, I felt that my role was to try to instigate as much nonviolence as I could in their activities—'cause they were clearly gonna be active. I spent lots of time there doing seminars and being an outside agitator, talking about how to do nonviolent action and make it work. And we were fighting a lot of very angry kids who didn't want to hear about that. I remember taking the microphone away from Mario Savio, who was getting this huge march full of kids into a fury with "they" this and "they" that and "They're gonna cut us down" and "We don't have a voice"—and I took the microphone away, and I said, "You have no right to talk that way. We *do* have a voice, and we can do anything we want to do. For instance"—it came in a flash—"if you felt like taking over Sproul Hall, which is *your* hall, you can *do* that." And then a week later, they decided they *would* do it, and they called me back up. I remember being thoroughly despised by a good portion of the crowd, because I said to them on the way into Sproul Hall, "Go in with as much love in your hearts as you can muster." They didn't want to hear from love, you know? And then I remember the police waited until Ira Sandperl and I had left the building at three o'clock in the morning, and then they moved in at 3:20 and started the arrests.

You were living in Big Sur by then, weren't you?

With my jealous boyfriend—isn't that horrible? [*Giggling*] The same jealous boyfriend. I lived in what is now Esalen, in that well-noted-by-*Time*-magazine "shack," for thirty-five dollars a month. Hunter Thompson was my next-door neighbor—he wandered by and took potshots at my kittens and stuff. I lived there for about a year. I would tour a little bit, you know, but I was still very afraid of that whole . . . *process* of whatever being a star was. And that was always agitated by the boyfriend, who didn't ever want me to leave, you know—wanted me sitting on the front porch watching him build his trimaran. And paying for it.

Exactly how long did that relationship last?

Four years—isn't that unbelievable?

Your career took some . . . interesting turns in the mid-Sixties. I remember, indelibly, your rendition of "You've Lost That Lovin' Feelin' " in a 1965 movie, 'The Big T.N.T. Show.'

Oh, my God. That was a mistake. I don't know how I got there. I remember vaguely being up at Phil Spector's house with all his karate security guards chopping bricks in half all over the place. Pretty loony. It was filmed at some hole-in-the-wall in L.A. There I was, and there was Phil playing "Spanish Harlem" on the piano, and everybody was loaded on drugs. I mean, I didn't even *understand* drugs, so I really didn't relate.

How about Woodstock? Has that retained its glow for you?

Oh, I had a lovely time at Woodstock. Flattered me, in a way—you saw all the big bands and their equipment, and yet they still let the little pregnant virgin walk out there with her guitar and do her thing. It was wonderful. I mean, it wasn't any fucking revolution; it was a three-day period during which people

were decent to one another because they realized that if they weren't, they'd all get hungry.

You seemed to be drifting away from the music business by 1979, the year you started Humanitas. What did you hope to accomplish with it?

I wanted my own organization. Instead of helping other people out with theirs, I wanted to be able to define what I did. It started with a study group in my house. We were visited by two boat people from Vietnam, and we decided to come out and openly criticize Hanoi on human rights. I'm still personally paying for that decision. People from the Left felt they'd been betrayed. What can I say? I had to make a choice between their feelings and the fact that there were between 200,000 and 800,000 political prisoners in Vietnam.

Radical lawyer William Kunstler attacked you at the time, contending it was impolitic to criticize any socialist government.

Well, I don't even know him. And from his statement, I wouldn't want to bother. I don't want to waste time on somebody who feels that way, because our whole emphasis at Humanitas is to drop ideology and learn to see repression for what it is. A rubber-hose beating is a rubber-hose beating, whether it's administered in South Africa or Latin America or Siberia. The Vietnamese people suffer because of their corrupt government. Never having had any illusions about governments *anywhere,* that was no big shock for me. For some godforsaken reason, I was given the gift of not having an ideology. I was associated with the Left because, of course, I worked mainly with the Left all through the Sixties. The right wing wasn't interested in stopping the war, so you worked with the left wing—and they're good people. I feel bad that they felt injured. But I feel worse that they don't see the picture in Vietnam for what it is. That government has betrayed its own people, and all of us, as well.

After all these years as a campaigner for peace and nonviolence, don't you ever despair?

Well, no. One suffers under a marvelous illusion that as long as you're working, something's still happening. Although I joke about having no illusions, that may be the one that I hang on to. I mean, I don't have illusions about other people—I really don't. I assume that we will blow ourselves up. I don't think people are gonna smart up in time. But, on the other hand, I don't deny the possibility of hope. Action is the antidote to despair.

Do you think the old peace movement of the Sixties can be revived?

I've gone back to people from my past who helped

teach me about nonviolence. I've met mostly with disillusionment, but that is simply because I know that what we need to move forward is something very, very new. I mean, dear, beloved pacifists, who are *the* salt of the earth—you cannot reach Middle America with those people. Their beards are too long. They don't look right. They scare off the front lines. Maybe you have to dress a different way. I mean, Gandhi was a stickler about it. He told the Indians—he *embarrassed* the Indian congress by standing up and saying that Indians have to stop spitting on the ground. Half the people got up and walked out, 'cause they didn't want to admit that Indians spit on the floor, you know, and made it dirty and made people sick. And he said they had to have their clothes spotlessly clean or they *shouldn't* be riding first-class.

So, I'm saying something has to be done about the peacenik image—and back in the Sixties, I was *furious* when people would say something like that to me. I'd say, "Well, goddamnit, we can look like what we please; it's what we do that counts." But it's a *style* that you either threaten people with or don't, and you can do it on no money or you can do it on lots. I'm going to sing for the French president's wife—she's willing to set up an organization that will fight for human rights in Afghanistan as well as El Salvador. That's a very important move. So when I visit her at the palace, I'll go dressed a certain way, you know? And when I go visiting the ghettos in Venezuela, I'll go dressed another way. Wherever it is, you make the people you are with comfortable with what you have on—'cause they're not gonna be comfortable with what you have to say. I'm sure I'll be criticized: "Well, Joan has enough money to buy the clothes...."

There is that.

My living standard is, um ... it's high. It's high, but it's relative. I mean, compared to most L.A.-style entertainers, it's modest. But compared with my friends in the movement, who live political lives, I live like a *queen,* you know? For me, if I've found a plateau where I'm happy, if I can keep that up, I don't care. I'm not concerned with *accumulating,* that's the difference.

Your ex-husband, David Harris, who sketched the years of your marriage in his book, 'Dreams Die Hard,' seems to have been unnerved by your celebrity and relative wealth. Are you on good terms today?

Very good terms. It's all based on whether he's a good dad and I'm a good mom. That's all we deal with. He's not very political anymore.

What's your love life like today? Are you involved with anyone right now?

Um, no. [*Laughs*] We were talking about this, and I said, "Well, maybe I'll tell ROLLING STONE; they'll help me out." You see, whatever it says on my imaginary T-shirt, I am absolutely deluged with homosexual women at my concerts.

Maybe it's because of that comment you made ten years ago about being bisexual because, as an adolescent, you'd had a brief dalliance with another girl.

Is that what it is? But they were there *before* that, too. And I am *not* interested. The other day, I was talking to some guys, and ... I am forty-two. It's not so bad; I should be able to pick up somebody [*laughs*]. And one guy said, "We wanted to come meet you, but my friend said, 'Oh, she's back there with about twenty-five lesbians.' " *Terrific.*

So Joan can't meet guys. . . .

Just don't put that in big print. I'd appreciate it. But it is curious. I'm aggressive, I'm strong, I hang out in the Nautilus [*laughs*]. So maybe I scare men away. Someday my prince will come.

Didn't you once have a passing fling with Kris Kristofferson?

[*Grimaces*] Yeah, we were great. He was an alcoholic at the time. He's gonna read this and just shit. Hi, Kris!

Will Bob and Joan ever get together again—when they're both sixty or something?

Spare us, please. Both of us.

Wouldn't be a good idea?

Why don't *you* ask Bob?

I came across this other piece of vintage gossip about you.

Goody.

You and . . . John Lennon?

[*Grimaces*] I traveled with the Beatles for four days on one tour and, uh, ended up with John at one point, but we certainly did not have anything. . . . I mean, it *was* wild times. This was their first or second trip to the States—the second, I think. I was performing in Red Rocks, above Denver, and they were on the next night, so I stayed over. There I was in this room full of *hundreds* of people, all scrambling around trying to figure out how they could get to *their* dressing room, and somebody came up and said, "The Beatles would like to meet you." And I just instantly went to jelly. I got to their door trying to think of something clever to say and finally just put out my hand—and one by one they introduced themselves. Now, they had been on the cover of every single newspaper for a month, and they're going, "Hullo, I'm George," and "Muh name's Ringo." I said, "Yes, yes, I know."

They were terribly funny and terribly sweet, and they invited me to stay on the road for their last three or four concerts. My tour was over, so I went with them—as I think *anybody* would have. You know, packed everything and, *whoopty-do,* off I went. I saw all the inner workings: how you climb into Volkswagen buses and then send the limousine out to be beaten to death by loving fans. All those things. I was fascinated. Then we ended up in this great big mansion in Los Angeles that somebody had given them. But big as it was, there weren't really enough master bedrooms for everybody. And poor John was the one who had invited this little Mexican waif along—I don't know what the hell they thought of me; they thought I was Florence Nightingale, because I used to tend to the wounded at their concerts.

Anyway, so here we are in the mansion in Los Angeles, and we've run out of bedrooms, and they've sent their people out to bring in groupies so they can pick who they're gonna, you know, hang out with. And these *poor girls,* just sitting downstairs waiting to see whether they're gonna be picked by somebody—they don't talk, they don't even *knit.* They just sit there in these little outfits that they've worked on for months waiting for this thing to happen. And eventually a Beatle will come by and pick one of them and, you know, drag her off to his lair. There was also a hotshot local somebody there—I didn't figure out exactly what she was, but she looked like a professional prostitute. Anyhow, John was stuck, having invited me and then not having anywhere to put me. So he offered me his room; it had a bed in it the size of a small swimming pool. I said, "Well, John, don't worry, I'm not fussy about these things—you just come in and use the other side of the bed when you're tired." I didn't want him to feel pressured, 'cause I figured they must feel pressured to perform all the time.

So I went to sleep, and he came in, in the middle of the night. And I think he felt compelled—"Well, I've asked her and she *is* a star and *oh, dear*"—and he started coming on to me, very unenthusiastically. I said, "John, you know, I'm probably as tired as you are, and I don't want you to feel you have to perform on my behalf." And he says [*adopts Liverpudlian accent*], "Oh, luvly! I mean, what a relief! Because you see, well, you might say I've already *been fooked* downstairs." [*Laughs*] So we had a good laugh and went to sleep.

Did you ever sit around and sing with them?

Yeah, when we first met we sat around and strummed. But they were in love with Bob Dylan's work, so I sang only Bobby's stuff. I think that the extent of their interest in me, really, was my connection with Bob.

And Dylan was equally interested in them, too, wasn't he?

I think so, sure. And then he and John went off on that wild trip to New York—John's first crack at smoking dope, or whatever it was. One of those old days.

You seem serene and secure in your maturity now. What does the future hold?

You know, I remember Martin Luther King telling us about going to the mountaintop; it was before he gave that speech. He said, "I've been to the mountaintop," and he told us how it happened. It was when he was in solitary confinement in Alabama or someplace. They had dumped him in the hole, and it was black, he couldn't see. And they shoved food into the room, but he was afraid to eat it. Starving, afraid—he said he got on his knees for hours. "And when I stood up," he said, "it didn't matter anymore."

We tried to hold ourselves together when we knew what he meant—we knew *he* knew he was going to die. And he was ready to die; and he was ready to make his commitment about Vietnam—which is *why* he died. "I've been to the mountaintop, and I've seen the promised land, and it doesn't matter anymore."

Oh, *shit*—I wanna be there! When somebody says to me—which they do like every five years—"How does it feel to be over the hill," my response is, "I'm just heading up the mountain." I want to get a look at the promised land, so don't bother me with the hill—*on* it, *up* it, *over* it, whatever. There are more important things.

10

Bob Dylan

INTERVIEWED BY KURT LODER (1984)

Bob Dylan hates to do TV, and he submits to print interviews with a profound reluctance. To call him mercurial is probably to understate his fundamental caginess. Since the release of his debut album back in 1962, he has been burdened with a series of unsought cultural roles—king of protest, father of folk-rock, the voice of youth in all its earnest indignation. His personal life has been scrutinized from so many inventive angles that one can understand how he might no longer care to share what's left of it with the succession of strangers that is the relentless press.

This is a shame, because in a relaxed mood, Dylan is a stimulating conversationalist—sly, playful, much into parry-and-thrust. A sweet guy, at heart, however reflexively guarded. He is endlessly interesting on the subject of American folk music, from country blues and mountain ballads to commercial pop and rock & roll. The fact of his fame, however, seems to hold little interest for him, and most of its trappings he endures with a glum resignation. At the time that we talked, in 1984, he was dealing with a constant drizzle of press speculation about his supposed spiritual beliefs. Dylan had always taken the long view, one might say, even in his earliest work, but by the early Eighties, when he was reported to be consorting with fundamentalists, his songs seemed to have taken on an Old Testament tone. This seemed disquieting news, and worthy of discussion. I'm not sure Bob agreed, but as you'll see, he humored me.

—K. L.

ON A TYPICALLY soggy March mess of a day in Manhattan, Bob Dylan, wearing black jeans, biker boots and a white sport coat over a white T-shirt, sat slouched on a stool at the far end of a small downtown studio. The crowd of cameramen, lighting technicians, makeup people and producers had withdrawn for a bit to consult their equipment, leaving Dylan to strum and hum on his own. As his long nails raked the strings of his Martin guitar, he began huffing softly into the harmonica racked around his neck, and soon a familiar melody filled the air. Could it be? I moved closer to cock an ear as Dylan cranked up the chorus. Yes, no doubt about it—Bob Dylan was running down the first-ever folkie arrangement of "Karma Chameleon," the Culture Club hit.

Soon, however, he was surrounded by tech

people again. The audio crew punched up the tape of "Jokerman," a song off Dylan's latest album, *Infidels,* and as the video cameras rolled, the star obediently lip-synced along. Dylan had been doing take after take of the number all morning and most of the afternoon without complaint. "Jokerman" would be the second video for *Infidels,* and he knew it had to be good. The first, for the lovely ballad "Sweetheart like You," had been a flat and lifeless embarrassment. So two of Dylan's most trusted friends—Larry "Ratso" Sloman, author of a book about Bob's 1975 Rolling Thunder Revue tour, and George Lois, a brilliant New York adman who met Dylan during the ill-fated legal-defense concerts for fighter Rubin "Hurricane" Carter a decade ago—were called in to assist.

It was Lois who came up with an agreeable video format for the stiff, camera-shy Dylan. Bob's face would only be seen onscreen during the song's choruses; the verses would be illustrated by classic art prints from Lois' own library: paintings by Michelangelo, Dürer, Munch—and, in a wry touch, a Hieronymus Bosch painting titled *The Musicians' Hell.* Lois' most innovative concept, however, was to superimpose the song's apocalyptic lyrics over the images throughout the video—a technique Lois laughingly dubbed "poetry right in your fuckin' face." The result, as it later turned out, makes most run-of-the-mill rock videos look like the glorified cola commercials they generally are.

But can a single thought-provoking video make Bob Dylan once again relevant to youthful record buyers? The man has been many things over the years: the voice of youth in the Sixties, the voice of aging youth in the Seventies and, now, in the Eighties—what?

Certainly, he remains a completely unpredictable character, as I discovered when we met a few hours later at a Greek café on Third Avenue. Smoking steadily from a pack of Benson & Hedges ("Nothing can affect my voice, it's so bad") and downing cup after cup of coffee with cream, he proved both guarded and gracious, sweet and sometimes acerbic. Not at all the arrogant young superstar who verbally demolished a *Time* magazine reporter in the 1966 documentary *Don't Look Back,* but still no dummy, either.

There was, of course, much to talk about. The man who had transformed the folk world with his raw, exciting acoustic debut LP in 1962, and who later alienated many folkies altogether when he appeared at the 1965 Newport Folk Festival backed by an electric rock band, was still, in 1984, as capable as ever of stirring controversy. Thirteen years ago, to the surprise of virtually everyone, he had turned up in Jerusalem at the Wailing Wall, wearing a yarmulke and reportedly searching for his "Jewish identity." Subsequently, he studied at the Vineyard Christian Fellowship, a Bible school in California, and shocked many fans by releasing three albums of fundamentalist, gospel-swathed rock. (The first, 1979's *Slow Train Coming,* went platinum, but the next two, *Saved* and *Shot of Love,* didn't even go gold.) Next, he became associated with an ultra-Orthodox Jewish sect, the Lubavitcher Hasidim, and last year returned to Jerusalem to celebrate his son Jesse's bar mitzvah. Then came *Infidels.* Although it continued the Biblical bent of Dylan's three previous albums (with an added overlay of what some critics took to be cranky political conservatism), *Infidels* was also one of his best-produced records ever—thanks to Dire Straits guitarist Mark Knopfler's ministrations at the recording console. With precious little promotional push from Dylan himself, the album had already sold nearly three-quarters of a million copies, and now he had not only wrapped up an excellent video but had also made a rare TV appearance on *Late Night with David Letterman*—a rickety but riveting event in which Dylan, backed by a barely prepared, young three-piece band, whomped his way through two *Infidels* tracks and the old Sonny Boy Williamson tune "Don't Start Me to Talking." (It could have been even more curious. At rehearsals, he'd tried out a version of the Roy Head rock nugget "Treat Her Right.") Bob Dylan was once again on the scene. And with concert promoter Bill Graham already booking dates, he was preparing to embark on a major European tour with Santana on May 28, four days after his forty-third birthday.

So here he is once more—but *who* is he? A divorced father of five (one is his ex-wife Sara's daughter, whom he adopted), Dylan divides his time among California, where he owns a sprawling, eccentric heap of a house; Minnesota, where he maintains a farm; and the Caribbean, where he island-hops on a quarter-million-dollar boat. While in New York—a city to which he soon hopes to relocate again—he caught a gig by his former keyboardist Al Kooper, dropped in on a recording session for ex–J. Geils Band singer Peter Wolf and hung out with old pals Keith Richards and Ronnie Wood of the Rolling Stones. Despite his spiritual preoccupations, he insists that he's no prude ("I think I had a beer recently") and that his religious odyssey has been misrepresented in the press. Although he contends he doesn't own any of his song-publishing rights prior to 1974's *Blood on the Tracks* ("That's Keith's favorite"), he is probably quite well-off—"Some years are better than others" is all he'll say on the subject—and is known to be extraordinarily generous to good friends in need. He apparently does not envision any future retirement from music. When I asked if he thought he'd painted his masterpiece yet, he said, "I hope I never do." His love life—he's been linked in the past with singer Clydie King, among others—remains a closed book.

As we spoke, a drunken youth approached our table for an autograph, which Dylan provided. A few minutes later, a toothless old woman wearing hot pants appeared at our side, accompanied by a black wino. "You're Bob Dylan!" she croaked. "And you're Barbra Streisand, right?" said Dylan, not unpleasantly. "I only wondered," said the crone, "because there's a guy out front selling your autograph." "Yeah?" said Dylan. "Well, how much is he askin'?"

A good question, I thought. How much might such a souvenir still command in these waning End Days?

*P*eople *have put various labels on you over the past several years: "He's a born-again Christian"; "he's an ultra-Orthodox Jew." Are any of those labels accurate?*

Not really. People call you this, or they call you that. But I can't respond to that, because then it seems like I'm defensive, and, you know, what does it matter, really?

But weren't three of your albums—'Slow Train Coming,' 'Saved' and 'Shot of Love'—inspired by some sort of born-again religious experience?

I would never call it that. I've never said I'm born again. That's just a media term. I don't think I've ever been an agnostic. I've always thought there's a superior power, that this is not the real world and that there's a world to come. That no soul has died, every soul is alive, either in holiness or in flames. And there's probably a lot of middle ground.

What is your spiritual stance, then?

Well, I don't think that *this is it*, you know—this life ain't nothin'. There's no way you're gonna convince me this is all there is to it. I never, ever believed that. I believe in the Book of Revelation. The leaders of this world are eventually going to play God, if they're not *already* playing God, and eventually a man will come that everybody will think *is* God. He'll do things, and they'll say, "Well, only God can do those things. It must be him."

You're a literal believer of the Bible?

Yeah. Sure, yeah. I am.

Are the Old and New Testaments equally valid?

To me.

Do you belong to any church or synagogue?

Not really. Uh, the Church of the Poison Mind [*laughs*].

Do you actually believe the end is at hand?

I don't think it's *at hand*. I think we'll have *at least* 200 years. And the new kingdom that comes in, I mean, people can't even imagine what it's gonna be like. There's a lot of people walkin' around who think the new kingdom's comin' next year and that they're gonna be right in there among the top guard. And they're wrong. I think when it comes in, there *are* people who'll be prepared for it, but if the new kingdom happened tomorrow and you were sitting there and I was sitting here, you wouldn't even *remember* me.

Can you converse and find agreement with Orthodox Jews?

Yeah, yeah.

And with Christians?

Oh, yeah. Yeah, with anybody.

Sounds like a new synthesis.

Well, no. If I thought the world needed a new religion, I would *start* one. But there are a lot of other religions, too. There's those Indian religions, Eastern religions, Buddhism, you know? They're happening, too.

When you meet up with Orthodox people, can you sit down with them and say, "Well, you should really check out Christianity"?

Well, yeah, if somebody asks me, I'll tell 'em. But, you know, I'm not gonna just offer my opinion. I'm more about playing music, you know?

Your views apparently seemed clear to many record buyers. Were you frustrated by the commercial resistance— both on record and on the road—to your fundamentalist-influenced music?

Well, after the '78 gospel tour, I wanted to keep touring in '79. But I knew that we'd gone everywhere in '78, so how you gonna play in '79? Go back to the same places? So, at that point, I figured, "Well, I don't care if I draw no crowds no more." And a lotta places we played on the last tour, we filled maybe half the hall.

And you don't think that was because of the material you were doing?

I don't think so. I don't think it had to do with *anything*. I think when your time is your time, it don't matter what you're doin'. It's either your time, or it's *not* your time. And I didn't feel the last few years was really my time. But that's no reason for me to make any kinda judgment call on what it is I'm gonna be. The people who reacted to the gospel stuff would've reacted that way if I hadn't done, you know, "Song to Woody."

You think so?

Yeah, I know it. I can usually anticipate that stuff —what's going on, what's the mood. There's a lotta young performers around. And they look good and they move good, and they're sayin' stuff that is, uh, *excitable,* you know? Face it, a lotta that stuff is just made and geared for twelve-year-old kids. It's like baby food.

Your latest album, 'Infidels,' is hardly subteen fodder. Some critics have even detected a new note of conservatism

in some of the songs—even outright jingoism in "Neighborhood Bully," in which the metaphorical subject is said to be "just one man" whose "enemies say he's on their land." That's clearly a strong Zionist political statement, is it not?*

You'd have to point that out to me, you know, what line is in it that spells that out. I'm not a political songwriter. Joe Hill was a political songwriter; uh, Merle Travis wrote some political songs, "Which Side Are You On?" is a political song. And "Neighborhood Bully," to me, is not a political song, because if it were, it would fall into a certain political party. If you're talkin' about it as an Israeli political song—even if it *is* an Israeli political song—in Israel alone, there's maybe twenty political parties. I don't know where that would fall, what party.

Well, would it be fair to call that song a heartfelt statement of belief?

Maybe it is, yeah. But just because somebody feels a certain way, you can't come around and stick some political-party slogan on it. If you listen closely, it really could be about other things. It's simple and easy to define it, so you got it pegged, and you can deal with it in that certain kinda way. However, I wouldn't *do* that. 'Cause I don't know what the politics of Israel is. I just don't know.

So you haven't resolved for yourself, for instance, the Palestinian question?

Not really, because I live *here.*

Would you ever live in Israel?

I don't know. It's hard to speculate what tomorrow may bring. I kinda live where I find myself.

At another point in the song, you say, "He got no allies to really speak of," and while "he buys obsolete weapons and he won't be denied, . . . no one sends flesh and blood to fight by his side." Do you feel that America should send troops over there?

No. The song doesn't say that. Who should, who shouldn't—who am I to say?

Well, do you think Israel should get more help from the American Jewish community? I don't want to push this too far, but it just seems so . . .

Well, you're not pushing it too far, you're just making it *specific.* And you're making it specific to what's going on today. But what's going on today isn't gonna last, you know? The battle of Armageddon is specifically spelled out: where it will be fought and, if you wanna get technical, *when* it will be fought. And the battle of Armageddon definitely will be fought in the Middle East.

Do you follow the political scene or have any sort of fix on what the politicians are talking about this election year?

I think politics is an instrument of the Devil. Just that clear. I think politics is what kills; it doesn't bring anything alive. Politics is corrupt; I mean, anybody knows that.

So you don't care who's president? It doesn't make any difference?

I don't think so. I mean, how long is Reagan gonna be president? I've seen like four of five of 'em myself, you know? And I've seen two of 'em die in office. How can you deal with Reagan and get so serious about that, when the man isn't even gonna *be* there when you get your thing together?

So you don't think there's any difference between, say, a Kennedy and a Nixon? It doesn't matter at all?

I don't know. Who was a better president? Well, you got *me*. I don't know what people's errors are; nobody's perfect, for sure. But I thought Kennedy— both Kennedys—I just liked them. And I liked Martin . . . Martin Luther King. I thought those were people who were blessed and touched, you know? The fact that they all went out with bullets doesn't change nothin'. Because the good they do gets planted. And those seeds live on longer than that.

Do you still hope for peace?

There is not going to *be* any peace.

You don't think it's worth working for?

No. It's just gonna be a false peace. You can reload your rifle, and that moment you're reloading it, that's peace. It may last for a few years.

Isn't it worth fighting for that?

Nah, none of that matters. I heard somebody on the radio talkin' about what's happenin' in Haiti, you know? "We must be concerned about what's happening in Haiti. We're *global people* now." And they're gettin' everybody in that frame of mind—like, we're not just the United States anymore, we're *global*. We're thinkin' in terms of the whole world because communications come right into your house. Well, that's what the Book of Revelation is all *about*. And you can just about *know* that anybody who comes out for peace is *not* for peace.

But what if someone genuinely is for peace?

Well, you can't be for peace and be *global*. It's just like that song "Man of Peace." But none of this matters if you believe in another world. If you believe in *this* world, you're stuck; you really don't have a chance. You'll go *mad*, 'cause you won't see the end of it. You may wanna stick around, but you won't be able to. On another level, though, you *will* be able to see this world. You'll look back and say, "Ah, that's what it was all about all the time. Wow, why didn't I *get* that?"

That's a very fatalistic view, isn't it?

I think it's *realistic*. If it *is* fatalistic, it's only fatalistic on this level, and this level dies anyway, so what's the difference? So you're fatalistic, so what?

There's a lyric in "License to Kill": "Man has invented his doom/First step was touching the moon." Do you really believe that?

Yeah, I do. I have no idea why I wrote that line, but on some level, it's like just a door into the unknown.

Isn't man supposed to progress, to forge ahead?

Well . . . but not there. I mean, what's the purpose of going to the moon? To *me*, it doesn't make any sense. Now they're gonna put a space station up there, and it's gonna cost, what—$600 billion, $700 billion? And who's gonna benefit from it? Drug companies who are gonna be able to make better drugs. Does that make sense? Is that supposed to be something that a person is supposed to get excited about? Is that progress? I don't think they're gonna get better drugs. I think they're gonna get more *expensive* drugs.

Everything is computerized now, it's all computers. I see that as the beginning of the end. You can see everything going global. There's no nationality anymore, no I'm this or I'm that: "We're all the same, all workin' for one peaceful world, blah, blah, blah."

Somebody's gonna have to come along and figure out what's happening with the United States. Is this just an island that's going to be blown out of the ocean, or does it really figure into things? I really don't know. At this point right now, it seems that it figures into things. But later on, it will have to be a country that's self-sufficient, that can make it by itself without that many imports.

Right now, it seems like in the States, and most other countries, too, there's a big push on to make a big *global* country—*one big country*—where you can get all the materials from one place and assemble them someplace else and sell 'em in another place, and the whole world is just all one, controlled by the same people, you know? And if it's not there already, that's the point it's tryin' to get to.

In "Union Sundown," the Chevrolet you drive is "put together down in Argentina by a guy makin' thirty cents a day." Are you saying he'd be better off without that thirty cents a day?

What's thirty cents a day? He don't need the thirty cents a day. I mean, people survived for 6,000 years without having to work for slave wages for a person who comes down and . . . well, actually, it's just colonization. But see, I saw that stuff firsthand, because where I come from, they *really* got that deal good, with the ore.

In Minnesota, in the Iron Range, where you grew up?

Yeah. *Everybody* was workin' there at one time. In fact, ninety percent of the iron for the Second World War came out of those mines, up where I'm from. And eventually, they said, "Listen, this is costing too much money to get this out. We must be able to get it someplace else." Now the same thing is happening, I guess, with other products.

What was it like growing up in Hibbing, Minnesota, in the Fifties?

You're pretty much ruled by nature up there. You have to sort of fall into line with that, regardless of how you're feeling that day or what you might want to do with your life or what you think about. And it still is like that, I think.

Were you aware of any anti-Semitism there when you were a kid?

No. Nothing really mattered to me except learning another song or a new chord or finding a new place to play, you know? Years later, when I'd recorded a few albums, *then* I started seeing in places: "Bob Dylan's a Jew," stuff like that. I said, "Jesus, I never knew that." But they kept harping on it; it seemed like it was *important* for people to *say* that—like they'd say "the one-legged street singer" or something. So after a period of time, I thought, "Well, gee, maybe I'll look into that."

I don't know. I never noticed it occurring with any other artists; I mean, I've never seen it about Barbra Streisand or Neil Diamond. But it *has* occurred with me. As a kid, though, I never felt anything, like, I had to fight my way through schoolyard crowds, you know? As long as I had a guitar, I was happy.

Was Hibbing an oppressive place? Did it just make you want to get out?

Not really. I didn't really know anything else except, uh, Hank Williams. I remember hearin' Hank Williams one or two years before he died. And that sort of introduced me to the guitar. And once I had the guitar, it was never a problem. Nothing else was ever a problem.

Did you get to see any of the original rock & roll guys, like Little Richard, Buddy Holly?

Yeah, sure. I saw Buddy Holly two or three nights before he died. I saw him in Duluth, at the armory. He played there with Link Wray. I don't remember the Big Bopper. Maybe he'd gone off by the time I came in. But I saw Ritchie Valens. And Buddy Holly, yeah. He was great. He was incredible. I mean, I'll never forget the image of seeing Buddy Holly up on

the bandstand. And he died—it must have been a week after that. It was unbelievable.

Late at night, I used to listen to Muddy Waters, John Lee Hooker, Jimmy Reed and Howlin' Wolf blastin' in from Shreveport. It was a radio show that lasted all night. I used to stay up till two, three o'clock in the morning. Listened to all those songs, then tried to figure them out. I started playing myself.

How did you take to the guitar?

First, I bought a Nick Manoloff book. I don't think I could get past the first one. And I had a Silvertone guitar from Sears. In those days they cost thirty or forty dollars, and you only had to pay five dollars down to get it. So I had my first electric guitar.

I had a couple of bands in high school, maybe three or four of 'em. Lead singers would always come in and take my bands, because they would have connections, like maybe their fathers would know somebody, so they could get a job in the neighboring town at the pavilion for a Sunday picnic or something. And I'd lose my band. I'd see it all the time.

That must have made you a little bitter.

Yeah, it did, actually. And then I had another band with my cousin from Duluth. I played, you know, rock & roll, rhythm & blues. And then that died out, pretty much, in my last year of high school.

And after that, I remember I heard a record—I think maybe it was the Kingston Trio or Odetta or someone like that—and I sorta got into folk music. Rock & roll was pretty much finished. And I traded my stuff for a Martin that they don't sell anymore, an 0018, maybe, and it was brown. The first acoustic guitar I had. A *great* guitar. And then, either in Minneapolis or St. Paul, I heard Woody Guthrie. And when I heard Woody Guthrie, that was it, it was all over.

What struck you about him?

Well, I heard them old records, where he sings with Cisco Houston and Sonny [Terry] and Brownie [McGhee] and stuff like that, and then his own songs. And he really struck me as an independent character. But no one ever talked about him. So I went through all his records I could find and picked all that up by any means I could. And when I arrived in New York, I was mostly singing his songs and folk songs. At that time, I was runnin' into people who were playing the same kind of thing, but I was kinda combining elements of Southern mountain music with bluegrass stuff, English-ballad stuff. I could hear a song once and know it. So when I came to New York, I could do a lot of different stuff. But I never thought I'd see rock & roll again when I arrived here.

Did you miss it?

Not really, because I *liked* the folk scene. It was a whole community, a whole world that was all hooked up to different towns in the United States. You could go from here to California and always have a place to stay, and always play somewhere, and meet people. Nowadays, you go to see a folk singer—what's the folk singer doin'? He's singin' all his own songs. *That* ain't no folk singer. Folk singers sing those old folk songs, ballads.

I met a lot of folk singers in New York, and there were a lot of 'em in the Twin Cities. But I ran into some people in England who *really* knew those songs. Martin Carthy, another guy named Nigel Davenport. Martin Carthy's incredible. I learned a lot of stuff from Martin. "Girl from the North Country" is based on a song I heard *him* sing—that "Scarborough Fair" song, which Paul Simon, I guess, just took the whole thing.

Could folk ever become big again?

Well, yeah, it could become big again. But people gotta go back and find the songs. They don't do it no more. I was tellin' somebody that thing about when you go to see a folk singer now, you hear somebody singin' his own songs. And the person says, "Yeah, well, *you* started that." And in a sense, it's true. But I never would have written a song if I didn't play all them old folk songs first. I never would have *thought* to write a song, you know? There's no *dedication* to folk music now, no *appreciation* of the art form.

Do you notice that you've influenced a lot of singers over the years?

It's phrasing. I think I've phrased everything in a way that it's never been phrased before. I'm not tryin' to *brag* or anything—or maybe I am [*laughs*]. But, yeah, I hear stuff on the radio, doesn't matter what kinda stuff it is, and I *know* that if you go back far enough, you'll find somebody listened to Bob Dylan somewhere, because of the phrasing. Even the content of the tunes. Up until I started doin' that stuff, nobody was talkin' about that sort of thing. For music to succeed on any level . . . Well, you're always gonna have your pop-radio stuff, but the only people who are gonna succeed, really, are the people who are sayin' somethin' that is given to them to say. I mean, you can only carry "Tutti Frutti" so far.

Like the current rockabilly revival?

The rockabilly revival was just about spirit and attitude.

Were you aware of punk rock when it happened—the Sex Pistols, the Clash?

Yeah. I didn't listen to it all the time, but it seemed like a logical step, and it still does. I think it's been hurt in a lotta ways by the fashion industry.

You've seen the Clash, I understand?

Yeah. I met them way back in 1977, 1978. In England. I think they're great. In fact, I think they're greater now than they were.

You mean since Mick Jones left?

Yeah. It's interesting. It took two guitar players to replace Mick.

How about Prince—have you ever run into him in Minneapolis?

No, I never have.

Have you met Michael Jackson yet?

No, I don't think so. I met Martha and the Vandellas.

Do your kids tell you about new groups: "You gotta check out Boy George"?

Well, they used to, a few years ago. I kind of like everything.

Are your kids musical?

Yeah, they all play.

Would you encourage them to go into the music business?

I would never push 'em or encourage 'em to. I mean, I never went into it as a *business*. I went into it as a matter of *survival*. So I wouldn't tell anybody to go into it as a business. It's a pretty cutthroat business, from what I've seen.

What do you tell your kids about things like sex and drugs?

Well, they don't really ask me too much about that stuff. I think they probably learn enough just by hangin' around me, you know?

You had a drug period at one time, didn't you?

I never got hooked on any drug—not like you'd say, uh, "Eric Clapton: His drug period."

Ever take LSD?

I don't wanna say anything to encourage anybody, but, uh, who knows? Who knows what people stick in your drinks or what kinda cigarettes you're smokin'?

When people like Jimi Hendrix and Janis Joplin started dropping away, did you look upon that as a waste?

Jimi, I thought, was a big waste. I saw Jimi . . . oh, man, that was sad when I saw him. He was in the back seat of a limousine on Bleecker Street, just . . . I couldn't even tell then whether he was dead or alive.

Do your old songs still mean the same to you as when you wrote them?

Yeah. Sittin' here, it's hard to imagine it, but yeah. Once you lock into that stuff, it's like it was just written yesterday. When I'm singin' the stuff, sometimes I say, "Wow! Where'd these lyrics *come* from?" It's *amazing*.

Do you still look back on some of it as protest material? Or did you ever see it as protest material?

I think all my stuff is protest material in some kinda way. I always felt like my position and my place came after that first wave, or maybe second wave, of rock & roll. And I felt like I would never have done the things I did if I just had to listen to popular radio.

At one point, didn't you disassociate yourself from the protest form?

Well, you see, I never called it protest. Protest is anything that goes against the ordinary and the established. And who's the founder of protest? Martin Luther.

Is it true that "Like a Rolling Stone" was done in one take?

Yeah, one take. It's amazing. It sounds like it's so together. That was back in the days when we used to do . . . oh, man, six, eight, ten tunes a session. We used to just go in and come out the next day.

Wasn't 'Another Side of Bob Dylan' the result of an all-night session, too?

Well, that was pretty quick, too. But that was easier to do; it was just *me*. But we used to do the same thing when there was a band in there. I don't think a song like "Rolling Stone" could have been *done* any other way. What are you gonna do, chart it out?

How do you maintain a balance between the requirements of the modern recording studio and the fact that a lot of your best stuff in the past has been done very quickly?

Right now, I'm changing my views on that. But I plan to do a little bit more acoustic stuff in the future. I think my next album is probably just gonna be me and my guitar and harmonica. I'm not saying all of it will be that way, but I'm sure a few songs will be. I *know* they will be.

What's your latest stuff like?

I just write 'em as they come, you know? They're not about anything different than what I've ever written about, but they're probably put together in a way that other ones aren't put together. So it might seem like somethin' new. I don't think I've found any new chords or new progressions, or any new words that haven't been said before. I think they're pretty much all the same old thing, just kinda reworked.

I heard an outtake from the 'Infidels' sessions called "Blind Willie McTell." Is that ever going to come out? It's a great song.

I didn't think I recorded it right. But I don't know why that stuff gets out on me. I mean, it never seems to get out on other people.

There's a lot of interest out there. You could put all

your unreleased stuff out in, like, a twenty-volume set or something.

Yeah, like *The Basement Tapes*. But it doesn't occur to me to put it out. If I wrote a song three years ago, I seldom go back and get that. I just leave 'em alone.

I never really liked The Basement Tapes. I mean, they were just songs we had done for the publishing company, as I remember. They were used only for other artists to record those songs. I wouldn't have put 'em out. But, you know, Columbia wanted to put 'em out, so what can you do?

You don't think that album has a great feeling to it? That material really has an aura.

I can't even remember it. People have told me they think it's very Americana and all that. I don't know what they're talkin' about.

So, then, it wouldn't occur to you to put out, say, the 1966 tapes of the Royal Albert Hall concert in London, another great bootleg?

No. Uh-uh. I wouldn't put 'em out because I didn't think they were quality.

That stuff's great. I'm amazed you wouldn't want to see it done legitimately and really do the tapes right.

Well, but you see, Columbia's never offered to *do* that. They have done that with *The Basement Tapes* and the *Budokan* album. But they've never offered to put that out as a historical album or whatever. And believe me, if they wanted to do it, they could.

Speaking of the 'Budokan' album . . .

The *Budokan* album was only supposed to be for Japan. They twisted my arm to do a live album for Japan. It was the same band I used on *Street Legal*, and we had just started findin' our way into things on that tour when they recorded it. I never meant for it to be any type of representation of my stuff or my band or my live show.

That was when the critics started saying you were going Las Vegas, wasn't it?

Well, I think the only people who would have said somethin' like that were people who've never *been* to Las Vegas.

I think it was the clothes you wore at the time. They said it made you look like Neil Diamond.

Well, it just goes to show you how times have changed since 1978, if you could be criticized for what you were *wearing*. I mean, *now* you can wear anything. You see a guy wearing a dress onstage now, it's like, "Oh, yeah, right." You expect it.

I've seen a lot of stuff written about me. People must be crazy. I mean *responsible* people. Especially on that *Street Legal* tour. That band we assembled then,

I don't think that will ever be duplicated. It was a big ensemble. And what did people say? I mean, responsible people who *know* better. All I saw was "Bruce Springsteen" because there was a *saxophone* player. And it was "disco"—well, there wasn't any *disco* in it.

It always seemed to me that you were sort of infallible in your career up until 'Self Portrait,' in 1970. What's the story behind that album?

At the time, I was in Woodstock, and I was getting a great degree of notoriety for doing *nothing*. Then I had that motorcycle accident, which put me outta commission. Then, when I woke up and caught my senses, I realized I was just workin' for all these *leeches*. And I didn't wanna do that. Plus, I had a family, and I just wanted to see my *kids*.

I'd also seen that I was representing all these things that I didn't know anything *about*. Like I was supposed to be on acid. It was all storm-the-embassy kind of stuff—Abbie Hoffman in the streets—and they sorta figured me as the kingpin of all that. I said, "Wait a minute, I'm just a *musician*. So my songs are about this and that. So *what?*" But people need a leader. People need a leader more than a leader needs people, really. I mean, anybody can step up and be a leader if he's got the people there that want one. I didn't want that, though.

But then came the big news about Woodstock, about musicians goin' up there, and it was like a wave of insanity breakin' loose around the house *day* and *night*. You'd come in the house and find people there, people comin' through the *woods,* at all hours of the day and night, knockin' on your door. It was really dark and depressing. And there was no way to *respond* to all this, you know? It was as if they were suckin' your very *blood* out. I said, "Now, wait, these people can't be my *fans*. They just *can't* be." And they kept comin'. We *had* to get out of there.

This was just about the time of that Woodstock Festival, which was the sum total of all this bullshit. And it seemed to have something to do with *me,* this Woodstock Nation, and everything it represented. So we couldn't *breathe*. I couldn't get any space for myself and my family, and there was no help, nowhere. I got very resentful about the whole thing, and we got outta there.

We moved to New York. Lookin' back, it really was a stupid thing to do. But there was a house available on MacDougal Street, and I always remembered that as a nice place. So I just bought this house, sight unseen. But it wasn't the same when we got back. The Woodstock Nation had overtaken MacDougal Street

also. There'd be crowds outside my house. And I said, "Well, fuck it. I wish these people would just *forget* about me. I wanna do something they *can't* possibly like, they *can't* relate to. They'll see it, and they'll listen, and they'll say, 'Well, let's go on to the next person. He ain't sayin' it no more. He ain't givin' us what we want,' you know? They'll go on to somebody else." But the whole idea backfired. Because the album went out there, and the people said, "*This* ain't what we want," and they got *more* resentful. And then I did this portrait for the cover. I mean, there was no *title* for that album. I knew somebody who had some paints and a square canvas, and I did the cover up in about five minutes. And I said, "Well, I'm gonna call this album *Self Portrait*."

Which was duly interpreted by the press as "This is what he is. . . ."

Yeah, *exactly*. And to me, it was a *joke*.

But why did you make it a double-album joke?

Well, it wouldn't have held up as a single album—then it *really* would've been bad, you know. I mean, if you're gonna put a lot of crap on it, you might as well *load it up!*

In the Sixties there was feeling that this society really was changing. Looking back, do you feel it changed that much?

I think it did. A lot of times people forget. These modern days that we know now, where you can get on an airplane and fly anywhere you want nonstop, direct, and be there—that's recent. That's since what, 1940? Not even that—after the war, it was. And telephones? *Forget* it. I mean, when I was growin' up, I remember we had a phone in the house, but you had to dial it; and I also remember there was a party line of maybe six other people. And no matter when you got on the phone, you know, there might be somebody else on it. And I never grew up with television. When television first came in, it came on at like four in the afternoon, and it was off the air by seven at night. So you had more time to . . . I guess to think. It can never go back to the way it was, but it was all changing in the Fifties and Sixties.

My kids, they know television, they know telephones. They don't think about that stuff, you know? Even airplanes: I never rode on an airplane until 1964 or somethin'. Up till that time, if you wanted to go across the country, you took a train or a Greyhound bus, or you hitchhiked. I don't know. I don't think of myself as that *old*, or having seen that much, but . . .

Do you have MTV at home?

No, I don't get that. I have to go to the city to see

MTV. And then, once I do find a set that has it, I'll just watch it for, you know, as long as my eyes can stay open. Until they pop out, I'll just watch it.

What do you make of video? Do you think it's all that important?

Uh, to sell records, yeah. But videos have always been around. David Bowie's been makin' 'em since he started. There was one thing I saw on a video, and I thought it was great. Then I heard the record on the radio, and it was *nothin'*, you know? But video does give you something to hook onto.

I was just talkin' to Ronnie Wood the other night. He went to the Duran Duran show at the Garden, and he said it was really funny, because they had a great big screen up over the stage with huge close-ups of the band members. And every time they showed a close-up of somebody in the band, the audience would just go crazy—they'd go *mad*, you know? So while they were showing a close-up of somebody in the band, the guitar player'd be playing a lick. So *he'd* think they were all doing it for *him*. Then he'd play the same lick again to get the same response—and get *nothing*.

I remember you were trying to get together with Ronnie and Keith [Richards] the other night. How'd it go?

It was pretty subdued actually. But I always like to see Keith or Woody or Eric or . . . There's a few people I like to see whenever I can. People who play like that. It has to do with a style of music, you know?

Do you ever collaborate?

Yeah, but usually it never happens. It's, "Okay, that's great, we'll pick that up later and finish it." But nothin' ever really gets finished.

Are your best friends mostly musicians?

My best friends? Jeez, let me try to think of one [*laughs*].

There must be a few.

Best friends? Jesus, I mean, that's . . .

You've got to have a best friend.

Whew! Boy, there's a question that'll really make you think. Best friend? Jesus, I think I'd go into a deep, dark depression if I were to think about who's my best friend.

There have to be one or two, don't there?

Well, there *has* to be . . . there *must* be . . . there's *gotta* be. But hey, you know, a best friend is someone who's gonna die for you. I mean, that's your best friend, really. Yeah, I'd be miserable trying to think who my best friend is.

What do you do with your year, aside from doing an album and maybe a tour?

Well, I'm happy doin' nothin' [*laughs*].

Do you spend a lot of time in Minnesota?

I get back there when I can, yeah. I got some property outside of St. Paul back in '74, a sort of farm.

Do you actually farm on this farm?

Well, it grows potatoes and corn, but I don't sit on the *tractor*, if that's what you mean. I'm usually either here or on the West Coast or down in the Caribbean.

Me and another guy have a boat down there. "Jokerman" kinda came to me in the islands. It's very mystical. The shapes there, and shadows, seem to be so ancient. The song was sorta inspired by these spirits they call *jumbis*.

Do you still have that house in California, that big, strange-looking place?

That's a story—you could write a baroque novel offa that. I had five kids, and I just couldn't find a house that was suitable. I liked this area because there was a public school in the neighborhood, and the kids could ride their bikes to it. So I bought this house on about an acre of land, past Malibu. And my wife looked at it and said, "Well, it's okay, but it needs another bedroom." So I got somebody to design another bedroom. You had to file plans, and they had to be passed—that's the way the red tape is out there. So we had architects come in, and right away they said, "Oh, yeah, Bob Dylan, right. We'll really make somethin' spectacular here." Anyway, it took six months to get the plans passed just to put on another room. I mean, *one room*. Jesus! So I went out there one day to see how the room was progressing, and they'd knocked down the house. *They'd knocked down the house!* I asked the guys who were workin', "Where's the house?" And they said they had to knock it down to restructure it for this bedroom upstairs.

Sounds like somebody was making a lot of money off you.

Ain't that the truth? I mean, has it ever been otherwise? So, one thing led to another, and I said as long as they're knockin' this place down, we're just gonna add more rooms on to it. And any time some craftsman passed by—hitchhiking to Oregon or coming back down to Baja—we'd say, "Hey, you wanna do some work on this place?" And they'd do woodwork, tile work, all that kinda thing. And eventually it was built. But then they closed the school out there, and the kids moved away, and Sara moved away, and, uh . . . So I was stuck with this place. As a matter of fact, I've never even put anything on the living-room floor. It's just cement.

Since you've spent a lot of time in the Caribbean, you must be familiar with Rastafarianism.

Not really. I know a lot of Rastas. I know they're Bible-believing people, and it's very easy for me to relate to any Bible-believing person.

Well, what if someone is born in a place where there are no Bibles—the Tibetan mountains, say. Could they still be saved?

I don't know. I really don't. Allen Ginsberg is a Tibetan—a Buddhist or something like that. I'm just not familiar enough with that to say anything about it.

Speaking of Allen Ginsberg, doesn't the Bible say that homosexuality is an abomination?

Yeah, it does. It says that.

And yet Ginsberg's a good guy, right?

Yeah, well, but that's no reason for *me* to condemn somebody, because they drink or they're corrupt in orthodox ways or they wear their shirt inside out. I mean, that's *their* scene. It certainly doesn't matter to *me*. I've got no ax to grind with any of that.

Were you up in Minnesota when they tried to pass that antiporn law in Minneapolis? The contention was that pornography is a violation of women's civil rights. What do you think?

Well, pornography is pretty deeply embedded. I mean, it's into everything, isn't it? You see commercials on TV that millions of dollars have been put into, and they look pretty sexy to me. They look like they're pushin' sex in some kinda way.

In a way, that's the real pornography, because the point isn't to get you off sexually, it's to sell you something.

Yeah, it's to stick the idea in your brain. But it's too far gone. I mean, if you start makin' laws against porno magazines and that kinda stuff, well, then where do you draw the line? You gotta stop the prime-time television shows also.

Any thoughts on abortion?

Abortion? I personally don't think abortion is that important. I think it's just an issue to evade whatever issues *are* makin' people think about abortion.

Well, I mean, when abortion's used as a form of birth control . . .

Well, I think birth control is another hoax that women shouldn't have bought, but they did buy. I mean, if a man don't wanna knock up a woman, that's *his* problem, you know what I mean? It's interesting: They arrest prostitutes, but they never arrest the guys *with* the prostitutes. It's all very one-sided. And the same with birth control. Why do they make women take all them pills and fuck themselves up like that? People have used contraceptives for years and years and years. So all of a sudden some scientist invents a *pill*, and it's a billion-dollar industry. So we're talkin' about *money*. How to *make money* off of a sexual idea. "Yeah, you can go out and fuck anybody you want now; just take this pill." You know? And it puts that in a person's mind: "Yeah, if I take a pill . . ." But who *knows* what

those pills do to a person? I think they're gonna be passé. But they've caused a lot of damage, a lot of damage.

So it's the man's responsibility? Vasectomy's the best way?

I think so. A man don't wanna get a woman pregnant, then *he's* gotta take care of it. Otherwise, that's just ultimate *abuse*, you know?

But the problem is not abortion. The problem is the whole concept behind abortion. Abortion is the end result of going out and screwing somebody to begin with. Casual sex.

But the abortion question is, Is it taking a life? Is it a woman's decision?

Well, if the woman wants to take that upon herself, I figure that's her business. I mean, who's gonna take care of the baby that arrives—these people that are callin' for no abortion?

In regard to these feminist sympathies . . .

I think women rule the world, and that no man has ever done anything that a woman either hasn't allowed him to do or encouraged him to do.

In that regard, there's a song on Infidels *called "Sweetheart like You," in which you say, "A woman like you should be at home . . . takin' care of somebody nice."*

Actually, that line didn't come out *exactly* the way I wanted it to. But, uh . . . I could easily have changed that line to make it not so overly, uh, *tender*, you know? But I think the concept still woulda been the same. You see a fine-lookin' woman walking down the street, you start goin', "Well, what are you doin' on the street? You're so fine, what do you need all this for?"

A lot of women might say they're on the street because they're on the way to their jobs.

Well, I wasn't talkin' to that type of woman. I'm not talkin' to Margaret Thatcher or anything.

Are you in love at the moment?

I'm *always* in love.

Would you ever marry again? Do you believe in the institution?

Yeah, I do. I don't believe in *divorce*. But I'm a strong believer in marriage.

One last question. I think a lot of people take you for a pretty gloomy character these days, just judging by your photos. Why reinforce that image by calling this latest album Infidels*?*

Well, there were other titles for it. I wanted to call it *Surviving in a Ruthless World*. But someone pointed out to me that the last bunch of albums I'd made all started with the letter *s*. So I said, "Well, I don't wanna get bogged down in the letter *s*." And then *Infidels* came into my head one day. I don't know what it *means* or anything.

Don't you think when people see that title, with that sort of dour picture on the front, they'll wonder, "Does he mean us?"

I don't know. I could've called the album *Animals,* and people would've said the same thing. I mean, what would be a term that people would *like* to hear about themselves?

How about 'Sweethearts'?
Sweethearts. You *could* call an album that. *Sweethearts.*

With a big smiling picture?
Yeah.

11

Desmond Tutu

INTERVIEWED BY
MARC COOPER AND GREG GOLDIN (1985)

In 1988, Nelson Mandela—for many the symbol of the struggle against apartheid—celebrated his seventieth birthday, and 70,000 people attended a concert in his honor at London's Wembley Stadium. Mandela, of course, could not attend, for he has spent the last twenty-two years of his life in South African prisons.

During Mandela's long imprisonment, his place at the head of the anti-apartheid movement in South Africa has remained vacant, and the organization he once guided, the African National Congress, remains outlawed, its leadership consigned to exile in Zambia. But in Mandela's absence, others have found themselves thrust to the fore in the battle against the brutal South African regime. Chief among these is Desmond Tutu, the Anglican prelate who was awarded the Nobel Peace Prize in 1984.

When young Americans were asked by ROLLING STONE in the late Eighties to name the public figure of the preceding twenty years whom they most admired, their answer was Martin Luther King, Jr. Much like Dr. King—another clergyman and Nobel laureate who was called to war with racial oppression—Bishop Tutu, as he makes clear in this interview, would have preferred to "carry on [his] work of being a pastor," rather than, as he puts it, "do [Mandela's] work." Today, however, there can be little doubt that Tutu speaks not only for his countrymen but also for millions of Americans who believe apartheid, and its suppression, to be one of the most pressing issues of this decade and, unfortunately, the next.

—S. H.

"HAVE YOU heard the latest story they're telling about me?" jokes Desmond Mpilo Tutu, the fifty-four-year-old Anglican bishop of Johannesburg, South Africa. "There's a new Kentucky Fried Tutu. You know what it's got? Two left wings and a parson's nose!" The winner of the 1984 Nobel Peace Prize sloughs off the criticism with a string of scornful "hmmphhs."

"What do they think they accomplish when they attack me personally?" Tutu asks, his smile turning into a look of puzzlement. "Do they think that by tarnishing my character they are changing the facts of the evil system that I am denouncing?"

That system is apartheid, the institutionalized system of racism that deprives 25 million blacks of the right to vote and subjugates them to the will of 5 million whites. "They" are the white regime behind one of the world's best-oiled police and military machines.

Apartheid became official policy in 1948, when the newly elected Afrikaner-dominated National Party codified 300 years of racial discrimination. Every South African was classified by race after a state-conducted inspection. Racial intermarriage was banned. Colored (mixed race) and Indian communities were stripped of political rights; blacks were stripped of their citizenship entirely. Nonwhites were prohibited from living in certain so-called white areas. Blacks had to apply for temporary permits to work in white areas and could expect as little as one-sixth of what white workers earned.

The government eventually designated ten areas—barren wastelands, really—as so-called homelands for blacks, and since 1948, nearly 4 million people have been forcibly removed from their homes and resettled. Most of those who have been permitted to remain in the white areas must live in squalid, segregated townships.

It is in one of these pressure cookers of humiliation and violence—Soweto—that Bishop Tutu lives today with an estimated 1.5 million other blacks. Just a fifteen-minute drive away from the city center, Soweto might as well be 10,000 miles away. Families live crammed into uninsulated shacks and bungalows, most with tin roofs. Unpaved streets meander for miles through the ghetto, never leading to a center, just on to another row of ramshackle houses. At dusk, a noxious cloud shrouds the township as tens of thousands of coal fires are lit, over which the daily fare of mealy-meal will be cooked.

For the last year, Soweto and dozens of other similar ghettos throughout the nation have been occupied by the white-led army, known as the South African Defense Force (SADF). The troops have been deployed to suppress the most serious revolt in the country's history. Ghetto youths armed with stones and gas bombs, militant black unions, boycotts of white-owned businesses and international condemnation of apartheid have shaken the regime to its foundations. Minor reforms have been enacted, others have been promised. But the basic system remains in place, as does resistance to it.

The SADF troops and security police have arrested more than 10,000 people over the last year, more than 3,000 of them detained without trial or charges. Hundreds have been killed in the streets. Others have died while in police custody. Forty-seven of the eighty top leaders of the anti-apartheid umbrella group, the United Democratic Front (UDF), have been killed, jailed or indicted in the past year. One of its founders (and a close associate of Tutu), the Reverend Allan Boesak, who also serves as president of the World Alliance of Reformed Churches, has been charged with four counts of subversion. And last July, in a pivotal move, the government of State President P.W. Botha declared a state of emergency in areas that have been the most rebellious.

From exile in nearby Zambia, the outlawed opposition group, the African National Congress (ANC), announced that its commandos operating inside South Africa will step up the war.

Amid this turmoil, Bishop Desmond Tutu has emerged as a leader whose self-assigned mission is to see that the liberation of black people, which he believes is inevitable, comes about peacefully. His anti-apartheid work, dating back to 1978, when he was leader of the South African Council of Churches, has thrust him into international prominence. What gives Tutu such strength and influence is his uncanny ability to look his Afrikaner opponents squarely in the eyes and laugh at the absurdity of their vision. Instead of indulging in a bit of sanctimony, for instance, in condemning the laws that, in effect, force black workers to live in single-sex hostels far from their homes and families, Tutu extends his arms, palms up, and says, with a bitter laugh, "Can you imagine that? This is the only country in the world where it is illegal to sleep with your own wife!"

The bishop was interviewed in his study— a room twelve-by-twelve that is dominated by a huge polished desk stacked high with papers, telegrams and lacquered plaques— his latest harvest of honorary awards. Tutu is always smartly dressed, but his well-cut suit, imported loafers and designer cuff links are never in conflict with his prominent silver cross and bright-purple rabat. Nor does this touch of flamboyance undermine his essential modesty. The diocesan offices of the Anglican Church on the edge of downtown Johannesburg are next to a rubbish dump, home to an occasional sleeping derelict. The adjoining church, where Tutu prays twice a day, has plastic chairs, no pews, an unpolished wooden floor, and a row of makeshift offices in one aisle along the nave. A pile of discarded furniture guards the chapel entrance.

Before becoming the bishop of Johannesburg, Desmond Tutu was the bishop of Lesotho. From 1978 to 1985, he was general secretary of the South African Council of Churches. Educated in his younger years in the segregated Bantu system of South Africa, he attained his master's in theology at King's College in London.

We were amazed by the manifest lack of security precautions taken by the bishop. His family has not been immune to reprisals; his son, Trevor, spent fourteen days in jail in August, detained under the state of emergency. Tutu may have office windows of reflecting one-way glass, and darkened windows on his Toyota, but apart from a lock on his office, he has no other protection. He relies on international vigilance and, as he says, on his faith in God, whose job it is to "jolly well look after me."

How has the system of apartheid personally affected you, Bishop Tutu?

Relative to the kind of life that many blacks lead, I have had a good time. I didn't have a particularly deprived childhood, nor was it particularly well endowed. My mother was a domestic worker; my father, the headmaster of a primary school.

We didn't think it was particularly odd that we were separated from white people. We thought that was the way that God had probably ordered things. I think my first experiences of awakening came when I used to ride my bicycle to town and had to run the gantlet of white boys taunting me racially. But even that was nothing thought to be out of the ordinary. It happened to every black boy. And I supposed that if we had caught a white boy in a similar situation, we might also biff him one!

A little later, I began finding things eating away at me. When I went walking with my father, we would get stopped for passes. What that does to you and your feeling as a human being is horrible. Or going to a shop with my father and hearing him addressed as "boy." [*Anguished*] I knew there wasn't a great deal I could do, but it just left me churned. I felt . . . I felt . . . I felt . . . [*takes off his glasses and passes his hand over his eyes*] poor man. What he must have been feeling. What he must have been going through, being humiliated in the presence of his son. Apartheid has always been the same systematic racial discrimination: It takes away your human dignity and rubs it in the dust and tramples it underfoot.

Even now you continue to be the target of government harassment. We have heard that the security forces try to humiliate you the same way those white boys did when you were a youngster.

Oh, yes. You are talking about the roadblocks. I was stopped at a roadblock and my car was searched, and the police wanted to body-search my wife and daughters, and this eventually happened at a police station, where they were stripped. A whippersnapper of a policeman asked me for some identification. Ha! [*Laughs heartily*] I am the bishop of Johannesburg. I am a Nobel laureate. Any policeman who says he does not know me does not deserve to be in the police force. If they treat me like that, what do they do to so-called ordinary people? What do whites know about tear gas, about police dogs, about armored vehicles rumbling through the streets of their suburbs, about rubber bullets that kill three-year-olds? What do they know about having the army deployed against a defenseless civilian population? What are they doing to our children, what are they doing to our beautiful land, what ghastly legacy are they building up for posterity? No country can afford to bleed as much as ours is, where black lives are dirt cheap.

You describe a situation in which whites have imprisoned themselves in their own physical and psychic ghettos, oblivious to what goes on in the black areas. Who then is the black man in the white man's mind?

I think it's easier to say what *most* whites think, because there are some splendid people among them. It's horrible to have to keep saying, "Some of my best friends are whites." [*He bursts into a belly laugh.*] By and large, white people think that we are humans, but not quite as human as they. That, I think, is the sum of it. They would say, "We *do* think you are humans." But if they really believe that, why do they think we get married and then would want to be separated from our wives for eleven months of the year? Why do they think when we come back home from work we don't like to be welcomed by our children? And why do they think that in the land of our birth we should have absolutely no participation whatsoever in the most important decisions affecting our lives—that they should legislate about us, that they should determine what is best for us? That's something you would only do for a moron or for little children. And if they think we are children—even when at fifty-four years of age we can be bishops and Nobel laureates, when we can meet up with all kinds of people all around the world—then they can tell themselves that an eighteen-year-old white child has more wisdom and more capacity to make decisions than I do. It must mean they believe that a black person, no matter how high he may go, no matter how educated he may be, is still less than an eighteen-year-old white child, because an eighteen-year-old white can vote and I can't.

And how does the black man see the white?

Many see the white man as something to fear—as one who is out there to squeeze the maximum out of you, and then when you have finished providing your labor, when he has squeezed all of that out of you, he then discards you. And that is what the whites have done. They get men to come and work, and as long as they are able-bodied and can provide labor, they are wanted. When they are no longer able to provide that labor, they are seen only as commodities, things. Things that were once useful and now are not so. One government minister said long ago, talking about these blacks who could no longer work, they were "superfluous appendages." Our mothers and fathers, "superfluous appendages."

Do you think that blacks hate the white minority?

I expect that there are many who do. They must, you know? What do they think happens to you? You work for the white person in a salubrious suburb of Johannesburg, in a huge house that probably has only got two people in it. You have had to leave your home when it was still dark because transport is so inadequate. You go back home to your ghetto, you haven't seen your children, and by the time you get home, they've probably fallen asleep. You are in your home, which is perhaps no larger than just the den of the home from which you have just come. What does that say to you? What do they think is happening to you as a human being? However, I think there is still the recurring miracle of blacks still talking to whites. There is an extraordinary fund of good will, still, despite all of what has happened here.

Who can legitimately claim to represent the blacks of South Africa?

The surveys show that Nelson Mandela [leader of the outlawed African National Congress] is consistently head and shoulders above everybody else. The man they put in a cold jug over twenty years ago, whose picture you are not allowed to publish in this country, whom you are not allowed to quote. Yet people who were not even born when he was sentenced see him as their hero, their leader. Ninety percent, every time. In comparison, let's take who might be considered the best of the lot who operate within the system that the people have rejected: Chief Gatsha Buthelezi [leader of the KwaZulu homeland]. He got barely six percent. Now, these surveys may not be very accurate, but what I am saying is that consistently Nelson is always right at the top and all the others come panting along a poor second, third or fourth.

What would happen if Nelson Mandela were released today? What would change here?

Ohhh! It would be electric. For one thing, Bishop Tutu would get on with his work of being bishop, man. [*Laughs*] I said to Winnie [Mandela], for goodness' sake, go and get that husband of yours out and let me carry on my work of being a pastor. I'm having to do his work, which I don't relish at all. Clearly, Mandela must be a remarkable man. He has done nothing—just sat there for twenty-four years—but he continues to be our leader. If he came out . . . well, how did you guys feel about JFK?

We're asking the questions today.

Hmmm. I'm answering them, I'm answering them. But I'm just saying that's more or less where we would be. It would change. It would be a different ball game.

And Mandela would be able to say—he's got that kind of authority—he would say, Stop that.

Stop the violence?

Yeah, whatever he wanted them to stop. He would be able to get them to do that. I mean, in comparison, we are just puny little things, man.

Are we going to see a black president in this country within a decade?

Yes. It is inevitable and obvious that we will have a truly democratic and majority government. I would not be as rash as to give precise timetables. It could be next year. It could be! You know this is a very strange country.

That's a mouthful. How do you get from white minority rule to black majority rule without an apocalypse?

Basically, there are only two ways. One is bloodshed, violence and chaos, which we are trying desperately to avert. The other is the route of negotiation, people sitting down together, a national convention, a constitutional conference, whatever you call it. That has been the call that the churches have been making now, for donkey's years, it seems, without making too much of an impression on the authorities. Now that the authorities are talking about negotiation, they speak of meeting with *elected* black leaders, knowing very well that the only elected black leaders are those operating within the government. Most of our people have rejected those so-called leaders.

You say negotiation is the preferred route. Is this likely, given an atmosphere of escalating violence?

We already have some of the necessary factors. Business leaders, startled by the run on the rand, have decided it is time to come out more forcefully and unequivocally against apartheid. A delegation of top business leaders went to Zambia to discuss issues with leaders of the African National Congress.

Are you saying that economic pressure may lead to a softening of apartheid policies?

If they don't get down to sitting and talking, they are going to be compelled by the business sector, who are seeing their profits slashed because the rand has lost so much of its value. A fifty-percent devaluation! The business community may be realizing that if they do not take action soon, they are going to the birds. It is impossible for a minority forever, and ever and ever, to rule over a vast majority. Business people are saying, "When the change comes, we don't want to be seen so have been part of the problem. We must indicate that we were part of the solution."

Was the meeting in Zambia with the ANC a hedging of bets by the business community?

Yes, I think so. But maybe not in a kind of cynical way. I think it has been drummed into their heads that no meaningful discussion about the future of this country can take place if you exclude the ANC. I mean, that is just a brutal fact of life.

You point to the meeting with the ANC as one sign of hope for peaceful change. But didn't the ANC itself give up on nonviolence when its leader, Mandela, was sent to prison?

No. They said they were forced to take the option of armed struggle because they were banned in 1960. I think many of the ANC leaders said, "If we can no longer operate legally and aboveboard, we still have to operate. We were set up as an organization to try and ensure that black people had a place in South Africa. It seems then the only way forward is through the armed struggle." I myself still believe—I am naive, of course—and I am not a politician, despite *all* appearances to the contrary, but I still believe that if this government says it intends to dismantle apartheid, it is releasing all political prisoners, it is allowing exiles to return home without any risk of persecution, and it wants to talk with those who are the authentic representatives of the black people, then I think the ANC would also be ready to talk.

Recently, the ANC announced a stepping up of its guerrilla war. What makes you so sure it would give up its guns?

If you are saying the only thing the ANC wants is to fight to the death, then why did they talk to the business leaders? The ANC is not bloodthirsty, despite what the government says about them. I know many of the ANC leaders personally. I met with them in December in Lusaka. I met with Oliver Tambo [the president of the ANC] in the archbishop of Canterbury's London residence, Lambeth Palace. [*Laughs*] Whites in this country would be shocked out of their skins if they got to know Tambo.

But Tambo is leading a declared war against the white majority government.

When you look how the ANC has operated inside this country, it is remarkable how restrained it has been. It hasn't been real terrorism, like you get in Beirut and Northern Ireland. The ANC still tends to attack only installations, only property, rather than persons.

If it is true that the ANC is not committed to violence for its own sake, what then can we expect from the government? Is there any willingness on its part to moderate its methods?

Let me make this point categorically. The situation

in South Africa is violent. And the primary violence is the violence of apartheid. It is the violence of forced population removals. It is the violence of detention without trial. It is the violence of mysterious deaths in detention. It is the violence that forces children to be stunted through a deliberately inferior educational system. It is the violence of the migratory labor system, which systematically destroys black family life. The catalog is endless. I have declared myself repeatedly as opposed to all forms of violence. But when opponents of this system have challenged it nonviolently, they have gotten it in the neck for their pains.

This government believes when people get obstreperous, why, just boink them one on the head and you will have sorted them out properly. My son was detained for fourteen days because he swore at the police. [*Laughs*] He told them what many of us believe about their actions, even though we might not have used equally picturesque language. I ask you, how does swearing at the police constitute a threat to the security of the state? Hundreds of children are arrested, from the age of seven, and many are kept overnight in jail, and there is hardly a squeak, not a semblance of outrage from the white community. An eleven-year-old boy is kept in jail with hardened criminals for fifty-seven days, and not too many are concerned. At a funeral in Bethal, a teenager's teeth were kicked out by the police, and our people are killed as if it were no more than swatting flies—just like swatting flies. There is no more than a whimper of protest from those altruists who are concerned that blacks will suffer most when sanctions are applied. They don't care a bean about our only too real suffering now. I don't know what they will make of the surveys indicating that an overwhelming majority of blacks favors sanctions.

The Reagan administration, employing what it calls its policy of constructive engagement, has been reticent to openly condemn the government of South Africa. The administration argues that its approach of quiet diplomacy has had a greater impact on apartheid than have strict sanctions.

When it was first announced, I said quite firmly that constructive engagement was going to be an unmitigated disaster for our people. I had no idea I was going to be so accurate in my forecasting. Since the Reagan administration took office, our country has seen a new constitution which has excluded the vast majority of us—that is, seventy-three percent of us—from political life. Forced population removal has continued. The pass-law arrests have continued, averaging something like 200,000 arrests per year in this period that

is supposed to be of reform. We still have Bantu education, the education that is designed simply for blacks, which has always been a sore point, a very real area of sensitivity. And what about deaths? How many people have died during the period of constructive engagement?

How many have died in the last year?

The figures vary from 600 to over a thousand. So many people have died that it actually isn't newsworthy. *They don't even give the names now. They just say, "Two people were killed."*

If constructive engagement is a disaster, then what, ideally, should be U.S. policy toward South Africa?

I would like to see a policy that would end apartheid.

And what would that be?

Oh, I think they know clearly what that would be. It is quite clear that the South African government has known that it can rely on the protection of Mr. Reagan and Mrs. Thatcher and Chancellor Kohl. But Reagan's protégé, the South African government, cocks its snoot even at him. Can anyone show me *one positive thing* that is the result of constructive engagement? All we have had is South African military attacks on Lesotho. Attacks on Botswana. On Angola. On Mozambique. It's unbelievable.

You obviously don't believe President Reagan has any sincere interest in doing away with apartheid.

I think that President Reagan's major concern is only for the white South Africans. Why did he not take so long to act against Poland as he did against South Africa? In Nicaragua, Reagan supports the *contras,* who, in the view of the Nicaraguan people, are terrorists. They are not terrorists in the eyes of America—they are freedom fighters. But Reagan is opposed to *our* freedom fighters who are trying very hard to change this system peacefully. For Reagan, our freedom fighters are terrorists.

I want to say to the American people: How about breaking your historical record? You have this extraordinary capacity of supporting the wrong side. Now, could you for once side with those who have right on their side and who are saying they would like to see this country be a genuine democracy where everybody, black and white, will have a stake?

Do you think anyone in the U.S. is listening?

I don't know why, but I seem to have some influence in your country. I guess it's just one of God's jokes.

President Reagan finally imposed sanctions on South Africa, yet you reacted by suggesting he was a racist.

Over the years there has been a fair degree of pressure suggesting that Reagan ought to take far more firm action against South Africa. And all along he has refused. He has made gaffes, like when he said this South African government has been a historical friend of the United States. But he's talking about people who supported the *Nazis* during World War II! Botha was a member of an organization that carried out acts of sabotage against the Allied cause. The people who really fought side by side with the Americans were blacks. Even then, because of the discriminatory policies, our blacks were sent to fight against Rommel's Desert Rats with spears because they were not to be trusted with arms. But our people died, and those are the ones that your president doesn't think about. He thinks about the wrong people, because his view of history is horrible. Let's face it, he doesn't know anything about South African history.

How do you know that President Reagan is so ignorant?

Certainly from the statements he makes! Of course, later he backtracked, but remember when he said that racial discrimination of the sort you once had in the South had been eliminated here? Many of us responded by saying, what's the point of eliminating whites-only signs that were put up by these guys in the government here—signs on park benches and toilets. [*Laughs*] I mean, who ever said that our ambition was to share a toilet with white people? That's not the height of our ambition.

But you can't deny that in the last few years some of the more outrageous prohibitions have been lifted.

They think that we are now supposed to be thrilled because we can marry across the color lines. Well, who introduced these laws in the first place? The government did. In its orgy of racism, it was separating everything like mad, left, right and center. Anyone who thinks that we should rejoice because the Immorality Act has been properly amended is like someone who wants you to celebrate because some guy no longer beats his wife. Why should we be thrilled when it was the government itself who established all of these obnoxious laws in the first place?

You had a personal meeting with President Reagan in Washington late last year. Did you have the impression that he understood what you were saying about apartheid?

My wife, who was sitting next to me, said she was looking at him, and you know white people have the disadvantage of their faces showing color more easily than ours do [*laughs*]. She said she saw what shook him, and it seemed like it was the first time he heard any of this. I produced the travel document that I was

using at the time—now I have a passport, but then I had this document. [*He stands up, walks to his desk and brings back a blue passport-sized booklet, Travel Document No. J 0270296, issued by the South African government. He opens it to the first page.*] "Undetermined nationality." Can you imagine that? That's what it says here. Undetermined nationality.

Did you show this to President Reagan?

Yes.

Well, what did he say?

I don't think he fully understood. But it shook him. At least that was my wife's impression, according to the look that registered on his face. But it was still early in the morning.

How did you feel when President Reagan's pal, the Reverend Jerry Falwell, came here for a few days this summer and then went back to the United States and called you a phony?

Ahhh, I have far more important things to be concerned about than wanting to respond.

We understand that people can be accused of a crime for merely advocating disinvestment. In this precarious legal context, can you tell us whether you favor economic sanctions and divestiture?

I think that although my official position is that I have not yet called for disinvestment, it's really academic. Disinvestment is happening in any case, without virtually any government having passed legislation to insist on it. It has happened because of where the rand is.

Where does this leave us in terms of foreign corporations? Should they be investing in South Africa or pulling out?

They should invest, but under very strict conditions. Not ones that merely ameliorate apartheid. We don't want apartheid made comfortable and acceptable. We don't want apartheid reformed. We want to be rid of apartheid.

You see, in the past these foreign corporations used to tell you that they were just visitors in South Africa. But I told them that their presence in South Africa was as much a political and moral issue as it was an economic fact. And they wouldn't buy that. They were more interested in trying to discredit me, really, as the South African government has been doing in its newspapers and television.

Discredit you personally?

Yes. They try to show that I am an awful guy in one way or another, that I have feet of clay. Why don't they just say I'm lying when I say apartheid is unjust, that it is immoral, that it is un-Christian. If that is a lie, then why don't they just say it's a lie and prove it?

The animosity toward you goes beyond the halls of government. On the streets of Johannesburg, we have met many whites who have called you everything from a bloody bastard to a communist. Many blame you directly for the unrest.

I am not the cause of all of this. If anything, some of us, like Allan Boesak and all these chaps they have been trying to vilify, have in fact been standing between them and the revolution! But they don't want to believe that. People like me are risking the danger of rejection by our young who say we are standing in our way. When I said that if some of our people go on burning collaborators, I will leave South Africa with my family, some of these young people said, "Good! Good riddance! Because you keep stopping us from finishing what we have started." So instead of white people—so many of them—being nasty to me and regarding me as some sort of ogre, they should be saying, "Oh, Bishop Tutu, we have a lot to thank you for." I don't really want them to thank me, but I want them to understand that even if they get rid of me, they will not have gotten rid of the problem.

There were brief-lived uprisings here in 1960 and again in 1976. What makes the current unrest deeper reaching and a greater challenge to the system?

Now I think the whole black community is basically at one in its opposition to apartheid. Given the way the authorities have been acting, especially against the young people, they have helped, perhaps unwittingly, to politicize and raise the consciousness of the older, more reluctant parents. Many of these young people do what they do now because of what their friends and colleagues did in 1976. There is a tradition of resistance. Also, the world has changed, it has awakened to apartheid. Most of Africa has become decolonized, and South Africa is surrounded by countries that have become independent. Just look at your country—it's a prime example of the change. If a year ago you had told me that *your* president would be signing a decree for sanctions against South Africa, and that your Congress, or at least the House, would vote so overwhelmingly in favor of sanctions, I would have answered, "Who is your psychiatrist? Don't you want to go visit him?"

What impression did you get on the U.S. college campuses when you traveled through our country in May?

For quite a while, people had been saying that the youth of the United States are not like they were in the Sixties, that most of them are worried only about getting on in the rat race. Then, suddenly, this South African thing came on, and now their fervor is something like during Vietnam. It is strange, because during Vietnam, they were worried about themselves being involved—they were likely to be drafted. There was a kind of self-interest being served. But on this issue of South Africa, there isn't, and that's what's remarkable. I was at UCLA, Berkeley, Davis. It was an incredible thing! Those students helped us recover our faith in humanity. They should have been busy with their final exams and worrying about grades. But at Davis there were 15,000 of them sitting in the sun, waiting for me to speak. Incredible. Incredible.

Does that sentiment get transmitted back, say, to the youths in Soweto battling apartheid?

They get reports here, but of course not the kind of major coverage that you would get in a free country. Nonetheless, young people are aware of what's going on outside.

Are white South African students any different than earlier generations?

Now you are getting young whites who are saying, "Man, if I go into the army, I may be sent to a black township. I may have to shoot someone who was my friend in the university. If I'm not defending my country against an outside enemy, what is it that I am defending? I'm defending this system."

I find young people to be a great sign of hope. And one needs to look for hope. [*Pauses*] I have a lot of time for young people. I think they are tremendous.

The mood of the black youth seems to be militant, if not explosive.

Many of the young people have, in my view, become determined to the point of recklessness. They believe the system will be changed only by violence, and they believe that they will die. And the frightening thing is, they don't care if they die. And we have authorities who do not appreciate and understand this. Or if they do, then they don't care, either. I think that the police and the army say to themselves, "Who cares? What is another black life?"

Your son has been arrested, you have been the target of many government media attacks. Do you fear for your personal safety and for that of your family?

I think you get to the point where you know if you oppose apartheid, you will at one point or another have to face government wrath. And while you will be concerned, there is not a great deal you can do. If they are after you, they're after you. And if they want to assassinate you, they'll assassinate you. If they want to boink you one, they can. If you begin worrying about that, you might as well just stay at home and sleep. Even then you are not safe, because they can petrol-bomb your house.

Is there any doubt in your mind that South Africa will one day be free?

Ohhh! We don't even discuss that, man! I mean, no, no, no! I say this also to people when I preach. Certainly in the black congregations. I ask them, "Do you doubt?" And they say, quietly, no—rather unenthusiastically. And I say, "*What?* Is that how you feel about it?" Then they really get warmed up about it. No. I may not be around, but I hope I will be here to experience it.

I am going to be talking at a major private school, and I'm thinking that I want to talk about what it will be like when apartheid goes. [*Pauses*] This will be a wonderful country. I will say to them that one of the things that will happen is that you won't have to listen to addresses such as this one anymore [*laughs*].

What are your greatest hopes and fears?

My greatest fear? That on the one side our people will get so impatient that they will say to hell with it. We are probably getting close to that point, to where we will have a bloodbath. On the other side, you'd have the authorities saying, "Let us hold on for dear life, let's hold on as long as we can." So you would have that classic situation of an irresistible force meeting with an unmovable object. That needn't be the case if these guys can still listen and be ready to sit down and talk with the genuine representatives and leaders. We can still get that.

What would it mean for the rest of the continent for South Africa to be free?

Ohhh. I was saying the other day, can you imagine Oliver Tambo sitting in the Union Buildings, the headquarters of government, and he calls on his intercom, "Eh, Nelson, could you please come here? What do you think we should do about this guy Botha?" [*Laughs*]

We would be the breadbasket for most of Africa. We would be the launching pad to propel not just Southern Africa but most of Africa into the twentieth century. I mean, can you imagine a time when most of our resources are not invested in protecting a system that is totally indefensible? When *all* the people of this country will be trained to their fullest capacity?

Okay. Last question. In that future free South Africa, where are we going to find Bishop Tutu? Somewhere in the government?

I will be a pastor. That is what I want. I am quite clear in my own mind. I don't want anyone to think that I have any public political ambition. I'm not as smart as these politicians. I'm really not. It's not that I'm trying to be modest. I just try to be a little bit of a visionary and to leave it to politicians to translate those visions into reality. I want to be around to maintain this critical distance so that I can say to them [the new government], "*That* is wrong." Just as I stand around and say something is wrong on the basis of the gospel, I want to be able to be around to say, "Just because *you* are doing the same thing doesn't make it right. If it is evil, it is evil, and I'm going to tell you so."

12

Jack Nicholson

INTERVIEWED BY FRED SCHRUERS (1986)

Fred Schruers is part of a great lunatic tradition at ROLLING STONE: *the writer who will do virtually* anything *in the service of a story. Jump out of a plane? Where's the chute? Out-talk, out-drink and maybe out-wrestle any self-swollen film star or five-man band in town? Make it an octet. Schruers' fearlessness (which extends, sometimes alarmingly, into his private behavior) is a vivid part of RS lore.*

Fred's techniques work best on fellow extroverts (the timid tend to cower), and Jack Nicholson surely qualifies as one of these. By the mid-Eighties, Nicholson had become the purest example extant of the classic Hollywood star. He was paid phenomenal sums of money to grace a film with his elemental presence, his exuberant gift for screen acting, his crackling marquee power. He could afford to pick his roles according to personal taste or inclination, and he didn't always opt for the safest choices. Whether ambling through the lackluster 'Heartburn' or careening across the screen in 'The Witches of Eastwick,' the sour confection that followed it, Nicholson was inevitably riveting. An actor of delightful physicality, he could also be quietly commanding, as he demonstrated in a relatively small role (as Eugene O'Neill) in his pal Warren Beatty's leftie epic, 'Reds.' Similarly, his cameo as the icy anchorman in 'Broadcast News' shifted the tone and focus of that movie for those few moments he was onscreen. And, of course, when Nicholson connects with a big part that affords full rein to his gift for invention—as he has over the years in such films as 'The Last Detail' and 'Terms of Endearment'—he embodies the magic that movies are all about.

Like many among the remote and celebrated rich, Nicholson is subject to spasms of pomposity and crankish spleen. This interview captures that, but it also percolates with his enormous vitality—the great motor of his art. And his art, and its sources, were what we had come to talk about.

—K. L.

J ACK NICHOLSON'S Hollywood Hills home perches above an empty ravine—a rare prospect amid these overbuilt hills of dirt and scrub. On the hot afternoon when I arrive, a chain-link fence is being installed (not, I'm later told, at Nicholson's instigation) on the winding driveway he shares with Marlon Brando. Despite the fence and an electronic inspection of visitors, Nicholson's complex—two houses, a row of carports topped by a basketball hoop and a deck equipped with a pool and a commanding view—doesn't have the aspect of a fortress. Inside, the walls are crammed with oils by the likes of Soutine, Matisse and Picasso, but the mountain breeze and the informality of the furnishings lend the house the air of a tropic bungalow. A cook is at work in the kitchen, and Annie Marshall, Nicholson's longtime pal and administrative assistant, who is the daughter of the late actor Herbert Marshall, fields calls in a study nearby. Alongside the dining-room table sit two cardboard posters bearing photos of Nicholson and Meryl Streep in their starring roles in *Heartburn*, the film version of Nora Ephron's *roman à clef* about her turbulent marriage to former *Washington Post* reporter Carl Bernstein.

I am informed that Nicholson is in the Jacuzzi, recuperating from an exercise session, and I take a stroll around the deck as John Coltrane's recording of "My Favorite Things" wafts from discreet outdoor speakers. When I turn toward the house, the man himself is in the shadowy interior. He shakes hands and apologizes assiduously for the delay. Dressed in baggy white slacks and a short-sleeved sport shirt, he looks unostentatiously stylish—even when he seats himself and his trousers hoist off his Adidas to reveal fluorescent-orange socks.

He'll talk here for the next three hours, using few gestures but often hunching forward in his seat to bear down on a point. The force of his passion when he's talking about things that make him angry can be a

mite scary: He begins to clip his words off, curl his lips back over his teeth and close sentences with "pal."

Jack Nicholson doesn't have a lot of competition as *the* modern movie star for America's everyman, a man who does his work spectacularly well largely without indulging in the pomposities and fits of temperament associated with other great movie actors. Often seen as a hard-partying, no-bullshit street guy from Jersey, he nonetheless maintains the seigniorial distance we expect of pop royalty. When the *paparazzi* catch him, he shrugs it off and lets the flashbulbs glint off his shades, telling us what he wants to with the set of his notoriously expressive mouth.

As the writer Derek Sylvester described him, Nicholson, "unlike the rising young stars who followed him . . . bestrode two distinct generations of acting styles. He possessed the pugnacity of a Cagney, the virility of a Garfield, the diabolic charm of a Gable. He could be as suavely droll as Cary Grant, as gee-shucks and gangling as James Stewart, as moody and introspective as Paul Muni . . . in other words, the most *indispensable* actor of modern American cinema."

He is also heir to the alienated brooding of Brando and James Dean, but having incorporated their inarticulate (if brilliant) posturing in his craft, he has gone on to stand up onscreen in service to the great *line,* from "You know, this used to be a hell of a good country," in *Easy Rider,* to "Heeeeere's Johnny!"—a marrow-chilling and hilarious ad-lib—in *The Shining.* In between, there's been plenty of time for other unforgettable outbursts, like his rebuke to the waitress with the problematic chicken salad in *Five Easy Pieces* ("Yeah, I want you to hold it between your knees") or his abrupt attack on a nasty bartender in *The Last Detail* ("I *am* the motherfucking shore patrol, motherfucker!").

His Oscars for Best Actor in *One Flew Over the Cuckoo's Nest* and Best Supporting Actor in *Terms of Endearment,* as well as his six other nominations, are official Hollywood's tributes to a maverick who has never pandered to it, and in 1985 he had the pleasure of watching his girlfriend of more than a decade, Anjelica Huston, win Best Supporting Actress for her role alongside him in *Prizzi's Honor.*

Heartburn was his fortieth film and his third for director Mike Nichols. He signed on just days before shooting began, after Mandy Patinkin had left the lead role of the philandering husband. "Jack is the guy," says Nichols, "who takes parts others have turned down, might turn down, and explodes them into something nobody could have conceived of. . . . All his brilliance at character and gesture is consumed and made invisible by the expanse of his nature—his generosity, his lovingness, his confidence, his positiveness—and because his nature is so generous, all technical decisions seem to have burned away. It's what makes him the great movie actor he is. You can't see any technique—it just appears to be life."

Nichols, who had been determined to keep Nicholson and Streep from meeting until their first moment before the camera, says that the day of his co-stars' first scene together was "electric with excitement." Streep concurs but points out Nicholson *had* broken the ice before shooting: "I'm sitting there getting my hair curled and looking like hell, and I get this knock on the door, and he said, 'Hi, this is Jack Nicholson. Can I use your toilet?' " The Nicholson who sat down to chat this afternoon was, unmistakably, the same free spirit Streep met that day.

In 'Heartburn,' your portrayal of "the Carl Bernstein character" seems fully rounded. But if I ask how much of the real-life Bernstein is in there, I suppose you'll tell me not much.

I'm gonna tell you—*nothing.* I was specifically hired *not* to play him. Mike and Nora and Meryl were very anxious to move the film into fiction. And since I had no desire on a couple of days' notice to do a biographical portrait, that suited me just fine.

Still, you must have had to cram a lot of preparation into less than a week.

I was working three days after I read the script . . . never read the book until partway into the shooting. This is my third film with Mike, and I'd always wanted to work with Meryl, and that made me want to do it—maybe a part I might not have done under other conditions. They kind of held their hands under my chin while I treaded water.

It was interesting for me at this stage to just go off on something. The framework is usually months of preparation. You don't get many unusual experiences at this level.

Mark, the columnist you play in the film, seems almost possessed—happy, but with a manic edge—in the scene where Meryl, as Rachel, tells him she's pregnant, and they both start singing and glomming pizza with a mason's trowel.

Well, that was maybe one of the last three or four things I did on the picture. The script for that is only the songs and the situation—where it's the first child and, you know, that kind of wacky head you get into at very high moments of your life. It's always an interesting choice as to where you pitch your musical ability. Meryl, for instance, sang worse than I did in a certain way—and of course she's almost as talented a singer as she is an actress. I saw her originally in a musical play, Brecht's *Happy Ending,* which I thought she was brilliant in. But where the scene continues into, one hopes, general hilarity, I elected to sing as well as I could without . . . [*his voice descends into a theatrical baritone*] dropping it into that John Raitt area. And Mike came up with the pizza, and Meryl, I think, suggested we eat it with the trowel—because the fact that the house is being built for years is a very big part of the story. This is the way you work on the set, adding dimension to a scene.

Another crucial moment in the film is Mark's appearance in New York to reconcile with Rachel. There's a particular, electric feeling between them, as if their entire future together depends on the next two minutes.

That scene was my most difficult. I felt something should happen, which I was trying to rev up to, and quite frankly, I never got there. When an actor is floundering, turgid or locked up, he's got to try and go outside himself. So I was watching Meryl very closely, and I'm thinking, "Jeez, I'm not getting there yet," but I could see she was really in great shape. So in order to feel positive, I told myself, "Meryl is great in this scene, and therefore it will cut well." I didn't do a great day's work for them maybe, but she covered that with her tremendous ability. As it turns out, that scene is quite good, and I'm not bad in it, and more interestingly, what I wanted in that scene actually occurred, out of nowhere, in a different one.

And that was?

In the scene where she has the second child. It came out in there.

What's the gist of their feelings? A kind of warmth, despite his betrayals of her?

Just the dead-on, primary openness of them within the relationship. No matter what happens in relationships, there are certain primary things—you can etch over them, make them obscure, but . . . there were some great connections there.

'Heartburn' is unusual in that it doesn't seem to have been packaged, like so many movies today, to appeal to a specific demographic group.

Well, these days the studios are constantly turning it toward the kinds of movies they believe will have maximum audience participation. I've got to find a way to get in at cross-purposes with what they're really after. This is why I like *Heartburn*. It's a real story about right now. It's neither an adult movie nor a child's movie—not an anything movie. It's just a movie about a subject that's germane now to everyone—man, woman, child. These kinds of movies don't come across your plate that often.

Do you feel that packaging is one of the reasons people are saying that movies are losing their magic?

There are millions of ways, but it's all—see, our country is becoming corrupted little by little by conglomeration and conglomerative thinking. Coca-Cola—look at Columbia [Pictures]. Coca-Cola owns them. Coca-Cola also owns part of Tri-Star. Coca-Cola runs its business based on market share. Period. That's the way they run it. And, baby, you or I ain't going to change it. Because it's back in Atlanta. It has nothing to do with any one movie. And that's where the business is being corrupted.

All these guys you read about in the newspapers who are the heads of the studios—I predicted this four or five years ago, when they were trying to cut my prices—all these deal makers are making themselves the stars now. They're on the covers of magazines. Their salaries are now quotable. Why? Because it isn't about movies anymore.

Hasn't the movie industry been flirting with that kind of conglomeration since it began?

When Harry Cohn and Louis B. Mayer and Darryl Zanuck and these people ran the business, I wasn't working—so I don't know if I would have been better off or not. But at least they were making *movies.* . . .

Every guy who was the head of a studio was also a gambler. They weren't making market shares with back-off sales and cross-financing and cross-collateralization. There's nobody that gambles now. Everybody's going for the big whamola all the time. Before this, the debate was whether you should go ahead and make a movie—whether or not you thought it was going to be profit making—because the movie made a valid statement. Well, that debate's not even on anymore. Anybody who tells you it is on is lying to you or doesn't understand the situation. Because there's nobody left to take that kind of chance.

Do you see a link between these new multiplex cinemas with their tiny screens and the banality of the studio film product?

You know, I like the big silver, I really do. The world is going to miss the movie-going experience. I know I still prefer going to a theater that's got a decent screen in it. If you can't see that it's more fun to sit and watch a movie at the Paramount Theater in New York than to sit in a bowling alley with this little postage stamp—well, then I can't explain my point. The point is, your life, the moviegoer's life, has been degraded by this thing.

Maybe that's why so many people would rather stay home and watch movies on television.

You know, television is not a support group for the movies; it's a competitive industry that's been devouring the movies like cancer since I came out here in the Fifties. And I happen to be anachronistically in love with the movies, so I deeply resent the whole video thing. Everybody says it's great for the labor pool. I didn't get in this to be in a union labor pool; I got in this to be an artistic, expressive person. The movies have sold their future so cheap for so long it's almost amateurish to comment on it.

Now that most of your films are out in video, do you anticipate seeing any more money from them?

Well, I almost don't give a fuck if I do. I mean, I'm so furious at video. *Prizzi's Honor* was one of the best-selling videos in Brazil, and no one even owns the rights. It's 100 percent pirated. They run my movies all the time. And I'm not compensated for it. That does nothing but hurt me. I mean, what would they have on cable by now if they didn't have movies? It's the end of the movie business.

You seem to be saying that the decline of the movies is an index to our descent into some kind of Orwellian nightmare.

It's so clear it's a joke. All you've got to do is drive across America. Go to Kansas City and see old Kansas City down *here,* and then there's this six-lane highway that goes around it, and you've got plastic light boxes that say Radio Shack and Chicken-Bicken and Roller Skate World. That's what America looks like today. I don't like what the light box has done to America at night—turned everybody into a fucking pinball-machine moth. If they had just outlawed these light boxes, the world would simply look bigger. But we can't even get them to stop acid rain—how can you get them to think about what's beautiful? Because what's beautiful is all that counts, pal. That's *all* that counts.

But the corporations that built those franchise strips will tell you they're creating jobs.

Okay. All right. Life used to be work until five o'clock and then you were meant to have some fun, some nourishment, some leisure. American don't understand leisure. They don't have a clue. They understand work; they understand play; they understand love; they do not understand leisure. Literacy is dropping. These are not redeemable things. These are our lives. I don't know what the minimum wage is today, but what you give up by putting up that light box, with bugs all over this world and graffiti up your keister . . . if you gave a kid the insight he would need to be a purer person at fifty, do you want to give that up for $200 a week?

Is labor God? Is a job God? People vote like it is. Ronald Reagan is a vote to return to the company store. People look at that guy Nicholson down there yelling and say, "What's he do?" Nothing—he sits around and complains. At least a guy in a nice pin-stripe suit down at the bank, he keeps the park clean, everything's cool. Who are these rabble-rousers? What do they do? Let's go back in there and let's buy shoes down at the conglomerate. Let's get our movie down at the conglomerate. Let's let the big guy in the pin-stripe suit run things—'cause it'll be quiet then.

Well, pal, that hasn't ever worked in the past. And it ain't gonna work in the future. Dream on, dream on. I can't do nothing about it. I understand numbers. I'm going to reach fifty years old next year. I just turned forty-nine. There ain't time for me to turn this around.

I did my part. I screamed my ass off for ten, fifteen years. I paid those dues, too. I'm not giving up. But I'm not going out there to try and rake people up. . . . The professional man says, "Hey, man, you can't take conglomeration out. The Japs got monopolies. . . ." The guy in the third grade knows if he gets a B minus on a spelling test what his job is going to be at Mitsubishi twenty years later. That's it—it don't change. That's what a monopoly is.

But, pal, if we're not a nation of idealists who fight against these things, I guess it's because we don't understand what it's costing us anymore. Anyway, I wasn't going to talk this wild. But you get the picture.

Don't you see your job as simply making quality movies about people's real emotional lives?

I still make the movies I want to make. I'm just talking about—where's the soil for them? Where's the informed intelligence? I'm doing fine. I have respect for myself and my collaborators, like Mike and Meryl. You know, you don't want to see this as so huge that you begin to dysfunction. But I have to whip up a foam in my spirit, or I'll just stop seeing where it's at, too.

Social graces don't come—they're not innate. You learn them, develop them. Once you're past the high-school prom, what you do on your own is what gives your life quality. *You* have to learn how to dance. *You* have to learn how to read a book. *You* have to learn how to appreciate music, to enrich your mind in order to have a conversation.

I heard someone call himself a conservative anarchist; I wonder where you feel yourself to be on the political spectrum.

I'm doing research for the movie I'm on now [*The Witches of Eastwick*, based on John Updike's novel]. I'm going to play the devil. I've read a lot of huge, studious books that deal with the Dark Ages. One of the things I came across is the big, long—seems like century-long—debate about the definition of God. And the only thing they could come up with is that anything definite you can say about God must be supported by its paradoxical opposite. And that's what life is all about, this paradoxical situation.

I guess you'd call me a liberal, certainly through my earlier years of involvement. I was flat-out anti–capital punishment. However, I agree with Reagan about terrorists. These people are not criminals against the United States. They're criminals against the world. And this is a degradation of all mankind. In World War II, you tortured the man; in Vietnam, you tortured the man's children in front of him. This is an indication of an overall decline in civilization.

Despite all this, friends point out your "positiveness."

There are many areas for optimism as well. I love the opportunity for working with Meryl Streep. For somebody who does what I do, you sit a lifetime yearning for that kind of feeling, and when it comes, you want to relish it.

I'm a simple person in my job, too. I don't want to do what I accuse other people of doing, not taking the time to smell the roses. Something very wonderful has happened to me. I don't want the fact that I see this endless din and gloom in the world to make me incapable of expressing something that's quite frankly wonderful. I'm a very fortunate—statistically impossible to describe how fortunate—person to be where I am and do what I do.

And you feel your work can help make a difference.

My first acting teacher said all art is one thing—a stimulating point of departure. That's it. And if you can do that in a piece, you've fulfilled your cultural, sociological obligation as a workman. What you're supposed to do is keep people vitally interested in the world they live in. The thing I originally wrote so pretentiously as a young person, *Ride in the Whirlwind*, was about the Sisyphean mountain. You push that boulder up, it rolls down. You push it up again. Man's dignity is in the trip down the mountain, returning to his labors. This is where artists are supposed to be of use, to make people, not necessarily happy, but enrich their vitality.

And, not incidentally, your own.

I start thinking, "Hey, Jack, nobody ever *needs* you." You've got to remember that. You're alone, that's it. Friendships are a boon, love is a boon, contacts with other human beings and events, these are all boons. You've got to do your part as well as you can.

My life is enriched by my friends—[screenwriter-producer] Don Devlin, my partner Harry Gittes. We've been communicating for thirty years. They're all still in my life—none of them has quit to become a hangman. They're doing these things I talk about. You don't talk to these people and get some pap. They're in there. They don't give a fuck—I mean, my closest friends probably have less of a consensus about adoring my movies than any other group. They fight with me about it. Now, I don't think that means they don't like me anymore, don't want to see me do anything. Quite the contrary. I hope I take what's positive, or at least stimulating, and grow from it.

I gather the collapse of 'Two Jakes,' the 'Chinatown' sequel you planned to make with screenwriter Robert Towne, left a bit of a rift between you, him and producer Robert Evans. It also left hanging a third film that would complete the saga. What undid the deal?

I haven't said anything much about it and don't intend to. Frankly, among other reasons, there's ongoing legal problems. I think it would be imprudent for me to say anything other than, creatively, we simply didn't get the film done. There are millions of reasons why movies go well and an equal number why they don't, and many of them are included here.

Let's talk about it in its purer state as a dramatic piece, then.

This is a kind of special theatrical covenant. I haven't

played any other detective out of deference to this character of Jake Gittes. What the three films always were intended to do was to show the history of Southern California—starting with the water issue—through this central character, an unarmed private detective, and the undercurrents of family and back streets. The water issue is real; the issue of *Two Jakes* is going to be the petroleum issue. Robert already knows, as I do, because he's told me, what the third film is. We always wanted me to play the part at the same age as the character. There were eleven years between the two stories, '37 to '48, and it was eleven years since we made *Chinatown*. This was something that hadn't really been done before.

But you're proceeding with other assignments until then.

Yes, I am going to do *The Witches of Eastwick*, which George Miller [*Mad Max*] is going to direct, and *Ironweed*, which Hector Babenco [*Kiss of the Spider Woman*] is going to direct. A lot of that has to do with Anjelica's working again. I might not have taken that much work on, but I don't want to sit around while she's working . . . so I'm taking on a little more than I might. I don't like to have that much acting work, because I still hope to direct movies, but these are interesting parts, both new directors, young directors, I'm excited about collaborating with. I'm going to work only with people I feel strongly about.

Your two years away from working before 'Terms of Endearment' involved a lot of skiing at Aspen—but what else?

I had a wonderful summer with one of my favorite people, who passed on this year, Sam Spiegel [the producer of *On the Waterfront* and *The African Queen*]. You know, I lost three of the really great men in my life this year—Sam Spiegel, Orson Welles and Shorty Smith [Nicholson's uncle]. They just happened to be three older dudes who I got along great with for a long, long period of time.

In that two years, I think I spent one whole summer with Sam, just like his sidekick. He was certainly an inspiration; those movies he made in the Fifties *were* the movies, just about. Sam's lesson to me was always to go for quality. This is not where producers are at anymore. I deal with guys who say, "Look, let me handle this, I know how the studio thinks. We've got a bing, we've got a bong, we've got a bing."

So you were woodshedding in a fashion, as well as enjoying Spiegel's company. But did you miss working during this time?

Everyone said, "Oh, God, you won't be able not to work for six months—you'll be a dead man." Well, I never missed it. And when I came back to work, great; I talked to Jim Brooks [the co-creator of the television series *Taxi* and director of *Terms of Endearment*], made the deal with him over the telephone. Never had seen his face and, I don't know if I ever told him this, didn't know what Jim *did* before—I sort of, as a formal thing, ignored television. But that didn't matter to Jim.

Brooks is a great genius, in my opinion. The minute I talked to him, I knew, "This is a guy I'm going to have a good time working with." He's a constantly questioning artist—he delves, argues with himself, and where you're concerned as an actor, he knows immediately if it's working. It's exciting to see these guys work. I'm glad that I saw Antonioni happy and excited while he was working, that I saw Stanley Kubrick delighted, saw John Huston commanding . . . this is the dessert of my job.

It's that upside you were talking about. It's almost like film sets represent a portable Utopia to you. Did you have that same sense of community growing up along the New Jersey shore?

I grew up through age five there in Neptune. I lived on Sixth Avenue in Neptune, and Fifth Avenue was Neptune City, so it's that close. But Mrs. Nicholson understood the difference, and when I got to a certain point of school age, she moved to Neptune City, this slightly . . . *affluent* is the wrong word, but just a little better situation for a kid.

To reiterate your situation so we've got things straight: You never met your natural father. Your real mother—June—was the woman you believed to be your sister. The woman you call Mrs. Nicholson—Ethel May, whom you called Mud—was in fact your grandmother, and her husband, presented as your father, was this hard-drinking guy who was never around. The third woman in the triumvirate that raised you was June's sister, Lorraine. Plenty of company, but no real father . . .

Well, I had Shorty. I had Smith around. He was married to Lorraine. That, believe me, is as good a father as anybody's ever going to get or need. I can be as hard on my family or friends as anybody—I'm fairly objective—but there's nobody much that's impressed me as much as Shorty. Simple guy, but many is the poem I've written in my mind to the higher feelings he promoted in me—which he would have no ability whatsoever to articulate. If I sat down with Shorty in the spirit world or something and said, "Look, Shorty, here's what you really mean, as a prince of the world," he'd look at me like I was talking a foreign language.

He took it for granted that he would become a protector of sorts for you?

Well, he wouldn't even assume that role. That would be pretentious to him, you see. He wouldn't take the credit. When I went to his funeral, I ran into people, sixty-year-old women, who had known him since he was in grammar school. And all they had to say is "Shorty had *all* the fun."

Now, Shorty's not what a civics class would pick out as a role model. He was a featherbedded railroad brakeman, you know, who went to gin mills and drank and sat around all day with his shirt off and bullshitted. Everybody did love Shorty. He was the first all-state football player from the region, and he stayed right there in Neptune. He wasn't a hidden man. It's not sentiment—this guy was advanced. Shorty just had a grasp—innate, not a conscious ability—about life. I hope I've got it.

Your natural father was someone you never met and didn't even know about till around 1975.

Both grandmother and mother were deceased before this particular group of facts came to my attention. I was very impressed by their ability to keep the secret, if nothing else. It's done great things for me. I mean, I don't have to question the abortion issue in my mind. It's an open-and-shut case where I'm concerned. As an illegitimate child born in 1937, during the Depression, to a broken lower-middle-class family, you are a candidate for—you're an automatic abortion with most people today. So it's very easy for me. I don't have to get into the debate of when does the thing come alive. And I'm very pleased to be out of it, 'cause it's not an easy issue.

They sound like a formidable group of women.

These were strong women—made their own way in a period of time when it just wasn't done that much. They did it without connections. In fact, Ethel May Nicholson was disinherited for marrying an Irish Catholic, because her family was Pennsylvania Dutch rock-hard Protestants, and that just wasn't done. I guess she got married very young, too. And never saw much of that very wealthy Pennsylvania family again in her life.

My basic model for women is an independent woman. There was no grandeur in that for me, because it was that way from the beginning. You know, here was Mud, and she carried everybody on her back like a tiny little elephant, and it didn't seem to faze her. She marched right through it. They all had a great lot of style, and a lot of fun. The neighborhood idolized all of them.

Mud was the patron saint of the neighborhood, and anybody who had a problem, they'd come running over to her beauty shop, and "Ethel, da-da-da," and she'd figure it out. I'm very fortunate to have had that very unusual environment to grow up in. Very free, very trusting. A lot of responsibility—not heaped on you, but just by definition of the situation.

You could talk out problems with them?

Had to, got to. They want to know. I'd get kept in sometimes, but . . . very Irish, very rational, nothing's-gonna-blow-anybody-out kind of environment to grow up in.

Once you moved on to Neptune City, what was the scene like there?

I started high school in 1950. Cool was invented in this period. Rock & roll did not start with Elvis Presley. In fact, to that age group, Elvis Presley was a secondary figure to Ray Charles. And, you know, Johnnie Ray. This is when all that stuff really got rolling. It wasn't as explosively widespread, but this is the seminal period of it. And peer group was everything. There was not a lot of visible rebellion, aside from the D.A. haircut and stuff. . . .

How did you dress?

I used to like to go to school in a pair of navy-blue cuffed pegged pants, a black or navy-blue turtleneck sweater, maybe a gray coat over it and a black porkpie hat that I'd gotten from the freeway in a motor accident that involved a priest. So it had a lot of juju on it. I wore it flat out like a rimmer. That was one way.

Now, when we had the dances and everything, you just got the greatest suit you could get a hold of. Always pegged, pleats, blue suedes, thinnest tie, shoulders, one button in front.

Anything like Jake Gittes?

Well, Jake Gittes' get-up . . . my grandfather-father [Ethel May's wayward spouse]—let's call him Mr. Nicholson so we don't give another hyphenated interview—before he had his problems in life, used to win the Asbury Park Easter Parade a lot as one of the best-dressed men. So he was a blade, and Gittes' style, which is the Thirties, rather more than the Forties or Fifties, is sort of after that man, who was very natty. You know, the hair combed. I've used him a lot actually—for a man I didn't see much. The glasses in *Easy Rider* were his glasses.

Not literally?

Not literally, but the same. I needed age for that character, I was considerably younger than what I was playing.

But we did everything—my friends, we'd go to New York on weekends, get drunk, see ball games, bang around . . . school was out, we just went to the beach all summer. And had fun, got drunk every night.

It was the age of the put-on. Cool was everything. Collars were up, eyelids were drooped. You never let on what bothered you.

And at the beach you'd try to pick up girls who came in from Camden or something?

Teaneck. And when you got to be a lifeguard, which I did later, why you were the prince of summer. You know, it didn't do me much good, but a lot of other guys made a lot of hay with it.

Did you wear oxide on the nose, sunglasses, the whole bit?

You bet. Where I worked in Bradley Beach, a boat stayed just outside the breakers and kept people in. You'd stand up in the boat, Mr. Cool, and look at everything. . . . I used to "boat" people, standing up with a black wool coat, no matter how hot it was, big white nose, big white lips and a prisoner's hat. They'd just gotten mirrored sunglasses in. Must have been the funniest sight of all time. I was sixteen years old, but I thought I was like death itself [*laughs*], guarding these people.

Then you got the girls. . . .

It was a great chance to impress the girls. But like most people of that generation, I didn't think I was adept at anything. It takes a while to find out all them people were lying to you. If you're a certain kind of guy, you don't lie about it. I could never make up any stories like that. It definitely was a different period, from the point of view of how adolescents go through the rites of spring.

You went straight from there to California at the age of sixteen.

I came here because it finally had occurred to me that I didn't want to work my way through college. I already thought I was lazy, and I had been working since I was eleven. I scored very high on the college-board examinations, so there was a certain interest in me academically, but I had a poor deportment record, and I never really hit the books or anything.

And since my only relative in the world was June, who was out here, I came out to look around. I don't think I left Inglewood the first six months that I came to L.A. I went to the race track, went to the pool hall.

June was living there with . . .

With her children, alone. So I'm wondering what I'm gonna do, and then I got a job in the cartoon department at MGM, and I saw every movie star known to man in that period. I had crushes on Grace Kelly, on Rita Moreno. . . .

What's striking about your early days is how the first friends you made are still in your life.

[Cartoonists] Bill Hanna and Joe Barbera, through the studio's talent department, got me started at the Players' Ring Theater as an apprentice, and from there I went into classes with Jeff Corey, where I met Robert Towne, [screenwriter] Carol Eastman, John Shaner, who wrote *Goin' South,* many of the people who are still in my life today.

Not long after leaving MGM you got the lead in 'Cry-baby Killer,' a picture produced by Roger Corman, king of the B movies.

And, I thought, "This is it—I'm meant to be an actor." Then I didn't work for nine months, a year. I didn't make another penny. I'm living on unemployment, this and that, and I went into Marty Landau's acting class, which is where I met Harry Dean Stanton. I'd seen Harry around just as a kind of Porsche-driving, troubled night person. We started hanging out together. I met my ex-wife, Sandra Knight Nicholson, in that class, and Millie Perkins. Again, people still in my life today. Don Devlin, Harry Gittes, came into my life around in here, in a house we ran over at Fountain and Gardner, which was the wildest house in Hollywood for a while.

Your family was transplanted to California by now?

By now Mud had come to California; she had contracted a fatal disease. She was sort of nursed by June, and then in the middle of it, irony had it, June got cancer and died before Mud did. I went away on *Ensign Pulver,* and June died while I was flying to Mexico. And the day I got back from that job, six or seven weeks later, was the day my daughter was born.

When did you end up in Laurel Canyon rooming with Stanton?

When Sandra and I elected to get divorced. I was doing two jobs at the time, and a lot of it was the pressure from that. I hadn't worked for a while, and I remember I was out on the lawn, doing a brake job on my Karmann Ghia . . . this massive undertaking to save fifty dollars, and that day I got two jobs. One to write a movie [*The Trip*] and one to act in one [*Rebel Rousers*].

The scene in *The Shining* comes out of this time, where I say, "Whenever I'm here and you hear me typing . . ."

The scene where he tells his wife to leave him alone when he's working?

Yeah. Later on, with Stanley Kubrick, we wrote that scene together . . . sort of the climactic scene of my marriage because I was under such pressure to get this script out, and I was acting in *Rebel Rousers,* an improvisational movie with Harry Dean and Bruce

Dern. . . . I think it's the only movie of mine I've never seen. Really the whole period was incredible long hours of work, meeting a writing deadline and getting up and doing an acting job. Most of my divorce is written into *The Trip.*

So I needed a place to stay. I tried moving in with Towne, but that only lasted one day. . . . I don't think either of us was particularly easy to live with. Harry Dean I found very easy. He'd already been living in his place at the bottom of Laurel Canyon a year or two when I moved in, and he still hadn't unpacked his boxes. The living room was completely barren. I wrote *The Trip* over in the corner at a desk. Bare floor with a record player on it, and I used to dance around, then go back and write like a fiend.

How old was your daughter when you divorced?

Jennifer was about five.

She's now about twenty-two?

Yeah. She went to high school in Hawaii, and I didn't see much of her. I see a lot of her now. She's starting to work now as an apprentice art director in movies. She's had an offer to go down and work as an assistant art director on *Miami Vice.* I don't know what she'll do about that, but I'm very impressed by her.

What have you told her about men?

Not too much, because she's been around me a lot, and I don't hide too much from her. So she oughta have a pretty good picture.

The overwork that precipitated your divorce kicked off a very productive period for you.

It's an overlapping thing. I guess from there I'm in. There were very few gaps. I'd been part of this very fertile underground film movement that really only existed in this period—I guess we kind of came up above ground and spread out.

I got in *Easy Rider* because I had done all these other nonunion or underground movies. I had produced the westerns [*Ride in the Whirlwind* and *The Shooting,* both 1965] in the middle of my marriage. Bert Schneider and Bob Rafelson [the co-producers of *Easy Rider*] thought I was a good actor but had me out with them all the time on locations, primarily to help with production.

I knew the movie was going to be huge, because I had done a motorcycle movie that did eight, twelve-million dollars, which was an enormous gross in those days. Dennis Hopper had had one, Peter Fonda had had one. Regular Hollywood hadn't tumbled to this yet. It was a progression in the genre, like *Stagecoach* was to the western—kicked it up one more notch.

That's putting it quite humbly; people at the time thought it defined the cold war between "straight" and "counter" culture.

Yes, my character was a bridging character.

In any event, 'Easy Rider' won Hopper the best-new-director award at Cannes and made you a hot property. You took full advantage of it.

I was ready. I was seasoned. I knew immediately—well, "I've worked so hard to become a known actor that now that it's happened, I've got to follow that line. . . ."

What's the one essential thing you would tell a novice actor today?

Well, I wouldn't give him any rules. Because . . . it would be like knowing a little law. In fact, I've directed actors who have never acted before in a movie, and what I learned to give them is . . . "If you get an impulse in a scene, no matter how wrong it seems, follow the impulse." Because we're not on a stage. It might be something, and if it ain't—take two. I try to tell them where the freedom lies, rather than the restraint. This is where unpredictability comes from, this is where the fortunate accident comes from.

Perhaps something like the famous chicken-salad speech in 'Five Easy Pieces'?

First-person autobiography. In those days, I used to do that sort of thing. So did Rafelson. Carol Eastman, who wrote the screenplay [under the name Adrien Joyce] knew about it.

Coffee-shop waitresses seemed to bust chops a lot back then.

Hey, I don't want to hear it *today*.

For most of your career there's been this dichotomy—your name is one of the synonyms for "box office," but you're seen as a maverick who seeks out off-beat films.

I always have to find a valid ethical reason for doing what I do. It's best if you agree totally with the ethical principles of a piece, but sometimes you're simply editorializing on where the ethics of it could lie. I mean, I played *The Postman Always Rings Twice,* let's say, in a much less romantically attractive way than it had ever been done before. I mean, this *is* a murder. That's why in the first scene, I steal cigarettes from the guy who's giving me a free meal, without even thinking about it.

Rafelson kept trying, which everybody does, to slim me down for that part. But I found it interesting to break the cliché of the gaunt, Depression-deprived man of the road. Because this guy gets hungry for five minutes, he'll just steal your food. He might be a bum, but he didn't miss no meals. He wolfed his meals down, and next thing, give me your wife.

There's a strong chance you'll do 'Ironweed,' from the William Kennedy novel, opposite Meryl Streep. You'll play Francis Phelan, a tragic drifter. Are you doing any long-distance preparation for that role?

One thing I don't do is two jobs at a time. I had to get a grasp of that character to know if I wanted to do it, and now I've sort of cut it loose again.

It's always the director that gets me going. One of the things I have to overcome as a director is that it's very hard for me to find a place to put my individual foot down where I don't know how one of the great masters does it already. So when I'm talking to someone, in this case we're talking about Hector, who has a kind of tone and relish about what he wants to do that's just different, I always respond to that. Once I'm in, all I want to know is what the director wants. I don't want to be the one who robs this guy of his chance to express his vision, whether or not it's mine. My whole craft is developed to be able to do what that guy wants.

Anjelica's working on the East Coast with Francis Coppola now on 'Gardens of Stone,' so you're a country apart. I imagine her Oscar had quite an impact—you were conspicuously delighted the night she won it.

I never had a greater moment. I've never experienced anything but anxiety and a kind of dreadful loathing when I've gone down to the Academy Awards. Life gives you very little time to extract pure pleasure from these kinds of things . . . it don't change the world, but you can't say it ain't there. One of the great delights for me about this was being able to behave in the way I would have had her do earlier on. I don't like to be involved with actresses, not because I don't think they're wonderful, which I do. I spend most of my life around them and I think they're great. I also know how demanding it is.

You see things proceeding happily ad infinitum?

I don't see any reason to see it any other way, sure.

Well, I hate to open a wound, but the Lakers' season ended rather abruptly with that crazy turnaround jumper by Ralph Sampson. I was peering at the television screen to try and catch your expression.

Babe, I was the first guy in the arena that knew it was gone. I'm sure if you look at the film, I'm the first guy in the arena that just turned away. The Lakers had history on the line—they lost that . . . but I don't use entertainment to depress myself.

What is it about pro basketball that fascinates you?

It's the most competitive thing on the planet. That's what I like. . . . Larry Bird is so monomaniacally focused. Bird's like me . . . somebody said about him that Bird don't come to play, he comes to win.

Have you ever talked with him?

I don't like backstage, and I don't like locker rooms. But last year I wanted to congratulate them, so I went in their locker room after the game, and I talked to him, yeah.

How did he seem?

Tough. *They're* tough. They have the most fun, they've got the least amount of dissension and cross-purposes on their club, and you can feel it.

Because of your notoriety as a basketball fan, you can change the temperature of an arena, perhaps even of the game itself. Have you consciously sought to do that?

Well . . . I don't do it much anymore sitting where I sit [at courtside, next to the opposition bench], be-cause it's *their* bench. So I'm not like a rabid fan in there. But, okay, last year the best thing we did was on K.C. [Jones, the Celtics coach]. He had been giving the officials a bad time, and when they came back down our way, we yelled at the officials, "Fuck you!" And they called a technical foul on the Boston bench.

We've talked a lot about that sterilized, buggy, overlit environment out there, and your hope that the work you do runs counter to that. Is there any other way to be a corrective to that?

Well, there is more that I do. . . . The main thing that I, that you, can do, is *be* it. *Be* it. That's the main thing you can do.

13
Sam Phillips

INTERVIEWED BY
ELIZABETH KAYE (1986)

Some interviewees are hard to get started. Sam Phillips is almost impossible to stop. Fortunately, his endless stories are mostly terrific. A sharecropper's son from Florence, Alabama, Phillips was deeply rooted in the Southern culture he set out to document at his Sun Studio, in Memphis, at the dawn of the Fifties. Always the iconoclast, he recorded great black blues and gospel as well as wild white country acts. He recorded B.B. King for the RPM label, in Los Angeles, and later cut seminal sides on Howlin' Wolf for Chess, in Chicago. His 1951 recording of the Jackie Brenston–Ike Turner opus "Rocket 88" is widely regarded as the first full-boot rock & roll record. And then, of course, there was Elvis Presley and, in his wake, Johnny Cash, Jerry Lee Lewis and Carl Perkins. The modern age. And that's just the beginning. (Did you hear about the time the Yardbirds came to town and shot holes in his studio ceiling?)

Phillips—apparently as much of a wild man as most of the blues-rocking bopcats he recorded—was born revved up and ready to go. Luckily, Elizabeth Kaye, a connoisseur of that combination of bullshit and brilliance that so often crops up in the music biz (and a survivor of even dizzier go-rounds with Jerry Lee Lewis), was no stranger to the pace.

—K. L.

THE HISTORY of rock & roll may have begun with a man known as Uncle Silas Payne. Uncle Silas was a black man, blinded by syphilis, who lived in Florence, Alabama, with the Phillips family, whose eighth child was named Sam. Uncle Silas used to tell Sam stories, stories that tempered the way Sam came to think, and perceive, stories that shaped his sense of possibility. "In Africa, Samuel," Uncle Silas would say, "we have the most beautiful molasses rivers, and we have bat-tercake trees that grow warm battercakes on them. And a young boy can pick those battercakes off the trees and sop them in those molasses rivers." This was a story that amazed young Sam, and it was based in magic and in alchemy. Much later, Sam himself would have the amazing idea that a white man could sing like a black one. And he would find that man in Elvis Presley, and together they would create the music that came to be known as rockabilly. Rockabilly would become a breeding ground for troubled souls and half-realized dreams. But before it was that, it was magic, and it was alchemy.

Sam Phillips is, at the age of sixty-three, a genuine eccentric, with the glowing, nearly wild eyes of a man whose gaze has been perpetually fixed on a point only he can see. Men of his type are often outcasts, but they are occasionally given, as Sam Phillips was, the opportunity to impress the peculiarities of their vision and quirks on history.

Phillips founded Sun studios in 1950. As a producer at Sun, he became one of the very first white Southerners to record the great Memphis bluesmen, like Howlin' Wolf and B.B. King, a truly revolutionary venture that annoyed and perplexed his peers. "You don't smell bad, Sam," they would say. "Guess you didn't have a session today." He discovered Elvis in 1954. He then went on to discover and record Johnny Cash, Carl Perkins, Jerry Lee Lewis and Roy Orbison, in the process creating a music so innovative and alive that the music itself became a revolutionary force that in turn changed everything.

In 1969, Phillips sold Sun (though he had stopped making records on the label in 1963) at a time when many independent companies were losing their battle for survival. He could have gone to work for RCA, but he had the good sense to recognize that he was far too stubborn, ornery and proud to answer to a corporate hierarchy. The music he had made and deeply loved was the manifestation of an untamable spirit; in the end, his independence mattered to him even more than his music.

He protected that independence by becoming a wealthy man. He was an early investor in the Holiday Inn chain, and today he owns five lucrative radio stations and plays the stock market with all the canny delight with which he once ran Sun.

This interview took place in one nine-hour session in the living room of Phillips' home in Memphis, a ranch-style house he bought in 1956 that has a small swimming pool in the back and Phillips' big blue and white 1976 Cadillac parked in the driveway. Throughout the interview, his two sons—Knox, 40, and Jerry, 37—sat on the modern beige couch facing their father, eyeing him attentively, laughing at his jokes, encouraging him with small nods of their heads, even prompting him by asking leading questions. They adore the man they call Sam and are passionately concerned that his place in rock & roll history be recorded with sufficient respect and that he be given the credit he deserves as the true patriarch of rock & roll. As for Phillips, he tells his version of the birth of that music with all the mesmerizing potency of a man who has a prodigious gift for oratory, no apparent modesty and a singular story to tell.

There are many stories about how Elvis came to Sun in 1954. I'd like to hear your version of it.

He was working for Crown Electric. I'd seen the truck go back and forth outside, and I thought, "They sure are doing a hell of a lot of business around here." But I never saw it stop anywhere. So Elvis had . . . he had cased the joint a long time before he stopped the truck and got out. And there's no telling how many days and nights behind that wheel he was figuring out some way to come in and make a record without saying, "Mr. Phillips, would you audition me?" So his mother's birthday gave him the opportunity to come in and make a little personal record. [Elvis claimed he was making the record for his mother, but her birthday was, in fact, months away, so perhaps he had other motives.]

The first song he recorded was "My Happiness." The story goes that it was recorded not by you but by your assistant, Marion Keisker. Is that your recollection?

Well, I would love to say Marion did it. She did an awful lot for me, man. I mean we painted floors together. I wouldn't take anything away from Marion Keisker. And I think she made the statement inadvertently. I don't want to make Marion look bad on the thing. I wish you'd just drop it, 'cause I don't care who it was. But it was simply me. That's all.

What did you think when you heard it?

There wasn't anything that striking about Elvis, except his sideburns were down to here [*gestures*], which I kind of thought, well, you know, "That's pretty cool, man. Ain't nobody else got them that damn long." We talked in the studio. And I played the record back for him in the control room on the little crystal turntable and walked up front and told Marion to write down Elvis' name and number and how we can get a hold of him.

Why would you want to get a hold of him?

Well, I told Elvis, "If I come up with any songs, would you be interested in maybe taking a shot at it?" And was he!

You called him back to cut a ballad called "Without You." That song was never released. What went wrong?

We got some pretty good cuts on the thing, but I wanted to check him out other ways before I made a final decision as to which route we were going to attempt to go with him.

And I decided I wanted to look at things with a little tempo, because you can really hang yourself out on ballads or when you go up against Perry Como or Eddie Fisher or even Patti Page, all of those people. I wasn't looking for anything that greatly polished.

After that, you put Elvis with a band, Scotty Moore on guitar and Bill Black on bass. Why did you choose them?

The two of them, they'd been around the studio, Lord, I don't know how many damned times, you know? Scotty had been playing with different bands, and although he hadn't ever done a session for me, I knew he had the patience, and he wasn't afraid to try anything, and that's so important when you're doing laboratory experiments.

Scotty was also the type of person who could take instruction real good. And I kidded him a lot. I said, "If you don't quit trying to copy Chet Atkins, I'll throw you out of this damn place." And Bill, he was just Bill Black, and the best slap bass player in the city.

Did you know by then that Elvis was the person you'd been looking for?

I sure did. I wouldn't have called him back and back and back again. I knew he had the fundamentals of what I wanted. He was the first one I had seen who had that potential. He had a different type of voice. And this boy had listened to a lot of different music, from the Grand Ole Opry to Bing Crosby to Dinah Shore to Crudup to Bill Monroe to Hank Snow.

What were you trying to achieve with Elvis?

Now, you've got to keep in mind Elvis Presley probably innately was the most introverted person that came into that studio. Because he didn't play with bands. He didn't go to this little club and pick and grin. All he did was set with his guitar on the side of his bed at home. I don't think he even played on the front porch.

So I had to try to establish a direction for him. And I had to look into the market, and if the market was full of one type of thing, why try to go in there? There's only so many pieces in a pie. That's how I figured it. I knew from the beginning that I was going to have to do something different and that it might be harder to get it going. But if I got it going, I might have something.

How did you come to cut "That's All Right"?

That night we had gone through a number of things, and I was getting ready to fold it up. But I didn't want to discourage the damn people, you understand? I knew how enthusiastic Elvis was to try to do something naturally. I knew also that Scotty Moore was staying there till he dropped dead, you know? I don't remember exactly what I said, but it was light-hearted. I think I told him, "There ain't a damn song you can do that sounds worth a damn," or something like that. He knew it was tongue in cheek. But it was getting to be a critical time, because we had been in the studio a lot. Well, I went back into the booth. I left the mikes open, and I think Elvis felt like, really, "What the hell have I got to lose? I'm really gonna blow his head off, man." And they cut down on "That's All Right," and hell, man, they was just as instinctive as they could be.

It's said that you heard him singing it, and you said, "What are you doing?" and he said, "I don't know," and you said, "Do it again." Is that true?

I don't remember exactly verbatim. But it was something along the lines that I've been quoted.

Scotty Moore says that when he heard the playback, he thought he'd be run out of town. How did you feel when you heard it?

First of all, Scotty wasn't shocked at any damned thing I attempted to do. Scotty isn't shockable. And for me, that damned thing came through so loud and clear it was just like a big flash of lightning and the thunder that follows. I knew it was what I was looking for for Elvis. When anybody tells you they know they've got a hit, they don't know what the hell they're talking about. But I knew I had it on "That's All Right." I just knew I had found a groove. In my opinion. And that's all I had to go on, honey. I mean I let people hear it. But I didn't ask them their damn opinions.

Then what happened?

I let Scotty, Bill and Elvis know I was pretty damn

pleased. Then I made an acetate dub of it and took it up to [Memphis disc jockey] Dewey Phillips and played him the tape. And Daddy-O Dewey wanted to hear it again. "Goddamn, man," he says, "I got to have it." Red, hot and blue. You'd have to know Dewey.

And two nights later, he played that thing, and the phones started ringing. Honey, I'll tell you, all hell broke loose. People were calling that station, and it really actually surprised me, because I knew nobody knew Elvis. Elvis just didn't have friends, didn't have a bunch of guys he ran with or anything, you know? Anyway, it was just fantastic. To my knowledge, there weren't any adverse calls.

Why did you decide to back "That's All Right" with "Blue Moon of Kentucky"?

This was before anybody thought of young people being interested in bluegrass. But we did this thing, and it just had an intrigue. And that's the one where I thought maybe there was a good possibility of getting run out of town, 'cause hey, man, you didn't mess with bluegrass. Bluegrass is kind of sacred, you know.

Once the record was released, there was an incredible furor. How did it affect you?

Rock & roll probably put more money in the collection boxes of the churches across America than anything the preacher could have said. I certainly know that to be a fact. Not only them. Disc jockeys broke the hell out of my records. Broke 'em on the air. Slam them over the damn microphone. Now if I *hadn't* affected people like that, I might have been in trouble.

Do you remember the session for "Good Rockin' Tonight"?

Oh, God, we all loved that song, man. I took Bill and I said, "I don't want none of this damned slapping. I want you to pull them damned strings, boy."

What about "You're a Heartbreaker"?

I had a little trouble with Elvis on that, because he wanted to move into a little heavier type of feel. And I didn't want to take him too fast. "You're a Heartbreaker" wasn't my favorite song of all time.

Would he balk at doing a song like that?

Elvis never really balked. But you could tell that maybe he felt we could find something better. And I had a little trouble with him on "I Forgot to Remember to Forget." I said to him, "Man, that is a classic. That is a play on words with a hook that'll knock your ass off."

Once you said that, there was no problem?

No problem. No bitching. No griping. No halfway doing it.

How about "Baby, Let's Play House"?

He loved that. We all did. That thing just hatched.

I would think you'd have worried about that one, though, in terms of sexual connotations.

Oh, we didn't mind sex around here and there.

But did you think of it as a marketing consideration?

Well, at that time it *was* controversial. But I mean, anything you said that wasn't "moon, june and something" was. But what's wrong with "Baby, let's play house"? Now, if he had said, "Baby, let's play doctor" . . .

On that song and several others, Elvis changed some lyrics. Would those changes generally be his idea or yours?

It was mainly him. I might suggest a different word to make it a little more hip.

What about "Milk Cow Blues Boogie," when Elvis says, "Let's get real, real gone"?

That happened because I wanted something on the front end of that thing. And I was very careful on narrations, 'cause that can kill a record on a jukebox. So we worked this thing out to where it would be a little bit different, and then when we went into our rhythm, honey, it took place.

Was it his ad-lib or yours?

I'm pretty sure I told him that.

What about "Mystery Train"?

That's my favorite record on Elvis. And when we did that take, he laughed because he thought it wasn't worth a shit. I mean that was the one, that was it, with that stupid laugh on him. He just knew I wasn't gonna be pleased with that cut, so he just acted silly as hell, and it turned out to be super.

You recorded four ballads with Elvis at Sun, but none was released. Why was that?

I wasn't going to release any damn ballads until he was ready as a ballad singer.

Did he know he wasn't ready at that point?

I don't think he did. But you need a person who will give you a judgment call no matter what it does to you.

Did you tell Elvis he wasn't ready?

No. I didn't tell him that. But I told him in so many ways. It was an insult to him if I had told him directly that he wasn't ready. I mean, I knew how to get around. But not only did I know Elvis wasn't ready for it, I knew the market wasn't ready then, because we had plenty of ballad singers that were super-duper.

Your contract with Elvis had him completely locked up, so the only way Colonel Parker could have become involved was as a concert booker. Why did you decide to sell his contract just a year and a half after he started with you?

I had looked at everything for how I could take a little extra money and get myself out of a real bind. I mean, I wasn't broke, but man, it was hand-to-mouth.

I made an offer to Tom Parker, but the whole thing was that I made an offer I didn't think they'd even consider—$35,000, plus I owed Elvis $4,000 or $5,000.

So you thought the offer was so high no one would take it?

I didn't necessarily want them *not* to take it.

But once you knew Elvis was going to be big, why didn't you try to expand your operation?

Number one, you couldn't borrow money. Not even after Sun Records was successful. The South knew nothing about the record industry and didn't believe in it. The only route I had was to go public. I didn't want the accountability. I would rather be my own boss and go down that way. I wanted to stay small.

Did you realize how much Elvis was worth?

Hell, no. I didn't have any idea the man was going to be the biggest thing that ever happened to the industry.

Were you ever sorry you let him go?

No. That was the best judgment call I could make at the time, and I still think it is. And Sun went on and did many, many things. I hoped the one thing that wouldn't happen to me was that I would be a one-artist or a one-hit label.

Did you give Elvis any advice when he left Sun?

The one real ammunition I gave him was "Don't let them tell you what to do. Don't lose your individuality."

Then how did you feel when he started making the type of movies he made?

They were just things that you could make for nothing and make millions off of, and Elvis didn't have anything to do with it. That was Colonel Tom Parker and the moguls at the different studios. I think it was almost sinister, I really do.

Did you ever think of becoming a manager?

I'm insane. But I'm not that insane.

Once Elvis was gone, were you banking Sun's future on Carl Perkins?

I banked it on me.

A few months after Elvis left, you released Perkins' "Blue Suede Shoes." Wasn't that the record that put Sun into the black?

Absolutely. And there was another one of those instincts. I knew I was giving up some kind of a cat, man, but, sure enough, I sold him, and that's what financed "Blue Suede Shoes."

Steve Sholes of RCA called you at the time "Blue Suede Shoes" was climbing the charts. RCA couldn't get anything going with Elvis, and Sholes asked you, "Did we buy the wrong guy?" What did you tell him?

I told him, "You haven't bought the wrong person." And I gave him the reasons. Number one, Elvis certainly had the talent. And unlike Carl, he was single and had no children and was a helluva-looking man. He said, "Well, would you be mad at us if we put out 'Blue Suede Shoes'?" Man, that staggered me. I said, "Steve, you all are big enough to kill me, you know." But they didn't put it out as a single. They released it as an EP.

Did it outsell Perkins' version?

Hell, no. Well, I guess over the years when it was put in nineteen packages. But the only reason Carl is not recognized for "Blue Suede Shoes" is that Elvis became so mammothly big.

When did you realize how big Elvis would be?

Not when I heard "Heartbreak Hotel." That was the worst record. I knew it when I heard "Don't Be Cruel." I was driving back from the first vacation I'd had in my life, and it came on the radio, and I said, "Wait a minute. Jesus, he's off and gone, man." I'd like to run off the road.

Were you jealous?

Hell, no, 'cause when I heard "Heartbreak Hotel," I said, "Damned sons of bitches are going to mess this man up." Then, boy, I heard "Don't Be Cruel," and I was the happiest man in the world.

What was the difference in what you were trying to achieve first with Elvis, then with Perkins?

With Elvis, I kind of wanted to lean more toward the blues. I wanted to get Carl more into modifying country music.

What was your favorite Perkins song?

This is the craziest thing, but one of the cutest songs I ever heard was his "Movie Magg." And "Boppin' the Blues."

When you started Sun, you were recording black bluesmen. Then you recorded country boys, like Perkins and Johnny Cash. It seems that you must have had a strong identification with downtrodden people. How did you develop that?

As a child, I was extremely physically unhealthy. I think that made me very sensitive to what life is all about, and more observant of the things that were around. Seeing kids who were so much more robust than myself had a profound influence on my feelings for people, my feelings for suffering. And it made me feel there had to be a certain belief in yourself.

Did the Depression affect you?

When the crash came in '29, I was six years old. My father was a tenant farmer and had managed to accumulate a little personal—well, we called it wealth. A few hundred dollars in the bank. So one night he goes to sleep and the next morning he wakes up and he has no money. He was almost fifty years old, and he had the great stamina and belief to not look back, 'cause there was not a lot he could do about that. That was a very inspirational thing to me.

When did you first hear the blues?

On our plantation—I call it that because it was 320 acres, which was one of the biggest farms then—very seldom did you go by the black mammas hanging out clothes or boiling clothes in a big old wash kettle that you didn't hear some humming, some singing. Certainly, in the fields that was absolutely their theme song. I saw that. I even felt that. So many people that went through relatively the same thing missed this because they thought of the black man as another mule or somebody not quite human. But I didn't, maybe because I was always loved by the black adults, like Uncle Silas Payne. They looked at me and had such a sympathy. And I'd see them work, and I mean the sweat and the heat and you walked every foot of the way behind those mules. And I saw how they kept their spirituality. They felt hope, and to me that said something. I can't say I knew at that immediate time what it said. I damn sure know what it means now.

What?

That they were the most creative people from a purely instinctive standpoint of any race in the United States. But had I not experienced what I did, it would be very difficult for me to feel that, or to feel the way I do about my kindredness with the black people, with music, with poor Southern whites, with the misunderstood peoples of the South. But because of that, I think the blues came very naturally to me.

You wanted to be a criminal lawyer, but your father died when you were young. Without enough money to be educated extensively, you became a disc jockey and an engineer. You worked in a number of places before settling in Memphis. Why did you choose to live there?

I first came through Memphis in 1939, in a '37 Dodge with a rumble seat. I'd heard about Beale Street. I'd heard it was the most unique street in the world. And we drove down Beale—it must have been five o'clock in the morning, and believe me, this street was busy. And I got to see how the blacks lived in their uptown social way. We drove up and down Beale half a dozen times, and God, it was so active and vibrant and alive. They were having a good time. To hell with what your head felt like the next day.

Then I saw the Mississippi River. I was born and raised on the Tennessee, a beautiful river, but here was this untamed damned river. Nice and muddy. And its

bank, man, was where it wanted to be at that particular time. You know? You didn't tell it what to do. So I fell in love with this old river town.

When you set up Sun in 1950, were you trying to attract a youth market?

Absolutely. From the beginning. There was just no music for young people then except for a few little kiddy records put out by the major labels.

And when you started recording black bluesmen, were you recording for young black record buyers?

I was recording to survive, honey. And I knew that my primary target would have to be black people. But Leonard Chess [owner of Chicago's Chess Records] and the Bihari boys [three brothers who ran the Los Angeles–based Modern Records] and I all talked to each other back then about the white youth market. And believe me, this is taking nothing away from anybody, but it hadn't occurred to too many people that white people would listen to black singers. But I wasn't in it just to record black music for black people alone. I was in it to record something I loved, something I felt, something I thought other people ought to have an opportunity to render a judgment on. And most especially young whites, young blacks and then the older blacks.

You got the idea for making very simple recordings when you were engineering broadcasts of big bands, like the Dorseys and Glenn Miller. How did that come about?

Because the rhythm section sounded better than the whole rest of them. Bass, drums, you know, piano, and the few bands that had guitars. Hell, yeah. And I'd always mix the rhythm section a little hotter than the horns. I kept it hot. I had fights with some of the bandleaders, but they all liked it after they heard it. And I'll tell you, every bandleader, when they heard my mix, they were a little surprised that the rhythm section was kind of pushing a little more than they wanted. They wanted the blend of their instruments to do the pushing, you know? And the accents of the arrangements. And hey, there's nothing wrong with that. But what I gave them was that plus. Because it felt natural.

One of the people you discovered at Sun was Ike Turner. What do you remember about him?

Ike was such a fantastic musician. But the only thing is, I had problems with Ike, because early on he wanted to get a little more sophistication into the music. See, he was a piano player when he came to me. And up to that time I never heard a piano player who could play with as much damn soul and feel in my life. Of course, later he switched to the guitar. And he had a good band. But I had to hold them down from trying to sound just a little bit too complicated, because his mind ran that way.

What part did he play in the recording of "Rocket 88," a song many people believe was the first rock & roll record?

Jackie Brenston [Turner's lead vocalist] had this song. And God, when I heard that thing, man . . . I have no doubt in my mind that this was the first true rock & roll record. Not because I cut it.

What do you remember about the session?

Well, when Ike and them were coming up to do the session, the bass amplifier fell off the car. And when we got in the studio, the woofer had burst; the cone had burst. So I stuck the newspaper and some sack paper in it, and that's where we got that sound.

Were you intentionally trying to create a new sound?

I would have been totally unfulfilled if I had just cut a good, conventional, beautiful hit record. I certainly could have used the money. But that type of music wasn't my interest at all. The more unconventional it sounded, the more interested I would become in it.

Of all the blues artists you worked with at Sun, who was your favorite?

Chester Burnett, the Howlin' Wolf. He was always so, quote unquote, unprepared. But so damn well prepared. No song was ever ready, and the closest analogy I can give to a white man would be a Jerry Lee Lewis. There ain't no way he's going to sing the song the same way twice.

And Wolf had the most god-awful voice that could be classified as a set of vocal cords I ever heard in my life. And that I knew had to draw attention. And if you get attention, hell, you can't ask for a better opportunity, can you?

One of the most interesting groups you worked with were the Prisonaires. What do you remember about their recording of "Just Walkin' in the Rain"?

The whole quartet was in prison, and so was Robert Riley, who wrote "Walkin' in the Rain." One of them, Johnny Bragg, had four 99-year sentences, and he went in there at sixteen years old, convicted for all the rapes in some county in East Tennessee that they couldn't solve or something. But I got this thing worked out with the warden to bring them over to Sun. And everybody was concerned with what precedent this would set. So we recorded the song, but then of course Johnnie Ray covered us, and that sure didn't help any. Later, they sang at the governor's mansion for President Truman. Sassy little dude. Loved him to death. And Truman told the governor after it was over, "Governor, pardon every one of them." And so every one of them are our taxpaying citizens now.

All the black men you worked with in the early days at Sun were poor men who had been taught to keep their place. What were the special problems of working with men like that?

When people are by tradition emotionally enslaved, they are looking for everything that might say you don't care about them. That was never my feeling, and I think they could feel that in me. I think they believed in me.

You once said that Elvis' sense of inferiority was markedly like a black person's.

Absolutely. That was true of all of the guys. Even Jerry Lee, except Jerry had something that I really like about him. He had that basic sureness about what he was doing. And he believed that what he was doing was good.

Jerry Lee once said that you and the other founders of rockabilly were nutty as fox squirrels. Is that a fair assessment?

We're all crazy. I'll admit to that. But it's a type of insanity that almost borders on . . . honestly, I believe it's on genius. I really feel that.

To be as free as you have to be for any kind of music, you almost have to be in another dimension. And to do the broad expanse of rock & roll, it takes an element of mind expansion that people less creative would term insanity.

Do you remember when you first heard Jerry Lee?

It was the day after I first heard "Don't Be Cruel." Jerry had come to Memphis with his cousin, staying at his house. He was a pretty determined person, and he made up his mind he was going to see Sam Phillips. Jack Clement [Sun's producer] was at the studio, and Jerry didn't even want to audition for him. But they cut this little audition tape. And when I went to the studio, Jack says, "Man, I got a cat I want you to hear." Well, I had been looking for somebody that could do tricks on the piano as a lead instrument. Lo and behold, man, I hear this guy and his total spontaneity.

Then, when you met Jerry Lee and he played for you, you're supposed to have told him, "You are a rich man."

I probably did. Not in the connotation of money, but of talent.

You've said that Jerry Lee was the most talented person you ever worked with but that you don't think he could have been bigger than Elvis. Why is that?

That gets into the thing of the total effect of the person. There is no question that the most talented person I ever worked with is Jerry Lee Lewis. Black or white. But Elvis had a certain type of total charisma that was just almost untouchable by any other human that I know of or have ever seen.

But this is a tough comparison for me to make. It looks like I'm drawing lines between two of the most talented people in the world, and I don't like to do that. But I would say that if they were both at their peak, and Elvis was booked for a show but Jerry Lee showed up, no one would be disappointed. Is there a better answer you can think of than that?

What do you remember about recording "Great Balls of Fire"?

That was the toughest record I ever recorded in my life. Otis Blackwell had done the demo. When I heard it, I said, "What in the hell are they doing sending me a record like this? It ought to be out." He'd written the damn thing on a napkin in a bar he owed a lot of money to. And we worked our ass off because those breaks . . . with Jerry having to do his piano, it had to be exactly synced with his voice.

You didn't do any overdubbing on it?

Hell, no. We didn't have nothing to overdub with.

It's been said that you were very tight-fisted with money. For instance, Jerry Lee played on sessions where he only got paid fifteen dollars.

Well, Jerry Lee was lucky to get to play for fifteen dollars when I didn't need him. I mean, I don't have a penny that's not mine, because hell, if I thought I had to cheat to win, forget it, honey. I'd lose everything.

Johnny Cash came to Sun in 1955. What was it about him that interested you?

When Johnny Cash came in, he sang his original country-gospel songs, and I have never been as moved in my life by anything to this day. But I was very honest with him. I told him, "Man, I love this, but God, I can't sell it, and if I can't sell it, you and me can't be in business." And I instructed him to use some of that talent in the secular world.

Didn't you tell him to write "a weeper with a tempo"?

Yeah. And he came back with "Cry! Cry! Cry!"

"I Walk the Line" was one of Sun's five biggest records, though Cash wrote it as a slow ballad. What made you change it?

Well, with a little tempo, here he was, a modern-day Burl Ives, with a commanding voice and a hell of a song. If I can't tell that, I mean, I better get out of the business.

It's an unusually minimalistic recording, with the guitar just playing bass runs. What else made it work so well?

I had a little piece of paper that I wove through Cash's strings. It had to be just the right width. I don't know how many times I ran it through those damn strings. And when I got it just right I told him, "Now you chord that damn guitar like you would with no paper in it." And do you think we didn't come up with a sound?

What do you remember about "Ballad of a Teenage Queen"?

I hate it to this day. Well, it's a good song, but we cut it on the wrong artist. I didn't want to cut it on Cash. I never wanted Cash on the pop charts except with "I Walk the Line." But there was nobody else I wanted to thrust it on anyway. It was a cute song. It's really lyrically a standard. But I still hate the damn thing.

Why did you release it?

Well, it was wrong to do, and it turned out all right.

What about "Folsom Prison Blues"?

I didn't know that that would have real mass appeal. But we got such a dynamic cut on that damn thing. And I got to thinking about it, that we all, in a way, are in prison, you know? I had to stretch my imagination, but I didn't expect the public to do that. But oh, God, I love that song. Great song, great rendition. Never been a better record made. Thank goodness [*laughs*].

What do you remember about Roy Orbison?

Basically, he could have been a real good songwriter. It didn't turn out that he was, but he could have been.

You don't think the songs he did after he left Sun, songs like "Crying" and "Only the Lonely," are good?

Oh, yeah, but I don't think he even scratched the surface. Roy is a very unusual musician. I like the way he picks the guitar. But he's been through so damn much, and seeing him wind up not as a big artist— even if he didn't have the most attractive physical appeal in the world, he has that power of communication because he just sings so damn good. I'm sure that if his mind hadn't been complicated by all the tragedies [the death of his wife and two of his children] maybe he could have written much more.

Who else came to Sun of real interest to you?

Charlie Rich is probably the most underrated musician to ever walk in my doors. His talent is almost boundless. But what he had to do was make himself get off his mind bent of jazz. But if he had had the fervor for rock & roll that he's got for jazz, this guy would have almost been limitless.

Do you think he was the best musician, singer and songwriter you ever recorded?

Without a doubt. The world has missed an awful

lot by not having Charlie's music available to them. And I would have liked to have been the one—because I adore Charlie.

You discovered all these men, and they all left you for bigger labels. You've said you were deeply hurt by that.

Well, yes. Because it's a child-bearing kind of situation, and you also feel you've given unselfishly and you've gambled on them from the front end with your talent, your time, with your energies. When they left me, I didn't blame them personally, because I knew the stories they had heard. And the stories were simply—no matter if I had been giving them ten percent—"Man, is that all you're getting?" These people were unsuspecting. It was their first contract. Their first adventure into the world of business and a little money. When they got a damned check for $50,000—can you imagine? They hadn't seen that much money in their lifetime or in their daddy's lifetime.

Do you bear them any ill will today?

Not at all. Never had any. I don't live that way.

Do you think any of the people you worked with at Sun achieved their full potential?

I think all of them missed me, I really do. Because I think eventually we would have had a small stable of artists. And I think they would have done better than they did.

When you were producing, how much control did you exert over your artists?

Fantastic amount. Number one, I didn't permit drinking at sessions, and I love to drink as much as anybody. I'd let Wolf have a little wine now and then—maybe a whole half pint for a session, 'cause he'd just go get it anyway. But overall, the control was an indirect control, because they knew I was very serious about what I was trying to do, not only for me but for them.

You used to say, "Do it one more time for Sam."

Oh, good God, I must have said that 100,000 times. And every artist, I don't care how much they might have cursed me, I think they knew what the hell I knew when I got behind that glass. And when I worked that floor, too.

How do you think your personality affected the creation of rock & roll?

A hell of a lot. Call it what you want, but the unseen factors—the psychological and spiritual factors, that is—always played one of the most important parts in every audition and session I had. You must have confidence in your ability to get the most natural response from artistically inclined people and especially unproven musicians and to be able to transfer this confidence subtly to them, to reassure them, often without actually saying anything.

This I believe I did. Maybe I'm a frustrated preacher with a flock I believed I could spot the best in.

Of the four major people you worked with, three became drug addicts and one became an alcoholic. What do you think happened to these guys?

You keep in mind that of all the enemies in the world there is no one potentially of greater harm to you than you yourself. And here we get into the elements of direction. We must never lose a focal point in our lives, regardless of the fame or fortune or adulation that comes forth from our talents and recognition. I think that these young people that came from total poverty, when they got into the big world and began to receive plaudits, they lost sight possibly of some of the basic values that are so necessary for us all to have. I think also that people have to take the time to think, "Who am I, what am I, and I'm still just me." It's sad that fame and fortune carries with it the potential for a heavy toll. It should be the other way around.

But since the music business takes so much from people, even as it gives them a lot, were you ambivalent about bringing these young country boys into it?

No. But I wished I could have kept them with me. I honestly believe that they would have drawn strength from the fact that nothing's ever affected me in the way of losing my center of perspective. The ladder of achievement is made of gold rungs going up, but it can have some very shaky rungs, if any rungs at all, coming down. I guess probably people need, quote unquote, parental advice.

And is that what you think they lost when they left you?

Oh, hell, there's no question of that. Though, God, you know, maybe I'll be reincarnated as the same thing I was. And some of these artists—they may be reincarnated as the same thing they were and let me do them over again.

When Elvis died, you said that he died of a broken heart. Can you amplify that?

When you really don't have something to look forward to with a good, sweet, beautiful attitude, you're in trouble. I don't care who you are. You're also in trouble if you're in bondage in any way. I'm talking about emotional entrapment. That's deep stuff. And it's serious stuff. And no matter what happens to you in this world, if you don't make it your business to be happy, then you may have gained the whole world and lost your spirit and maybe even your damned soul.

But wasn't Elvis entrapped by circumstance?

Absolutely.

What could he have done differently?

Been hardheaded like me and said, "I will break your damned neck. I don't care—you can't scare me. Monetary factors can't scare me. Starvation can't scare me. Threats can't scare me." I mean, you have to have that attitude.

Elvis also knew that success wasn't enough. It's like Mac Davis said, man, and I think this is one of the greatest quotes, Bible included: "Stop and smell the roses." Now that's where we can all find ourselves if we don't stop and smell the roses.

And the sad thing about it is dying before you actually physically die. I mean, you know, bless his heart.

In 1969, you decided to sell Sun. Why?

I had been approached by I don't know how many people to buy my masters. When I saw the big companies were going to eat me alive—I didn't want to face that fact, but I saw what was coming. Not that they could out-produce me, but they were buying all the artists from the independent companies. I knew this was going to make the structure of distribution very unhealthy. They had the ability to do it. They had that glamour over you. And artists had felt for many years that if you weren't on a major label, you just weren't very good. And that's sad, because there should be room for the majors, room for the independents, but the independents are just about extinct now. And unfortunately, without the independent labels, a lot of the real initiative gets taken out of people. That may not sit so well with the Rock & Roll Hall of Fame board, but it's the truth.

So I saw the writing on the wall. I knew it was time to sell, and Shelby Singleton [who had once been the head of production for Mercury Records] approached me on buying. Shelby loved the old Sun records, and I just wanted the Sun label to be bought by somebody who would take it under his wing and love it like I had loved it. I sold to Shelby for way less than half of what I could have gotten.

Who are the people you admire now?

You remember Creedence and Fogerty, don't you? And listen, I never liked "Born in the U.S.A.," but have you heard "My Hometown," by Springsteen? You think that cat can't sing? He doesn't have to holler all the time, does he? And the Del Fuegos and the Blasters. And, of course, Bob Dylan is doing better stuff now than he's ever done. And Willie Nelson is a total classic. And Merle Haggard. And have you heard "Lost in the Fifties Tonight," by Ronnie Milsap? I want to tell you something, honey, all that shit is clas-

sic. None of it is overly complicated. None of it is synthesized.

You've said you think Willie Nelson is the greatest entertainer of our time. What sets him apart?

It's that he's always kept his music right to the point. Totally uncomplicated. So uncomplicated, it's complicated.

What do you think of sexually explicit performers who could be called the heirs of Elvis?

Now wait just a goddamn minute. Jesus Christ! What they are doing versus what Elvis was doing— you bring him up here today and he'd look like a virgin. Now I understand that what Elvis did, shake his hips, man, probably had the same connotation then as what's going on today. But when you substitute just the sexuality of individuals—I mean, explicit sex has a place, I like it. But not with my damn music.

Why do you think people do it?

It's total *M-O-N-E-Y*.

Do you think rock & roll is dead?

Rock & roll has just been asleep too damn long. I think if we don't begin to create that true atmosphere of experimentation, things are going to suffer greatly. Or if the people in the industry don't take a chance on things that are not what the last thing they released is like, or what this label over here is doing. I think we run a real risk of losing that beautiful thing called creativity.

Who would you most like to work with?

Bob Dylan. There are very few originals, and certainly Bob was one of the original originals. Dylan is a true free spirit. I would have loved to work with him. And Bob has written me how many letters, and I ain't answered a damn one of them.

If Dylan wanted to do an album with you, would that get you out of retirement?

It wouldn't take me out of retirement. I might take a little *time* out of retirement.

What do you think the legacy of rock & roll has been?

I said many years ago that all the diplomats in the world could not do more than rock & roll has done to bring us closer together. Rock & roll played an important part in the way we think about each other. We didn't go across the waters and try to sell them rock & roll. The State Department didn't do that. It was just the sheer simplicity of communication and the freedom they felt in those records that made them know there was a bunch of damn hillbillies, thinking, feeling people—and made them say that America sounds free. Have you ever seen an influence in your life like rock & roll?

It's been said that you perceive yourself as a prophet. Is that a fair estimate of you?

I think prophet is an awfully strong word. Let's just make it *messiah* [*laughs*]. No, I think *highly intuitional* is a more accurate description. I think that I was able to see probably further down the road, and as it worked out in most cases, I was right.

Do you have any regrets?

I seriously regret not spending time with Elvis in the later years. I'm not a doctor, I'm just an individual who's believable and sincere and has experienced an awful lot of things. And I feel that there was an awful lot I learned through those processes that I could have shared, mainly in an indirect way, with Elvis, and that might have been helpful.

How would you like to be remembered?

I'd like to be remembered as the sexiest . . . no, I actually don't want a lot of remembrance on a person as such. I want a remembrance on the fact that maybe I brought a little pleasure to people, and even probably more than that: gave people an opportunity to be themselves just a little bit more. I want a remembrance on the fact that maybe I was one of the people who dared. That would give me the greatest marker I could have.

Some people say you're America's real Uncle Sam. What do you think of that?

Well, now, that's an awfully high compliment. I think in a way that I am. I guess I really do think that I did an awful lot—not alone—but an awful lot to help people become better acquainted through an international type of language: music.

14

The Everly Brothers

INTERVIEWED BY KURT LODER (1986)

If there is any journalistic experience more melancholy than discovering an unhappy underside to a beloved legendary life, it's having to go home and write about it for public consumption. The Everly Brothers were known to have a volatile relationship, but the depth of their unhappiness was still a surprise to me. Their great hits were among rock's foremost glories in the late Fifties and early Sixties; and yet this stellar success, both artistic and commercial, brought the brothers themselves no peace.

As with the Bo Diddley interview on page 181, the Everlys' story—intimately entwined as it is with earlier forms of American music as well as the evolution of the American pop scene—required a considerable amount of stage setting and period recreation. The sheer bulk of interview and research materials dictated a straightforward chronological structure, with short narrative bridges interspersed where necessary. For all its fascination, it was not a happy task.

This is a sad story but one to which a happy ending may yet be appended. The Everly Brothers continue, in their quiet way, to make glorious records together. One can only hope that harmony will one day reign in their troubled lives as well.

—K. L.

O F THE ten acts inducted into the Rock & Roll Hall of Fame in 1986, three are deceased, one's virtually forsaken rock for religion, and most of the rest seem comfortably settled into legend, far from the madding charts, champions to be cherished in dignified repose. Only the Everly Brothers, out of this galaxy of pioneering stars, glow on at something close to their original artistic voltage.

This is ironic, because the Everlys, with their clean-cut looks, pristine country harmonies and string of early teen hits largely written to order by Nashville tunesmiths, have in the past seemed to some the embodiment of domesticated white-boy rock—well-mannered worlds away from the rowdier stance of Chuck Berry or Jerry Lee Lewis, the lunatic rumpus of Little Richard, the raw soul of Ray Charles. And yet, here they are, twenty-nine years after their first hit, "Bye Bye Love," creating whole new worlds for those heart-melting harmonies to inhabit. Their voices are richer now, and more complexly intertwined. Their songs no longer celebrate the bird dogs and little Susies of their original success, but neither do they flirt with the musical middle of the road. Although they have always been nonpareil balladeers, the Everlys remain, at heart, root-level rock & rollers. Their "comeback"—the 1983 reunion concerts at London's Royal Albert Hall and the two extraordinary studio albums they've released in their wake—has escaped all suggestions of a "rock revival." (As Don says, explaining why he and Phil have never played an oldies show, "Rock & roll should never have to make a comeback.")

The Everlys have actually been making records for thirty years, if one counts their first effort, a quickie single called "Keep A'Lovin' Me," which was released and forgotten in February 1956. They have seen rock & roll evolve from a despised pop cult into the American musical mainstream—in which, after years of tears and trials, they are once again aswim. In late February, the Everlys got together in Los Angeles—where Phil has lived since 1960 and where Don was visiting, from his home in Nashville—to savor the critical response to the second album of their revitalized career, the recently released *Born Yesterday*. Interviews with the brothers were conducted separately, which seemed appropriate, for they are very different men. Donald (as his brother and friends call him), now forty-nine, is the darker-haired and bulkier of the two: rootless, restless, mercurial, a lover of good food, fine Beaujolais and beautiful women. Phil, a slender and weathered forty-seven, is diffident, reclusive, a homebody happiest away from the stage in his San Fernando Valley digs. Both are courteous and unaffected in a way that's more common among country performers than rock & rollers.

In the beginning, with their crisply thrumming guitars and vibrant harmonies, the Everlys conjured a world of shimmering innocence eternally on the verge of experience, of First Love forever. By now, between them, they have notched up five divorces and can testify to the chillier realities of love's long later seasons. When Don sings, in the superb title song he wrote for the new album, "He lost his mind today/She threw his clothes away/A love they thought would last/Just flew away," the new lyrics' import is perhaps as intimately pertinent to the Everlys' original audience, now deep in middle age, as were the dewier odes of their common, now-vanishing youth. In this new land of lengthening shadows, innocence is an ancient memory.

"It's hard to get fluffed up above love anymore," says Phil. "I've lived it. I try to avoid it. If I'm extremely fond of a woman, if I think I might really wind up walking down the aisle again . . . I go in another direction."

The women have come and gone; so have the drugs that disrupted their lives in the early Sixties. They've survived the years of endless gigs, the long, dead nights on the road, the claustrophobic togetherness. Through it all, the wheel of musical fad and fortune spun on, oblivious to their art, to the beauty of two voices chiming as one, clicking on through Beatlemania, acid rock; the disco of the wretched Seventies. And through it all, they remained the Everlys—until one bottomed-out night in Southern California, after which they were lost even to each other for ten blood-denying years. Now they're back, older, maybe wiser, trying once again to hold the craziness at bay and to sing their song for a new generation.

Isaac Donald Everly was born on February 1, 1937, in Brownie, Kentucky, the son of a coal miner, Ike Everly, and his wife, Margaret. Ike, who was himself a coal miner's son and was determined not to end his days in the mines, had picked up the rudiments of a hot thumb-picking guitar style (one he would later pass on to the celebrated Merle Travis) from a local black guitarist by the unlikely name of Arnold Schultz, and polished it after work and on weekends with his two musically inclined brothers, Chuck and Len. Like other white country musicians, from Bill Monroe (also tutored by Schultz) to Hank Williams, Ike Everly was inspired as much by black traditions as by the enveloping hillbilly idiom.

DON: Country's not the right word for what he played. It was more uptown, more honky-tonk. I'll tell you the right word for it: blues. White blues.

Before Don was two, the Everlys relocated to Chicago, to a teeming Italian neighborhood on Adams Street, where Ike obtained employment with the Works Progress Administration and by night set out with his guitar—now equipped with a De Armond electrical pickup and cabled to an amplifier—to play the workingmen's bars along Madison Street. It was in Chicago, on January 19, 1939, that Phillip Everly was born. Before long, Ike was appearing with a country group, the North Carolina Boys, on KXEL radio.

DON: He loved black music, too. We'd go down to Maxwell Street and listen to all the blues singers down there. Dad also had one of the first amplifiers on Madison Street. I remember he played this Greek-owned white club that catered to migrant workers from Kentucky, Tennessee, all those places. They had pool tables in the front and then the club in the back, with a little stage. And they would open the club door, put the amplifier in the doorway and fill the place up. One time around Halloween, I went down there with him, and we took along this little papier-mâché pumpkin I had, and he put a sign on it, and that was the kitty, where you'd put the money for requests. People would walk in off the street and just ask for whatever was on their mind, and Dad and the band would try to play it. I was just amazed, seeing my little Halloween pumpkin up there on the stage.

Dad wouldn't let me fool with his guitar much, because I'm left-handed, and I'd pick it up upside down. But I remember learning to sing "Paper Doll," the Mills Brothers song—this was during the war—and I remember my dad taking me down to one of those little record booths where you could make spoken letters to send home. He took me down there with his guitar, and we recorded that song: "I'm goin' to buy a paper doll that I can call my own. . . ." A little after that, we moved to Iowa.

It was the radio age, and broadcast musicians were in demand. Seasoned by his stint on KXEL—and budding as an amateur songwriter—Ike Everly decided to pursue his radio career in Iowa, first at a station in Waterloo, then at KMA, in Shenandoah. A welcoming notice in the KMA program guide in the fall of 1945 announced that Ike had written a "hillbilly lyric" called "Have You Forgot Your Joe?" It also took note of the Everly siblings: "When he grows up, Donald, 8, wants to be an entertainer like his dad so they can form a vocal and musical team. Phillip, 6, hasn't decided on his future yet."

Shortly thereafter, at a KMA Christmas party, it was learned that young Donald actually could sing. Soon he was given his own spot: 'The Little Donnie Show.'

DON: It was just a ten- or fifteen-minute show, part of another show, actually. I had a little theme song: "Free As a Little Bird As I Can Be." Dad had all these songs in the back of his mind—he was the instigator behind it all. He and a fellow on accordion and another on clarinet would back me up. I'd sing three or four songs, read a commercial and go home. I remember I had a picture taken, too, for promotion: "Sincerely, Little Donnie, KMA Radio." I don't know how long that lasted—long enough to make an impression on me. Then we started working as the Everly Family in the early mornings, and that lasted for a long time. We brought Phil in. He was too young to sing harmonies at first, so he just sang lead and I sang harmony until he learned how. Dad did it. He sat us down every day, and we would rehearse and practice all day long. We also played a local barn dance on Saturday nights, and occasionally we'd get up on the back of a flatbed or pickup truck with speakers and go play for various little harvest-jubilee-type things. We never made a lot of money at it, but enough to get through, to get by.

With the rise of records and television over the next ten years, live radio music began dying out. The family moved to Knoxville, Tennessee, where they had found another gig, but Ike Everly saw the handwriting on the wall. He held on to his musical dreams but began to accept the fact that they might have to be realized vicariously. As a guitarist, he much admired Chet Atkins, the Tennessee picker who had risen as an accompanist for the Carter Family to become a member of the Grand Ole Opry, on WSM, in Nashville—the ultimate live-radio gig—and, on the side, a hotshot session guitarist for RCA Records' C&W outpost in Music City. Ike had been writing admiring letters to Atkins, and in 1954, when the guitarist paid a visit to Knoxville, they had actually gotten to talk. Ike had played up the talents of his teenage sons, who were starting to write songs. Atkins expressed interest. Don and Phil visited Atkins and ran through their tunes, and Atkins became very interested. He placed Don's "Thou Shalt Not Steal" with Kitty Wells, a major country star since she'd scored with "It Wasn't God Who Made Honky Tonk Angels" two years earlier. In 1955, Anita Carter cut another of Don's songs, "Here We Are Again." Don Everly, still in high school, was suddenly showered with more money—from royalties—than either he or his parents had ever seen all in one piece.

Nineteen fifty-five was the year of "Maybellene" and "Bo Diddley," 'Rebel Without a Cause' and 'The Blackboard Jungle,' featuring Bill Haley's epochal "Rock Around the Clock." Times were changing fast, and the Everly Family was working what turned out to be its last gig, its radio show in Knoxville. By the time that petered out, Ike Everly, in need of a new trade, was studying to be a barber; Margaret was studying to be a beautician. Their son Don, a high-school senior with new dreams of his own, decided to pursue them.

DON: I was never really good at school, and here I had made a thousand-some dollars in royalties from my songs. So as soon as I graduated from high school, we packed the car up and high-tailed it for Nashville.

The Everlys and their mother moved into a little house in Madison, outside of Nashville, and Phil, who was sixteen, enrolled in the private Peabody Demonstration School. (Later, when the hits started coming, he would finish his education via a correspondence course.) Ike Everly joined the family a short while later but eventually had to move north to find work. Meanwhile, Don signed as a songwriter with the music-publishing company Hill and Range, from whom he obtained a much-needed advance, and the Everly Brothers began auditioning around town as an act. Don Law, an A&R man at the local Columbia Records branch, gave them a sliver of studio time at the end of somebody else's session, and the brothers, backed by country star Carl Smith's band, laid down four tunes in record time. Two of them, "Keep A'Lovin' Me" and "The Sun Keeps Shining," credited as joint compositions by Don and Phil, were released on a single on February 6, 1956, and promptly went nowhere. The Everlys continued auditioning. After being turned down by about ten execs, they finally encountered Wesley Rose.

A college-trained former oil-industry accountant, Rose was the president of Acuff-Rose, a C&W publishing company founded in the Forties by his father, Fred, and country star Roy Acuff. The firm had prospered publishing material by Acuff and Hank Williams, and Wesley Rose had been instrumental in promoting hit pop covers of Williams' tunes by such mainstream singers as Tony Bennett and Joni James. When Elvis Presley erupted out of Memphis and rock & roll began making inroads into the country market, Rose decided to get a piece of the new action. By the time the Everlys met him, he was busily putting together a stable of hot new songwriters—a group that would come to include John D. Loudermilk, Roy Orbison and Marty Robbins. Rose told the Everlys he would get them a recording contract if they would sign with him as songwriters. Don didn't mention his tie to Hill and Range, but he quietly slipped out of it, and soon the brothers signed with Acuff-Rose.

The record contract Rose had mentioned turned out to be with Archie Bleyer, proprietor of a New York City label called Cadence. Bleyer was seeking to branch out into the country field, and the Everlys eagerly ran off to record a demo tape for him.

PHIL: We were friendly with this one girl, and she arranged for us to make a tape in a little audition studio at this hotel. But we didn't have the money to do it, so after we finished, she had to talk the guy who owned the place into giving us the tape without paying. He said, "Yeah, go ahead." And then when we went downstairs, we found the police had towed away our car. So we had to go back in the studio, and the girl talked the guy into lending us enough money—which was twelve dollars—to get the car out of the pound.

Bleyer liked the Everlys' songs but also wanted them to try a tune that he and Rose had been holding for some time. It had been written by two of Acuff-Rose's most prized staffers—the team of Boudleaux Bryant, a Georgia songwriter who'd started out as a classical violinist, and his wife, Felice, a former Milwaukee elevator operator. The Bryants had crafted hits for Carl Smith and Eddy Arnold, but the song now proffered to the Everlys had been turned down by just about every other artist in Nashville. It was called "Bye Bye Love."

DON: Archie Bleyer and Wesley Rose and Boudleaux were there, and they sort of sang the song to us, a rendition of it, and we learned it right away—just like that. I had an arrangement of one of our songs, called "Give Me a Future," and it had this guitar riff in it. Archie said, "Why don't you put that to this," you know? And it worked.

"Bye Bye Love" was recorded and released in March 1957. It was the beginning of the Everly Sound, created in RCA's Studio B by guitarists Chet Atkins, Ray Edenton, Hank Garland (composer of "Sugarfoot Rag") and Don himself, pianist Floyd Cramer, drummer Buddy Harmon and bassist Floyd "Lightning" Chance, among others.

Having cut the record, the Everlys, still on a tight budget, signed up for a tent-show tour of Mississippi and Louisiana with bluegrass king Bill Monroe (whose "Blue Moon of Kentucky" had been transformed three years before by Presley) and Florida songwriter Mel Tillis, whose career as a singer was stalled in the shadow of Opry star Webb Pierce, who kept covering Tillis' songs out from under him and having hits with them. For the Everlys, touring with Monroe—whose own Opry connections assured maximum turnout—signified their arrival in the big time. They would perform straight country for the crowds that packed in under the canvas—Delmore Brothers hits, radio stuff—then be featured in a mini–rock & roll show (attendance fifty cents extra), during which they'd belt out such current rock and R&B hits as Gene Vincent's

"Be-Bop-A-Lula" and Ray Charles' "Leave My Woman Alone."

PHIL: It was so crazy. We all rode in Bill's limo—thirteen people in this big old Cadillac. The stage was just a wood platform, and the tent cut it in half, so "backstage" was actually outside, in the dark, and there was a slit where you would step through to go on.

DON: It was a wonderful experience, that tour with Bill Monroe. I got my first beer down there, saw the Gulf of Mexico for the first time. I remember in Gulfport, Mississippi, we arrived late at night and stayed in one of these wooden-shingled places right on the beach. I got up the next morning and walked down to the ocean—I had never seen it before in my life. A wonderful thing. We got ninety dollars a week apiece and we were in hog heaven.

The record came out while we were on the road down there. Then one day, Mel Tillis came up to us and said, "Hoss, I got some bad news for you. Webb Pierce has covered your song."

PHIL: Mel just looked down and shook his head, like, "It's all over boys, forget it." It was like, Jesus, such bad luck, you know?

DON: Disaster. I almost fainted. I called Archie Bleyer up in New York. I said, "Something terrible's happened." He said, "What?" I said, "Webb Pierce has covered our record." And he said—I'll never forget this—he said, "Webb who?" He didn't even know who Webb Pierce was! He said, "Forget about that—the record's hittin' pop." I didn't have a clue what he was talking about.

PHIL: Driving back to Nashville, when we got within radio distance, they had this pop station on in the car—and it was playing our record. That was, like, big juju. It really was.

DON: Then we became members of the Grand Ole Opry for about a year. We were hot then. The audience loved our music; we got an encore every time. There were no barriers between country and rock, you know? Nobody thought about it. It was the first time I felt appreciated as a musician.

Phil and I bought our first car then—a brand-new blue 98 Olds—and we drove it to Chicago. Dad was working up around there. They had just opened the first freeway to Chicago, and there was no speed limit on it yet, so we barreled up there at 100 miles an hour. That Olds would fly, boy. We picked Dad up, and we said, "You don't have to do this anymore. Come on back to Nashville."

In August 1957, the Everly Brothers cut their second single: the Bryants' "Wake Up Little Susie" (Boudleaux had dreamed it up on the way to a meeting with the brothers), backed with a song Don and Phil had written, the hauntingly beautiful "Maybe Tomorrow." Like its predecessor, it would quickly capture the number one spot on the country chart and also go top pop ("Bye Bye Love" had made it to number two). On September 6, the Everlys embarked on an eleven-week, seventy-eight-city tour—a classic rock & roll roadshow that also featured Chuck Berry, Fats Domino, the Crickets (fronted by the as-yet-unbilled Buddy Holly), the Drifters, LaVern Baker, Clyde Mc-Phatter, Eddie Cochran, Paul Anka and Frankie Lymon and the Teenagers, all backed by a hot black orchestra from New York led by Paul Williams. It was an unforgettable trek.

PHIL: We rode in buses—not like today's tour buses, with the microwaves and videocassette players—just regular buses. Paul Anka and Frankie Lymon used to sleep up in the luggage racks, you know? And LaVern Baker stretched out across the aisle with suitcases in between the seats. Now, LaVern was as sweet as anybody could be—she'd sew buttons on for us and things. But nobody would ever wake LaVern if she was sleeping, because she got . . . well, a little cranky. I remember once, we were crossing the border into Canada and everybody stepped over her real gingerly to get out at the customs station. The customs officer said she had to get out, too. He went on to wake her up, and she called him words—*combinations* of words—I'd never heard.

DON: We also played for Alan Freed at the Paramount Theatre in New York, and boy, it was hysterical. Five shows a day, and everybody was on them: Jerry Lee, Fats, Buddy. We got to be very close friends with Buddy Holly and the Crickets, because we all had the same kind of country-blues background. He wrote a couple of things for us—"Love's Made a Fool of You" might have been one of them, I forget now. We had a little problem with things like that, because we were signed to Acuff-Rose. But we did give Buddy "Raining in My Heart," which Boudleaux had written for us, but we didn't think was right. And we took him and the Crickets down to our clothes stores in New York, too: Phil's Men's Shop, Lefcourt's for shoes. We had just learned to dress a little sharper ourselves, and they noticed it, so we took them to all the places. If you look at pictures from back then, you'll see all of us in the same jackets—Ivy League, like. Same photographer, too: Bruno of Hollywood.

PHIL: They were good buddies, the Crickets. The

last time I was really with Buddy was at the Park Sheraton in New York—that was the hot hotel, where all the rock & rollers used to stay. Eddie Cochran was in town, and we were all up at his room there. Buddy was having a drink, and he asked me to make sure he got home that night, and I did. We used to do that kind of thing. I don't mean to make it sound like we were a bunch of drunks—that wasn't anywhere near the case. But once in a while you'd go out and tie one on, you know—always knowing what you were doing, though. In the Fifties, we were all pretty sane, compared to the Sixties. And New York was great then, too. I remember walking through Times Square with Chuck Berry, and him buying us our first cheesecake at Lindy's.

When Buddy died, I flew down to Lubbock for the funeral. Went down and sat with his parents and Maria Elena. I wasn't a pallbearer, though. I didn't want to see him put down in the earth.

DON: I didn't go. I wouldn't go. It just freaked me right out when Buddy died. I took to my bed. Quit riding planes for a while, too.

From their first hit on, the touring never stopped for the Everlys, because the hits kept coming: "All I Have to Do Is Dream" (with Chet Atkin's then-novel tremolo guitar chording), "Claudette" (donated by Roy Orbison between shows one night), "Bird Dog," "Devoted to You" and "Problems" in 1958 (the year they first went to Europe); "Take a Message to Mary," "Poor Jenny" and "('Til) I Kissed You" in 1959. By this time, Don was married, to Sue Ingraham, his first sweetheart, and Phil was going with Archie Bleyer's stepdaughter, Jackie Ertel, who would later become his first wife. But the farther away their touring took them, the more strain was put on their relationships.

DON: I wrote "('Til) I Kissed You" about a girl I met in Australia. Her name was Lilian, and she was very, very inspirational. I was married, but . . . I wrote the song about her on the way back home.

PHIL: The first time we flew to Australia was by prop, and it took thirty-two hours. You shaved twice, it was ridiculous. Eddie Cochran got laid on one of our Australian flights. Only person I ever knew that knocked a stewardess off. Got her in the back of the plane. The flight was so damn long, they got well acquainted.

"Let It Be Me," released in December 1959, reached the Top Ten, but the Everly Brothers were feeling artistically stifled at Cadence, so the duo left Archie Bleyer's label and signed with Warner Bros. Records. Their con-

tract was, at the time, the fattest ever offered a rock act: $1 million guaranteed, to be paid out over ten years. Their first Warners single was Don's "Cathy's Clown." It turned out to be their biggest hit.

DON: Part of the inspiration for "Cathy's Clown" was the *Grand Canyon* Suite: *domp-de-domp-de-da-da-da, boom-chaka-boom.* And then I had this girlfriend called Catherine. That was the formula for that one.

On signing with their new label, the Everlys—feeling increasingly out of place in the anti-rock environs of Nashville—moved to Los Angeles. There, the brothers briefly took acting lessons, but they turned down, in disgust, the rock-exploitation films they were subsequently offered. They busied themselves helping their pals (passing on "Let's Think About Living," a song written for them by Boudleaux, to singer Bob Luman, who had a 1960 hit with it) and launching side projects such as their own Calliope label (on which Don and arranger Neal Hefti scored in 1961 with an orchestral update of "Pomp and Circumstance"—credited to "Adrian Kimberly").

They soon became preoccupied with the deteriorating state of their relationship with Wesley Rose, who had become their manager in the Cadence years. They say that, in poring over their Warners contract, they were surprised to discover that Rose—who had helped them negotiate it, ostensibly in order to protect their songwriting interests—had written himself into the deal, complete with veto power over the songs they could release. As the conflict with Rose escalated, the Everlys found themselves cut off from the Bryants' material. (Rose, while acknowledging that his name was included in the contract, denies that he had veto power over the Everlys' releases but allows that they did part company with him in a disagreement over the suitability of the song "Temptation," which the brothers were determined to release.)

Fortunately, the Everlys had their own resources, and they proceeded conclusively to prove themselves superb songwriters, not mere puppets of the pop production line. Their last Top Ten hit for Cadence, "When Will I Be Loved," released in May 1960, after their departure from the label, had been written by Phil in a car parked outside an A&W root-beer stand. And their second Warner's single, another Top Ten entry, was Don's "So Sad (to Watch Good Love Go Bad)." Still, the brothers began casting about for outside tunes. "Walk Right Back," written by early Buddy Holly guitarist Sonny Curtis, and "Ebony Eyes," written by John D. Loudermilk, continued the string of hits into 1961.

It was around this time that Don, depleted by years of constant touring, became involved with Ritalin therapy—

essentially a program that mixed an amphetamine-like stimulant and vitamins to restore a patient's general perkiness. There was nothing illicit about Ritalin at the time—John Kennedy, then president, reportedly saw the same doctor for a similar treatment. But in short order, Don became addicted.

DON: People didn't understand drugs that well then. They didn't know what they were messing with. It wasn't against the law: I saw a picture of my doctor with the president, you know? But it got out of hand, naturally. It was a real disaster for a lot of people, and it was a disaster for me. Ritalin made you feel energized. You could stay up for days. It just got me strung out. I got so far out there, I didn't know what I was doing.

Don's first wife divorced him in 1961, by which time he was consorting with Venetia Stevenson, a model he'd met on the Ed Sullivan TV show. In 1962, to avoid the draft, the Everlys enlisted together in the Marine Corps reserves, doing six months with a howitzer unit at Camp Pendleton. Don emerged from this drugless stint considerably strengthened. He married Venetia, a new beginning. But soon he was back on Ritalin. Phil, meanwhile, had been briefly involved with a different program of drug treatments. And, increasingly, the brothers were at each other's throats.

PHIL: What we needed was to take a long vacation, to get off the merry-go-round. There were too many people making too much money off us, keeping us going. Things were too confused. We should have taken a long rest. But in those days we couldn't. The tensions between Don and I . . . well, we're just a family that is like that, I guess. Everything that was happening then contributed to it. But you could just as easily say that the tension between us existed from day one, from birth. And will go on forever.

The Everlys' 1962 hits, "Crying in the Rain," a Brill Building song written by Carole King and Howard Greenfield, and "That's Old Fashioned (That's the Way Love Should Be)," were to be their last two to reach the Top Ten. Don was by then obsessed with Ritalin—and, in his growing paranoia, feeling smothered as an individual artist within that fading entity called the Everly Brothers. One crazed day in a London hotel room, during a fall tour of England, he attempted to kill himself by taking an overdose of barbiturates. Venetia got him to a hospital, where his stomach was pumped. Released, he returned to his hotel and tried again, gulping more pills. This time, his rescuers put him on a plane back to the States, where he was committed to the mental ward of a New York City hospital and given electroshock therapy.

DON: They say shock therapy is good for some things, but it didn't do me any good. It was a pretty primitive treatment at the time—once they gave it to you, you couldn't remember how long you'd been there. It knocked me back for a long time. I thought I'd never write again.

With the help of a psychiatrist, Don slowly conquered his addiction to Ritalin over the ensuing months. But it was too late to halt the slide of the Everlys' career. They only made the Top Forty two more times: with "Gone, Gone, Gone" in 1964 and "Bowling Green" in 1967. Suddenly, all in a rush, it seemed, there was Beatlemania, the British Invasion, Vietnam, psychedelia, hippies, Nixon. The new youth music was outspoken, engaged, acknowledged as art. There was no place in it for the sweet sound of the Everly Brothers. They didn't starve—"There was always some place in the world where we were hot," says Phil—but they did play Las Vegas a lot. Don began to feel shut out of the new scene.

DON: When Phil and I started out, everyone hated rock & roll. The record companies didn't like it at all—felt it was an unnecessary evil. And the press: interviewers were always older than us, and they let you know they didn't like your music, they were just doing the interview because it was their job. Then along came the Sixties, and everyone suddenly got real young, and if you were over thirty, they didn't trust you.

The Sixties, boy. I remember meeting Jimi Hendrix one night at the Scene, Steve Paul's club in New York. I was working the Latin Quarter at the time, right? And I had never been to Greenwich Village before, so Steve and Jimi took me on a tour. Here we were, Steve wearing a bathrobe, the three of us smoking a joint in the back seat of his limo. I was still worried about getting busted, but they didn't seem to be. We went to the Bitter End, and there was Joni Mitchell, whom I had already fallen in love with via records. My life changed. I wanted to play these places, too. I wanted to be a part of this music scene. I became friends with Jimi, liked him a lot. He invited me to sessions, even came around to the Latin Quarter to see me, can you believe it?

It was all very strange. I took LSD—the best, Owsley's orange sunshine—but I was wearing tuxedos at the same time. We'd be playing a country show one night, then the Fillmore West the next, with the Sons of Champlin or somebody. Played the Bitter End, too, finally. Met Bob Dylan there one night. We were looking for songs, and he was writing "Lay Lady Lay" at the time. He sang parts of it, and we weren't quite sure whether he was offering it to us or not. It was one of those awestruck moments. We wound up cutting the song about fifteen years later.

We played Saigon once, a benefit for the Tan Son Nhut orphanage. That night we sat on the roof of this house and watched them napalming stuff outside the city. We played a lot of hospitals in the Philippines, too, full of Vietnam casualties. That's when it began to dawn on me that something was dreadfully wrong with that war. I became very political in my mind, totally anti-Nixon, but there didn't seem to be much I could do about it. We were working nine, ten months out of the year; we were really out of touch with what was going on in the world.

PHIL: The Sixties weren't my cup of tea. I never bought that philosophy that, you know, we're all brothers and that'll solve everything. And I never believed that music dictated the times. I always thought it reflected them. We were against the grain in that period, and there was a lot of confusion about our direction. Maybe we were just losing the freshness of it all, losing interest.

Adrift in the Sixties, the Everlys released, among other records, an album of country hits, two albums of rock oldies, a Merseyish LP called 'Two Yanks in England' (which featured a stirring version of Manfred Mann's "Pretty Flamingo") and, in 1968, the extraordinary 'Roots,' a harbinger of a country-rock explosion to come. In 1970, there was a live LP recorded at the Grand Hotel in Anaheim. That summer, they hosted a ten-week variety series on ABC, replacing 'The Johnny Cash Show.' The series was loaded with hot guest stars—Stevie Wonder, Linda Ronstadt, Ike and Tina Turner, even their dad, harmonizing with his sons—but when it ended in September, the network didn't renew it. In December came the release of 'Don Everly,' the first solo album by one of the brothers. Perhaps reflecting Don's state of mind at that point, it was a somewhat woozy effort, recorded with the assistance of much booze and reefer.

By 1971, Phil's first and Don's second marriages had ended. Phil took a new wife, Patricia Mickey; Don met his third-wife-to-be, Karen Prettyman, the following year. In June 1973, Phil released his first solo album, 'Star Spangled Springer,' with his wife joining in on two songs.

The split came one month later—inevitable but nonetheless ugly. Don gave Phil two weeks' notice: the Everly Brothers' show at the John Wayne Theatre at Knott's Berry Farm near Los Angeles on July 14 would be their last. "It's over," he told a reporter on the eve of the gig. "I'm tired of being an Everly Brother." The next night, Don got so drunk that a Knott's manager stopped the show midway through the second of three scheduled sets. Phil, furious, stormed offstage, smashing his guitar to the floor before disappearing. Don carried on alone for the third set. When a spectator asked, "Where's Phil?" he replied, "The Everly Brothers died ten years ago."

DON: It was a flip statement. I was half in the bag that evening—the only time I've ever been drunk onstage in my life. I knew it was the last night, and on the way out I drank some tequila, drank some champagne—started celebrating the demise. It was really a funeral. People thought that night was just some brouhaha between Phil and me. They didn't realize we had been working our *buns* off for *years*. We had never been *anywhere* without working, had never known any freedom. We were just strapped together like a team of horses. It's funny—the press hadn't paid any attention to us in ten years, but they jumped on that. It was one of the saddest days of my life.

PHIL: It was silly, you know? But Donald had decided. It was a dark day.

For the next ten years, apart from seeing each other at their father's funeral in 1975, the Everlys basically didn't speak. Don eventually moved back to Nashville, went fishing, practiced his pasta cookery, joined Les Amis du Vin and generally kicked back. He and his mother didn't speak much (she recently sued him to acquire full title to a house Don partially owned), but otherwise the Nashville years were a time of healing; Don had a new, stabilizing romantic relationship, with a woman named Diane Craig. By 1983 he was ready to consider the prospect of a rapprochement with Phil, who, like Don, had continued to release solo LPs, with only moderate success. Their reunion concerts in London, filmed for a TV special and recorded for a double album, were hailed as a triumph of undimmed talent. Dave Edmunds, the British guitarist and rock scholar, was chosen to produce their comeback album. Searching for some hit-worthy material, and realizing that the Beatles had been major Everly Brothers fans in their youth, Edmunds rang up Paul McCartney to ask for a song.

DON: Dave said it was the hardest phone call he ever made, because McCartney is always being asked for something. Paul said if he could come up with anything, he'd give a call. Dave forgot about it, but about six weeks later the phone rang and it was McCartney. He said, "I think I've got one."

McCartney's contribution, "On the Wings of a Nightingale," was the centerpiece of the ensuing album, 'EB '84.' The Everlys set off on a world tour and were received with great enthusiasm. With the release of 'Born Yesterday,' it looks like the brothers are back for good. In an era of rampant gimmickry, they sound as fresh and up-to-date as ever. There are still minor problems, such as record-company-selected album covers so tackily unimaginative that some retailers have unthinkingly filed their recent LPs in the reissue bins. And on the domestic front, while both brothers dote on their children (Phil's two sons, Don's son and three daughters—one of whom, under the professional name Penelope, is a high-fashion model with the Wilhelmina agency in New York), complications persist for the ever-restless elder brother.

DON: My personal life now is sort of strange. I really don't know what to say about it, hardly. I guess I'm with a girl called Victoria right now—but I'm still with Diane, too. I don't know how to describe this situation. You get your career straightened out, and all of a sudden your personal life goes.

But he is an artist, that's the main thing. And the Everly Brothers are an American institution, oblivious to musical fads and fashion.

DON: We just open our mouths and we sing. I figure we've got another few years at that. We're not going to work ourselves into a frenzy this time . . . but we're gonna take it as far as we can.

15

Paul McCartney

INTERVIEWED BY KURT LODER (1986)

By the time I talked to Paul McCartney, John Lennon had been dead nearly six years. But his memory glowed brighter than ever, while McCartney's artistic stock had dropped precipitously. After all those post-Fab solo albums filled with silly love songs, he had finally come to seem . . . well, kind of silly. 'Press to Play,' the album whose imminent release occasioned our encounter, would soon become one of his biggest bombs.

I think one can assume that this was a confounding state of affairs for a man as vastly talented as McCartney. In the Sixties, with the Beatles, he had redefined the role of the electric bass in pop music, and his virtuosity on that instrument remained breathtaking. He was a fluid and sophisticated crafter of songs, as well, and one of rock's sweetest singers. (A pretty great screamer, too.) If he had never written another note, his place in pop history would have been spacious and assured.

But over the nineteen years since the breakup of the Beatles, McCartney and his music had settled into a cozy domestic torpor, while Lennon, in death, remained the ageless upstart. And this situation, as it turned out, was very much on McCartney's mind when we met.

After a quarter century of Q&A, McCartney is a total interview pro, elaborately adept at deflecting any question that threatens to discomfit. His charm is a bit too studied to be entirely credible, but his humor is real, as is his talent. And his status as a living legend remains uncontested.

—K. L.

I T IS Monday in London, two days before the royal wedding, and Soho Square is filled with flowers, sunshine and fresh-faced young tourists. Some loll on the grass, sharing joints. Others peer up expectantly at the etched-glass windows of an art-deco-style town house across the street, where, in an airy third-floor office, Paul McCartney presides over the bustling affairs of MPL Communications, the company that manages the professional projects of the singer and his wife, Linda.

McCartney is in from his country home in Sussex—where he has a brand-new, state-of-the-art recording studio—to promote his latest album *Press to Play*. It is the fifteenth album he has released since he announced the breakup of the Beatles back in 1970, and the years are beginning to tell: his hair is mostly gray these days. But he's as buoyant as ever, bubbling with enthusiasm. After eight years of largely lackadaisical releases on Columbia, he is back with Capitol—the Beatles' old label—and he seems serious about rehabilitating his somewhat tattered artistic reputation.

Press to Play features some good new songs and a tough new pop sound, courtesy of Hugh Padgham, who co-produced it. Linda McCartney's background vocals are the only aural remnant of Paul's erstwhile band Wings; this time out he's backed by guitarists Eric Stewart and Carlos Alomar, drummer Rick Marrotta and such drop-in rock-star pals as Pete Townshend and Phil Collins. Pouring tea from a china pot, McCartney talks up his new tunes (one song, "However Absurd," is a stream-of-consciousness stew of non sequiturs lifted from the works of such poets as W.H. Auden) and his ambitious plans for the future. But he cannot ignore his celebrated past and the persistent tug of its emotional undertow. Will he ever again be seen in as sweet a light as that which illuminated the Beatles twenty years ago? The subject seems open for discussion. Paulie passes the cream.

*O*n *your new album, there's an almost punkish song called "Angry." That's not an attitude usually associated with Paul McCartney. What are you angry about?*

Well, the same things a lot of us are angry about.

Traffic jams, stuff like that?

Well, there's that—the day-to-day piss-offs. But I was thinking more about, um, British trade unions withdrawing coal when there's old ladies dying, and we kind of just go, "Yeah, well, the union's got a right." And Britain's attitude toward apartheid at the moment, which is just so crazy. I mean, *still,* after all those years of Martin Luther King and everything, they're *still* buggerin' around with black and white. It's so *insane.* Couldn't they just wise up? But there's Maggie saying, "We don't need to do sanctions," while everybody else—all the civil-rights groups—are saying, "But you *do.*"

Given such views, it's ironic that a London tabloid, 'The Sun,' recently questioned whether you were a racist after hearing bootleg Beatles outtakes from the 'Let It Be' sessions that feature you referring to Pakistanis—unflatteringly, it seems—in a rendition of "Get Back."

Sensational journalism—*The Sun* is not a highly reputable newspaper. What this thing is, I think, is that when we were doing *Let It Be,* there were a couple of verses to "Get Back" which were actually not racist at all—they were *anti*-racist. There were a lot of stories in the newspapers then about Pakistanis crowding out flats—you know, living sixteen to a room or whatever. So in one of the verses of "Get Back," which we were making up on the set of *Let It Be,* one of the outtakes has something about "too many Pakistanis living in a council flat"—that's the line. Which to me was actually talking out *against* overcrowding for Pakistanis. *The Sun* wishes to see it as a racist remark. But I'll tell you, if there was any group that was not racist, it was the Beatles. I mean, all our favorite people were always black. We were kind of the first people to open international eyes, in a way, to Motown. Whenever we came to the States, they'd say, "Who's your favorite artists?" And we'd say, "Well, they're mainly black, and American—Motown, man. It's all there—you've got it all." I don't think the Beatles ever had much of a hang-up with that.

What about sensationalism in rock & roll—the alleged surfeit of sex and violence that many of the music's critics seem to find these days. Do you worry that your children are being influenced by this sort of thing?

No. I think they're into pretty good music, actually—Simple Minds, Dire Straits, Tears for Fears, stuff like that. I've never tried to favor anything, 'cause I figure I wouldn't have liked my dad to sort of *tell* me to like Elvis, you know? It would have put me off it.

Are you familiar with the PMRC in the States—the group of Washington wives who want ratings for pop records?

Oh, the lyrics thing. Uh . . . I kind of see their point, you know? I think there is a point, like with newspapers, where you start to want to censor stuff. I don't *really* think you ought to, but . . . Let's say a really great group emerged—and you tend to think they'd be heavy metal, although that's probably "heavy metallist" to say [*laughs*]—and say they were advocating, I don't know, killing, Satanism. And they came out with a really great album and turned a lot of people on to Satanism. There's got to be a point where you're gonna say, "Look, guys, we're all for artistic freedom, but maybe we just don't want *de debbil* trampling across America at the moment." I mean, what would you do? I don't know. I think censorship's very dangerous. . . .

But things are getting farther and farther out. I saw a show the other night on television which . . . I was not *offended* by—I mean, it doesn't really bug me—but it made me start to wonder whether people were going slightly far out. It was a gay thing, and a couple of guys were really gettin' to it. Now, I have no objection to anyone getting their rocks off in *any* way they want. But maybe public telly isn't the forum for it. And video nasties—*I Drill Your Brain, I Spit on Your Grave.* I haven't seen those movies myself—I'm gettin' to be an old fruit, you know?—but how far ought they to let that go? I think, in a way, that it doesn't really hurt to have someone keepin' an eye on all this stuff. It's not a bad thing to have watchdog groups; you just mustn't let them get too much power.

In a more positive vein, you've actively supported other causes you believe in, such as Live Aid.

I'm not a great joiner, but I do support a lot of things. I've supported Amnesty International for a while, and of course Live Aid, obviously, was—*is*—a great thing.

Are you troubled by reports that the money Live Aid raised for Ethiopia ultimately benefits that country's military regime and not the starving people?

Well, before Live Aid, there was going to be another concert of that sort, and Dave Gilmour and myself were going to get involved in it. Then a neighbor of mine, David Astor, who was quite big in Amnesty at the time, told me that his son was in Eritrea at that moment and that there was very worrying news coming out. He said, "If you do charity, it's going to go straight to the military. They say, 'Thank you very much for helping our country. *We're* not buying food for our people—we're spending our money on guns.' " So, at the time of Live Aid, I did a little bit of work on that, checked it out—me, Astor, Pete Townshend, a few other people. And we decided that Bob Geldof had enough good people on the case. We wanted to do *something,* even if there was some risk—I mean, we were seeing people on television just *dying* in front of the camera.

So I was glad to have done Live Aid. Someone's always gonna bitch. There's always gonna be a bad side to everything you do. When I did "Ebony and Ivory" with Stevie Wonder—which was a perfectly harmless attempt at pinpointing the need for racial harmony—some people said, "Oh, it's just pap." Well—*sez you,* you know? I mean, tough. The point

is, there *is* some kind of black-and-white problem—certainly in South Africa, probably less now in the States, but there's still tension, it still erupts. You can't deny that. I just wanted to do something good, to do a song that I thought might take a little tension out of the situation. And there were a few great things I got off it. Like, there's a great black sax player in Los Angeles, Ernie Watts. I think he's got a white wife, and he came up to me at a session we did, and he said, "Oh, man, thanks for that song." And that made it all worthwhile for me, you know—just if one person's situation was alleviated to the tiniest degree. I don't care what *all* the critics say then; that's really enough. Ernie Watts plays a hell of a lot better than any critic I ever heard.

But do you think there's any merit to the frequent charge that your post-Beatles music has gotten too soft?

Yeah, I'm sure it's true. You can't get it right all the time. If there's been a fault with my stuff, I think some of it was unfinished. Looking back on some of it now, I think, "You didn't finish the bloody thing." So . . . yeah, I might have been a bit soft, and some of it might have been a bit unfinished. And sometimes a critic will say, "That's really lousy"—and I'll tend to agree with him: "He's right, it's not very good, that one." I know there are quite a few tracks on my albums that I just don't like now. Like "Bip Bop," off *Wild Life*—oh, God, I can't listen to it; it just *goes nowhere.* But occasionally a good one comes along, and occasionally there's a little wave on the little millpond, and that makes it all worthwhile.

Critics may be pleased by the harder pop sound of 'Press to Play.' Some of the tracks have an almost experimental tilt to them.

The funny thing is, there was a time when *I* was the avant-garde one in the Beatles—around the time of *Sgt. Pepper,* 'cause that album was largely my influence. I thought of the idea, the concept of pretending we were another group. I was trying to get everyone in the group to be sort of farther out, and do this far-out album. John was living out in Weybridge with his wife and child at the time, and *I* was bein' the bachelor in London—living on my own, going to the theater, checking out the *International Times,* Allen Ginsberg. It was a pretty rich period. I used to make 8-mm home movies and show them one frame at a time—*flick, flick, flick*—which made them last about an hour, when they only should have been ten minutes, you know? I remember showing them to Antonioni—I think he was in town filming *Blow-Up*—and Keith Richards. We had some nice evenings—quite *stoned* evenings, I must admit—just watching these movies. I still have them. And I was into Stockhausen, and I used to make a lot of home tape loops and just send them to friends for, like, a buzz. I remember sayin' to John once, "I'm gonna do an album of this and call it *Paul McCartney Goes Too Far.*" And he said, "Yeah, you've gotta do it, man!" So *I* was the one who introduced John, originally, to a lot of that stuff. In fact, not many people know this, but Yoko came to my house before she met John. There was a charity thing—it was rather avant-garde, something to do with John Cage or something—and she wanted lyrics, manuscripts. I hate to tell you, but I really didn't want to give her any of my lyrics—you know, selfish, or whatever, but I just didn't want to do it. So I said, "But there's a friend of mine who might want to help—my mate, John."

So you were the catalyst for John and Yoko's relationship?

Well, I don't know that. But I kind of put her on to John, and then they really hit it off—it was like a *wild fire,* you know? John was certainly in love. Um . . . a little *insecurely* in love, 'cause he warned me off Yoko—sort of said, "Look, no, no." 'Cause he knew I was a bit of a lady's man—I liked the girls, no doubt about that. And I said, "Yeah, okay." I mean, I wasn't *about to,* anyway, but he didn't know that.

You became involved with Linda Eastman instead. Has it been difficult to sustain such a controversial union over the last sixteen years?

Well, we've been up, we've been down, we've been in love, we've been out of love—we've been every which way, you know? It's certainly not been as idyllic as it looks on the surface. It's a *real marriage,* believe me—as real as any other marriage. The bottom line is that we love each other, and what's more, we *like* each other. It sounds corny, but what else can I say?

Thinking about you and Linda, and John and Yoko, inevitably recalls the end of the Beatles. After all this time, the cause of the group's breakup still seems murky. What really happened?

The actual story in my mind is that it was all getting a bit sticky during the White Album. And *Let It Be* was very sticky—George left the group then, and so did Ringo, but we managed to patch that back up. The dates are all purple haze to me, but at some point—after *Let It Be* was finished, and about the time I was wanting to put the *McCartney* album out—we had a meeting at the Apple office, and it was like "Look, something's wrong, and we've got to sort it out." I had my suggestion: I said, "What I think we ought to do is get back as a band—get back as the

little unit we always were. I think we ought to hit small clubs and do a little tour." I just wanted to *learn* to be a band together again, 'cause we'd become a business group. We'd become *businessmen.* So that was my big suggestion. And John looked me in the eye and he said, "I think you're daft. In fact, I wasn't gonna tell you . . . but I'm leavin' the group." To my recollection, those were his exact words. And our jaws dropped. And then he went on to explain that it was rather a good feelin' to get it off his chest—a bit like when he told his wife about a divorce, that he'd had a sort of feeling of relief. Which was very nice for him, but we didn't get much of a good feeling.

At first we agreed not to announce it. But after three or four months, I got more and more guilty about people saying, "How's the group going?" when we sort of knew it was probably split up. So I did a kind of dumb move in the end, and when I look back on it, it was really . . . it looks very hard and cold. But I was releasing the *McCartney* album, and I didn't really want to do much press for it; so I told a guy from the office to do me a list of questions and I'll write the answers and we'll print it up as a pamphlet and just stick it in with the press copies of the album. The questions were quite pointed, and it ended up being like me announcing that the Beatles had broken up. John got quite mad about that, apparently—this is one of the things he said really hurt him and cut him to the quick. Personally, I don't think it was such a bad thing to announce to the world after *four months* that we'd broken up. It had to come out sometime. I think maybe the manner of doing it I regret now—I wish it had been a little kinder, or with the others' approval. But I felt it was time.

Weren't the others also upset that your album, 'McCartney', was released a month before 'Let It Be'?

Yeah, I think John thought I was using this press release for publicity—as I suppose, in a way, I was. So it all looked very weird, and it ruffled a few feathers. The good thing about it was that we all had to finally own up to the fact that we'd broken up three or four months before. We'd been ringing each other quite constantly, sort of saying, "Let's get it back together again." And I think me, George and Ringo *did* want to save things. But I think John was, at that point, too heavily into his new life—which you can't blame him for. He'd always wanted to be a little more avant-garde, and so living in New York, and Yoko's influence, obviously helped him do that. It was very exciting for him on a lot of levels. So it became clear about that time that the group wasn't gonna get back together. And that was it.

Did it sadden you to see Lennon subsequently drift off into heroin addiction?

Yeah, I really didn't like that. Unfortunately, he was driftin' away from *us* at that point, so none of us actually *knew*. He never told us; we heard rumors, and we were very sad. But he'd embarked on a new course, which really involved anything and everything. Because John was that kind of a guy—he wanted to live his life to the full as he saw it. He would often say things like, "If you find yourself at the edge of a cliff and you wonder whether you should jump off or not—try jumping." And I am afraid I would always say, "No, man, I'm not gonna jump off that cliff; I don't care how good it is." I remember we had dinner one night—just a friendly dinner, just bein' mates—and I remember John saying he was thinking of having this trepanning thing done: drilling a hole in the skull. The Romans or the Greeks or somebody used to do it, so that gave it a validity in John's mind, I think. And he said, "Would you be up for that? Do you fancy doin' that? We could go and get it done." I said, "Why?" He said, "It relieves the pressure on your brain." I said, "Look, *you* go try it, and if it's great, you tell me, and maybe I'll do it."

That was the kind of stuff that was floatin' around then. I just feel very lucky to have said no to those things. 'Cause at the time, I felt *bad* about sayin' no. I thought, "Oh, here I go again, look at me, unadventurous, I'm always the one, they're gonna make such fun of me." I mean, I got such pressure when I wouldn't take acid the first time. I got a *lot* of pressure there.

Was it like the group sitting around all dropping acid, and you . . .

Yeah. They were sayin', "What's wrong with him?" *Now,* looking back on it, I think, *Jesus,* I must have had some courage to actually resist that peer pressure. But at the time, I felt really goody-goody, you know: "Hey, Mr. Clean, squeaky clean," you know? It was like "Aw, come on, fellas, I'm not *really* squeaky clean, but, you know, acid is maybe gonna do our heads in."

But you eventually did try LSD.

Yeah, finally. In actual fact, it was because John had done it by mistake one evening. We turned up for a session at Abbey Road, and he thought he'd taken a pep pill—speed, or whatever—to sort of wake him up for the evening, but it turned out to be acid. He had a little pillbox, and he'd taken the wrong pill. This was around the time of *Sgt. Pepper.* Well, we didn't get a lot done that night. John came over and said, "Jeez, I'm trippin'." And we all went, "Ahhh . . . okay. Keep cool, lad. Now, is this a good place to be tripping?"

He said, "No, not really." Okay. George Martin didn't know. We said, "George, John's not feeling too well"—so George took him *up on the roof!* We said, "Maybe that's not a good idea, George." I said, "Tell you what, I'll take him home." So I took him home, and that was my first trip, that night, because I figured, you know, I can't leave the guy on his own—he was all *aowooommm. . . .*

Your apparent preference for marijuana has made many headlines over the years. Do you still indulge?

I don't talk about stuff like that no more—it's too crazy. Where I *was* lucky was with my avoidance of heroin. I went through most of the other stuff, and I had a friend in the Sixties who was getting into heroin. He said to me, "Man, the thing about heroin is that it's okay as long as you've got the money to support the habit—there's no problem as long as you can pay. And you're not likely to have a problem with that, so it's cool." But something in my brain went *djing!*—a little light went on—and I said, "No, this is wrong." So I was very lucky. I said, "No thanks," and avoided that scene. And I thank God that I did, because a lot of my friends *didn't,* and they went through some *horror zones,* you know? Some of them didn't come out of it.

It's sobering to realize that the recreational drug taking of the Sixties, which seemed so lighthearted, has resulted in the wall-to-wall drug scene of today—which is anything but.

I think a lot of it's been caused by people's ignorance of the drug scene—like lumping marijuana with heroin, saying, "Well, one leads to the other." I always say to them, "Well, booze leads to it just as easily, and cigarettes lead to booze, and so on. It all leads to each other." I personally think that if the older generation had been more sensible, instead of busting people and using scare tactics . . .

Like the scare stories about cocaine in the States recently.

I'm not sure about coke. I'm not into that. Again, I was lucky, because I *was* into that just before the entire record industry got into it. I was into it at the time of *Sgt. Pepper,* actually. And the guys in the group were a bit, kind of, "Hey, wait a minute, that's a little heavier than we've been getting into." And I was doing the traditional coke thing—"No problem, man, it's just a little toot, no problem." It was all very lightweight, really. But I remember one evening I went down to a club, and somebody was passin' coke around, and I was feelin' so great, and I came back from the toilet—and suddenly I just got *the plunge,* you know? The *drop.* And somebody said, "Have some more. Come on, get back up again." I said, "No, man, this isn't gonna work." I mean, anything with that big a downside . . . Anyway, I could never stand that feelin' at the back of the throat—it was like you were chokin', you know? So I knocked that on the head. I just thought, "This is not fun."

I must say, since we're gettin' into drugs—and at the risk of sounding goody-goody again—that I do personally feel, from this perspective, today, that my favorite thing is to be clean and straight. I think you can enjoy your life better that way. I mean, when we were very straight in the Beatles, we did music that was pretty much as far out as the stuff we did later. Maybe it wasn't *as* far out, but actually, beneath the surface, it was every bit as meaningful.

On a more trivial but similarly ancient note, a new biography of you claims that Paul McCartney, the world's most famous left-handed bassist, is actually right-handed. True?

No, I'm quite definitely left-handed. When I first got a guitar, I couldn't understand what was wrong with it, 'cause I really couldn't get it together. I felt so unrhythmic—so *white,* you know? Suddenly I was, like, whiter than I'd ever been. I just had no rhythm in my hands. Then I saw a picture of Slim Whitman —now *there's* a name to conjure with—and he had his guitar the wrong way round. He was the first lefty I'd ever seen, and I said, "Hey, shit, that's it: turn the guitar upside down." After that, my strumming hand got a little blacker again.

Did you feel similarly reassured when Jimi Hendrix turned up on the London scene?

Yeah, Jimi was brilliant. I knew him and loved him. The first time I saw him was down at a club—I think it was the Bag o' Nails—and I was just completely blown away. I'd never seen anyone turn their amp up that high. He'd wind up a hundred-watt Marshall and hit his guitar, and it'd go *beyowww-whoot-rowww!* Fantastic! Townshend and Eric Clapton were in the audience, and me—all checking Jimi out—and our jaws were just droppin'. He had such expertise—he really knew his way around a guitar. And he was a very sweet guy, very quietly spoken, very enthusiastic. The greatest compliment he ever paid me was when the Beatles did *Sgt. Pepper.* The album was released on a Friday night, and on Sunday Jimi played a little gig that Brian Epstein used to run called the Savile Theatre—and he opened with "Sgt. Pepper's Lonely Hearts Club Band": *boom-boom-bahhhm, boom-boom-bahhhm!* Oh, man, that was so good. I mean, it had only been out for two days!

So, yeah, I have very fond memories of Jimi. I mean,

Van Halen's great—I love Eddie Van Halen—but I still think Jimi was the best.

After John Lennon conquered his drug problem, did the two of you finally patch up your personal relationship?

We were submerged in business troubles at the time. There was incredible bitterness. At one point, to get some peace in the camp, I told my lawyers I wanted to give John an indemnity he had been seeking against a certain clause in one of the Apple contracts. I said, "Someone's gotta make the first move. I'd love to be the voice of reason here." I happened to be on my way to the Caribbean, so, passing through New York, I rang John up. But there was so much suspicion, even though I came bearing the olive branch. I said, "Hey, I'd like to see you." He said, "What for? What do you *really* want?" It was very difficult. Finally . . . he had a great line for me: He said, "You're all pizza and fairy tales." He'd become sort of Americanized by then, so the best insult I could think of was to say, "Oh, fuck off, Kojak," and slam the phone down. "Pizza and fairy tales"—I almost made that an album title.

That was about the strength of our relationship then—very, very bitter—and we didn't get over that for a long, long time. But thank God, at the very end, we suddenly realized that all we had to do was not mention Apple if we phoned each other. We could talk about the kids, talk about his cats, talk about writin' songs—the one paramount thing was not to mention Apple. So then the last couple of phone calls we had were getting very nice. I remember once he said to me, "Do they play me against you like they play you against me?" Because there were always people in the background pitting us against each other. And I said, "Yeah, they do. They sure do." That was a couple of months before he . . . it's still weird even to say, "before he died." I still can't come to terms with that. I still don't believe it. It's like, you know, those dreams you have, where he's still alive; then you wake up and . . . "Oh."

It was all so tragic. But I do feel thankful that the last few years of his life were very happy, from what I can gather. He was always a very warm guy, John. His bluff was all on the surface. He used to take his glasses down—those granny glasses—take 'em down and say, "It's only me." They were like a wall, you know? A shield. Those are the moments I treasure. I suppose we hurt each other and stuff, but I keep looking at all the evidence of how I hurt him, and I don't know—it doesn't seem quite as bad as I think he was making it.

I just read about this thing that's going on sale at

Sotheby's—this Apple booklet with John's comments in the margins in his own handwriting. It is *so* bitter. Like, there's a picture of Paul and Linda's wedding—and John's crossed out "wedding" and written in "funeral." I think it starts to tell there. Another caption says, "Paul goes to Hollywood"—and then he's apparently written in the margin, "To cut Yoko and John out of the film." He often thought that we were tryin' to cut Yoko out of things, to cut her out of *Let It Be*. I suppose we were, in some degree; because she wasn't in the Beatles, and it was a Beatles film, and it wasn't absolutely necessary to have long footage of her in there. She certainly *was in there,* but obviously they felt she should be in there a little more. I bent over backward trying to see John's point of view. I still bend over backward trying to not malign him.

You do seem to have been cast as the heavy in the Beatles' breakup.

It isn't pleasant. A lot of the accusations John made in public were slightly wild. I mean . . . maybe we should've taken to Yoko a little better. I often *do* feel not too clever about not taking to her, because we didn't get on too well. She was very *different* from anything we'd encountered. A lot of people still find her a little difficult to take. I figure, well, he loved her, so it's nothin' to do with me—I should respect her through him. And I felt that I tried to do that. But we were being so set against each other that his unreasonable bitterness was almost inevitable, I think. It's such a pity he felt that way. But the bottom line is we loved each other. And I'm glad to be getting back to some semblance of sanity with George and Ringo now—we can meet and hug and say we love each other, you know?

Might the three of you ever record together again?

I don't know. I'd like to. But it's a touchy affair. I think all of us, rather than get the world's press on our backs, would rather just play that aspect down for now. But I'd like to. And I know George and I have talked once or twice about maybe just plonking a couple of acoustics together. So that whole scene is warming up a bit, which is nice. It's such a breath of fresh air—and it's been a long time coming, you know? So I see hope for the future in that direction. But I don't

want to rush it. I don't want to put anyone off. I'll just play it by ear. Just let it happen.

We were talking about doing a Beatles movie a couple of years ago: slinging in home movies and old outtakes, adding narration—the definitive Beatles story. We were going to call it *The Long and Winding Road.* We asked Dick Lester to direct it, but he said no one would be interested. Two months later, *The Compleat Beatles* came out on video—and it's still in the video charts. So Dick was wrong: There's quite a big market. And we have all the *Let It Be* outtakes. And I have a beautiful piece of footage from that Dezo Hoffmann photo session with the Beatles on the beach in old-fashioned bathing suits. It's fabulous, 'cause John is doing this beautiful Charleston—which his mother taught him how to do. I love it. I'd still like to do that movie. I talked to Steven Spielberg about it, and he was much more encouraging than Dick Lester. He said Martin Scorsese might be a good person to talk to.

Meanwhile, I'm thinking of getting a band together myself. I know the Beatles used to say, "We won't be rock & rollin' when we're forty," but I still love it. The Prince's Trust benefit just zonked me out: looking around and seeing Eric Clapton, Mark Knopfler, Bryan Adams, Elton, Tina—there was such a buzz on that stage. I think they were glad to see me sort of vaguely gettin' it on. I sang "I Saw Her Standing There" and "Long Tall Sally," too—in the original key! It really felt great. I could do that every night. So I'd like to get a band. I don't know if I'll call it Wings—maybe some new incarnation.

Whatever may happen, will you be leaving the gray in your hair? It looks very distinguished.

Yeah, I'm leaving that. When you're past forty, the game is up, you know? My wife actually likes it. Ringo told me off about it, though—he reckoned I ought to color it. I think he's kind of gaugin' himself by how old I look—like I make *him* feel old if *I* look a bit old. But what the hell, you know? This is life. We're all gettin' older every second. My main thing is just to try and enjoy it. And I'm very surprised to find that, more often than not, I really do.

16

Bill Graham

INTERVIEWED BY
MICHAEL GOLDBERG (1985)

Bill Graham brought professionalism to the presentation of live rock music. This statement will only sound ominous to those who have never sat through a poorly produced rock concert, complete with lousy sound, lax security and long waits between bands. Graham was a fan of the music, but he was also—just as proudly—a businessman. And his pioneering insight was that quality was a key component of the rock music business. The sound had to be right, or else why put on a show at all? Security had to be organized, because otherwise, in an imperfect world, simple good will would not be sufficient to deal with brawls over seats and bad acid trips. And that was just the beginning. Someone had to arrange hotel accommodations, catering, sound checks, lights, posters, advertising and post-show parties. Somebody had to do all this business. Bill Graham was just the man.

Graham became one of rock's greatest screamers. He wanted things done right, and he wanted them done right now. No options were entertained. The result of all this backstage psychodrama has been the creation of what may very well be the finest concert-promotion agency in the world. When Amnesty International began planning a logistically unprecedented, five-continent Human Rights Now! concert tour for the end of 1988, Bill Graham was given the job of actually pulling it off. Who else was there?

Graham's personal life has been, if anything, even more extraordinary than his professional history, and Bay Area native Michael Goldberg knew all the right questions to ask.

—K. L.

TWENTY YEARS ago, on November 6, 1965, Bill Graham produced his first concert. It was a benefit for the San Francisco Mime Troupe, and it featured an eclectic group of artists: the poets Lawrence Fer- linghetti and Allen Ginsberg, the Jefferson Airplane and the improvisational comedians the Committee. The show was held at the troupe's Howard Street loft, and thousands of people showed up. In the ensuing months, Graham held two more Mime Troupe benefits. By then, he had discovered an auditorium in San Francisco's Fillmore District—and his calling. "I came to realize what I could do with my life," he said. "I am not an artist. But I had found a means of expression."

Graham was born Wolfgang Grajonca in Berlin on January 8, 1931. His father died in a construction accident two days later; his mother placed him and his youngest sister in a Berlin orphanage so she could work. His earliest memory is of being taken to an orphanage in France, which is where he was in 1939 when war broke out between France and Germany. Two years later, a Red Cross representative helped Graham and sixty-three other children flee the Nazis. It was a nightmarish journey that eventually landed him in New York. Graham's mother died in a Nazi concentration camp.

Today, the fifty-four-year-old Graham is a multimillionaire who rules over a music-business empire that grosses more than $100 million a year. Though still best known for the hundreds of concerts his company, Bill Graham Presents, stages each year, he also has a management division (Santana and Eddie Money are two of his clients); a technical division; a merchandising company; record-production, music-publishing and film-production wings; and even a food and beverage company, Fillmore Fingers. In addition to presenting nearly every major rock and pop act that comes to the San Francisco Bay Area, Graham has promoted national tours by Bob Dylan and the Rolling Stones, and was the producer of the Band's farewell concert, the Last Waltz, and the American portion of Live Aid.

Graham, who has two sons (David, 17, and Alex, 8) and a stepson (Thomas, 18), has been married once, and is now divorced. His spacious, million-dollar Marin County home, which is where these interviews were conducted, sits on nearly nine acres in the hills thirty minutes north of San Francisco. A quarter-mile driveway, lined with eucalyptus trees, leads up to the house and past an immense, slowly spinning lighted globe and a gigantic skull—both props from some Grateful Dead show—set on the hillside. There's a swimming pool, basketball court and volleyball court. A silver Mercedes 280SE and a brown Jaguar convertible sit in his garage.

Inside the house, Graham is surrounded by his past. Framed Fillmore posters. A painting of the stage from the Rolling Stones' 1981 world tour. Photos of Keith Richards, the Grateful Dead, Marlon Brando, Bob Dylan. A shredded black vest that once belonged to Richards hangs in his study. And, in a frame, a tambourine and microphone used by Janis Joplin.

Graham has mellowed considerably since the late Sixties and early Seventies, when he could often be found outside the Fillmore East or Fillmore West shouting down some hippie who wanted free admission. Yet he remains extremely sensitive to the accusations that he was, as Graham himself puts it, "a capitalist-pig rip-off."

"The minute somebody starts attacking me in that area, something happens to me," said Graham. "I'm like a cobra whose head is rising, and *sss* . . ." Late in the second session, he talked about what makes him happy these days. At one point, in his deep, gruff voice, he said, *"Not to be accused."*

*Y*ou've been involved with rock & roll for twenty years now. How have things changed since you started out?

Rock & roll is now the music of the land. Broadway. Movies. TV commercials. *Miami Vice.* It's the music of America. It's certainly not the music of the alternative society. Somebody, a guy who used to go to the Fillmore East all the time, had a comment about Live Aid. He said, "Isn't it amazing, Bill. In twenty years, the outlaws became the heroes." Hall and Oates at the Statue of Liberty. Live Aid. Farm Aid. Royalty at Wembley. Rock & roll is in the White House!

Did you ever think, back when you first opened the Fillmore in 1965, that twenty years later you'd still be in the music business, and on such a grand scale?

The scene at that time was in its embryonic stage. Did I know that it was going to be that lucrative? Impossible. I went into it not so much as a way to earn a living—although I had to earn a living—but as a way of life. It was a means of expression. There was no conception of what the whole thing would be like twenty years later.

How did you learn how to put on a rock concert?

We have to leapfrog back in time to the mid-Sixties, when there were no rules, no blueprints. The rock & roll business—the weekly concerts, the Fillmore, the Avalon—that all started in 1965. All of a sudden, there was the Fillmore, and there was the Avalon. And, oh, those are agents? Is that who you talk to? And the posters and the light shows. There was no rock & roll college. And yet, the promoters that followed . . . I know a major promoter back East, for example, who stood in the lobby of the Fillmore East and made notes and notes and notes. Well, we didn't take notes.

So you didn't know much about the concert business when you put on the benefit for the Mime Troupe?

I want to show you something. [*Graham leafs through a scrapbook from 1965 and stops at a small handbill advertising the Mime Troupe benefit.*] A few weeks before the benefit a man called me, and it turned out to be Chet Helms, who told me he was with the Family Dog [a communal group that later became Graham's chief competition]. He said, "We'd like to donate our services."

Well, when he arrived the night of the show, I asked him where the dogs were. I didn't mean it as a joke. I actually thought that they were a dog act. And the proof is that they're listed right here among the other entertainers: Jefferson Airplane, the Committee, *the Family Dog!* At the time, that was the extent of my knowledge of the scene.

When you first started presenting concerts at the Fillmore, you co-produced one show—featuring the Paul Butterfield Blues Band—with the Family Dog. But it seems they rubbed you the wrong way.

They ran their business differently than I did, and in a way that in the long run couldn't make it. You can't invite so many people in as friends and then be able to conduct your business. . . . If an artist travels thousands of miles, he's owed something. He's owed your awareness that he needs to eat and needs shelter. I'm not relating it to Chet. I'm relating it to anybody. Chet meant well. His image was the exact counterpoint to mine.

On the one hand, this hippie—flowery, long-haired Chet Helms. And on the other, Bill Graham—the guy with the clipboard who knew how to deal with city hall.

Chet was a product of that era; I was a product of an earlier era. At our company, at that time and today,

you can't do drugs on the job. Why? Somebody has to be clearheaded. And that's us. What I'm trying to do, indirectly, is tell you the difference between Chet and me. I wish the utopian theory of life could work. But to cross a bridge, you gotta have a coin for the toll. And I think sometimes that was forgotten.

For a long time, the Grateful Dead were trying to dose you with LSD. Eventually, they succeeded. What exactly happened?

That was at the Fillmore West, during my 7 Up era. We'd put plastic barrels full of sodas and ice in the dressing rooms. And they took the 7 Up cans on top in these barrels and used a hypodermic needle to put in their goodies. They figured that sooner or later I'd pick one up. And on one of my trips, just as I habitually would do, I picked up a can of 7 Up. Just about the time they were going onstage, it hit. Rather heavily.

One of the guys, [drummer] Mickey Hart, asked if I would like to come onstage with them. He gave me a drumstick and said, "Feel free to play anything you like, and hit the gong whenever you like." Now, I've always felt as the producer that the stage belongs to the artist. But that night I felt no inhibitions about staying up there. I spent the next four and a half hours onstage with the Dead. I didn't think I'd made an ass of myself. I just had one of the great evenings of my life.

How do you feel about drugs in general?

I have never been a heavy drug user, ever, except there was a week, maybe ten years ago. I was in New York, and it was very late, and I had to get up early the next morning. A friend was with me, and I said, "I don't know how I'll get up." He said, "I've got some coke. Take a little hit." I have never enjoyed coke the way other people have or seem to have. It's just like a bamboo pole up my ass. It will wake me up, but it doesn't take me away. But he gave me a small vial of it. That first morning, I took some, and I felt good. I had a very tough day. The next day, I had another tough day, and I thought, "Thank God I have got a little bit of this stuff." I did that four mornings in a row. The fifth morning, I found myself getting up and automatically going for it. I stood in front of a mirror with a nail file, and I put the nail file into the little vial. I saw myself in the mirror, and I knew that I had done it automatically. That woke me up forever, I think. I hope.

You've presented almost every major rock act except the Beatles. Did you ever try to get them to do a show?

In the first year and a half that I was in business,

on three different occasions, I wrote letters to Brian Epstein, saying, This is who I am, you visited the Fillmore, ta-da-da-da. . . . I said, If you are ever going to come back to America, I now have so much money saved, and I offer you this amount of money. . . . Just to have the Beatles play here would be an honor. And when I had saved $10,000, I wrote to them again. I remember the highest amount I offered them was $28,000. But I never got a response.

How much money did bands usually make when they played the Fillmore?

Well, the most significant early-day figure that I remember is for a week of shows with the Jefferson Airplane, Gabor Szabo and Jimi Hendrix, who was the opening act. Jimi made $750 for the week.

How much did the Airplane make?

The headliner would make $2,500, perhaps, or $3,000, something like that. For a weekend—three nights.

For years you felt you were forced to assume, as you put it when you announced the closing of the Fillmores, "the role of Antichrist of the underground." People hated you because they thought you were ripping them off, charging too much for tickets and so on. They called you names. Swore at you. How did that make you feel?

When people shit on you, it stinks. Who wouldn't be affected by that? To be verbally attacked, psychologically attacked. In the early days of this business, I retaliated very strongly against accusations by challenging people verbally rather than trying to make them really understand. I'd get into a screaming match with the person. There were hundreds of situations where I didn't feel good about what happened. The anger came on so strong. I was engrossed in "you have no right to do this"—whatever you were doing. If you would show me an instant replay of some of those incidents, I could look at myself and say, "What an asshole."

How do you deal with your anger now?

It's almost nonexistent. There are still times when I'll snap, but I'm not as possessed, obsessed. And something happened: The audience changed. The promoter no longer was "the capitalist." In the early years, I would walk through the crowd, waiting for some negative things. Somebody would say, "Money." Or just, "Fuck the pigs! Why do you charge so much? Capitalist rip-off!"

If I had this conversation once, I've had it a thousand times—where somebody says, "Well, why is the ticket price so high? I know if it was up to the artists, they'd play for nothing." And then I would say, "How much do you think the artist makes a night? Their take

was twelve times mine." Still, they weren't satisfied, because they weren't concerned with how much the artist made. The artist was a member of their family. I wasn't. I was a businessman. I don't experience that anymore. Now, more often than not, it's "Hey, Bill, great show!"

What's the most memorable show you've produced?

The Mime Troupe benefit was, is and always will be the most exciting night of my life in theater. Here were these filmmakers who met these poets for the first time. And jazz musicians and rock & roll musicians. It was a totally different thing than I'd ever seen. People dancing with people they had never met before. Men and women and kids were just dancing. And all of a sudden, it was six o'clock in the morning—it started getting light—and Allen Ginsberg was doing his mantra chants.

When I think about the past twenty years, I think about the Stones tour, the Dylan tour or Live Aid. I think about the Last Waltz or the closing of the Fillmore or the opening of the Fillmore East. And, of course, the early days. There was a gig with the Butterfield Blues Band and B.B. King, and both Albert King and Freddie King showed up and played.

When the power structure was different, we were able to put on Howlin' Wolf with Janis Joplin, or two one-act plays by Leroi Jones at a Byrds concert at the Fillmore. To see the faces of Grateful Dead fans listening to Miles Davis; to watch a roomful of really hyper Who fans being blown away by Woody Herman. Turning the houselights on with Aretha Franklin and Ray Charles and the King Curtis band, and the band went into twenty minutes of laying down this incredible beat, and Aretha and Ray both stopped playing and singing, and Aretha just held Ray's arm, and the two of them just rocked back and forth on the stage. [*Laughs*] That was pretty much nirvana.

Those kinds of shows—where you present a soul or blues or jazz act to the rock audience—rarely happen these days. Rock & roll is much more segregated now. Does that bother you?

More than any single aspect of this business, it bothers me the most, and I miss it the most. In the first six or seven years, I was able to do that. It gave me pleasure, it gave the public pleasure, and it also educated the public and me at the same time. I'd never seen these people perform. I couldn't believe Howlin' Wolf the first time I saw him. The effect of Mavis Staples keeping time by snapping her fingers. Rahsaan Roland Kirk walking through the audience like a Pied Piper, playing two saxes.

But gradually, the struggle was with the power system of our industry.

I can sit here as a producer and say, "Wouldn't it be nice to see Talking Heads and King Sunny Ade on the same bill," but that also takes the artists' doing. If two artists really want to get together, they could. Nothing stops them.

How would you compare the big stars of today—say, Madonna or Prince or Michael Jackson—to the stars of the Sixties? Are there more prima donnas today?

The obvious problem we have with that type of question is that as a producer who's dealing with these people, if I start tearing anybody down by name, I'll lose that relationship.

The days of insisting on a white limousine are gone. Because the stars found out that people pound on limousines. So let's not take limousines; let's take station wagons. They learned through the years. In between, it was difficult. There was an artist we lost because I would not get him a white limousine; the only white limousine was in L.A., and I wasn't about to schlep to L.A. for a white limousine.

There was a certain English group some years ago that asked us for bottles of a highly expensive vintage wine. But I found out after a few visits that they never opened them. So one time I went into the dressing room and said, "Hello, how are you? God, that's a nice wine." And I picked up a bottle as if I were going to open it. And someone said, "Don't touch that bottle!" And I realized one of the leaders of this organization was a wine collector. And he was just gradually amassing this amazing wine collection. From then on, I said, "Why should I be feeding your wine collection?"

Let's talk about some of the rock stars you've known. What's your favorite memory of Janis Joplin?

Janis and Grace Slick were the two queens of rock & roll in the Sixties. Dual royalty on the feminine side, both living in San Francisco. Once in the late Sixties, Janis came off her second set and said, "Bill, you wanna hang out, get something to eat?" She had never said that to me in her life. We weren't friends, and therefore it was very unexpected.

We got into her car, which was a psychedelically colored Porsche, and went to an all-night place where you could get food. She had some booze; we got some cheese and salami and crackers and Oreos—just garbage food. Then we went driving across the bridge to an area where you can look at the Golden Gate Bridge from the Marin side. We sat down and talked about how insane life was, how tough it was to pull down the blinds and just be off on your own.

Janis had just become really huge. She'd done a few tours, and she talked about the horrors of the road. The key sentence was, "You know, you're in Des Moines, in the middle of a tour, and at the end of a gig, the guys go back to the Holiday Inn, and they can go down to the bar and see what's happening. What does a *woman* do in this society?"

Janis made me realize that in spite of "making it," you could still have great difficulty balancing work and play and joy. In the end, a truck driver can be luckier than Janis Joplin.

What about Jimi Hendrix?

There was a night in New York that is among my favorite incidents of all time. He played New Year's Eve and New Year's Day at the Fillmore East—two shows a night—and they were recording it for an album. It was the Band of Gypsys, with Billy Cox on bass and Buddy Miles on drums. During the first show, he was really having fun, humping, grinding, putting the guitar behind his back. Usually, he would do that later on in the set. First, he would really play. But that night, that stuff started very early on, and it bothered me.

While we were clearing the house before the second show, Jimi came down to my office and said, "How are you doing, man? What did you think?" *He never did that.* Jimi Hendrix was a very quiet, private person.

There were other people in the office, and I asked them to leave. Then I said, "I'll tell you something. I saw you humping and laying down, playing behind your back. You did all that shit, but you forgot one thing. You forgot to play." And he looked at me like he couldn't believe what I said. He didn't really say anything; he just sat a minute or more. Then he turned to me and very seriously and gently just pointed to me and said, "Bill, you are here for the second show, right?" I said, "Yeah." And he said, "Okay, man. Thanks."

At the second show, he proceeded to play eighty minutes of the most brilliant music, emotionally and technically, that I have ever seen. He moved very little. The audience sat there as if they were watching a ballet. He came off, and the people were applauding, and he saw me standing there. He came up to me and looked very serious and very drenched in perspiration after giving energy that was awesome. He looked straight at me, maybe three inches from my face, and said, "All right?" And just stared at me. "All right?"

And then he went out and did a fifteen-minute encore of nothing but shit, nothing but circus. All the bumps, the grinds, the fire, the humping, guitar behind the neck, somersaults—all of it—as if to say, "Okay, you got yours; now I'm gonna just have fun."

What do you remember about Jim Morrison?

A funny incident happened when he was at the Fillmore. He took the microphone and started swinging it like a lariat, letting more and more of it go. It started swinging over the audience, and I immediately went through the crowd and tried to stand in front of the stage, because I could see that sooner or later he was going to lose it, and I didn't want it to hit anybody. I was standing maybe ten people back, waving my arms, trying to catch his attention, and then he loses it. And out of 2,000 people in the hall, it hits me right in the head. There's this lump on my head. Afterward, I went downstairs, and we joked about how ironic it was.

The next time he came to the Fillmore, he gave me a gift. It was a psychedelically painted pith helmet—a protective pith helmet that I should wear during the show.

The Who?

In 1970, the Who were playing a week at the Fillmore East. There was a grocery store on the corner of the theater, and during the latter part of the performance one night, someone threw a Molotov cocktail into the store. It started to go up in flames. Some of the flames started coming in through the side door of the Fillmore, and all of a sudden, with maybe three or four minutes of the performance left, the fire department started coming in through the front doors. The audience was totally convinced that this was part of the show, and they cheered. Nobody left the building. And then they saw the smoke coming in and thought it was special effects.

The first fireman went down the aisle and jumped up on the stage. Roger [Daltrey] didn't know who they were, and he goes and kicks the guy off the stage. Pete [Townshend] comes over and wants to hit the guy with his guitar. The audience was going crazy and applauding—thought it was the greatest thing they'd ever seen.

Well, everyone was finally evacuated from the building. But the fire department was pissed: Who were these guys kicking us off the stage? And the police were looking for the members of the Who. So I took them to my apartment, which was around the corner. The next afternoon, their lawyer surrendered them to the police. They held them at the station for a number of hours, took some statements. The end result was that they were released about a half-hour before it was time for them to go back onstage at the Fillmore the next night.

How about the Stones? There's a beat-up pair of Keith

Richards' boots sitting in a cabinet in your dining room. How'd they get there?

Every time Keith walked onstage during the Stones' 1981 tour, he wore a different outfit, but he always wanted to wear these handmade Spanish boots. After a while, after playing many cities, a little piece of suede came loose, and they had to glue it down. In another city, the stitching or the sole might come loose, and they'd put some tape on it or nail it together. There was tape here, gauze there, glue there, nails . . . But it got to a point where the boots became a major concern of mine, because he loved them and wanted to wear them all the time. Finally, at Candlestick Park [in San Francisco], the Stones were just about to go on, and the heel snapped off and broke.

I said, "Aw, jeez, do you really want to wear those? Do you have something else?" He said, "Yeah, but I just feel like . . ." He didn't go crazy. And I said, "Well, I'll try." So I leave the trailer and go out and ask everybody who works for me, "What are you wearing? Let me see your heel." "What do you want?" *"Let me see your heel!"* I couldn't find anything.

But then there was a guy at a table in the other backstage area who had a pair of boots on, and the heel was just about the same size—a little higher, but the same shape. And I said to him, "Do me a favor. I can't explain it to you now. Let me have your shoes for fifty bucks." He didn't know what I was doing. I got them and took them back to the tech area. Two of the guys got a nail and hammer, shaped the heel down a little and put it on Keith's boot. Up and away it went. He used it. After that date, there was more paper, more glue, more spit, more rubber bands. He always wanted to wear those boots.

On the plane back to New York after the last date, he said, "Hey, Bill, I want to see you for a minute." And we stepped into the toilet area. "Man, I just want to tell you, I really drove you up the wall. Sometimes it was insane. But . . ." And he had this package wrapped in newspaper with a rubber band around it and a rose attached, and he just said, "Thank you." And I knew what it was. It was the boots.

What was it like working with Dylan in 1974?

At the beginning of the tour, I said to my staff, "I'm not assuming that you don't know who Bob Dylan is, but he's going back out, and he's going to be looked at in every town with adulation and respect and love and affection. It's really going to come at him. He's going to get that all the time. We should just be loose. Some of you may say, 'Hey, Bob, good morning.' But don't make him answer, because he's going to get that in every city. He's going to get, 'Hey, Bob, hey, Bob, hey, Bob.' So just know who he is, and let him have his space."

On the third date, in Cleveland, late one night, Bob called and asked if I could come to his room. Everything seemed quite nice the first few days—getting the kinks out of the lighting and so on. He was blown away by the public acceptance. The encores. So it was the middle of the night. I went up to his room, knocked on the door, walked inside, and he said, "Why isn't anybody talking to me?"

Around that time, you also produced national tours for George Harrison and Crosby, Stills, Nash and Young. In doing that, you essentially took on the roles of both agent and promoter. Agents, as well as other promoters, didn't like that. They felt you were stepping on their turf.

After a few tours, some agents and managers and promoters invited me to a luncheon up in Long Island to discuss the industry. Knowing what this meeting was going to be about, I wanted to make it a little more merry. So I hired some people from Central Casting. And as we're getting into it, these black limousines drive up, and this group of gentlemen—about twelve of them—gets out. They were all dressed in *Untouchables*-style clothes—Prohibition-era suits, Stetson hats, spats—and they all had musical-instrument cases.

The door to the room we were in opened, and the first guy, a very large man, stepped in and said, "Everybody sit down. Nobody moves!" The guys spread themselves out around the room, and within fifteen seconds, the first guy leans across the table—and just before they came in, I lit a cigar—and says, "Excuse me, Mr. Graham, is everything satisfactory?" And I just nodded my head. And they all got their musical-instrument cases and opened them, took their jackets off, stuck them in the cases and started to leave. And on the back of each of their shirts was written "Bill Graham Presents." I wanted to take the edge off. As if to say, "If you had my shot, wouldn't you take it if you were smart enough?"

In 1971, you were famous. The Fillmore West and Fillmore East were both great successes. Yet you closed them both. Why?

Running the Fillmores had begun to take its toll. I was flying back and forth across the country. I was beginning to lose some acts to bigger places. The business of rock & roll got so big, and the managers said, "You can make as much in one night at the Garden as you can in three nights at the Fillmore."

But one day I got a phone call from Sol Hurok,

the great Russian impresario. He was the only person that I really looked up to, so I went to see him in New York. I went in, and there was Mr. Hurok, sitting behind this large marble table with a lot of press clippings on his desk. He looked at them for another few minutes. Then he looked at me and said, "Yes? Oh, you've come." He shook my hand. He looked at me, he looked down at the papers and said, "It says here you've got lots of guts and balls. Is true?" First thing he ever said to me.

His reason for asking me to come was that he had a contract to do a month with the Stuttgart Ballet at the Metropolitan Opera House, and they had canceled. He had a free month, and he didn't know what to do with it. He had paid the rent. So the idea was that we would present a month of the best rock & roll we could get into the Metropolitan Opera House. Well, I was flabbergasted—this was the citadel of the arts and music world, the most popular facility in the world.

In the ensuing months, some groups said yes, some said maybe, some said no. But I wanted the great artists, and I was having difficulty with a lot of the managers. One night, I was in my office at the Fillmore East, and the manager of an up-and-coming group returned my call. I tried to explain to the manager: "The band has to do five nights, and this is all you are going to make. But this is the Metropolitan!" I went through the whole thing, and he finally said, "Bill, you expect my boys to play all week for a lousy fifty grand?"

That was the trigger. This was the Metropolitan Opera House! Look at the opportunity you've got to break through to that fucking yo-yo world out there that doesn't trust you. And you have the balls to say to me that I have no right to ask you to play for a lousy fifty grand a week? You piece of shit. I just said to myself, it's not worth it. If I was totally healthy at the time, totally free of problems, it might not have affected me that hard. But it blew my mind. I just said, Fillmore East, Fillmore West—that's it.

Michael Jackson initially wanted you as tour consultant to help run the Jacksons' 1984 tour. One of the Jacksons' advisers told me they decided not to use you because you were "too egoed out." Were you?

For me, that criticism has no foundation. You can always use somebody's personality against them: Well, Bill isn't soft-spoken; Bill may speak his piece if you ask him a question. Your ego, as best as I know what ego means, is a feeling that you have a particular gift for something. I think we are good producers; I think we are ethical people.

Many people's names came into the picture. Mine

fell out somewhere early on. The end result was that, as we know, other people were involved in that project. Everybody lost. The show lost, the public lost, and Michael Jackson lost. . . .

How would you have produced the Jacksons' tour?

One thing I would have done was made the ticket price more commensurate with the going price for any major superstar. Maybe twenty dollars, but not double the going rate. I would have used local promoters, and I would have had community involvement because of who the Jacksons are and who Michael Jackson is. At the time, I mentioned *x* amount of dollars to go toward sickle-cell anemia.

As the tour progressed, the word got out that it wasn't such a hot show. Dates weren't selling out. There was a bad feeling about the tour.

It started at the beginning, with the handling of the tickets. You couldn't buy two tickets. *You couldn't buy two tickets.* And you had to send your money in way in advance to some place back East, and they sat on your money for months. Sooner or later, an aura surrounds everything.

Woodstock was heralded as a major countercultural event. You were there, but you didn't see it that way.

It was great for some people, but it was a horrific experience for others. I met many people ten, fifteen miles away who pitched their tents or sat in the back of a truck and didn't get any closer 'cause the roads were jammed. And some had driven from Iowa.

I felt badly for those who didn't get what they came for. But it was the forerunner of them all. I always imagined that as Woodstock took place . . . I had this image of sleeping corporate giants waking up and waxing their mustaches and saying, "Aha! Rock & roll. Very interesting." If hundreds of thousands of people would get together on a farm in upstate New York, that's *big business*. And Woodstock, more than any single event, heralded the era of big-business music.

Do you think that Band Aid and USA for Africa and Live Aid have brought back some of the Sixties spirit?

Yes, I do. Bob Geldof should be remembered in history for suggesting that a lot can be done if we tap this power source. And the power source is music and the people who make it. Give me another element of our society that could have drawn as many people as Live Aid. A sporting event? An international soccer match? I don't know. I'm trying to show what a rare position these artists are in—that a group of people can say: You want to raise $10 million?

When I first saw that film [about the famine in Ethiopia], I thought of doing something, but I never really thought I could do what Bob did. And I realize

why. He's an artist, asking another artist. To follow that mania and do what was seemingly undoable—I take my hat off to him.

You were born in Germany around the time of the Second World War. What was your childhood there like?

Other than what my sisters have told me, I have absolutely no direct memory of the first nine years of my life. When my father died, my youngest sister—there were five girls and one boy—and I were put into an orphanage. My mother made and sold hats in a hat shop in Berlin, because she had to go to work after my father died. And she would take care of the other four girls. And on the weekends, we would come home or they would visit the orphanage.

In the summer of 1939, a group of French-Jewish orphans went on a two-week exchange with the children that were living in the Berlin orphanage. And this orphanage was southeast of Paris, in Chaumont. During the two weeks that we were in France, war broke out between France and Germany, and the French children perished in Berlin.

Eventually, we were moved onto the grounds of a château. When the raids really started in Paris and the surrounding areas, we dug shelters beneath the grounds of the château. And I remember when the air raids came, we went into these shelters. In the rainy season they became almost flooded full of water, and we stood in water up to our waists. The biggest fear of my life—I feared them forever and ever—was a little snake and a toad that jumped up at me. This little short snake. I've had a fear of snakes, and anything in the reptile family, all my life.

The raids were pretty constant. And then, as the Germans broke through the lines and it was inevitable that France was going to fall, the International Red Cross sent a man to our community to take all of us south. The whole nation was moving south. The roads were full of cars and carts and people, just walking with their belongings. It was just like in the movies. Everybody fleeing. I remember, outside Lyons, the Germans had these suicide parachuters to demoralize the public. And I saw this happen. These fanatics would parachute into an area of the country that wasn't yet occupied, and they would be throwing hand grenades as they came closer to the ground. I saw the French Resistance forces capture one of these men and put him against a wall two streets away and riddle him with bullets.

And as we were moving, some children ran away. And the group became smaller and smaller. And very little food. We got to Madrid and then went to Lisbon, and in Lisbon they put us on a freighter to Casablanca and eventually across the Atlantic to Bermuda. And on the crossing we were stopped by a German U-boat. We were on the freighter for nineteen days. All we had to eat were cookies and oranges. When we got to New York, they put us in a bunch of barracks run and funded by the Foster Home Bureau. What they did was ask people, preferably Jewish homes, to take young people in.

On weekends, the families would come up to these cottages, looking at us as though they were picking out a pet in a pet shop. And all of us wanted to be taken by somebody. Nine weeks passed. Finally, on the last weekend in November, a family came, a couple with a boy who was two years older than I was. I've always felt that the primary reason that they took me into their home was that the two languages their son was studying were French and German. I was taken by them and began my life in New York City.

Growing up in the Bronx, you spent a lot of time in the streets.

When I first got to the Bronx, I didn't speak English. But to the kids in school, it didn't mean anything that I was a refugee. To them, I wasn't a Russian Jew. To them, I was a German. All they knew was that I spoke German, and Germany was the enemy. And I used to get my head kicked in all the time at school. They would goose-step in front of my house and say, "Nazi go home." My foster brother, who was two years older, said, "Not only are you going to have to learn how to speak English very quickly, you also have to lose that accent." So on a daily basis, he and I sat down and read the newspaper headlines, and I practiced every day with a mirror. *Getting rid of za accent ven you go down ze street to ze store.* Within six months, I learned English, and I lost my accent.

Later, you were in the Army, fought in Korea and were awarded a Bronze Star and a Purple Heart. You also had started to fine-tune your business skills.

I was on board a ship, headed overseas. I was working in the kitchen. The crossing was, I think, eleven days. Well, I started running a little crap game. And the first night, people had cookies from home to eat. By the second night, nobody had anything. So I made a couple of sandwiches, took them down—people got hungry in the middle of the night—and sold them for a dollar each. I figured out roughly that from apples and oranges and sandwiches and whatnot, I took in about $1,400. And from the crap game, I was up about $1,300. I was twenty-two years old, and I had $2,700 in my pocket. When we pulled into base, they started a game on deck. Well, I lost all the money. I got off in Tokyo without a dime on me.

You also worked as a waiter at resort hotels in the Catskills.

What I learned as a busboy and a dishwasher and a cabdriver, and then eventually as a waiter, is how to be a qualitative surface conversationalist. You get an instinct: Does this person want to talk? Or not talk? You learn to say: How are the greens today? I can't spell *golf.* I know nothing about golf. But you learn certain words. How many laps did you do? Did you ride the horses today? Whatever it is.

Every morning, I would buy three copies of *The New York Times* and three of the *Daily News.* And my guests would come in, and I'd say, "See the paper today?" "Oh, thanks." What did it cost me? Twenty cents or thirty cents. I know nothing about real estate, but I can have a conversation with real-estate people. They leave the table feeling, you know, Bill is really interested in my business.

That must have come in handy later on.

You meet performers for a night, and it's not that you're conning them, it's not that you're playing games with them. If there are 60,000 people out front, 99 times out of 100 the act will do an encore. And if they don't, I will find the one way to get them to do that encore. I'll tell stories until the cows come home to get them to do an encore. Or if there are 10,000 people outside making noise, I'll say, "Let me tell you the last time this happened . . ."

It's like an honest con game. I've always thought of myself as an honest con. Meaning, if it's not going to be bad for you and bad for anybody else—it looks like a con to you, but it's okay.

Your son David, who is seventeen, is a big rock fan. Would you want him to become a musician?

Probably not, because I've seen very few musicians who truly live a balanced life. Most famous artists have difficulty on the private side. And I gave up something that I shouldn't have—the breakup of my family.

For twenty years, you have been totally consumed by your work. One wonders, though, if there's more to life for you than putting on the next concert?

Yes, there is. If there is something—not to conquer but to experience—it's the man-woman experience. The ultimate other expression in life. What do you do with your life, and who do you share it with? There is nothing else I really need. I'm fifty-four years old, and I'd like to share what I and one other person could have. That stuff, it's been difficult because of the life. It's just obviously not nine to five, and obviously it's time consuming, and obviously, for many years, it's taken the form of the consummate mistress.

17

Eric Clapton

INTERVIEWED BY ROBERT PALMER (1985)

Eric Clapton has made the blues his own. The same might be said of Jeff Beck and Jimmy Page, Clapton's stellar contemporaries, both of whom, like Clapton, served time in that seminal British Invasion group the Yardbirds. But whereas Beck, at his most exhilarating, revels in flash, Clapton achieves some of his most piercing effects by adhering to the sense of strategic restraint that is at the heart of the blues. And while Page (along with Pete Townshend) essentially redefined the role of the guitar in blues-based hard rock, as an improviser he has never matched Clapton's sense of extended structure or his effortless fluidity.

Like Beck and Page, too, in their different ways, Clapton has truly had the blues. *Of the three men today, however, Clapton—having been involved in one of rock's most celebrated romantic entanglements (with his best friend's wife) now seems the most in control of his talent. That little more need be said by way of preface to what follows is a tribute to the empathy and the expertise of the interviewer, and to Clapton's own rare candor.*

—K. L.

ERIC CLAPTON joined the Yard-birds in 1963 and was recognized almost immediately as one of the most dazzling guitarists in popular music. Like Charlie Parker and a few other virtuoso improvisers before him, he was deified by his most devoted followers, who scrawled CLAPTON IS GOD around London. Also like Parker, he attempted to deal with the adulation, and with the pitiless creative urges that drove him, by deadening his nerve endings with drugs and drink. But unlike many who go down that road, he lived to tell about it.

From John Mayall's Bluesbreakers to Cream, from Blind Faith to Derek and the Dominos, from his first solo album to *Behind the Sun,* Clapton has consistently maintained exacting musical standards. His audience, expecting superhuman playing from him no matter what the context, has sometimes been disappointed by his records and, to a lesser extent, by his shows. But if his music has sometimes lacked fire, it has never lacked consummate craftsmanship. And on his two most recent albums, *Money and Cigarettes* and *Behind the Sun,* the fire and intensity have been rekindled.

Clapton is an intensely private man who

was never a talkative interview subject. He hadn't been interviewed in depth in some seven years when we first talked, by telephone, during his 1983 tour. I figured that it might pleasantly surprise him to talk to a journalist interested in music rather than in scandal, and sure enough, when he was rehearsing in England for an American tour this spring, I was invited over.

I got the impression that Clapton still found the idea of an interview about as appealing as a trip to the dentist, and for a week he kept putting off our first meeting. When we finally sat down to talk, in a comfortable room down the hall from his manager's London office, I told him we could start anywhere he liked. "Let's start at the beginning," he said, and for most of the next week we met every afternoon for a three- or four-hour session. His manager, Roger Forrester, seemed positively shocked by Clapton's sudden loquacity.

Clapton is still married to the former Patti Boyd, whom he wooed away from her first husband, George Harrison, more than a decade ago. At the time of the interview, however, their relationship was in a rocky phase. "The one thing I will not discuss," Clapton had announced before we began, "is my personal life." After several days of talking about Clapton's heroin addiction and period of alcoholism, openly and often in clinical detail, I risked asking him how things were with Patti. "She's the only woman I have ever really loved," he said deliberately. And that was that.

Clapton met every other subject unflinchingly, and we took a long, careful look at his major musical involvements. The man has always been his own toughest critic, and along the way we opened some old wounds and raised some formidable specters—guilt, fear, challenges that were not squarely faced. But when all was said and done, and despite Clapton's frequently harsh assessments of his own achievements and worth, he seemed to emerge from the grilling with a certain feeling of pride. "I think he's finally discovering," one of his associates said, "that his life hasn't been such a bloody waste after all."

Since we're starting at the beginning, why don't you tell me a bit about the town of Ripley, where you grew up.

It's only about thirty miles outside of London, but it's very country—Ripley is not even a town; it's a village with farms all around it. And very few people ever leave there. They usually stay, get jobs, get married.

What kind of music did you hear when you were growing up?

Pop music, first. Mostly songs that were still hanging over from wartime—"We'll Meet Again," that sort of thing, melodic pop music.

There was a funny Saturday-morning radio program for children, with this strange person, Uncle Mac. He was a very old man with one leg and a strange little penchant for children. He'd play things like "Mule Train," and then every week he'd slip in something like a Buddy Holly record or a Chuck Berry record. And the first blues I ever heard was on that program; it was a song by Sonny Terry and Brownie McGhee, with Sonny Terry howling and playing the harmonica. It blew me away. I was ten or eleven.

When was the first time you actually saw a guitar?

Hmm . . . I remember the first rock & roll I ever saw on TV was Jerry Lee Lewis doing "Great Balls of Fire." And that threw me; it was like seeing someone from outer space. And I realized suddenly that here I was in this village that was never going to change, yet there on TV was something out of the future. And I wanted to go there! Actually, he didn't have a guitarist, but he had a bass player, playing a Fender Precision bass, and I said, "That's a guitar." I didn't know it was a bass guitar, I just knew it was a guitar, and again I thought, "That's the future. And that's what I want." After that I started to build one, tried to carve a Stratocaster out of a block of wood, but I didn't know what to do when I got to the neck and frets and things.

I was living with my grandparents, who raised me, and since I was the only child in the family, they used to spoil me something terrible. So I badgered them until they bought me a plastic Elvis Presley guitar. Of course, it could never stay in tune, but I could put on a Gene Vincent record, look in the mirror and mime.

When I was fourteen or fifteen, they gave me a real guitar, an acoustic, but it was so hard to play, I actually didn't even try for a while. And pretty soon the neck began to warp. But I did invent chords. I invented E, and I invented A. I thought I had discovered something incredible. And then I put it down again, in my later teens, because I started to become interested in being an artist. The bohemian existence beckoned; actually, the good-life part of it beckoned more than the work. And at that point, when I was about sixteen, I started making weekend trips to London.

From hanging around in coffee bars and so on, I met a certain crowd of people, some of whom played guitar. One was Long John Baldry, who was then playing a twelve-string, doing folk and blues. Every Friday night, there would be a meeting at someone's house, and people would turn up with the latest imported records from the States. And shortly, someone showed up with that Chess album, *The Best of Muddy Waters,* and something by Howlin' Wolf. And that was it for me. Then I sort of took a step back, discovered Robert Johnson and made the connection to Muddy. For me, it was very serious, what I heard. And I began to realize that I could only listen to this music with people who were equally serious about it.

Did getting involved with this music send you back to the guitar?

Yeah. Baldry and these other people would just sit in a corner, playing folk and blues while everyone else was drinking and getting stoned. And I saw that it was possible to actually, if you like, get on with it— to just sit in the corner playing and not have everyone looking at you. I saw that it wasn't something to be frightened of or shy in doing. So I started doing it myself.

Playing what, folk-blues?

Yeah, things by Big Bill Broonzy and Ramblin' Jack Elliott, "Railroad Bill," "Cocaine." But then I was drawn more and more toward electric blues, along with a few friends, a select few people. And, of course, then we had to be purists and seriously dislike other things.

When I was about seventeen, I got booted out of art school, and I did manual labor for about a year for pocket money. And during that time, I met up with a guy, Tom McGuinness, who was going to get involved with a band, and I knew just about enough to be able to play and keep up that end of it. So I got involved in that band, the Roosters, and that was a good feeling.

What kind of music did the Roosters play?

We did "Boom Boom" and a couple of other John Lee Hooker things, "Hoochie Coochie Man" and some others by Muddy, I think. We did whatever we could get on records, really, on up to rock & roll things like "Slow Down" by Larry Williams, because you had to have the odd rock & roll number in there.

Then Tom McGuinness brought in "Hideaway" by Freddie King, and the B side was "I Love the Woman," which is still one of the greatest. And that's the first time I heard that electric-lead-guitar style, with the bent notes—T-Bone Walker, B.B. and Freddie King, that style of playing. Hearing that Freddie King single was what started me on my path.

According to rock historian Pete Frame's family tree of your various bands, the Roosters only lasted from January to August 1963.

Yeah, some of the people had day jobs that were more important to them than the band. Practical considerations brought the band down. But by that time, I had no other interests at all. I practiced a lot.

After the Roosters, I got a job with Tom McGuinness in another band, Casey Jones and the Engineers. That folded pretty soon, too, and then I heard the Yardbirds had started up.

The Stones had been playing at the Crawdaddy Club, and when they moved on, the next band in was the Yardbirds. I had met two guys from the Yardbirds at some bohemian parties, and at that time they were playing music by Django Reinhardt, "Nuages" and so on. We became friends. I went down to hear them at the Crawdaddy and was fairly critical of them, especially the guitarist they had. And I don't really remember how it came about, but I replaced him. I was watching one week and playing the next.

I know you were already playing those Freddie King kind of leads, but with the exception of your solo on "I Ain't Got You," the Yardbirds things I've heard were mostly raveups, band improvisations rather than a lead player fronting a rhythm section. Were the live gigs also in the nature of raveups?

Yeah, building up to musical climaxes, trying to develop crowd frenzy. Paul [Samwell-Smith] would start it on the bass, going up the fretboard, and everyone else would go up and up and up, and then you'd get to the leading pitch and come back down again. If you do that on just about every number, there's very little time for reflective or serious playing.

Is that why you became disenchanted with being in the Yardbirds?

Partly. At first, if we could get a good gig and make the crowd happy, that was enough. But then the Stones came out of that whole scene, and it sparked ambition in some members of the band. The Stones were getting on big package tours, they were on TV, they got a Chuck Berry song onto the charts. And some of the Yardbirds and Giorgio [Gomelsky, their manager] began to see a future in being internationally famous. I couldn't see what was so wonderful about competing with the Liverpool sound and all of that, trying to jump on the bandwagon; there was still a great part of me that was very much the blues purist, thinking, "Music is this; it's not that."

Were you really listening to nothing but the blues?

No, I listened to some modern jazz. I would put on a John Coltrane album after a John Lee Hooker album. I don't think I understood Coltrane, but I listened to him a lot. I loved his tone, the feel of it.

Were the Yardbirds' gigs with Sonny Boy Williamson the first chance you had to play with an American bluesman?

Yes, and I think that's when I first realized that we weren't really being true to the music—when Sonny Boy came over and we didn't know how to back him up. It was frightening, really, because this man was real and we weren't. He wasn't very tolerant, either. He did take a shine to us after a while, but before that he put us through some bloody hard paces. In the first place, he expected us to know his tunes. He'd say, "We're going to do 'Don't Start Me to Talkin'' or 'Fattening Frogs for Snakes,'" and then he'd kick it off, and of course some of the members of this particular band had never heard these songs.

There was a certain attitude in the band, a kind of pride in being English and white and being able to whip up a crowd on our own, and there was a sort of resistance toward what we were being asked to do— why should we have to study this man's records? Even I felt a little bit like that, because we were coming face to face with the reality of this thing, and it was a lot different from buying a record that you could take off when you felt like it. So we were all terrified of him, me most of all I think, because I was really making an attempt. Years later, Robbie Robertson of the Band told me that Sonny Boy had gone back to the South and hung out with them and had said he'd just been over playing with these white guys who didn't know how to play anything at all.

Yeah, Robertson once told me that Sonny Boy had said, "Those Englishmen want to play the blues so bad—and they play it so bad!"

Right. At the time, I thought we'd done pretty well. But by that time, the momentum of the band was toward becoming a pop group, and this man arrived and took it all back down to the basic blues. And I had to almost relearn how to play. It taught me a lot; it taught me the value of that music, which I still feel.

It's a very subtle language, blues. Much more than a matter of licks, it's a matter of sound, and how much you bend or flatten a note is directly related to the feeling you're trying to convey.

Yes. I got so obsessed with that that I forgot another essential, and I still do. And that is time—when you hit the note and when you stop. How you place it

exactly. I thought I'd learned very early on all about sound, about how with one note, if it sounds right, you can create everything. But I kept forgetting about where you put the note. I discovered when I went back and listened to some of the live Cream records, a year or so after making them, that I sometimes turned the time around, played on the wrong beat, because I was so into the sound of it.

What caused you to leave the Yardbirds just when they were on the brink of success? You're supposed to have been grossed out by that first pop hit, "For Your Love."

Yeah. At a certain point we started getting package tours, with the Ronettes, Billy J. Kramer, the Kinks, the Small Faces, lots of others, and we lost our following in the clubs. We decided to get suits, and I actually designed suits for us all. Then we did the Beatles' Christmas show, and at that point we really began to *feel* the lack of a hit. We'd be on for twenty minutes or half an hour, and either you were *very* entertaining or you did your hits. A lot of times the raveup bit got us through, and a lot of times it didn't. It became very clear that if the group was going to survive and make money, it would have to be on a popular basis. We couldn't go back to the clubs, because everyone had got that taste and seen what fun it would be to be famous.

So a lot of songs were bandied about, and Giorgio came up with a song by Otis Redding. I thought that would make a great single, because it was still R&B and soul, and we could do it really funky. Then Paul got the "For Your Love" demo, and he heard it with harpsichord. Whoa, harpsichord. Where does that leave me? Twelve-string guitar, I suppose. So we went in the studio to do both songs, but we did "For Your Love" first. Everyone was so bowled over by the obvious commerciality of it that we didn't even get to do the Otis Redding song, and I was very disappointed, *disillusioned*, by that. So my attitude within the group got really sour, and it was kind of hinted that it would be better for me to leave. 'Cause they'd already been to see Jeff Beck play, and at the time he was far more adaptable than I was. I was withdrawing into myself, becoming intolerable, really, dogmatic. So they kind of asked me to leave, and I left and felt a lot better for it.

Is this the time when you did nothing but practice every day for a year? Or is that story apocryphal?

Well, it wasn't a year, it was only a few months. I had never really practiced seriously, just practiced as I worked, until I got edged out of the Yardbirds. Then I went up to Oxford to stay with Ben Palmer, who had played piano in the Roosters and was a close friend, and during that time I began to think seriously about playing blues. And then, while I was there, I got a call from John Mayall, who'd heard I was serious, if you like, and not money orientated or popularity orientated, and he asked me to come and audition, or just come around and play. I got the job, and I actually got to feel like I was a key member of that band from the minute I walked in. Right away, I was choosing material for the band to do.

And Mayall went along with this? He has a reputation for being kind of autocratic.

Well, I think in me he met a soul mate who liked the same things. With the guitarist he'd had before, he hadn't been able to do certain numbers he wanted to do—the Otis Rush songs, for example, which I really wanted to do. We were really together on that.

"Double Trouble" and those other Otis Rush things were on Cobra, a really obscure label, and at that point I don't think they'd ever been reissued. I've always thought your playing had a lot in common with Otis'—you both really get off on minor-key blues. But where did you hear his stuff?

John was quite a collector. I went down to his house to audition and saw this record collection that was beyond my wildest dreams. It was almost all singles, and every one I put on, I would right away start saying, "We should do this."

Otis Rush is very intense. What did you think when you first heard him?

I always liked the wilder guys. I liked Buddy Guy, Freddie King and Otis Rush because they sounded like they were *really on the edge*, like they were barely in control and at any time they could hit a really bad note and the whole thing would fall apart—but, of course, they didn't. I liked that a lot more than B.B. I got into B.B. later, when I realized that polish was something, too.

You were with Mayall for a while and then, before making the 'Bluesbreakers' album, you left to go to Greece. What was that all about?

I was living in a place with some pretty mad people—great people, really. We were just drinking wine all day long and listening to jazz and blues, and we decided to pool our money, buy an estate wagon and take off round the world. The job with Mayall had become a job, and I wanted to go have some fun as well. So we ended up in Greece, playing blues, a couple of Rolling Stones songs, anything to get by. We met this club proprietor who hired us to open for a Greek band that played Beatles songs.

Then the Greek band was involved in a terrible road accident in which half of them were killed, and I found myself obliged to play with *both* bands. I was a quick learner then; I learned all the Beatles and Kinks songs they were doing, and I began to realize I was trapped, that the proprietor wouldn't let me go. He fired the rest of our band, and I was stuck there, with this Greek band. A couple of weeks of that, and I escaped somehow, headed back up here.

When I got back with Mayall, Jack Bruce was on bass, and we hit it off really well. Then he left to go with Manfred Mann, and Mayall got John McVie back. I decided that playing with Jack was more exciting. There was something creative there. Most of what we were doing with Mayall was imitating the records we got, but Jack had something else—he had no reverence for what we were doing, and so he was composing new parts as he went along playing. I literally had never heard that before, and it took me someplace else. I thought, well, if he could do that, and I could, and we could get a drummer . . . I could be Buddy Guy with a composing bass player. And that's how Cream came about.

But before that happened, you made the 'Bluesbreakers' album, which really has become a classic. How do you feel about it now?

At the time, I just thought it was a record of what we were doing every night in the clubs, with a few contrived riffs we made up kind of as afterthoughts, to fill out some of the things. It isn't any great achievement. It wasn't until I realized that the album was actually turning people on that I began to look at it differently.

Were you already thinking about starting Cream, or at least starting a band with Jack Bruce?

Well, after I had the experience of meeting and playing with Jack, the next thing that happened was that Ginger Baker came to this John Mayall gig. We'd worked the same circuits as the band Ginger was in, the Graham Bond Organization, and I'd liked their music, except it was too jazzy for me—the jazz side of Ray Charles, Cannonball Adderley, that's what they were playing. But then Ginger came backstage after this Mayall gig and said to me, "We're thinking of breaking up, and I like the way you play. Would you like to start a band?" I said, "Yeah, but I'd have to have Jack Bruce as well," and he kind of backed off that. It turned out that he and Jack were really chemically opposite, they were just *polarized*, always getting into fights. But we talked some more, and then we had a meeting at Ginger's house, where he and Jack immediately had an argument. I had no foresight whatsoever; I didn't think it was really serious. I left Mayall pretty soon after that.

What were your original ideas for Cream? You became known for those long jams, but on your first album, 'Fresh Cream,' there was a lot of country blues and other songs, all of them pretty compact.

I think our ideas about what we were supposed to be were pretty abstract. At first, I was throwing in Skip James and Robert Johnson songs, Jack was composing, and Ginger was composing. The American thing with "flower power" was filtering over, and I started seeing us as the London version of all that. I had an idea of how we could look good as well as be a good band. We were just scrambling for the forefront, and we didn't get much feedback until we played in front of an audience. That was when we realized that they actually wanted to go off somewhere. And we had the power to take them.

I heard Cream play one night at the Cafe Au Go Go in Greenwich Village, on your first trip over to the U.S. It was really loud—big stacks of amps in this little room! And you'd go off into these twenty-minute jams. I wasn't really aware that Jack and Ginger had such strong jazz backgrounds, but it did seem like they were going off into a much freer thing and sort of playing around your blues, which was like the music's backbone. Were you comfortable in that role?

Very occasionally, when my purist side got the better of me, I might get a little insecure. But if you think about it, if I had formed a trio, say, with a blues drummer and a blues bass player, we would have gone on imitating, as I had been doing with John Mayall. I would never have learned how to play anything of my own. In Cream, I was forced to try and improvise; whether I made a good job of it a lot of the time is debatable.

The three of us were on the road all the time, trusting one another, living in one another's hearts, and I found I was *giving*, you know, more than I had ever done before, and having faith in them. Jack is such a musical genius, there was no way he could be wrong about anything. I had to trust these people, so I did, I went with it. Of course, when we got back to our hotel rooms, we would all be listening to something different. And then I would sometimes have doubts, because a part of me still wanted to duplicate. That's the fear, you know, the fear of actually expressing and being naked.

There seems to have been a change in your listening tastes between the recording of 'Fresh Cream' and the second album, 'Disraeli Gears.' You started using some effects, like wah-wah, and you must have been very impressed by Albert King, because your solos on "Strange Brew" and several other songs were really pure Albert.

The big change was that Hendrix had arrived. Cream was playing at London Polytechnic, a college, and a friend brought this guy who was dressed up really freaky. This was Jimi. He spent a lot of time combing his hair in the mirror. Very cute but at the same time very genuine and very shy. I took to him straightaway, just as a man. Then he asked if he could jam, and he came up and did "Killing Floor," the Howlin' Wolf tune. And it blew me away. I was floored by his technique and his choice of notes, of sounds. Ginger and Jack didn't take to it kindly. They thought he was trying to upstage me. But I fell in love, straightaway. He became a soul mate for me and, musically, what I wanted to hear.

We were hanging out in some London clubs not long after that, and we started listening to the singles Stax was putting out by Albert King. We were both very, very attracted by that.

Even after you'd been hanging out with Hendrix, your playing and his were still really different.

He was the leader of his band, and that was that. What I felt with Cream was that I owed it to the other two not to try and dominate too much, even though I did. Apart from that, I didn't—and still don't—like to rely on effects that I can't create myself. It's what you're going to *play* that matters.

This was the period when you ascended to godhood.

All during Cream I was riding high on the "Clapton is God" myth that had been started up. I was flying high on an ego trip; I was pretty sure I was the best thing happening that was popular. Then we got our first kind of bad review, which, funnily enough, was in ROLLING STONE [RS 10, May 11, 1968, by Jon Landau]. The magazine ran an interview with us in which we were really praising ourselves, and it was followed by a review that said how boring and repetitious our performance had been. And it was true! The ring of truth just knocked me backward; I was in a restaurant, and I fainted. And after I woke up, I immediately decided that that was the end of the band.

There toward the end, we'd been flying with blinkers for so long, we weren't aware of the changes that were taking place musically. New people were coming up and growing, and we were repeating ourselves, living on legend, a year or two years out of date.

We didn't really have a *band* with Cream. We rarely played as an ensemble; we were three virtuosos, all of us soloing all the time.

You must have been in an acid phase toward the end of Cream. Some of the playing had that sort of . . . flavor.

Yeah, we did a lot of acid, took a lot of trips, in our spare time. And we did play on acid a couple of times.

There are still plenty of people around who think Cream was rock's absolute zenith. A lot of what's now called heavy metal came out of stuff you were doing, by way of Led Zeppelin. What can you say to those people?

You have to move on.

You were also doing some sessions—"While My Guitar Gently Weeps" with the Beatles, for example. And you played that gig in Toronto with John Lennon and Yoko Ono and the Plastic Ono Band. What was that like?

I'd met John and would see him a lot around the London clubs. I got the impression that he was a very shy, slightly bitter but also very sweet young man. There seemed to be a sort of game going on between John and George [Harrison], partly, I suppose, because John was a pretty good guitar player himself. When I was with Cream, George became interested in my playing, and I think he might have told John that he liked my work. So John assumed that if George liked me, I was probably better than George. So we got into these sessions.

John called me one Saturday morning and said, "Do you want to go to Toronto?" I said, "Sure. When?" And he said, "In a couple of hours." I happened to have my equipment at home, so I met them at the airport, with [bassist] Klaus Voormann and [drummer] Alan White. We all got first-class seats on the plane and learned the repertoire on the way. There was a guy there who was a Gillette salesman—I'll never forget that—and he was trying to give us free razors, 'cause we all had beards.

I got slightly disillusioned when we landed at the other end and John and Yoko were whisked off in a limousine and all the band was left standing in the rain. We didn't know how we were going to get to the gig or anything, but that wasn't their problem. Then before the gig, we did so much coke that I actually threw up and passed out. They had to take me out and lay me on the ground. And at the last minute, we realized that we were going on between . . . I think it was Jerry Lee Lewis and Chuck Berry, and we were terrified. We were shaking. But it turned out to be a great experience.

You were getting involved with some heavyweight people.

Well, I'd been with Jack and Ginger, and those were heavy people. I remember one gig in the north of England where Jack had what appeared to be a semi-epileptic fit because of the adrenaline. He got in such a state that he actually passed out. Ginger and I played for about half an hour without any bass. And Ginger was using [heroin] pretty heavily; he would sometimes just throw up while he was playing a solo.

I know you haven't had much good to say about Blind Faith, but I actually think the album holds up really well.

Well, there was a lack of direction in Blind Faith, or a reticence to actually declare among ourselves where we were going. Because it seemed to be enough just to be making the money, and that wasn't good; the record company and the management had taken over. I felt that it was too soon for Steve [Winwood]. He was feeling uncomfortable, and since it had originally been my idea, I was uncomfortable. I started looking for somewhere else to go, an alternative, and I found that Delaney and Bonnie [Bramlett] were a godsend. After the Blind Faith tour, I lived with Delaney for a while.

The first night we met, we were in New York, and we went down to Steve Paul's club, the Scene, and we took acid. From there we went to see Mac Rebennack [Dr. John] and hung out in his hotel room, and then we went back to our hotel, to one of the rooms, his or mine. And Delaney looked straight into my eyes and told me I had a gift to *sing* and that if I *didn't* sing, God would take it away. I said, "No, man, I can't sing." But he said, "Yes, you can. Hit this note: *Ahhh . . .*" And it was suddenly like the most impossible thing I could do was to hit that note, because of the acid. So it quavered, but I did hit it, and I started to feel that if I was to gain his respect, I ought to really pursue this. That night we started talking about me making a solo album, with his band.

Didn't you sing back when you were playing folk-blues for the beatniks?

Yeah, I started singing in the pubs, but I had a very weak voice. I still have a small voice, 'cause I have no diaphragm to speak of. Then I sang a couple of backup things with the Yardbirds, but that was it. Most of the time, I concentrated on the guitar. Which is a shame, 'cause maybe I'd have been better if I'd managed to balance out the singing and playing at an earlier stage of my career.

Sounds like Delaney, being from Mississippi, got into a Baptist-preacher bit to get you singing again. So what happened after the Blind Faith tour? Did you start working on the solo album?

No, first of all we did a tour of England and Europe, as Delaney and Bonnie and Friends with Eric Clapton. And having got me to sing, Delaney started trying to get me to compose, as well. So we were writing a lot.

And that was great. He'd start something off, and when I came up with the next bit, he'd say, "Look what you can do." Some of the time, I think, it was so he could get fifty percent of the songwriting, but it was also inspiring me. By the end of that tour, I was ready to make the album and felt very sure of myself.

This must have been the first time you were able to work with a band of American musicians. Did you notice a difference?

When we finished the album [*Eric Clapton*], I thought it was a great record, for me. I'd never sung like that before. Though all I was doing really was copying Delaney, doing my best to sing those licks and project like him.

It's funny, because on the 'Bluesbreakers' album, your vocal on the Robert Johnson tune ("Ramblin' on My Mind") seems to me like better blues singing than almost anybody coming out of England at the time, because you didn't just torture every syllable like just about everybody else. You must have lost confidence in your singing after that.

I felt a lot of insecurity about it in Blind Faith, because I felt that Steve was probably the finest singer in England. His range . . . see, my range isn't very good, and he can really get up there.

Toward the end of the Bonnie and Delaney thing, I started to feel a lot of pressure, to feel trapped. Certain parts of the concert audiences had come to see me, and I'd do one solo number, and they'd all applaud and say, "More Eric Clapton." That created a kind of tension inside the group, and I sort of felt I was spoiling it for them. At the same time, Delaney didn't want to let me go, because I had the popularity and the status to carry the whole thing a lot further. It was heart-rending, but finally I extricated myself from it and came back home, without any kind of idea of what to do next. Then at that point, [drummer] Jim Gordon and [bassist] Carl Radle got in touch with me; they'd asked Delaney for a raise, and he'd fired them all. And I hired Jim and Carl and Bobby [Whitlock, a keyboard player]. And they came to England, and we lived together at my house for a year, and we played night and day and took all kinds of dope. We did a club tour in England as Derek and the Dominos, which was funny, because no one knew who we were. But the word spread very quickly, and we had good crowds most of the time.

Why did you go to Miami to record 'Layla'?

The attraction was Tom Dowd. I'd worked with him in Cream, and he was to me—and still is—the ideal recording man.

Yeah, he engineered all those great early Atlantic R&B and soul sessions and practically invented stereo.

Right. And he can guide you in a very constructive way. So we got there, we were doing a lot of dope and drinking a lot and just partying. It was great times. After about a week of jamming, I wanted to go hear the Allman Brothers, who were playing nearby, because I'd heard Duane Allman on Wilson Pickett's "Hey Jude," and he blew me away with that. After the concert, I invited him back to the studio, and he stayed. We fell in love, and the album took off from there.

The first time I ran into you was during those sessions at Criteria Recording Studios. There was a lot of dope around, especially heroin, and when I showed up, everyone was just spread out on the carpet, nodded out. Then you appeared in the doorway in an old brown leather jacket, with your hair slicked back like a greaser's, looking like you hadn't slept in days. You just looked around at the wreckage and said, to nobody in particular, "The boy stood on the burning deck/Whence all but he had fled." And then you split.

Yeah. We were staying in this hotel on the beach, and whatever drug you wanted, you could get it at the newsstand; the girl would just take your orders. We were on the up and the down, the girl and the boy, and the drink was usually Ripple or Gallo. Very heavy stuff. I remember Ahmet [Ertegun, chairman of Atlantic Records] arriving at some point, taking me aside and crying, saying he'd been through this shit with Ray [Charles], and he knew where this was gonna end, and could I stop now. I said, "I don't know what you're talking about, man. This is no problem." And, of course, he was dead right.

I guess you have to work that stuff out for yourself.

I don't know about that. When I started using [heroin], George [Harrison] and Leon [Russell] asked me, "What are you doing? What is your intention?" And I said, "I want to make a journey through the dark, on my own, to find out what it's like in there. And then come out the other end." But that was easy for me to say, because I had a craft, music, that I could turn to. For people who don't have that, there's a lot of danger; if you haven't got something to hold on to, you're gone. It's no good just saying, "Well, that person is gonna go through it, no matter what." You've actually got to stop them and try to make them think.

The music you and Duane got into on 'Layla' was really special, a once-in-a-lifetime thing. Did you tour after you finished recording?

Not with Duane, of course, but the Dominos did a very big tour of America. We copped a lot of dope in Miami—a *lot* of dope—and that went with us. Then I met up with this preacher from New York who was married to one of the Ronettes, and he asked if he could come along on part of the tour. The spiritual part of me was attracted to this man, but he immediately started giving me a very hard time about the dope. I felt very bad about this, and after the first week on the road, I put everything I had in a sack and flushed it down the loo. Then, of course, I was going to the other guys, trying to score off them.

By the end of the tour, the band was getting very, very loaded, doing way too much. Then we went back to England, tried to make a second album, and it broke down halfway through because of the paranoia and the tension. And the band just . . . dissolved. I remember to this day being in my house, feeling totally lost and hearing Bobby Whitlock pull up in the driveway outside and *scream* for me to come out. He sat in his car outside all day, and I hid. And that's when I went on my journey into the smack. I basically stayed in the house with my girlfriend for about two and a half years, and although we weren't using any needles, we got very strung out. All that time, though, I was running a cassette machine and playing; I had that to hold on to. At the end of that period, I found I had boxes full of playing, as if there was something struggling to survive.

I guess that's what kept you alive.

I had no care for the consequences; the idea of dying didn't bother me. Dying from drugs didn't seem to me then to be a terrible thing. When Jimi died, I cried all day because he'd left me behind. But as I grow older, as I live more, death becomes more of a reality, something I don't choose to step toward too soon.

So then, in January 1973, Pete Townshend organized a concert for you at the Rainbow, in London, with Ron Wood, Steve Winwood and others.

I did that very much against my will. I wasn't even really there. It was purely Townshend's idea, and I didn't know what I'd done to earn it. It's simply that he's a great humanitarian and cannot stand to see people throw their lives away. It didn't matter to him if I was willing or unwilling; he was making the effort so that I would realize, someday, that someone cared. I'm always indebted to him for that.

If that didn't draw you out, what did?

Carl Radle sent me a tape of him playing with Dick Sims and Jamie Oldaker in Tulsa. I listened to it and played along with it, and it was great. So I sent him a telegram saying, "Maintain loose posture, stay in touch." And at some point after that, I started to get straight.

Then you made '461 Ocean Boulevard,' your resurrection album. Are you happy with that record?

Yeah, very. I'd wanted to do "Willie and the Hand Jive" since my childhood, and the Robert Johnson song ["Steady Rollin' Man"] and "Motherless Children" for almost as long. George Terry was there [in Miami], and when we were hanging out before the band arrived from Tulsa, he played me this Bob Marley album, *Burnin'*, and "I Shot the Sheriff" was on there. I loved it, and we did it, but at the time I didn't think it should go on the album, let alone be a single. I didn't think it was fair to Bob Marley, and I thought we'd done it with too much of a white feel or something. Shows what I know. When I went to Jamaica after that, a lot of people were very friendly because of the light it had thrown on Bob Marley, and Marley himself was very friendly to me as well.

Your Tulsa band could play everything from reggae to blues to pop. What happened to that band?

Toward the end of that particular band, we were gettin' out of it again, and I was in the lead. I started to get straight, but I was drinking maybe two bottles a day of whatever hard stuff I could get my hands on. And there was real bad tension in the band that was aimed at me. Then I hired Albert Lee. We became friends, and there was a division between these two Englishmen and the Tulsa boys. And at the end of this particular tour, I think it was in '78, I fired everybody. Not only that, I didn't even tell them—I fired them by telegram. And I never saw Carl again. He'd saved me at one point, sending me that tape, and I turned my back on him. And Carl died. It was, I think, drugs, but I hold myself responsible for a lot of that. And I live with it.

Bobby Whitlock is a songwriter in Nashville, right? And I read recently that Jim Gordon had been convicted of murdering his mother. I heard that you were among the few people from his past who got in touch and tried to help.

I did try. When I was last in L.A., I kept making inquiries about how to get in to see him. But then I spoke to [drummer] Jim Keltner about it, and Keltner said it probably wouldn't be a good idea, that they had him on so much Thorazine he didn't really know what was going on.

Your next band was all English. Had you become disenchanted with crazy Americans?

Yeah. The idea of being with English gentlemen was a break. They weren't ambitious. They just wanted to play good music, and that was really easy for a while. Unfortunately, there were some things they just couldn't do. And one was to play the blues.

I guess I was underachieving a little bit, putting a certain kind of playing to one side, because I didn't think the band would be able to do it. But there were things they did bring out in me, especially a wish to be more of a composer of melodic tunes rather than just a player, which was very unpopular with a lot of people.

But if you're a blues player, which I am by my birthright, it seems, you can't face it all the time. Sometimes you need to hear some harmonic softeners, some quiet, some subtle, to kind of quench the fire and calm yourself. Don Williams' music and some of the other things I was into were very calming to me. When I got back to being *me*, it was almost a shock to realize how tough my stuff was in comparison.

When you were touring England in the late Seventies with that band, you urged one audience to support Enoch Powell, a member of Parliament who had a decidedly racist bent. Somehow I had trouble picturing you as a racist.

I was drunk, and a drunk will blab off about anything to as many people as he can; you cannot believe anything a drunk says. The funny thing is that I was able to play through all that. The old survivor, the automatic pilot, still managed to help me play. But there were many occasions around that time when I had to be led offstage and given some black coffee or some oxygen. I was really on the edge of collapse, completely insane.

I remember your coming to America in 1981 for a tour and landing in the hospital about eight days into the tour. Was that when your drinking started to come to an end?

Not quite. But it was pointed out to me while I was in hospital that I had a drink problem, and I think that was the first time anyone had ever said something like that to me. But I was still happy drinking and actually quite terrified of not drinking. I had to go further down that road to complete insanity before I stopped. It wasn't until it finally hit me in the head that I was killing other people around me, *as well as* killing myself and going insane, that I decided to stop.

What is the lure there, the attraction, of addictive behavior, whether it's using dope or booze?

It's obsessive. Part of my character is made up of an obsession to push something to the limit. It can be of great use if my obsession is channeled into constructive thought or creativity, but it can also be mentally or physically or spiritually destructive. I think what happens to an artist is, when he feels the mood swings that we all suffer from if we're creative, instead of facing the reality that this is an opportunity to create, he will turn to something that will stop that mood, stop that irritant. And that would be drink or heroin or whatever. He won't want to face that creative urge, because he knows the self-exploration that must be undertaken, the pain that must be faced. This happens most, or very painfully, to artists. Unless they realize

what it is that is doing that to them, they'll always be dabbling in something or other to kill it.

You reorganized your band again before you recorded 'Money and Cigarettes,' trading your English rhythm section for an American one. Do these things come in cycles?

I started working on that album with the English rhythm section, but I found that I couldn't get any kick out of them for some reason. The thrill was gone, and there was a feeling of paranoia in the studio because they sensed it, too. I spoke to Tom Dowd about it, and he said, "Just be brutal. Fire them all, send them all home. They'll understand. And then we'll bring in some people." He brought in [bassist Donald] "Duck" Dunn and [drummer] Roger Hawkins, and the first day they came in, we set up and played "Cross-Cut Saw" all day.

I found I was really getting stretched, and it was the first time I'd been stretched for several years, simply because I'd been playing with people who were laying back, and the more I laid back, the more they laid back. Whereas this rhythm section, they counted themselves off and started playing, and I didn't have to be there. If I wanted to get in on it, I had to work fucking hard. And that's when I decided I was getting back to where I should be.

Yeah, hearing the best stuff on that album was like welcoming back a long-lost friend. "Ain't Going Down," in which you sang, "I've still got something left to say," and got the guitar screaming, was the most exciting thing I'd heard you do since 'Layla.' And on that tour, with Jamie Oldaker back on drums and Duck really pushing you, you were playing like a new man. Which, in a lot of ways, I guess, you were. Though, in certain ways, I think the best records you made in the Seventies were the live albums, 'E.C. Was Here' and 'Just One Night.'

Yeah, there's always been a big difference between the stage and the studio for me. The studio has always been an alien place you have to be in temporarily. If I did just studio work, I think I'd learn how to do it one day. But I'm mainly a road musician. The music I always feel is the best is the music you make for the gods and for the audience that night. And usually the best music you make in the studio is the music you make when the machines are turned off.

When we talked after 'Money and Cigarettes' came out, and I said I liked it, you said the next album would be better. And 'Behind the Sun' is better, especially the stuff you did with Phil Collins. It's both you and a real contemporary kind of sound. I like the three Jerry Williams tunes you recorded in L.A., but I'm not sure they mix with the rest that well.

Well, I'd really wanted to work with Phil, but when

Warner Bros. heard what we'd done, they felt there wasn't enough hit-singles material. They sent me some of Jerry Williams' tunes, and I was so impressed with them that I went out to L.A. and recorded three of them. I think Jerry Williams is phenomenal; I'd very much like to work with him in the future.

What about other current music? Has anything you've heard in the last year or so impressed you or done something to you emotionally?

I'd like to say that Prince really took me by storm.

I happened to be in Montreal, touring with Roger Waters, the day *Purple Rain* opened there. Because of the dryness of that [Waters] show, the rigidity of it, if you like, I was feeling a bit stifled. So I went along to see *Purple Rain,* because I've always liked Prince's records. And when I saw that film, it made me feel that something very powerful was going to happen again in popular music, and *was* happening with that man. That gave me a lot of hope for the future of music.

18

Bo Diddley

INTERVIEWED BY KURT LODER (1987)

By today's standards—and maybe by any standard—many of the black performers who pioneered rock & roll were screwed out of much of the money made off their music. Chuck Berry didn't co-write "Maybellene" with Alan Freed, the white deejay—Freed simply sliced off some of the writing credit as part of his entrepreneurial due. Similarly, one wonders if the great Elmore James ever even met Morris Levy, the notorious record mogul—and yet they, too, mysteriously share the credit for one of James' tunes. The music business of the Fifties was rife with such chicanery—to some extent, it was standard business practice, acknowledged, however grudgingly, by all parties. But with the passing of years, and the continual (and highly profitable) repackaging of early rock music, many of the aging artists involved began to get angry enough to consider taking legal action. Bo Diddley was one of these.

What follows is an example of a Q&A that required a relatively long introduction—to set the cultural stage of the Fifties for Eighties readers, many of whom are too young to remember that now-remote decade—and a considerable amount of firsthand research, especially in attempting to track the transcorporate peregrinations of the much-abused Chess Records catalogue. After this piece appeared in ROLLING STONE, I heard through a PR intermediary that Bo was somewhat unhappy about the way in which he had been depicted—as if he were eking out his final days in backwoods poverty. It was not my intention to do this. Bo Diddley is a man of great dignity, and well off by his own reckoning. The fact that he feels no need for a mansion is much to be admired. The fact that he couldn't walk out and buy ten of them if he so desired, however, is—given the influence of his music—painful proof of the epic shortchanging he's suffered at the hands of an industry he very much helped to set in motion.

—K. L.

THE LITANY of Bo Diddley's great hits is one of the fundamental incantations of original American rock & roll. From the characteristically self-celebratory "Bo Diddley" in 1955 (which featured "I'm a Man" on the flip) through "Diddy Wah Diddy," "Who Do You Love," "Hey! Bo Diddley," "Mona," "Crackin' Up," "Say Man" (his pop peak: Top Twenty) and into the early Sixties with "Road Runner" and "You Can't Judge a Book by the Cover," Bo's music is one of the true wellsprings of rock.

If Bo Diddley were in his artistic prime today, with sharp lawyers and management, he might well be—like so many fey pop youths of the moment—a very wealthy man. Instead, one of the fathers of rock & roll lives in a trailer at the end of a long and bumpy white-sand path deep in the woods around Archer, Florida, about half an hour outside of Gainesville. Pulled up in front of the double-width mobile home is a gold-toned Ford pickup with a brass duck mounted on the hood. Parked off to the side is a long, white '64 Cadillac in some disrepair ("It's an antique," Bo says). A small but clamorous pack of semi-domesticated dogs guards the trailer's entrance—souvenirs, like Bo's Aussie-crafted guitars, of his world travels.

Inside, all is tidy. There's a sofa covered with a flower-print quilt, side tables neatly decked with towels and a coat stand topped with a collection of Bo's trademark lids. On the floor are two disconnected TVs and a VCR, all blown out in a recent electrical storm. Nearby lies Bo's guitar case, encrusted with Coors-beer stickers and road mottoes along the lines of GIRLS WANTED. The square-bodied Kinman guitar inside is tuned, of course, to an open chord. There is a large Bible, opened to Job, and on the walls a scattering of posters emblazoned with slogans: BEAM ME UP, SCOTTY, THERE'S NO INTELLIGENT LIFE DOWN HERE. And IF YOU THINK ROCK & ROLL STARTED WITH ELVIS, YOU DON'T KNOW DIDDLEY. Bo's girlfriend, Marilyn, a cheerful, thirty-year-old white woman, sits at a dining table near the kitchen, sipping a Pepsi.

It is still morning, but Bo has been up since daybreak and has just returned from a maintenance visit to the seventy-two-acre piece of property he owns in Hawthorne, about forty miles away. Until recently, he lived there, in an elaborate log cabin, with his second wife, Kay, who is also white. But after some two decades of marriage, they've just divorced, and now Bo has to sell the Hawthorne spread. He's still too pained by the split to say much else about it. He is wearing work pants and a pair of dusty brogans, and his full, graying hair is swept straight back on his head. He seems weary as he takes a seat by Marilyn at the dining table, although whether from his morning's labors in Hawthorne or from the general weight of his fifty-eight years is not clear.

Bo says he lied so much about his age when he was young that he's sometimes forgotten what it actually is. He agrees that he was in fact born on December 30, 1928, in a house in McComb, Mississippi—deep-blues country. His father, about whom he knows little, was a man named Bates. His mother was named Ethel Wilson. She couldn't afford to keep her child, so in a scenario common to rural black life at the time, she placed her eight-month-old son with her first cousin Gussie McDaniel. Thus, says Bo, his full legal name is Ellas Bates McDaniel.

Gussie's husband, Robert, died when Bo was little. At about age seven, Bo moved with Gussie, her two daughters and her son to Chicago, to live with an Uncle Herbert and Aunt Janie—the latter a churchgoing woman who took the boy on regular visits to the Ebenezer Baptist Church. Those were the Depression years—"*hard* times," Bo says—and the family scraped by on occasional stockyard jobs and government relief. When he was about eight, Bo saw a man "dragging a stick across some strings" and decided that he, too, wanted to play the violin. The congregation at Ebenezer Baptist took up a collection to buy him one, and soon he was studying with the church's musical director, Professor O.W. Frederick, from whom he also learned trombone. "I used to read all this funny music, like Tchaikovsky," Bo says. "But then, I didn't see too many black dudes playin' no violin."

His nickname, Bo Diddley, was given to him by grammar-school classmates, he says; he has no idea what, if anything, it means. In the early Forties, he taught himself to play guitar the easy way—open tuned—and began performing on street corners with guitarist Earl Hooker, a fellow student at the Foster Vocational High School. Bo wrote his own tunes even then—songs with titles like "Hey, Noxzema" and "Dirty Muthuh Fuh Yuh." He left school at sixteen, and between jobs at a punchboard factory and as an elevator operator at a seat-cover company (along with occasional amateur boxing matches), he continued playing the streets through the end of the Forties with a group that included Little Joe Williams on second guitar, a washtub bassist named Roosevelt and Jerome Green on maracas. ("Jerome couldn't carry a tune in a bag," says Bo, "but that sucker could shake those maracas.") He also married a woman named Ethel Smith, with whom he had two children, Tanya and Anthony.

By the early Fifties, with the now legendary Chicago blues scene exploding all around them—Muddy Waters, Little Walter, Howlin' Wolf—Bo and his band had moved off the streets and into the city's booming South Side clubs. In 1955, he was signed to Checker Records, a subsidiary of Chess, the renowned blues label run by Leonard and Phil Chess. His classic Checker sides—not just the obvious hits but such terrific nuggets as "Diddley Daddy," "Hush Your Mouth," "Bring It to Jerome" (with Green singing lead) and the moody blues-violin opus "The Clock Strikes Twelve"—revealed Bo to be a raw and powerful talent. There were Latin and even African elements in his music, but his roof-shaking vocals were straight out of the Delta-blues tradition. He was a rock & roll hitmaker before Chuck Berry—a Chess stable mate—had even released his first record.

Along with the classic singles came a series of classic albums: *Go Bo Diddley*; *Bo Diddley Is a Gunslinger*; *Have Guitar, Will Travel*. The titles occasionally alluded to transient musical trends—*Bo Diddley's a Twister, Surfin' with Bo Diddley*—but the music remained, even through the Sixties, inimitably his own. By 1967, however, when he scored his last entry in the pop Top 100 with a song called "Ooh Baby," the glory days were over. He relocated to Los Angeles and then—at the suggestion of his pals the Everly Brothers—to New Mexico. There he settled in a town called Los Lunas and even became a deputy sheriff for Valencia County. By the end of the Seventies, though, he'd moved to Florida, where, when he's not on the road—as he pretty much still is most weeks, flying off to play with pickup bands across the country—he's content to remain.

Bo is a bitter man in many ways—bitter about what he sees as the financial injustices he suffered, first at the hands of Chess Records, then at the hands of the New Jersey–based Sugar Hill label, which bought the Chess catalogue in the mid-Seventies. Like many black artists of the Fifties—Chuck Berry, for example, or Frankie Lymon and the Teenagers, acts that sacrificed songwriting credits to the white deejays and label executives who helped make them stars—Bo feels he was exploited throughout his career.

Was he? Details are difficult to come by at this remove. Leonard Chess is dead, and his brother, Phil, who lives in Arizona now, was unavailable for comment. According to Marshall Chess—Leonard's son, who grew up around the Chess studios from the mid-Fifties—Bo was "always coming in every three weeks for advances. He was one of those guys who would five-hundred you to death; then, at the end of the year, he'd see a statement where he owed $30,000, and he'd say, 'I don't owe that.' "

Marshall Chess acknowledges that "black artists in that era had a problem"—record-company royalty payments were generally low, from two to four percent and only half that much for foreign sales. But, says Chess, "we never cheated any artists. We weren't that kind of company. I'm sure that Bo got paid on every record sold, minus returns." The Chess catalogue was sold in 1967 to GRT, a tape-retailing company that has since gone bankrupt. Sugar Hill Records bought the catalogue in 1974, but Joe Robinson, head of Sugar Hill, declined to discuss any Chess-related business while he is embroiled in a civil suit against MCA, the company that entered into a distribution agreement with Sugar Hill in 1983 and now owns the Chess catalogue. Bo hopes that MCA, at last, will "do the right thing" and pay him the royalties he feels he's owed. Says an MCA spokesman, "MCA is paying royalties whenever a contract calls for it."

To straighten out his tangled business affairs, Bo has retained the services of the New York–based Artists Rights Enforcement Corporation, which also represents such other dissatisfied Chess acts as Etta James.

In the meantime, Bo continues to crank out albums on his own. One, *Ain't It Good to Be Free,* has been released on the French New Rose label, but Bo is unable to get a U.S. recording deal. He remains a marvel in performance—as raucously riveting as ever —but he is frustrated by the tastes of today's kids, who, he feels, have never known real rock & roll; they seem to prefer the screaming guitars of modern rock and perceive his music, if at all, as simply old-fashioned. "I feel like I'm bein' led to the slaughterhouse," he says grimly.

But Bo Diddley is a survivor, still the same man who sang, a quarter of a century ago, "You got your radio turned down too low— turn it up!" The message remains the same, and just as salutary, however many people are still able to hear it.

The Forties and early Fifties, when you started out in Chicago, were the years when Muddy Waters was electrifying the Delta blues and playing around town with people like Little Walter. What was that scene like?

I knew 'em all. They used to play the 708 Club all the time. At first, when I was still a teenager, I used to sneak in and hide behind the cigarette machine, and the bouncer would catch me and throw my tail in the streets.

But you'd sneak back in?

Yeah, because I figured, you know, Muddy Waters had somethin' goin', and, man, I was tryin' to find out what it was. Muddy Waters had everything sewed up around Chicago—I mean, *sewed up.* Big time. I liked what him and Walter was doin'. Walter . . . there'll never be another harmonica player like Little Walter. He created something that will live on.

Were these guys nice to you—a young kid sneaking into clubs to catch their sets?

Nope. I'm not gonna lie about it, no. Muddy wasn't an easy guy to learn about, you know? He had his thing, and he didn't associate too much with cats like me.

What about when you made it into the clubs yourself?

No. See, everybody had a little bit of professional jealousy—they felt, like, threatened, you know? They were blues cats; I was a little bit different. So we didn't hang together, 'cause if you played some other kind of music, you didn't hang with the blues dudes, you know? Because you didn't have anything in common. Anybody came along doin' somethin' new was almost like a threat. But in reality, it wasn't a threat. It was just a new dude came along with something—this is the way you keep the bandwagon rolling, you know? So they thought I was the weird one. But I was the one that nobody wanted to go onstage behind. They'd say, "Man, I don't want to follow you." I'd say, "Well, bring your fire extinguisher onstage with you, 'cause I'm gonna set that sucker on fire. You put it out."

When did you come up with the Bo Diddley beat?

Oh, in 1952, 1953, something like that. It was just something that I put together. Everybody tried to give me this bullshit that "Bo Diddley" is public domain. They tried to say it was "Hambone"—"Hambone, Hambone, have you heard/Papa gonna buy me a mockin' bird." But "Bo Diddley" ain't that. And they say you can't copyright a beat. But "Bo Diddley" is not just a beat; it's a melody *and* a rhythm pattern. The same as "Harlem Nocturne" or anything else. So what is this bullshit everybody tries to tell me?

How did you hook up with Chess Records in 1955?

I went to Vee Jay first with this song I had, "Uncle

John." Vee Jay was across the street from Chess. And they didn't like the song. They said it didn't sound right—said it was "jungle music." So one day I was breakin' bottles in the alley over there, and this cat opened a door and was throwin' old broke records out the back. And I says, "Is there a record company up in here?" He says, "Yeah—Chess Records."

So you were ushered in to see the Chess brothers?

I wasn't ushered. I *walked* in there. I said, "Man, you all make records in here?" And Phil was there, he said, "Yeah, whatta you want?" I said, "Well, I got a song." He said, "Let us hear it." And when I started playin', Phil called his brother Leonard in and said, "Listen to this."

Did they take you right into the studio to record it?

Uh-uh. They told me to rewrite it. The words was a little rough. It had lyrics like "Bowlegged rooster told a cocklegged duck/Say, you ain't good-lookin', but you sure can . . . crow." The old folks didn't understand that. It took me about seven days to rewrite it, and that song became "Bo Diddley."

What about the flip side of that record, "I'm a Man"?

That took about thirty takes. Because they wanted me to spell *man*. We'd get to that spot in the song, and they'd say, "Okay, now spell it—m-a-n." Real quick, like that—you know how some white guys is out of time? They couldn't tell me exactly what the hell they were talkin' about. So I said it the way they had: "M-a-n." They said, "Goddamn, just spell it." This went on all night. Finally, I was getting tired, and I said it real slow: "M . . . a . . . n." And they said, "That's what we're talkin' about!" I said, "Why in the hell didn't you coulda told me that the first?" That's the truth, I ain't lyin'.

"Bo Diddley" went Top Five on the R&B charts and got you onto Ed Sullivan's TV show—where I gather Sullivan wanted you to sing "Sixteen Tons," a big Tennessee Ernie Ford hit that you were performing onstage at the time, and you refused.

Ed Sullivan did everything in his power to shut Bo Diddley down, because he claimed that I double-crossed him on that song. What happened was, they had my name written on a piece of paper; my name is Bo Diddley, and I had a song called "Bo Diddley." He heard me singin' "Sixteen Tons" and wanted me to sing it on the show. So I thought I was supposed to do two tunes. I went out there and sang "Bo Diddley" first—that's what I was *there* for, y'understand?—and he got mad. He says to me, "You're the first colored boy ever double-crossed me on a song," or a show, or somethin' like this. And I started to hit the dude, because I was a young hoodlum out of Chicago, and I

thought "colored boy" was an insult. My manager at the time grabbed me and said, "That's Mr. Sullivan." I said, "Who is that?" I didn't know who the hell he was, man. Shoot.

When I did the Ed Sullivan show, they gave me a check for 750 bucks. CBS cat say, "You gotta sign it, but you gotta give me the check back. This is a formality." I says, "Uh . . . formality—who's that?" He says, "We get you on the show, but you gotta kick the check back." I said, "What kind of crap is this?" I done signed my name to that sucker, you understand? Who was gonna pay taxes on that? But all right, I gave him the check back. Then a few years later, I picked up a book and read where they paid Elvis Presley, for his first appearances on Ed Sullivan, $50,000—and I got sick.

That told me what was happenin'—what rock & roll really was, and rhythm & blues. Rhythm & blues was for *me*—"ripoff & bullshit." It was to keep me from gettin' my hands on any money, and anybody else that looked like Bo Diddley—meanin' black cats. Elvis himself didn't have anything to do with this—he was only takin' whatever he could get comin' up. But, see, the people that was dealin' in this was much older. And they'd say, "We're gonna take *him* to the back, but we're going to take *him* to the front," you understand? We were dealin' with this type of thing. So rock & roll was for the Caucasians, and R&B was for the black cats. And I was black, so I got hung up in the R&B, which . . . the money wasn't the same. If you're R&B, you don't make the big money. If you're rock & roll, you make all the money, or your price is a lot different, one way or another. It was basically all the same music, but if you could get a white boy to record it, certain stations would play it. "We'd break it if you get a white boy to do it"—some radio-station people told record companies this.

How about on the road—what kind of money could you make touring back in the Fifties?

Would you believe—hold on to your ass—would you believe I made as low as $375, and I had the biggest fuckin' record ever? This is 1955, 1956. Who got the money? *Somebody* got the money, but we didn't have any way of knowin' it. Say a club owner wanted me in a club. The booking agency might say, "Yeah, we got Bo Diddley. He's gonna cost you $1,250." And they'd send me, say, $550, you understand? When I started catchin' dudes doin' this kind of stuff, they didn't want no more to do with me, you know? And this hurt.

What about those big package tours they had back then?

Oh, man. They didn't pay us nothin', you know?

185

We were told the budget was so-and-so, the man's got six acts, he can't pay no more than that. And nobody never walked up to us and said, "Hey, man, the tour was great, I made a little money, here's a thousand dollars." Or, "Here's $200." Or, "Here's $50 for you and the band." Not a fuckin' quarter. Nothin'.

The music business is a *good* business, but why do we have to have all the fuckin' thieves that rip off cats? *We* have it bad enough runnin' up and down this damn highway, ridin' these airplanes, stayin' up all times of night, tryin' to get to a gig to make people happy.

What about record sales? Did you see much money from "Bo Diddley," for example?

Say what? Shit. I got a brand-new Chevrolet station wagon, two door; it cost $2,800, and I think I paid for it about three times. The car was an advance on royalties. I think I saw another check for about $1,200.

Did you ever ask Chess about your record sales?

I got some counts, but I know damn well they wasn't right. But you didn't ask questions. If I'd have asked questions, I would not have lasted this long. They would have figured out how to stop me right there, before I got started. "You're gettin' too smart," you know? "We're gonna shut you down, pull your plug." And then they'd shut off your juice, you understand? And that means you ain't workin' no more. So I just shut up, played it smart and learned all I could.

What did you think of the Chess brothers?

Well, they gave me a break. Me and Chuck Berry, Little Walter, John Lee Hooker—we *was* Chess Records. We were the beginnin' of rock & roll, and Chess Records should be labeled as that—it deserves that honor. People wouldn't even bother with no stuff like "Bo Diddley" and "I'm a Man" and stuff like that ten years earlier, or even a year earlier. Then Leonard and Phil Chess decided to take a chance, and suddenly a whole different scene, a different kind of music, came in. And that was the beginning of rock & roll. I thought Leonard and Phil were very nice until I found out what I found out.

Which was?

Well, Bo Diddley ain't got shit. My records are sold all over the world, and I ain't got a fuckin' dime. If Chess Records gave me, in all the time that I dealt with them, if they gave me $75,000 in royalty checks, I'll eat my hat. Boil it and eat it. *Somebody* got some money—everybody in this business has big mansions and stuff, you know? I got a log mansion. When I left Chess Records, they said I owed them $125,000.

How come?

That's what I'd like to know. How? And whatever it was, it should have been paid off in, say, two years. It don't take eight years or somethin'. My stuff is selling all over the world—everywhere. Where is the money? Bo Diddley did not get it. I would like for the government to find out: Where is the money? Now, if the publishing company got it, that's cool, because I sold all of my catalogue to the publishing company, Arc Music—that's Gene Goodman, which is Benny Goodman's brother. He's the publisher. Gene has been pretty nice. But there were things that went on that Gene can't explain, because he wasn't involved—it was Leonard Chess. And Leonard Chess is dead.

Why did you sell Arc your song rights?

Because I didn't have no money—this was back in the Sixties or Seventies. And since I was in show business, the only place I could get any money from was the record company or the publishing company. I *should* have been getting it from the record company. I should have had *checks*. But I didn't. And they wouldn't lend me none, so the publisher jumped up and said, "We'll buy your catalogue." So I said, "Okay, I'll write more songs." You dig? You get into trouble, you got two or three kids to feed, you don't think about nothin'. Everybody says, "You did the worst thing in your life, sellin' your songs." Well, I couldn't *find* these people that's tellin' me that when I had two or three kids with their mouths running and openin' the refrigerator and there ain't a goddamn thing in there to eat. You'll sell the shirt off of your back if you're tryin' to feed your kids and pay your rent and everything else that's goin' on. You'll do it to keep from goin' out and blowin' some sucker up, turnin' into a criminal. This is what you will do.

What kept you going?

Well, you know, some people say to God, "God, you said you'd be with me if ever I needed you. You said if I made a step, you'd make a step. Well, where was you yesterday, when I was sick and down and out? Because there wasn't but one set of steps, and I didn't see yours." And God says, "Well, that's when I carried you on my back." You dig? And I think God's been carryin' me a long, long time. I think he made it possible for me to be Bo Diddley. Now, a lot of people jump up and say, "But you play the blues." But why couldn't it be God that gave me this talent? Why does it always got to be the devil? I've heard that from some of my own people. But I think my music is God's gift. Because I am not a highly educated person, and I was trying to figure out how to survive in this cruel world that I was comin' up in.

"Bo Diddley" was released three months before Chuck

Berry's debut single, "Maybellene," which, unlike your record, became a Top Forty pop hit. Were you and Berry already friends then?

No, no, lord, we wasn't friends right away.

Why not? Was there a rivalry?

No, we wasn't enemies, either. We just didn't have nothin' in common. At one time, somebody wrote up that we had a feud goin', and that was the biggest lie ever told. It was a feud we didn't know about. We've always been runnin' buddies ever since we kind of got to know each other. Chuck and I are different, but he's a very nice person, and he's a good friend of mine, and I hope that he'll always be a good friend of mine. But Chuck has his ways, just like I got mine. No two people are alike. I don't care if they're twins, you know?

One of your strangest records was "The Clock Strikes Twelve," recorded in 1958, on which you played violin. What did the Chess brothers make of that?

Freaked out. See, they didn't know I played violin. I just brought it in there and did it. I've always got a secret hid somewhere. I keep a secret weapon.

Oddly shaped guitars have always been your trademark. When did you come up with that idea?

I just started designin' 'em. Gretsch was makin' 'em at first. Tom Holmes, in Nashville, makes my guitars now.

Do you still use the fur-covered one?

Somebody ripped that off. That wasn't nothin' but rabbit hair, but whoever stole it, I guess they thought they had some mink. It tickles me that they got a damn bunny rabbit.

Sylvia Robinson, who was part of the duo Mickey and Sylvia back then, told me that she got "Love Is Strange" from you—the song that became a Number Two R&B hit for them and that also went to Number Eleven on the pop charts.

That's right.

She said she and Mickey Baker, her partner, wrote the words for it, that it was originally an instrumental called "Paradise" that your guitarist, Little Joe Williams, would pick out at—

Backstage. Yeah. *They* called it "Paradise." I wrote the words, and I named it "Love Is Strange."

Leonard Chess didn't want you to record it yourself?

No. He told me I thought I was Perry Como. That's why Sylvia got the song. I let her record it, and I published it under my first wife's maiden name, Ethel Smith, to keep Leonard and them from messin' with me about it. And they *still* tried to get it. I got some change off of that. I get BMI money off of it now, every once in a while.

Did you encounter much racism in the early days?

In the Fifties, you ran into some ignorant people down South—down behind the ignorant curtain, I call it. You was a sad son of a bitch if you couldn't fix your own car then, 'cause if it broke down, you'd be sittin' off in the bushes, and the service-station cat would just be sittin' up there lookin' at you. The crap that we went through to try to bring rock & roll to people. And all these dudes that's running around now tryin' to claim the shit—they ain't got no business claimin' nothin', 'cause they didn't do it. We were the pioneers, and we went through hell and high water to make this shit happen. We went through some heavy changes. I had guns put up to my head, man; run out of town, and I still don't know why.

Where was that?

Right goin' into Arkansas, the day after President Kennedy got shot. We were runnin' out of gas, so we parked at this gas station at night and we were waitin' for it to open up in the mornin'. So by 7:30 or 8:00 there were four or five white guys standin' on the corner, like they were waitin' on somebody to pick 'em up, and we were sittin' there in this big, long, stretched-out Chevrolet with eight doors on it. They ain't botherin' us, and we ain't botherin' them. The gas station still ain't open yet, so me and the driver decided to mosey across the street to look at this thrift shop over there. Just about the time we got to the middle of the street, I heard this guy hollerin', "Hey, you! Whatta you lookin' at?" I looked around and didn't see nobody, so we went on across the street. Then we walked back, and just as we got maybe ten feet away from the car, we could see this old man runnin' out across this field and down this hill, hollerin', "Hey, you all, whatchoo doin' there? What're you lookin' for?" So I stopped and looked at him, and I pointed—"Me?" He said, "Yeah, you. Wait a minute." And when he got there, this old man pulled out this great big old gun and stuck it up to my head. Now, if you've ever had a gun put up to your head, the barrel of a .38 looks like a wind tunnel or somethin' when somebody stick it in your face—it gets *real* big, you understand? And this old man told me, "I want you to get out of town. Ain't none of y'all around here, and y'all get a-movin'."

See, again, that was a time when God carried my booty on his back. Because this was the most horrible experience a man could ever have, for no particular reason. Nothin' should have been that bad. But, see, people back then, this is what they thought—they were taught this. They were raised that way. They didn't know. They thought they were right. It's different now. The people down here in the South now is got their shit together. Everybody's fine; everybody gets along beautiful, and I'm so happy that that's what's happened. But you can always find a fool—you can find a fool in *church,* you understand? And there's some runnin' around right now, man, that's still fucked up, and it shouldn't be. I don't see color, you know? But that was the thing we had to go through. And not just black people; white people, too, if they let their hair grow long or something. I don't understand why Americans do this—they love to pick at one another, you know? I think we'd be better off if we exercised the idea that that man's a free man, just like I am, and if he want to wear his hair down to his asshole, that's his business. It ain't botherin' me—I ain't gotta sleep with him, you dig? Leave him alone. And if you don't want him in your house, just say, "Hey, you can come in, but the hair gotta stay out."

One white person who didn't share those prejudices was Elvis Presley, who's said to have once caught your shows at the Apollo Theatre in New York for a whole week straight.

Oh, yeah, that I know about. I didn't know who in the heck he was, but him were there. He wasn't there a week, though, not that I know of. He'd have had to be crazy—to come into Harlem, bein' *white,* in 1955, and hung around there for a *week?* No way. *I* was there for a week and was scared to death, and I was *black.* Because I wasn't from around there, man, you know? And if you don't walk like them dudes in New York, they know you a stranger right quick, see, and they look at you funny. So I know doggone well that Elvis wasn't there for a week.

One white act that did see a lot of you—because you toured together—was the Everly Brothers. Phil Everly once told me that of all the original rockers, you were the most amazing live performer.

Those are my buddies, man—the Everlys, Frankie Avalon, Ricky Nelson, Bobby Vee, Freddy Cannon . . .

All the white teen idols? That's strange.

Well, we just spoke the same language. Even Jerry Lee Lewis. And Bobby Rydell, all of them, yeah. Fabian [*laughs*]—that's my *pardner.*

Fabian?

Yeah, [*sings*] "I'm a *tiger* . . . [*laughs*].

In the fall of 1963, you toured Britain with the Everly Brothers on a bill that also featured the Rolling Stones making their first tour of their homeland. What were they like then?

They were good people. They treated me like a king. Good people. I never will forget that.

Was their music at the time pretty close to what you were doing?

No, no, no, no. They were playin' like Muddy Waters then. They played so good that I thought it *was* Muddy. They was not doin' anything like Bo Diddley at all. That didn't come till later, after I went over there, and they found out what I was doin' and decided to copy it. I think they did "A Hard Day's Night" . . . no, wait a minute—that was the Beatles.

Ever meet them?

No. I never really wanted to, because I never understood what the hell they was doin'. They had music that you couldn't really dance to. I still ain't figured out what it is. They just caught the fancy of a generation. It was almost like me, but I was ten years ahead of myself, you know? I had to back up, slow down and then come back around.

Your music has certainly been influential. It was even featured on the soundtrack of Ralph Bakshi's 1971 animated film 'Fritz the Cat.'

I had nothing to do with that, never seen no money from that. I freaked out when I heard it. I was in the theater, settin' up there lookin' at it, and all of a sudden—*ching-a-ching-ching, a-ching-ching.* I said, "Wha'? That's me." [According to one of the film's producers, all music rights were duly contracted for at the time.]

You were also featured in a somewhat classic 1966 concert documentary, 'The Big TNT Show,' along with such pop acts as the Byrds, the Ronettes and the Lovin' Spoonful.

Yeah, that's another rip-off. I don't even remember how much they gave us to do that thing. It's just rip-off, rip-off, you know? Look at this album I ran into. [*He pulls out a reissue EP featuring old Bo Diddley and Billy Boy Arnold tracks on the British Red Lightnin label—titled, ironically, 'It's Great to Be Rich.'*] Now, who had the nerve to do this? I ain't never seen a fuckin' dime from it. [Peter Shertser, head of Red Lightnin, says the tape of Diddley's performance was legitimately acquired; that the record has sold minimally to date; but that when royalties do accrue, they will be paid.] See, my fans think they been buyin' a product from Bo Diddley; they don't know I ain't got a dime of that money. I have so many copies and bootlegs out on me. I thought bootleggers were supposed to go to jail, but they don't. But if I did something wrong, like a traffic ticket, there'd be twenty cops at my door tryin' to lock me up. I'm terrified, man, about what happens to you when you work your ass off to try to become somebody, and you got a son of a bitch sittin' around the corner rippin' you off.

What do you think should be done?

I feel there should be a special court that knows about the music business, a special judge that nobody can buy and lawyers that watch other lawyers and make sure the shit come out right, you understand? Because I feel I deserve that. But there's one bad law in this country—the statute of limitations. That's a damaging thing to a cat like me or the Coasters or anybody else. These cats all know they been ripped, but they can't get no lawyer, because they ain't got no money to hire one. I ain't got no $10,000, $20,000, to cough up to a lawyer, or $5,000 to give him as a retainer. I ain't even got no *parts* of it, you dig, to give him to go to bat for me and start searchin' for stuff. And then, ten days later, he needs another $5,000. I don't *have* this. So in the meantime, statute of limitations is creepin' up on my booty, you understand? And before you know anything, seven years is *there,* and you *still* ain't got no money. So you in a trick bag—you just fartin' in the wind. And *they know*—when Chess Records decided not to pay me and a lot of other artists, they knew what they were doin'. If you ain't got no money, you can't fight them.

But I'm goin' to court. If I don't go, my kids are goin'. Because, see, the money belongs to them. *They* have been deprived of college, when I made enough money that they could've went, you understand? And I got grandkids now that needs to get ready to go to college. Maybe the kids didn't make it, but maybe I can get the grandkids through, you dig?

See, I'm tired of havin' a big name and nothin' to go along with it. I am a monument without a pedestal to sit on; a millionaire without a dime. I'm fifty-eight years old. I might die. I want what was due to me thirty years ago—and I want the *interest* off it. I done waited half my motherfuckin' life, you understand? Ain't no more dummies, man. I used to be scared, but I ain't scared anymore.

Bo, if someone from Mars came down to Earth and wanted to know what rock & roll was, how would you define it?

What did you say?

If someone from Mars wanted to know what rock & roll was, what would you tell them?

That's what I thought you said.

What I mean is, What is rock & roll in your opinion?

It's music, baby. Happy music. And classical music is music-music. In other words, classical music is the stuff by cats that have deceased, but their music lives on. Rock & roll is the other range, the other step. And I feel like my music will live on after I decease, too. But wait a minute—I ain't plannin' on goin' nowhere too *soon,* you dig? 'Cause I'm feelin' like the Rock of Gibraltar, brother.

19
Robert Plant

INTERVIEWED BY DAVID FRICKE (1988)

Nineteen eighty-eight was the year of Led Zeppelin—again. Of course, the awesome specter of Zeppelin never actually disappeared after the group broke up in the wake of drummer John Bonham's death in 1980. New metal bands continued to ape the Zeppelin sound, while FM deejays beat the records to death in the name of "classic rock."

But 1988 was different because it was the year Led Zeppelin singer Robert Plant decided to invest in the ongoing revival himself. Chagrined by the outright thievery of sampled Zeppelin riffs by the rap brigade and impressed by futurist applications of the trademark Zeppelin roar on records by Hüsker Dü and Let's Active, Plant dug into his old bag of lemon-squeezing vocal tricks, turned up the guitars and came up with his best solo effort to date, 'Now and Zen.' By the time Plant hit the American concert trail a couple of months after this interview, which was conducted in London in January 1988, he was blowing away old Zep heads and neophyte fans alike with killer stage versions of "In the Evening," "Misty Mountain Hop" and "Communication Breakdown."

This interview was unique in that it was the first time Plant had spoken in depth about Zeppelin since the demise of the group; the old records; Bonham's death; and the aborted attempt in 1986 at a full-scale Zeppelin reunion. Later that year, in May, Plant, guitarist Jimmy Page and bassist John Paul Jones (with Bonham's son Jason on drums) took another crack at reconciliation when they climaxed Atlantic Records' fortieth-anniversary concert at Madison Square Garden with a monster set. They subsequently went their separate solo ways. But with this interview, Robert Plant provided a rare opportunity to see, through his eyes, what it was like for a decade to hold the hammer of the gods in one's hands.

—D. F.

I N A BRIGHTLY lit corner of an otherwise dark and cramped set at the studios of London Weekend Television, Robert Plant settles comfortably onto the sofa where he is about to be interviewed and glances at a monitor to his left. A faint smile of bemused recognition spreads across his distinctive hawklike features as he watches vintage black-and-white footage of a young man, barely out of his teens, wailing into the camera like a heavy-metal Mongol, thrusting his bare chest forward, filling the screen with a golden avalanche of shoulder-length blond curls. The turn-of-the-Seventies image—bell-bottom pants, a skimpy open floral blouse, exaggerated sex-warrior stage moves—seems strange, even quaint, on the small screen. But the singer's voice and the roar of the band behind him are unmistakable.

"You need coolin'/Baby, I'm not foolin'," the young blond buck howls. "I'm gonna send ya/Back for schoolin'/Way down inside/Uh, honey, you need it/I'm gonna give you my love/I'm gonna give you my love/*Wooooaaaah!*"

The band, of course, is Led Zeppelin. The song is "Whole Lotta Love." And the singer is a much younger Robert Plant, then all of twenty-one years old. As the video fades out, the TV interviewer turns to the present-day Plant with a sly grin and asks, "How does it feel to see that again, you sticking your chest out and throwing your hair back?"

Plant doesn't blink an eye. "Oh," he says with a sly grin of his own, "I *still* do that every night."

Back at his manager's London office later that afternoon, Plant is still grinning as he discusses his old stage image. "It looks a little camp," he says sheepishly, swigging at a bottle of Perrier water. "But it was honest, and there was nothing camp about it at the time. It was a young man, feeling his feet."

Now approaching his fortieth birthday, Plant is an older and wiser man, and still feeling his feet. With the death of drummer John "Bonzo" Bonham in 1980 and Led Zeppe-

lin's subsequent low-key dissolution, the singer lost not only his band and his best friend but also the axis around which his musical world had spun for more than ten years—guitarist Jimmy Page. Scorned by the punks and embarrassed by cheap Zeppelin imitations, Plant spent his first three solo albums roaming the shifting terrain of Eighties rock in search of an identity that had nothing to do with lemon squeezing or "Stairway to Heaven."

He never found it. He had a couple of hits along the trail, like "Big Log," from his 1983 album *The Principle of Moments*. But for all of their adventuresome drive and hip future-rock angularity, Plant's solo records in general lacked the unbridled passion and risky spontaneity of Zeppelin in full flight.

Now, after seven years of Zeppelin denial, Plant has come to his senses. His new album, *Now and Zen,* is the biggest leap forward of his solo career—and all it took was two steps backward to Led Zeppelin.

You can hear the old snap, crackle and pow all over "Tall Cool One," a high-tech rockabilly raver featuring ingeniously deployed computer samples of platinum Zeppelin wax like "Black Dog," "Dazed and Confused" and "Whole Lotta Love." At the end of "White, Clean and Neat," Plant slips in a brief vocal reprise of the 1970 Zep blues "Since I've Been Loving You." The album is also a Zeppelin reunion of sorts; Jimmy Page plays guitar on both "Tall Cool One" and the single "Heaven Knows." Even those *Now and Zen* songs lacking overt Zeppelin references, like the surging "Dance on My Own" and "The Way I Feel," pack a familiar wallop.

"I've stopped apologizing to myself for having this great period of success and fanatical acceptance," Plant declares. "It's time to get on and enjoy it now. I want to have a great time instead of making all these excuses."

Plant has, in fact, been surrounded by echoes of Zeppelin for some time. Goth-rock bands like the Cult and the Mission U.K. have racked up hits with shameless but clever rewrites of

"Kashmir" and "The Immigrant Song." Def Jam major-domo Rick Rubin boldly lifted the core Page riff from "The Ocean" for the Beastie Boys' "She's Crafty." But it took a demo cassette of "Heaven Knows," written and performed by an eccentric British outfit called the Rest Is History, to shake Plant out of his anti-Zeppelin mind-set.

The song itself was a knockout, a refreshing change from the derivative demos that usually arrived in his mail. Plant soon found out that Phil Johnstone, who co-wrote "Heaven Knows" and played keyboards on it, was also a dyed-in-the-wool Zeppelin freak. "We immediately wrote 'Tall Cool One' and 'White, Clean and Neat' in the same afternoon," Plant raves. "It was *bang!* The guy had been a Zeppelin fan, and I suddenly remembered that, yeah, so had I." Plant and Johnstone went on to co-write seven of the nine tracks on *Now and Zen*. Johnstone also rounded up a band of like-minded young compatriots, including guitarist Doug Boyle and drummer Chris Blackwell, to heat up the songs in concert and on record.

As part of coming to terms with his past, Plant and the band have cooked up new versions of "Misty Mountain Hop," "Trampled Underfoot," "The Wanton Song" and "In the Evening" for the *Now and Zen* tour.

Johnstone says Plant's reconciliation with history did not come easy. "We were working on 'White, Clean and Neat,' and I had this neat riff to go with it. He said, 'But, aw, man, that's *bluesy*.' And I said to him, 'But that's what you are. You're a blues singer.' He'd denied that he was a blues singer for so long."

In fact, Plant had spent his teens bellowing the blues in folk and rock clubs up in the English Midlands. By age eighteen, he'd already cut three singles for CBS in Britain, mostly Jack Jones cabaret pop dosed with cheap hippie kitsch. He was back in Midlands clubs, this time singing "White Rabbit" and Moby Grape's "Omaha," when Jimmy Page signed him to the fledgling Zeppelin. More than anything else, it was, Plant says with a smile, "just a chance to get paid by the week. I opened a bank account in June 1968 and put in thirty-five dollars."

Though Plant is far richer today, he hasn't lost his open mind and eager ear. The owner of an enviable collection of classic blues, R&B and rockabilly records, he is also constantly checking out pop's Next Big Things. Among his recent faves are Hüsker Dü, the rising Irish star Sinéad O'Connor and the San Francisco funk-metal band Faith No More. He also digs Prince—for "sheer entertainment and audacity." He adds with a wink, "Prince and Page together would be great."

Plant and Page back together is enough to send most of the world's rock populace swooning. Plant returned the favor of Page's contributions to *Now and Zen* by singing and co-writing a song, "The Only One," on Page's forthcoming solo album [*Outrider*]. There are also plans afoot for a live Plant-Page reunion this spring at a gala celebration marking the fortieth anniversary of Atlantic Records, Zeppelin's original label.

If nothing else, the Zeppelin revival has certainly loosened Robert Plant's tongue. "If you had asked me a year ago about Led Zeppelin or my relationship with Pagey," he says, "I'd have just beat around the bush, given you the runaround." He smiles broadly. "But it feels okay to talk about it now."

*D*oes it feel strange, after years of deliberately distancing yourself from the Zeppelin legacy, to be working with younger musicians, like Phil Johnstone, who are essentially Zeppelin's spiritual descendants? They grew up on Zeppelin and absorbed it into their own thing; now they've turned you on to it all over again.

That's exactly what happened. I was turned on to what I'd done in the past by people saying, "That stuff was great." And as soon as my eyes were opened again, Zeppelin was everywhere. Everybody was saying, "It's all over the place," and all this time I was going, "Well, I've never heard of them."

Didn't you feel foolish, having renounced Zep for so long?

No. I had to do that. I remember poor old Clapton, years and years before, having had this phenomenon with Cream. Every time he tried to play "Layla," people would scream for "Crossroads."

I wanted to establish an identity that was far removed from the howling and the mud sharks of the Seventies. So if I go onstage now and sing "Misty Mountain Hop," it's cool because I've given it the time in between. I can come out and do it without having traded on it all the way down the line.

"Tall Cool One," with its computer samples from "Black Dog" and "Whole Lotta Love," is the first overt reference to Zeppelin you've made on record since the band split. Although the song was done with tongue firmly in cheek, a sense of affection for your past comes through.

Especially as throughout every verse there is this sonic-dive-bomber guitar sound. I played it to Jimmy Page, and he didn't even know what it was. It's the guitar that goes into the middle bit of "Whole Lotta Love." He thought it was just something we'd written in. Then he played the solo on it, and we put all the Zeppelin-record bits on at the end. We played it for him, and I wish I'd had a camera to catch the expression on his face.

Pleasant surprise?

It was more like tiresome wonder. Like, "What is he doing, and why is this essential for him? Is he taking the piss out of it?" I'm not taking the piss. I'm showing that his riffs are the mightiest the world has ever heard.

How did you choose which Zeppelin records to sample?

I just picked what I thought was appropriate. In fact, onstage now, we finish "Tall Cool One" with about a minute of "Custard Pie" because it sounds so good. "The Ocean" was an important one to use because it's been a hit with "She's Crafty," by the Beastie Boys.

Whereas you were basically borrowing from yourself.

Well, I borrowed from Jimmy, truth to tell. I've decided that's what I want. I want it to be a bit harder. I want to play stuff that's exciting again.

How much did the Led Zeppelin reunion at Live Aid spark this reconciliation with your past?

Not at all. In fact, it was horrendous. Emotionally, I was eating every word that I had uttered. And I was hoarse. I'd done three gigs on the trot before I got to Live Aid. We rehearsed in the afternoon, and by the time we got onstage, my voice was long gone.

It was very odd. Everyone was congratulating themselves for being there because that's what they'd always wanted. Yet there are a lot more important things to want than Page and I staggering around in Philadelphia, me hoarse and him out of tune.

Did you get a buzz from being onstage with Jimmy again?

Yeah, of course. Every time I play with Jimmy, it's great. Jimmy and I, to be perfectly honest, we've played together for various reasons over the last two years, but we haven't really *gotten* together. We don't go out together, we don't sit around together. Our preoccupations and priorities are quite far apart.

Was that true when you were together in Zeppelin?

Our relationship deteriorated, but this is what we've got now. Live Aid was like having the umbilical cord there for me to see again. Because even if it was just a musical umbilical cord, at least the power was there to wake up certain parts of me. But it also smacked of the shambles and shoddiness that Zeppelin could never get away with, right now in 1988, if we were out touring.

What's the real story about the secret rehearsals you, Page and John Paul Jones reportedly held with drummer Tony Thompson after Live Aid? How far did you really get in forming a new Led Zeppelin?

We had a week together with Tony Thompson. This was the following January, '86. The guy who's now my tour manager was brought in to look after the drums, to help Tony Thompson leave Heathrow Airport and travel to this secret destination.

Where was this secret destination?

Isn't it crazy? "Secret destination." It was just off the motorway near Peter Gabriel's house in Bath. We took a village hall, filled it with parachutes to take all the angles and corners off the room and set up the equipment. Pagey duly arrived, and we plugged in. But as much as he wanted to do it, it wasn't the time for Pagey to do that. He had just finished the second Firm album, and I think he was a bit confused about what he was doing.

And the interesting thing is that after seven years of being without him and fending for myself, I'm a lot more forthright. When I reach a conclusion, I immediately react to it. Way back in the old days, this might have taken a week of mutual discussion. One person couldn't make the decision for four people.

Did you have serious, or at least cautious, hopes about what you could accomplish?

Yeah, I think so. But it wasn't to be. There was this little club we used to go to in this little town. Tony was a celebrity because he had played on Belouis Some's hit record. So he was invited to parties and stuff; we were, too, because we'd been famous once. Jonesy and I often chose to walk back to the place we were staying, at two in the morning. Pagey wouldn't come out, which is hardly the way to get everything back together again.

Meanwhile, Tony became a celebrity and was metaphorically carried around on everybody's shoulders. He ended up in one of these small minicars with five other people. They took a corner too fast and ended up in somebody's basement, went off the road, through some iron railings and down a few steps.

So I was called at five o'clock in the morning by the Bath Royal Infirmary by a rather short-tempered matron saying, "We have your Mr. Thompson here. He states you, Mr. Plant, as next of kin." I said, "But you can't do that. He's *black!*"

So after arguing about him having African descent, I went there, and Tony was lying in the hospital going, "Oh, man, oh, man." So that was the end of him.

Did the band actually get any playing done?

Yeah, we did about two days.

What did you play? Did you have any new material to start off with?

No, nothing. It was the most bristlingly embarrassing moment, to have all that will and not knowing what to play. Jonesy played keyboards, I played bass a bit.

It sounded kind of like David Byrne meets Hüsker Dü, I guess, sounding good and quite odd, because of Jonesy's tendency to play these jolly, rollicking keyboards, Jimmy cutting right across the whole thing with these searing, soaring chord mechanisms and me plotting the routes on the bass. It was pretty good. And there were two or three things that were very promising.

Then Tony left the road with his merry band. One of the roadies, who is now my tour manager, played drums. He was quite good, too, but the whole thing dematerialized. Jimmy had to change the battery on his wah-wah pedal every one and a half songs. And I said, "I'm going home." Jonesy said, "Why?" "Because I can't put up with this." "But you lived with it before." I said, "Look, man, I don't need the money. I'm off." For it to succeed in Bath, I would have had to have been far more patient than I have been for years.

Do you think you have also outstripped Jimmy in terms of your ambition and creative drive?

No, I don't think so at all. Jimmy needs a community workshop, and he needs to put his trust and his faith and his vulnerability into someone. We shared

something, and that's fine. It's just that the way that we do things now is different. And I don't know if the two ways of doing it are compatible.

You've worked up some Zeppelin songs to do on your 'Now and Zen' tour. How does it feel singing the old numbers again?

I feel regenerated singing them. I feel that power and simplicity, like "Misty Mountain Hop." The lyrics are so hippie-dippie—"Lots of people sitting on the grass with flowers in their hair/Saying, 'Hey, boy, do you want to score?' " It's very hard to sing that now, but at the same time it's *great* to sing it. It's very powerful stuff.

Have you considered doing "Stairway to Heaven"?

I wouldn't dream of it. I actually wouldn't enjoy doing it. I could do it, I suppose, with Page now and again.

How was it written?

We were working at Headley Grange, an old almshouse, with Ronnie Lane's mobile recording truck. We had been playing all day, and Bonzo and Jonesy had gone off to the Speakeasy Club . . . to "relax" I think is a good term for it. Jimmy and I stayed in, and we got the themes and thread of it right there and then. It was some cynical aside about a woman getting everything she wanted all the time without giving back any thought or consideration. The first line began with that cynical sweep of the hand—"There's a lady who's sure all that glitters is gold/And she's buying a stairway to heaven"—and then it softened up after that. I think it was the Moroccan dope.

Were you surprised that it came to be regarded as the definitive Led Zeppelin song?

It's not. I don't think it is.

Everyone else seems to think it is.

Because they missed the point. It's a nice, pleasant, well-meaning, naive little song, very English. It's not the definitive Led Zeppelin song. "Kashmir" is.

In what way?

It's the quest, the travels and explorations that Page and I went on to far climes well off the beaten track. Of course, we only touched the surface. We weren't anthropologists. But we were allowed, because we were musicians, to be invited in societies that people don't normally witness. It was quite a remarkable time, to open your eyes and see how Berber tribesmen lived in the northern Sahara. My interpretations lyrically are not that fantastic; they never have been. But that's what it was like for me then. That, really, to me is the Zeppelin feel.

Do you have a single favorite Zeppelin album?

Physical Graffiti. Strong stuff. And it sounded good, too. It sounded very tough, but it was also restrained, exhibiting a certain amount of control as well.

The last Zeppelin studio album, 'In Through the Out Door,' marked the start of what would have been your second decade together. How did you feel about Zeppelin at that point?

I was developing my own independence, and I didn't feel tied to them anymore. But I wanted to be. There was a lot of love there. But I didn't want to do anything a minute longer than was necessary if I didn't like it.

So after a lot of shuffling, it came out all right. Jimmy's role wasn't as predominant as it was before. Jonesy and I worked a lot more on things. But by the time we were playing Knebworth and the 1980 European tour, Jimmy was back in his commanding position.

Describe your immediate post-Zeppelin life, particularly coming to terms with John Bonham's death in 1980.

The band didn't exist the minute Bonzo had gone, to me.

Was that a group consensus?

I don't know what they thought or how strongly they thought it. But that's exactly how I felt. Sometimes I still shout up there at that mass of blue and go, "That was not a very good trick."

How much did the senselessness of the way he died—death by alcoholic misadventure—affect you?

It was devastating. It's relative, isn't it? All deaths before senility are senseless. All I could think was that there was a great big hole there. Suddenly, your idea of the rock & roll musician takes second place to the fact that he was my pal for so many years.

Oh, we used to fight. It was an honest relationship, where he would say, "Look, you can't sing, but just go out and look good and I'll look after everything else behind you." [*Laughs*] We always had this antagonistic relationship—and I miss that. Nobody's actually giving it back to me like that now. People are either nice and humble to me or completely the opposite. You don't get that fun, the windup. Every time I got a bit like, "Hey, I'm the star," he'd be back there in the middle of a concert growling, "You're fucking hopeless. But don't forget, I'm here!"

So I couldn't care two hoots about Led Zeppelin. How was the family going to cope with it, and how were we going to cope with it on a personal level? Fuck the music. The music can go to hell.

Because of the band's stormy relationship with the media, the primary source of biographical info for most Zeppelin fans has been the unauthorized biography 'Hammer

of the Gods.' Your road manager, Richard Cole, provided the author, Stephen Davis, with some rather intimate details—mud sharks and the traveling groupie circus. How much of what he revealed is true?

I haven't read the book. I read the end to see what the summary of the whole thing was, to see whether or not my solo career was mentioned.

Yeah, they were wild times, without having to go into the names of the recipients or the makes of televisions that went out the window. But the exaggeration that Cole used—I figure he thought the more sordid he made it, the more money he'd get out of it. Because it does go beyond reason in places. I've met him since, and he seems very embarrassed and uncomfortable about it. I can't blame him.

Did you talk to him about the book?

Maybe for about two sentences. I said something like, "However much you got, you didn't get enough, Richard."

In the end, he did have kernels of truth. There was a lot of wildness going on. I think he missed some of the best bits, though. I can't remember them, but sometimes I'll meet somebody in New York or whatever, and they go, "Hey, do you remember Swingo's, in Cleveland, on such and such a night?" And I remember, uh, romps.

There's no sense in waffling about them now. It was like a traveling football team really, except somewhere in the end you become masters. So John Paul Jones, who was never a physical man and was very laid-back, if he was feeling the frustrations of the goldfish-bowl life, he'd take a television set to pieces and glue it upside down on the ceiling in the correct order. There was a good sense of humor there.

How much of your denial of Zeppelin in your early solo days was a byproduct of being embarrassed by the band's reputation for X-rated road debauchery?

I don't deny it. A lot I can't remember, unless someone brings it up to me.

That's an easy out.

But it's true. There were so many things. Think about it—we spent so long in America. I can remember a stream of carpenters walking into a room as we were checking out. We'd be going out one way, and they'd be going in the other way, with a sign, "Closed For Remodeling," being put on the door.

It's kind of embarrassing. But without being too facetious, that's what people *wanted*. Once the seed had been sown, it would be terrible if it was just once a week. It had to be all the time. But you don't serve urine cocktails all the time.

The real lame thing is—and it has to be said—the singer went to bed. Not necessarily alone. But there was a lot to be said for trying to keep the voice in shape. I've used that as a cop-out, but at the same time it was a fact. At a certain point, I had to say, "Oh, the sun's coming up, I'm off." And the best fun is usually in the first five minutes.

How did it feel, on that first solo tour in 1983, to be up there onstage without the three guys you'd spent the past decade with?

I immediately found out that I missed a partner. Robbie [Blunt] had the toughest job of all. He is a great guitarist, and he didn't want to have to step into Page's shoes. As much as I was proud of the fact that he had his own style and was very good, I missed the volatile showmanship which was second nature to Jimmy. He didn't have to think, "Can I do this? Should I do that?" It was just there. His performance was stunning.

Suddenly, I was without anybody from those days, holding the whole thing on my own. But we did well. I was so proud of the hard work, of the refusals to pander. There are enough guitarists out there now, leaning back with their tongues wagging, playing "Black Dog" every night.

Not only did you go out with an entirely new repertoire, you also played for predominantly young Zeppelin fans who'd never seen the real thing. You were the totem for them.

But I was only part of the totem, and they had to get that right. That however much one might want to make me Led Zeppelin, I'm not. And I've never had the power, nor would I ever attempt, to emulate or re-create that thing. And I know darn well if Jimmy and I were to travel America and Coca-Cola wanted to stuff money up our bum, it would be deceit to try and bring it all back. By me just chuggling along on my own, I don't expect to try and fill that gap. I can't go into every project thinking, "Oh, my goodness me, what about 'Boogie with Stu'?"

You say that you miss Page a lot. Yet on record and in previous interviews, you've taken pains to emphasize that you're a contemporary artist, making Eighties music, implying that you've left Jimmy and what he represents—the ultimate in Seventies guitar heroism—back in that Zeppelin time warp.

I've ferreted around, working incessantly, trying different things out. If I made a record tomorrow that sounded like parts of R.E.M.'s *Document,* I'd be really pleased.

I also listen a lot. I don't know whether Jimmy goes out and listens. It's his business. But all he has to do is play guitar on a contemporary-sounding track, like "Heaven Knows," and it sounds great.

Having done the Live Aid gig and worked on each other's new albums, do you foresee doing any more studio or stage work with Page, even on a semi-regular basis?

Yeah, I'd like to work with him until we're really comfortable. And when we're really comfortable, we'll write all new songs. Because we've never been really comfortable anyway.

Jimmy and I got along well with Jonesy and Bonzo. But between ourselves, there was a lot of unspoken rivalry. Jimmy had already gotten a name when I was trotting out "White Rabbit" in some dance hall in Newcastle with Bonzo. He employed a very democratic approach to the whole thing. He encouraged me a lot.

Then, suddenly, we were side by side. And he didn't quite like that. Occasionally, I could feel it. If the shoulders were a little close, you could feel the flinch a bit. Especially if we were sitting at the same table and one woman went by and we both liked her. It was "Oh, no, here we go."

What is the status of your R&B–cover project, the Honeydrippers?

Asleep.

You did put 'Volume I' on the EP.

Well, of course I would. There is a little bit of humor in my existence. If there was a next one, I'd call it *Volume III.*

But it didn't work. It worked, but it didn't work.

How didn't it work? It was a big hit.

It was just another tangent. Which was great. But I want to keep this "Heaven Knows" department. When I get a good album together with at least seven really good songs, I feel really good. And I'm messing around with these Sixties songs by the Remains and the Knickerbockers. They're much more appropriate for me. Because I can actually deliver them, rather than crooning over violins, like "Sea of Love."

What's your opinion of the current reincarnations of Led Zeppelin—bands like the Cult, Whitesnake, Bon Jovi and the Mission U.K.?

They're all different, aren't they? I can't tell you honestly whether Bon Jovi is better than anybody else. I know that the success ratio is fantastic. And I think that's what counts to them. The aesthetics of the thing have nothing to do with it.

So are they just imitating Zeppelin, or are they getting it right, the whole package with the risks as well as the noise and the strut?

The Mission are getting it right to me. The Sisters of Mercy, too. They're trying it, and they mean it. It's not just a parody of a pastiche of a parody. If they nick a few chord shapes, that's okay. But at least they're doing it in the spirit of it. I prefer that to the pretty-boy-wailing department.

These guys, the Bon Jovis and company, when they weren't selling anything, they saw the mechanism working. They saw they had to follow the now strongly dictated lines of the commercial process, to come up with the choruses and wiggle your ass at the right moment. There is nothing impromptu or accidental about it. It's immaterial whether it's hard rock or not. It could just as easily be—who's that geezer with the really big nose you've got over there?—Barry Manilow. Fortunately, I had success before a lot of these new rules, so I can say, "Fuck it."

What's your opinion of producer Rick Rubin and what he did with the Led Zeppelin sound on the Beastie Boys' album? He seems to be one of the few people trying to take that thing out on a different tangent.

Maybe he ought to write his own riffs then. He's not particularly an innovator in that way. There's loads of house music from Chicago and rap stuff that steal Zeppelin in far less obvious ways. I guess if he's going to nick something, he might as well nick something good.

He contacted my office and said he'd like to produce my new album. It would be right round full circle. Jimmy could come around and guest on that, and he could just sample the riffs we got this time. Take 'em over to those three guys. But I can't have any sort of anger towards Rick Rubin. He's made a lot of money. Maybe he'll buy me a drink. He owes Page more of a drink than he owes me.

How do you relate to the continuation of Led Zeppelin's fantastic popularity? It's probably the ultimate compliment, that what you did with Zeppelin still blows young minds.

There were some neat little moves, but I was stuck in the middle of them. Now, when I look back, I don't get any sense of great achievement out of the fact that people still like it a lot. I get achievement out of the fact that it was good.

The ironic thing about that adoration is that, to some degree, it is responsible for the malaise in current pop and rock. It seems that so many fans—and bands—are looking

back to bands like Zeppelin because they have no better idea how to go forward.

But we were, too. Everybody looks back, glances sideways, peeps over shoulders. It's like cheating during examinations. Jeff Beck and Rod Stewart were out there doing a double act, and we were right behind them. Beck's always moaned about Pagey: "He knew what we were doing, Rod and I. He got this guy from the Midlands. They were doing 'You Shook Me.' " We were *all* doing "You Shook Me" at the same time. It was more famous than "God Save the Queen" in England at the time.

So when I listen to Mitch Easter's work, I hear a bit of Zeppelin. I heard a steel-guitar bit on the Let's Active album *Big Plans for Everybody* that sounds just like "In My Time of Dying." And I was flattered, even though I didn't play the guitar part. That's looking backwards. But it's looking backwards with such gentility and taste.

If Led Zeppelin—with the same personnel and musical aspirations—were formed today, what would your chances for success be?

It's impossible to say.

Granted, that set of circumstances in 1968—the time, the energies—was a kind of cosmic accident.

There was still this consciousness around which musical appreciation was built. There were a lot of players around, people playing well. There were people like Barry Melton and Jack Casady experimenting happily, so you had to be able to stand up alongside a lot of really good musicians.

Right now, the structure is built on different priorities. A different altar is there to be consecrated. Different idols. I don't know how Zeppelin would have got on. If the Cult and the Mission were copying something that sounded like Led Zeppelin and then we came flying in with the real goods, we'd do great business. I often think I'd just like to rehearse until I was really good with Page and then do one very quick blast through.

But it would have to be some incredibly good music. And that's what I'd need to be able to go out and call it Page and Plant. That's how it would have to be, the *real* new Zeppelin. And the possibility of that is years away—if at all.

20

Stanley Kubrick

INTERVIEWED BY TIM CAHILL (1987)

Stanley Kubrick's greatest films have been prophetic. 'Dr. Strangelove,' his 1963 antiwar classic, established black comedy as an integral component of Sixties artistic style. '2001: A Space Odyssey,' released in 1968, became the ultimate "trip" film for the psychedelic era. And 'A Clockwork Orange,' in 1971, anticipated the explosion of punk sensibility that would follow five years later. At his best, Kubrick has seemed to be almost preternaturally in synch with his times.

Whether his best work is behind him remains to be seen. Kubrick made only two films in the Eighties, both of them problematic. The first of these, 'The Shining,' was based on a straightforward horror story by Stephen King, which Kubrick transformed into a harrowing (and somewhat discombobulated) meditation on domestic psychosis. 'Full Metal Jacket,' the shot-in-England Vietnam opus that followed seven years later, seemed to break down into two very different parts, the first of which—set in a Marine Corps boot camp—at least had the virtue of not being entirely dull. But Kubrick appeared to have lost some crucial link to his time: in his hands, Vietnam seemed a spent subject—he had nothing new to say about it.

But then, as interviewer Tim Cahill points out, critics have often misapprehended Kubrick's work at first. Not surprisingly, this was one of the subjects that Cahill found the director ready, however reluctantly, to talk about.

—K. L.

HE DIDN'T bustle into the room, and he didn't wander in. Truth, as he would reiterate several times, is multifaceted, and it would be fair to say that Stanley Kubrick entered the executive suite at Pinewood Studios, outside London, in a multifaceted manner. He was at once happy to have found the place after a twenty-minute search, apologetic about being late and apprehensive about the torture he might be about to endure. Stanley Kubrick, I had been told, hates interviews.

It's hard to know what to expect of the man if you've only seen his films. One senses in those films painstaking craftsmanship, a furious intellect at work, a single-minded devotion. His movies don't lend themselves to easy analysis; this may account for the turgid nature of some of the books that have been written about his art. Take this example: "And while Kubrick feels strongly that the visual powers of film make ambiguity an inevitability as well as a virtue, he would not share Bazin's mystical belief that the better film makers are those who sacrifice their personal perspectives to a 'fleeting crystallization of a reality [of] whose environing presence one is ceaselessly aware.' "

One feels that an interview conducted on this level would be pretentious bullshit. Kubrick, however, seemed entirely unpretentious. He was wearing running shoes and an old corduroy jacket. There was an ink stain just below the pocket where some ball point pen had bled to death.

"What is this place?" Kubrick asked.

"It's called the executive suite," I said. "I think they put big shots up here."

Kubrick looked around at the dark wood-paneled walls, the chandeliers, the leather couches and chairs. "Is there a bathroom?" he asked, with some urgency.

"Across the hall," I said.

The director excused himself and went looking for the facility. I reviewed my notes. Kubrick was born in the Bronx in 1928. He was an undistinguished student whose passions were tournament-level chess and photography. After graduation from Taft High School at the age of seventeen, he landed a prestigious job as a photographer for *Look* magazine, which he quit after four years in order to make his first film. *Day of the Fight* (1950) was a documentary about the middleweight boxer Walter Cartier. After a second documentary, *Flying Padre* (1951), Kubrick borrowed $10,000 from relatives to make *Fear and Desire* (1953), his first feature, an arty film that he now finds "embarrassing." Kubrick, his first wife and two friends were the entire crew for the film. By necessity, Kubrick was director, cameraman, lighting engineer, makeup man, administrator, propman and unit chauffeur. Later in his career, he would take on some of these duties again, for reasons other than necessity.

Kubrick's breakthrough film was *Paths of Glory* (1957). During the filming, he met an actress, Christiane Harlan, whom he eventually married. Christiane sings a song at the end of the film in a scene that, on four separate viewings, has brought tears to my eyes.

Kubrick's next film was *Spartacus* (1960), a work he finds disappointing. He was brought in to direct after the star, Kirk Douglas, had a falling-out with the original director, Anthony Mann. Kubrick was not given control of the script, which he felt was full of easy moralizing. He was used to making his own films his own way, and the experience chafed. He has never again relinquished control over any aspect of his films.

And he has taken some extraordinary and audacious chances with those works. The mere decision to film Vladimir Nabokov's *Lolita* (1961) was enough to send some censorious sorts into a spittle-spewing rage. *Dr. Strangelove* (1963), based on the novel *Red Alert*, was conceived as a tense thriller about the possibility of accidental nuclear war. As Kubrick worked on the script, however, he kept bumping up against the realization that the scenes he was writing were funny in the darkest possible way. It was a matter of slipping on a banana peel and annihilating the human race. Stanley Kubrick went with his gut feeling: He directed *Dr. Strangelove* as a black comedy. The film is routinely described as a masterpiece.

Most critics also use that word to describe the two features that followed, *2001: A Space Odyssey* (1968) and *A Clockwork Orange* (1971). Some reviewers see a subtle falling-off of quality in his *Barry Lyndon* (1975) and *The Shining* (1980), though there is a critical reevaluation of the two films in process. This seems to be typical of his critical reception.

Kubrick moved to England in 1968. He lives outside of London with Christiane (now a successful painter), three golden retrievers and a mutt he found wandering forlornly along the road. He has three grown daughters. Some who know him say he can be "difficult" and "exacting."

He had agreed to meet and talk about his latest movie, *Full Metal Jacket,* a film about the Vietnam War that he produced and directed. He also co-wrote the screenplay with Michael Herr, the author of *Dispatches,* and Gustav Hasford, who wrote *The Short-Timers,* the novel on which the film is based. *Full Metal Jacket* is Kubrick's first feature in seven years.

The difficult and exacting director returned from the bathroom looking a little perplexed. "I think you're right," he said. "I think this is a place where people stay. I looked around a little, opened a door, and there was this guy sitting on the edge of a bed."

"Who was he?" I asked.

"I don't know," he replied.

"What did he say?"

"Nothing. He just looked at me, and I left."

There was a long silence while we pondered the inevitable ambiguity of reality, specifically in relation to some guy sitting on a bed across the hall. Then Stanley Kubrick began the interview:

I'm not going to be asked any conceptualizing questions, right?

All the books, most of the articles I read about you— it's all conceptualizing.

Yeah, but not by me.

I thought I had to ask those kinds of questions.

No. Hell, no. That's my . . . [*He shudders.*] It's the thing I hate the worst.

Really? I've got all these questions written down in a form I thought you might require. They all sound like essay questions for the finals in a graduate philosophy seminar.

The truth is that I've always felt trapped and pinned down and harried by those questions.

Questions like [reading from notes] *"Your first feature, 'Fear and Desire,' in 1953, concerned a group of soldiers lost behind enemy lines in an unnamed war; 'Spartacus' contained some battle scenes; 'Paths of Glory' was an indictment of war and, more specifically, of the generals who wage it; and 'Dr. Strangelove' was the blackest of comedies about accidental nuclear war. How does 'Full Metal Jacket' complete your examination of the subject of war? Or does it?"*

Those kinds of questions.

You feel the real question lurking behind all the verbiage is "What does this new movie mean?"

Exactly. And that's almost impossible to answer, especially when you've been so deeply inside the film for so long. Some people demand a five-line capsule summary. Something you'd read in a magazine. They want you to say, "This is the story of the duality of man and the duplicity of governments." [*A pretty good description of the subtext that informs 'Full Metal Jacket,' actually.*] I hear people try to do it—give the five-line summary—but if a film has any substance or subtlety, whatever you say is never complete, it's usually wrong, and it's necessarily simplistic: Truth is too multifaceted to be contained in a five-line summary. If the work is good, what you say about it is usually irrelevant.

I don't know. Perhaps it's vanity, this idea that the work is bigger than one's capacity to describe it. Some people can do interviews. They're very slick, and they neatly evade this hateful conceptualizing. Fellini is good; his interviews are very amusing. He just makes jokes and says preposterous things that you know he can't possibly mean.

I mean, I'm doing interviews to help the film, and I think they do help the film, so I can't complain. But it isn't . . . it's . . . it's difficult.

So let's talk about the music in 'Full Metal Jacket.' I was surprised by some of the choices, stuff like "These Boots Are Made for Walkin'," by Nancy Sinatra. What does that song mean?

It was the music of the period. The Tet offensive was in '68. Unless we were careless, none of the music is post-'68.

I'm not saying it's anachronistic. It's just that the music that occurs to me in that context is more, oh, Jimi Hendrix, Jim Morrison.

The music really depended on the scene. We checked through *Billboard*'s list of Top 100 hits for each year from 1962 to 1968. We were looking for interesting material that played well with a scene. We tried a lot of songs. Sometimes the dynamic range of the music was too great, and we couldn't work in dialogue. The music has to come up under speech at some point, and if all you hear is the bass, it's not going to work in the context of the movie.

Why? Don't you like "These Boots Are Made for Walkin' "?

Of the music in the film, I'd have to say I'm more partial to Sam the Sham's "Wooly Bully," which is one of the great party records of all time. And "Surfin' Bird."

An amazing piece, isn't it?

"Surfin' Bird" comes in during the aftermath of a bat-

tle, as the Marines are passing a med-evac helicopter. The scene reminded me of 'Dr. Strangelove,' where the plane is being refueled in midair with that long, suggestive tube, and the music in the background is "Try a Little Tenderness." Or the cosmic waltz in '2001,' where the spacecraft is slowly cartwheeling through space in time to "The Blue Danube." And now you have the chopper and the "Bird."

What I love about the music in that scene is that it suggests post-combat euphoria—which you see in the Marine's face when he fires at the men running out of the building: He misses the first four, waits a beat, then hits the next two. And that great look on his face, that look of euphoric pleasure, the pleasure one has read described in so many accounts of combat. So he's got this look on his face, and suddenly the music starts and the tanks are rolling and the Marines are mopping up. The choices weren't arbitrary.

You seem to have skirted the issue of drugs in 'Full Metal Jacket.'

It didn't seem relevant. Undoubtedly, Marines took drugs in Vietnam. But this drug thing, it seems to suggest that all Marines were out of control, when in fact they weren't. It's a little thing, but check out the pictures taken during the battle of Hue: You see Marines in fully fastened flak jackets. Well, people hated wearing them. They were heavy and hot, and sometimes people wore them but didn't fasten them. Disciplined troops wore them, and they wore them fastened.

People always look at directors, and you in particular, in the context of a body of work. I couldn't help but notice some resonance with 'Paths of Glory' at the end of 'Full Metal Jacket': a woman surrounded by enemy soldiers, the odd, ambiguous gesture that ties these people together. . . .

That resonance is an accident. The scene comes straight out of Gustav Hasford's book.

So your purpose wasn't to poke the viewer in the ribs, point out certain similarities. . . .

Oh, God, no. I'm trying to be true to the material. You know, there's another extraordinary accident. Cowboy is dying, and in the background there's something that looks very much like the monolith in *2001*. And it just happened to be there.

The whole area of combat was one complete area —it actually exists. One of the things I tried to do was give you a sense of where you were, where everything else was. Which, in war movies, is something you frequently don't get. The terrain of small-unit action is really the story of the action. And this is something we tried to make beautifully clear: There's a low wall, there's the building space. And once you get in there,

everything is exactly where it actually was. No cutting away, no cheating. So it came down to where the sniper would be and where the Marines were. When Cowboy is shot, they carry him around the corner—to the very most logical shelter. And there, in the background, was this thing, this monolith. I'm sure some people will think that there was some calculated reference to *2001*, but honestly, it was just there.

You don't think you're going to get away with that, do you?

[*Laughs*] I know it's an amazing coincidence.

Where were those scenes filmed?

We worked from still photographs of Hue in 1968. And we found an area that had the same 1930s functionalist architecture. Now, not every bit of it was right, but some of the buildings were absolute carbon copies of the outer industrial areas of Hue.

Where was it?

Here. Near London. It had been owned by British Gas, and it was scheduled to be demolished. So they allowed us to blow up the buildings. We had demolition guys in there for a week, laying charges. One Sunday, all the executives from British Gas brought their families down to watch us blow the place up. It was spectacular. Then we had a wrecking ball there for two months, with the art director telling the operator which hole to knock in which building.

Art direction with a wrecking ball.

I don't think anybody's ever had a set like that. It's beyond any kind of economic possibility. To make that kind of three-dimensional rubble, you'd have to have everything done by plasterers, modeled, and you couldn't build that if you spent $80 million and had five years to do it. You couldn't duplicate, oh, all those twisted bits of reinforcement. And to make rubble, you'd have to go find some real rubble and copy it. It's the only way. If you're going to make a tree, for instance, you have to copy a real tree. No one can "make up" a tree, because every tree has an inherent logic in the way it branches. And I've discovered that no one can make up a rock. I found that out in *Paths of Glory*. We had to copy rocks, but every rock also has an inherent logic you're not aware of until you see a fake rock. Every detail looks right, but something's wrong.

So we had real rubble. We brought in palm trees from Spain and a hundred thousand plastic tropical plants from Hong Kong. We did little things, details people don't notice right away, that add to the illusion. All in all, a tremendous set-dressing and rubble job.

How do you choose your material?

I read. I order books from the States. I literally go

into bookstores, close my eyes and take things off the shelf. If I don't like the book after a bit, I don't finish it. But I like to be surprised.

'Full Metal Jacket' is based on Gustav Hasford's book 'The Short-Timers.'

It's a very short, very beautifully and economically written book, which, like the film, leaves out all the mandatory scenes of character development: the scene where the guy talks about his father, who's an alcoholic, his girlfriend—all that stuff that bogs down and seems so arbitrarily inserted into every war story.

What I like about not writing original material—which I'm not even certain I could do—is that you have this tremendous advantage of reading something for the first time. You never have this experience again with the story. You have a reaction to it: It's a kind of falling-in-love reaction.

That's the first thing. Then it becomes almost a matter of code breaking, of breaking the work down into a structure that is truthful, that doesn't lose the ideas or the content or the feeling of the book. And fitting it all into the much more limited time frame of a movie.

And as long as you possibly can, you retain your emotional attitude, whatever it was that made you fall in love in the first place. You judge a scene by asking yourself, "Am I still responding to what's there?" The process is both analytical and emotional. You're trying to balance calculating analysis against feeling. And it's almost never a question of "What does this scene mean?" It's "Is this truthful, or does something about it feel false?" It's "Is this scene interesting? Will it make me feel the way I felt when I first fell in love with the material?" It's an intuitive process, the way I imagine writing music is intuitive. It's not a matter of structuring an argument.

You said something almost exactly the opposite once.

Did I?

Someone had asked you if there was any analogy between chess and filmmaking. You said that the process of making decisions was very analytical in both cases. You said that depending on intuition was a losing proposition.

I suspect I might have said that in another context. The part of the film that involves telling the story works pretty much the way I said. In the actual making of the movie, the chess analogy becomes more valid. It has to do with tournament chess, where you have a clock and you have to make a certain number of moves in a certain time. If you don't, you forfeit, even if you're a queen ahead. You'll see a grandmaster, the guy has three minutes on the clock and ten moves left.

And he'll spend two minutes on one move, because he knows that if he doesn't get that one right, the game will be lost. And then he makes the last nine moves in a minute. And he may have done the right thing.

Well, in filmmaking, you always have decisions like that. You are always pitting time and resources against quality and ideas.

You have a reputation for having your finger on every aspect of each film you make, from inception right on down to the premiere and beyond. How is it that you're allowed such an extraordinary amount of control over your films?

I'd like to think it's because my films have a quality that holds up on second, third and fourth viewing. Realistically, it's because my budgets are within reasonable limits and the films do well. The only one that did poorly from the studio's point of view was *Barry Lyndon*. So, since my films don't cost that much, I find a way to spend a little extra time in order to get the quality on the screen.

'Full Metal Jacket' seemed a long time in the making.

Well, we had a couple of severe accidents. The guy who plays the drill instructor, Lee Ermey, had an auto accident in the middle of shooting. It was about one in the morning, and his car skidded off the road. He broke all his ribs on one side, just tremendous injuries, and he probably would have died, except he was conscious and kept flashing his lights. A motorist stopped. It was in a place called Epping Forest, where the police are always finding bodies. Not the sort of place you get out of your car at one-thirty in the morning and go see why someone's flashing their lights. Anyway, Lee was out for four and a half months.

He had actually been a Marine drill instructor?

Parris Island.

How much of his part comes out of that experience?

I'd say fifty percent of Lee's dialogue, specifically the insult stuff, came from Lee. You see, in the course of hiring the Marine recruits, we interviewed hundreds of guys. We lined them all up and did an improvisation of the first meeting with the drill instructor. They didn't know what he was going to say, and we could see how they reacted. Lee came up with, I don't know, 150 pages of insults. Off-the-wall stuff: "I don't like the name Lawrence. Lawrence is for faggots and sailors."

Aside from the insults, though, virtually every serious thing he says is basically true. When he says, "A rifle is only a tool; it's a hard heart that kills," you know it's true. Unless you're living in a world that doesn't need fighting men, you can't fault him. Except maybe for a certain lack of subtlety in his behavior.

And I don't think the United States Marine Corps is in the market for subtle drill instructors.

This is a different drill instructor than the one Lou Gosset played in 'An Officer and a Gentleman.'

I think Lou Gosset's performance was wonderful, but he had to do what he was given in the story. The film clearly wants to ingratiate itself with the audience. So many films do that. You show the drill instructor really has a heart of gold—the mandatory scene where he sits in his office, eyes swimming with pride about the boys and so forth. I suppose he actually is proud, but there's a danger of falling into what amounts to so much sentimental bullshit.

So you distrust sentimentality.

I don't mistrust sentiment and emotion, no. The question becomes, Are you giving them something to make them a little happier, or are you putting in something that is inherently true to the material? Are people behaving the way we all really behave, or are they behaving the way we would like them to behave? I mean, the world is not as it's presented in Frank Capra films. People love those films—which are beautifully made—but I wouldn't describe them as a true picture of life.

The questions are always, Is it true? Is it interesting? To worry about those mandatory scenes that some people think make a picture is often just pandering to some conception of an audience. Some films try to outguess an audience. They try to ingratiate themselves, and it's not something you really have to do. Certainly, audiences have flocked to see films that are not essentially true, but I don't think this prevents them from responding to the truth.

Books I've read on you seem to suggest that you consider editing the most important aspect of the filmmaker's art.

There are three equal things: the writing, slogging through the actual shooting and the editing.

You've quoted Pudovkin to the effect that editing is the only original and unique art form in film.

I think so. Everything else comes from something else. Writing, of course, is writing, acting comes from the theater, and cinematography comes from photography. Editing is unique to film. You can see something from different points of view almost simultaneously, and it creates a new experience.

Pudovkin gives an example: You see a guy hanging a picture on the wall. Suddenly you see his feet slip; you see the chair move; you see his hand go down and the picture fall off the wall. In that split second, a guy falls off a chair, and you see it in a way that you could not see it any other way except through editing.

TV commercials have figured that out. Leave con-tent out of it, and some of the most spectacular examples of film art are in the best TV commercials.

Give me an example.

The Michelob commercials. I'm a pro-football fan, and I have videotapes of the games sent over to me, commercials and all. Last year Michelob did a series, just impressions of people having a good time—

The big city at night—

And the editing, the photography, was some of the most brilliant work I've ever seen. Forget what they're doing—selling beer—and it's visual poetry. Incredible eight-frame cuts. And you realize that in thirty seconds they've created an impression of something rather complex. If you could ever tell a story, something with some content, using that kind of visual poetry, you could handle vastly more complex and subtle material.

People spend millions of dollars and months' worth of work on those thirty seconds.

So it's a bit impractical. And I suppose there's really nothing that would substitute for the great dramatic moment, fully played out. Still, the stories we do on film are basically rooted in the theater. Even Woody Allen's movies, which are wonderful, are very traditional in their structure. Did I get the year right on those Michelob ads?

I think so.

Because occasionally I'll find myself watching a game from 1984.

It amazes me that you're a pro-football fan.

Why?

It doesn't fit my image of you.

Which is . . .

Stanley Kubrick is a monk, a man who lives for his work and virtually nothing else, certainly not pro football. And then there are those rumors—

I know what's coming.

You want both barrels?

Fire.

Stanley Kubrick is a perfectionist. He is consumed by mindless anxiety over every aspect of every film he makes. Kubrick is a hermit, an expatriate, a neurotic who is terrified of automobiles and who won't let his chauffeur drive more than thirty miles an hour.

Part of my problem is that I cannot dispel the myths that have somehow accumulated over the years. Somebody writes something, it's completely off the wall, but it gets filed and repeated until everyone believes it. For instance, I've read that I wear a football helmet in the car.

You won't let your driver go more than thirty miles an hour, and you wear a football helmet, just in case.

In fact, I don't have a chauffeur. I drive a Porsche

928 S, and I sometimes drive it at eighty or ninety miles an hour on the motorway.

Your film editor says you still work on your old films. Isn't that neurotic perfectionism?

I'll tell you what he means. We discovered that the studio had lost the picture negative of *Dr. Strangelove*. And they also lost the magnetic master soundtrack. All the printing negatives were badly ripped dupes. The search went on for a year and a half. Finally, I had to try to reconstruct the picture from two not-too-good fine-grain positives, both of which were damaged already. If those fine-grains were ever torn, you could never make any more negatives.

Do you consider yourself an expatriate?

Because I direct films, I have to live in a major English-speaking production center. That narrows it down to three places: Los Angeles, New York and London. I like New York, but it's inferior to London as a production center. Hollywood is best, but I don't like living there.

You read books or see films that depict people being corrupted by Hollywood, but it isn't that. It's this tremendous sense of insecurity. A lot of destructive competitiveness. In comparison, England seems very remote. I try to keep up, read the trade papers, but it's good to get it on paper and not have to hear it every place you go. I think it's good to just do the work and insulate yourself from that undercurrent of low-level malevolence.

I've heard rumors that you'll do a hundred takes for one scene.

It happens when actors are unprepared. You cannot act without knowing dialogue. If actors have to think about the words, they can't work on the emotion. So you end up doing thirty takes of something. And still you can see the concentration in their eyes; they don't know their lines. So you just shoot it and shoot it and hope you can get something out of it in pieces.

Now, if the actor is a nice guy, he goes home, he says, "Stanley's such a perfectionist, he does a hundred takes on every scene." So my thirty takes become a hundred. And I get this reputation.

If I did a hundred takes on every scene, I'd never finish a film. Lee Ermey, for instance, would spend every spare second with the dialogue coach, and he always knew his lines. I suppose Lee averaged eight or nine takes. He sometimes did it in three. Because he was prepared.

There's a rumor that you actually wanted to approve the theaters that show 'Full Metal Jacket.' Isn't that an example of mindless anxiety?

Some people are amazed that I worry about the theaters where the picture is being shown. They think that's some form of demented anxiety. But Lucasfilms has a Theater Alignment Program. They went around and checked a lot of theaters and published the results in a [1985] report that virtually confirms all your worst suspicions. For instance, within one day, fifty percent of the prints are scratched. Something is usually broken. The amplifiers are no good, and the sound is bad. The lights are uneven. . . .

Is that why so many films I've seen lately seem too dark? Why you don't really see people in the shadows when clearly the director wants you to see them?

Well, theaters try to put in a screen that's larger than the light source they paid for. If you buy a 2,000-watt projector, it may give you a decent picture twenty feet wide. And let's say that theater makes the picture forty feet wide by putting it in a wider-angle projector. In fact, then you're getting 200 percent less light. It's an inverse law of squares. But they want a bigger picture, so it's dark.

Many exhibitors are terribly guilty of ignoring minimum standards of picture quality. For instance, you now have theaters where all the reels are run in one continuous string. And they never clean the aperture gate. You get one little piece of gritty dust in there, and every time the film runs, it gets bigger. After a couple of days, it starts to put a scratch on the film. The scratch goes from one end of the film to the other. You've seen it, I'm sure.

That thing you see, it looks like a hair dangling down from the top of the frame, sort of wiggling there through the whole film?

That's one manifestation, yeah. The Lucas report found that after fifteen days, most films should be junked. [The report says that after seventeen days, most films are damaged.] Now, is it an unreal concern if I want to make sure that on the press shows or on key city openings, everything in the theater is going to run smoothly? You just send someone to check the place out three or four days ahead of time. Make sure nothing's broken. It's really only a phone call or two, pressuring some people to fix things. I mean, is this a legitimate concern, or is this mindless anxiety?

Initial reviews of most of your films are sometimes inexplicably hostile. Then there's a reevaluation. Critics seem to like you better in retrospect.

That's true. The first reviews of *2001* were insulting, let alone bad. An important Los Angeles critic faulted *Paths of Glory* because the actors didn't speak with French accents. When *Dr. Strangelove* came out, a New York paper ran a review under the head "Moscow Could Not Buy More Harm To America." Something like that. But critical opinion on my films has always been salvaged by what I would call subsequent critical opinion. Which is why I think audiences are more reliable than critics, at least initially. Audiences tend not to bring all that critical baggage with them to each film.

And I really think that a few critics come to my films expecting to see the last film. They're waiting to see something that never happens. I imagine it must be something like standing in the batter's box waiting for a fast ball, and the pitcher throws a change-up. The batter swings and misses. He thinks, "Shit, he threw me the wrong pitch." I think this accounts for some of the initial hostility.

Well, you don't make it easy on viewers or critics. You've said you want an audience to react emotionally. You create strong feelings, but you won't give us any easy answers.

That's because I don't have any easy answers.

21

Woody Allen

INTERVIEWED BY
WILLIAM E. GEIST (1987)

Not since the truncated heyday of Orson Welles has there been so complete and sovereign an American filmmaker as Woody Allen. He started out as a comedy writer and stand-up funnyman, but over the past quarter century Allen has become the laureate of urban existential anguish—although he no doubt would be more pained to hear it put that way than most critics are willing to concede. Apart from a few early oddities, such as 1967's 'Casino Royale' (an expensive mess in which he participated peripherally) and 1976's 'The Front' (another director's film, to which he contributed a memorable, and largely straight, performance in the title role), Allen's films have come to constitute a genre all their own. Each can be described—meaningfully to his many admirers—as "a Woody Allen film." They are movies that reflect the long-running obsessions of their auteur—the passage of time, the transience of love, the search for life's meaning in art. And, of course, they are made in New York, far from Hollywood and nearer, in spirit, at least, to the Europe of Bergman and Fellini, two of Allen's idols.

Allen began the Eighties in a bit of a bog: 'Stardust Memories' (1980) and 'A Midsummer Night's Sex Comedy' (1982) are not likely to be numbered among his most spirited works in any foreseeable future. But by 1984, he had regained his unique stride and, in annual succession, turned out 'Broadway Danny Rose,' 'The Purple Rose of Cairo', 'Hannah and Her Sisters' and 'Radio Days.' Of these four, 'Hannah' was the most diaphanous, shall we say (lest we say insubstantial*), and so the Hollywood Academy, with its usual infernal logic, named it the Best Picture of 1986. Woody didn't show to pick up his Oscar, of course. He was already hard at work on another film. Fortunately, he did have time to give a rare interview, and Bill Geist—a deep-dyed New Yorker himself—got it.*

—K. L.

I DON'T KNOW, Woody Allen seems sane to me. Maybe I've been in New York too long. But it goes further than that: Woody Allen is one of the most well adjusted people I've met in New York.

Could this be one of the seven warning signs that New Yorkers are even more deranged than had previously been imagined? And should the governor place the National Guard on full yellow?

It could also mean that characterizations of Woody Allen have been somewhat extreme over the years. Or maybe Woody Allen has changed some.

On the way to the interview in his film-editing studio in a Park Avenue hotel, I passed a door marked SERVICE ENTRANCE and almost went in. I was feeling humble and nervous, about to encounter a man described as a comic genius, a modern existential hero and a filmmaker on the level of Bergman and Fellini.

But Woody Allen put me at ease. He answered the door himself, dressed in a garage-sale-style sweater and a wrinkled shirt. His hair was unmanaged. And he was nice—very casual, not at all condescending, and self-unimportant. He wasn't cynical. He didn't even try to be funny, although his brutal honesty and extraordinary seriousness about the smallest of things made me laugh a lot.

He insisted that he was not obsessing over the essential nothingness of the universe at the moment and invited me to sit down. He sat down, too, and not at all in the fetal position. It was Saturday. He was working. His newest film, the nostalgic *Radio Days,* was about to open. He had finished shooting another film just the day before [*October*] and had begun work on yet another.

For a man often depicted as a tormented neurotic, Woody Allen appeared remarkably relaxed, "centered and directed," as pop psychologists say, honest and sincere. And also quite rich. In addition to fortune, he has fame but somehow doesn't get bothered much by fans, while always getting a good table at Elaine's.

True, he is troubled by morbid introspection (he sees the concentration camp as a metaphor for life, a thought you'll never see on a greeting card) and by an inordinate fear of bushes and woodchucks. Yet he *does* have a blond movie star for a girlfriend.

He loves New York, where he seems to lead a charmed life. In his only brush with crime, burglars broke into his apartment, were scared off before they took anything and left a TV set from a previous break-in.

Born Allen Stewart Konigsberg in the Flatbush section of Brooklyn and raised in a home where, he says, the basic values were "God and carpeting," he is now fifty-one. His appearance hasn't changed in twenty years. Ours has.

He is also more amusing than we are. He began writing jokes for gossip columns at the age of sixteen and barely managed to graduate from high school.

He is at once remarkably productive—he's written and directed fifteen films since 1965 and written or acted in five more—and the only person I have met in New York with Leisure Time. Time for walking around, watching the Knicks, seeing friends and browsing—remember browsing?—in bookstores. He also plays clarinet at Michael's Pub, where he plans to be on Academy Award night, even though his film *Hannah and Her Sisters* has been nominated for seven Oscars.

He has the joy of children—Mia Farrow, the aforementioned star, has eight (five of them adopted)—but he lives across Central Park from her and doesn't have to change diapers.

Unlike most New Yorkers, he recognizes his neuroses, obsessions, phobias (could be the three decades, off and on, of psychoanalysis), and seems to be living comfortably with them now in a large duplex apartment overlooking Central Park.

On this day, Woody Allen seems almost . . . *happy*.

You *are making a film a year. What drives you?*

It's not a big deal. There have been times when Sidney Lumet or Bergman have done three films in a year. It takes me a couple of months to write a film, several months to shoot and edit it.

A guy who drives a cab or works in an office works more than I do. I have time to practice my clarinet, see films, go out to dinner and see people. And my work doesn't have the sense of labor about it.

But if I worked at a different job, I couldn't wait until I got home to write. I enjoy it. It's like being paid to play baseball or something. It's like I'm on a constant vacation.

This doesn't sound like Woody Allen talking at all, actually enjoying *yourself. Normally you are portrayed as a basically neurotic, workaholic, tormented—shall I go on?—recluse who is incapable of enjoying yourself. Is this something new?*

Probably the truth about me lies somewhere in between. Writers have tended to . . . *emphasize* certain characteristics, because it makes good copy.

I'm being paid to do what I like. And that is essentially to write and occasionally perform. I do have some trouble with my nonwork time, that is true. I'm not a person who gets too much of a kick out of traveling, country houses, boats, vacations or things most people do have a good time with.

So you're happier when you're working.

Yes, it's an important distraction. I've always felt if one can arrange one's life so that one can obsess about small things, it keeps you from obsessing about the really big things. If you obsess about the big things, you are impotent and frightened, because there's nothing you can do about aging and death. But the little things you can spend days obsessing about, such as a good punch line for the third act. And this is a nice problem to obsess over, because it's not surgery. . . . I'm a little more morbid than the average person.

Do you envy the guy who goes to work and goes out on his boat and drinks beer, and all this stuff never occurs to him?

No. I do occasionally envy the person who is religious naturally, without being brainwashed into it or suckered into it by all the organized hustles. Just like having an ear for music or something. It would just never occur to such a person for a second that the world isn't about something.

And I wouldn't go out in a boat. I'd hate the boat. I've been out on a boat twice, and I got seasick and sunburned and windburned, and I was trapped. That would be hell for me.

Are you agnostic?

Agnostic—I mean, I know as little about it as anyone, you know?

You seem to be approaching your work in a more relaxed manner.

I think as the years go by, and you gain more confidence, you become more secure about it. My first couple of films, I would have been more frantic and nervous.

Do you ever worry that you are doing things because they are easier and that the film will suffer a bit?

I'm aware that I'm doing it because it's easy. I mean, I'm completely aware that I'm shooting in New York because it's easy.

But maybe the finished product is worse because you take it easy. Is that a concern?

Yes, I do think it. And I'm happy to go along with it, even though it's worse. I think, "This may be worse, but it's easy."

I can't make that—doing things the easy way—fit with your continuing to work so hard and make so many films.

I do say to myself, you know, "This scene would be much better if we went to, say, Philadelphia to shoot it." But I don't really want to go to Philadelphia to shoot it, because it's a two-hour car ride. So let's find a street downtown that we can fob off as Philadelphia, and it won't be as good. I won't have the vista. I won't make a great shot of the Liberty Bell or something.

But you are trying to make great films, are you not?

I'm trying to make as wonderful a film as I can. But my priorities are always in order, and they're never artistic. Artistic accomplishment is about third or fourth.

I'm not sure I buy that.

I swear.

But you are such a perfectionist. You pay such close attention to every detail. There is a story about an extra in 'Radio Days' wearing a 1940s-style garter, even though it won't show onscreen.

Still, I wouldn't put making a film above inconveniencing myself where I shot it or an important engagement or appointment.

What's more important?

Oh, for instance, I've wrapped films early in the day so I could get home in time to see a Knicks game on television. Sure. They'll say, "But there are two more hours of light."

It sounds like the obstetrician who induces labor so he can make his tee time on the golf course. Is that an important Knicks game you're talking about or just any Knicks game?

Important. There have been times when I'd be out with a beautiful woman, and I would think to myself, "Do I really want to stay up all night, till four in the morning?" Because I've got to go in at six o'clock in the morning and shoot the next day.

And I think of my priorities. I think, "What's more important?" The time spent with the beautiful woman is much more important to me than the other time—being on top of it the next day.

Is this a new approach?

It might be. It might be the gruelingness of the filming that has worn me down to a degree. If you were to hang around the set of a picture of mine, you would see that it's all work, even if it happens to be a comedy of the broadest type, whether making *Hannah and Her Sisters* or *Bananas*. It's hard work and has a grim, businesslike quality to it. It's not a gang of guys joking and having a lot of fun. Maybe the films would do better if it was, I don't know.

I want to make more intimate films, which are easier and faster to do, shot indoors, with no bad weather, fewer actors and fewer sets.

But 'Radio Days' doesn't reflect that approach?

No, but that was the last straw. That was such a hard job physically for me. It was exhausting to direct. Not all the film made the picture; originally there were 200 speaking parts. You have to do musical numbers and crowd scenes and nightclub scenes.

When I was doing *Hannah,* you know, that was an intimate picture, and I was dealing with small numbers of people, filming in Mia's apartment, and it was a physically easy picture to do. And then I wanted to do a completely different kind of picture. But while I was in the midst of *Radio Days,* I thought, "God, what did I get into?"

I said to myself, "*Forget* it!" I just want to do some nice intimate pictures, a couple of people in a room with some nice personal conflicts.

Nice personal conflicts?

Yeah. Just in terms of sheer physical exhaustion, it's more fun for me to make a small film than a big film. Cecil B. De Mille or Stanley Kubrick or [Franco] Zeffirelli—they love getting a hundred people out there. They love moving them around, and they do it beautifully. But to me, getting two people in a room to talk is more relaxing filmmaking.

Is the film you just finished shooting like that?

Yes, it's a much-smaller-scale thing, sure. It's a one-set, virtually.

Can you tell us anything about it?

Well, I can only tell you a couple of things. Mia's in it, of course, and Dianne Wiest. I'm not in it.

Not even as a narrator, which you are in 'Radio Days'?

No, no. And it's a small film, a small idea, a small, intimate kind of film, principally dramatic but hopefully with some laughs in it.

And you've begun writing another one?

Yes, planning it. That's ninety percent of the work—pacing the floor, thinking it out, the plot and structure. The actual writing just takes two to three weeks. Writing it down for me is the easiest part.

You use what almost amounts to a repertory company, with many of the same actors—many of them close friends of yours, such as Mia, Diane Keaton, Dianne Wiest and Tony Roberts—in each film.

It's much easier to work with my own friends and acquaintances, because if I'm shooting with Michael Caine [who was in *Hannah and Her Sisters*], when I finish, he goes to India or England to do another picture. But Mia or Dianne Wiest or Tony Roberts, I can call them up on a moment's notice and say, "Listen, I've got a great idea for a new scene, let's meet and shoot it."

Does that really happen?

All the time, on every picture, constantly on *Hannah.* In the original version of *Hannah,* there was only one Thanksgiving party, at the beginning of the picture. And when I saw the picture and started to get ideas about how it could be developed and amplified in a good way, I thought, you know, "Let's make it end with Thanksgiving, too. That would be a nice thing." I did that. And I said, "You know what would really be great too? If we had one more Thanksgiving party in the middle of the picture."

So you just all gathered back at Mia's apartment?

Right. Shooting at her apartment made things easier, too.

Also, you sometimes use friends of yours who aren't even actors.

Yes, because I'm aware of them as good types. In a relatively minor acting part, it's not so risky.

Are you more contented, too, in your personal life?

Well, for the last seven years I've been seeing Mia, and things have been stable. And I've been introduced through her to a lot of children and all the activities with them.

How do you get along with them?

Fine, fine.

Well, you are also portrayed as someone who probably wouldn't get along with pets and children.

Oh, pets I hate. Mia has many pets. I hate them. I do everything I can to avoid them. She has a dog and cats and fish and a parrot and hamsters. She's really got the full complement of creatures. But I've never had problems with children.

What is the latest count of her children?

Eight.

And you think that children have had an effect on you?

It's, it's a . . . pleasurable dimension. And it's extra pleasurable for me because she has always done all the hard work, and I sort of live across the park and get to have the fun of the kids without having to raise them and do all of that stuff.

Do you function okay when you leave the city to visit Mia's country home in Connecticut?

No, I don't function okay. I'm like a fish out of water. I'm just not comfortable. When the evening comes, it gets dark and there's no place to go. A walk in the woods at night or something is not very appealing to me.

Why not?

There's nothing to do or feel or see. I'm definitely a child of the city streets, and I feel at home on my own two feet, you know, not in a car or a train or anything like that.

In Manhattan, I know the town. I know how to get places. I know where to get cabs. I know where to duck in and go to the bathroom if I have to. And what restaurants to eat at and which ones to avoid. I just feel at home in the city.

I don't go swimming in her pond because I've seen snakes in the water.

You know how to swim?

I was always a good swimmer, a good athlete.

Really?

I really was, in many sports. Baseball and basketball and track.

That's something a lot of people wouldn't guess.

But I never know what to do in the country. I like to be able to be in a place where, if I want to, I can go downstairs and there's stores and people around. I like to look at people. I like to watch people. I like to look at stores.

You can go around in New York and do that fairly easily without being bothered, can't you?

I can do it because I'll wear a hat, and that will cut down hugely on my recognition. I enjoy it, but as soon as I go to the country, I find it so quiet.

What is it you don't like about the quiet?

I don't find there's a lot of things to do. I'm there, and yeah, sure, I can read a book for a while. But I can read a book in my apartment, too. Mia and I are always arguing about this. I don't mind on a given day—let's say a beautiful fall day or something—I can see getting into the car and driving up to the country and getting out and walking around and looking at the lake and leaves and that kind of thing and then getting back in the car and coming home. That I can see. To go and spend two hours, five hours in the country, something like that. I can't see bedding down in the country overnight. I see nothing in that.

I like to know, although I've never done it, I like to know that if at two o'clock in the morning I get a sudden urge for duck wonton soup, that I can go downstairs, find a taxicab, go to Chinatown, get it and come back home. This is important to me.

You're not telling a joke here, are you?

No, I mean it sincerely.

Why would that be important to you?

It makes me feel comfortable to know that I'm in that atmosphere. You know, after dinner if I want to take a walk, for instance, and go look in the bookstores and maybe drop into a movie theater or go up to Elaine's or something, I know that I have the options. I eat dinner out 360 nights a year.

I like the idea that it's a live, active city. I don't like to know that if I go outside, it's all trees and bushes and paths.

Just because it's dull, not because it's threatening.

Both. I find it threatening, too. I find that while it may be true statistically that the city is more dangerous, I feel less endangered in the city. This may be a false feeling of security, but it's still psychologically helpful to me. I feel that in a crisis situation, I'd at least have a chance. I know where to go and how to avoid certain things and where to seek refuge.

In the country, as I said in *Annie Hall*, if Dick and Perry—you know, the guys in *In Cold Blood*—if they show up at the house at night, I mean, you've had it. That's the end of it.

So you aren't just afraid that a woodchuck might come at you?

I wouldn't like that, either. I would not like to be in the country and come face to face with a rabid possum or rabid woodchuck. I don't appreciate that stuff.

When was the last time you were outside New York City?

Except for Mia's place in Connecticut? A few years

ago, when Mia and I went to Paris and Rome for a week.

You don't go out of New York to America?

Sometimes I get to thinking New York is America, but that is wrong. Once I was in the suburbs, and I drove by one of those theaters with about eight movies playing at once, and I almost couldn't imagine one of my films playing there.

You could almost be a target for the House Committee on Un-American Activities. Do you have a valid driver's license?

I do, but I haven't driven a car in many years.

In how long?

Oh, I'd say twenty-five years.

Twenty-five?

With the exception of once I had to make a shot in *Annie Hall*, so I drove. . . .

Not very well.

That's why I don't drive in real life.

Do you watch television? Do you own a television?

I watch sports and films and news.

Do you ever watch your own films on TV?

No, I never watch my films, anyplace, ever. They disappoint me.

Do you watch 'The Love Boat'?

No.

'Dallas'?

No, I don't watch what is purported entertainment. Not that I watch highbrow stuff. . . . I watch baseball and basketball.

But I don't watch the junk stuff. I don't find it even *remotely* rewarding, on any level. It seems to me if I happen to see it while dialing through on the way somewhere, it just looks like elevator music, the height of soulless, plastic, brightly lit, antiseptic, you know . . . stupidity. I don't think it is worth anybody's time.

Have you ever been in a shopping mall?

I don't know that I've ever been on a shopping mall.

You said "on a shopping mall." Shopping malls are enclosed, you know.

Oh, are they? Then I've never been in one, no. Then what am I thinking of? When I visit Mia in Connecticut, sometimes she'll go to buy something, and I'll be in the car with her, and I'll get off, and that's where I think I've been on a mall.

And you don't get off a car either. You get out of a car.

Okay.

At the opening of your film 'Manhattan,' there is a statement that the lead character loves New York, even though he views it as a metaphor for the decay of civilization. Is this your view?

Yes. But I think of it often as it used to be. When I was growing up and could ride the subways with impunity at age ten . . . it was coming to the end of the really golden age. My guess is that in the Twenties and Thirties there was probably nothing to equal Manhattan ever in the history of the world. When you think that there would be a hundred plays at once, you just can't get your mind around that. And the movie houses and nightclubs and speakeasies.

Is it depressing for you to look at some of it now?

It's crushing to me. I speak to people that were in Broadway shows, older actresses, and I was speaking to one woman who was saying to me she and her girlfriend would do a show, and the curtain would come down at 11:15, and they would get dressed and go out for dinner in Times Square—two girls about nineteen years old, totally unescorted—and then go to a movie house on Forty-second Street after dinner and see a Katharine Hepburn or Spencer Tracy picture. And then walk home through Central Park. I wish I could have lived in New York in a different period.

Is the film you just shot set in New York?

Well, no, it's set in Vermont. But I shot it in New York.

How do you make New York look like Vermont?

It all takes place in one house.

What do you enjoy about filmmaking?

I enjoy the writing most. It always seems great in the writing. You're at home alone in your apartment and you know it's just wonderful. Then reality suddenly starts to creep in. You start to realize that this actor is unavailable, so you're going to have to settle for that actor, and you really can't afford $200,000 for a set, you're going to have to get one for $15,000. Gradually the compromises come in. And those lines are not so funny that you thought were so great back in your apartment.

Or too funny? Too funny can obliterate all else.

Or it's too funny, yeah, although too funny is usually one of those problems like too rich.

Do you enjoy the directing?

No. I would like to conceive of the film and then press a button and have the film master. Directing is enervating, and very often you're standing around on freezing-cold street corners at six in the morning, and I don't think anyone would find that much fun. And it's long hours, and often the results are very disappointing when you see them the next day in the screening room, in terms of lighting and acting and that your idea was not so good. And you directed it too slow or too fast and you're going to have to go back the next day and do it again.

'Radio Days' was warm and funny, but it didn't seem as ambitious as some of your others.

Well, I don't want to do a series of films that always seems to make profound statements. That would be really limiting. You want to do a certain number of films and try to do that, and I would like, in the course of my life, to do some broad comedies and a musical. You want to mix it up.

When I did *Annie Hall*, everyone wanted *Annie Hall II*, and the same with *Hannah*. But it's very important for me not to do that. After *Annie Hall*, I made *Interiors*, and after *Hannah*, I made a completely different kind of film, because it's important not to get suckered into the success syndrome because the public likes something.

Why this picture, 'Radio Days,' at this time?

I spend almost a year on a film, and by the time you've lived with something for a year, you want to get on. You get bored with that subject matter and that style of film, so you want to get into something different.

Hannah was a living-room picture. It becomes dull, so you look for something different to do, just to break the monotony. And so I thought it would be fun to do something that was episodic and full of music and cartoonlike and nostalgic.

Why do you do so many films? Couldn't you do fewer and make them all great, important works that would go down in film history?

No. I wouldn't want to make those kinds of films. They'd be expensive and they'd be hard work and you'd have to emotionally commit yourself for years to the same project.

I'd much rather make small pictures and just make many of them. I don't find any correlation between size and greatness. You take some of those Bergman films that are enormously complex, enormously complex. He shoots those things quickly, like in four weeks', five weeks' time. They're the best films in the world, I think.

I just do as many films as I have ideas for, just as fast as I can. And when I'm finished making films in my life, I will have made whatever number of films, and some of them, if I'm lucky, will be very good films, and some of them won't be good films, and some will be entertaining.

Something people always want to know: How much of 'Radio Days' is autobiographical?

Some of it is loosely autobiographical, but very loosely. The radio programs, such as *The Masked Avenger*, were generic because it would be such a nuisance to get clearance on actual radio shows.

The film painted a grim picture of Hebrew school.

Public school was equally bad. I went to both. Double horror.

Were you funny in school? Did they send you out in the hall a lot?

There'd be periods when I was really quiet and never said anything and other periods when I was amusing and we'd get into trouble constantly. But it was never a pleasurable experience. It was a spectacular treat to be sick, because you could avoid school, which was the blessing of all times.

What was so awful about school?

Everything. First of all, there were the natural things that kids would not like: sitting still, being disciplined, not being able to talk and not being able to have fun. It was a loathsome thing. The teachers were backward and anti-Semitic.

In your neighborhood in Flatbush? There weren't a lot of Jewish kids in school?

Almost all.

But the teachers were just anti-Semitic anyway?

Uh-huh. And they were stupid and mean. They were unpleasant people, and one never wanted to go to school.

Did you write in high school?

Yes.

Things that were not always appreciated by teachers?

I used to write things that they thought were dirty.

Were they?

No, they were dirty by the backward, ignorant standards of my teachers. My mother was called in to school so often because of that and other problems.

Like what?

Truancy, bad marks, causing disturbances. She was called to school so frequently that into her sixties, when my mother was still in the old neighborhood, kids who went to school with me would recognize her and say hello to her.

My mother's eighty now. My father's eighty-six. They live just a couple blocks from me. My sister lives ten blocks from me.

Has any of the stuff that borders on the autobiographical ever bothered them?

No, because the stuff that people insist is autobiographical is almost invariably not, and it's so exaggerated that it's virtually meaningless to the people upon whom these little nuances are based. People got it into their heads that *Annie Hall* was autobiographical, and I couldn't convince them that it wasn't. And they thought *Manhattan* was autobiography. Because I make the lead character a comic or a writer, I play it myself. I can't play an atomic scientist. I'm not going to make the lead a mechanic. I know the language of certain people.

Although you say you were never the schlemiel you have made yourself out to be, does it feel good to make films where you get the girl and all of that?

I've had a certain amount of successes and failures in every aspect of life. My life where I grew up in Brooklyn and in Long Beach was completely average. I was a perfectly good schoolyard athlete. And I had friends and dated some girls and was rejected by others.

Do you ever reflect on your situation now and say, "Wow, I'm having relationships with movie stars"?

I've been in the movie business the last twenty years. So it's logical that I would be seeing an actress or screenwriter or someone in my related field.

My life began being special when I was sixteen and got a job writing comedy. But even then I went to school in the daytime. I had lower-than-average marks and only went to NYU for a very short time to please my parents.

I was dropped by NYU after less than one year because of bad marks. I was a film major at NYU but couldn't even pass my major. I took what was called the limited program—three subjects.

You failed the limited program?

And I couldn't care less, because I'd ride the train to NYU from Brooklyn and I'd think to myself, "Don't get off here. Keep going." And I'd go right up to Forty-second Street, cutting school to go to the movies, hang out at the automat, buy the newspapers and go to the Paramount—and then go in to work in the afternoon.

By then you had a job and an inkling you might do well.

I felt very confident. . . . And again, to please my parents, who were so crushed by this because all of my friends were becoming lawyers and doctors and going to college and doing well, I also went for a very, very short time up to City College.

Have you changed along with your films?

I don't know that *I* have changed. The films have. I've become more interested in doing what for me is intellectually more difficult and more challenging.

How do you respond when people ask you, in effect, "Why don't you cut the crap and just be funny?"

Well, it has never really meant a thing to me what anyone said. I'm just sort of going the route I've chosen to go. If people like it, they like it, and if they don't, they don't. Crowd pleasing just never interested me.

This kind of goes back to your school days, when what teachers said apparently didn't mean anything to you. What then do you tell the youth of America? Is it okay for them to goof off and just do what interests them?

It's hard to give advice, in that sense. You see, I was lucky. I don't think you can count on being lucky. I was lucky in that I had a talent to be amusing. If I didn't have that talent, I would have been in great peril. You can only be independent that way if you luck out. But you can't count on it.

But people have always told me what to do. And I always listened politely, and I'm always nice to them, but I always do what I want to do.

The world is full of people who are quick to tell you films you should be doing and what to cut out and what to put in. There is an old proverb: "He can't think, but he knows all about it."

Or, in more recent history, as you said on film, "Those who can't do, teach, and those who can't teach, teach gym."

Yes, that was in *Annie Hall*, and I always felt people are very quick with advice, fast advice from the man on the street and profound advice from your peers. You read your books and you live your life and you see your friends and make your own evaluation as to what you want to do.

People are forever telling me, well, don't do this joke, or don't dress that way, or don't do this subject matter, or don't do that kind of film. You don't want to do *Take the Money and Run.* You want to do a different kind of film. You don't want to do *Annie Hall,* you know, because it's really less funny than *Bananas.* You don't want to do *Interiors* because of this and that. And I always listen politely, because they are nice people, but, you know, I do what I want to do, because your *body* demands it. You feel it. It's not so much a conscious decision. You go your route.

Have you ever thought afterward that those people were right?

That could never be, because I've always done what I wanted to do at the time. This doesn't square itself, necessarily, with commercial success. But who cares about that?

I've done films that were not commercial successes that I think were much better than ones I've done that were tremendous commercial successes.

For example?

I think *The Purple Rose of Cairo* was a *much* better

film than *Hannah and Her Sisters*. Much better. Much more imaginative. It's just a better film.

How about 'Radio Days'?

It was the best I could do at that time. As with all my films, you know, when I see it, I always feel disappointed, because I have such grandiose notions at first. But when you get into the very, very difficult world of having to translate those grandiose fantasies from a piece of paper and your mind to reality, and it requires props and people and huge crews and music and everything, it's very hard to transfer it with the same perfection that you conceive it in your mind, where everything moves beautifully. So, I'm always disappointed.

How did 'Radio Days' fall short?

Well, the concept in my mind was more glorious, was grander and more beautiful and funnier and more profound and more moving. It fell short in every important way. But this is not infrequent for me. It is quite usual.

And when you say this, you are not being falsely modest. The fact of the matter is that when you approach something, its potential is very often tremendous. And it's not an easy job to milk the potential from something, to realize that potential. And the more challenging the project is, a movie like *Zelig*, the harder it is to get the potential out of it.

As one who thinks about mortality, have you ever thought in terms of perhaps only living long enough to do ten or fifteen or twenty more films, and that they'd better be good and they'd better be this kind or that?

No, only because it really doesn't matter to me. It wouldn't matter to me if I stopped making films tomorrow. I'd be just as happy to write books.

Do you get any enjoyment from fame?

No, I'll tell you what I do like. The perks of being well known are very good, because I can always get a hotel room or a plane reservation or a table in a restaurant. And you do get good service.

That's it? You know, you really don't have to keep doing a film a year and be compared to Bergman to get a table.

Yeah. One of the reasons I don't travel more is because I'm bothered by the *paparazzi*. That's one of the drawbacks of being well known.

You're really more free to walk around New York than you are in Rome?

Yes, or Paris, absolutely. There's no satisfaction in the fame. When you're a kid, you think there would be. But as soon as you become an adult you see that there's nothing outside of these practical purposes like . . .

Getting a table.

And good theater tickets.

Is there some way that you want to be remembered?

No. Someone once asked me if my dream was to live on in the hearts of my people, and I said I would like to live on in my apartment. And that's really what I would prefer.

Forever.

Exactly. Nothing short of changing the human condition would be worth it. You drop dead one day, and it means less than nothing if billions of people are singing your praises every day, all day long.

Oh, come on.

You wouldn't know it. It would mean less than nothing.

You wouldn't like it if once a year there was a Woody Allen ticker-tape parade up Broadway?

You'd be better off with a couple of years' extension.

22
Billy Joel

INTERVIEWED BY
ANTHONY DeCURTIS (1986)

Historically, rock & roll never left much room for growing old with grace. In the Eighties, however, rockers who survived the excesses of the previous two decades began to seek a life beyond the studio and stage. For Billy Joel—one of the angriest young men of the Seventies—this meant a second marriage, a child and a reexamination of his identity as a rock & roll star.

These personal changes naturally influenced the music Joel made, from the heady sense of possibility captured on 'An Innocent Man' (released in 1983) to the exploration of emotions and relationships at the heart of 'The Bridge' (1986). "I have found that the better human being I can be, ultimately the better writer I am," says Joel, who was thirty-seven at the time he was interviewed. "So the human being has to come first."

In this interview, which took place in Montauk, Long Island (where Joel was vacationing with his family), and at the interviewer's apartment in Astoria, Queens, Joel talks about the challenge of progressing musically; the genesis of his relationship with model Christie Brinkley; the responsibilities of fatherhood; and a future beyond being an "entertainer" who does arena tours.

"You know, I like to think I'll be able to live like a normal human being," Joel says, looking ahead. "I'm not going to be a celebrity forever." Setting aside the defensiveness that had so often characterized him in the past, Joel begins to reveal in this interview just who that "normal human being" might turn out to be.

—A.DeC.

T HE ATMOSPHERE at Kaufman Astoria Studios in Queens combines all the giddiness and physical discomfort of a back-to-school shopping spree. Billy Joel has interrupted rehearsals for his first tour in nearly three years to sample the latest fashions for potential stage wear—and he's getting expert advice from his wife, model Christie Brinkley, who's sitting on the floor with their nine-month-old daughter, Alexa Ray.

The short, broad Joel—whom Christie always calls Joe—waddles into the room, decked out in a flashy, double-breasted gray suit. "Do

I look like an English rock star?" he queries in a mock-British accent, while bumping and grinding his hips and growling out the riff to Robert Palmer's "I Didn't Mean to Turn You On." Christie, meanwhile, is up on her feet, walking around Billy, examining the look. "When you get that suit made in your size, don't get it made too small," she advises. "And don't do that short-sleeves routine. . . . Those pants make you look really slim, honey, and they lengthen your legs."

When Christie leaves the room, Joel slips into absurdly tight black jeans and a fluffy white shirt open to the waist with the collar turned up. When he's got the get-up together, he looks for Christie in the next room. "Honey, *this* is the look, right?" he asks gleefully. "*Yeah*," she agrees, playing along, her eyes dancing around his chest as if the sight of all that body hair had stripped her of self-control. "But I think you need some gold chains." Joel nods thoughtfully in agreement and strikes a dramatic, lounge-act stage posture. "Don't go *changin'* . . . ," he begins to croon, and the room erupts in laughter.

These days, Billy Joel is a happy man. His new album, *The Bridge,* is a smash, but that's just a small part of it. His marriage to Christie and the birth of their daughter seem to have settled him in a profound way. He's still feisty and combative, but what the world thinks of him or expects from him—which once seemed his total obsession—doesn't appear to matter as much now. And though he sometimes denies it—"I'm supposed to have mellowed," he says wryly; "I have *not* mellowed"—his own expectations have taken on a more human scale. Following his own advice from "You're Only Human," Joel seems to have remembered his "second wind," and its momentum is carrying him along quite nicely.

*W*hen you first became popular, people used to think of you as a scrappy rock & roller. That image seemed to change dramatically after you got involved with Christie Brinkley.

Oh, yeah. Right off the bat, the recognition factor doubled. What I found was that I didn't change, Christie didn't change, but people's reaction to us changed drastically: "Oh, well, he married this fabulously notorious model, and now he's changed." As if I married her *because* she was famous or wealthy.

Did that characterization bother you, or did you just feel distant from it?

No, it bothered us, because it made us seem as if we were these social butterflies, and we're not like that at all. We're pretty low-key people. We enjoy very simple things. We do our own shopping, we do our own cooking.

How are you able to do that? Don't people come up to you all the time?

Yeah, people will do a double take in a supermarket. When I'm in the diaper section trying to figure out which one my baby uses and I ask somebody, "Is the purple box for the sixteen-month-old?" they'll do a double take, like "Hey, you look like Billy Joel!" I'll say, "Yeah, I hear that all the time."

Has having a child changed your life much?

Completely. It shifts your focus completely from yourself. All your life, you're consumed with yourself and your own priorities. Even when you get married, I still believe you're focused on yourself—you're marrying this person because they make *you* happy.

But when you have a kid, you see everything in terms of the child. It's very healthy in a way. You get away from yourself. All you worry about is the child. Health, finance, the emotional impact of things. It's a wrenching process. You have to mature rapidly.

You grew up on Long Island, your own background was blue-collar. Your daughter will obviously have a much more privileged upbringing. How do you feel about that?

Well, I think she's going to get a lot of love, that's for sure. And she'll be able to grow up in a nice place. But other than that, she's not going to get anything handed to her on a silver platter. She's not going to get to a certain age and come into fabulous wealth. We want her to go through a character-building process like we all did.

I'd like the kid to have as much of a normal life as possible, because it's not fair for her to be thrust into the limelight. The *paparazzi* are after her, taking pictures already. If Christie goes out with the baby, and they manage to get her picture, they caption it, "Christie poses with the baby." Christie doesn't pose with the baby. We don't want people to become too familiar with what the baby looks like, because the kid won't have a chance to live a normal life.

Your own father left when you were about seven. Do you think much about what kind of father you want to be to Alexa Ray?

I missed having a father very much. I went out and did crazy things to discover what my masculinity was. I got into trouble, I got into fights. I had to go out and box to discover my masculinity. Stupid stuff.

One thing I knew when I had a kid was I was going to be very much present as a role model. I definitely want to be very much present in my daughter's life. Not just as a male but as a father. And I don't mean in the old sense of *Father Knows Best,* with the pipe and the slippers.

But won't a long tour, like the one you recently started, separate you from your family?

Christie's going to be coming out on many of the dates. We're trying to set it up, like, if we play a certain area in the Midwest, we'll base ourselves out of a place like Chicago and fly in and out. On the West Coast, we'll do it from Los Angeles, and so on. So we won't have to be separated that much. Still, that's something that's going to be hard on a baby.

How did you and Christie meet?

I took a week off in the winter of 1982–83, the first vacation I'd taken in years. I was going through a separation and divorce. I had just finished a tour, and I was exhausted. Paul Simon had rented a house down in a place called St. Bart's, this island in the Caribbean, and he said, "Look, it's great down here. It's real quiet. Just take a break." It sounded like a good idea.

When I was making the transfer flight—you go down to St. Martin, then you take a commuter plane—I saw Christie Brinkley. I recognized her immediately. She was more beautiful than she was in her pictures—"Oh, wow, that's *Christie Brinkley.* I wonder if she knows who I am." So I did what I call an album cover—I tried to look like me on an album cover. I gave it every angle I could. She didn't recognize me from a hole in the wall.

And then I was on St. Bart's, and I went to this bar in the PLM hotel. They have a little piano there, and I had a couple of drinks. I was feeling, you know, a little melancholy. And there's Christie Brinkley. *And* Whitney Houston and another girl, Elle [Macpherson], who is now also a famous model. I met them *all* at the same time.

I can't imagine how you managed to keep playing.

I'm sitting there going, "I don't *believe* this." So, everybody's having a couple of drinks, no one was feeling any pain, and we started having a sing-along.

I was making believe I was Humphrey Bogart in *Casablanca,* and I was playing "As Time Goes By." Eventually, a little crowd gathered, and we were singing. Christie was sitting next to me. Whitney was standing in front of the piano, singing. Elle was there. And that's how we met. I started playing some old rock & roll songs. Platters songs, Little Anthony and the Imperials, mushy stuff.

She told me afterward she had just split up with a guy she had been seeing, and all of her friends were trying to encourage her to meet other guys.

She'd broken up with the French racing-car driver Olivier Chandon?

They had split up months before that, and she hadn't been seeing anybody. I guess she was kind of down, too. And they said, "How about Billy Joel?" And she said, "Nah, he's not my type."

Why was that? What was her impression of you?

I guess her first impression of me must have been this guy sitting at a piano with a Harley-Davidson T-shirt, looking like a bloated, puffy lobster. I had this incredible sunburn.

The music was the key to the introduction. She sat down and started singing, too. She was laughing about it, saying, "I don't have much of a voice." And I was *encouraging* her, "Oh, no, you have a *great* voice. Come on, sing, sing, sing." And I got a crush on her right then and there.

What was she like?

Real down-to-earth, you know, down-home kind of girl. Not stuck-up or anything, and not very self-conscious about her looks.

I didn't see much of her on the island after that. We chitchatted and said, "Well, maybe I'll see you when we're back in New York." And when I was back in New York, I was living at the St. Moritz hotel, and she was living on Sixty-seventh Street by Central Park West, which is right around the corner. I picked up the paper one day, and I saw that Olivier Chandon had been killed. I called her up and said, "Look, I know you're going through a hard time. If you just need someone to talk to, I'm here."

Had you been thinking about her since you met her?

Yes. Actually, I had been seeing a couple of different women. Sowing a few wild oats. I was going out with this girl Elle, as a matter of fact. But she stayed in my mind. She was such a nice person. And she seemed to like me. I thought about it—"Maybe this isn't a good time, but what she needs right now is a friend." I was in a good position to be a friend at that point, because I was feeling a certain amount of simpatico.

She said, "I can't believe you called, because I just called you." She called me the exact same day. The St. Moritz operator had been getting a lot of funny calls for Billy Joel, so she had been putting everybody off. So we got together as friends at first—we started to date. Then we saw more and more of each other and fell in love.

At what point were you able to stop thinking of her as "Christie Brinkley"?

I was not in love with her fame or her notoriety—we kind of met on equal terms that way. I know a lot of men who saw her were impressed with her celebrity. I'm not, and she likewise with me.

We were not at all prepared for the impact of our getting together—"Beauty and the Beast" or "Opposites Attract," that kind of thing. When the first articles came out, we were kind of hurt by it. "Well, she needed a shoulder to lean on, and he couldn't believe his astounding luck at meeting this stunning beauty." Wait a minute, we're just two people who met and got together.

How did you and Christie decide to get married?

I popped the question. I think we'd been going out something like two years. I was on the road—I think I was in Dallas. I hadn't even thought about it. I'm sure it had crossed my mind, but I really didn't know I was going to do it then. We were in a hotel. I said, "Will you marry me?" I think she was very moved by the fact that I asked.

A couple of weeks after that, we were home. We had kind of not said anything after that. I got her this diamond ring. I had this whole candlelight dinner planned, but I couldn't wait. It was the middle of the afternoon. She was upstairs painting—she had a little art studio. I had the ring, and it was burning a hole in my hand. I ran upstairs, and I put it on her easel table. She broke up, and she said, "Yeah, let's get married."

The relationship seems to have had a big impact on your work. 'An Innocent Man' seems like a valentine to her.

It started being written while I was dating other women. The whole idea came about because of the joy of finding myself to be an innocent man all over again. I was new to dating and romance and all that stuff, and that's where the seed of the album began. With Christie, the album became focused, all those feelings going toward one person. It became the valentine.

In "This Is the Time," on 'The Bridge,' you seem to be imagining future memories of the two of you together.

That's a strange song, in that part of it is the past, part of it is the present, and part of it is reminiscing about what the future will be. "I'm warm from the memory of days to come."

It's like the relationship itself is a "bridge" connecting the past, the present and the future.

Right. There's also a maturation of the relationship, because the character says, "You've given me the best of you, and now I need the rest of you." Now I'm ready to go beyond the infatuation stage. I'm ready for more depth. The relationship has to move, it has to be constantly progressing. And there's always a danger in progression of losing some things. "I know we've got to move somehow, but I don't want to lose you now." There's a certain amount of surrender, a certain amount of acceptance.

The song is also reassuring in its assumption that relationships can last.

I do believe relationships can last. I see these old people who are together in their eighties, holding hands. I think that's really neat. I think that's probably one of the hardest things to do in the world, to be a human being, maintain a relationship, be a decent person. They talk about the difficulties of being an artist and the difficulties of being successful in business. These things you can work on. The toughest thing is to do the things that are very human and make them work, because everything seems to be against it a lot of the time. A lot of temptation, a lot of pressure in other directions.

You know, I like to think that I'll be able to live like a normal human being. I'm not going to be a celebrity forever. I don't have any great grand plan to be a famous personality when I'm older. I hope to retire from it somewhat.

Really? It seems unlikely that you won't always be very well known.

Well, I don't see me being an *entertainer* forever. I don't see me being a recording artist forever. I can see me working in music and composition and maybe songwriting, but sort of retiring from the forefront of the celebrity part of it.

Do the demands of your career and Christie's put a lot of pressure on your relationship?

I think it's a matter of knowing, just *knowing*, what your priorities are. I would walk away from being a rock & roll star in a shot if it was a choice between my wife or my work. I know what's important. So does she. She never embraced modeling as some kind of successful career to strive for. She fell into it by accident, and she's never looked at it as an end in itself. She's an artist in her own right. She's a very good painter and illustrator. She has a flair for comedic acting. We have other things that we're interested in, besides the particular fields we're in right now.

That seems like quite a shift. You've always made such a point of defining yourself as a rocker.

That's very true, because my whole introduction to popular music was through rock & roll bands. The initial process was playing—playing in a bar band, Top Forty bands, garage bands. But it's sort of like being an athlete. Eventually, you have to become a coach. It's just a natural extension. The live performing thing, now that it's gotten to a level where all we do is 20,000-seat hockey arenas, where do you go from there? You do stadiums. To me, that is no longer progressing musically, that's progressing body-count-wise. For me to be challenged musically, I have to find other mediums. You can get stagnant in any form of music, unless you challenge yourself.

From that standpoint, how does the prospect of doing an extensive tour seem to you?

I've made myself available. I said, "All right, I'll go out on the road, because I believe in the album, and I want to support the music." The thought of going and living in hotels for months, now that I've got a family, is not pleasing. As a matter of fact, this is probably the last tour of this kind I'm ever going to do. That is not to say that I'm never going to play again, but for this particular kind of touring, this is probably a swan song.

You have to have an extraordinary ego to get up on a stage in front of 20,000 people and think that they're going to sit there and listen to you for two and a half hours. You must have this incredible confidence, and this drive to perform. And I can feel that starting to go. I think, eventually, the performing thing is going to take a back seat. The writing is going to become more and more prevalent.

How do you hear new music? Do you watch MTV or listen to the radio? Do you go out and buy records?

Every way you mentioned. I go to the record store and I'll buy twenty cassettes at a shot. New stuff, old stuff, whatever I see. I look around. I got the Peter Gabriel album a couple of months ago. He's great. I've liked Peter Gabriel for a long time.

What about Prince? Did you hear the last Prince record or see 'Under the Cherry Moon'?

I didn't go see it. I like his *1999*-era stuff. That may be my own block. There was such a personality cult that arose around him—that put me off.

What about Sting?

Yeah, Sting, definitely. I think the two greatest songwriters right now are Elvis Costello and Sting. Elvis Costello specifically for lyrics, and Sting specifically for music. Those two guys have definitely had an impact on me and how I perceive the writing I'm doing. Sting brought a jazz consciousness out.

"Running on Ice," from 'The Bridge,' seems to have a Police feel to it.

Yeah, I think that and "Mulberry Street," where my voice is real high. I'd walk around the house singing Police songs, Sting songs, and say, "Gee, I didn't realize I could sustain that kind of high note. Maybe I should try singing a song in that key." I never would have thought of it if it hadn't been for Sting.

What about Costello?

Well, he's such a literate writer. It's not the cleverness that gets to me, it's his use of the English language—it's a beautiful and also a tough language. Costello has tied them both together. I think he's had an impact on every group that followed him—he's the godfather of that whole New Wave. I don't think you can be a thinking writer and not have been affected by him.

How about Bruce Springsteen?

In the old days we used to see each other's gigs a lot. I think we went in different directions. I try to use economy, where Bruce can expound. I think he uses *a lot* of words very well. I like to use as few words as I can, because efficiency is something I like. He's also taken performance to its height. He lives to perform. I don't think Bruce's music has impacted my music. I like his purity, I admire that spirit of purity. I mean, he's living his rock & roll dream. Rock as religion, rock & roll as heroism. And he's proved it. He is the essence of it.

The Beatles have consistently influenced your music. What sort of impact did they have on you as you were growing up?

The main thing that hit me was that they played their own instruments. That made them legitimate musicians, whereas a lot of pop stars were just singers. They wrote their own songs. They wrote their own lyrics, they did their own arrangements, they sang their own harmonies.

For me, they were the rock & roll band that showed the most growth of any band I've heard before or since. It was almost like seeing *into* them. Every time there was a record, there was an incredible amount of progression.

There seems to be a strong John Lennon presence on 'The Nylon Curtain.' Were you thinking about him a lot when you did that LP?

I wasn't aware that I was doing a Lennonesque type of music—it only came out in the vocals when I listened back to it. It was kind of scary. He had been shot right around the time I was writing that album. It was a shock, not only because John Lennon had been killed, but because it signaled the true end of the Beatles. It was almost like a father figure had been taken away. I remember taking out the *Help* album. There's a picture of John—they're on this island or something—and he's got this funny hat with the brim turned up, and he's got this stupid grin, like he hated taking pictures and he was going to make as much fun of it as he could. I just broke down crying when I saw that.

What Beatles records particularly affected you?

There was a very exciting time with the Beatles. It was the era of *Sgt. Pepper* through *Abbey Road,* when they were doing these extended pieces. George Martin, I suppose, was doing a lot of the orchestration. No one did it as well as the Beatles. And all of a sudden it ended, and along came the California sound, the singer-songwriter era. I always felt cheated that that era got cut short. I always wanted to see how it would progress. I suppose some of the writing of *The Nylon Curtain* was trying to go back and pick up a string.

With "Allentown," "Goodnight Saigon" and "Pressure," the album seemed like an attempt to address some very American themes, like unemployment in factory towns and the legacy of Vietnam.

I thought it was kind of ironic that a few years later you had *Born in the U.S.A.,* you had John Cougar Mellencamp's album, you had very much awareness of American music. My timing was off, I guess. My timing is not the greatest, but I don't think in terms of how to time a career.

Even though you've addressed those kinds of topics in your songs, you seem to be somewhat ambivalent about the issues-oriented events that have taken place over the last couple of years. You did the "We Are the World" session and the first Farm Aid concert, but you decided not to do Live Aid.

I didn't decide not to do it. I couldn't do it, because I didn't have a band. The band was out doing different things. There's no way we could have got everybody together. I told Bob Geldof, actually, "If I can get the band together, I'll do it." Otherwise, I don't think I have the cullions to get up onstage and play the piano by myself in a stadium. I don't have *that* much confidence.

Also, you know, I do a lot of local charity. I keep it very low-key. You won't see me putting in my tour book that I've donated *x* amount of dollars to this, that and the other thing, even though I know it's good to bring attention to a cause. I don't like blowing my own horn about charity.

Do you believe music can help change things politically or socially?

I see that when music is stretched to be anything other than music, music loses. These great gatherings of musicians for charitable organizations are just gatherings of rock stars. The quality of the performance of the artists is not the greatest. You don't really get to see an hour-and-a-half show, you get to see fifteen or twenty minutes. The facility itself is kind of iffy.

Are those things the point?

I think that when you think you're going to see an artist do a definitive performance, you should see an artist do a great performance. This is not putting any of this stuff down. What I'm saying is, people know what they're going to see—they're going to see a festival. And it's not always the greatest concert you can see.

I think music in *itself* is healing. It's an explosive expression of humanity. It's something we are all touched by. No matter what culture you're from, everyone loves music.

You seem to be suspicious, however, about the role musicians can play on social issues.

I tend to question any sort of mass movement. I tend to question any sort of fad, trend. I'm a real believer in individual thinking, and I always look at both sides of things. When something is immensely unpopular, I'm always trying to figure out, well, what's on the other side of that? Why do *they* believe in that?

On "The Night Is Still Young" you sing, "Rock and roll music was the only thing I ever gave a damn about," yet you seem to be moving away from that now.

I found that to be a successful artist, to be a rock & roll star, you must be very self-centered. You must be totally devoted, tunnel vision, narrow-minded. And I found that that lessens you somewhat in human relationships. You must sacrifice much of your personal life to fulfill your vision. And I'm not willing to sacrifice human relationships, my personal life, in order to be a successful artist or rock star.

"Not willing" or "no longer willing"?

I'm no longer willing. But I don't think I ever pursued being a "rock star." I was always interested in being a consummate musician, a good composer—that was what was consuming me. And it still does, to a very great extent. I have to control it sometimes, because it can become all-consuming. If you become an artist too much, you become an elitist, and you live in this rarefied atmosphere, and you begin to accept it and believe it. That's why there's this problem with drugs and drinking and ego tripping with people who are extremely successful. And I don't want that to happen. I have found that the better human being I can be, ultimately the better writer I am. So the human being has to come first.

Did all those issues get confused in your first marriage, when your wife also worked as your manager?

She was more focused on my career than I was. Her function as my manager was to make me a rock star, and I think that's where our paths diverged. I might have become a commodity to an extent, and she might have become the enemy, which is business, capitalism, exploitation. I think as human beings, we went in different directions. It was fruitful and successful in terms of what the music business is supposed to be, but it was ultimately damaging in terms of a relationship.

You seemed like an angry man back then, when you first started achieving massive success. For example, you used to blast critics onstage when they gave you bad reviews.

I suppose I overreacted to some reviews. It probably wasn't the coolest thing in the world to do. I don't regret my impulse, but I regret acting on the impulse. It just drew more attention to the negative review than there would have been normally. Also, I was taking it too seriously. But then again, sometimes I had to, because the reviews questioned my motives, my integrity. A lot of reviewers, they don't review the album, they review me. Everything is colored by their perception of Billy Joel. Therefore, the album never really gets an objective look.

You went through a bad emotional period when you were twenty-one. A relationship had broken up, your career wasn't going well, and you felt suicidal. You checked yourself into a psychiatric ward for observation. Do you ever feel that same level of anxiety or frustration now?

Yeah, I feel things very deeply. I can get very angry, I can get sad. I don't get into self-pity—I was cured of that by going to this observation ward and seeing people who really had deep-seated problems. I'll only give myself about thirty seconds of good self-pity, and then this button switches on and goes, "Get off it."

What was it like in the observation ward?

It was just a real shock to be in a ward where there were bars on the window and electric sliding doors. You were given a robe—no clothing, no laces, no belts. You weren't allowed to carry matches or razors. And you couldn't leave. You're in the snake pit. And

I would go to the nurses' station and knock on the window, just like in *One Flew Over the Cuckoo's Nest,* and say, "Hey, look, I'm okay. These people are crazy, but I'm really okay. Let me out of here." They'd say, "Sure, Mr. Joel. Here's your Thorazine."

They gave you Thorazine?

Yeah, they were giving everybody Thorazine. I didn't take them. I put them under my tongue and then spit them out. I met with these shrinks at the end of a couple of days, and they said, "How do you feel?" I said, "Get me out of here!" I said, "I checked in because I was feeling suicidal. I no longer feel suicidal. I made a big mistake." I suppose it was a healthy answer—you're supposed to want to get out.

I was led out, the door slid shut behind me, and I ran and I never looked back. I said, "Wow, that's the end of that chapter. I will never, never think that I have problems that I can't resolve," because I saw people who couldn't, and it was scary. It scared the hell out of me.

Looking back over all the years you've been making records, how do you think your music has changed?

I'm not afraid to be Billy Joel. I'd kind of stayed away from that on purpose after *52nd Street.* I thought he'd had his say. I think I write certain things better than I write other things, which doesn't mean that I think my main strength is ballads. I think my main strength is melody. And I'm not afraid to sing more like me now. I've gotten used to the fact that, well, that's what my voice sounds like. Let's not have to hide it so much.

Do you have any favorites among your own records?

I think if I had to pick an album that I was most proud of, as a recording, it would be *The Nylon Curtain,* because I'm still amazed at the stuff that's in that record, the work that went into it. The stuff I enjoy hearing, believe it or not, is *Glass Houses,* because that album was written, not to prove that I was a rock & roller, as I've read in a lot of places, but to be a performance album. We were playing in these big arenas, and I started writing arena-oriented pop and harder-edged stuff because it works better in those places. I enjoy listening to that album, because I know the fun it was done in. The same with *An Innocent Man. An Innocent Man* was written so quickly, really, without a lot of laborious effort going into it, that I still enjoy the spontaneity of it.

What would you like the legacy of your work to be?

I would like the music to have meant something during the time in which I lived. It doesn't necessarily have to represent what was going on, but I would like to be thought of as *of that time*. And to be able to transcend that time. I think that a piece of music that is written well enough can continue. I don't even know if the lyric has to. I think if a jazz musician thirty years from now could play "Baby Grand," "Just the Way You Are" or "New York State of Mind" as a standard, then the music still will have a life.

Does it feel different to be so successful and so affluent at this point? Do you feel different about yourself?

It still surprises me that I'm this very naive, non-capitalist type of person dealing with what is the American dream. It scares the hell out of me, because I don't know what's going on. I wouldn't know how to invest money. I've never been in a bank in ten years. I don't know what it all means. I mean, I go to a bar in Manhattan, and there are these Wall Street brokers sitting around talking earnestly, in detail, about achieving exactly the kind of thing I've achieved. I sit there thinking, "I got more money than everybody at that table, but I don't know *what* they're talking about." It scares me. I'm kind of glad I've retained a lot of that innocence.

23

Clint Eastwood

INTERVIEWED BY TIM CAHILL (1985)

In the middle Sixties, as the elemental protagonist in a trio of so-called "spaghetti westerns" by the Italian director Sergio Leone, Clint Eastwood brought to the screen a dense and effortless iconic presence of a sort previously associated with the primal cowpokery of John Wayne. But where Wayne was merely terse, Eastwood seemed—to some, at first— virtually post-verbal. He could convey assessment and intent with the twitch of a lip or the glowering shift of a cigarillo, but the lack of conventional elaboration in his portrayal of Leone's Man with No Name led many critics to dismiss Eastwood the actor as a stiff. More distasteful aspersions followed in the Seventies, when he achieved mainstream stardom as that tarnished and snarling avenger of the SFPD, "Dirty" Harry Callahan.

Although sometimes tacitly equated with these two violent roles, Eastwood the man—a lover of jazz music and film art—is hardly a social Neanderthal. As a director, he has made a practice of quietly incorporating substantive roles for women and blacks into his films; and despite the absence of political ambition expressed in the following 1985 interview, he did subsequently serve a one-term stint as mayor of Carmel, California, that was unmarred by public lynchings or pistol-whipping epidemics. Like Callahan the detective and the nameless drifter of the Leone movies, however, Eastwood has always kept his own counsel, both as an actor and director, and he has consistently gone his own way. A pragmatic artist-star, he has utilized his ultra-bankable box-office clout in the service of the smaller, more personal pictures that constitute some of his most appealing work. Perhaps his most personal film to date—in that it drew on his lifelong fascination with jazz, as well as on the period of his own youth—has been the 1988 'Bird,' a near- three-hour paean to the late jazz-saxophone legend Charlie Parker, which also marked a new critical peak in Eastwood's directorial career.

Critical accolades will no doubt continue to accumulate as Eastwood goes on forging his singular artistic path. And chances are that he will remain, as a man, pretty much as Tim Cahill—one of ROLLING STONE's oldest hands—found him in 1985: a nice guy, a restless and questing star . . . an American original.

—K. L.

TWO DECADES ago, a friend of mine insisted I go see a movie about the American West, a film made in Italy and shot partially in Spain. At the time it was intellectually acceptable to be passionate about Italian films that limned the sick soul of Europe; the idea of an Italian western was oxymoronic—at best, like, oh, a German romantic comedy. What's more, in America the western as a genre seemed bankrupt, and going to see *A Fistful of Dollars,* which featured an international no-star cast headed by Clint Eastwood, some second-banana cowboy on an American TV series called *Rawhide,* promised to be entertaining in a manner the director, another unknown named Sergio Leone, probably never intended.

My friend was a graduate student in philosophy, and she'd seen the movie three times because she thought it was "existential." The Clint Eastwood character was called the Man with No Name, and he went around rescuing people for no stated reason and outdrawing ugly, sweating bad guys who insulted his mule.

A lot of the violence was stylized, tongue-in-cheek comic-book mayhem, and you couldn't take it very seriously, though several critics did just that, describing the film as "simple, noisy, brutish." This sort of abusive critical reaction didn't keep audiences away, but it did rather dampen the enthusiasm of philosophy majors who had seen smatterings of Sartre in the Man with No Name.

Clint Eastwood starred in two more of the movies that came to be called spaghetti westerns, then he went back to Hollywood in 1967 to make *Hang 'Em High,* another popular success in spite of critical reactions like "emetic and interminable."

By the early Seventies, an interest in Clint Eastwood movies among film buffs was considered a shameful and secret vice, like masturbation.

In 1971, Don Siegel directed Eastwood in the enormously popular *Dirty Harry,* a movie that sent some critics into fits of apoplectic name-calling. "Fascist" was one of the kinder descriptions.

That same year, Eastwood directed his first movie, *Play Misty for Me.* The studio had warned him against the project. Universal was reluctant even to pay him for a film in which he would play an easygoing, soft-spoken, jazz-loving disc jockey who inadvertently gets involved with a psychotic young woman. The movie opened to lukewarm but favorable reviews. Pretty good directorial debut, was the consensus, for some damn cowboy.

Eastwood went on to star in three Dirty Harry sequels, all of which minted money at the box office. He directed nine more films, including the classic western *The Outlaw Josey Wales* (1976). And though Eastwood could count on box-office success simply by whispering, "Dirty Harry," he often made choices that confounded his studios, critics and fans.

The 1978 film *Every Which Way but Loose*—a PG-rated comedy featuring an orangutan named Clyde—was another film the studio foresaw as an instant flop. The studio was partially right: Nobody liked the film but the public. Clearly, Clint Eastwood knew his audience better than anyone else, and his box-office success has allowed him to direct what he calls his "small films." *Bronco Billy* (1980) features Eastwood as a none-too-bright Easterner who runs an anachronistic Wild West show. In the pivotal scene, Bronco Billy allows himself to be humiliated by a gun-toting sheriff rather than betray a friend. The message might be that loyalty supersedes macho on the list of desirable modern virtues, a concept some critics interpreted as "punning on points of identity." Maybe, the critics seemed to be saying, Clint Eastwood isn't actually Dirty Harry after all. Another small film, *Honkytonk Man* (1982), is a character study, set in the Depression, of a self-destructive country singer. *Tightrope* (1984), Eastwood's depiction of a troubled cop in New Orleans, was both a critical and popular success.

By the mid-Eighties, critics were having a

difficult time defining Eastwood. *Sudden Impact* (1983), the fourth Dirty Harry movie, got strangely mixed notices. "The picture is like a slightly psychotic version of an old Saturday-afternoon serial, with Harry sneering at the scum and cursing them before he shoots them with his king-size custom-made '44 Auto Mag,' " scoffed one reviewer, while another felt that "many who have long dismissed Eastwood's movies as crude cartoons now suddenly understand that the violence has always been infused with self-irony and moral intelligence."

The weight of opinion seems to be shifting toward the latter viewpoint. In an article in *Parade* magazine, Norman Mailer was adamant in his admiration: "Eastwood is an artist. . . . You can see the man in his work just as clearly as you see Hemingway in *A Farewell to Arms*. . . . Critics had been attacking him for years over how little he did onscreen, but Eastwood may have known something they did not." The *Los Angeles Times* noted that women in Eastwood's movies have always been strong, interesting as both heroes and villains, and that "Eastwood may be not only one of the best, but the most important and influential (because of the size of his audience) feminist filmmaker working in America today." The French film review *Cahiers du Cinéma* noted the "self-parodying subtlety" in Eastwood's movies, while the London *Daily Mail* noted that Europe was discovering "hidden depths" in Dirty Harry. *The New York Times Magazine* ran a cover story on Eastwood the artist, appropriately titled "Clint Eastwood, Seriously."

It would be pleasantly ironic to report that this reassessment of Eastwood's career has come on the heels of declining popularity at the box office, but the man who formerly had No Name is, by some accounts, the most popular movie star in the world. Theater owners named him the top moneymaking star of 1984 and 1985, a distinction he also won in 1972 and 1973. Since 1955, his forty films have grossed more than $1.5 *billion,* a figure that

rivals the gross national product of some nations. Moreover, a recent Roper poll found that Americans aged eighteen to twenty-four picked Clint Eastwood as their number-one hero. Ronald Reagan was a distant third (behind Eddie Murphy), which may account for the fact that the president of the United States has begun quoting from Clint Eastwood films when issuing challenges to Congress.

For all his renown, Clint Eastwood in person is affable, a gentle man who speaks in a whisper-soft voice. At six-four and 190 pounds, he is physically imposing, but there is none of the coiled-spring tension one senses in Dirty Harry. Of all the roles he has played, Eastwood in person seems most like the mild-mannered California jazz deejay he portrayed in *Play Misty for Me,* a man happily out of step with the times and secure in his private enthusiasms. He lives alone in Monterey, California, where he jogs, works out with weights, plans his next projects and is sometimes seen in the company of actress Sondra Locke. He has two children by his former wife, Maggie: a daughter, Alison, 14, who appeared in *Tightrope,* and a son, Kyle, 17, who co-starred in *Honkytonk Man.*

Clint Eastwood is, as Norman Mailer noted, "a nice guy," a fifty-five-year-old man who has taken his chances and seems distantly amused by the sudden storm of critical acclaim after having weathered thirty years of dismissal and abuse. And, like many of the characters he's portrayed on screen, he is often more interesting for the things he doesn't say than the things he does. Listen:

Y̰ou are, by some accounts, the world's most popular movie star. Do you sometimes wake up in the morning, look in the mirror and say, "Can that possibly be me?" I mean, does it surprise you?

If I thought about it enough, it might. Yeah, I guess so. I guess you'd look back and say, "How did a kid from Oakland get this far?" I'm sure other people do that to some degree. It's like waking up with a hooker—how the hell did I get here?

Let's start with 'A Fistful of Dollars.' How did that come about?

Well, at that time I'd done *Rawhide* for about five years. The agency called and asked if I was interested in doing a western in Italy and Spain. I said, "Not particularly." I was pretty westerned out on the series. They said, "Why don't you give the script a quick look?" Well, I was kind of curious, so I read it, and I recognized it right away as *Yojimbo*, a Kurosawa film I had liked a lot. When I'd seen it years before, I thought, "Hey, this film is really a western." Nobody in the States had the nerve to make it, though, and when I saw that someone somewhere did have the nerve, I thought, "Great."

Sergio [Leone] had only directed one other picture, but they told me he had a good sense of humor, and I liked the way he interpreted the *Yojimbo* script. And I had nothing to lose, because I had the series to go back to as soon as the hiatus was over. So I felt, "Why not?" I'd never been to Europe. That was reason enough to go.

You've said that in the original script, the Man with No Name shot off his mouth more than his gun.

The script was very expository, yeah. It was an outrageous story, and I thought there should be much more mystery to the person. I kept telling Sergio, "In a real A picture, you let the audience think along with the movie; in a B picture, you explain everything." That was my way of selling my point. For instance, there was a scene where he decides to save the woman and the child. She says, "Why are you doing this?" In the script he just goes on forever. He talks about his mother, all kinds of subplots that come out of nowhere, and it goes on and on and on. I thought that was not essential, so I just rewrote the scene the night before we shot it.

Okay, the woman asks, "Why are you doing this?" and he says . . .

"Because I knew someone like you once and there was nobody there to help."

So you managed to express ten pages of dialogue in a single sentence.

We left it oblique and let the audience wonder: "Now wait a minute, what happened?" You try to let people reach into the story, find things in it, choice little items that they enjoy. It's like finding something you've worked and hunted for, and it's much more enjoyable than having some explanation slapped into your face like a wet fish.

So you have a lot of faith in your audience.

You have to. You don't play down to people—you don't say, "I'd better make this a little simpler, a little more expository." For instance, in *Josey Wales,* when he rides off at the end of the picture, the editor and I had wanted to superimpose the girl's face over him. He said, "We want the audience to know that he's going back to her." Well, we all know he's going back. The audience wills him back. If he rides off on the other side of town, the audience will say, "Well, he's gonna turn left." It's really looking down on an audience to tell them something they already know. Or tell them something they can draw in because it arises out of the story. I try to make that part of their job.

To . . .

To think about it a little bit.

You did two more of the Italian westerns with Leone: 'For a Few Dollars More' and 'The Good, the Bad and the Ugly.'

Yeah. The other two, the productions were glossier, more refined. The stories didn't mean a whole lot. They were just a lot of vignettes all shuffled together. I enjoyed them, they were fun to do. Escapism. And the American western at that point was in a dull period. But when Sergio approached me about being in some of the subsequent westerns, I thought it would be going too far. So I came back to Hollywood and did *Hang 'Em High.* Sergio was interested in expanding the size and scope of his films, and I was more interested in the people and the story line. I guess, selfishly, because I am an actor, I wanted to do something with more character study.

You've described yourself as introverted. Do you think that's because you moved so much as a kid?

Maybe, yes. We moved around California a lot. We lived in Redding, Sacramento, Hayward. My parents were married around 1929, right at the beginning of the Depression. It was a tough period for everybody, and especially a young guy like my dad who was just starting out. In those days, people struggled for jobs. Sometimes jobs didn't pan out, or they couldn't afford to keep you. We drove around in an old Pontiac, or something like that, towing a one-wheel trailer. We weren't itinerant: It wasn't *The Grapes of Wrath,* but it wasn't uptown, either.

It gives you a sort of conservative background, being raised in an era when everything was scarce. Once, I remember, we moved from Sacramento to Pacific Palisades because my father had gotten a gas-station attendant's job. It's still there, the station. It's at Highway 101 and Sunset Boulevard.

Were you involved in any school activities?

Yeah. I played a little basketball. Some football in

junior high. I didn't really get involved in team sports, because we moved so much. I did some competitive swimming, and one of the schools I went to had a great gymnastics program, so I diddled with that for a while. I wasn't particularly suited for it, because I was so tall, but I liked it.

I suppose one of the biggest things when I was a kid—I always liked jazz. A wide spectrum of jazz. Back in the Forties and Fifties, I listened to Brubeck and Mulligan. And I loved Ellington and Basie. I'd get books on everybody: Bix Beiderbecke, King Oliver, Buddy Bolden. I used to be very knowledgeable.

Then, up through the Forties, I used to go to those Jazz at the Philharmonic things. One time, they had Coleman Hawkins, Lester Young, Charlie Parker and a whole group of classic players. In fact, nowadays, when I talk to composers that are maybe ten years younger than I am, they're all jealous about that concert: "You saw those guys live!"

You play some jazz piano yourself.

Yeah, when I was a kid, I played. Fooled around with some other instruments, but I was lazy. I didn't really go after it. I just started again in the last few years. I've been diddling around with composition. Five or six things. I used one as my daughter's theme in *Tightrope,* and I also did the theme for the young girl in *Pale Rider.*

I have some regrets that I didn't follow up on music, especially when I hear people who play decently. I played on one cut on the album for *City Heat.* After the session, Pete Jolly and Mike Lang and I were all talking about how we started out playing piano. We all started the exact same way, only those guys went on to really play. We began by playing blues: blues figures at parties. I was such a backward kid at that age, but I could sit down at a party and play the blues. And the gals would come around the piano, and all of a sudden you had a date.

You had a country hit, "Barroom Buddies," a duet with Merle Haggard. When did you get interested in country music?

Well, I think you can say that Merle Haggard had a hit and sort of dragged me along. I was never terribly knowledgeable about country music. The first real good taste of it I got was when I was eighteen or nineteen, working in a pulp mill in Springfield, Oregon. It was always wet, really depressing. Wintertime. Dank. I really didn't know anyone, and someone told me to go out to this place where there was a lot of country music. I wasn't very interested, but this guy told me there were a lot of girls there. So I went. I saw Bob Wills and his Texas Playboys. Unlike most country bands, they had brass and reeds and they played country swing. They were good. It surprised me a little bit, how good they were. Also, there were a lot of girls there, which didn't surprise me at all. So I guess you could say that lust expanded my musical horizons.

Why didn't you follow up on the music?

I was going to. I tried to enroll in Seattle University, where they had a good music program. I got my draft notice before I got in there, though, and ended up at Fort Ord [California]. And I guess I just failed away from music.

I served my two years and went down to L.A. City College, where I enrolled in business administration. In the service I had met some guys who were actors —Martin Milner, David Janssen—and when we got out, a cinematographer got me a screen test. I got an offer to go under contract with Universal, seventy-five bucks a week to start. They threw me out a year and a half later. But it was a pretty good deal for a young guy. We had acting classes every day.

Is that when you realized that being introverted could be an asset for an actor? That you could play on it?

I don't know if I played on it consciously. I know that for many years before I became known for the way I act now, I played characters that were not terribly talkative. Economical characters. Some books— even Stanislavsky's people—discuss the fact that sometimes less can be best. Sometimes you can tell more with economy than you can with excess gyration.

The *Rawhide* series was a great training ground. All of a sudden, everything you ever studied about being an actor you could put into play every day. It's one thing to work for a week in a Francis the Talking Mule picture—which was how it had been going for me— and another thing to be doing it all day for eight years.

It's like the story of the great classical trumpet player they found one day playing in a baseball orchestra at Wrigley Field. Somebody recognized him and said, "My God, Maestro, what is the greatest classical trumpet player in the world doing playing in a baseball band?" He said, "You must play every day."

In *Rawhide,* I got to play every day. It taught me how to pick up and run, how to make things up, wing things in there.

'The New York Review of Books' recently ran an article about you that said, "What is most distinctive about East-wood . . . is how effectively he struggles against absorption into mere genre, mere style, even while appearing, with his long-boned casualness and hypnotic presence, to be nothing but style." Do you want to comment on that?

Well, yeah, style. Take guys like Kirk Douglas and Burt Lancaster. They're terrific actors, but their style is more aggressive. Both of them did some marvelous things and some films that weren't big hits but were great all the same: Douglas in *Lonely Are the Brave* and *Paths of Glory*; Lancaster in *Trapeze*. But their style was a little different than, say, Gary Cooper's or Henry Fonda's, because those guys were more laid-back, more introverted, and you were always leaning forward, wondering what they were thinking. With the Lancaster-Douglas school, there was never any doubt. Fonda or Cooper: You were never quite sure with them. They had a mysterioso quality.

Which is something you strive for: that little taste of ambiguity.

Exactly.

Let's go over a few of your films. 'Dirty Harry.'

There was something there I felt some people missed. One critic said Dirty Harry shot the guy at the end with such glee that he enjoyed it. There was no glee in it at all—there was a sadness about it. Watch the film again and you'll see that.

'Every Which Way but Loose.'

All of a sudden, Norman Mailer comes out and says he likes this film, and because he's such a well-thought-of writer, people think, "Wait a second, maybe that wasn't such a bad movie after all." I thought it was kind of a hip script myself when I read it. Here's a guy pouring his heart out to an ape and losing the girl. I like the correlation with some of my westerns, too. The guy purposely loses the big fight at the end because he doesn't want to go around being the fastest gun in the West.

'Bronco Billy.'

It's about the American Dream, and Billy's dream that he fought so hard for. And it's all in the context of this outdated Wild West show that has absolutely no chance of being a hit. But it's sweet. It's pure.

In the pivotal scene, Billy allows himself to be humiliated by the sheriff rather than allow his friend to be arrested. That played so against your established image: it must have been fun to do.

Really fun. It was suggested that Billy come back at the end and punch this guy out. That would have ruined the picture, the whole theme of loyalty. Billy doesn't approve of this kid being a deserter, and he doesn't know enough to intellectualize what his friend's feelings were about the war in Vietnam. He just knows he doesn't approve but he's going to stick by his friend. Now if Billy had come back and kicked the crap out of the sheriff at the end, it would have wrecked all that.

There's no real excuse for being successful enough as an actor to do what you want and then selling out. You do it pure. You don't try to adapt it, make it commercial. It's not *Dirty Bronco Billy*.

'Honkytonk Man.'

Red Stovall is based a bit on some self-destructive people I've known. He's wild and funny, but he's been a coward in his time. He won't face up to his ambitions. He's not that great a singer, but he writes some interesting things. When he gets his moment, he's already destroyed himself.

And the studio suggested that it might be a good idea if Red didn't die in the end?

I resisted that.

'Pale Rider.'

It's a western. One of the earliest films in America was a western: *The Great Train Robbery*. If you consider film an art form, as some people do, then the western would be a truly American art form, much as jazz is. In the Sixties, American westerns were stale, probably because the great directors—Anthony Mann, Raoul Walsh, John Ford—were no longer working a lot. Then the Italian western came along, and we did very well with those; they died of natural causes. Now I think it's time to analyze the classic western. You can still talk about sweat and hard work, about the spirit, about love for the land and ecology. And I think you can say all these things in the western, in the classic mythological form.

You're not generally credited with having any sense of humor, yet certain of your films get big laughs in all the right places. The first half of 'Honkytonk Man,' for instance, was very funny.

That's the way it was designed: a humorous story that becomes a tragedy. A lot of the humor is not in what you say but in how you react. Comedians are expert at that. Jackie Gleason in *The Honeymooners*: Alice zaps him, and his reaction—just the look on his face—cracks you up. Jack Benny could do that. Comedy isn't necessarily all dialogue. Think of Buster Keaton: the poker face and all this chaos going on all around him. Sometimes it's a question of timing, of the proper rhythm.

Does it amuse you that the president is quoting from 'Sudden Impact'?

Yeah, it was kind of amusing. I knew that "Make my day" would have a certain amount of impact in the film, but I didn't realize it would become a sort of "Play it again, Sam."

I've read that you occasionally speak with Reagan on the phone.

Well, I don't know where that came from. I think

some secretary or someone mentioned it. I've talked to him a couple of times, but they make it sound like I'm some great adviser.

I want you to meet my secretary of state, Dirty Harry . . .

Yeah, right [*laughs*].

You're not going to tell me what you talk about with the president?

I haven't really said that much. I was in Washington not too long ago, and I walked to the White House for lunch. We didn't discuss much of anything except the National Endowment for the Arts medal we were passing out. There were some former members of the NEA there, of which I was one. It was a small luncheon, a few laughs.

I mean, he doesn't ask me for advice. I could suggest some better places to go than that cemetery in Germany.

And you're not going to run for political office.

That's something nobody has to worry about.

You have a reputation for shooting your films quickly and bringing them in under budget. Do you think that has anything to do with having grown up in the Depression?

I would like to say it's just good business, but it may be that. It may be a background of not wanting to see waste.

There's a rumor that people work quickly on your sets because you don't provide chairs.

That rumor derived from a comment I made. Someone asked why I liked shooting on location as opposed to in the studio. I said, "In the studio, everyone's looking around for a chair. On location, everyone's working." But there are chairs on the set and on location.

You also have a reputation for bringing in young or underappreciated talent. 'Thunderbolt and Lightfoot,' for instance, was Michael Cimino's first film. Some people might say that you do that because you get these folks cheap.

Nothing's cheap, and I don't think I'd cut off my nose to spite my face. I don't think I'd get somebody cheap just because I thought he was cheap. I think I'd want the film to be the best possible. Otherwise you're selling yourself short. An awful lot of directors are expensive, but you don't know how they got to be that way. Sometimes it's just a matter of salesmanship and agenting.

I haven't worked with a lot of big-name directors, but I came up during an era when they were all beginning to retire: I never worked with Hitchcock or Wyler or Stevens or Capra or Hawks or Walsh. I missed all that.

I suppose the most expensive director I've worked with is Don Siegel. I think I learned more about directing from him than from anybody else. He taught me to put myself on the line. He shoots lean, and he shoots what he wants. He knew when he had it, and he didn't need to cover his ass with a dozen different angles.

I learned that you have to trust your instincts. There's a moment when an actor has it, and he knows it. Behind the camera you can feel that moment even more clearly. And once you've got it, once you feel it, you can't second-guess yourself. If I would go around and ask everyone on the set how it looked, eventually someone would say, "Well, gee, I don't know, there was a fly 600 feet back." Somebody's always going to find a flaw, and pretty soon that flaw gets magnified and you're all back to another take. Meanwhile, everyone's forgotten that there's a certain focus on things, and no one's going to see that fly, because you're using a 100-mm lens. But that's what you can do. You can talk yourself in or out of anything. You can find a million reasons why something didn't work. But if it feels right, and it looks right, it works.

Without sounding like a pseudo-intellectual dipshit, it's my responsibility to be true to myself. If it works for me, it's right. When I start choosing wrong, I'll step back and let someone else do it for me.

The critics are beginning to say that you've made some pretty good choices.

Some of them. But it's luck. It's instinctive. It comes from the animal part of the brain: the instinctive, intuitive part. The analytical brain can kill you as an artist. You want to stay in touch on a deeper level.

Why do you think the critics have begun to reassess your career?

I think it just finally got to the point where people said, "Well, he does quite a few different things. Maybe it isn't all some cowboy or cop who happened to click." It's easy to dismiss those kinds of films unless you're consciously looking for the best in them. Then again, I've changed. I've done films, like *Bronco Billy,* that were unusual for me, unusual for anyone. At a Museum of Modern Art retrospective in New York, they liked *Bronco Billy* and worked back from there. The French worked back from *Honkytonk Man,* which was one of the best-reviewed English-language films of the year there. In Montreal, at the film festival there, they liked *Tightrope.* All those films accumulate, and after thirty years, people are beginning to look at a body of work.

But how do you feel about it, this critical reassessment?

It's gratifying.

24
Neil Diamond

INTERVIEWED BY DAVID WILD (1988)

Neil Diamond? you ask incredulously. How did the man whom some consider the king of schlock-rock achieve admission to the company of, well, more fashionable pop icons such as Robert Plant, whose visage graced the cover of ROLLING STONE when this interview first appeared? Even Diamond seems to have had his moments of doubt. After all, the headline for this interview was originally a question he himself had posed: "Am I a rock person, or what the hell am I?"

Judging by the company Diamond has kept throughout his long career, pop snobs may have misjudged him. He was once employed as a songwriter by Jerry Lieber and Mike Stoller, now members of the Rock & Roll Hall of Fame. Later, he was given his first chance as a performer by Ellie Greenwich and Jeff Barry, part of the Brill Building elite that sustained rock & roll during the darkest hours of the pre-Fab Sixties, and he delivered with a series of unforgettable pop-rock gems. And in the Seventies, soon after Robbie Robertson produced 'Beautiful Noise,' one of Diamond's finest albums, he held his own with far hipper superstars at the Band's Last Waltz concert. Less persuasive to the cognoscenti but impressive nonetheless is the brute fact of those millions and millions of records sold. It's not called popular music for nothing.

After this interview took place, the governor of Massachusetts appropriated one of Diamond's compositions as the theme song of his campaign for the presidency. The song was "America," but America, of course, had other ideas. At about the same time, UB40 took another Diamond composition "Red, Red Wine," to the top of the charts.

So even if some choose to write him off as a mass-culture joke, Neil Diamond is no doubt having the last laugh.

—D.W. and S.H.

NEIL DIAMOND is sitting in his elegant Los Angeles office, noshing on a Danish and amiably considering the depths of his unhipness.

He is recalling a night more than a decade earlier when he shared the bill at the Band's Last Waltz show with infinitely more chic artists such as Bob Dylan, Joni Mitchell, Neil Young and Van Morrison. When his turn came to join the Band for a number, Diamond turned in a dramatic version of "Dry Your Eyes"—a song he and Band leader Robbie Robertson wrote for Diamond's 1976 album *Beautiful Noise*. So there he is, one of the most popular musical entertainers in the world, and all most people watching him can think is, "*What the hell is Neil Diamond doing here?*"

"I don't fit in," says Diamond, 47, before breaking into a wide grin. "But you could put me in *any* show and I wouldn't fit in. You could put me in a rock show and I wouldn't fit in. You could put me in a country show and I wouldn't fit in. You could put me on-stage with Sinatra and I wouldn't fit in. I just do *not* fit in. . . . I'm sorry. I apologize to everybody. But I never tried to fit in, because that meant conforming what I could write or what I could do to a certain set of rules. . . . The last group I remember joining was the Boy Scouts, and *they* threw me out for non-payment of dues. So I suppose you could say that I've always gone my own way."

It's been a tremendously popular, often intriguing route. Neil Diamond was born in Brooklyn, New York, on January 24, 1941, to Kieve and Rose Diamond, first-generation Americans of Polish-Russian ancestry. Except for a couple of years in the mid-Forties when the family lived in Cheyenne, Wyoming—where Kieve was stationed in the Army—Diamond spent his childhood in the working-class neighborhoods of Brooklyn. A visit by Pete Seeger to his summer camp got the fifteen-year-old Diamond interested in songwriting. In his junior year he switched from Erasmus Hall High (which Barbra Streisand,

his future "You Don't Bring Me Flowers" partner, attended at the same time) to Abraham Lincoln High, the student body of which included precocious teens like Neil Sedaka and Carole King.

Though he cut his first single (as part of the Everly Brothers–inspired duo Neil and Jack) shortly after graduating from high school, Diamond went on to attend New York University on, of all things, a fencing scholarship. Just ten credits short of graduation in 1962, he dropped out to become a fifty-dollar-a-week apprentice songwriter with Sunbeam Music, a small publishing company. By his own admission, Diamond was struggling, a washout at writing hits for other people, until one day in 1965 when Ellie Greenwich—who along with her husband at the time, Jeff Barry, wrote such pop classics as "Da Doo Ron Ron," "Leader of the Pack," "Be My Baby" and "Then He Kissed Me"—was asked by Gil-Pincus Music to sing on the demo of one of his songs.

"When he was teaching me the song, I thought, 'Gee, this guy really has an interesting sound,' " Greenwich says. "I loved his songs. And Jeff loved the way he sang. So we thought, 'There must be something here that we can do with him.' " With the couple's help, Diamond was soon signed to the fledgling Bang label.

Before "Solitary Man," his Bang debut, was released in 1966, Diamond—thinking his real name too bland—briefly considered calling himself either Noah Kaminsky or Eice Cherry. That near disaster averted, Diamond was soon racking up hit after hit with inspired pop tunes like "Cherry Cherry," "I Got the Feeling," "You Got to Me," "Girl, You'll Be a Woman Soon" and "Kentucky Woman."

Suddenly, people wanted to cover Neil Diamond songs. "I'm a Believer" and "A Little Bit Me, a Little Bit You" became smashes that helped establish the Monkees, and across the Atlantic, artists like Cliff Richard and Lulu hit the charts with Diamond's songs. Diamond's relationship with Bang soured when label founder Bert Berns refused to release "Shilo"—a song that pointed in the more serious, introspective direction Diamond wanted to move in—as a single. In 1968, Diamond signed with the Uni label. And even though his first Uni albums, like *Velvet Gloves and Spit* and *Brother Love's Traveling Salvation Show/Sweet Caroline,* saw him experimenting, sometimes successfully (the latter's inspired *Elmer Gantry*-like title track) and sometimes not (the former's bizarre antidrug anthem "The Pot Smoker's Song"), the hits just kept on coming: "Sweet Caroline," "Holly Holy," "Soolaimon," "Cracklin' Rosie," "I Am . . . I Said," "Song Sung Blue" and "Play Me."

In 1972, Diamond recorded *Hot August Night*—one of the most popular live albums of all time—at the Greek Theatre, in Los Angeles (Diamond had moved to the West Coast in 1969, where he now lives with his second wife, Marcia). By this time, Diamond—who Greenwich says was "terrible," "nervous" and "uptight" onstage in the early days—had turned into a charismatic live performer. In 1973, Columbia signed Diamond to one of the most lucrative contracts up to that time, guaranteeing him more than $4 million for ten albums. Interestingly, Diamond chose this time to begin a nearly three-and-a-half-year sabbatical from touring; he spent time with his family, entered a period of spiritual and psychological introspection and worked on the soundtrack for the film version of Richard Bach's *Jonathan Livingston Seagull.* Though the film was a critical and box-office disaster, the soundtrack album became a smash hit, selling more than 10 million copies.

In 1975, Diamond approached Robbie Robertson, a Malibu neighbor, to produce his next studio album. The result of the unlikely pairing was *Beautiful Noise,* an evocative musical tribute to Diamond's Tin Pan Alley days that remains his best album.

"I thought his early stuff was fantastic," says Robertson of Diamond. "He thought up these melodies that you couldn't get out of your head. And sometimes it was aggravating

that you couldn't get one of those songs to go away, but that just proved how infectious they really were. . . . My theory is that there was a musical vacuum out there between Elvis Presley and Frank Sinatra. And there was this huge audience that said, 'We gotta have something,' and they adopted Neil. And when you go to see him perform, it's like 'What is going on here?' These people are *hypnotized.* He can probably sell out more seats than Bruce Springsteen, you know? And it's not because it's the hip thing to do; it's because there's an audience there that needs this fix."

Since *Beautiful Noise,* Diamond has moved increasingly to the middle of the road, becoming a staple of the adult-contemporary-radio diet and scoring such occasional pop hits as "Forever in Blue Jeans," "You Don't Bring Me Flowers," "Heartlight," "September Morn," "Love on the Rocks," "Hello Again" and "America." The last three songs are from the soundtrack of *The Jazz Singer,* the 1980 movie in which Diamond made his film-acting debut opposite no less a figure than Laurence Olivier. As with *Jonathan Livingston Seagull,* the soundtrack did spectacularly, the movie less so. The film also underscored the fact that for a devoutly mainstream performer, Diamond was unusually open about his religion; who else but this Jewish Elvis could go multiplatinum with an album that featured a version of "Kol Nidre"?

Diamond may sometimes have been dismissed as a schlock-rocker—in some cases deservedly so—but his massive following has never wavered. And if critics have slighted his songs—often unfairly—he has had the supreme compliment of having them covered by everyone from Sinatra to UB40, Presley to Deep Purple. And even if his albums don't sell in the quantities they once did, his glittery, S.R.O. 1986–87 national tour (documented on the recent *Hot August Night II* album) proves he is still an unparalleled crowd pleaser.

Back in the Bang days, Neil Diamond wrote a song called "The Non-Conformist Marching Song." And for better and for worse—hipness be damned—he's been walking to its beat ever since.

The subject of loneliness—of the solitary life—comes up again and again in your songs. "Shilo," for instance, is about a child's imaginary friend. Were you a particularly lonely child?

I look back at the 8-mm films that my father took of me when I was a kid, and I *look* as happy as any other kid. I had my parents with me, and my kid brother; when I got bored, I could always beat him up [*laughs*]. Maybe I do have a little bit of a tendency to go off by myself and do my own thing. . . . I often wonder if anybody would ask me if I had a particularly lonely childhood if "Solitary Man" hadn't been my first chart record. Maybe I felt solitary that day, and maybe I just liked the way the word sounded with that melody.

Did the time you spent in the West as a child have an influence on you musically?

I think Cheyenne had a big influence on me. That's where I got to love cowboys. Because I always thought I was one after I came back from Cheyenne. I was a Brooklyn cowboy [*laughs*]. When I was a teenager, I used to take people riding at the Brooklyn Riding Academy. And I always loved the singing-cowboy movies. And on the back of comic books there was always that ad where kids could get free gifts if you sold enough greeting cards, and my eyes always went right to that guitar—there was always a guy on a horse with a cowboy hat and a guitar.

Is it true that a visit by Pete Seeger to your summer camp inspired you to start writing songs?

Yes, Surprise Lake Camp. It was a very liberal camp. We went for a winter get-together at Surprise Lake, and Pete Seeger came up and played for us. Some of the kids played their songs for him, and they were all singing about causes, you know, whatever causes meant something to a fourteen-year-old. That was the first time I realized that my peers could write songs. And that I could do it, too, maybe, just for fun. Not thinking that, *hey*, this would be my life.

The old record-company bio says when you were ten, you formed an a cappella group called the Memphis Backstreet Boys and ran away from home.

That biography was made up by the folks at Bang. I think they wanted to make up a fascinating history for Neil Diamond. See, what they wanted was more like a Bob Dylan or a Van Morrison, you know? But what they got was a Jewish kid from Brooklyn, and

they didn't think that was interesting. And so they made up something else.

Why do you think so many Sixties pop stars came out of a few Brooklyn high schools? Was it something in the water?

Every school kid in Brooklyn learns at some point that George Gershwin was born in Brooklyn and that he became a very respected musical prodigy around the world. So there's a tradition there. Also there just happened to be a couple of teenage geniuses who lived in Brooklyn then. It was like a little clique there, people competing with each other. Sedaka came back and played my high school, and he was great. But why Brooklyn? First of all, I think that it's a way to get out.

What was the Tin Pan Alley scene like when you got there?

Everybody wanted one of those geniuses. You had Carole King and Gerry Goffin, Phil Spector, Jerry Leiber and Mike Stoller, Doc Pomus and Mort Shuman, Barry Mann and Cynthia Weil, Neil Sedaka and Howie Greenfield, Jeff Barry and Ellie Greenwich, Burt Bacharach and Hal David. These people were the geniuses, and everybody wanted to be like them and to write as well as them. Together they probably had more of an effect on American contemporary music than anybody. So that's what you aspired to. And beneath that level there were hundreds of other writers—young, middle-aged, old and leftover from different periods—all trying to have their music heard.

That whole interplay was very simplistic at the beginning, because rock & roll was very simplistic. But then things became more complicated when people like Bob Dylan and John Kennedy came along. Suddenly the childlike nature of the music coming out of that area had an opportunity to change and to grow. And over the next few years—with the introduction of the Beatles and the whole invasion of British groups—things changed almost completely, because only those writers who were performing their own music had a chance at having their music heard. And a lot of people were kind of lost for a number of years. I think the thing that saved me was I had no hits at that point. So I was an unknown factor.

Was it hard to write songs in a cubicle with other people banging out tunes all around you?

Well, it sure didn't work for me. I was always conscious that people were listening to what I was doing. Now, of course, I realize that they couldn't care *less* what I was doing. So usually I did my writing at home or on the subway, anywhere but at an office.

When I finally left the system, I took a little office

of my own above Birdland [a New York City jazz club]. It wasn't really an office. It was a storeroom that I sublet from a printer. I paid like forty dollars a month. I put in a chair, a desk, an old piano. I put a pay phone in. I lived in that room for a year. And there—for the first time working without some kind of specification about what I could write—I wrote some of the best songs I had written up to that point.

So many of the Brill Building greats wrote in pairs. Why didn't you have a partner?

It's not like I had a lot of people beating down my door to work with me [*laughs*]. But, yes, most of what I did, I did on my own. I guess that's part of who I am.

You worked as a staff writer for Leiber and Stoller in the early Sixties. What kind of bosses were they?

I hardly saw them. They were always in their room and very apart from the writers. They were writing Drifters songs. What do they want to know about some jerk with a guitar? *Nobody* wrote with guitar in New York. It was all piano writers. So when I walked in with a guitar, I was like a hayseed, despite the fact that I was from Brooklyn. . . . I had some staff jobs, but they didn't end happily. Actually, I was fired from all of them, which is a pretty good record [*laughs*].

What do you think was lost when the Brill Building era ended?

Well, I would have loved to have heard another ten years of creative, successful music from the writers of that time. But I'm not so sure if I would trade it for what was to come.

Were you a fan of Jeff Barry and Ellie Greenwich before you started working with them?

Oh, yeah. I would have given a toe to have written one song as good as some of the things that they were just knocking out. They'd write a song right before they were supposed to meet the artist. It was . . . unbelievable. They didn't have to spend a lot of time writing "do wah diddy diddy." Those songs became that way because they never took the time to finish them [*laughs*]. The songs were accepted before they were actually completed. Two bars of Jeff and Ellie, and you'd want it.

Why would you consider changing your name to Eice Cherry or Noah Kaminsky?

While the label was writing a new biography, I thought maybe I should have a different name. This was all going to be some kind of a giggle that I'd be able to show my grandchildren. At the last minute, I just couldn't do it. So I flirted with using a pseudonym. But needless to say, I'm very relieved that I didn't.

But do you think that you would have made it as Noah Kaminsky?

Yeah, of course. I mean, if Simon and *Garfunkel* could do it, Noah Kaminsky could do it, you know? [*Laughs.*]

Why do you think people are still drawn to the Bang records?

There was definitely a simplicity to the Bang songs, because I didn't have anything to live up to. I didn't have a year to ponder a lyric. I always tried to get back to that simplicity, but it's harder and harder, because you want to keep trying something new to keep yourself interested.

When you first started having hits, did you feel part of the rock scene?

I was aware of being the only single artist out there, certainly the only American single person, as opposed to a group. People didn't know exactly what to make of me. There's the LSD scene in San Francisco, and there's the folk scene in New York. There's all kinds of English music coming over, and here comes a guy with a guitar, and I didn't really fit into what was happening in music. The critics and the press absolutely paid no attention to me. I did a show at Carnegie Hall as a way to showcase myself. No reviewers showed up. People weren't looking to some guy with a guitar who, while nobody was looking, had ten hit records in a row. It was like I didn't exist.

You must have been aware when you formed Performers Against Drugs and released "The Pot Smoker's Song" that it wasn't going to help matters.

Yeah. You know, part of me is rebellious. And part of me will do something like that just to say, "Hey, fuck you." That's all it is. Fortunately that side of me doesn't come out too often. I'd met some people who were running the Phoenix House drug-abuse program in New York. And I just got fascinated by it. I think probably in retrospect it was misnamed, calling it "The Pot Smoker's Song," because the fact is that none of these people were on pot. They were mostly on heroin. So to the hip community, you know, it was more evidence that Neil Diamond was not one of their kind of guys. It was genuine; it was heartfelt. But it also confirmed a lot of people's feelings that I wasn't hip.

Was there a moment when you realized you weren't really part of the rock world?

I never thought I was, so I never felt that I wasn't. It wasn't until recently—this year in fact—that I began to ask myself, "Am I a rock person, or what the hell am I?"

And what was the answer?

Well, the answer is yes, my music is based on rock

music. But I also have a tremendous love for the romantic music that came before rock, partially because it's in my tradition. But all of my music is based on rock, you know? If Roy Orbison is rock, if the Everly Brothers are rock, if Elvis Presley is rock, if the Beatles are rock, then yes, I am.

What do you remember about the Last Waltz?

I had fun. Forget that my style was not the same as theirs. How about just to be like a fan and hang out backstage with people like Bob Dylan and with Robbie and Joni Mitchell. They knew who I was. I wasn't a stranger to them. I did feel like odd man out . . . but I saw Bob Dylan perform for the first time there. I was standing right on the side of the stage, and Bill Graham couldn't get me off. He wanted to throw me off. He didn't have the nerve to do it. So he asked the stage manager to do it. His stage manager asked *my* stage manager to do it. My stage manager said, "You do it!" And so I just stood there. Before Bob went out, I was kidding with him backstage. I said, "You'd better watch it, because this is my audience, and I'm going to kick them in the ass." Knowing, of course, that these people probably didn't have the vaguest idea who I was. And he kind of looked at me. But he went out there and he really kicked ass.

So hipness has never been a problem with other musicians?

No. No way. With other musicians, I'm right there and they're right there. Those are the easiest kinds of relationships that I can possibly have. Because look at the common ground we have to talk about. Look at what we live through together, you know? We live and die with chord changes. I find the respect that I need from those people. Whether it's Miles Davis, who says, "Hey, I really love this song," or it's Bobby Dylan, who sends me his version of "Sweet Caroline," or Stevie Wonder, who says, "Here's a song that I think you'll sing great." So maybe that helps to ease the criticism a little bit, that my peers accept me and respect me, and that's enough.

What's it like to hear people like Dylan, Presley and Sinatra cover your songs?

It was great, because you know, some people collect trophies. Some people collect stamps. To me, to have a dozen different artists that you really love record a particular song, it's fantastic.

Any favorite covers?

Sinatra did "Sweet Caroline" with a swing band, and he *killed* the song. I mean, he just did it better than anybody, including me, ever did. I love that. That's probably my favorite cover version. And I loved UB40's "Red, Red Wine," which came out of the blue.

What about least favorites? For instance, what's it like to hear your songs done as Muzak?

Muzak is . . . difficult, but you don't really listen to it. It doesn't try to grab your attention. The *really* bad thing is when something tries to grab your attention, and it does, and it stinks. Then you've got a problem. But the things that I haven't liked? Yeah, there have been things that I haven't liked over the years, but how can I possibly complain?

Did you ever hear Deep Purple's version of "Kentucky Woman"?

I think I must have heard it. It was pretty . . . radical. They may have even kept some of the melody [*laughs*].

Do you feel a kinship with Paul Simon, another New York–bred singer-songwriter?

I always thought of Paul as much more of an intellectual than I was. I was just a sheer emotional guy. But our backgrounds, I guess, are similar. He started much earlier than I did, you know? He asked me when I did my first Dick Clark show, and I said '66, and he did his in like '56 or '58. He must have been twelve years old at the time. So he was further ahead than I was along the evolutionary scale. He's also a talented guitar player, which I'm not. He's a standard of excellence, you know?

Did you and Simon and Garfunkel attract the same sort of audiences?

Uh-uh. Their audience was much more intellectual, liberal, you know? Hipper. But then *everybody's* audience was hipper than mine, you know? What can I say? I was left with the rest of America [*laughs*].

Have you ever resented being lumped in with other MOR favorites like Barry Manilow and Kenny Rogers?

Not really, as long as I'm the number one, you know?

Do you feel you fit in that category?

I don't. I think some of that was created around me, and they kind of came into it. But it's kind of nice to be lumped. I never was lumped. I always felt kind of lonesome out there by myself. I was a solo male singer in a world of groups. Elton John was the first one that I remember. Up until then, I was completely alone. And then John Denver and then . . . maybe Barry Manilow? For boy singers it's been pretty lonesome out there. So I'm happy to see a single guy come along and keep it happening out there while I'm resting [*laughs*].

What do you think when people dismiss you as being "slick"?

Well . . . when I hear "slick," it's like a Broadway show would be slick. Everything is like a machine; it works to perfection. And that would be pretty boring after a while. I think if I were slick, I couldn't do it for twenty years. There always has to be an unknown element. Something that makes this night or this record different from all others. A professional, yes. Extraordinarily particular, yes. . . . Hard working, intense, focused, serious, yes. Slick? . . . I don't see it.

It's not my place to say if something I do is "brilliant" or "schlock." 'Cause I know some of it is brilliant, and I know some of it is schlock. But I followed my own dumb little zigzaggy progression over the years. From "Cherry Cherry" to "The African Trilogy" to *Jonathan Livingston Seagull* to "America," I've had a very strange kind of a weird path. It hasn't made very much sense at all, but at least it's been my path. I think I probably would have been driven crazy if I'd taken any of it seriously. I certainly would not be doing this the way I am today, because they all told me to get out of the business when I started. From the music publishers on to my very first review, which said that I should stick to songwriting.

Do you think you were a born performer?

No, I think if anything I was kind of thrown into it. You have a hit record, and you can't just sit there. You better show your face. So I went down to the Village, and I got myself what I considered to be appropriate stage costume, which was a pin-striped suit and a tie [*laughs*]. I already had my Everly Brothers guitar. I took an extra set of strings and chord charts for the band. And I went out and did it.

Why does the man who did "Forever in Blue Jeans" go onstage in outfits with all that glitter and all those sequins?

Not sequins.

Not sequins?

No, those are glass beads. There's a *big* difference [*laughs*]. Well, I love to be flamboyant onstage. I'm not very flamboyant offstage, so it's my one chance to really let 'em have it between the eyes. And also, when you're playing large arenas, it's nice for the audience to know *approximately* where you are.

When you wrote a song like "Sweet Caroline" or "Song Sung Blue," did you have any sense you were writing pop standards?

I knew that I loved them. But when I was writing them, I don't think that I knew they would be hits. As a matter of fact, "Song Sung Blue" was my second choice for a single from that album. And Russ [Regan, who ran Uni] said, "No—'Song Sung Blue.' It's going to be your biggest copyright ever." I mean, the song had two verses; I never got around to writing a bridge for it. And although the lyric says everything I wanted it to say, there's not much meat to it, you know? But it turned out to be a major, major copyright.

"Done Too Soon" is certainly the only time a songwriter ever mentioned Sholom Aleichem, Albert Camus and Caryl Chessman in a pop tune.

It was kind of esoteric, especially at that time. But it's just me trying to say something a little different, just try and jog something in a person's memory, or to elicit a reaction. That's what my job is, to do something a little bit different and yet something that's me and something that's you.

Which song that you wrote came the slowest?

"I Am . . . I Said." It took four months every day, all day. I'd go into my room, I'd lock the door, and I'd struggle with this song. It came out of a screen test that I did for a movie they were going to make on Lenny Bruce's life. And somehow I did one of the scenes in the morning, and I went back to my dressing room during lunch. I was really depressed, 'cause I knew I had done a miserable job. And I had my guitar there, and I started to play this thing. There were a couple things there I really loved. So I went in every day and I fought with it. I cursed it out. It was like a person who wouldn't submit. I got as close as I could get it.

Which song came the quickest?

I have to say "America." The lyric and the form of that song came very quickly. I almost wrote it directly on the paper, because it was like so close to me. I knew all the information already. It was just a matter of putting it down.

And what song are you proudest of?

I have to say "America." Because so many people are moved by it and feel a sense of association with it. Interesting groups that have picked up on that song. All of the foreign-born parking-lot attendants and people from other countries know me and think I'm a big star. They saw *The Jazz Singer,* and they loved it. It was their story, the story of an immigrant. It pleases me so much that it got such exposure. Not only when it was a hit record and through the movie, but in so many situations since then. Like with the hostages coming home from the embassy in Iran. On the news that night they're playing [*sings*], "They're coming to America," you know? And it was so easy to write, because it was so me, you know? I had to talk for myself; I had to talk for my people.

When you speak of "my people," it makes me wonder if there was a concern that making 'The Jazz Singer' was not a good career move for you, that it was "too Jewish?"

Of course. That's a fear, because most of the world is not Jewish, I have found [*laughs*]. And people have different prejudices against Jewish people. A lot of which I don't understand. Some of which I do understand. All of which hurts. And so I had a responsibility with that movie. First, to get up enough nerve to play that kind of a part as opposed to a western hero, which I was offered. As opposed to a science-fiction kind of a guy, which I was offered. And I was very protective of how this character was portrayed. The only argument I had at all with Olivier was about one of the lines which I wanted changed. In this scene, his character—my father—is saying you have to stay and be a cantor. And my character was supposed to say, no, I have to go out and make a living and make some money. And I said, "I can't say this line. This character is not doing this music for money. And Neil Diamond is not doing this music for money and never did." And Olivier said, "Well, I worked when I was a youngster to try and make money." Well, he's not Jewish, so how could he understand my sensitivity to having someone base his whole life on chasing after money? It's the stupidest thing in the world to do, to try and make money with music, because it doesn't happen that way. It only happens by accident. So I changed it.

Is it true that when you went to the White House dinner for Prince Charles and Princess Diana a few years ago, you discovered that the Marine Corps had more than a dozen of your songs in its repertoire?

I didn't know I would be asked to do anything. I should have gotten a hint when we made our entrance, because there was a string quartet playing "Song Sung Blue." And Mrs. Reagan's secretary came over and brought me to Mrs. Reagan, who was dancing with her husband at the time. She dropped him like a hot potato [*laughs*]. And she came over directly to me. I felt so terrible. "My God, lady, this is the president." She said, "Would you sing for the princess?" And I said, "I'd love to, but I haven't rehearsed with the orchestra." And she said, "Come with me." And she brought me over to the conductor. He opened the book, and he showed me a list of fifteen or twenty songs of mine that they had orchestrations in my key. In my key! And I said, "Okay, I'll take that one and that one." And they played beautifully. I mean, it was mind blowing.

Are you optimistic about the future of rock?

Sony was willing to pay $2 billion [for CBS Records] to have a piece of the rock, you know? You tell me if it's in trouble.

And are you looking forward to being a Sony artist?

Well, the letter we got from the president of Sony that said all the artists were going to have to do exercises every morning before going into the studio was a little disturbing [*laughs*]. No, I think it'll be fine. Sony got, I think, a tremendous bargain. If I'd had the $2 billion, I would have bought it myself.

So, after all this time, who's the average Neil Diamond fan?

My fans are all well above average [*smiles*]. When you have done so many songs over the years, one of them has got to have attracted at least somebody, you know? If you haven't liked one song that I've written, then I should probably hang it up. I tried for twenty years to get everybody to like at least one song. And if I haven't done that by now, I'll just have to spend the next twenty years trying to do it.

25

John Cougar Mellencamp

INTERVIEWED BY DAVID FRICKE (1986)

Few rockers have been as reviled and revered in equal measure as John Cougar Mellen-camp. For years after his disastrous debut as the glitter-punk hype Johnny Cougar, critics dissolved in fits of spiteful laughter at the mere mention of his name. Bitter and disillusioned, he stripped down his sound and toughened up his songwriting for a comeback crack as John Cougar, only to be dismissed as a cheap Springsteen imitation with a bad attitude.

Today, it is hard to believe Mellencamp was ever such a scourge on popular music. A founding member of Farm Aid, an outspoken critic of corporate sponsorship in rock and a songwriter of rare poignance and grit, Seymour, Indiana's, favorite rock & roll son is now a national hero. His four platinum albums—'American Fool', 'Uh-Huh', 'Scarecrow', and 'The Lonesome Jubilee'—testify to his popularity as well as the evolving power, social urgency and emotional appeal of his parables of ordinary people coping with extraordinary frustration and heartbreak. Not bad for a guy who once titled an album 'Nothin' Matters and What If It Did.'

—D.F.

J OHN COUGAR MELLEN-CAMP had every right to be angry. Nearly 20,000 fans had paid $17.50 a ticket to see the small-town boy play the biggest room in New York, Madison Square Garden. And on this, one of the most important nights of his career, his expensive, highly sophisticated sound system went kaput not once but twice, thanks to a faulty fifty-dollar circuit breaker.

But Mellencamp didn't blow any fuses. He didn't throw drummer Kenny Aronoff's kit into the crowd the way he did during a legendary tantrum at a London, Ontario, concert in 1982. He didn't storm offstage muttering obscenities, as he did that same year during an on-camera fracas with a CBS News interviewer. The thirty-four-year-old Indiana singer just sat in his dressing room until the sound problem was solved and then returned to the stage, where he told the crowd, "I feel so bad about this that if you got your ticket stub, you got your money back." He sweetened the deal by playing for another two hours, venting his anger through ferocious renditions of his biggest hits and a long medley of Sixties nuggets. (Financially, he stood to lose nearly $350,000 from his refund offer, but only half the fans returned their tickets.)

"If this had happened to me five years ago, I would probably have passed out," Mellencamp said, laughing, a few days after the December 6 concert. "There would have been so much blood rushing to my head, I would have just blacked out." But this is a different John Cougar Mellencamp from the bantamweight hothead who topped the charts in 1982 with "Jack and Diane" and had the biggest-selling album of that year with the cynically titled *American Fool*. Cursed with a corny stage name given to him by his first manager, David Bowie's former svengali Tony DeFries, he was a man who loved to hate—his record company, the critics who dismissed him as a minor-league Springsteen, even his own songs.

"If you'd come in here then, I wouldn't have wanted to like you. It was safe for me. This guy might not like me, so I'm going to not like him first. It's a real juvenile way of thinking, but that's the way I functioned in my life for years."

"I don't think he enjoys that emotion anymore," says guitarist Larry Crane, who has played with Mellencamp for almost fifteen years. "He liked the rush of getting angry, but not anymore. If something's not right at a sound check, John will look at me and say, 'Aw, do I really have to get mad at somebody today?' " Indeed, considering his reputation, Mellencamp was unexpectedly relaxed and thoughtful during the two sessions for this interview, backstage in Binghamton, New York, and in his Manhattan hotel suite.

Sobered by success (*Scarecrow* is his third straight platinum album), Mellencamp has replaced the chip on his shoulder with the weight of private and public responsibility. Instead of relocating to a superstar community like New York or Los Angeles, he stays in Indiana, where he keeps tight with relatives, old school buddies and biker pals. He turned down an offer to play at Live Aid—"Concerts that just raise money aren't a good idea"—but he has devoted much of his nonmusical energy to publicizing the plight of American farmers. He helped organize the September 22 [1986] Farm Aid concert with Willie Nelson and Neil Young, and in his own shows he asks fans to write to their congressmen demanding legislative action.

"Yeah, John Mellencamp has a history of being the biggest joke in rock & roll, right?" he snaps. "But you can't take away the fact that as far as what's going on right now, I care about it."

Born in Seymour, Indiana (population 15,050), on October 7, 1951, the second of five children, John Mellencamp wanted to be a rock & roller in the worst way, and that's exactly why he made it. He scuffled through a series of hard-luck bar bands, including a glitter-rock outfit with Larry Crane called Trash, which played only four gigs over a whole year. In 1976, Tony DeFries hyped him as a Bowie-Springsteen hybrid called Johnny Cougar, a transparent hustle (made worse by a limp debut album, *Chestnut Street Incident*) that poisoned Mellencamp's image for years. Even after he signed with Rod Stewart's then-manager Billy Gaff, the going was rough. Larry Crane remembers one gig the Cougar band played on a 1978 U.K. tour in a broken-down soccer stadium—under the bleachers. "We were in a room that was like a refreshment stand. You wonder why John was miserable then?"

The no-frills *American Fool*, which contained the first hints of his garage-rock instincts, along with plenty of Springsteen-Petty-Seger references, pulled Mellencamp sharply out of his commercial nose dive. For his 1983 album, *Uh-huh,* Mellencamp wrote his bittersweet state-of-the-nation address, "Pink Houses," and machine-gunned the tunes to tape in little more than two weeks. But on *Scarecrow*, his equation of the farm crisis with the general deterioration of the American Dream, Mellencamp comes much closer to his dream fusion of lyric commitment and Sixties energy. He actually had his four-piece band prep for the sessions by learning a hundred old Sixties hits note for note, from Lou Christie and Four Seasons records to Beach Boys classics and even "Talk Talk," by the Music Machine. "I thought he was giving us busywork," confesses bassist Toby Myers, "but he wanted us to understand what made those songs tick so we could put some of that grit into his songs."

When he isn't on the road or lobbying for Farm Aid, Mellencamp lives on twenty-three acres in Bloomington, Indiana, with his second wife, Vicky, and his three daughters—Michelle, 15 (by his first wife, Priscilla); Teddy Jo, 3; and Justice, who arrived less than six months ago. Their home is a spacious old Cape Cod–style house renovated by John and Vicky two years ago—a modest luxury paid for in full with a decade's sweat and pain, no matter what you might think of his art. During a recent video shoot, a technician stood on Mellencamp's porch and muttered sarcastically, "Okay, little pink houses for you and me." Mellencamp turned to him and said, "Listen, pal, don't you pass judgment on me until you've walked a mile in these shoes."

Your latest stage show is a lot like a Bruce Springsteen concert. There's no opening act, you perform for nearly three hours, and you include several Sixties covers in the set. After so much Brucemania, weren't you worried about the comparisons?

I didn't even think about the Springsteen comparison. What Springsteen does is a marathon. What we do is a sprint. But I'm becoming convinced that the comparison is good. I feel like I'm giving something back to the people, and if Springsteen is doing that, too, well, great. If rock & roll took a bigger cue from what he's doing and what I'm doing, I think rock & roll, at least in the arenas, would be better for it.

Yet for years you were crucified by critics as a pale echo of Springsteen, an AOR hack ripping off Bob Seger and Tom Petty as well.

I had never even seen Springsteen perform live until last December in Indianapolis. I remember saying to one magazine, "I can't wait until I meet Bruce Springsteen so I can tell him what a problem he's been for me." So when I met him at that show, I told him. He acted like he was my big brother, which was nice. He said he really liked "Pink Houses." And I said, "Well, I stole it all from you." We laughed and shook hands.

Somebody once said to me, "When Jon Landau said he saw the future of rock & roll in Bruce, he was right." Look at all these guys who do the exact same fucking thing. Me, Petty, Seger, a whole bunch of us who are American singer-songwriters. We're all the same age, we all listened to the same music. What do people expect?

When you were getting off the tour bus the other day, you shouted, "Look out, Binghamton, here we come, the second-best rock band in the world!" How much of that is really self-doubt, not just kidding around?

I know I can do better than I'm doing.

What's missing?

Talent! Some people are born with it. Some people have to work at it. In school, I had to work my ass off just to get C's. I flunked sophomore English in high school three times. I'm not a poet.

Take "Jack and Diane." I was so disgusted with people thinking the line "Hold on to sixteen as long as you can" meant to stay a teenager forever. What I meant was keep doing whatever makes you feel alive. I could have put any number in there: "Hold on to ninety-nine." Then I realized I shouldn't be disgusted with those people because that's the signal I was sending out. That song taught me a lesson, that you can connect with a line—"Life goes on/Long after the thrill of living is gone"—and, in the same song, lose it with "Hold on to sixteen" because I didn't write what I was thinking.

What were you thinking when you wrote "Pink Houses"?

I was just a reporter. A black guy was sitting in front of a pink house, and that's all there was to it. It was at a highway interchange in Indianapolis. We were on an overpass. I looked down and saw this old man, early in the morning, sitting on the porch of his pink shack with a cat in his arms. He waved, and I waved back. That's how the song started.

I wasn't that happy with the ending of "Pink Houses": "And there's winners and there's losers/But they ain't no big deal/Because the simple man, baby, pays for the thrills, the bills, the pills that kill." Kind of negative, isn't it? I could have put more thought into it. But I wrote that song in about as much time as it takes to play it. I sat down with a tape machine, described the black man and never stopped.

Do you write all your songs that quickly?

I used to write a lot of songs like that. We had an exercise in speech class in school, impromptu speaking, that I was always real good at. And I used to sit around with hippies—we were all stoned—and make up funny songs about anybody who might be in the room: "Look at David/He's falling off his chair/He's got slobber in his hair." I'd just go on like Dylan. I used to be good at doing that.

But with *Scarecrow,* I typed out the lyrics. I never used a typewriter before. I used to just write them down on a piece of paper and never change them. I thought, "This is the spirit of the song, that's the way it's going to stay." But with this record, I typed and rewrote, typed and rewrote.

In 1982, you described your own songs as "real insignificant bullshit." Did you honestly believe that?

A few years ago, it was hard for me to accept the responsibility that I had to all these people buying my records. I couldn't believe it when people said, "You've got kids copying you." Now I understand that it's true. When I say kids, I don't mean fourteen-year-olds. I'm talking about nineteen- and twenty-year-old guys who see me as some sort of role model. They know I've come from the dregs of rock & roll to where I am now.

"Jack and Diane" was a significant step. I was arguing until I was blue in the face that I didn't mean anything by that song, that I didn't take my songs seriously, and every night I'd have 10,000 kids tell me the opposite by the looks on their faces and the way they reacted. They were sending the message loud and clear.

On 'Scarecrow' you have made a serious attempt to write about significant issues, like the farm crisis in "Rain on the Scarecrow." Why did you hold back for so long?

I've always been issue oriented. In the Sixties, I wore a black armband in high school, and I was at the Vietnam War moratoriums in Washington, D.C. I was there cheering. But I never wrote songs like that because I felt, until recently, that it was too pretentious. When I think of the Sixties songs that I liked, they were never politically or socially oriented. For a long time I thought, as far as my career goes, it would have been ridiculous for me to make a record and talk about anything other than "Hurts So Good." People just

didn't see me that way. I didn't think anybody would take it seriously.

Now you seem to be sending out mixed signals. Songs like "The Face of the Nation," on 'Scarecrow,' and "Pink Houses" are anti-national anthems describing the erosion of the American Dream. Yet at your show in Binghamton the other night, two girls in the audience unfurled an American flag and waved it back and forth during the "Ain't that America" chorus in "Pink Houses."

I've had people throw American flags onstage. But I don't need that false rah-rah. The reason the audience does it is because they want to relate to me. And they think this is one thing we have in common.

President Reagan also reportedly expressed interest in using "Pink Houses" as a campaign theme.

That got blown out of proportion. One of his aides knew my West Coast attorney. He asked if we would be interested in having Reagan hear "Pink Houses," and we just said no. He asked why, and we said, "None of your business." It was a one-day conversation and a fifteen-minute laugh.

How would you describe your political position?

My politics are pretty much what they taught us in fifth-grade history, the old values, the very nuggets of this society. When a guy comes on my TV and tells me he's going to do something for me if I vote for him, he better fucking do it. Because if he doesn't, he's a liar and a manipulator.

When was the last time you voted?

I've never voted. I've never registered to vote. But I will this time.

Why didn't you vote?

Same thing most Americans say: I don't make a difference. I don't matter. I realize now that I do. Until now, who would I vote for? Mondale or Reagan? But I never thought about this local legislator who's going to make a difference in Bloomington, Indiana.

You were very active in Farm Aid, even though you don't come from a farming family. How did you become so concerned about the farm problem?

My grandfather was a carpenter. His father was a farmer. See, farming is not really in my family, but my younger sister married into a big farming family in Dudleytown. Let's take Mark, her husband. He works eighteen hours a day. Last year, he figured out how much money he made. His wage was $1.15 an hour. And he's got hundreds of hogs. Here's a twenty-eight-year-old kid who has a very heavy debt hanging over his head. I know he's scared to death of that. He doesn't sleep at night, worrying about it. That's my understanding of farming—my friends, the guys I went to high school with. There was one kid whose parents had a huge chicken farm. He works in a grocery store now. He's not the same guy he was after his family went out of business.

That song, "Rain on the Scarecrow," came from months of table talk about the farm problems and seeing it on television. All George Green [Mellencamp's frequent lyricist] and I did was act as reporters on that song. The "ninety-seven crosses" was straight out of the news. Every time a farm foreclosure would take place in a certain state, they planted a cross in the courthouse yard.

What did you say to Willie Nelson when he asked you to help plan and promote the Farm Aid concert?

I talked about no corporate sponsorship. I talked about low ticket prices for the concert. I talked about not making this a concert for the rich. I said, upfront, my education on this is limited. I'll help because I know a lot of people in rock bands. But I didn't want to get into a situation where people would be asking me about what happened to the money for Farm Aid. I told Willie, "I don't want to know about this money. It's not why I'm doing it."

Probably the biggest problem with Farm Aid—besides coming so soon after the spectacular success of Live Aid—was the confusion over exactly what people were being asked for. Was it money? Political action? Or simple understanding?

Live Aid appealed to people's emotions. Farm Aid tried to appeal to logic. What were we going to show? We couldn't show our problem as vividly as Bob Geldof could. He was talking about starving individuals. It was easy to show a baby with flies all over its face. We couldn't appeal to people emotionally. It's such a logical business transaction that's going on with these people. You goddamn near need a legal pad and a computer to figure it out.

There were also right-wing overtones to the presentation of the Farm Aid concert. A familiar refrain during the TV broadcast was "It's time to do something for us," which was a rather jingoistic snub of Live Aid's demonstration of global unity.

I got a little confused, too, when I heard Merle Haggard's "Amber Waves of Grain" song. That's not why I was there. But you can't go shootin' all the dogs 'cause one's got fleas. I know why I was there. And I feel like I know why Willie was there.

During your concerts, you've been asking audiences to write letters to their congressmen asking what they are doing to help the small family farmer. What has been the response?

I don't know. It's too early to tell. Every day after the show, I take out an ad in the local paper and give the senators' names and where to write to them. I don't know if it's going to mean anything at all. I mean, some guy in a rock band isn't going to make a hell of a lot of difference with these guys.

You resisted corporate sponsorship at Farm Aid, and you have continually turned down sponsors for your own tours. Why?

I don't need to make money that way. I didn't write these songs or play these shows so they can offer me money in return for sticking their logo above my name. The beer ones get to me. I don't even drink! Cigarette ones gall me, too, because I hate that I smoke.

My parents can't understand why I don't take these corporate sponsorships. "You're turning down millions of dollars, John," my old man says. "Strike while the poker's hot."

Have you been approached about licensing your songs for commercials?

That's another war. That's one of the reasons my last manager, Billy Gaff, and I parted company. He couldn't understand why I wouldn't let some ketchup company use "Hurts So Good." It was for a hot sauce. I didn't write the song for that reason. However good or bad the song was, it was entertaining. But it wasn't written for ketchup to pour out to.

You dedicated 'Scarecrow' to your grandfather Speck Mellencamp, who died in 1983. How important was he in your life?

He was a much larger inspiration to me than Bob Dylan or Woody Guthrie ever were. He taught me the value of dedication and trying to do the best you can with the tools you've got. He'd say, "It's a poor workman who blames his tools."

He never had more than a seventh-grade education. He chain-smoked Camel cigarettes and hammered nails and planks. But he just loved to live. He was not afraid of anything. You asked me if I voted. My grandfather never voted. This is how proud he was. He went to register to vote, and the woman said, "Name?" "Harry Perry Mellencamp." The woman started laughing. He just walked out. He said, "I'm not going to go in and have people laugh at my name just to get the opportunity to vote." He was real stubborn.

Would you say you picked up your own stubborn nature from him?

Yeah. I always found that I made my biggest mistakes when I compromised myself—the Johnny Cougar name, some of the records I made, the producers I was talked into using. Whenever I compromised, I should have listened to Grandpa. Don't ever compromise yourself, right or wrong. That's something he always told us, to always believe in yourself.

Were you a troublemaker as a kid?

When I was eight years old, I got put in jail for breaking and entering. There was an old barn that this rich woman in Seymour had. She was an artist. A whole bunch of us vandalized her art, took her oil paints and threw them around the pictures, stuff like that. Every kid in the neighborhood was in on it. They took sixteen of us to jail. But we weren't arrested. It was our parents trying to teach us a lesson. So they put us behind bars for three hours.

You were also picked up for narcotics in high school.

Me and another kid were high in school, right? Just amphetamines. We'd been up for like three or four days. A teacher turned us in, and the narcotics agents from Indianapolis came down.

They didn't have anything to arrest us for. We went out to the parking lot where the other kid had a Volkswagen. When I opened the door of this old beat-up Volkswagen, all the pills ran out onto the sidewalk. Which was a blessing in disguise, because they weren't in our possession at that point. They were on the sidewalk. The agents didn't have a search warrant, either.

Of course, I made the mistake of telling my parents. Got my ass beat for it. I should have kept my mouth shut. The school never contacted them.

Were you a heavy drinker then as well?

Oh, man! You think I have a temper now. You should have seen me when I was drunk. When I had a half pint of whiskey in me, I was a wild man. I was so obnoxious I couldn't stand myself. I was always getting beat up when I was drunk. I just had to quit.

I quit drinking in '71 and quit doing drugs in '72. I didn't like the feeling of not being in control. When I was high on pot, it affected me so drastically that when I was in college, there were times when I wouldn't get off the couch. I would lie there, listening to Roxy Music, right next to the record player so I wouldn't have to get up to flip the record over. I'd listen to this record, that record. There would be four or five days like that when I would be completely gone.

You graduated from Vincennes University near Seymour, where you registered as a communications major. Were you trying to get a job in radio?

My problem was I couldn't read on the radio. And the Vietnam War was going on. It'd be time to do the news, and there would be some Vietnamese name, Colonel So-and-so, whose name I couldn't pronounce right. People would call up and laugh at me. Then I'd play *The Crazy World of Arthur Brown,* the entire album. People would call: "Would you get that junk off?"

See, after I got out of high school, I laid out a year because I was already married and had a kid. But I went to college because the job market was real poor. Everybody I knew that didn't go to college was drawing unemployment. Once, when I was married to Priscilla, I landed a job as a carpenter's helper. She was working as a phone operator, and we had a kid, car payments and all that crap. We ended up with eighteen extra dollars one week. I remember walking home from the construction site with the eighteen dollars. I went into a record store and spent every cent of it. I remember I bought a Ten Years After album.

When did you first start playing in bands?

The first band I was ever in was in fifth grade. We played along with records, miming the music. I sang at a student convocation in seventh grade. Me and a guy named Sam Abbott did the song "Abilene." He played guitar, I sang, and this other kid played congas. It was horrible. But the first real band I joined was Crepe Soul. I was in that band for a year and a half. I decided bands don't work, this idea of everybody voting on everything, because nothing ever got done and we never played anyplace. After I quit Crepe Soul, I joined a band called Snakepit Banana Barn and got kicked out because I couldn't sing. Then I bought an acoustic guitar and just started playing songs. I even told my mom and dad I wrote Donovan's "Universal Soldier."

What a bald-faced lie!

Right, it was. Do you know the reason I did it? Because my parents kept saying, "These guys with long hair, they're just ruining American society." I got tired of hearing it. I knew if they would just listen to one of these songs, they'd change their minds. They weren't going to listen to Donovan, but they'd take an interest in their own son, right? So I played "Universal Soldier," and my mom just went nuts. "That is beautiful, John!"

Finally, I had to tell them I didn't write the song. I just wanted to show them it wasn't all nonsense.

The long Sixties set you play at the end of your current stage show runs the gamut from the Miracles' "Mickey's

Monkey" to Creedence Clearwater's "Proud Mary" and the Human Beinz' garage-punk version of "Nobody but Me." Is that medley reflective of your musical roots?

The interesting thing about those songs is that they are all by American artists. I find comfort in heritage. And I feel like I understand the Human Beinz. I understand their energy, what they were doing.

I love the spirit of that music. I would never be as presumptuous as to say I write anything remotely as exciting as that. But that is the spirit of what I do. If you turn on the radio, what I do is so far away from other bands that I see are popular. The only person that is close is Springsteen. And that's because we both have guitars and drums and scream over them.

What current music have you been listening to?

The last record I bought was Joni Mitchell's new one. Also that band from Los Angeles, Cruzados. I hear a couple of new acts every now and then, like Los Lobos. I love that song, "Will the Wolf Survive?" I'll tell you what, though. I just can't get away from those old records.

When Tony DeFries launched his ill-fated Johnny Cougar campaign in 1976, he wasted no time in comparing you to Springsteen, David Bowie, Bob Dylan and Elvis Presley. Then he staged a big Johnny Cougar Day concert and parade in Seymour. How did your friends and neighbors react to the hype?

They couldn't believe it. Some of them thought, "Well, this must be the way it's done. This is the music business." Others thought, "Why are we supposed to be applauding John all of a sudden? Because some English guy wants to throw a bunch of money around?"

I can remember me and Larry [Crane] getting in the limo for Johnny Cougar Day to drive through town and wave at these people. Both of us went, "Wait a minute," then went behind a garage and threw up. I looked at him and thought, "We're not gonna make it—this is too fucking stupid." But we went out and did it.

Did people say "I told you so" when the 'Chestnut Street Incident' album stiffed and you returned to Indiana?

I don't think anybody was overtly catty about it. Most people were pretty respectful. It was like somebody died. They'd send their condolences. "I feel sorry that things didn't work out for you, John." At least that's what they'd say to my face. Nobody ever goaded me.

Why didn't you drop the Cougar name after you split with DeFries?

I should have. If I'd been a little bit secure with myself, I would have. But I would call record people up and say, "This is John Mellencamp. I'd like to speak to . . ." "Sorry, he's not in." I'd call back ten minutes later and say, "Hi, this is John Cougar." "Okay, hold on."

They didn't know the name Mellencamp, so to get my foot in the door, I had to use that horrible thing that happened to me. I had also talked myself into thinking that it wasn't so bad after all. Dylan even said, "My name, it means nothing/My age, it means less." Surely that's right.

Do you think you'll ever drop it?

Why should I? People accept it. Most people know the story of why it's that way. It doesn't mean squat to me anymore. I thought at one point I could run away from it and found out I couldn't do that. So it is what it is, and I imagine it'll remain.

Considering the DeFries disaster, you made a remarkably swift comeback. In 1977, you signed with Rod Stewart's manager at the time, Billy Gaff. Then Pat Benatar's cover of "I Need a Lover" was a hit, and in 1980 you scored with "Ain't Even Done with the Night," from the 'Nothin' Matters and What If It Did' album.

I wasn't even *at* that record. *Nothin' Matters* was my worst attitude phase: "Going to the studio today, John?" "Fuck it. Tell me what happened." I was sick of it. I'd been on the road for three years straight, playing every bar in the world. I couldn't understand why the public kind of liked me and the critics hated me so much. They were going to hold that DeFries mistake against me forever?

I was at my most hateful, rebellious time. There is stuff on that album that is so embarrassing, things I'd do on purpose just to piss people off. I wrote a song called "The Record Company Song" [for the album, appropriately retitled "Cheap Shot"]: "The record company's going out of business/They price the records too damn high." There was a line about ROLLING STONE in it. I took a shot at everybody and everything. I figured, "What do I have to lose? This is it for me." Hence the title—*Nothin' Matters and What If It Did.*

Were you surprised by the multiplatinum success of 'American Fool'?

I was surprised to even be on the radio. When I was making that record, the record company told me, "This is the biggest mistake you're ever going to make. This record sounds like the Clash." I ended up throwing the A&R guy out of the studio in Miami: "Get the fuck out of here. I don't need you coming in here, telling me this shit." They didn't even want to release

255

the record. Billy Gaff went nuts. He told the record company, "Put the record out, or let me out of the contract."

Did you believe songs like "Hurts So Good" and "Jack and Diane" were hit-single material?

Here's how smart I am. I thought "Hurts So Good" was a hit, but "Jack and Diane" wasn't even going to be on the record. If it hadn't been for Mick Ronson, who worked on the record with me, that song wouldn't have ever made it. He kept saying, "It's a great song, you gotta put it on." I thought it was the silliest, dumbest song. It was the only number-one record I've had, and I didn't want to put it out. That's how smart I am.

How did you get the nickname "Little Bastard"?

From the record company. It was during the *American Fool* record. Their suggestion to me was they might be able to save the record if we got the Memphis Horns to play on it. My remark was "Horns belong in marching bands, not on this record."

Did someone from the company actually call you a little bastard?

I heard it. "The guy's an asshole, that little bastard Mellencamp."

Do you know who said it?

Yeah, but I don't want to say. They're funny, record companies. They're always there to say, "Yeah, we were with you in the beginning." I just let them say what they want to. I can still remember all the record companies that turned me down. I remember the guys that did it. And I run into them sometimes. And sometimes I'm not too shy about bringing it up.

Are you taking on more production jobs like Mitch Ryder's 'Never Kick a Sleeping Dog' or the track "Colored Lights" you did for the Blasters' last album?

I don't really want to. I get asked to do a lot of stuff, but I don't really think people want me to do it as much as they think I can get 'em a hit record. The Neville Brothers asked me to do an album for them a couple of years ago. They wanted me to do it because they thought it would be "cool." And, you know, when I worked with Dave and Phil Alvin and the rest of the Blasters, they didn't need me there. They're going to do the same thing I did. They're going to wake up one day and say, "Hey! Let's just do it ourselves." Because nobody's going to come in and be able to arrange the Blasters' house the way they want it.

You were reportedly writing a screenplay a couple of years ago. What happened to it?

I wrote it the summer before last. It's called *Ridin' the Cage*. The story I wrote was about guys our age, trapped—in a light way, but also in a sad way. The story wasn't that great, but the characters were really cool. This guy that I play, Dud, has two kids, he's unemployed, thirty-two years old, hates the fucking world and everybody and everything in it. But his friend, this numskull kind of guy, turns Dud's thinking around.

When I was done with it, I gave it to Warner Bros. They wanted to make the movie with me; they just wanted someone to rewrite it. It turned out that Larry McMurtry [*Terms of Endearment*] knew who I was, so I called him up and asked if he'd be interested in seeing it. He agreed it was a poor story, but he liked the characters. So he rewrote the story, with these same characters but in different situations. And I don't play Dud anymore. He wrote a new character for me.

The movie company was also upset because I don't sing in the movie: "So what the hell's he in it for if he doesn't sing?"

What was the company's final verdict?

It's still being discussed.

Have you been offered other movie roles?

You name it—from the silliest to ones *so* serious. Like, "Hey, John, why don't you come and be a singer in this movie?" You know the cliché. This guy's in a band, and he's a rebel.

What about the serious ones?

Real dark roles. I get knifed in the neck with a fork in one of them.

The reality is I'd probably make a better actor than anything else, because I am so emotional. But right now, I'm a singer. I'm just starting to catch on to doing that.

If you weren't in the music business, what do you think you would be doing now in Indiana?

I'd be a construction worker. Other than this, that's all I know. I also know how to saw wood and nail it together, because Grandpa taught me. He always let me work for him in the summer. He'd pay me ten dollars a day. I did that until damn near when I got married. Even though I was a lazy, lousy worker, he'd still let me work for him.

With all the money you've made in rock & roll, you could live anywhere in the world. Why do you choose to stay in Indiana?

The reality is I'm not interested in any place else. All my friends are there.

What do you do when you're home?

I see a few people that I know, family, friends. I never go out. George Green and I sit in my kitchen, drink tea, smoke cigarettes and talk about the world.

Whenever I go to another city, I'm there to work. I'm not there to shop or see the sights or go to bars. I'm there to play a concert. My world is in Indiana and this, here, is what I do for a living. I wish I could do it better sometimes than I do. That's the same as anybody that cares about their job. Imagine if all of a sudden I said, "Thank you very much. 'Pink Houses' is the best song I can write. I'm just gonna write a whole bunch of songs like 'Pink Houses.'" What if I said that about "Hurts So Good"? You writers would have lost your minds reviewing those songs. You would have run out of shit to say about me.

Even people that don't like me realize that I could be safe. I could do just what I know how to do and rake in the money. They have to say, "God, he did it without us, he did it without record-company support, and he did it on a minimum amount of talent. You gotta hand it to the guy."

26
Tip O'Neill

INTERVIEWED BY
WILLIAM GREIDER (1986)

When we listen to Tip O'Neill, we hear the America of Franklin Roosevelt and John Kennedy speaking. First as a legislator in Massachusetts, later as a congressman and finally as the Speaker of the House, Tip O'Neill shared the New Deal vision of FDR and the Camelot optimism of JFK: an America where no one went unfed, unclothed, unhoused.

These ideals seem strangely old-fashioned in the late Eighties, a time when prosperity for the lucky has been achieved at the cost of misery on back roads and in city streets. In a decade that has seen the spiritual descendants of the nineteenth-century robber barons—Boesky and Trump—celebrated, and rewarded, as pop heroes, O'Neill's remembrance of a time when government promised to work for all the people seems at best grandfatherly, at worst a sign of encroaching senility.

For many readers of ROLLING STONE, *however, the goals, if not the methods, of the New Deal and LBJ's Great Society have yet to be tossed aside with the bell-bottoms and the tie-dye of the Sixties. Nor are these readers a minority of Americans. After all, despite the personal popularity of Ronald Reagan, his message has largely gone unheeded at the polls, if one is to judge by the results of the congressional races in 1986, when the Democrats regained control of the Senate, and 1988, when they increased their majorities in both houses. If, as O'Neill says, "All politics is local," then the president who may well be remembered chiefly for tripling the federal deficit has been no more successful at capturing the electorate for the forces of reaction than he was at sustaining his career as the Errol Flynn of B movies.*

Nonetheless, when this interview appeared in the fall of 1986, Tip O'Neill still seemed, at least to some, out of place in the pages of ROLLING STONE. *One imagined him listening, if he listened at all, to Count Basie, not the King (much less Prince). But William Greider, the national editor of the magazine, recognized that as O'Neill's retirement from the House neared, the Speaker might have something of importance to say to a generation of Americans that had benefited from the liberal legacy and was then suffering from Ronald Reagan's attempt to despoil its birthright—a free, generous and open society. The resulting interview was sometimes moving and always amusing.*

—S. H.

TIP O'NEILL could not have planned a more graceful exit. The November 1986 elections gave his beloved Democratic party a majority in both houses of the Congress. His own seat in the House of Representatives, which he is relinquishing after thirty-four years, passed with his blessing to Joseph P. Kennedy II—the nephew of John F. Kennedy, whom O'Neill succeeded in the seat in 1953. Only five years after the lowest point of his career—when he was openly ridiculed by the Republicans, the press and some members of his own party—the Speaker of the House came down from the Hill to tell the American people, "The Reagan revolution is over."

The rise of Thomas P. O'Neill is a story of the old politics. His grandfather came from County Cork, Ireland, to settle in North Cambridge, Massachusetts, where he found work as a bricklayer. His father started a small contracting business there and was elected to the city council. O'Neill entered the Massachusetts state legislature at the age of twenty-four.

In 1952, JFK ran for the U.S. Senate; a year earlier he had privately informed O'Neill of his plans, giving O'Neill enough time to expand his political base, then win a narrow victory in the contest to replace Kennedy in the House. O'Neill served his first nineteen years in the House as a loyal soldier of the party—except for publicly breaking with LBJ over the Vietnam War. He became the majority leader in 1972. The next step was Speaker of the House, four years later.

O'Neill's political philosophy, forged during the Depression and the New Deal, has remained constant throughout his public life. It is a vision of the nation as a neighborhood, of the innate decency of men and women, of the duty of a prosperous country to help its have-nots. Since O'Neill was first elected to the state legislature, in 1936, several generations of government programs—from social security to the GI Bill to Medicare—have brought that vision closer to reality.

For O'Neill, politics wasn't about macroeconomics, demographics or academic theories about the electorate. Politics meant taking care of people, especially your own. It meant doing favors and asking for votes. He joyfully stumped the ethnic neighborhoods in his district and remembered every name. Though never a gifted speaker, he contributed his own homely maxim to Washington lore: "All politics is local."

O'Neill was forty years old when he came to Congress in 1952, a cigar-smoking Red Sox fan with a thick Boston brogue and a generous physique. His district encompassed Harvard, MIT and O'Neill's alma mater, Boston College, but the heart of his constituency was always the working-class Irish and Italian neighborhoods of North Cambridge and Charlestown. He knew what the people in every precinct needed, and he got it for them.

In Congress, O'Neill was never occupied by crusades. Instead, he served on the Rules Committee, the traffic cop that controls the action on the House floor. From this position, a shrewd operator can learn to track every issue, rewarding friends and punishing enemies. O'Neill learned. He also played a lot of cards—thousands of poker games over the years with other pols around town—where his natural Irish warmth brought him lasting friends while his politician's eye took their measure.

Then came the Reagan revolution of 1980. The Republicans mocked O'Neill viciously during the election campaign: One TV ad featured a slovenly look-alike who recklessly drives a car until it runs out of gas. A freshman GOP congressman named John LeBoutillier sneered, "He's just like the federal budget—fat, bloated and out of control." To the Speaker's dismay, some of the younger Democrats agitated for his early retirement. But when the dust settled after the Republicans' victory, Tip O'Neill was the only major Democrat left to articulate his party's opposition to Reagan's agenda.

"I had a hard time of it," O'Neill admits now, "but I had the advantage of forty years in public life and knowing what my party had done, and I didn't think we should ever leave the basics."

Today, Tip O'Neill ranks nearly as high as the president in the public-opinion polls, but the Speaker knows his day is passing. The old politics of the city neighborhoods and the New Deal liberalism that once united the Democratic majority are history. But O'Neill, partisan to the end, believes that the conservative movement has peaked and the pendulum is now swinging back to the Democrats. If the 1986 elections are any indication, the Speaker will have the last word.

You've said that there won't be flaming liberals like Tip O'Neill anymore, that those days are over. You don't really believe that, do you?

Those days have gone. I'm the old type of liberal. I was a working-wages man, a belly liberal. My philosophy was based around the home and the family—keeping it together—because when I was a kid, things weren't like that. Your father probably worked six days a week. A fireman worked 108 hours a week; a police officer, 84 hours a week. My father was a bricklayer. He worked six days a week, and my mother died when I was nine months old. You never got to see your dad. And that wasn't what life was all about. So we—from the state to the national levels of government—changed the life of America in response to the will of the people.

Now there are liberals more concerned with the environment, with clean air, clean water—and we always have to have people watching those things. I'm

all for Save the Whales, and I'm for the snail darter, but not at the expense of the American family. I was a Roosevelt liberal, a people's liberal—keep the family together, help the American people get a better home, a better education.

Do you think that America doesn't need that kind of politician anymore?

Sure, we need them, but right now we're going through a conservative trend. It started with Goldwater in 1964—when twenty percent of America was living in poverty—and it went all the way through to '80, when Reagan was elected, and '84, when he had his sweep. It's continued through part of '85, but the pendulum is swinging the other way. By the time '88 comes around, the conservatives will be dead. The country will either be moderate or progressive. But it will be a long way from liberal, too.

What do you think will turn the tide against the conservatives and their values?

Eighty percent of America, the new leaders of America, were educated in community colleges, state universities on the GI Bill of Rights, Eisenhower grants, Pell grants. Now that they're the leaders, why should they pull the ladder up from the poor guys who are coming along? It's basically wrong, and they're going to change their policy when they see that. [Because of Reagan's budget cuts] a million students or better in the last couple of years haven't been able to go to college. That's wrong, and it's wrong when you shut the door on a poor kid whose most nutritious meal of the day is the free breakfast that he gets at school.

While the conservatives were gaining power, the Democratic party was going through fundamental changes. Did that begin in 1974, with the first post-Watergate election, with seventy new congressmen and senators joining the party?

There's no question about it. The leadership wasn't as powerful as it had been in the past, and at the time the [political] organizations were almost over the hill, except for Chicago. If the Democrats had truly believed that they could win those seats any other way, the young Watergate candidates never would have been the nominees. In their place, there would have been people who were active in politics, who had been in the state legislature, in county office, been the town mayor.

That was the first group, since the founding fathers, in which better than sixty percent had never served in public office. They never came through the party system, and they knew no discipline. And when they arrived, they said, "Hey, all I have is the label of Democrat. I financed my own campaign. The party didn't do anything for me." There were almost fifty that had won Republican seats that year, and I think there were seventy-odd new Democrats in all, and they came here with great independence.

They were the most highly educated group that we'd ever had in the history of the Congress—Sorbonne graduates, Oxford people, junior executives, young lawyers. Tremendous talent, and tremendous independence. We had a hard time with them. They immediately formed the freshman caucus, as they called it, and you know, that particular year, we had just changed the law of the [Democratic] caucus that elected committee chairmen. They knocked three of them right out of the box. I was majority leader at the time. I used to have to meet with them every week—had to keep an eye on them and listen to their gripes and their griefs and listen to their ideas.

Did they treat you like you were another old party hack?

No, I got along with them very well, to be perfectly truthful. I have a pretty good ability to judge men, and I could see who were the born leaders—like Paul Tsongas, who was in that group—who were babbling at the mouth and who had substance. So when I came along two years later as Speaker, I had no problems. Nobody opposed me.

You wound up as the Speaker of the House in the age of televised government. For better or worse, you've become something of a celebrity and a symbol.

Well, that's true. I'm probably better known nationally than any of the other Speakers. The Republicans thought I was a pretty good target—you know, I'm easy for a cartoon. The *Times* had a cartoon the other day, about all these people weeping about my retirement. Who are they? The cartoonists of America. Well, the job they've done of me. Six-foot-two, 265 pounds, big nose, cabbage ears, white hair—what the hell, I'm easy to portray. They made me the symbol for the party—the target—and the president stayed with it.

Did that hurt, when the Republicans and the press were sticking it to you?

I would have to say the saddest days in my life were in 1981. Along with all the caricatures, you had people in your own party who were kind of revolting. I took the abuse, and I gambled that I was going to be vindicated in the '82 election. My wife used to say, "Put on a good tie, and put your best foot forward. Have a smile on your face. You believe in your heart, and you're right, and you're going to win in the end."

How much damage did Reagan actually do to the Dem-

ocrats' social programs with the 1981 budget cuts? You have said yourself that some of these programs would have been cut by your own party anyway.

Well, there's no question about that. You have to take into consideration that when I went into public life, fifty percent of the country was living in poverty. By the time Reagan became president, the poverty rate was eleven and a half percent. We had changed America. And if Carter had been reelected, we would have had a tax reduction. Not the unfair tax reduction that gave more to the wealthy in America and the loopholes in the '81 tax bill. We would have had an increase in the military budget, but nothing of the scale that we have. There was never any window of vulnerability. We would have increased military spending, and we would have cut back on the programs, because many of those programs were obsolete. But we wouldn't have meat-axed the programs in the manner in which we did.

Where is the country headed? Things are going pretty well for most people these days. And when that's the case, who needs Democrats?

When people start to think we've been going down the wrong road for the last eight years, that we've hurt too many people, they'll say, "I didn't mean that those things should be cut." Americans are basically a family people. They love their neighbor. They want their neighbor to be successful. If they live on one side of the town, they go through the old neighborhood and they remember. And if it's still the same people there, they want them to have success, too.

In 1932, under Roosevelt, the original philosophy of the Democratic party brought together all types of Democrats—liberals, progressives, moderates, conservatives and ultraconservatives. For one reason: to save the family unit. We had to work together, no matter what your philosophy was, to get food on the table, to save the farmer, to save the manufacturer, to pull ourselves out of the doldrums we were in. In any other country in the world, we'd be five splinter parties.

How do you see the future for the party?

Now, I see nothing but great victories for the Democratic party. After January 1981, they were saying, "There's a realignment in America—first time in fifty years. There are going to be fewer Democrats in America than Republicans." Well, we were expecting a tremendous offensive by the president. There was no offensive. What does he come out for? He comes out for nothing. He picks the tax reform of [Richard] Gephardt and [Bill] Bradley—and they're Democrats. And he launches into it. Now, that's going to be the spearhead of his whole eight years as president. He picks up the *contras*—$100 million for the *contras*—that's the big issue that he wants. I don't think that's a policy that America should be following. And a majority of Americans feel the same way. He's with the SDI, Strategic Defense, the Star Wars. Sixty percent of the scientists of America say it will never work. So the great offensive never happened. These are the three things that he came forward with. Everywhere you go everybody tells you how much they love the president, but they don't love what he stands for—on South Africa, on Central America. They think there's tremendous waste and fraud and abuse in the Pentagon. Go down the line, they don't like his attitude.

What do you tell young people who might be thinking about going into politics?

You've got to have a feeling for politics. Just because you think you're going to change the world doesn't mean you're going to like it. It's like going in the military or the clergy. You've got to be thick-skinned, and you've got to have a set of principles which you believe in—and that you can save the nation by being there.

I always say, "People like to be asked, and people like to be thanked." Once you make your decision, go out all the way. And ask people. There are four elements in every campaign—the candidate, the issue, the organization and money. If you can't finance a campaign, don't get into the fight. Regrettably. But those are the elements that you've got to face.

And if you're a politician, don't go to sporting events and let yourself be introduced. Don't give them a target. No matter where you go, people love to boo politicians. It's an American trait, and they enjoy it. The Red Sox called me the first of the year, and they said, "You coming to the opener?" My wife, Millie, and I haven't missed an opener in years, and all my life I wanted to throw out the first ball, but I didn't because I know what's going to happen. So Millie threw out the first ball. She got a hell of a hand.

But I threw out the first ball at the World Series. And the reception was very good. Made a good pitch, too. So I felt good about it.

You were one of the first major Democrats to come out against Lyndon Johnson and the war in Vietnam, in 1967. What made you change your mind?

At that time, the president could do no wrong as far as foreign policy was concerned. It was a bipartisan policy, the realm of the White House, and you just followed along. I used to go out to all of the colleges in my district—there's twenty-one of them—and speak,

advocating the foreign policy of Johnson and the American government.

On a Wednesday, the Defense Department comes over and gives me a briefing. Thursday morning the White House gives me a briefing. Thursday afternoon the State Department. They'd tell me all the questions they were asked at the University of North Carolina, University of Wisconsin, Berkeley—wherever the hell it was—"and here's the answers." I went over to Boston College. Remember, I've been briefed by [General William] Westmoreland, I've been briefed by Johnson, I've been briefed by [Ambassador Ellsworth] Bunker, and they have credibility in my eyes. One of the students gets up and asks me if I've ever been briefed by the other side. That night I'm thinking, and I said, "You know, I never looked at it that way."

So I started out with State Department people. And I started to ask assistant secretaries of state, people like that, and our ambassadors. Well, I get to talking with the admiral of the Mediterranean fleet. He kicked the living bejesus out of our policy. He's head of the American fleet! Now I started asking Army generals. I'm asking everybody along the line, and I can't find *anybody* who agrees with our policy, even though they advocate it publicly. You know, "Don't quote me on this, but our policy is awful."

I had a telephone call from a fella at the CIA. I met a few of them, and we had supper, and they said, "You know, we advocate the policy of the president all around the world. Everywhere we go the people say that we're wrong. We make our reports of what they say in every different nation in the world, we put them on the president's desk, and the president never sees them." "What are you telling me for?" I ask. "Well, we heard that you were making a study on the war and that you were going to come out against it." I said, "Yeah, that's right, I am." "We'd like you to tell [Speaker of the House John] McCormack that the president doesn't get the CIA reports."

So I came out against the war. About three months later, *The Washington Star* writes, "First of Established Democrats Leaves President, McCormack's Personal Friend Opposes the War." Actually, I'd done it six weeks earlier in a newsletter to my district.

How did Johnson react when he found out?

He went through the roof, they tell me. I got in that night about 1:30, and I get a call from a guy I used to live with. And he said, "Where in the hell were you? The president has been looking all over town for you. How the hell did you get by those Secret Service guys? They've been waiting outside." I said, "What

Secret Service? I put the car in the garage at the back and came up the back elevator." So I called the White House. It's now half past one, quarter to two. "The president wants to see you at nine o'clock," I'm told.

Well, when I went in and I saw the president, he says, "You! You, Tip O'Neill! Jesus, I cannot believe this. I've known you since the day you arrived. To think that you'd do this to me. I wouldn't care," he says, "about burying the rest of those assholes, but you're part of my own crowd. To think you'd do this to me." And I said, "Well, Mr. President, I tell you, I've made a study on it, and you're absolutely wrong. How the hell can we run a war when you can't walk north of the line, and you can't shoot when you're shot at, and you don't mine the harbors, and you don't knock out the bridge coming in from China and the power plant. What the hell kind of a war are we in? I've talked to your generals, I've talked to your admirals, I've talked to your State Department people." And I said, "Furthermore, I've talked to the CIA, and you don't even see the CIA's messages. They don't even get through to you." He says, "You think I'm wrong? You think you know more about this war than I do?" Then he brings me into a room. And, Jesus, there's a whole board with lights all over the place telling where everybody is. I said, "I'm sorry, Mr. President, but that's my feeling. It's a wrong war, and we shouldn't be there."

After a while, he said, "You know, I gotta tell you something, Tip. I thought you'd changed your mind because of the students at Harvard Square. I thought that they'd got to you." I said, "Eighty-five percent of my district believes in your policy. When I walk down the street, the Irish, French-Canadians, Italians, cross the street when they see me coming. You don't know what I'm going through. They look at me, and they say, 'He's joined those guys in Harvard Square.' I don't get elected by students—I get elected by the guy on the back street, and he's mad at me at the present time."

The president put his arm around me. "Tip," he says, "I thought you did it for political reasons, to satisfy that *cult* in Harvard Square. If you did it within your heart, and you think within your mind that it's the right thing to do," he says, "well, I'm opposed to you, and I think you're wrong. But always we will be friends." Put his arms around me. That was the conversation.

Have you got that in your mind when you look at the situation in Central America?

I've talked to every leader in Central America and every leader in South America—twenty or thirty oth-

ers around the world—and I haven't met anybody who thinks our policy is right. They all say we ought to go the Contadora route. After all, they're the same heritage, the same background, the same culture, the same language. What the hell are *we* doing down there? I've talked to people who say Ortega—I haven't met Ortega—but they say there's only one man in the world dumber than Ortega, and that's Ortega's brother. And their government is going to fall of itself because the economy is so bad down there.

When you follow that issue through the last five years in Congress, there're about twenty or thirty swing votes that are with you one time and against you the next. What is it that pulls those votes back and forth?

People back home. You know, they're unbelievable. In many areas where you still have the VFW and the DAR and the American Legion as the social blood of a town, a congressman comes in who hasn't voted properly, you know, and they'll meet him wearing the old American Legion hat, *and they got it tilted*. They're with Uncle Sam all the way, and the president can do no wrong.

It's home pressure that makes them change. Plus the fact that it's pretty hard to turn this guy Reagan down. He knows the avenue—where the block of votes is that you have to work on. So you're getting worked on from home, and you're getting worked on from the White House. And it's been tough. [Alexander] Haig hadn't been secretary of state three weeks when he said to me, "We ought to be in Nicaragua cleaning it out." And I can say, "Hey, six years later we're not in Nicaragua. I played a part in that, and I feel pretty good about it."

You got burned on that same question—the question of sending in U.S. soldiers—with Lebanon, though.

They only told me sixty percent or seventy percent of the story. I got a telephone call about half past six, seven o'clock—[George] Shultz on the telephone. I'm down at Cape Cod. Sunday morning, I believe—[KAL flight] 007 was knocked out of the sky. He says the Army plane'll be down in an hour. We're going to have a meeting, I think, at ten o'clock, something like that, in the White House. So I get down there, and we talked about 007. And after 007, Robert McFarlane gave a review of what was happening in Beirut. He had just come back. All parts of the puzzle were put together. He said, "Everything is going to fall together beautifully. Gemayel is going to form a new cabinet; and all sects and creeds and ethnic types are going to be represented." Israel was going to pull its troops, and Syria was going to pull its troops out. And now they wanted us over there. The French and the Italians and, just as a symbol, a contingent of Americans. We were only going to be there for assembly purpose. Well, the Syrians didn't pull out, so the Israelis weren't going to pull out. And we were never informed that we were to be the guardians of the airport. Nobody told us at that point. You know, when I acquiesced, everything was looking fine. But later they said, "Well, you know, they're defending the airport. That's why we've got them there." But they never told us that the morning Jim Wright and I were there.

Do you wish that you could undo that decision to let the Marines go into Beirut?

After the Marines got killed, you know, we were all wanting the boys back, wanting the boys back. And the walls have ears in Washington. There isn't much that I don't know about that's going on. I may go to the University Club, or I may go and play a little gin. I may go to some other place and have a drink, and I may go to some kind of social event. People like to come up and tell you how much they know. They assume that you know this, and they want to let you know that they know it, too. I remember a fellow from the White House comes up and said that the decision was made the night before that the president was going to bring the Marines home—one-third, one-third and one-third—for the next three months. He assumes that I know that. He doesn't know he's leaking. I didn't know it, and I'm furious. I've been screeching for the boys to come home anyway. When the chips were down, I put myself and my party on the line by saying, "Sure, we're going to be the American symbol. Sure, we want to help bring peace over there." And so I came up about two days later, and I kicked the hell out of the administration to get the boys home. Reagan's accusing me of cutting and running. And I already had information that we're going to go out one-third, one-third, one-third. So I didn't tell that to anybody, I hit the press with it. Right after he's accused me of cutting and running, I called the White House, said, "I know what your plans are. That's hitting below the belt, and it's lousy." I said it to McFarlane or Mike Deaver or somebody like that. Yeah, they treated me a little bit shabby there.

But isn't that just good old hardball politics? Reagan's done that to you on the arms-control question. He does it on taxes all the time.

Listen, America loves this man. If the Democrats were to do the things that he did, they would be lynched. Three days after Beirut, what did he do? He turns the ship around and goes into Grenada. What's the object of going into Grenada? History is going to show that we didn't have to go into Grenada to straighten that thing out. It was to get Beirut off the front page. They were supposed to go in there thirty-six, forty-eight hours, clean up. We send 6,000 soldiers, Marines and sailors. It ends up we lose 19 lives. Three years later—we still have something like 500 people there. And it's cost us hundreds of millions of dollars. So America waved the flag, and the president waved the flag, and the students get off the plane and kiss the ground. They get down there, what do they have? Forty-three Cubans. Pretty plain, huh? And it still plays.

You can't tell the American Legion that, you know?
What do you think about what happened in Iceland?

He was a *bust* up in Iceland. A bust! Before he went to Iceland, everybody, the State Department people, workers at Geneva, thought that the intermediate missiles were going to be cut back. That's agreed to. Gorbachev makes a second issue offer. He makes a third offer. He should have said, "Hey, wait a minute. We're only going to be up here for a day and a half. Let's put this together, and anything else we put on the agenda for the next meeting." But then he comes back with all this nonsense about SDI—you know, it fell apart over SDI. Why does he come back and make that an issue? Because of the plight of the farmer, the plight of the textile worker, the plight of the manufacturer—the fact that there are, at the present time, fourteen states with unemployment rates over eight percent.

You've been across the table from Ronald Reagan, negotiating budgets and so forth. What is he like to deal with up close?

Well, he comes in with his three-by-five cards. He reads his little piece on the three-by-five. Then, if it's defense, he turns it over to the secretary of defense. If it's something about policy in Central America, China, he turns it over to Shultz. If it's something about the environment or something like that, he turns it over to the secretary of the interior. He always makes a three-minute opening statement and never participates from then on. But you've got to take into consideration that when I'm sitting across the table from him, I'm not negotiating. I'm there because we happen to control the House. I'm not there as an adviser to the president of the United States.

Often he will gas off about, you know, workmen's compensation. You know—"These fellows are earning more than they did on the job, and they ought to be paying taxes on it." Or unemployment—"As soon as they find employment for this one fellow, they couldn't find him to give him the job. You know how many of those people are out there?" I said, "Look, I'm sick and tired of this, Mr. President. Have you grown in the period of five years?" Now I don't intend to argue with the president, but when he makes statements like that, I'm not down there as an adviser to him. I'm down there because I'm the leader in one branch of government, in which they have to get legislation, and they're informing me what their program is going to be. So I don't want to have a confrontation with him. But if I were to sit there and say nothing, they'd say, "Well, the president said this, and the president said that, and Tip O'Neill didn't say anything. So he acquiesced."

Is Reagan dumb?

Oh, I'm not going to make a statement like that, but I've been with eight presidents, and he has less talent and less ability and less knowledge about the Congress and about the laws of this land than anybody else. But I'll say this about him: He's got charisma, and he's got leadership. He's hardheaded.

Is he a nice person up close?

Oh, yeah.

You said once he's got ice water for blood.

When he was talking about cutting the social programs. And the reason I said that is because he's more influenced and more interested in the greedy people of America than he is in those who are trying to work themselves up from menial jobs and get an education and help the rest of their family.

So why does the country love this guy?

I can't understand it. A fella came into my office in a wheelchair. He was from North Cambridge, a roofer. He said, "I've voted for you all my life." "I'm very, very grateful," I said. "What can I do for you?" He said, "I'm on unemployment compensation, I'm on workmen's compensation. I'm going to be in this wheelchair the rest of my life. They want to tax us in a new bill down in Washington, and I hoped that you would be opposed to that." I said, "Let me tell you something. That's Reagan that wants to do that." He said "Oh, no, Tip, not Ronald Reagan. He may have some mean bastards around him, but he doesn't know about it, because he would never be for that."

I was going through a sausage factory. Little old lady stuffing sausages says, "Mr. Tip," she says, "I love ya! Fifty years I vote for you, we all vote for you. But you're mean to Mr. President. I love him," she says. "Don't be mean to the president." Here she is getting minimum wage. I can't explain it.

How much has the press got to do with it?

The press has got everything to do with it. Jimmy Carter was defeated for president for only one reason—he was unpopular. Everything went wrong. Iran went wrong. The saving of hostages went wrong. The hostages being there. Oil went from thirteen dollars a barrel to forty dollars a barrel—that caused inflation, that caused a rise of interest rates. He couldn't articulate on television. And, Jesus, till the night of the debate he was even in the polls with Reagan. America wanted to know whether this guy who believed in a voluntary-social-security system was for real. This guy who'd keep telling stories about a woman from Chicago having 108 welfare checks, this guy who said that the rich were being taxed too much. He got on television, and he looked like a sensible American. He was well groomed, and he handled himself pretty well. Within forty-eight hours, Jimmy Carter's down twenty points. The election is over. Reagan got elected not because of any change in fiscal policy.

The press loved Jack Kennedy, but they were mean to Johnson. They were mean to Nixon, to Ford. That's the type of style America likes, you know? Everybody is a Sam Donaldson out there. Squeeze the nuts off them and all that. Anyway, the press said, "Well, we've got to give the guy a honeymoon. He was elected because we want a change in the fiscal policy of America." That wasn't what the election was all about, but the press said that's how he won.

Is Jimmy Carter ever going to get over his reputation as the Democratic Herbert Hoover?

History is going to show Jimmy as a much better president than he was. After Truman, Carter was the only one who really spoke up to the Russians. He did the right thing after they went into Afghanistan, pulling our Olympic teams out, stopping shipments of soybeans and wheat and grain, stopping their airplanes from landing here.

It cost him, too, didn't it?

It cost him, but I think he sent them a pretty good message. At Camp David he did a good job. He was right about the humanitarian issues. I think he's going to be treated better than he's being treated right now. His biggest problem was that he couldn't communicate with the American people. You know, that famous statement, the "malaise" thing. He probably was telling the truth, but the people don't like to hear the truth.

Did you have trouble talking to him?

I love Jimmy Carter. He's the most able and talented man I ever met. But he did a lot of things wrong. His staff was terrible, parochial. Carter was so able, whether it was on human affairs, foreign affairs, domestic issues, on the problems of farmers. On missiles, he was absolutely brilliant. He had a bad staff around him. They came into town with a chip on their shoulder. He had a tough press out there, and everything that could go wrong went wrong. But he was a beautiful person.

During Watergate, did Richard Nixon ever try to come at you personally?

Never did. I played poker with Nixon, and he was a very gregarious individual in that kind of company. When he got to the White House, he was solemn. He had no trust and faith, and he had a bad group around him.

Who's the best politician you've served with in Washington?

I think probably Jack Kennedy. Jack Kennedy was an amazing guy. He had a tremendous amount of talent and knowledge and know-how. One day after the 1958 election, he came into my office, wanting to know how he did in my district—precinct by precinct. "How'd I do with the French-Canadians, with the Irish, with the blacks, the Italians? How did every religious group vote?" He was always asking questions. "How do we register blacks? How do we handle city buses? How do we go and set up parades?"

You know, I remember when he first got elected to Congress. I opposed him. I was with Mike Neville. Kennedy was the most bashful kid that I ever saw. I never saw anybody grow the way that guy grew. People don't classify Kennedy in the realm of politician, but he was a master pol.

I would have thought you'd say Lyndon Johnson.

That's a different story. Lyndon was one hell of a majority leader. But where Kennedy looked with absolute distrust on West Point, the Navy, Air Force, Johnson was absolutely thrilled and taken in by them completely. As far as operating in the Congress, though, he was the best, no question about that.

In ten years as Speaker of the House, you presided over many reforms. You were instrumental in abolishing secret voting in the House and passing an ethics code. You made committee and subcommittee chairmen truly elective and therefore accountable. Did you see yourself as a reformer?

I always believed that people were entitled to a report on their congressmen. I never hid a vote in my life. If they didn't agree with me, I went home to my people and explained why I voted the way I did. I had a very early experience my first year in the state legislature of 1937. I voted against the Teacher's Oath,

because I thought it was morally wrong. Well, Jesus, after I didn't vote for it, you couldn't believe it. At the election polls, the American Legion stood up there with their uniforms on opposing me. And I'm running for reelection, and I won. I won big. And I said to myself, "You know, if you've got the guts to vote the way you think, and you go home, and you explain to your people why you voted, they'll believe you and trust you." And, Jesus, I've had a career of trust. I never hid from a goddamn vote. I never walked out on a vote in my life. The tougher the vote—doesn't bother me.

How does the House work? The public's perception is that Congress can't get its act together on budgets and everything else.

Pretty hard to get its act together on budgets, especially in the last half a dozen years. You've got to take into consideration when you talk about Congress, you always refer to the Democrats. That's what the average mind of America thinks. I think we passed all the appropriations this year, sent them to the [Republican-controlled] Senate. I don't think the Senate passed four of them. But nobody says the Senate passed the bill. They think of Democrats. And we don't run this government.

Why did you decide to retire?

I was talking about it with my wife, Millie, and she said, "You make your own decision. Don't quit because of me, and don't ever say that I asked you to quit." And I sat there and I thought, "McCormack was around too long, Reagan's around too long." I've been here eight years. Jim Wright is a great guy, a loyal soldier and a strong right arm. The truth of the matter is that I didn't want to stay around too long. I've got ambitions. I'd like to be ambassador to Ireland, go back to my roots. I've got relatives over there.

I always knew my abilities as far as politics was concerned were organizational, likability, great instincts. I was unbeatable. A lot of people have said, "Tip O'Neill's never been a legislator." But I was on the Rules Committee. I knew enough about the broad language of every piece of legislation that's ever been here. Everything comes through there. So I have an overall knowledge. And I always figured someday I was going to be Speaker of the House.

Twenty years from now, what do you think history will say about Tip O'Neill?

I don't know about history. All I can say is, I've never forgotten from where I came. And I've seen a changing of America that's been absolutely beautiful. And I played a part.

27

David Bowie

INTERVIEWED BY KURT LODER (1987)

Like most long-running stars, David Bowie has become a master at manipulating the media (in showbiz, it's a matter of survival). That he is able to do so with such flair and general likability is a tribute to what I think is his essentially amiable nature. Bowie lives the luminary lifestyle to the max: sleek limos and ladies and ultra-luxe suites; a château remote from the madding tax bite. Yet he also appreciates the irony of a man in his forties setting forth every few years to disport himself as a rock star and, in fact, will be happy to join you in having a laugh about it. This, believe me, is refreshing behavior.

The occasion of the interview that follows was a cover for a special issue on "rock style," which should serve to explain all the fashion blather leading up to the actual Q&A. Fortunately, style is an issue of some substance in Bowie's case—and, what the hey, he had an album to flog.

Bowie had been passing his nights in Los Angeles pursuing a new-found interest in billiards with his old pal Iggy Pop. In the mornings, he went roller-skating. We met around noon and sipped cranberry juice while listening to vintage R&B records by Irma Thomas and Benny Spellman. The ensuing conversation took a chronological trajectory and flowed pretty much as follows.

—K. L.

F OR FIFTEEN years, David Bowie has been the ringmaster of rock style, whipping up new fashions and attitudes with every flick of his public image. A prodigy of self-invention, he has been at various intervals Art Man, Dance Man and Pioneer Androgyne. Today he's just plain David, but the contemporary urban clubscape is still littered with Bowie replicants bearing painted witness to the lingering influence of his past personas: whole tribes of bleached and preening Ziggys, plucked and pallid Aladdins, sleek, cadaverous Euro-lizards. But the man behind those masks has long since moved on.

As he sat down for an interview in a suite at a Westwood hotel one recent afternoon, Bowie was wearing simple black jeans, a snug tank-top T-shirt and steel-toed Gaultier brogues. It was February, one month after his fortieth birthday, and Bowie was in Los Angeles to shoot videos for his seventeenth studio album, *Never Let Me Down*. Clear-eyed and lightly tanned beneath a generous thatch of blond-plus hair, he looked astonishingly fit and professed his eagerness to wade back into the rock-biz fray. He'll kick off a world tour in June, performing songs drawn from the breadth of his twenty-year recording career, backed by a band featuring his old pal Peter Frampton—the son of Bowie's high-school art teacher—on lead guitar. It will, he said, be something special.

The subject was rock style, of which Bowie is pretty much the reigning embodiment. Born on January 8, 1947, and raised in the London districts of Brixton and Bromley, he is old enough to have witnessed firsthand the arrival of rock & roll. As a kid, he marveled at the brawling, zoot-suited antics of the Teddy boys, England's first rock-oriented youth cult. In the Sixties, he took up the saxophone, joined a school band (the Kon-rads) and felt himself drawn toward the clothes-obsessed mods, who shared his musical taste for American R&B. He idolized such British beat legends as the early Who and the Yardbirds (whose lead singer, Keith Relf, inspired him to grow his hair down to his shoulders). As Davy Jones, he hacked around with a succession of groups—the King Bees, the Manish Boys, the Lower Third—to little avail. Advised in 1966 that another Davy Jones had hit it big as a member of the Monkees, he adopted the stage name Bowie and went solo. He recorded his first album in 1967 and scored his first hit single—the trippy "Space Oddity"—two years later.

Bowie's breakthrough came in 1972, with the release of *The Rise and Fall of Ziggy Stardust and the Spiders from Mars*, an album of hard, snarling guitar rock pumped out by what may have been the best band he has ever had (Mick Ronson on lead guitar, Trevor Bolder on bass and Woody Woodmansey on drums, three musicians from the north of England, with American keyboardist Mike Garson added to the lineup a bit later). The main attraction, though, was Bowie's pancaked, mock-mincing Ziggy persona—a character that came to define the glitter-rock era of the early Seventies. (Bowie occasionally appeared in public wearing dresses and at one point even told a reporter that he was gay—a statement he disavowed in a 1983 interview with ROLLING STONE.)

Ziggy grew ever more alien over the course of such subsequent albums as *Aladdin Sane* and *Pin-Ups* (a terrific collection of oldie remakes). By the time of 1974's *Diamond Dogs*—the cover of which depicted David with the body of a dog—Bowie was feeling burned out: wasted by heavy cocaine use and increasingly isolated by the MainMan organization, a production office set up by his drug-disdaining manager, Tony DeFries, but staffed by high-living trendies recruited from Andy Warhol's Factory axis, among them ex-groupie Cherry Vanilla and his future biographer Tony Zanetta. Weary and confused, he hired a new personal assistant—Corinne "Coco" Schwab, the multilingual daughter of a noted French photographer, who had been raised in India, Haiti and Mexico and thus shared Bowie's own general sense of statelessness. He then split from MainMan and in 1975, with disco on the rise, suddenly slicked back his hair, suited up and released the ultra-danceable *Young Americans*, an album of what Bowie called "plastic soul." The following year came *Station to Station* and yet another new character: the skeletal and decadent Thin White Duke. Bowie also starred in Nicolas Roeg's movie *The Man Who Fell to Earth* (inaugurating an erratic film career that includes 1978's *Just a Gigolo*, a resounding bomb; 1983's *The Hunger*, a campy vampire flick directed by Tony Scott, and *Merry Christmas, Mr. Lawrence*, a memorable prisoner-of-war movie directed by the esteemed Japanese filmmaker Nagisa Oshima; and 1986's *Labyrinth*, a goblin fantasy directed by Jim Henson, and *Absolute Beginners*, a musical fiasco by video wiz Julien Temple). Bowie moved to Berlin, began listening to such German synthesizer groups as Kraftwerk and in 1977 released the first of a trio of largely brilliant art-rock collaborations with former Roxy Music synth avatar Brian Eno (*Low, Heroes* and *Lodger*).

By 1980 a new cult of fashion-crazed kids—the New Romantics—had sprouted up in London. Bowie walked among them (they were his stylistic children, in many ways) and came back with *Scary Monsters* (*and Super Creeps*), an album that, unfortunately, yielded no major hits. Was he running out of steam? Bowie answered that question with an emphatic no in 1983, when he dropped all his guises and went dance-pop with *Let's Dance*, the biggest-selling album of his career.

Bowie was married for nearly ten years to Angela Barnet, an Anglo-American woman with whom he had a son, Zowie (now called Joe). Their union, hardly strengthened by David's dalliance with such girlfriends as black singer Ava Cherry, dissolved in divorce in 1980. Today, David lives with Coco and Joe—who'll be sixteen in May—in a house in Switzerland, not far from the jet-set resort of Gstaad, where Bowie frequently skis. He also works out and roller-skates in his spare time—of which there's never much: he remains a workaholic. Despite his now-moneyed seclusion, he remains an artist with one ear—and one shrewd fashion eye—ever cocked toward the street, ever alert for the latest innovations. At last glance, however, no likely usurpers had appeared to challenge Bowie's position as the king of rock style.

*F*irst *of all, a belated happy birthday.*
Thank you!
Has turning forty made you reflective?
No, not at all. Now I feel I can do and say what I want [*laughs*].
Were you aware of style as a kid?
Yes, I *liked* how things went together, and it interested me how it all worked. But I think I was always drawn to the crass [*chuckles*], so that saved my ass, really: I was never very hot on sophisticated taste when it got *too* sophisticated. I didn't mind a sense of elegance and style, but I liked it when things were a bit off—a bit sort of fish-and-chips shop.

Were you aware of the Teds when they appeared?
Yeah. There was a bloke who lived down the road from us who was a Ted—Eric, I think his name was. He had brilliant, curly ginger hair and razor blades in his collar—for purposes of not being molested, I guess, by other Teds. That I found very impressive. But he was slightly potty—he would just stand on the corner for hours, swinging a chain manically.
Were you ever inclined toward Teddishness yourself?
Yeah, a lot of kids my age got into those things. But I didn't really like the Teddy clothes too much. I liked Italian stuff. I was *really* early into Italian stuff. I liked the box jackets and the mohair. You could get *some* of that locally in Bromley, but not very good. You'd have to go right up to Shepherd's Bush or the East End. And once I'd left school, you could save a little money and go find a tailor who would make it up really well. There were some good tailors. The one I used to go to was the same one that Marc Bolan used to go to, a fairly well known one in Shepherd's Bush. I remember I saved up and got one suit made there, but that was really all. The rest of my money I put into equipment and saxophones and things.
There's a picture of you with the Kon-rads where you have this sort of upswept crew cut....
Oh, yes, yes. I loved the hair-style stuff, yeah.
And the band is wearing, like, little candy-striped ties....
We wore gold corduroy jackets, I remember, and brown mohair trousers and green, brown and white ties, I think, and white shirts. *Strange* coloration.
Was there a particular rock performer who had really turned you on as a kid? Someone you saw and said, "That's what I want to do"?
Little Richard. I saw him at Brixton Odeon. It must have been 1963, 'cause the Stones opened for him. I'll tell you who else was on that bill as well. Oh, it was wonderful—listen: The Stones opened, then there was Bo Diddley and, if I remember rightly, Duane Eddy, and it closed with Sam Cooke. That was the first half. Then the second half . . . Who else was on that thing? Somebody else unbelievable was on, and *then* Little Richard. And Little Richard was *just unreal.* Unreal. Man, we'd never seen *anything* like that. It was still mohair suits then—I mean, just *great* suits—baggy trousers and all that. And he was workin' with a British band called Sounds Incorporated—our only horn band, the only band that knew anything about saxophones. There was one other, Peter Jay and the Jaywalkers, but they weren't as good. Sounds Incorporated were the one. And I think it was probably Red Price on tenor sax, guy with dark glasses. I used to love all those

sax players, 'cause that's what I wanted to do. And he led Lord Rockingham's XI, too [*laughs*]. Remember them? "Hoots, mon, there's a moose loose about this hoose!" You don't remember that?

Anyway, that show was unreal. And the Stones were so funny. They had, like, four fans at that time, who *rushed* down the aisles to the front. These four chicks in the front there—it was *so* funny. Keith was dynamite, 'cause he did that aeroplane stuff in those days, whizzing round and round—he really made an entrance. And Brian was kind of dominant in the band then; he really was. It's amazing the progress that Mick's made, thinking back, because as stage personalities, Mick and Brian were equal. And some bloke—I'll never forget this—some bloke in the audience looked at Jagger and said, "Get your hair cut!" And Mick said, "What—and look like *you*?" It was *so funny!* I went with the Kon-rads, and we just collapsed in our seats.

What kind of stuff did the Kon-rads play?

Lotta covers. And then . . . the band broke up because of me, actually. Yes, folks, I broke the Kon-rads up—now it can be told!

Why did you do that?

I wanted to do rhythm & blues songs, and nobody was interested. I remember the first one I really tried to get them to do—and I wish we'd done it, 'cause it would've done rather well—was "House of the Rising Sun," off an old blues album that got released in England.

In 1963? You were ahead of your time.

Eh! It was so great, and I wanted to put a beat to it. But I rather got beaten to that.

What about the Manish Boys, that seven-piece group you were in till early 1965?

That was just survival. I didn't really like that band at all. It was rhythm & blues, but it wasn't very good.

Nobody ever earned any *money*. The band was so huge; it was dreadful. And I had to live in Maidstone. That's where the Manish Boys were from, and so I had to go and live there, because we were gonna rehearse and work outta there. I don't know if you know Maidstone. Maidstone Prison is one of the biggest in England. It's all criminals round there—one prison and a few suburban houses. It's the only time in my life I've ever been beaten up.

By whom?

By some ex-prisoner, I suppose. I don't know. It was just this big herbert walkin' down the street just knocked me on the pavement, and when I fell down, proceeded to kick the *shit* outta me. For no reason

that I could fathom to this day. I haven't got many good memories of Maidstone.

That wasn't a long-lived band, though, the Manish Boys. But I affected a Keith Relf haircut, I believe, at the time. I was quite keen on Keith. I thought he was pretty cool—my favorite R&Ber. I liked the Who's sound but Keith Relf's look. I thought, "If I can get that down, wow—watch out world." [*Laughs.*]

Was the Lower Third, your next band, a happier affair?

The Lower Third was very Who inspired.

Did you do Who covers?

No, we wrote our own stuff. I was fully into writing by then. I was absolutely convinced that I could write anything as good as anybody else, have a go at it.

And proved yourself right, eventually.

Yeah, that's right—see, Pete! [*Laughs*] I took my first single to Pete Townshend. It was at a Who concert in 1969—must have been around there—and I took it and I got backstage and I gave it to him. I said, "Play that and let me know what you think of it one day." And it was many years later he said, "By the way, son, I remember you bringing me that single. I meant to let you know—I *did* like it." Lyin' bastard! [*Laughs.*]

Were you much of a mod?

Yeah. Oh, absolutely.

I mean, were you deeply into it?

Not deeply into the lifestyle. Superficially. Because I didn't like riding scooters. And I was never too much of a club guy—never really went clubbing very much.

Really?

No. Like once a week or something. Which actually, in that time, was not very much. I mean, those kids used to go every night and hang out till seven in the morning. I liked going to art museums and bits of theater, things like that. I wasn't really that concerned with *that* many clubs.

But you picked up on the mod clothes?

Yeah.

Where would you buy them?

Let me see. At that time, I suppose sport shops and things. Like now. See, that's come back full cycle. A lot of mods used to wear sports clothes—Fred Perry shirts and things like that. Um . . . Carnaby Street was *briefly* popular, for like a three-month period or something; then it fast became . . .

What it is today—a sort of tourist slum?

Yeah, exactly. And then of course the Kings Road also had its time, you know? But they were all sort of very fast. I didn't really have a hangout for clothes. I didn't wear much that was fashionable, actually. I mean,

I was quite happy with things like Fred Perrys and a pair of slacks. Not very loud clothes.

Did flower power pretty much sweep everything else away, fashionwise?

Yeah, I think everybody did become psychedelic, at least. I don't really remember the people that I knew being that affected by the love-and-peace things about it. They were *definitely* affected by the mushroom aspects, and the colors and all that—the clothes and the psychedelic music. But love and peace, I felt, was very much the American part of it all. It certainly made its impression in the hit parade, but it was very commercial oriented—you know: "If you're going to San Francisco," that kind of stuff. And we had bands like the Flowerpot Men. There was a lot of that about. But the best aspects of it were some of the early things that Jeff Beck did, you know? Now, that's what I liked about it—that was really good stuff.

Your Ziggy Stardust persona was a daring departure for rock. What were those early shows like?

What was quite hard was dragging the rest of the band into wanting to do it.

They were pretty much rock & roll, pub kind of guys?

Yeah, we always had that problem. That was the major problem, that we really didn't think alike at all. It was like, "Jesus, come *on*, you lot—let's not just be another rock band, for Christ's sakes." [*Laughs*] But they were a *great* little rock band, you know? And they caught on to it as soon as they found that they could pull more girls. Then it was, "Hey, they *like* these boots." I thought, "Yeah, there you go." That's what it needed. God—get a bit of sex into it and they were *away*, boy. Their hair suddenly got . . . oh, it was every color under the sun. All these guys that wouldn't get out of denims until two weeks ago [*laughs*].

Where did the clothes for the Ziggy period come from? Did you design them yourself?

No, that was a designer whose clothes I saw, a guy named Kansai Yamamoto. Now, of course, he's an international designer, but he was very experimental at that time—his stuff was way off the board. So the very first things were influenced by him, and then I got to know him, and he made all the stuff you really know—the suits, the pull-apart stuff, all those things. He said, "Oh, this band are weird—*tee-hee-hee*—they wear my clothes."

How did audiences respond to the early Ziggy shows, before the 'Ziggy Stardust' album actually came out?

There was quite a bit of antagonism. Nothing like, say, the Pistols got when they started. But the first couple of months were not easy. The people did find it very hard, until we had a musical breakthrough. The actual look and everything, I mean, it was, "Aw, a bunch of poofters," you know? Which was kind of fun. I mean, we played it up—well, I did, anyway—played that up a lot. Because it was the most rebellious thing that was happening at the time.

Is it true that when Ziggy and the Spiders played Santa Monica on the first tour, the band went off to a Scientology meeting and got converted?

Well, two of the band *are* Scientologists now. Mike Garson always *was* a Scientologist. I mean, Mike was a real hard nut to deal with, a very strange cat. I mean, he spent *all* his time tryin' to convert everybody—it was kind of difficult to work with him, you know? And he converted Woody Woodmansey, the drummer. Mike got him. He tried it on me for a bit, until we had a bit of a fight about it. He said, "Oh, well, you'd never understand, you're a druggie." I said, "Yeah, that's it—drugs are keepin' me away from Scientology." He was so po-faced. Very serious guy.

You had conceived Ziggy as the ultimate plastic rock star; ironically, the music that "he" made was really great.

I know, I know. It sounds all right now, yeah. I find it ironic when I look at a band, say, like Sigue Sigue Sputnik, where it's *so outré*, so *absolutely* in the Ziggy court, you know? All this time later, it still raises its brightly colored head.

Like psychedelia: It never goes away.

Yeah. That whole period, I guess. They keep recycling *all* of us—Roxy, me, Gary Glitter, Marc Bolan. I guess those four were the big ones from England, the champions of the early Seventies and all that. But it really seems to have permeated every area of rock now—something that one of us did is somewhere in all modern music. Which is *great*. I think that's fabulous.

Like Prince, maybe?

Prince, yeah, sure. I mean, he's probably *the* most eclectic artist I've seen since *me* [*laughs*]. I think he's a *great* stealer.

Was Aladdin Sane meant to be a conscious modulation on the Ziggy character or something completely different?

It was meant to be . . . a crossover: getting out of Ziggy and not really knowing where I was going. It was a little ephemeral, 'cause it was certainly up in the air.

Did you design the Aladdin Sane makeup yourself?

I came up with the flash thing on the face.

What was that meant to be?

Lightning bolt. An electric kind of thing. Instead of, like, the flame of a lamp, I thought he would probably be cracked by lightning. Sort of an obvious-type thing, as he was sort of an electric boy. But the teardrop was Brian Duffy's, an English artist-photographer. He put that on afterward, just popped it in there. I thought it was rather sweet.

And how did Aladdin Sane then mutate into the 'Diamond Dogs' period?

Christ knows! I know the impetus for *Diamond Dogs* was both *Metropolis* and *1984*—those were the two things that went into it. In fact, *Diamond Dogs* was gonna be a rewrite of *1984*—I wanted to try to get the musical rights for it and turn it into a stage musical for touring. But my office, MainMan, didn't bother to do anything about it, and then I found out that if I dared touch it, Mrs. George Orwell would sue or something. So I suddenly had to change about in midstream, in the middle of recording, you know? But, I mean . . . well, it wasn't a real office in those days. Nobody did anything.

In 1973, midway between 'Aladdin Sane' and 'Diamond Dogs,' you released 'Pin-Ups,' a collection of cover versions of your favorite oldies. A lot of people still think it's one of your best records. Might you ever do another one like it?

Yeah, I'm dying to do that. But I'd want to do it properly, not just as a filler between albums, you know? I really want to do it. 'Cause I've always made lists of things that I want to cover one day, and those lists go on and on and on. So it would be easy to just drop one in. I think the best time to do it would be at the end of a tour, when you're really up and you've still got the energy to do some high-energy performances. I'm so tempted—*this* is the time.

What songs would you like to cover?

I'm not gonna tell ya! [*Laughs*] 'Cause I've got some beauts that nobody'd ever *dream* of doing.

'Young Americans,' the studio album that followed 'Diamond Dogs' in 1975, marked a brand-new artistic direction for you—deep into black American dance rhythms. What do you make of the current state of black pop?

There's nobody that's knockin' me out. I'm not in there with Lionel anymore. I liked Cameo's "Word Up," and then I heard the album and I just went to sleep. Rap is really the only cutting edge at the moment—Run-D.M.C. are my favorites. But I have a tough time with a lot of black music now—it's all a bit dancey, and there's no real underbelly there, you know? I think Prince is probably the best of the current crop.

Did you see his second movie, 'Under the Cherry Moon'?

Yeahhh . . . I saw it. I'm not gonna say a thing. I mean, I've had so many of those myself, I wouldn't even *dream*. It'd be the pot callin' the kettle black, you know? *Whoops!* [*Laughs.*]

In 1976, you moved to Berlin, and the following year, you began a new avant-garde period with the release of the 'Low' and 'Heroes' albums. What's your impression of the state of the musical avant-garde today?

Well, in America, it seems to have died.

It does seem very career oriented here.

That's an interesting thing. There's Philip Glass, who's now at the zenith of his professional bit, and Laurie Anderson, who does TV and stage shows. In Germany, that period is over. I think it was starting to fold up on itself just around the time I left Berlin. The stuff that's coming out of Düsseldorf now is really boring.

What about Kraftwerk? You named one song on 'Heroes' after that group's Florian Schneider. What do you think of its latest music?

It's its usual pristine self. And it's good, in its genre. But they're like craftsmen—they've decided they're gonna make this particular wooden chair that they designed, and each one will be very beautifully made, but it will be the same chair. It's like a cottage-industry thing. They're craftsmen.

Despite all the touring you did—and the critical acclaim you amassed—through that early part of your career, you wound up in considerable debt. How come?

It was all the MainMan tribe. Most of them wanted to be stars; so a lot of them were usin' the money that was comin' in—if it wasn't for drugs, it was to put their own stage productions together and things like that. I mean, there were more drugs goin' around—*unbelievable*. I thought I was bad, but it was just incredible how many drugs there were. And that's what happened to all the money.

You finally got the business side of your career together in 1983, when you signed a very lucrative contract with a new label and released your biggest album, 'Let's Dance.' How do you look at the music business today—as a game you've sort of mastered?

I had a few problems with it a couple of years ago, at the time of *Let's Dance* and just after. I suddenly had this huge audience that I'd never had before. I didn't quite know what I was supposed to do. So I just cut out last year—stayed in Europe, up in the mountains most of the time, writing and working, just doing the things that I really like. And that put me back on course. That's why I guess this new album sounds so much more . . . as though the continuity hasn't been broken from *Scary Monsters*. It's almost as though *Let's Dance* and *Tonight* were in the way there. And I'm going to do a stage thing this year, which I'm incredibly excited about, 'cause I'm gonna take a chance again.

Can you say what it might be?

No! [*Laughs*] Too many other acts are goin' out. I'll just be doing what I always did, which is keeping things interesting.

What do you actually do at home in Switzerland? It's a pretty quiet place, isn't it?

I work. All the time. If I'm not working, I ski. That's my only other preoccupation. I paint if I have the time or if I feel in the mood. And I read extensively.

What have you read recently?

I've just finished reading Joe Orton's plays. I also read Harold Pinter's *The Dumb Waiter*, which is a fabulous short play.

Have you ever met Pinter?

Lord, no. I'd love to meet him. Well, I *think* I'd like to meet him. Actually, I *hate* meeting famous people. It's always a letdown. They're a lot shorter than they look on television [*laughs*]. Charlie Sexton's the only bloke I've met recently who's taller than I thought he was. No, hold on—there's a Duran who's like that as well: John Taylor. He's quite tall, yeah.

What do you make of the Durans? Are you buddies with them?

I had a hard time with them when I first met them a few years ago. I thought they were really sort of a bit arrogant. But I guess we all go through that. They've really got okay over the last year or two. Simon [LeBon] seems to have changed an *awful* lot since he seriously got back into sailing again. And since he changed his hair color [*laughs*].

Have you read these two recent books about you, 'Bowie,' by Jerry Hopkins, and 'Stardust,' by journalist Henry Edwards and your old MainMan employee Tony Zanetta?

The *two* books on me? Do you know that at last count there are thirty-seven? Thirty-seven, at the moment. I stopped reading those things after about the fourth or fifth one. Because once one saw the cast of characters, it became obvious that they were making a career out of it. The inevitable names would just keep coming up: the ex-wife, Ava Cherry, Cherry Vanilla, Tony Zanetta. Basically, all the people who had such a good time in the early Seventies and now are broke.

Have you ever been approached about doing your own book?

A *million* times. For *amazing* amounts of money.

Ever been tempted to do it?

Not in the least.

You started a feature-film career in 1976 with 'The Man Who Fell to Earth,' and there've been five more movies since then. Are there any new films in the works that you can talk about?

Not really. Mick and I are always talkin' about doing one. I guess that probably will come off, but only if we can arrive at a story that we believe in doing, and not just being put together for an on-the-road movie, or something like that.

You've been looking at scripts?

We're more concerned in writing something. That's what we're endeavoring to do. I think we've got to play it very carefully. It's got to be a story of some considerable substance, and inevitably it should have a lot of music in it. But I don't think it should have performance. Otherwise, it falls into that abyss of, you know, the celebrity rock & roll movie.

It's a difficult one, but I think we're cracking it. We are workin' on something, I've got to admit. We're working in conjunction with a writer that we respect a lot, so we'll see how it goes.

Is it difficult for someone like you—who deals in masks and personas onstage—to do film acting, to reveal himself to the camera?

No, it's not difficult for me. I don't know enough about it, so it's quite pleasant for me still. I don't have the burden of thinking, "I've got to better my last performance," you know? [*Laughs*] So I just enjoy it.

Were you happy with the way 'Absolute Beginners' came out?

I *liked* that movie. I see it as another *Rocky Horror Picture Show*. I was in Tower Video the other day getting a couple of things, and they said that that film is one of *the* most rented movies. And kids come back sayin' they've learned the entire script of it. If *that* starts, and it starts goin' out into those late-night theaters, I can see it becoming one of those kinds of movies.

Well, it's not like any other movie.

[*Laughs*] No, it's not like any other movie. And Julien Temple, like Tony Scott . . . I mean, I had the pleasure of workin' with Tony on *The Hunger*—fortunately, we're still friends—and after *The Hunger*, he had *such* a tough time. People wouldn't even look at him. I mean, nobody ever suspected—least of all him, I think—that he would become the biggest director in America. One *Top Gun* [*snaps fingers*]—suddenly he's got *Beverly Hills Cop II*, and he's *it*! I *knew* he had incredible talent as a director. And I feel the same way about Julien—Julien *will* break through.

I always thought 'The Hunger' would become a cult movie.

That rents pretty good, too. It's in that book, *Cult Movies.* Along with *Absolute Beginners.* Listen: *Absolute Beginners, The Hunger, The Man Who Fell to Earth*—they're *in* there, boy. [*Laughs*] Of *course* I looked!

Which of your films are your favorites?

The Man Who Fell to Earth I still think is a fascinating movie. And *Merry Christmas, Mr. Lawrence,* I guess. Those are the two I like the best. Although I do feel quite sympathetically towards *The Hunger* now. Yeah, there's some quite interesting stuff in that. I tell you, the first twenty minutes rattle along like hell—it really is a great opening. It loses its way about there, but it's still an interesting movie.

Everything lives on on video now. I think that's great.

Yeah. Well, for *some* it's great [*laughs*]. They can lose *Just a Gigolo,* as far as I'm concerned [*laughs*].

That's probably in 'Cult Movies,' isn't it?

I didn't even want to gaze at the *J* section [*laughs*].

Not a pleasant memory?

Well, it was, actually. I had more fun on that than any of them. Because we all looked at each other after a couple of weeks and said, "This is a piece of shit, isn't it?" "Yes." "Okay, let's just have a good time." So we had a great time in Berlin for the five or six weeks. But we *knew.*

Did you ever meet Rainer Werner Fassbinder during your time in Germany?

I never met him. I saw him once, in a bar.

Drunk?

No, he was all right. He was standing up. With a bunch of *really* heavy-looking guys. The kind of guys that the Hell's Angels would stay away from. I mean, he hung with a heavy crowd there—a heavy dude! But he was a fascinating guy. Extraordinary use of film, and the symbolic messages in it. Just incredible. I must say, I do have a penchant for the German filmmakers. Herzog is just fabulous as well.

Tina Sinatra recently said that you and Robert De Niro are the two people she has in mind to play her father, Frank Sinatra, in a film biography she's doing.

Which part of him would I play?

The English part, I suppose. She said that Frank "respects" you as an artist.

That's very decent. What an extraordinary thing.

Have you ever been offered the lead in any other biographical films?

Oh, funny things—like Byron, stuff like that. I don't

know, I think Mick would do a better Byron. I'd probably be a better Shelley [*laughs*]. But I don't think I'd like to do those kinds of things. I'd much prefer to do originally created stories for the screen—things that I could treat more seriously than some of the stuff I'm offered.

Do you think there are any movies that have really captured rock & roll on film?

I think probably *Sid & Nancy,* in a strangely macabre way. Those are the aspects that seem to grab people's attention, and it was a great film in those aspects. I thought the characterizations of some of the people around Sid were awful. I thought Iggy was ridiculous. I mean, did you see that as Iggy? It was incredible. The guy was like Neil Diamond or something, in this big apartment with all these girls round him. I've never seen Iggy like that in *my* life, and I'm sure the Pistols never saw him like that, either. And Johnny Rotten was terrible. But Gary Oldman was good as Sid. I only met Sid twice, I think.

How did he strike you as a person?

Just a mindless twerp. I didn't find anything at all romantic about him, or even interesting. I think he was just *completely* under the charisma of Rotten. Whatever Johnny said, Sid would jump to it.

Did you ever see the Pistols live?

No. I just saw them because of my involvement with Iggy, on his 1977 tour, when I was playing piano. And Johnny and Sid—they all individually turned up to different shows, you know? 'Cause, I mean, they just worshiped the ground that Iggy . . . spat on [*chuckles*].

Ah, the old nihilism. You used to be very apocalyptically minded, it seemed, back in the 'Diamond Dogs' days. Do you still feel that way—that the end is near?

No, I don't feel that at all. I *can't* feel that. I always *have* to look for some kind of light at the end of the tunnel. Having a son does that. You change a lot. I think when you're young, you feel it's kind of exciting to have that kind of negative feeling about things. But that changes as you get older. That's the one thing that *does* change. The *energy* doesn't change; it just gets channeled in a different direction.

Do you think rock & roll has changed?

Rock & roll is for *us*—it's not for kids. *We* wrote it, *we* play it, *we* listen to it. *We* listen to rock. Kids listen to something else—they have a new need for music, in a different way.

Do you think rock is dead?

Purely on release of high spirits, it's still just as important as it was. But *socially,* it's changing its calendar; it's changing its vocabulary continually. Which is what makes it the most exciting art form, really. Because it *is* social currency; it actually has a place in society. It's a living art, and it is undergoing constant reevaluation and change. Which makes it *far* more interesting than, say, painting, or any of the plastic arts, which are so much for the few. And there's quite as much money attached to painting these days as there ever was in rock. . . .

I think there's a refocusing in rock now. I think the emphasis is off videos—which is great—and it's returning back to stage, to interaction between the audience and the artist. It's entirely physical and dangerous at the moment, but I think artists and audiences are coming together again in a different way. Video was very much in the way between the artist and the audience over the last few years.

Which is your favorite new band?

The Screaming Blue Messiahs. I love them. I think they're terrific. . . . And I've always had a penchant for the Psychedelic Furs. I think they're a great band. I've always wanted to produce them, and they've often asked me to, but I never had the time. I would never be forward enough with most bands to suggest producing them, because I always like what it is they have themselves. It would never occur to me to suggest to, say, the Messiahs that I want to get involved with them. Because they seem to be so right on course with what they're doing that they need me like a hole in the head.

Does your son turn you on to groups?

Yeah. I got this band I've got to listen to, called the Stupids. I never heard of them. It's a band in England that Joe quite likes. He really liked PiL, until he saw them, which was unfortunate. I thought the last album was great, but we went to a bad show. The whole thing was so tired. There was no enthusiasm in the band or the audience. . . .

I don't like many of the English bands at the moment. And the older ones, who *were* exciting, like the Fall . . . I mean, that new album by the Fall is such rubbish, such fourth-form poetry. It's really sophomoric.

Your own latest album has a certain recherché feel to it, with sitars and Mellotron, even some harmonica. And on one song, "Glass Spider," the backing vocal sounds remarkably like John Lennon.

Well, actually, the album *was* reflective in a way, because it covers every style that I've ever written in, I think. And also all the influences I've had in rock.

On one song, "Zeroes," I wanted to put in every cliché that was around in the Sixties—"letting the love in," those kinds of lines. But it was done with affection—it's not supposed to be a snipe. I just wanted the feeling of that particular period, the very late Sixties.

What inspired the title track, "Never Let Me Down"?

It's basically about Coco, more than anybody else.

Is there a romantic relationship there?

No, it's platonic. But there *is* a romance in it, I guess, inasmuch as it's hard for two people to feel totally at ease in each other's company for that period of time and not expect too much from each other. Always being prepared to be there if the other one needs someone, you know? There's not many people you find in life that you can do that with, or feel that way with.

Any other long-term friendships?

Yeah, I've got three or four friends that I used to go to school with. One of them I've known since I was five. I see them every year. In fact, we all came together again when I was forty—'cause they're all gonna be forty, too, you see. So we all met, and we just went back: "Oh, do you remember . . . ?" And "Did you ever think . . . ?" It was really something.

Do you think you've changed a lot over the years?

I'm more like I was in 1967 now, say, than I was in 1977. I *feel* like I am, anyway. I feel as bright and cheerful and optimistic as I was then—as opposed to feeling as depressed and sort of nihilistic as I was in the Seventies. I feel like I've come full circle in that particular way.

Well, you don't wear dresses anymore.

Do you know, the only time I wore dresses . . . There was that funny little white thing with white boots.

And I did three drags for the "Boys Keep Swinging" video. And I wore a dress on *Saturday Night Live,* which was based on a John Heartfield photo montage—sort of a Communist Chinese air-hostess look. But I never wore dresses as much as Milton Berle did.

Do you feel relieved that you don't have the sort of burden of outrageousness on you anymore?

Why, no, not really. It's a bit of a disappointment [*laughs*]. I'll keep tryin'. I've got a few things up me sleeve.

Any final fashion statement?

Wide shoulders are the flared trousers of the Eighties.

28
Michael Douglas

INTERVIEWED BY
LYNN HIRSCHBERG (1986) AND
FRED SCHRUERS (1988)

Michael Douglas still seems much too nice a guy to be a big shot in the picture business, but that's exactly what he is. Best known to the moviegoing public as the star of such hit films as 'Romancing the Stone', 'Fatal Attraction' and 'Wall Street,' Douglas is most meaningfully approached as the producer of 'Romancing the Stone' and other such box-office bonanzas as 'The Jewel of the Nile,' 'The China Syndrome' and the Oscar-winning 'One Flew Over the Cuckoo's Nest' (his maiden production, a property purchased from his father, Kirk Douglas). Hollywood producers don't generally turn out to be pussycats, but Douglas virtually purrs through interviews. Can this guy be for real? The answer, as we've found out on more than one occasion, is yes.

—K. L.

I T IS a week before *The Jewel of the Nile* opens, and Michael Douglas, the producer and star of the movie, has just decided to try to quit smoking. "It's not exactly the best time," he says, sounding tired, "but I was up to three packs a day." Douglas started smoking three years ago while making *Romancing the Stone*, 1984's surprise hit comedy-adventure-romance. The success of that movie prompted a nerve-racking rush job on the sequel, *The Jewel of the Nile*, which is destined to be another hit. In fact, Douglas is getting to be easily predictable: every movie he's produced—*One Flew Over the Cuckoo's Nest* and *The China Syndrome* are the other two—have been big hits. Yet to the public he isn't really known as this hugely successful producer. He's simply a movie star.

It is possible that this balance between backstage and onstage roles has saved Douglas from becoming either power mad (as a producer) or wildly egotistical (as an actor). He can see the traps on both sides, but Douglas doesn't dwell on that sort of thing—he is not an analytical thinker. He is reflexive, savvy and, most of all, very charming. His charm is easy, it works: It is simply the most effective way to do business. And Douglas pulls it off—he deftly shifts the spotlight away from himself, focusing instead on his audience.

Douglas's charm also protects him. By deflecting the spotlight, he is able to maintain his privacy. For someone who does over forty-five interviews in a day, a sense of privacy is crucial. To charm is to be gracefully distant.

Douglas, who is forty-one years old, learned this at an early age. After his parents were divorced when he was only five, he lived with his mother on the East Coast and spent summers on movie sets with his father. Douglas went to the University of California at Santa Barbara and then went on to become a television star, beamed into millions of homes via *The Streets of San Francisco.* He left that show in 1976, having already made his debut as a producer the year before with *One Flew Over the Cuckoo's Nest.* The next year, Douglas got married (he had lived for years with actress Brenda Vaccaro), and he and his wife, Diandra, had a son, Cameron. Then came *The China Syndrome* in 1979 and, five years later, *Romancing the Stone.* At some point, Douglas earned the reputation for being a quintessentially nice guy. Douglas *is* nice, but the word, which is used more than any other to describe him, isn't quite accurate. *Nice* is a charming word—it isn't complex enough.

At the moment the right word would perhaps be *overwhelmed.* Or, simply, *exhausted.* Douglas is sitting on a couch in the Parker Meridien hotel in New York, not far from a ringing telephone. Last night was the premiere of *Jewel;* tonight is the press screening. Douglas is upset about the quality of last night's print, as well as the sound levels. He asks if I've seen the video for the theme song from the movie, "When the Going Gets Tough, the Tough Get Going," in which he and costars Kathleen Turner and Danny DeVito do a Temptations *hommage.* He asks the movie's publicist if he has a copy of the new television commercials for the movie. His mind appears to be racing over a thousand niggling details, and he looks weary. Nobody said producing was fun. Douglas smiles. "But who would want to do anything else? I meet intelligent people, travel around the world. What a great job!"—L.H.

Do you need a certain knack, a talent, to produce movies?

The only knack, I guess, is to like a piece of material. When I started producing, with *Cuckoo's Nest,* I was fortunate enough, from *Streets,* to be financially secure.

So when I made *Cuckoo's Nest,* it was a labor of love. I'd never really thought about producing. My father was about to sell [the rights to] *Cuckoo's Nest.* It had been a labor of love for him for a long time, for eight years. He'd had a tough time getting it made. I loved the book, so I just said, "Dad, you're gonna sell this thing, let me take it and run with it." It took about four or five years, but I finally got it made.

So the combination is to have a love of the project and then the stamina and the tenacity to see it through. Because what happens a lot is, you like a project, and the studio tries to make a suggestion to change it, and you're beaten down so much that you're just desperate to make the deal, so the project changes. The point is, you don't want to waffle, you want to remember the virgin instincts you had when you first got a taste of the project. You want to remember three years ago when you used to lie awake at night thinking about the picture. Remember, so that after the years of knocking on doors, trying to get it made and saying, "Well, maybe I could do that," when you know in your heart that's just not right, you recall that spirit and still get the picture made. I don't develop a lot of stuff. I've got a ratio of less than two things in development for every one that gets made.

Were there points during the making of 'Cuckoo's Nest' when you just felt like it was not worth all the hassles?

Oh, sure there were. But what kept me going was the revenge factor. That's a key part of producing. It's like, "Someday, someday, I'm going to get that sonofabitch. I'm going to have a hit picture." I think revenge is a very good motivation if you can direct it. It's healthy. Very healthy.

'One Flew Over the Cuckoo's Nest' won five Academy Awards, including Best Picture. You were thirty-one years old at the time. How was that for revenge?

I must say, they're real happy to see you when you win five Academy Awards. They're *real* happy. I milked that for a year. Everyone was happy to see me. It was great. But I thought, first of all, I wasn't a producer, really. I was just an actor who made that movie. And goddamn it, it turned out great. And you know, I was going to enjoy it. I learned this from my father's career. They used to make many more films back then, and sometimes you didn't get a chance to stop. He'd finish one picture and have to start another. He never got to enjoy his success. My big thing in life is, whatever you do, you have to stop when things are good and taste it. So I took a year.

But I remember when we were all sitting around after the Academy Awards—Milos Forman [the director], Saul Zaentz [Douglas' co-producer] and me —and I said, "Well, it's all downhill from here."

Did you really think that?

Oh, yeah. Well, come on! [*Laughs*] Five Oscars? You're not going to top that. I said "It's all downhill from here" to psyche myself up. I wanted to set an attitude so that life would not be a disappointment. And for me at that early an age, it was important. Otherwise, let's say it had been a total fluke—that would have been depressing.

Is moviemaking instinctive for you?

Yes. I think that my biggest strength is instinct. I feel like I'm really lucky. I have good instincts, and I trust them. My first instinct is right a large amount of the time. And when I get into a bind, I try to remember what my first instinct was in the situation and go with that.

You have a reputation for being a nice guy. Is it possible to be a nice guy in Hollywood?

I think so. I try to be diplomatic. But if it gets ugly, I'll mix it up with anybody. I've got no problems with that at all. And I do, on occasion. It's not my style, but if I've got to, I do it. I didn't get this far just from being a nice guy. It may have taken me a little longer or whatever, but, you know, there is also something else. I don't just produce, I also like to act. I'm an actor first and a producer second.

Is it difficult to switch from one to the other within a picture?

Not really. I love the fact that on one side, with acting, you can be a child—acting is wonderful for its innocence and the fun—and I think it helps you with producing.

On the other side, producing is fun for all the adult kinds of things you do. You deal in business, you deal with creative forces. As an adult who continues to get older, you like the adult risks. It's flying without a net, taking chances and learning. I was never good in economics or business—had no business background, you know—and I like it. By producing, you learn all these different areas.

Is it possible to keep doing both?

What's the difference between the games people play in the privacy of their house, in the privacy of the bedroom, versus how they conduct themselves in their business world? You don't have to choose. You can have both.

Do you ever feel torn between your reviews as an actor and how the movie does at the box office?

We're all vain, so sure you care. Do I think, in hindsight, that I should have protected or developed my part more for *Romancing the Stone?* Maybe yes. *Romancing the Stone* made Kathleen Turner's career. She's a big star now. But the picture was about her character, so if you're going to wear both hats, you've got to be a producer first. *Romancing* was about the growth of a woman, a young woman going from this to that, meeting this guy, and the adventure she had. It was her story. If we had screwed around with that, I wouldn't have made myself a star, because maybe the picture would have been a turkey. And stars are made out of pictures that are successful.

Look, I've got a healthy ego. And we all have our own ways and styles of approaching things. The best, most satisfying way for me is to make the best picture.

Do you read scripts differently as an actor than as a producer?

Yes and no. You read the script to see if it's a good story, if it's a good picture or not. As an actor, I would then focus in on the part, seeing if it's the kind that I want to play. As a producer, I go back and try to picture it in my mind and see if, impulsively, I like it. Then I try to make sure that I haven't been seduced by what's written on the page and find out if I can translate it to the screen. I read it like I'm looking at it on the screen.

Do you go to a lot of movies?

No. I'm way behind. I'm not like a historian. I'm not really knowledgeable about old-time films. I feel guilty about films I have not seen.

As a producer, you have a reputation for being hard on ideas, meaning you make a decision based on what's best for the story, and you stick with it.

It's what I call throwing away your lovelies. My job is very much like that of an editor, to try to be unbiased. I may make a suggestion and then say, "Forget it. It sucks." And then I throw it out. It's very hard, but somebody's got to do that. It comes with the territory. I find the problem with a lot of pictures is they don't do that, they don't look at their ideas. There's no commitment. There's a waffling in films, a muddiness. I try to find the character's motivation, the visceral, the emotional, the through-line. Does it keep people connected? And then, execute that. Then, hopefully, your picture's like an arrow. It's got a thrust, it's clean, it's straight. The audience knows they're in good hands.

You found 'Romancing the Stone' by reading the screenplay by Diane Thomas. You liked it immediately and bought it. Why'd it take over five years to get made?

Romancing took a long time because people would not understand that you could juggle adventure, comedy and romance. People kept saying, "What is it?" I'd say, "Well, it's an action adventure picture, it's a comedy, it's a romance." They'd say, "You can't do that. What's the concept?" And so I lost a lot of time. *Raiders of the Lost Ark* helped *Romancing* get made.

Had you always planned to do a sequel if the first movie was successful?

No. I was recuperating in April or May [of 1984] after the picture came out, and in June people started asking me if I wanted to do a sequel. I had never thought about it. A lot of people said, "Well, what happened to Jack and Joan? What's going to happen?" I approached the studio, and they said, "Well, we don't know. We're watching the figures." And the studio was going through all sorts of changes in administration. Then in August—the new regime was not in yet—they finally decided, "We want a sequel, and we need it pronto. We want a sequel by Christmas of '85." And I said, "I don't know. I've got no script, nothing."

Did you have an idea for the script?

A little bit, but mostly it was about how to avoid the jungles and the rain and mud rather than what happened to Jack and Joan in *Romancing the Stone.* The opposite would be sun and sand. The only thing I could come up with that looked different would be Nepal or Africa. You can't get a lot of laughs out of the Middle East, so I started focusing on the Sudan area, looking at maps, at African cultures and Arab cultures and all that. We decided it would be a good idea to bring Danny DeVito back. He was a pretty integral part in our balance of comedy, adventure and romance. Then I started thinking about the characters and what happened and how they got their dream and they got the boat. They're off in the boat, they've been sailing on the boat for six months, and you know, Joan Wilder's in love with this guy. It was great for a week, and two weeks was fine, stopping off in the Caribbean, they went down and around and headed over to the Mediterranean.

We pick them up in the South of France about six months later, and Jack thinks this is just hot shit, we're having a great time. And she's not sure. We'd already done the growth of Joan Wilder's character; she'd already gone from this meek, doubtful, insecure woman living through fantasies to a full-fledged woman. The next step would be for her to start thinking she could do something more with her life. She had this taste and at the same time wasn't sure of this whole boat thing, definitely not knowing where they were going next or when they were going to leave. She's trying

to keep up her success in romance novels, but they're not quite working out. She could write the novels before because it was a fantasy. Now, with the reality of a relationship, it's different. So, I mulled over that and started meeting writers.

How did you find them?

You read scripts. First of all, you find out who's available. There was no time, so you've got to know who's available now, right this second, which is not the way you'd like to go about it. You meet with different people and pitch your story outline and then you see if they can elaborate on it. I locked on to two writers. What I usually do is index cards or just an outline form. In other words, I know I've got a beginning, a middle and an end. I'm sort of old-fashioned that way. So we outlined the thing, and then they went off to write a first draft. In the meantime, I moved my family back to New York in time for my son to begin school in September and then went into *A Chorus Line* in October, set up my little office upstairs in the Mark Hellinger Theatre, where they were filming the movie. While I'm waiting for the first draft, I start getting together my team—all the logistics stuff you have to do. But still you don't have a go-ahead with the studio. The studio was leaving me alone until I got a script. I get one in early November, they say, "Let's go, we're gonna go for Christmas." I say, "I don't know if I can do it, I don't know if I can do it. It's really tight." Then I had a Christmas break, a December break. I took my son to Santa Barbara for the holidays and at the same time worked with the writers on the rewrites. After that, I told Kathleen, and at the end of the vacation I came back to New York. Around January 3, I flew to England to meet with the production staff I had put together.

By this point, Lewis Teague had been set as director because Bob Zemeckis, the director of *Romancing,* wasn't available. We all met in England to decide where we were going to film. It appeared that Egypt was sort of dicey and spread out, and they didn't have everything. Israel didn't have everything. We could shoot part of it in Morocco and part of it in Israel. I was a little nervous about that. I didn't foresee getting many long-distance telephone calls through to Morocco from Tel Aviv because of the whole Arab-Jewish situation. We decided on Morocco. Then I said, "Okay, you guys go down with Lewis, lock up the locations." I came back to New York and finished *Chorus Line.* I went back to Morocco, and that was when I realized I was in deep shit.

What happened?

I arrived in Casablanca, where we're going to shoot eighty percent of our picture, and this one Moroccan production manager meets us at the airport. I had the production designer and the director with me. The Moroccan production man is running around getting cars, and all of a sudden I realized this is it. *I've got to drive a car; Lewis,* my director, is driving a car, and I died. *I died.* I said, "Where's your office?" He said, "What office?" Nothing had been set. A day later, I realized locations hadn't really been firmed up, and that was the beginning. I went to my hotel room and just cried. Yeah, crying is good for openers. I thought I had to call the studio up and say we weren't ready. I deliberated about a day whether to call it off, whether to postpone the picture. The problem was that because of the weather, I would have had to postpone it for three or four months. I would have had to wait until after the summer or the fall.

It was horrible. But I decided, all right, let's go for it. I called in all our department heads. Our wardrobe and prop departments came from England. And everybody came to Casablanca.

How did you keep your faith?

Well, it wasn't a question of faith anymore. It was blind ambition. You have to act once you make the decision. I was scared to death. I didn't see how I could do it, but you have to look like you know what you're doing. And you have these very good, responsible meetings with executives. You make decisions one after another, boom, boom, boom, and then you go back to your room and—AAAAAH!—you cry.

So we ran around, we firmed up locations. I ultimately fired the production manager. We were set to start shooting in April. I went back to California to work on the script, to do casting. I would do the Academy Awards and then leave the next day to go back to Morocco.

About a week before the awards, I get word that we'd lost our production designer, our location manager and their pilot in a plane crash. That was a very, very sad time, because they were missing for four days. It was hard for everybody. I didn't know whether to go over there. My brother was telling me, "We're doing everything we can, you've got to keep going ahead with the script. There's nothing you can do here." But it was a very, very sad and uncomfortable time, trying to continue with the picture, having meetings, and you kind of drift off for a while and look out a window, and out there somewhere they're still missing.

I felt like we were going against the gods. I knew in my gut that the rhythm of this was totally wrong.

And yet I was going ahead, pushing ahead. It really bothered me. After the tragedy, we lost a couple of people who just wanted to leave the picture because they felt it was doomed.

Really?

Yeah. But I got back over there right after the Academy Awards and kept plowing ahead. But we still had disastrous problems: We had no accommodations. We had the crew coming, so we had to get rooms, and nobody would double up—the English refused to double up. And that's when I called the head of the studio, the head of production in the studio, because we had mutual approval on the production manager and I wasn't happy. I cleaned house.

Was there any point when you felt this is just too much to handle, I'm going to go home now?

You can't. You just do it. You have to fight—you're jabbing, you're ducking, you don't want to get knocked out.

When did you even have time to think about your character?

The acting wasn't hard. Acting's play, you know. Producing is work.

What saved you amid all this?

I think I'm a good logician. The art of logic is reducing everything to the lowest common denominator, and I think I have a good ability to see what the priorities are.

But this was just one nightmare after another. There were terrible customs problems. We had a long list of military equipment for which we had contracted with the Moroccan government, but we got a shipment of blank guns, rifles, that were not on a requisition order with the military. So somebody in customs decided that if we were going to bring weapons into the country, they had to call a military tribunal. In other words, if one of the divisions, either the air force, army or navy, has a requisition for weapons, the king calls the leaders of the military together because he wants to make sure that one division doesn't get too strong and let him have it. Checks and balances.

Meanwhile, I need the guns, because the guys in the train scene are shooting little rubber guns, which looked okay on the long shots, but now they've got to really go bang-bang. Plus, we'd been having all the problems with the accommodations. So I had a flip-out day when I had to take a plane, track these government officials down in Rabat, which is the capital, and Marrakech, where one of the king's forty-two-odd palaces are. And that got ugly. I had a really ugly meeting and decided no more Mr. Nice Guy. I basically said, "Look, I'm dying here. I'm going down, and you're going to go down with me." I said, "I'm going to get every international press person I can to come in here." I said, "You know *Good Morning America?*" "Yeah." I said, *"Good Morning America* is going to have their crews out to watch us get kicked out of our offices and the hotel." The only thing that really appealed to them was the international press. They were scared of the international press. And I got my guns.

This whole movie was like a battle. It was a war, but in the end, we were intact. Every day it was attack, attack, attack. But we started getting a pride going, and everybody was helping one another out. They were reaching out more than you normally would, even when you're tired or sick. And that's what you hope for. That's the magic or chemistry that as a producer you hope for. Because then you got something that nobody can take away from you. You've got family, you've got stories, you've got memories. It makes me doubly glad the picture worked out. This is one where they can wear their T-shirts proudly.

Would you ever want to do a small movie?

My only dream is to find a great script that's a three-room comedy or drama. Something like that would be much easier to produce. These two movies were very heavy back-to-back things. What I have to learn to do is to allocate responsibility.

Would you like being a full-time producer?

I go back and forth on it. I can see gearing up with the producing, but I've been watching all the people who are doing it and, you know, I've been doing okay. I'd still like a few months off to sort it out. I'm emotionally drained now. I haven't had a break in how long? It's not the best time to try to make some rational decision, because you just feel like you want to rest.

I think there's a way—an executive-producer-type situation—that I can be as effective and not necessarily have to be picking up the cables and doing every single thing, every step of the way. I think by now I've found a lot of proper people after having made all the mistakes, and I can still be directly involved but not strung out quite so much.

Are you interested in doing more movies like 'The China Syndrome,' as opposed to the last two, which were sheer entertainment?

It all depends on the material. I tell you, after *China Syndrome* I was getting so depressed. Every serious-problem-in-the-world script was being sent to me, and at that time I was recently married and had a son and wasn't in that kind of mood.

If 'The Jewel of the Nile' is successful, will you make another sequel?

I ain't cheap, but I can be had.

Where are you going to do it? Underwater? I mean, you're running out of . . .

Paris. [*Laughs*] I have no idea. I really can't think about it. My dream is right now. I dream of being here in New York in January and being in my bathrobe for about four days. I do that. I just go prenatal, and I get up early, and I see my kid, and I have breakfast with him, and I look out the window a lot. And sports, all the sports—I've got great sports stations on cable. They play sports around the clock. I love watching sports. I love anything where I don't know what the ending is going to be.

You haven't lost yet as a producer. Do you feel like you're an everyman who understands what people will like?

I think I'm a chameleon. I think it's something that I possibly inherited early on as a child going back and forth between two families. I know that whether it's right or wrong, I have an ability to sort of fit into a lot of different situations and make people feel relatively comfortable in a wide range without giving up all my moral values. I think that same chameleon-like quality can transfer into films. I think if you can remember the reason you got involved with it in the first place and try to keep that impulsive, instinctive feeling even when you're being beaten down or exhausted or waylaid, you'll be successful. It certainly is more effective if one can be charming to get the best out of whomever you're working with and use it to your best advantage. However you choose is your own moral dilemma and responsibility. That's all I try to do.

H E HAS driven his gray '78 Ferrari into Hollywood with but a few minutes to spare before he faces the television camera. But it's a taping, not a live spot; the interview will be broadcast later that day in Australia to support two films of his that will land there shortly. One's a little item called *Fatal Attraction,* which has made, um—the studio man right over there should have that figure—yes, over $94 million as of week 9. The other, *Wall Street,* features what may be be the pivotal performance—as a bad guy, yet—of his acting career.

So even as Michael Douglas is ushered into an overbright cubicle; a camera poking into his face and a disembodied Aussie voice filling the room via satellite, he looks perfectly calm. He and his interviewer talk about the weather down under while the sound levels are adjusted.

Always the soul of cooperation, Douglas seems to be subtly soothing the interviewer, setting an easy conversational pace even though their audio exchanges sound a fraction of a second off. "If we're not talking, there's a device called a noise gate that comes in and shuts it all off," says the Aussie. "That's why it sounds a bit strange." "Noise gate?" says Douglas, as they count down to rolling tape. "I'd like to put one on my son sometimes."

In fact, Douglas will cut short his West Coast business the next day so that he can be back home in New York for the weekend with his eight-year-old son, Cameron, and wife, Diandra, but with that line, his eyes flick toward the control room, where the engineers titter, and then back to the camera for show time. Australia is clearly abuzz with the sociological import of *Fatal Attraction,* in which a husband's impulsive act of infidelity backfires horrifically on his family. Douglas says that in the States "it seemed to uncover a deeper sort of anger and hostility going on between the sexes. . . . The initial impression we got was that women were dragging their husbands or boyfriends to see the picture."

He and the interviewer go on to talk about the rewards for him of playing a villain in *Wall Street,* and the Aussie asks if people will soon be referring to Kirk Douglas primarily as Michael's father. "Well, I think I have a way to go before that happens," he replies, adding that his dad is getting a kick out of his success. "We're looking for a picture to do together." Michael pauses for a sly grin that implies he's sitting down to a whole new card game. "We just can't decide who's gonna be the bad guy."

An accomplished producer, Douglas has until recently earned only grudging respect for his work on the other side of the camera. *The China Syndrome, Romancing the Stone* and *The Jewel of the Nile* were hits partly because of his acting work, but they made him only Hollywood's favorite young producer—leaving him frustratingly short of being on the leading-men A list. When director Oliver Stone made Douglas his first choice to play the tough, edgy corporate raider Gordon Gekko in *Wall Street,* it was considered a gutsy pick from a field that included Warren Beatty and Richard Gere. "It wasn't really casting against type," says Stone. "He lives in that world [of financiers], knows that world."

Sherry Lansing, who co-produced *Fatal Attraction* with her partner, Stanley Jaffe, has been a supporter of Douglas' ever since he was cast in *Coma,* which she'd worked on as executive story editor at MGM some twelve years before.

"I remember watching him in the dailies for *Coma,* and thinking that man was extraordinarily gifted," Lansing says, "because he had such sympathy—you just liked him on camera. When Stanley said, 'Let's give [the leading role in *Fatal Attraction*] to Michael,' I said, 'That's a fabulous idea, because not only are we getting this really vulnerable, funny, hang-loose guy who'd be uniquely right as Dan Gallagher, but he thinks like a producer.' He gave us invaluable creative input, and when we were being rejected by studios, rejected by directors, who almost without exception said you couldn't sympathize with a guy who did *that,* he would always say, 'Don't worry, Sherry, look at *Romancing*'—it took him years to get it made— 'I finally got old enough to play the part.' "

But it's Douglas the actor whom Lansing cherishes. "He can both produce and act," she says. "Of that there's no doubt—and maybe he could run the Bank of America, too. But as someone who loves films, I would hope acting would be his priority. It's like a ballerina who says, 'But I can choreograph,' and you say, 'Yes, but you can dance.' "

Douglas has been one of the best-liked people in his business for some years now, but even his friends didn't always talk this way. There's a revelatory aggressiveness in his portrayal of Gordon Gekko in *Wall Street*. He owes that in part to Stone's stern, even goading directorial style. But in this interview, he shows a new willingness to step forward in the mantle of a full-grown actor.—F.S.

I heard you and Oliver Stone had a rocky start on the 'Wall Street' set.

I was on the ropes for a while, doing a lot of homework, sorting things out. I was struggling early on the first day with a lengthy monologue, and I thought I had it down. But he just wasn't happy, and he made it clear he wasn't, so I said, "Christ, if you're unhappy, let's reshoot it." He looks me in the eye and says, "John Ford never reshot." I said to myself, "All right, okay, so he's a character."

Then I went to dailies—I never go to dailies when I'm acting in a picture, except when there's a problem—and I said, "This is pretty good," and I went back and said this to him, and he says, "It is, isn't it?" And I said, "You fucker."

In hindsight, I think probably what he was doing was toughening me up for the kind of role I was playing. He's not outwardly supportive, but he believes in you very strongly. His style is "Let me see whether you can cut it." He's brutally honest.

He's not the kind of man you can tell that you like him, but I do. I've got a lot of respect for him, and I always reminded myself, "Hey, he offered you this part. This is a great part." Both on and off camera, I was developing that Gekko mystique—"If you want to go eyeball to eyeball, that's fine"—and I think it probably was a toughening-up process that was helpful. . . . I drew upon my producing background, all the years you spend on projects, getting turned down and rejected. . . . I always try to be as congenial and cordial as possible, but at the same time, the word was out that if I had to mix up, I'm more than happy and willing to do so.

Quite different from your image, till now, among the moviegoing public.

My father has always said, "You're gonna do a great killer sometime. You're such a charming guy, but they're gonna find out the prick you really are."

Some people will probably always think of you as that nice cop in the corner of the frame in 'The Streets of San Francisco.' How difficult did you find the switch from the little screen to the big one?

I'm still learning about that. I'm not sophisticated about it, even with as much camera work as I've done. I think there are certain actors—predominantly *actresses*—who like the camera. I was always impressed that Kathleen Turner picked up a real knowledge of the camera very early in her career. I just recently began looking at the camera like it's not a howitzer [*laughs*].

There was a time when you were traumatized by the camera?

Oh, yeah. I basically started out struggling with stage fright. Acting's nothing that came naturally to me. I really wasn't able to relax until I could benefit from the repetition of doing *Streets*—where even though I was struggling with insecurities, I'd remind myself they were stuck with me for the run of the series, or at least for the year.

But I find you'll always have pangs, you'll always have insecurity running rampant. You begin to try to analyze why it happens. I've come to accept it now as a red flag going up that something is not right, even though I may not know what it is.

A sign that something's amiss in your own feelings about a scene or a shoot?

Yeah. I used to fight through it, whereas in the last three years, I've begun to recognize that it's some kind of signal and have dealt with it. I try to find out why it's happening. It may be as simple as your own tension. It may be a scene that I know is coming up that's affecting everything else. I think sometimes it can be diet. Sometimes you get a late start, and all of sudden you realize, "Well, I've had too many cups of coffee." You've got to go through a checklist of different things. Sometimes it's easy to discover and sometimes not.

Where did it arise on 'Wall Street'?

I do a fair amount of preparation. And a lot of times you arrive on a set with an idea of how you think it's going to go. Then all of a sudden it's either an entirely different location or an entirely different setup. You're thrown off in some way. In *Wall Street*, I begged them to please resolve the names, because of the size of Gordon Gekko's speeches. And in the eleventh hour, all of a sudden Cromwell Papers is now called Teldar. And you go, "No, no." [*Laughs*] You've got this whole long rhythm of these speeches—just throwing these names off the tip of your tongue—and now in the back of your mind, all you're thinking of is trying to remember the name change.

Do you think your early feelings of stage fright and camera shyness had to do with the fact that you were following in the footsteps of your father and his eminent career? Or would you still have had stage fright if he'd been an electrician?

I think it's a combination. You gotta remember, I went into theater because I didn't have a major. It was my junior year in college, and I really didn't know what the hell I wanted to do. I really had never thought about acting at all. So when I jumped in, I hadn't done any high-school plays or anything. Still, I was able to get some pretty decent roles. When you're an offspring of the same sex and have a vague resemblance, I think in their heart of hearts, people really would like to see an immortal Kirk Douglas.

He's not just an accomplished actor but an icon of American cinema, of American culture.

I think earlier in my career, I couldn't perceive playing the kind of dynamic, larger-than-life characters my father did. I think I was somebody who was basically struggling for confidence. I watch my eight-year-old son now, and he's much more outgoing, more gregarious, more apt to speak his mind than I was at that age. I was a little more withdrawn. I would say that insecurity came from not enough foundation work. Certainly when I did become a drama major at the University of California at Santa Barbara, it turned out to be a surprisingly good program. And after that, in 1967, I went to the National Playwrights Conference for the first time, which was this great opportunity to work with all these playwrights—Sam Shepard, Israel Horovitz, Lanford Wilson, John Guare. I went to New York and studied for about six months, but before very long, I came out to California. I didn't have a lot of training. I was always running on raw instinct rather than knowing some of the basic classical techniques of how to ground yourself, and I was a little lost as to how to approach characterizations. I relied a tremendous amount on my own sense of honesty, which is a painful, uncomfortable way to work—and also limiting in terms of playing different types of characters.

What types of roles did you get early on? Were there any where you had to be a stretcher-bearer or somebody like that?

I was discovered on a *CBS Playhouse*, in which I had the lead. And then I did an anti-Vietnam, antiwar picture called *Hail, Hero!*, in which I was in every scene. The best work that I actually did was a *Medical Center* in which I got to play a retarded boy. It was my first opportunity to play someone other than a sensitive young man. I was real, real pleased with it.

Playing that part was a step in that process of learning how to create a character?

Exactly. I did my homework, spent some time in hospitals and homes in L.A. getting the voice, the movements, everything like that.

There are two ways you can paint on a mask. One is you work and make this character—once you have that mask painted on, it allows you the freedom to do anything. *Wall Street* was that—creating this character who certainly had elements of myself but really was a creation. The other way is you wipe everything off, getting down closer and closer to yourself. Which is painful. And that was one of the techniques that I had to use in *Fatal Attraction*—all of a sudden you look and say, "Man, this is me." So the moments are real.

How important was a background story for you in playing Gordon Gekko in 'Wall Street'? When you were shooting, did you have to sit there and think, "Okay, get me into Gordon now?" Did you ever mentally revisit his past?

Not on a daily basis. For me, the wardrobe was the key—the hair, things like cuff links, suspenders, immediately gave me a costume. Gordon was what you might call a counter puncher—he'd always give the jab while the other guy was winding up, so he was always in your face one beat before. A city guy, very *clean*. Just like a white shark, you know, swimming and eating, swimming and eating. Anything that's in the way, just go right through it. His idea of being really well dressed is probably a little flashy. He didn't come from a well-to-do family.

In the script, he mentions his parents—he feels they were stepped on in a certain way by the world.

Maybe it boils down to how much drive came out of feeling the hurts inflicted on his parents—that feeling of being lower-class and fighting upward. He sure was not a hippie back in the Sixties. Gekko was always going to make it, you know? I think he started hustling at an early age. He was a real good reader of people. He surrounds himself with devotion, and he's very supportive of people around him. I think he found out early on what the true value of information was —this whole question of inside information is very much a gray area. This phenomenon of deregulation really happened in the last seven years, the Reagan era. So this guy probably exploded in the last five or six years.

And he becomes a kind of idol to Bud Fox, played by Charlie Sheen. This was Sheen's second outing with Oliver Stone.

Charlie actually gave me a little more insight into

Oliver. I asked him a couple of times about Oliver, and he gave me a few anecdotes about being in the Philippines [making *Platoon*]. I was real impressed with Charlie's professionalism, and he was very kind to me. I'd heard all this Brat Pack talk. All I saw was a young guy who was very hip to the fact that he had this wonderful opportunity. Not like these guys on TV series who assume that because the show's a hit, they're big stars.

For a scrapper, Gekko's also quite an aesthete.

He collects paintings and art because they connote some degree of culture and taste. But I really do think he has an ability to read into people and objects. He can look at a painting or look someone in the eye and judge.

When he's sparring with Terence Stamp's Wildman character, there's a kind of grudging respect, even as they trade dirty tricks.

Well, I was just thinking about that. The other thing that I drew upon—from my produciary background [*laughs*]—is that revenge is wonderful. Gekko thrives on the energy of anybody who's ever crossed him. He cherishes holding grudges. It gives him the fuel to keep going. I know that during all the years when I dealt with rejection on film projects, it was an emotion that gave me the endurance and stamina that I needed to get a picture made. Or in Gordon's case, to get deals done.

I suspect I'm not going to hear any names, but are there people around you'd still like to pay back?

No. Because to me, it was only a question of proving to them where the pictures they wouldn't make went—the great joy of seeing them in a restaurant about the fourth or fifth week after the picture was out, when it was number one, a big hit. Stopping by their table, just as nice as could be. Saying, "Hi, how you been? Good to see you."

Walk softly and carry a big hit.

With the success of *Cuckoo's Nest*, I was able to control my own destiny a little bit. One of the beauties of producing was that it took away the insecurity of never knowing where my next job was coming from.

That particular dish of revenge was shared by a bunch of you—there were five Oscars.

We were the dark horse; we were the independents with a picture nobody wanted to make. And we did it. So we took great satisfaction in the fact that it was great for all of our careers and that we all liked each other.

I've had a similar situation with *Fatal Attraction*. Sherry Lansing was one of my early supporters when she was an executive at MGM, when I was doing *Coma*. And then when I was doing *The China Syndrome*, at Columbia, she was the studio executive assigned to that picture. When she was president at Fox, we did *Star Chamber* together. I always tease about when they used to have meetings, and she'd suggest, "Well, what about Michael Douglas?" One day somebody said, "Can I ask you something? Are you fucking him?" [*Laughs*] And she said, "No, no, I just think . . ." She believed. I think it's apropos that tomorrow night I can have dinner with her, her partner, Stanley Jaffe, and [*Fatal Attraction* director] Adrian Lyne and celebrate—enjoy a success with friends who were part of it. Because you realize it's not true that a lot of people are real happy for you. So you have your handful of friends, and you have those people who are actually involved with that picture who you're still friends with. And that's about it.

Was that a lesson you learned as a young man about Hollywood?

My stepfather told me, when I was running around hysterically in junior high school, worrying who my friends were, "Look, you know, you'll be lucky in your lifetime if you can count your good friends on one hand." I remember being very shocked. And I think he's right. He's absolutely right. So I've got a lot of acquaintances.

One of the difficulties we have in this business is that our kind of lifestyle makes you go away for periods of time, or you have erratic schedules, and you don't seem to have continuity. You're incredibly busy, so you've got these large gaps of time during which you're not able to maintain friendships. But the beauty of it—and I guess it's really a sign of the good friends—is that when you do get together, it's like not a day has passed. I was also very fortunate being second generation and learning about the failures as well as the successes—which allows you to keep a better balance than a lot of people coming into this business from the outside.

In many ways, Hollywood still seems to be a small town. 'Fatal Attraction' came about after a chance encounter with Stanley Jaffe; you told him that you wanted to make a movie about lust.

Many, many years ago, I had been really attracted to a book called *Virgin Kisses*, written by Gloria Nagy. It was basically about how lust destroyed a married man's life. Then about four years ago, I ran into Stanley Jaffe on an airplane. We were comparing notes, which you do a lot. Sherry and Stanley develop projects, and they'd been working on this one for a while, and it had not been received well. I mean, Dan Gallagher [Douglas' character in *Fatal Attraction*] is not a sympathetic character. And at that point they said to me, "Well, here, we'll send you a draft, and if you're interested, we'll write it for you playing this part. And, you know, why don't you look at the drafts. You can throw in your two cents' worth and all that." So that's what happened. I looked and said, "Yeah, it's got a lot of promise." We worked on about two or three more drafts and started to try to find a director.

When you get involved in a script that way, what do you look for?

Number one, whether I think the movie works. Then I look at my part, see how I like it. I also see what my responsibility is, what my part's responsibilities are to the movie. So when I worked with them on the script, it was not in terms of my part. It was like working on making the picture better. And what ultimately happens is it becomes a collaborative form.

I remember there was a lot of discussion about the ending—we've had nine different endings in the script. In earlier drafts, the marriage was in much, much worse shape than it was in the movie. But the basic structure was there. The real problem was that we could not judge what the moral tenor was. And the tone had changed from when the marriage was bad. And there was a question about having sort of a nihilistic ending in which everybody lost—Alex [Dan's lover] killed herself, Dan went to jail, his wife, Beth, and the kid would be alone. One exciting thing for me was to take a character who initially was unattractive to the audience, who was an adulterer, and somehow switch the audience's allegiance around. That came about in terms of how strong the family unit was. That, and with the steady deterioration of Glenn's character. Yes, you can be sympathetic about a psychotic woman who is alone. But as soon as that woman begins to attack a family unit, then your sympathy for a mentally ill person is gone. So this was a natural evolution.

I've taken a lot of offense with certain people who jumped on the bandwagon that it was a marketing ploy that we reshot the ending. It really disregards the hundreds of hours spent by relatively intelligent people discussing and debating. A lot of Broadway plays first go out of town to try the play out. With a psychological thriller, there has got to be some kind of emotional release. The previous ending had an intellectual resolution—valid, but you didn't get off.

People are coming back to see this movie a second time. Was that part of your intention as filmmakers?

Christ, no. All you want to do is get them in seats. I just figure that if it's a story I really like and it's executed well, there's going to be a few other people out there who might want to go see it, too. I've never tried to second-guess what the market is.

That first time you make love with Glenn Close's character, Alex—to what degree were you going for some laughs in the middle of this outrageous sex?

I always thought that if you succeed in making the sex work on film, you always need some kind of a release. 'Cause if it's really working, audiences get uncomfortable. After the hot thing, I wanted to get a laugh. I think it's important to mix comedy with sex.

Glenn Close has usually been seen as this pure, prim figure.

And that's why we cast her, because no one's really going to suspect her after the roles she's played.

Because you've been a producer, you're used to having a good deal of input from producing. Do you think you will always want that kind of participation in writing the script, casting—those decisions?

I would hope that even as an actor for hire, I would be working with people who were confident enough that I could always share all my thoughts with them. Not necessarily get my way. I mean, we had lots of debates making *Fatal*. But we had a healthy balance between the two producers and the director and myself. That's the way I like to work. When I'm the producer, it's not much different, other than the actual physical chores. I've never had a situation where I've had to pull rank. It's always been resolved. Any discussion. My cut has always been the director's cut.

What about directing one of these days?

Yeah, some day. I've worked so hard and long just to get my acting career in this kind of position that I can't imagine taking the mandatory eighteen months off to direct a picture in the next four or five years. And I've also been fortunate enough to be included in the creative process, so that I haven't ever felt deprived of my input.

Do you think the fact that Adrian Lyne's last picture, '9½ Weeks,' was rebuffed critically and commercially made him hungrier for a success this time around?

Yeah. I saw a vengeance. I saw an obsession. I saw a blind conviction that was real exciting.

It's hard to find male directors who don't have a feeling of either competition or slight jealousies about wanting to act themselves. Adrian adores actors. He's supportive and encourages them to take chances. He really was instrumental in letting me believe that my screen presence alone was enough. Which is something

I think I was insecure about—your ability to react without jacking it up, pumping it up.

Yeah, because Dan Gallagher is a passive guy.

It was a frustrating part. The picture used to really drive me nuts. It's his inability to act. And it was structured that way. There were places where I felt handcuffed—you want Dan to do something. I shared this with my dad: "All this is making me nuts, this inability to act." He says, "Well, listen, Mike, you do nothing better than anybody I know." He used to watch me on *Streets of San Francisco*, when I would just stand there and have nothing to do. He was saying my presence—just being there, having to do nothing—was adequate.

There is a political component to your life that you don't talk about that much. Do you feel that now that you are more visible, you have more of a duty to be a spokesman for causes you believe in—like the Committee of Concern, which tries to educate the American public about the players and policies in Central America?

Well, it's not a question of a duty. I just run out of time. I feel frustrated that other than making financial contributions and lending my name, I haven't been that involved the last couple of years. I liked to think that some of our efforts over the last six years in Central America have had some input into the American public's perceptions. Reagan has isolated himself to a certain degree on Central America and does not really maintain the kind of popular support that he would have liked to have had.

Do you feel optimistic about the economy?

No, I'm not optimistic. We accused Jimmy Carter of presiding over a big deficit, but it was a fraction of what's happened in the last seven or eight years. We've lost our middle class in the last few years.

'Wall Street' has a political message—it questions this country's values. And you and Oliver Stone share similar political views. When you and he first met, did you broach any issues, or did you talk purely about the character and the script?

We just talked specifically. I mean, we all have our political views. He teases me about my not getting my fingers dirty anymore—about my being a producer and financing films on Wall Street. I tease him that his career *did* exist before *Salvador*. I like to remind him of *The Hand* and a few other films he made [*laughs*]. See, he likes to barb. He likes to mix it up in a nice way. I'm fond of that.

I had been at a loss in the late Seventies, early Eighties, as to what was an issue. And Oliver's raised two of them well with *Salvador* and *Wall Street*. And I'm really impressed with that. He's a hell of a writer and a fine director. But in my case, I don't think it was a loss of political energy. *Romancing* was an effort to get away from social issues, because I wanted to do something lighter. And my life, my career, got excessively busy. I do feel the strings being pulled to get back to some more socially redeeming projects. Although *Fatal Attraction* and *Wall Street* do basically deal with the key moral issues of our time: lust and greed.

29
Sting

INTERVIEWED BY DAVID FRICKE (1988)

This was a very special encounter with Sting: his first major interview in years with absolutely no references to obscure German philosophers, no extended discussions of advanced psychoanalytic theory and no classical or jazz music name-dropping. Frequently pasted by critics as pop's most pretentious star, as well as a man who knows too much in a genre that is supposed to be 95 percent inspiration, Sting sat down with ROLLING STONE *in November 1987, in Rio De Janeiro, Brazil, and talked plain and straight about the Police, politics and being pretentious and proud of it.*

"I'm being cast in this idea that rock stars should be idiots and should only be allowed on stage," he bristled. "And anyone who tries to break that mold is supposed to be pretentious."

Indeed, Sting embodies the very model of the Eighties pop god: photogenic, aligned with all the right social causes, disdainful of the crass immaturity of the music business, literate in his songwriting and well-versed in world music. But if he does often wear an intellectual mask to distinguish himself from the talking haircuts that crowd him on the charts, he proved here to be a frank and earnest interview subject, as open and articulate in discussions about the recent deaths of his parents as he was about the acrimonious collapse of the Police and the songwriting process.

After this interview, Sting did his talking from the stage for almost an entire year, first on an extensive world tour of his own, then as part of the Amnesty International's Human Rights Now! *rock revue with Peter Gabriel, Bruce Springsteen, Tracy Chapman and Youssou N'Dour.*

—D.F.

R O-O-OX-A-A-ANNE . . . . A-A-Anne. . . . You don't have to put on the red light . . . red light . . . red light . . ."

Sting's cool, bracing tenor cuts through the fierce midday heat, shooting across the seemingly endless soccer field in Rio de Janeiro's giant Maracana Stadium, ricocheting off the faraway balcony back toward the stage. The words, intertwined with Steve Coleman's eerie sax breaks, echo once, twice, sometimes even a faint third time in the expanse of this huge concrete frying pan, the largest stadium in the world.

Right now, during a sound check, Maracana is empty except for the star, his seven-piece band and a small army of roadies and local stagehands sweating buckets under the merciless Rio sun. But tonight, to witness the official opening night of Sting's 1987–88 world tour, an estimated 200,000 Brazilians will pack the Maracana field and bleachers, the largest single concert audience of Sting's solo career and the second largest of his entire life (the largest was with the Police at the Us Festival). Hell, this isn't an audience; it's a city unto itself, Rio de Sting, and the population absorbs Maracana's monster echo with its own hearty roar—"Stingé! Stingé!"

Statistics may not be the most accurate measure of his achievements, but the Cecil B. De Mille–like immensity of Maracana and its undulating waves of wall-to-wall humanity are testimony to the worldwide success Sting has attained less than two years after the breakup of the Police. Strangely enough, his former fellow officers, drummer Stewart Copeland and guitarist Andy Summers, are touring Brazil at the same time, in a band with bassist Stanley Clarke. The night before, in Porto Alegre, they played to 10,000 people—hardly small potatoes. For Sting, though, Maracana is just the beginning. The other dates on his South American tour are nearly all in supersized venues. The smallest show on the Brazilian leg is an arena date in São Paulo—capacity: a paltry 60,000.

"I don't really see giantism as success," Sting says the morning after Maracana, lounging in his hotel suite, which overlooks the quarter-moon curve of Copacabana Beach. "We went through that with the Police. We played Shea Stadium and these other massive places. Having done it, it doesn't mean that much anymore. Last night, I enjoyed it, and it was quite emotional at times. But it's not the goal."

The goal, it seems, is to avoid the predictable at all costs. Subvert the obvious. And, whenever possible, confound the skeptics. As

the voice, the face and the principal songwriting brain in the Police, Sting, né Gordon Sumner, was never shy about lancing the Top Forty with third-world grooves, literary allusions and twisted romance. On his own, he has been even bolder, deliberately testing the limits of his artistic license and the patience of his fans with deeper forays into jazz, ethnic music and highbrow scholarship.

This experimentation makes the payoffs that much more impressive. Sting's 1985 solo debut, *The Dream of the Blue Turtles,* abounded with musical and lyrical references to Prokofiev, Weather Report, Shakespeare and the British coal miners' strike—and sold more than 2 million copies. His current album, . . . *Nothing Like the Sun,* is like nothing else in the upper reaches of the charts. Dedicated to his mother, Audrey, who died during the making of the record after a two-year illness, it is a smorgasbord of high-stepping reggae, lilting Hispanic rhythm, big-band jazz and the whispery strum of Brazilian samba, linked by the theme of maternal strength in the face of male-triggered social and political disaster. Particularly powerful in this regard is "They Dance Alone," a moving tribute to the Chilean wives, mothers and daughters of "the disappeared."

Sting's ambition has earned him the disdain of jazz purists, who claim he taints jazz with pop banality, and a number of rock critics, who dismiss him as an aristocratic rockstar dilettante. Sting remains unfazed.

"What have I got to worry about, really?" he says. "Rejection? I can always say, 'They didn't understand.'" He laughs. "The audience of one, that's it. That's all I've ever had. Basically, it's nice to make pop music without necessarily following to the letter the formula that's presented. That's what makes pop interesting. Anything can happen."

"The thing I admire most about playing with Sting is that he has a very definite idea of what he wants, not what his *ego* wants," says saxophonist Branford Marsalis, a charter member of the *Blue Turtles* band who has rejoined Sting for his current U.S. tour. "To expect pop to have the same freedom that jazz has is ludicrous. But in the context of what we're doing, we have more freedom than any other pop group I've heard."

In addition, Sting has put his money where his mouth is by forming his own record label, Pangaea, which he hopes will be a home for inventive, otherwise uncategorizable music. A joint project with his co-manager Miles Copeland and Christine Reed, formerly an A&R exec with CBS Masterworks, Pangaea is, Sting says, "an extension of this thing that music shouldn't agree with what's imposed on it—the labels, the ghettos." In that spirit, initial Pangaea releases will include albums by Steve Coleman (who has played with bassist Dave Holland and leads his own group, Five Elements) and a Nashville-based duo, Kennedy Rose ("a female Everly Brothers," claims Sting), and the reissue of renegade composer-arranger Kip Hanrahan's critically acclaimed American Clavé catalog. Sting has a very full plate for '88: there are two imminent additions to his film *oeuvre* (*Julia and Julia*, with Kathleen Turner, and *Stormy Monday*, with Melanie Griffith and Tommy Lee Jones) as well as the Amnesty International world tour with Peter Gabriel.

The Brazilian kickoff had a bitter twist for Sting. The day before the Rio show, his father, Ernest, died after an extended illness, barely six months after the passing of Sting's mother. Yet during the three sessions for this interview, Sting—himself the father of four children, two by his girlfriend, Trudie Styler, two by his ex-wife, Frances Tomelty—is thoughtful and straightforward about both his fame and his misfortune. He is also unapologetic about his work, confident it has a resonance even beyond the echoes of Maracana Stadium.

He's soon proved right about that. After the second session, he's called to the phone. There's a brief moment of silence as he listens to Kim Turner, his other co-manager, on the other end of the line. Then he suddenly shouts,

"Hurray!" It turns out the Chilean government board of censors has banned . . . *Nothing Like the Sun* because of the subject matter of "They Dance Alone" and its criticism of the Pinochet regime. Score one for the dilettante.

It's ironic that you're playing these Brazilian shows at the same time your former Police mates, Stewart Copeland and Andy Summers, are touring the country with Stanley Clarke.

That's macabre! They left this hotel the day I got here; I don't know what that means. Actually, I'm glad they're working. I'm glad they're playing. Andy's on my record, and I think he was really great. We got on. Our relationship is fairly easy, musically.

And otherwise?

It's okay. Being outside of the Police, I find it much easier to relate to them; we all do. Those little things we were stuck with, this grungy little group. Never again. It's much more pleasant now.

How unpleasant was it when the Police regrouped in 1986 to do that remake of "Don't Stand So Close to Me"?

It didn't work; you can never go back. It was awful. My idea was that rather than cashing our chips in and saying, "Here's a greatest-hits album, stick it out there," I wanted to put some effort into it. Okay, here we are, three musicians, ten years on. We have to be better musicians, we're better at making records. Let's see if we can make the songs better.

I don't know whether we did or not. But I thought it was worthy to try. Someone in the group described it as cynical, that we would do that, as if the original hits were sacrosanct. Which is utter bullshit. They're just songs.

Was the idea to do just that one song?

I wanted to do the whole album that way, redo all the hits we'd had. I wasn't supported in this belief.

How far did you get?

We did two songs, "Don't Stand So Close to Me" and "De Do Do Do, De Da Da Da."

The latter was never released. How did it turn out?

It was all right. I'd always felt that song had basically been dismissed as garbage.

As baby talk.

That was the whole idea! I was trying to make an intellectual point about how the simple can be so powerful. Why are our favorite songs "Da Doo Ron Ron" and "Do Wah Diddy Diddy"? In the song, I tried to address that issue. But everyone said, "This is bullshit, child's play." No one listened to the lyrics. Fuck you! Listen to the lyrics. I'm going to remake it again and put more emphasis on what I was talking about. [*Laughs*] It's very painful to be misunderstood.

You are frequently accused by critics of being pretentious. How painful is that?

What is pretension? I'm being cast in this idea that rock stars should be idiots and should only be allowed onstage. They shouldn't be allowed to speak or hear, they shouldn't be able to write prose or lead reasonable lives. It's the dictatorship of the critic. And anyone who tries to break that mold is supposed to be pretentious: pretending to be human, pretending to be thoughtful, pretending to be caring, pretending to be weak, pretending to be strong.

What saves you from pretension is the idea of metaphor. If you hit issues head-on—let's make the world a happier place, let's all love each other, let's stop war—there's no art to it. If you approach the issue through a metaphor, it's not pretentious—it's powerful. I don't think I can write without one. And if I am pretentious, it's because I haven't got a metaphor.

Was it hard coping with your mother's terminal illness while using it as a metaphor to create a body of work—the songs on your new album?

I felt my mother dying was something we had no choice about. She was going to die; it was a given. And how were we to approach it, my brothers and sisters and myself? The way I deal with it is to express it in terms of songs. I think it was much easier for me because I had this valve I could turn on. It was almost like exploiting it, which sounds awful, exploiting it for your own sanity.

My father died three days ago. I walked onstage the other night in front of all those people and felt like I had to celebrate him. It was like a wake for me, so it was kind of joyous. Why do we perform? One of the reasons I became a performer was to get attention from my parents. So the ultimate kind of attention you can get is to become a celebrity. Your parents *have* to take notice of you at that point.

One of the sadnesses is that that gig was a confirmation of beingness—and my parents were dead. At the same time, I feel very strongly that they were with me in a way. Every time I've been onstage since my mother died, I thought she was with me. Because she was trapped in this body that was increasingly useless to her. She was stuck in bed, she couldn't move. So I felt that my freedom and my life were hers. I'd phone her up and tell her what I'd done, and you could tell

she was living through me. That's what I wanted on Friday night, to do it for my parents, to do it for my father.

In "The Lazarus Heart," there is a striking contrast between the blood-and-flowers imagery and, in the last verse, your mother's deathbed courage. The song also has a surprisingly jubilant rhythm, considering the somber subject matter.

If we agree that the album is about mourning, then I needed to start it off in this special, joyful way. It's about rebirth, hopefully. I didn't want to just cry in my beer, do this moaning record about how awful life and death are. I wanted to say that, yes, we have to face death and there is a way to do it that isn't just moaning. We have to rejoice, in a way. It's a victory song.

That's the way my mother was. That's what she gave to me when I said goodbye to her. It was her incredible sense of humor and her sense that all was not lost. She was joking and she was loving. She gave me such an example of courage that I had no choice but to rejoice. That's why the record is happy. It's not a mournful record; it's an up record.

"They Dance Alone" is a mirror image of your own situation, with its portrait of the Chilean women dancing alone, not just in memory of the fathers, sons and husbands they lost but also in proud defiance of Pinochet's regime.

There is a certain victory implicit in what those women do, which is so much more powerful than throwing petrol bombs or burning cars—that negative loop. It's not terribly positive to say the end is nigh and all is terrible. I don't want to write songs that just confirm that nihilism and gloom, that there is no future. If I write about issues that are sad or horrific, I want there to be light at the end of the tunnel. And there will only be light at the end of the tunnel if we want it. That song reflects that. It is a very sad song, but at the end it is victorious. One day that country I'm singing about will be free. I hope so.

Your last tour of South America was with the Police. How aware were you at that time of the politics and the oppression in the countries you visited—Chile, for example?

I was already a member of Amnesty International, and I asked them about their position on bands going there. They said, "You should go. It's not like South Africa. You're not there to uphold an elite section of society." If anything, at the time, Chile was a closed society. If it's closed, they can get away with anything. By us going, they felt we could help open it up.

I was very depressed, frankly. I went along with all this information that Amnesty had given me about what was happening there. We got to this big gig; I looked at the audience, and I didn't see any torturers out there, or colonels. It was kids. Yet on every street corner there was a tank. It was really awful, and yet a really beautiful country, with a wonderfully spontaneous audience, like last night. There was so much passion in the audience. Yet outside there were all these fucking guns. Chile is something that has stayed with me for a long time.

Before you joined the Police and saw the world, what was your songwriting like? What did you write about?

It was pretty much like what I write now. I see songwriting very much as a craft, which is learned by trying to handle almost every style. And once you've got your chops together, songwriting is a modular system. You chop, you change. I'm quite adept at writing songs. What you can never be adept at is being in tune with inspiration. That's the Great Accident, the Great Imponderable. I used to get so terrified of not being able to write a song. "What am I going to write about? I'm totally empty of ideas and inspiration." And then I realized after about five years of this terrible block that some of the time you have to be on "input." You just have to receive and then retransmit it and hope it comes out as something else.

Did you suffer from writer's block with the Police?

Yeah, all the time. I used to have awful sleepless nights, that any talent I had was gone.

Was it the pressure of being expected to write all the songs? Intraband jealousies over your being the principal songwriter?

The real pressure was not having the time to sit and think. Just being on this roundabout, touring all the time, TV appearances. I didn't have time to be on input. It wasn't rivalry in the band. Maybe there was, but I never thought about it. The songs spoke for themselves. In the end, I didn't have to defend myself that much.

Were there particular songs that reinforced your confidence as a songwriter?

When I wrote "Every Breath You Take," I knew immediately it was a hit. When I wrote "Don't Stand So Close to Me," I knew that was a hit. There was no arguing with those songs.

Was that the idea, to write hit singles?

Yes. We were a hit band. Our albums were supplements to the hits. We did some good album work, but it wasn't consistent. The albums were uneven.

For example?

Now we're going to get into band politics. I don't want to discuss this.

How would you compare '. . . Nothing Like the Sun' to a Police album, like 'Zenyatta Mondatta' or 'Ghost in the Machine'?

When we first started out, we had a fairly common idea of what we wanted to be—"the thing." We polished this jewel, and that was it. But as we developed as people, and as celebrities, as individuals, by natural law nobody could hide behind me and say, "Whatever Sting says is right." They had different views and ideas. So the whole thing had to explode. Except I always had a clear idea of what I wanted to do. I'd write twelve songs, have the album title sorted out—I knew what I wanted. Then I was presented with this other group of ideas. I just could not see it. And of course it caused friction.

It's much easier now. I don't have to deal with the bullshit. If you don't like someone's song, it's a bit like saying their girlfriend is ugly. There is no tactful way of saying it. But at the end of the day, if you want to have something that works, you have to do that.

Are you worried about repeating yourself? Some of your recent songs sound very much alike: "Sister Moon," on the new album, bears a suspicious resemblance to "Moon over Bourbon Street," from 'The Dream of the Blue Turtles.' "Rock Steady" has the same jazzy strut of "Consider Me Gone."

I kind of like it. The analogy is that of a painter doing various studies of the same still life, changing the angle slightly. I like the idea of sequels. "If You Love Somebody Set Them Free" is a sequel to "Every Breath You Take," lyrically the mirror image. "Sister Moon" and "Moon over Bourbon Street" are kind of sequential. Album by album, you keep referring to things. I can take a line from one song, stick it in another and move on.

You've admitted that "Every Breath You Take" was in fact an aggregate of every timeworn rock & roll riff and phrase you could think of. Where's the originality in that?

What's unique about it is the sound of my voice. There's no one else who sings like me. They might sing better than me, but no one sings exactly like me. My voice sticks out on the radio by a mile. And as long as I have this voice, what I do is original.

So I don't worry about originality. As long as it comes through me, it will have that stamp on it. "Every Breath You Take" is an archetypal song. If you have a major chord followed by a relative minor, you're not original. A million songs have been written that way. But you can't take away from the power of "Every Breath You Take," because it was *us*, the Police.

On '. . . Nothing Like the Sun' you seem so interested in musical cross-pollination that you skip over the basic charms of simple guitar riffs and song hooks.

Having made some of the simplest and most direct pop music, I don't know whether I want to do it again.

But this music, taken to a logical conclusion, can only get more complicated and, maybe, indigestible. In the Seventies, they called it art rock.

When this record was first completed and handed to the record company, they threw up their hands. It wasn't simple enough or directed toward the charts. And I said, "Why underestimate the record-buying public? Why do you imagine that they have to be spoon-fed all the time? Does it have to be so utterly simple? I don't think so." Now the record is doing well on the radio and in the shops; the concerts are selling well. It confirms my belief that sophistication, or intended sophistication, is not the kiss of death. As long as you're grounded somewhere in common sense.

In the chorus of "Englishman in New York," you sing, "I'm a legal alien." How can someone who aspires to be so worldly still feel so out of place?

The song is about someone else. It's about Quentin Crisp [a British writer, the author of *The Naked Civil Servant*]. I think he is one of the most courageous men I've ever met, and one of the wittiest. He was flamboyantly gay at a time when it was physically dangerous to be gay. He lives near the Bowery, and he has an unbelievable sense of humor and joy in life that everybody can draw a lesson from. It was my song to appreciate his singularity.

But it's about me, too. It's very important for any kind of writer to have a period in exile. One, it makes you see the country you're in a little clearer than the people there see it. Two, it makes you see the place you come from a little clearer. And I do regard myself as an exile. I've chosen to live in New York for the past two years because of the musicians I play with, because I find it inspiring, because I meet interesting people much more easily than I do in London. It's less phobic here.

At the same time, I know I'm not an American citizen. There are certain things about America that terrify me—its foreign policy, religion—and there's a lot about America that I love. But I'm not assimilated. I don't want to belong anywhere. I come from a place I'm proud to come from. That's almost enough. To settle down somewhere for me seems to equate with a sense of decay.

Last year you did a movie in Newcastle, England, with Melanie Griffith, 'Stormy Monday,' in which you play a sleazy jazz-club owner. What was it like going back to your hometown?

It was great fun to go back, to see people I'd been to school with, to walk the streets I used to walk. I went past all the schools I'd ever been to and all the houses I'd lived in. I basically spent three weeks there assessing my life and how it had changed, for better or worse. I don't think I got any real answers I could write down, but there was certainly something profound about the experience. My mother had just died, my father was dying. It was just the right time to do it.

When you walked down those streets, was it with a sense of fondness, nostalgia? Or triumph, that you'd escaped and beaten the system?

Living there gave me a sense of politics, a sense of poverty, a sense of identity, a sense of beauty and also a sense of what's ugly, because they're all there in Newcastle. Going back there, I saw very clearly why I wanted to be an artist, why I wanted to express ideas and why I started very early.

I lived in this street, and at the bottom of this street was a shipyard with enormous tankers. In 1967, they built the biggest ship in the world, which was a million tons, the *Northumbria*. This thing blotted out the sun. It was at least four times the height of our house. All my life I had a symbol of this thing they'd built up, this massive, monstrous creature. The men would be like little ants, putting pop rivets into it, thousands of men walking down the street to work on this thing.

I don't know what it means, but I know it means something very special to me. It gives you a sense of enormity. If I'd been brought up on a housing estate, a featureless place, then I'd no doubt be a very different person. But I was brought up in this Ridley Scott movie: acetylene lamps going off all the time, huge cranes swinging over me. I guess I got a taste for things that are big, on a large scale.

How would you assess your film career to date? High-profile projects like 'Dune' and 'The Bride' weren't exactly boffo at the box office, even less so with the critics.

There's no actor who's been in nothing but great movies, nothing but successes. You can make a few lousy movies in relative obscurity. But my celebrity, if you like, means people hang a movie on me, even if I'm just doing a cameo in it. It becomes "Sting's movie." I agreed to do this cameo in *Dune* because I like David Lynch's work. Then it becomes *my* film. And because it wasn't a mammoth hit, it was marked down as my failure.

How serious are you about acting?

It's a way of throwing a curve. When I made *Brimstone and Treacle,* I was the golden boy of English pop. I was the George Michael–Simon LeBon of the time. I had blond hair, a family. Everything was nice. So I took this role as a fucking pervert who screws paraplegics. Suddenly it's "Ugh!"

I love playing the bad guy. It frees me. The role of pop star is the troubadour, the good guy. You're on the side of wholesome things; it's boring. After a whole day of being good and liberal and wonderful, it feels so good to be able to take your shoes off and be downright evil.

You were quoted two years ago in 'Playboy' as saying, "I hate most of what constitutes rock music—which is basically middle-aged crap." Given that you're getting toward middle age yourself, whose crap were you referring to?

Anybody older than me! [*Laughs*] I'm not sure what I meant then. What I mean now is people who are in their late thirties or forties pretending to be teenagers. There are a couple of groups on MTV at the moment who are clearly in their forties singing love songs to strumpets in high heels. This isn't middle-aged music. It's menopausal music. Own up. You're forty-five years old. You've got children who are twenty. Why the fuck are you chasing after these floozies? Why are you wearing this corset, for a start? That's undignified. It devalues the whole exercise. I can take bands like Poison and Mötley Crüe. They're aggressive and full of machismo and warrior chic. But they're young; it makes sense. But these old farts—please!

Meanwhile, the mantle of responsibility and adult expression in pop is being passed down from the Beatles and Dylan to your generation—you, Peter Gabriel, U2.

I think we're wiser than that generation; we're cleverer. And we're more cynical, just as the generation that has evolved from us. We can't be the same as the Beatles are, and the bands that follow us won't be the same as us. We'll be irrelevant and obsolete in time. Every day you practice for your obsolescence and hope you can still be laughing.

After all these years, aren't you tired of the name Sting? It started out as a nickname, but it's a public identity now. If you want to, say, write a string concerto, calling it Sting's First Concerto in A-Flat hardly lends it a ring of authority.

It's no sillier than Beethoven or Mozart. What's in a name? It's my name now. Gordon Sumner is a name that I don't ever use. I will sign a check with it, and my passport says that. But it's not a name I use with anyone who knows me. My children call me Sting, and they have no questions about it. It's also very useful. It's very graphic. It creates a kind of mystique, although that wasn't the original intention. It was a nickname, given to me. But it created a curiosity which is [*smiles mischievously*] well founded.

You've never regretted it or considered changing it?

Once you've established a certain identity, like Johnny Rotten, which was wonderful, to back off from it is a problem. Elvis Costello tried it and realized it wasn't right. It's too self-conscious. If I ever back off from it, I'll have a real good reason. But right now I don't feel like it. Again, it's a spanner in the works. Can this man really be taken seriously with such a ridiculous name?

30
Robin Williams

INTERVIEWED BY BILL ZEHME (1988)

Stand-up comedy is a performance art that is often forsaken by its most gifted practitioners in favor of film. Richard Pryor, Steve Martin, Eddie Murphy, Robin Williams—each of these men started out in stand-up, and each has eventually heeded Hollywood's talent-hungry call. The results have varied. Murphy's sensational appeal as a screen performer has obliterated traditional assumptions about race as a box-office issue. Martin's film career, while low-key by comparison, has been distinguished by his taste and intelligence, as well as by the humane glow with which he has managed to imbue even the broadest of farces. Pryor, on the other hand—who may be the most monumentally talented stand-up artist ever to take a stage—has never found a screen vehicle that came anywhere near matching his potential.

And then there's Robin Williams. An actor of considerable charm, Williams' screen oeuvre was largely a mess until 1988, when he broke through as a speed-rapping military deejay in 'Good Morning, Vietnam.' Ironically, the film had much less to do with its real-life subject, ex-Army radioman Adrian Cronauer, than it did with Williams' own well-established facility for dazzling flights of comedic invention. As we have seen with Pryor, this is not the sort of talent that translates easily or often to movies, and the question of whether Williams will continue to grow as an actor remains open. (He spent the fall of 1988 in New York appearing with Steve Martin, F. Murray Abraham and Bill Irwin in a Lincoln Center revival of Samuel Beckett's stage classic, 'Waiting for Godot.') On the other hand, he may never be more astonishing than when he simply stands up behind a microphone and free-associates his way into the comedic stratosphere. The man has an amazing brain, and on a good night, his torrential improvisations can outstrip even those of his pioneering idol, Jonathan Winters—an astounding feat, indeed.

Williams was just beginning to promote 'Good Morning, Vietnam'—and to reflect on his new drug-free and nonpromiscuous lifestyle—when Bill Zehme was assigned to interview him in California. It was one of those interview situations that requires a certain amount of hanging out. Fortunately, Williams, as you'll see, is always on a roll.

—K. L.

H E IS STILL a Kamikaze of The Night. In the cockpit of his blue four-wheel-drive vehicle, he purrs through the hushed, sloping arteries of San Francisco, seeking out comedy huts to raid, improv stages to commandeer. He never strikes before midnight, never allows word of his attack to leak out in advance. He likes it that way. It is the only instant gratification he permits himself nowadays, the only vice he has not sworn off. "Joke 'em if they can't take a fuck," he has said, not a little ruefully. Laughs are all that is left, and laughs are what he craves most. Okay, maybe laughs and a thriving movie career, but we'll get to that.

Robin Williams lives in San Francisco. His family migrated to the Bay Area from the Midwest when he was a teenager, and now he has come home to stay, to reclaim normalcy in his life. He has vanquished the demons that had ravaged his reputation: drugs, liquor, womanizing. His primary motivation was the birth of his son, Zachary, who is now nearly five. But despite fatherhood's cleansing effect, his nine-year marriage to Valerie Velardi is in disrepair. They have been separated—on amicable terms—for more than a year, with no resolution on the horizon. (Williams' father died last October, compounding the inner turmoil.) Williams now keeps company with his personal assistant, Marsha Garces, a petite brunette. It is she, in fact, who unfailingly rides copilot during his nocturnal comedy missions.

On successive nights in mid-January, they zero in on a pair of favorite targets: an upscale north-of-North-Beach club called Cobb's and a scruffy Richmond District walk-in closet called the Holy City Zoo. The latter is where it all began for Williams, where he worked his way from behind the bar to the stage. These days, Williams, ever the polite interloper, will not lunge for the microphone until all of the scheduled comics have finished their sets. He lingers outside or on a secluded bar stool—usually with a hood yanked down over his forehead—nursing his anonymity before moving in for the kill.

The kill, as perpetrated by Williams, has always been a thing to behold. His brain fires off a synaptic staccato of lunatic *frissons*. His rubbery face twists and congeals. Marauding voices take his tongue hostage. And on these chilly nights, his antics are as fecund as ever. He switches mineral-water bottles from table to table, announcing, "It's a little game we like to call San Francisco roulette." He is Bernhard Goetz taking a Rorschach test ("Is it Oprah Winfrey?"); a male lesbian ("I feel like a man trapped inside a man's body"); a channeled spirit called Limptha, "an 8,000-year-old retail salesman that somehow speaks English perfectly"; and a swishy gumshoe ("The fog wraps around me like a cheap mink coat—that's the way I like it").

Late in his set at the Holy City Zoo, a back-row inebriate begins to chant, *"Popeye! Popeye!"* Williams, a bit agitated, leans forward and solicitously lectures him: "No, Lumpy, no more Popeye. But I have a new movie that just might work, and if not, I'll be off somewhere shouting, *'Show me a vowel!'* There's a scary thought, boy."

He refers, of course, to *Good Morning, Vietnam,* the Barry Levinson film that has been hailed as the first big-screen project properly suited to the comedian's frenetic genius. More important, it also promises to be Williams' first unqualified box-office bonanza (in its three weeks of limited release, *GMV* earned $1 million playing on only four screens; in its first weekend of wide release, it earned nearly $12 million).

It has been a long time coming. After exploding upon the scene ten years ago as a hyperkinetic extraterrestrial in ABC's hitcom *Mork & Mindy,* Williams embarked on a meandering film career. Only his canny performances in George Roy Hill's *World According to Garp* and Paul Mazursky's *Moscow on the Hudson* earned critical huzzahs for the Juilliard-trained actor. The rest of his *oeuvre* has become the soggy mulch of dolorous cable programming: *Popeye, The Survivors, The Best of Times, Club Paradise.*

Now, as military deejay Adrian Cronauer in *Good Morning, Vietnam,* Williams is at last happily typecast as an exultant anarchist. Handling the Saigon morning-drive shift on Armed Forces Radio in 1965, he is the father of shock radio, stirring platoons in the fields with non-issue sarcasm. Williams, sans constraint of script, pursues his inimitable manic riffs behind Cronauer's microphone. He becomes, in quicksilver turns, Walter Cronkite, Gomer Pyle, Elvis Presley, Mr. Ed, Richard Nixon and a host of chowder-head officers. As a fey military fashion consultant who disapproves of camouflage: "You know, you go in the jungle, make a statement. If you're going to fight, *clash!*" As LBJ, explaining his daughter's ornithological middle name: "Lynda *Dog* would be too cruel."

The role fits. "It's amazing to me that some people have seen this and said, 'Well, that's what Robin *does,*'" says director Barry Levinson. "That's a bit like saying Fred Astaire dances well."

The Levinson-Williams dynamic has proved so copacetic that already there is talk of a second collaboration, possibly on a film entitled *Toys,* which would explore the eccentricities of the toy industry. And there are plans for Williams and Steve Martin to share the stage this fall in Samuel Beckett's *Waiting for Godot,* directed by Mike Nichols, at New York City's Lincoln Center.

These are bittersweet times for Robin Williams: personal life in flux, professional life in the ascendant. Yet, as his longtime manager, Larry Brezner, explains, "he is handling the crises in a really mature way. There was a point at which Robin would have simply run off and refused to face difficulty. Now, maybe for the first time in his life, he is an adult."

The newly introspective Robin Williams was in evidence throughout this interview. During the discussion, he swallowed a gallon of coffee ("Betty Ford speed balls"), flounced perkily upon a couch and summoned the usual menagerie of comic voices. And when the interviewer brandished a vintage 1979 plastic Mork doll at the outset, Williams barely blanched.

*D*o *you recognize this guy?* [*Hands Williams the doll.*]

[*In a geriatric warble*] Oh, *look,* from the *old* days! Here, let me check the nose to see if there's anything up his nostrils! [*Inspects doll.*] This way we'll know if it's authentic. This is amazing. This is the doll that had the bad voice backpack where you pull the string and hear garbled sentences. Some people sued because some dolls in the Midwest actually said, "Go fuck yourself."

Strangely enough, its body is dated 1973 and the head 1979.

Oh, that's scary. Then the body is obviously from an old G.I. Joe doll or maybe a Ken or a Barbie. Yes, it's probably from a *Barbie* doll. "Mommy, look, Mork has tits!" It's very strange to see this again. It was also strange to see them dismembered after the show was canceled. You'd see 'em hanging out of garbage cans, burned. It's so weird.

I don't know whether I'm experiencing nostalgia or nausea looking at this. It's like a combination of both. But that's a great way to start an interview. "I handed him the Mork doll." Well. Let's put this away for now, shall we?

All right. Do you think Mork complicated your progress in Hollywood?

Hardly. You can't say that something that took you from zero to a hundred was damaging to your progress. It certainly wasn't a hindrance economically, either. And no matter what happened on the TV series, I always had the other image: the nightclub comedian. If I'd just done Mork and nothing else, it might've been dangerous. But I always had a total other outlet beyond that character. I thank God for cable TV. Without it, I think it would be death for comedians.

Did you ever find the transition from TV to films unwieldy? It seemed in some ways like bringing a Tasmanian devil into captivity.

Some of the reviews have indicated that. I've had an odd habit of choosing projects that were the opposite of me, sometimes to the detriment. People are now saying about *Good Morning, Vietnam,* "This film is basically you and what you do best. So why did you wait eight years?" Well, I made other choices. I wanted to go against what I was doing on TV—not just with *Mork & Mindy* but the cable stuff as well. I was saying, in effect, "I'll *act*. I'll show you *I can act*."

If 'Good Morning, Vietnam' hadn't worked out, what do you imagine the status of your film career would be? Did you feel like "If this one doesn't hit, I'm hosed"?

You're not hosed, totally. You simply slip down the comedy food chain, that list of people who get scripts. It exists. From the top there's Eddie Murphy and Bill [Murray] and Steve [Martin]. I guess on the next level there's Tom Hanks, myself, John Candy—there's a lot of us. It all kind of works that way.

If this film had failed, I'd go down another couple of notches. So you have to work your way back up again or do character parts—or you fall back and punt. Now, with this, I knew I had this open field to run through. The radio broadcasts obviously afforded me the freedom to improvise, yet the story had dramatic elements that provided some interesting turns. It was a chance to fuse those two things together.

Hasn't it confounded you that Eddie Murphy can sniff out sure-fire parts almost effortlessly?

Very much so. He's instinctual, like a shark who knows where the blood is. He's only made a few mistakes. He knows what his area is and what he does. That's why he's on top of the script food chain.

Do you agree with those who feel that you'd never found the right role onscreen?

Well, like I said, it was part ego, part stubbornness, in trying to do something unexpected. Then there were other times when I took on slight projects, thinking, "I can fix this." I got suckered into a couple films like that—*The Best of Times, Club Paradise*. I thought, "Well, they'll give me the freedom to do my thing," but it turned out they didn't.

Also, for the first time I didn't have fear or tension. Barry Levinson kind of took away the onus of being "on." He would surreptitiously roll cameras and not go through the whole thing of "We've got speed and—*action!*" I could *ease* into a scene, and it helped me a lot. I started to relax.

The real Adrian Cronauer wasn't exactly the radio desperado you portrayed him as.

No, he's a very straight guy. He looks like Judge Bork. In real life he never did anything outrageous. He did witness a bombing in Saigon. He wanted to report it—he was overruled, but he said okay. He didn't want to buck the system, because you can get court-martialed for that shit. So, yes, we took some dramatic license.

But he did play rock & roll, he did do characters to introduce standard army announcements, and "*Goooood* morning, Vietnam" really was his signature line. He says he learned whenever soldiers in the field heard his sign-on line, they'd shout back at their radios, "*Gehhhhht* fucked, Cronauer!"

I heard you improvised several characters on mike that we never saw in the movie. Do you remember any?

We left out a lot of stuff because the jokes just took too long to set up. Some other stuff might have been too rough. I was trying a riff on booby traps and said [*as black GI*], "Now, if it was a pussy trap, people would line up to get in." Armed Forces Radio used to give out winning bingo numbers, so I tried this: "Our lucky bingo winners are 14, 12 and 35. If you've been with any of these girls, call your medic immediately!"

Do you think Bob Hope approved of you moving in on his territory? It looked like he gave you the cold shoulder on the Carson show a few weeks ago.

[*As Hope*] "Yeah, *wiiiiild*, isn't he?" I don't know. Certainly, there's that line about him in the film: "Bob Hope doesn't play police actions. Bob likes a *big room*." I think Hope knew about that, because he leaned over to me at one point and said, "You know, I was there in '65, but they didn't want to get all the guys in one place." At one point he was talking about going to the Persian Gulf, and I said, "I'll go if you like." He said, "Yeah, *right*." Translated: "I'd no sooner have you there than a third testicle."

Let's try mounting a brief retrospective reconsideration of your filmography. What did you think of 'Popeye'?

Popeye was a sweet-enough character. I had to dub that movie over twice, though, because people couldn't understand what I was saying. I sounded like a killer whale farting in a wind tunnel. The weirdest thing of all was to watch it at one of those Hollywood premieres, which are rough to begin with. But when a film doesn't work—[*simulates a seizure*] *oooh!* I remember walking out and seeing this fifty-foot can of spinach. It was like *2001*, but on bad acid.

What about 'Garp'?

I think *Garp* is a wonderful film. It may have lacked a certain madness onscreen, but it had a great core. It had a wonderful sense of family. Maybe if I had known more about children at the time, I could have done more with it. I would love to take now what I know about my son and the powerful feeling of parenthood and play Garp again.

'Moscow on the Hudson'?

I loved doing it. Immersing yourself into another

language and culture is wonderful. Oddly, it was a little bit like Mork in that I was looking at the American culture from the outside. People may have thought the ending broke down and got a little saccharine. Maybe. I'll always remember leaving some screening where a woman came up and said, "You are really hairy." She was referring to that scene in the bathtub where my body just looked like fur. She went, "Jesus, are you some sort of monkey?" "Thank you, thank you very much, glad you enjoyed the film. . . ."

For the first time ever you're seeing a therapist. People around you are saying you're saner than ever.

[*Grinning*] Yeah, they bought it.

Has inner peace been difficult to achieve?

Oh, I don't have inner peace. I don't think I'll ever be the type that goes, "I am now at one with myself." Then you're fucking *dead*, okay? You're out of your body. I do feel much calmer. And therapy helps a little. . . . I mean, it helps *a lot*. It makes you reexamine everything: your life, how you relate to people, how far you can push the "like me" desire before there's nothing left of you to like. It makes you face your limitations, what I can and can't do.

The hardest word of all to say is *no*. Bette Davis told me, back when I was doing the revival of *Laugh-In* about ten years ago, "The one word you'll need is *no*." The secret is to be able to turn things down, to not take on projects like *The Best of Times* or *Club Paradise* just because they say they want you. If they can't get you, they'll get anybody, so wise up. They'll take Gary Coleman.

You don't audition on a regular basis, do you?

I have recently. I'm not going to play that game of [*indignantly*] "What do you mean, *audition?* I'm *Robin Williams!*" Fuck it, I'll go read. It's worth it to try. And it felt better to read with somebody than to get hired and not have the chemistry work out. It's sobering, too, because a couple of parts have fallen through.

I read for a movie with DeNiro [*Midnight Run*], to be directed by Marty Brest. I met with them three or four times, and it got real close, it was almost there, and then they went with somebody else. The character was supposed to be an accountant for the Mafia. Charles Grodin got the part. I was craving it. I thought, "I can be as funny," but they wanted someone obviously more in type. And in the end, he *was* better for it.

But it was rough for me. I had to remind myself, "Okay, come on, you've got other things."

Sounds like Robin Williams has grown up.

[*Facetiously*] Yeah, right. [*As Freudian analyst*] "But you still talk about your dick a lot, though, don't you?"

It's been a tough year with the death of my father, the separation from my wife, dealing with life, with business, with myself. Someone said I should send out Buddhist thank-you cards, since Buddhists believe that anything that challenges you makes you pull yourself together.

You used to refer to your father as Lord Posh—he was an uncommonly elegant man, a powerful automobile executive. Did you see him any differently at the end?

I got to know another side in the last few years. I saw that he was funkier, that he had a darker side that made the other side work. He was much older than me; he died at eighty-one. Up until four or five years ago, I kept distance out of respect. Then we made a connection. It's a wonderful feeling when your father becomes not a god but a man to you—when he comes down from the mountain and you see he's this man with weaknesses. And you love him as this whole being, not as a figurehead.

Were you with him when he died?

I was here in San Francisco, and he died at home, out in Tiburon [a nearby suburb]. So I was close. He'd had operations and chemotherapy. It's weird. Everyone always thinks of their dad as invincible, and in the end, here's this little, tiny creature, almost all bone. You have to say good-bye to him as this very frail being.

At least he was at home and died very peacefully in his sleep. My mother thought he was still asleep. She came downstairs and kept trying to shake him. She called me that morning and said [*calmly and evenly*], "Robin, your father's dead." She was a little in shock, but she sounded happy in a certain way, if only because he went without pain.

Is it true that you scattered his ashes?

[*Chuckles*] Yeah, it was amazing. It was sad but also cathartic and wonderful in the sense that it brought my two half brothers and me together. It kind of melded us closer as a family than we've ever been before. We've always been very separate.

That day we gathered right on the sea in front of where my parents live. It was funny. At one point, I had poured the ashes out, and they're floating off into this mist, seagulls flying overhead. A truly serene moment. Then I looked into the urn and said to my brother, "There's still some ashes left, Todd. What do I do?" He said, "It's Dad—he's holding on!" I thought, "Yeah, you're right, he's hanging on." He was an amazing man who had the courage not to impose limitations upon his sons, to literally say, "I see you have something you want to do—do it."

What has fatherhood taught you about yourself?

That most of your actions have consequences with the child. And I've learned to have the security not to worry that he will love me—as long as I keep the connection strong enough. I've learned not to try to force the love. You can't. All you can do is try to set up a world for him that's safe and stable enough to make him happy. I want to protect him and shield him from public sight. I want him to have his own life.

How is he handling your separation?

Very well. He's more comfortable with it now. He understands it. He sometimes gets confused and calls someone by the wrong name. But we have a good custody agreement, so he comes and goes freely. He knows exactly how many days he's here and how many days he's there. Children at his age do not want to deal with the anger and the volatility or whatever would develop. As long as things are peaceable, he's fine switching back and forth. Also, he doubles down at Christmas: "Look, I got this many dinosaurs."

Do you find yourself performing for him?

Yeah, and sometimes he'll love it. I did a Señor Wences thing for him. I dressed my fist in a napkin and was Mother Teresa. I played her drunk and made her drink water, which I'd spill down my arm. He liked that.

The hard part is when you really have to back off and provide him with the time to play alone. Children are a drug. I used to say they beat the shit out of cocaine: You're paranoid, you're awake, and you smell bad. It's this constant metamorphosis. This is a precious time. Some of those lines in *Garp* ring true. I never thought I would literally sit and watch a child sleep. But you can. I never thought that would be real.

You've been drug free for how long now?

Five years. Six months before Zach was born, I basically stopped everything.

Do you remember the last time you were on the cover of ROLLING STONE, *in 1982?*

Wasn't the basic premise that I'd cleaned up my act?

The headline was "Robin Williams Comes Clean." Was that honestly the end of the self-abusive chapter in your life?

There was no going back. I realized that the reason I did cocaine was so I wouldn't have to talk to anybody. Cocaine made me so paranoid: If I was doing this interview on cocaine, I would be looking out the window, thinking that somebody might be crawling up fourteen floors to bust me or kick down the door. Then I wouldn't have to talk. Some people have the metabolism where cocaine stimulates them, but I would literally almost get sleepy. For me, it was like a sedative, a way of pulling back from people and from a world that I was afraid of.

Going from zero to a hundred on the American fame-ometer, I take it, was a bit harrowing.

I was twenty-six or twenty-seven, and then, *bang,* there's all this money, and there are magazine covers. Between the drugs and the women and all that stuff, it's all coming at you, and you're swallowed whole. It's like *"Whoooaaa!"* Even Gandhi would have been kind of hard pressed to handle it well. [*As Gandhi on cocaine*] "Just one line, if you pleeeze. I'll just do a little and save *the world*—fuck India!"

Talking about your marriage five years ago, Valerie said, "If I had said, 'Don't cross this line,' he would have been long gone." In retrospect, was she too tolerant of your indulgences?

Maybe. I don't think I would have been long gone. I think I was crying out for someone to say, "Enough." In the end I had to make my own line. Anybody who finally kicks himself in the ass and wants to clean up makes his own line. You realize the final line is the edge.

Is the failure of your marriage a great disappointment to you?

It's not disappointing. That's why therapy helps a lot. It forces you to look at your life and figure out what's functioning and what isn't. You don't have to beat your brains against a wall if it's not working. That's why you choose to be separated rather than to call each other an asshole every day. Ultimately, things went astray. We changed, and then with me wandering off again a little bit, then coming back and saying, "Wait, I need help"—it just got terribly painful.

Would you admit you're tough to live with, even cleaned up?

Oh, God, yes. I'm no great shakes. It's the "love me" syndrome combined with the "fuck you" syndrome. Like the great joke about the woman who comes up to the comic after a show and says, "God, I really love what you do. I want to fuck your brains out!" And the comic says, "Did you see the first show or the second show?" One hand is reaching out and the other is motioning to get back.

Couldn't you have gotten therapy sooner and circumvented a lot of the trouble? Were you afraid of it?

A little bit. My mother is a Christian Scientist, whose tenets maintain that you can always heal yourself. So I said, "Well, I'll fix myself." But there are certain things you can't fix in yourself. You can get yourself healthy. I kicked drugs alone—I never went to a hospital.

You may be the only celebrity who beat dependency without the benefit of the Betty Ford clinic. What's your secret?

With alcohol, it was decompression. The same way I started drinking, I stopped. You work your way down the ladder from Jack Daniel's to mixed drinks to wine to wine coolers and finally to Perrier. With cocaine, there is no way to gently decompress yourself. It took a few months. Someone said you finally realize you've kicked cocaine when you no longer talk about it. Then it's gone. It's like pulling away and seeing Pittsburgh from the air. People come up to you with twitching Howdy Doody jaws, and you think, "Hmmm, I looked like that." You realize that if you saw by daylight the people you'd been hanging out with at night, they'd scare the shit out of you. There are bugs that look better than that.

How much money do you think you ultimately spent supporting your drug habit?

The weird thing about the drug period was that I didn't have to pay for it very often. Most people give you cocaine when you're famous. It gives them a certain control over you; you're at least socially indebted to them. And it's also the old thing of perfect advertising. They can claim, "I got Robin Williams fucked up." "You did? Lemme buy a gram then." The more fucked up you get, the more they can work you around. You're being led around by your nostril. I went to one doctor and asked, "Do I have a cocaine problem?" He said, "How much do you do?" I said, "Two grams a day." He said, "No, you don't have a problem." I said, "Okay."

How often does John Belushi cross your mind these days?

Not a lot. I mean, he crosses my mind. I've been through the grand juries, I've talked about it. And I know, in the end, I was only there [in Belushi's bungalow at the Chateau Marmont the night of Belushi's death] for five or ten minutes. I saw him and split. He didn't want me there, really. He obviously had other things he was doing. I do think I was set up in some way to go over there. A guy at the Roxy said John wanted me to stop by his bungalow. But when I went by, he wasn't looking for me. He wasn't even there. When he arrived, he said, "What are you doing here?" and offered me a line of cocaine. I took it, and then I drove home. If I had known what was going on, I would have stayed and tried to help. It wasn't like he was shooting up in front of me.

The next day, on the set of *Mork & Mindy,* Pam Dawber came up to me and said, "Your friend died." Here was a man who was like a bull. I didn't talk about it immediately at the behest of some people. But not talking about it only created more controversy.

What motive would there have been in setting you up?

I don't know. You could say it would have been a great bust if it had happened.

Robert DeNiro, along with Belushi, supposedly had summoned you there, right?

I called DeNiro's room upstairs, but he was with company. And John wasn't around. It just didn't seem like I was really called there. Obviously, all the elements didn't fall into place, because I didn't stay long.

Have you harbored some guilt over his death?

It took me a couple of years to go, "Wait, there's nothing to feel guilty about." I was there, yes, but a lot of people saw him that night, did drugs with him or talked to him. Yeah, there's a feeling that if you could have known, you would have stayed and talked with him or dragged him out to get something to eat. I wasn't close enough to say, "Hey, don't be an asshole!"

I mean, I admired the shit out of him. I'd had a wonderful time with him. One time he took me to a heavy hard-core punk club, and I was scared shitless. People were slam-dancing, which I'd never seen before, and there was a band playing called the Bush Tetras. He said, "Guess which one is the woman." I said, "The guy on the right?" And he said, *"They all are! Ha, ha, ha!"* It was like being on a tour with Dante, if Dante were James Brown. He took great delight in seeing me go, "Whoooaaa!" I was like Beaver Cleaver in the underworld.

Do you think you can ever deal autobiographically with your drug problem onstage the way Richard Pryor has?

I can now, I think. It's because he did it so well that I choose to talk about it almost in a third person. I've hinted at it. I mean, everyone knows exactly what I've done; it's implied.

Moreover, can I really stop people from doing drugs? I can't proselytize. Bob Goldthwait probably hit on the best antidrug campaign ever. He said that he'd read a quote where Bob Hope said he smoked marijuana once. Can you imagine a picture of Hope toking weed, going, *"Wiiiild,* isn't it? This hooch is wild! This Mary Jane really drives me nuts! Ya know, I'm so hungry, I can't tell you!" Some fifteen-year-old would see that and go, "Oooh, fuuuck, man!"

You recently played the Prince's Trust concert, in England. Did you clean up your act for Charles and Diana? I suppose you had to lose your royal-incest material.

Yeah, the royal-family shaving routine. "Oh, hemophilia!" There's a fear there. You're not allowed to talk about what might be happening in their lives. So how do you keep your anarchy and still keep your respect? You have to talk about cultural differences, about how their newspapers make the *National Enquirer* look like Pulitzer Prize material. [*As a page-3 girl*] "My name is Betty, and I don't like bombs—but look at *these* missiles!"

Meeting the princess was amazing. She's exquisite. I knew *he* would have a certain presence, but with her you go [*long wolf whistle*], "Wow!" She's obviously been trained to do certain things, one of which is this look: She'll look at you, then turn away, then look at you again. It's beyond coquette. It makes you go [*as Goofy*], "Oh-ho, shucks, ma'am, you're so purrrty!" Before the show she asked me, "Do you know what you're going to do tonight?" I said, "No, I really don't know, but after you see it, I don't think you'll want me back." She said, "Oh, don't tell me that." And she gave me one of those looks. "*Whoooaaa, golly,* ma'am."

As a comedy professional, are you going to miss the Reagan presidency?

Am I going to miss Reagan? Or is that *Miss* Reagan? That's a great movie title: *Miss Reagan.* [*As Butterfly McQueen*] "Oh, Miss Reagan, I don't know nothin' 'bout balancin' no budget!" People say satire is dead. It's not dead; it's alive and living in the White House. He makes a Macy's Thanksgiving Day float look ridiculous. I think he's slowly but surely regressing into movies again. In his mind he's looking at dailies, playing dailies over and over. Nancy's kind of in another world, too. She's pushing for him to get a Nobel Peace Prize, but she's out arm-wrestling with Raisa on the lawn.

Did the recent rash of religious scandals surprise you at all?

Sam Kinison, who was once an evangelist himself, has always said that these people have dark lives. Still, who would have the balls to say, "God will take me away unless I get $8 million"? As if God's a large man named Vinnie, going, "*Where the fuck's the money?*" They're selling the promise of hope on the strength that there's no such word as *audit* in the Bible. The Lord was not audited. Jesus did not have an accountant, even though *he* was Jewish. That would be great,

to play Jesus' accountant: "Okay, we've got nails, that's a valid expense. How many dinners did you have this week? One? Okay, we can write that off."

Did you see the item about the pope supposedly wanting to meet Madonna?

And she said, "If he wants to meet me, let him come see the show." Yeah, that's nice when she gets herself confused with her predecessor. [*As Madonna, snapping gum*] "He wants to say hello? Sure, tell him to come backstage." [*As a black bodyguard*] "Madonna! Madonna! John Paul's here!" [*Madonna*] "The Beatles?" [*Bodyguard*] "No, just one guy. He's wearing a yarmulke. Okay, Yo' Emmense, she be out in five minutes. She gotta get outta her lace thang. Can I get you somethin'? Some wine? Crackers? So, you got two names. You from the South? That's ermine you're wearin', right? You a little light in the sandals? Ha, I'm kiddin' you. *Madonna, come on out here!*"

A few years ago, you ended one of your cable shows with a vignette about Albert Einstein. You quoted him, saying, "My sense of God is my sense of wonder about the universe." What do those words mean to you?

It's like Mel Brooks's great line as the 2,000-year-old man [*in a Yiddish accent*]: "There's something bigger than *Phil.*" You can't help but see it when you deal with nature in the extreme. Like when you're body-surfing on Maui and a storm suddenly makes a ten-foot wave come at you. It gives you a sense of your mortality. Or it's when you see something incredibly beautiful. I get it when I see Zachary changing. Here's this being who is you but *not* you slowly growing and forming opinions of his own.

It stems, too, from a sense of horror at things that go on in the world. The planet's climate is changing at such a drastic rate, causing the worst blizzards and droughts in history. Now there is an incredibly large hole in the ozone layer. Like Shakespeare said, this place is such a delicate, fragile firmament. It's a one-in-a-billion crapshoot. And we're fucking it up.

Einstein is your idol, isn't he?

Yeah. Good old Al. [*Chuckles*] Imagine Al doing stand-up. [*As Einstein*] "So, it's *relative.* Does that mean I have to make love to my mother? No, I'm *keeding,* please! I gotta go. . . . I came back to make a bomb. *Nagasaki!* Who's there? It was a *joke!* Hey, I gotta go!" Wasn't he *wiiiild?*

31
The Edge

INTERVIEWED BY JAMES HENKE (1988)

More often than not, the trio format has proved an unwieldy one for modern rock guitarists. Jimi Hendrix made it work in the studio (by dint of extensive overdubbing), and so, to a considerable extent, did Eric Clapton in his days with Cream. But on a big concert stage, backed only by bass and drums, even the most resourceful guitarist may be hard-pressed to fill in enough holes to replicate a group's recorded sound. Only Pete Townshend of the Who, that great conflator of lead and rhythm lines, was able to really pull it off—until U2 came along.

Like the Who, U2 is a guitar-trio-with-lead-singer. And like Townshend, Dave Evans (nicknamed "the Edge"), U2's guitarist, has found a way, through the prodigious use of echo and big, chiming riffs, to approximate the group's soaring studio sound onstage. That sound, first widely heard in this county on U2's 1980 album 'Boy,' had by 1988 helped make the Dublin-based band one of rock's most formidable, and best-loved, live acts. At the same time, the group's social idealism—bred in the specific torments of strife-torn Ireland—had risen to such a pitch on recent albums like 'The Unforgettable Fire' and 'The Joshua Tree' that it seemed to decry All Bad Things. This is a hard stance to argue with, inasmuch as there's no argument. But such rampant virtue can be burdensome. As U2 was greeted with a crescendo of renown in early 1988, the group's much-interviewed singer and chief lyricist, Paul "Bono" Hewson, seemed drawn ever closer to that dodgiest of rock roles, the Spokesman for a Generation. No one questioned his sincerity, but seven months after the following interview appeared, 'New York Times' critic Jon Pareles would sum up the next U2 album, 'Rattle and Hum,' as an exercise in "sincere egomania."

Fortunately, Jim Henke, a longtime admirer of U2's music and its messages, realized that in a guitar band—however noble its lyrical ideals—the guitarist is key. (There's been no clamor for a spoken-word Bono album yet.) And, as it turned out, Evans proved to be thoughtful, perceptive and eloquently self-aware.

—K. L.

NESTLED AMONG warehouses in the drab Dublin dockside, Windmill Lane Studios would, under normal circumstances, hardly qualify as a tourist attraction. Since the ascension of U2 to the highest levels of rock stardom, however, the scene outside Windmill Lane has changed dramatically. The building, which functions as a sort of command center for the group's activities, has been covered with graffiti—ITALY LOVES U2; EDGE, I THINK YOU'RE BRILL; DEAR U2, I'VE BEEN HERE '40' TIMES AND 'I STILL HAVEN'T FOUND WHAT I'M LOOKING FOR'—while dozens of faithful fans patiently stand watch along the street, hoping to catch at least a glimpse of rock's reigning heroes.

On one particularly rainy, windswept day in mid-January, their perseverance pays off when U2's guitarist, the Edge, arrives in his 1971 Volkswagen Beetle. As a security guard looks on, Edge rolls down his car window and obliges a few fans with autographs. Then another fan, in his mid- to late twenties, approaches and asks for money to get home. Edge gives him seven pounds, then realizes it's time to move on. "It's kind of hard to deal with," he says of the adulation. "I find it a little embarrassing."

Though Bono is the more public face of U2, Edge—whose nickname resulted in part from his tendency to observe things from the sidelines—has quietly played a key role in the band's journey to the top. His minimal, echo-laden style of guitar playing has virtually defined the group's sound and spawned a legion of imitators. He is also responsible for writing the lion's share of the group's music, as well as contributing a few key lyric ideas.

Born Dave Evans in East London in 1961, Edge moved to Dublin with his family when he was a year old. Settling in the middle-class suburb of Malahide, the Evanses, Protestants of Welsh heritage, felt a little like outsiders in largely Roman Catholic Ireland. That sense of not quite fitting in led Edge to music—

he took up guitar when he was nine—and when U2 was formed in late 1978, he finally found a focus for his energy. "It became an obsession pretty quickly," he recalls. "We all realized that we really liked doing it. We loved playing together and writing songs together."

And that feeling is now stronger than ever, Edge insists. "I've found out recently that I really want to be in this group," he says. "I don't want to write screenplays or soundtracks or do anything else. I want to write songs, and I want to record them, and I want to go on the road with those songs."

Before embarking on another road trip, though, U2 has to complete work on its feature-length concert movie, which was filmed during last year's American tour, as well as an accompanying soundtrack double album, which will feature four or five previously unreleased studio tracks. Those projects will take Edge to London and the United States, away from his wife of four years, Aislinn O'Sullivan, and their two daughters, Hollie, three, and Arran, two.

"Keeping a marriage going can be kind of hard, and you gotta work at it," Edge says. "But I think it's so much more true of anybody in a band, because being in a band is almost like being married anyway. I'm so close to the other three guys in this group that sometimes it feels like a marriage."

Over the course of two days, Edge elaborated on that second marriage in interview sessions at the group's offices and in a nearby pub. "It's only in later life that the lure of the pint of Guinness has really drawn us into the pubs," he says, adding that, especially on the road, "a few drinks can really put things in perspective."

When the band was starting out, did you ever imagine that U2 would become this successful?

Well, I don't know if I ever really thought about it too hard. You know, this year's been a dangerous year for U2 in some ways. We're now a household name, like Skippy peanut butter or Baileys Irish Cream, and

I suppose that makes us public property in a way that we weren't before. And that's a bit weird, because we're getting so much mass-media attention. We've seen the beginning of the U2 myth, and that can become difficult. Like, for instance, Bono's personality is now so caricatured that I worry whether he'll be allowed to develop as a lyricist the way I know he can.

What's the greatest danger U2 faces?

Going cold. Because there are too many distractions now. I spend most of my time trying to avoid distractions.

What kinds of distractions?

All sorts of things. Financial things. Once you have money, it has to be taken care of. As much as you try and forget about it and let someone else deal with it, there are times when it just has to be faced up to. I think it was Eno who said that possessions are a way of turning money into problems. And so I've tried to cut down on anything like that.

My lifestyle, and that of the rest of the band, is pretty straightforward. I don't want to get fat. I don't want to get lazy. Money can bring great freedom, because it means you can travel, you can go into the studio whenever you want. You can pretty much do whatever idea comes into your head. But a lot of groups have not survived financial success. So there's a potential problem.

I also think being taken too seriously is a problem. It seems that no matter what we do, people place this huge weight of importance on it. Importance out of the realm of music, whether it's political importance or something cultural or whatever. I think that can be bad.

I assume that's what you were talking about when you referred to "the U2 myth." In the past year you've suddenly become "the spokesmen for a generation."

[*Laughs*] Well, it gets tough, you know, running Amnesty International, organizing summits between superpowers. It gets pretty exhausting. I sometimes feel sorry for Bono, because he seems to get the worst of that. But we try and not let it affect us, because we'd probably be inclined to do something really stupid in order to prove that we're just like ninety percent of the musicians in other bands.

But ninety percent of the musicians in other bands don't wind up on the cover of 'Time.' What was that like?

[*Laughs*] I was king for a week, I suppose. I don't know, it felt good. What I liked about it was not just that it was U2, but that music was there that week. That felt good. You know, it's nice for rock & roll to cause a stir from time to time.

You complain about being taken too seriously, but U2 certainly cultivated a more serious image than most bands. Everything from the songs to the interviews to Anton Corbijn's black-and-white photographs made it clear that this was a "serious" band.

I just never liked my smile. That was the problem. [*Laughs*] I mean, we just write songs. That's what we do. And the idea of being a leader is just so horrible. That's the last thing we ever wanted to be. But I love Anton's shots. They're kind of European. He gave us a sense of being European.

It's funny, but when you leave where you are, you get a perspective on it. When we first started touring Britain and Europe, we started seeing how Irish we were. Suddenly, Ireland became big in our songs. When we first toured America, we sensed our Europeanness. Now, with *The Joshua Tree,* I suppose we sensed the charm of America, the writers and the music.

How has your perception of America changed over the past seven years?

I like it a lot more. I didn't like it much when I first went there. We were really just passing through, and we didn't get the full picture. I left with only a superficial sense of what America was about, and that superficial level really didn't interest me. During the second couple of tours, I purposely avoided things like the radio and TV because I thought they were bad. But on the last couple of tours, we've seen what I call the hidden side of America, the side that's not obvious if you're only in town for one night.

What have you found there?

Well, for instance, music that never gets played on the radio, that never gets exposed to any extent—blues and country music. And American writers, like Raymond Carver, and some Indian writers. Also the openness. American people are very open. In most big cities in Europe, people are aloof, very unfriendly. It's not an Irish thing, but you find it in London and Paris. I don't find that in America, and in that way it's more like Ireland.

What do you think of the state of America now, politically, culturally?

Well, it scares me. It scares me a lot, this kind of "let's forget the Sixties" mentality, the new fascism, the new conservatism. But America's always been the best and worst rolled into one, and it's going to be very interesting to see how it goes in the next couple of years.

I'm a little fearful, but it's as bad in Europe. It's as bad in England, as far as I can see. I think in years to come, people will look back at the Sixties as a very peculiar era. We think of it as the way people should be. But if you think about the years that went before and the years that have come after, it's the Sixties that are weird, not the Seventies, not the Eighties.

Many of U2's songs, like "Bullet the Blue Sky," convey less-than-favorable impressions of America and its policies. Yet, in concert, it sometimes seems that your fans don't have a clue as to what you're trying to say.

It would be great to think that people understood what we were talking about, but the fact is that probably about half of them do—or less. The rest pick some of it up, or none of it. I think we have a pretty good balance. Some people come to shows because we're a great rock & roll band. And some people come to the shows because everyone else is going. And some people come because they understand exactly where we're coming from and they agree.

But rock & roll to me is communication. I don't just mean communication of ideas, but communication of feelings. The bands I was into when I was younger were the ones where you'd listen and get a feeling about the person, whether it was John Lennon or Marvin Gaye or Patti Smith or Lou Reed. That's the most important thing in rock & roll. It's not necessarily that your idea is great, but that it's *your* idea. That's why when we write songs, we don't sit down and say, "Let's write a song about this because this is an important issue now." We write a song because we feel we have something to say.

People always ask us if we think our songs can really change anything. And I always say that's not why we wrote the songs. We didn't write them so they would change the situation. I think it would be too much to expect that. But they might make people think for a second, in the same way that we stop and think.

It always seemed that U2 was determined to become a big group. When I interviewed Bono in 1980, he told me, "I do feel that we are meant to be one of the great groups," and he compared the band to the Beatles, the Stones and the Who.

Well, Adam [Clayton] and Bono used to say that a lot—and I used to believe them. We assumed it, in a weird way, and I don't know why. We assumed that we would achieve commercial success, and we never had any kind of problem in going out and working for success, going for it. And therefore that really wasn't a big issue. What was more important was achieving musical success, and we're still trying to get that. I mean, we're getting closer with each record.

Though Bono writes the bulk of the band's lyrics, I understand that it was your idea to write a song about the strife in Northern Ireland, which turned out to be "Sunday Bloody Sunday."

Yeah, Bono was away on holiday—I think it was his honeymoon. And I wrote the music and hit on a lyric idea and presented it to the guys when they got back.

Belfast is only about fifty miles up the road from Dublin, and I'd read about it in the newspapers and seen it on TV. But going there was a bit of an education. What was incredible was that the people of Belfast had the most incredible warmth and friendliness and sense of humor—and there was this thing going on that was just tearing the whole community apart.

And "Sunday Bloody Sunday"—I can't remember exactly what incident sparked it off, but I just remember sitting in this little house I had on the sea, just bashing out this music, and it just came to me, that this should be about Northern Ireland. And I wrote down a few lines, and Bono instantly improved on them when he came back.

How often do you come up with ideas for lyrics?

Not that often. I might give Bono a title, like "I Still Haven't Found What I'm Looking For." And that'll light a spark, and he'll write a song about it.

You and Bono seem like exact opposites—he's loud and outgoing, while you're quieter and more reserved.

Generally speaking, that's true. He's more at home in the public eye. It's kind of hard for the rest of us, Larry [Mullen] and me, in particular, because we're not naturally gregarious.

As kids, Bono was the exact opposite of me. I was a very quiet kid in school. I think we shared a sense of humor, though, and when the band came together, it was kind of natural that we would get on.

What was your childhood like?

Being Protestant and being English—or Welsh, in fact—in what is ostensibly a Catholic country, it felt a bit strange at times. There were times when I really did feel like a bit of a freak, and I spent a few years where I was pretty quiet. I didn't go out an awful lot. Those are the years when I listened to the most music.

When was that?

I suppose between the ages of fourteen and sixteen. That was when albums like *Horses,* by Patti Smith, came out. There were some good records around that time—Lou Reed, Bowie, the first Talking Heads records. Nobody else was really listening to those records, but they really meant a lot to me. I always remember that when someone who's sort of fifteen or sixteen comes up to me and talks about our records. I remember how I felt about records at that age.

Have there ever been any periods when you've had second thoughts about U2 or about being in a rock & roll band?

Yeah. I lost sight of what it was all about for a period. I think when a band goes on the road, unless the band is very strong, things get a bit cloudy. And that happened with us. We had to figure out who we were musically and what we were doing and where we were going. And once we had that all together, then we were fine. But for a while there, I really wasn't sure what we were up to and whether I wanted to be a part of it all.

It was kind of just after the *October* album, coming up to writing the *War* album. We'd come off the road, the album had done reasonably well, we'd done an awful lot of hard work, and we kind of had to just take stock of what was going on. I thought it was pretty healthy, actually, and I think that without that, I would be in serious trouble at this stage.

In his recent book 'Unforgettable Fire: The Story of U2,' Eamon Dunphy spends a lot of time discussing a crisis the band went through a little earlier than that, when you were making the 'October' album. He suggests that you, Larry and Bono struggled with the question of whether it was possible to reconcile your Christian beliefs with the more decadent lifestyle that has come to be associated with rock & roll.

Well, the book deals with it in a very simplistic way. It's something that's so complicated that I really feel quite inadequate to explain it fully. The *October* album was kind of our statement in that area. Maybe we're a little clearer now about what we want to be, whereas that album was probably a search. It was us trying to find out what we were doing and where we were going. And now we just want to be a great rock & roll band. And everything else is personal in a way. But it's still there, unspoken, in the music. And it should be there in the way we do things and what we are as a band.

Have you been able to come to terms with what rock & roll represents in many people's minds—the sort of "sex and drugs and rock & roll" image?

My feelings are a whole series of contradictions, and I certainly haven't been able to reconcile them. I just know that when I pick up that guitar and Bono starts to sing, I feel good about it. And that's as far as I think it needs to be justified. I'm not pretending that I've got it all sorted out. I don't think I ever will. But this band's special, and that's all I need to know.

Have you gone through any other rough periods, when you've questioned what you're doing?

No. For a while, I wanted to be this sort of Renaissance man in the group, doing soundtracks and producing other people and that kind of thing. But I tell you, being a great rock & roll band is not easy, and I've realized that if we want to be a great rock & roll group, there's little time for anything else, really.

What's the hardest thing about it?

Being brilliant. [*Laughs*] That's a bitch! No, seriously, though, there are very few brilliant rock & roll bands around. There have been a handful since rock & roll was invented. There are a lot of really average groups out there who get away with it. But that never would be good enough for us.

So you consider U2 to be a brilliant rock band?

Well, I think *The Joshua Tree* is a brilliant album. But it's not brilliant enough for me. I'm very proud of that record, though. It's the closest we've come to what we wanted to do. *The Unforgettable Fire* was a very mixed record, a lot of experiments. But with *The Joshua Tree* we really set out to write songs and work with the song as a sort of limitation. And now I don't feel nearly as much need to innovate as I would have earlier on. I feel more at home with the idea of working within classic areas.

But doesn't the magnitude of your success pose a problem for the band creatively? Now people expect a certain "U2 sound" or a specific "Edge sound."

That makes us immediately want to change it. Instantly. When we recorded the *War* album, even at that stage we were trying to kill this idea of the U2 sound. I don't mind having a characteristic style of playing, but the idea that this is a band with a sort of formula sound really appalls me. So *The Joshua Tree* had a lot of songs that were really very untypical, and that will continue, probably more so, on the next few records.

What about your guitar playing? There certainly seem to be a lot of Edge imitators out there these days.

Well, you're always going to get that, and it's flattering in a way. But I think anyone who tries to sound like me has already missed the point, really. What I'm interested in is what new guitar players sound like. It's great to hear somebody coming out with something new. Like Johnny Marr—I thought that was an interesting thing he was doing with the Smiths. That high-life-y quality was something I hadn't heard before. I always thought the guy with Magazine [John McGeoch] was good. Again, it was something different.

I'm not a fan of the million-miles-per-second guitar player. That's more a form of athletics than anything else. It's not really about music. . . . Peter Buck from R.E.M. is also good. Good in that nothing he ever does really bowls you over—until you've heard it about twenty times. I think that's a sign of music that really has longevity, when it grows on you like that. I like R.E.M. Maybe it needs a few more records to be brilliant, but it's great now.

What guitarists did you listen to as a kid? Did you like people like Eric Clapton?

I was probably a bit young for him. My brother had a couple of Cream albums, but I really missed Clapton. I missed most of those guys. I mean, I would have been eight when Woodstock happened. So it kind of went by me. But I've been playing guitar for some time now. I got my first guitar when I was about nine years old. It took me five years to learn how to tune it. [*Laughs*] But it was easy from there on.

Was that the guitar your mother bought you?

It was the one before that. The one my mother bought me I learnt how to tune. The one I had before that was like this little Spanish guitar. It looked good. That was part of it. I mean, I liked guitars at that stage. I stopped looking at them for a while. But I've started to notice how amazing they look again.

That's one of the things that attracted me to rock & roll. Initially, there's that feeling of potential, of power, when you strap on an electric guitar. And then you learn that what it's really about is controlling that power. I mean, the guitar has been a big part of rock & roll. I just can't imagine Elvis holding a violin!

How did you develop your style of playing?

I can't really pick out influences. It's very hard. I used to mention Tom Verlaine a lot. I like him—I mean, *Marquee Moon* was a great album—but I think what I took from Verlaine was not really his style but the fact that he did something no one else had done. And I liked that; I thought that was valuable. I mean, I knew more what I didn't want to sound like than what I wanted to sound like early on, when we first formed the group.

In some ways that's why my playing is so minimal. Play as few notes as you can, but find those notes that do the most work. It became a whole way of working. If I could play one note for a whole song, I would. "I Will Follow" is almost that.

How did you start using the different effects, like echo?

Oh, yeah—the discovery of the echo unit. When we first started writing songs, I started working with what I later found out to be very Irish musical ideas,

like using open strings, alternating those with fretted strings to produce drone type of things. And then when we went in to do some demos, I thought it might be neat if I got hold of an echo unit. Actually, it was Bono's idea for me to go and get it.

So I borrowed some money from a friend and got this really cheap Memory Man echo unit. We wrote "11 O'Clock Tick Tock" and then "A Day Without Me," and it just became an integral part of my guitar parts. It was really an enhancement originally, but I quite naturally got into using it as part of the guitar itself.

I tend to use effects that don't change the tone of the guitar. I don't like phasing or flanging or anything like that. I like echo. I like reverb. And Eno's been a big help in adding new sorts of treatments to my repertoire. I really think that the use of treatments and effects is one reason why U2 works so well outdoors and in these big arenas. The sound just seems to resonate through these big arenas. We've never had any problem making our music work in a big space. In fact, I think I feel more at home in a big space than I do in a small club or theater now.

U2 played quite a few stadiums on the last leg of its U.S. tour. How did you feel about that?

It was a difficult decision for us, because we've always tried to create a feeling of intimacy in any show. People said we couldn't do it in arenas, and I really believe we did. When it came to stadiums, we really had to make the move, because if we didn't, it meant playing twenty nights in an arena, which we just couldn't face. Bruce Springsteen seems to be able to do that and retain his sanity, but any more than about six shows in one town and we start going totally wacky. It becomes like a job.

There were times when I felt that we really succeeded spectacularly at the stadiums and times when I really felt disappointed. I remember one great show, in Olympic Stadium, in Montreal. It was great. That's when I thought, "Hey, this can work."

But what about the fans? Do you really think someone at the back of a 60,000-seat stadium is feeling "intimate"?

With U2, it's the music that makes the atmosphere. There's no laser show, no special effects. And we always make sure that the sound is as good at the back end as it is right down in front. If we succeed or fail, it's definitely down to our own ability to communicate the music. All I can say is that some of those shows have worked really well, so it's not impossible, just kind of difficult.

Mark Knopfler recently said that any decision to play

stadiums really comes down to money. You can make x million dollars by playing stadiums as opposed to only y million by playing arenas—that in the end it really has little to do with how many fans will be able to see you.

There's no doubt that if you do exclusively stadium shows, you make a lot of money if they sell out. But what we did was a mixture of stadium shows and arena shows, which is the most uneconomic thing you can do. We didn't feel confident enough to play only stadiums, but we also didn't feel that we wanted to spend six or seven months just touring the United States. I don't know what we'll do next tour. I think we could take on the stadiums. But I also feel that we've proven that we can do it, and we don't have to go any further.

In fact, two terrific stadium appearances—at Live Aid, in 1985, and at the final Amnesty International show, in New Jersey in 1986—played a big role in establishing U2 as a major-league band. Do you sometimes worry that U2 has gotten too closely identified with those types of benefit shows?

Well, being the Batman and Robin of rock & roll has its disadvantages. I think we realized in the last couple of months that you can't continue to be involved in charity events. What we are, first and foremost, is a rock & roll band. If we forget that, people are going to stop listening. So at the moment my feeling is that I don't really want to do any charity shows for the moment. I think it would devalue anything else we've done.

As far as being responsible, I feel no need to be anything other than what we are. I don't feel we need to be in some way virtuous or whatever. When you reach the stage we're at, you have to learn to say no a lot more. I mean, we could do charity events solidly for the next ten years. But I don't think it would really do any good.

What about Amnesty International?

That's the one charity we really feel we can support, because its aims are so basic. You know, who can argue about human rights? It's fundamental.

In the last year it seems U2 has done everything in the book—had a number-one album and single, graduated to playing stadiums, and now a book, a movie and a live album are planned for 1988. What can you do for an encore?

Break up [*laughs*].

But seriously, how do you avoid the traps that have destroyed almost every other rock band?

By still being in love with music. I think a lot of groups that fell by the wayside just got distracted. At the moment, we're so into where the band is going and what the band can do musically that the other things have really had little effect on us. It's really like we've let it wash over us without messing us up. And also because there are four of us in this group, we're all in the same position.

It must be hard being, say, Bruce or Bob Dylan. Because it's just you. There's no one else you can check with and see how they're feeling or who can keep an eye on you when you're going through a rough period. With us, when we get into the limousine and there's the four of us, it's a good feeling. There are just those four people—but it makes it a lot easier to handle, no matter what happens.

I think we're more committed to being a great group now than we ever were. For years we were insecure about our playing, about how good a band we were. But I've no doubt anymore. We're a lot less insecure. But there are still a lot of musical goals that we haven't achieved. I'm personally very excited about what's going to happen in the next three years.

So what's left for U2 to do?

I think we're about to reinvent rock & roll. That's our challenge.

32

David Byrne

INTERVIEWED BY
ROBERT FARRIS THOMPSON (1988)

Who better to interview David Byrne, the leader of America's most consistently interesting preppie band, than a practicing academic? Robert Farris Thompson, a professor of African and Afro-American Art at Yale University (known with some bemusement around the ROLLING STONE *offices as Professor Mambo), was obviously an enthusiast, as well as an expert, in the field of what he called Afro-Atlantic culture. Cynics might be permitted a sigh when he starts rattling on about spirit possessions, but there was no question that Farris was uniquely qualified to talk with Byrne about the sort of "world music" that, over the preceding decade, had transformed his work with Talking Heads.*

Talking Heads was a band of art-school types that blossomed in the beer-soaked loam of CBGB, the Bowery punk pit, in that transitional New York year of 1975. Although Byrne's onstage persona—a sort of shell-shocked science dweeb—inspired a wave of nerd chic, the Heads were never really punks in any true sense. Their music was smart and artful three-piece minimalism, anxious but tuneful. Its parameters were gracefully expanded with the addition of Jerry Harrison on guitar and keyboards in 1977, and largely remapped following the arrival of producer/collaborator Brian Eno in 1978. Eno's dedication to pushing beyond traditional rock forms and assumptions, and his fascination with non-Western music, dovetailed with Byrne's own interests along those lines, and together they made a record spiced with found exotics called 'My Life in the Bush of Ghosts.' Eno also collaborated on three albums with the Heads and helped launch Byrne into the international pop avant-garde. In the Eighties, Byrne wrote for ballet and film. He made movies. He immersed himself in the expatriate Afro-Atlantic musical scene in Paris and, in 1988, emerged with a new Heads album called 'Naked', a record aboil with hot, tropical rhythms. What next? Professor Mambo was dispatched to inquire.

—K. L.

I N 1980 a reporter for a Los Angeles newspaper called to tell me that Talking Heads had mentioned my book *African Art in Motion* in the press kit for their album *Remain in Light*. She wanted to know my reaction. I told her I was intrigued. And I was. I began to track the group's music more closely. I was especially impressed by the Afro-Atlantic excursions—*My Life in the Bush of Ghosts* (with Brian Eno) and *The Catherine Wheel* —by the band's singer and chief songwriter, David Byrne.

In the spring of 1987, I met Byrne for the first time. Jonathan Demme, who had directed *Stop Making Sense*, Talking Heads' concert film, invited us both to dinner at a café on Manhattan's Upper West Side. David came dressed immaculately in white, appropriately evoking the image of an American initiate into the Yoruba religion. Throughout that first conversation, Demme and I did most of the talking, waxing poetic about Haitian *vodun* (*vodun,* not *voodoo,* is the respectful way to refer to this much-maligned African-rooted religion). But I could see that David genuinely dug Haiti and her arts.

Several weeks later, I invited him to accompany me to a Haitian *vodun* initiation ceremony. It was a *canzo,* a ceremony in which two blacks and two whites (one was an administrative assistant for a major magazine) would pass the fire test, holding their hands briefly in a scalding-hot mixture without feeling anything, as proof of self-control and oneness with the spirit. The successful completion of the *canzo* would be celebrated with dancing and spirit possessions.

The dancing was scheduled for five in the afternoon in a basement *hounfor* ("shrine") in the Morrisania area of the Bronx, not far from the George Washington Bridge. We arrived on time, but the ceremony didn't get under way until nearly four hours later. David passed this impromptu initiation test. Instead of stirring restlessly or pointedly glancing at his wristwatch, he simply plunked himself down in a chair and watched a television that someone had left on. Around nine, the drummers finally came and set up, and the rhythms for the gods resounded. Several women and one man became possessed by the gods and goddesses of ancient Dahomey, in Africa. Ghede, one of the most powerful deities, came down in the flesh of a woman and—wham!—fell right into David's lap before lunging ecstatically to the altar. David hardly blinked an eye. It was as if the intense non sequiturs of his songwriting—not to mention the unpredictability of rock stardom—had prepared him well for this kind of experience.

Other outings with David in Afro-Latin New York have confirmed, for me, that he has an abiding connection with the arts of the black Atlantic world. At a New York jazz club called Carlos I, for example, I've seen David in the audience, righteously rocking along with Ayizan, a New York Haitian band that plays the one-note bamboo trumpets of Haiti over rock and jazz. I've also realized from these encounters that David is always "on." He knows how to dress, move, sit, gaze—how to augment, with gesture and attitude, any given creative context. I would guess that when he switched from studying art to performing music, he carried the insights of line, form and color to the world of grooves and silences. But also, wherever he is, whatever he is doing, he is on in the ethnographic sense of being a participant-observer.

One night at S.O.B.'s, the New York nightclub specializing in African, Brazilian and Caribbean black music, Celia Cruz, the queen of salsa, invited David onstage to play guitar for her. It was, of course, an exciting minievent for the performers and the audience. But David Byrne, the musician-ethnographer, was also there, and he was on. That night he met Angel Fernandez, Cruz's trumpet player, and commissioned his talents as an arranger. Consequently, "Mr. Jones," a brilliant cut on the new Talking Heads album, *Naked,* swings with the kind of classic horn lines made famous by the Cuban mambo king Perez Prado; it cleverly complements the Afro-Cuban sounds and rhythms that percolate throughout the rest of the record.

I've also learned that David's love affair with these cultures is not only sincere, it's pervasive. The conversations from which this interview is taken would usually start at a New York restaurant and wind up at Byrne's home, a loft in SoHo, where he lives with his wife, Adelle Lutz, a Eurasian designer. The loft's outside corridor is guarded by two *drapeaux de vodun* ("*vodun* flags"), which salute the deities Bossu and Erzulie. In the living room, the sofa is draped with a multicolored Akan *kente* cloth. To the side of a state-of-the-art television is a table set with several miniature wedding couples frozen in a dance of love over a *bogolanfini* cloth from western Africa. There is also a wooden Nimba statue, a striking feminine image from the Baga people of Guinea, and an amazing fusion sculpture—with David doing the fusing—made of a cake studded with red power figures purchased in a *botánica,* a Yoruba-American herbal store. Of course, not all of the accents are African or Afro-American. The bedroom area, with its translucent sliding walls, is Japanesque. And although Byrne has very hip, up-to-date catalogues of African, Afro-Brazilian and North American visionary art on his coffee table, his current john literature is an important work on film theory by Jay Leyda.

So one could say that David Byrne is nowadays as much ethnographer as he is rock artist. All of these interests propel him more and more into the making of film. (The *vodun* sequence in his first film effort, *True Stories,* foreshadows his next big project, a film on the Yoruba religion in Brazil.) All his imperatives seem to be blurring, one into the other, and probably just in time. The continuing upsurge of black-based popular musics—such as reggae, *compas direct,* mambo, merengue, *cadence,* zydeco—which is being reinforced by hyper-tech, means that we are going into a new era. Put it this way: I think David Byrne points the way to the future, when rock masters will be noted for extraordinary acquisitions of multiple cultures in sound.

"Mr. Jones," on *Naked,* is a kind of declaration of independence for all these tendencies and more. It's an answer to Bob Dylan's "Ballad of a Thin Man," which has the immortal lines about Mr. Jones. That song made a fetish of being snobbish toward out-of-it elders and beer-drinking, football-loving America. Now Byrne is saying that there is something happening out there, and it's Señor Jones (Willie Colón, Ray Barretto, Roberto Roena), Señora Jones (Celia Cruz) and, in Portuguese, Senhora Jones (Denise Delapenha, Gal Costa, Alcione). It's also Monsieur Jones and his Haitian colleagues (Ayizan, Troupe Makandal, Coupé Cloué), who will one day be to New York what the Mississippi Delta bluesmen were to Chicago. The showdown music for the showdown decade of the 1990s is already here. And David Byrne not only hears it, he makes it. He's keeping up with the Joneses—the right ones.

*W*hen *were you first turned on to African music?*
I think it must have been around 1978. I heard a South African jive instrumental record, something I picked up in a record store. I had no idea what it was.

What was it about that record that turned you on?
It was that I heard elements of sounds that I was sort of familiar with. I heard a little bit of Cajun, a little bit of Caribbean—gosh, what else? It was just something different. I guess I might've heard Fela before that. But the South African jive and Fela's Afrobeat were close to the R&B that I was already familiar with, so it was kind of an easy entry.

It seems you and Brian Eno opened up that area of exploration for other rock artists, like Peter Gabriel and Paul Simon.
Well, I'd rather not get into who did what first. I know Peter Gabriel was doing something around about the same time, but it had a different flavor.

What moved you to incorporate these new elements into your own music?

At first, it was probably just instinct. I liked it. Later on, when I started breaking the beats down and putting them back together again, I saw how African and Afro-American songs were put together in similar ways. I saw there were social parallels to the music and a kind of sensibility and philosophy and even metaphysics that's inherent in the way the music's constructed and the attitude in which it's played. Then I started to understand *why* I liked it. And it seemed to me a way out of the dead end, the one-sided philosophical binder, that Western culture has gotten itself into.

Back in '79 and '80, when we were doing that, a lot of people thought, "Oh, did you go to Africa?" And they were surprised to find out that we hadn't—and I hadn't—and still haven't really. I'd love to, but I just haven't. But I think what happened was we'd found that the same sensibility existed right next door. There were American musicians playing from the same foundation. As different as the styles are in Paris, for instance, there's still a lot happening here.

Paris is where you recorded most of the new album, 'Naked,' working with a host of African musicians. What kind of relationship did you have with them?

It was very relaxed. It didn't seem exotic. It was very natural and comfortable. In 1979, 1980 or whenever, when we were first playing around and trying to learn some other kinds of things, I think we really felt like students then, although we were often feeling our way on our own. But now I think that there's less of that relationship and more of a direct interplay. Everybody learns from everybody else and whatnot.

What about the Afro-Americans you've worked with?

Bernie Worrell and Alex Weir and Steve Scales, all those guys, we were learning a lot from them. Bernie's a kind of philosopher; something that would take me a page to say, he can say in a couple of words and hit the nail right on the head. Like his general attitude of playing with other musicians—you know, listening to what the others are playing and leaving spaces for each other, instead of everybody getting in their own seat of the car and then driving off.

You made your first African-influenced music with Brian Eno. What was the nature of that relationship? Was he both mentor and collaborator?

We first met him in London, and we'd hang out with him whenever we were there. This was all before we'd made any records together. So it kind of evolved in a very organic way, in the same way that when Talking Heads first got together, we weren't getting together because any of us were virtuoso musicians.

We just kind of got along as people, and music was the way we could work together. Then we started getting into some stuff that had other beats in it, that kind of thing. I know, for Eno and me, it was a shared interest and enthusiasm. We were friends, and we'd exchange tapes. I'd have a tape of something from Africa, and so would he, without any idea of doing something with it but just saying, "Have a listen to this; you might like it," or vice versa. And pretty soon, you know, we realized that something's happening here.

Do you think that this openness—with Eno and all the guest musicians—is the source of strength that's kept Talking Heads together for more than a decade?

That's a big part of it. Once we established that we weren't gonna always stick to one thing—although we always kept it more or less within a song framework —it was wide-open; it was almost like you could do anything. So it's pretty hard to get bored. Yeah, that would be a good reason we could continue.

You're obviously very protective of your privacy. Are you also attracted to the romantic image of the lone artist, or do you prefer being part of the extended family of a band like Talking Heads?

Well, I really love working with other people, whether it's the band or whether I'm working on a film or a video or whatever. In my creative endeavors, it's the most enjoyable. But I don't know—I just don't hang out with a whole entourage or anything like that all the time.

A lot has been made of your preoccupation with alienation. What do you think of that?

I certainly find it kind of exaggerated. I think it's probably true in some of my material. To me, songs like "Road to Nowhere" are about surrender, not alienation. Maybe people are taking the words apart from the music. That's a possibility. Or they isolate my body language or the tone of my voice without looking at it as a whole. It's like, in terms of African sculpture, most people look at a sculpture that's got 100 nails driven into it, and they go, "Oh, my God, what a horrible demon." What can you say? It's a reflection of their own sensibility. The thing is acting as a mirror.

They miss the moral judgment in that mirror. Speaking of subjective perceptions, there's also a popular view of David Byrne as a rather cool and detached performer.

I sometimes find it disturbing or unfortunate. My intention has always been for the musical structures or the stage performance or even the lyrics to acknowledge their structure, to kind of let you see how they're put together. Maybe for that reason people find it detached. But my intention has always been to have a lot of feeling in it. When I was perceived as detached or whatever, I often took that to be a criticism, and thought, "Well, how can I improve what I'm doing, what the band's doing, so that that's not the case?" I think that the *Stop Making Sense* movie made it pretty obvious that if that was the case at one point, it wasn't the case anymore.

You've definitely turned in some wild performances. Do you see performing as a means of releasing your passion?

I suppose it is, but it's more complicated than that. Maybe in the early ones it had to do with passion, which is, in its simplest form, an emotional outburst. But the later stuff became more about a sense of community and the whole catharsis that came from injecting some of your individuality into a group and getting something bigger back. And that's a very different kind of passion from the passion of somebody screaming in your ear.

At an ideal level, do you think the performance of rock could become a form of religion for you, and even for the audience?

Yeah. I mean, that's true. But like any religion, it always has the danger of becoming—oh, what's that Zen saying about pointing at the moon and mistaking your finger for the moon? There's always the danger of mistaking the thing in front of you for what's behind it.

Is this implied religiosity bound up in your fascination with TV and radio preachers and gospel singers [in 'True Stories'] and the Afro-Atlantic religions?

Yeah, I think all of those involve performances with real passion in them. Or the kind of passion where in many cases I can see a parallel with musical performances, where one loses oneself, that kind of thing. Even the TV evangelists who are probably completely jive—they might be just going through the motions, but I think some of the people in the audience, the congregation, are not.

What were your childhood religious experiences? You were born in Scotland.

Yes. And my parents.

Where in Scotland?

It's above England.

Oh, yeah! You turn left at Liverpool. No, I mean, where "in" Scotland?

Oh. Dumbarton. It's near Glasgow.

What was your parents' religion? What were you brought up as?

Let's see. They would go to church, and it was—

what was it? It was either Presbyterian or Methodist. Something like that; it was along those lines. I kind of lost interest when I was a teenager. It's a pretty dour kind of spirituality. Then, being transplanted to the States, you're confronted by this incredible variety of spirituality, and some of it is very physical and very passionate in a really obvious way, which was very different from that. So that was an eye-opening experience.

One of your Celtic cousins, Van Morrison, was able to combine his religious passion with rock & roll.

Yeah, he went straight to R&B and found a common thread between R&B and Celtic spirituality.

And now you're investigating the Afro-Atlantic religions. You've studied Haitian vodun and Cuban and Brazilian orisha [Yoruba deities]. What do these religions mean to you?

I think the first thing you discover is that they are benign, they're healthy. They're not some kind of creepy cult that's casting spells. After that, what you do with it is up to you, I guess. I don't know where to go with it from there. I mean, one thing I want to find out is if—as they would say in some TV commercial—it touches the parts that the other ones miss.

Artistically, you notice that this is the route where a lot of music and sensibility and attitude finds its way into pop music and popular culture. So it's a pretty natural thing to want to find out where all this came from: Let's get back to whatever it is.

Do you think that America at large can learn from these religions?

Oh, yeah. Of course, in a way I think it filters in through music and speech patterns, all kinds of ways, even without people knowing that it has its roots in Africa. I mean, rock & roll probably owes as much to that tradition as it does to country & western and anything else. So it's already in there, and it's already had, and probably will continue to have, a big influence. It's just a question of how much it's acknowledged. And that's maybe where things will change.

The strong part about that kind of spirituality is that a lot of it is improvised. Because of that, it can mutate into something that has a direct bearing on contemporary life in America. It doesn't have to remain as something exotic.

So you think rock & roll will fuse more deeply with the spirit of Afro-Atlantic religions?

Well, they all come from the same roots, which is where the hope lies. Even us white kids who grew up on rock & roll have a common linkage with rhythms from Kongo.

Well, rock comes from blues. Blues comes from work song. Work song comes in part from Kongo. But how do you define rock & roll, and where do Talking Heads fit in?

This guy named Timothy White said that rock delivered a personal truth. That the musician and the singer were delivering a personal truth to the listener. In that sense you could say that reggae is the rock & roll of Jamaica because it performs the same function: It delivers a personal truth. That's a nice, broad definition. But I tend to think of rock & roll as being a specific musical form: Chuck Berry, Little Richard, Elvis Presley and Eddie Cochran, who were blues based and embodied a kind of attitude—body attitude and stance. Now that's a much narrower definition. If you take that definition, then a lot of what Talking Heads have been doing is outside of that tradition, trying to break out of it. But if you take the broader definition, then we're in, we're inside the definition.

When did you get hooked on rock & roll?

I think it was in my teens, when a lot of us felt that rock was a very direct kind of communication and not just music. There was also a lot of visual things that went along with it, a lot of the things that were making very direct connections and bypassed any need for translation. For me it was stuff in the mid- and late Sixties, which happens to have been the time when I first heard certain things. And I think it was just the sound. Sometimes the words would be good, but it almost didn't matter.

I tend to think of the pop music I grew up with as communicating through texture. The Miracles, the Temptations and the Byrds were pretty separate kinds of things, but to me it all had the texture of bells ringing; it sounded very metallic, like ringing metal. Which is what it was: striking the strings. You'd think of a pleasant sound as coming from a violin or something softer. And here was all this clanging!

Where were you picking up on it?

In the bedroom, you know, on the radio. And then I'd go to local dances.

Where did you hang out in Baltimore?

At that time, it was called a teen center. I think it was one of the school cafeterias. Then, in the evenings, there was this place where local bands played. Kids my age would sometimes, you know, drink more than they should have [laughs].

Let's review some Talking Heads songs. How about "Psycho Killer," from 'Talking Heads: 77'?

This song is about the psycho killer's mental state. It's not about a violent act. It's about how he imagines

himself and how he feels. Tina [Weymouth, Talking Heads' bassist] was most involved in the French; her mother is French. I talked to her about what kind of thing I wanted it to say, and she came up with the words. There's a little Otis Redding in there, too.

"I Zimbra," from 'Fear of Music'?

To tell you the truth, I couldn't think of words, in this instance, that beared repeating. A lot of the music was based on some African records I'd been listening to. The melody came from Brian [Eno], and he noticed that this dada poem fitted the melody. It's a dada sound poem—poems that were meant to be read aloud. The dadaists were doing the same thing we were doing: trying to get behind the language to the meat of the expression. It was all in the sound of what was being said.

"Once in a Lifetime"?

This is one of the songs where you do a cinematic jump cut, an abrupt transition from one sensibility to a completely different one. Then you put the two next to one another, and they play off one another. In this case, the man was bewildered: Where and how did I get here? And in the chorus this same man seems to have found blissful surrender coming out from under water, water washing over him—blissful surrender in the Islamic sense.

Now let's try some riffing, a bit of call and response, starting with God.

Oh, my goodness.

You said at the outset that you wanted to deal with deep, metaphysical questions. Here they are. How do you envision God?

Well, I certainly don't believe in an old bearded man up there. I see God as a force that guides and unites our finest actions and sensibilities. We might call it God because we have no other way of explaining it. And it doesn't fit causal rationality, where you say, "Well, this happens, and that causes this, and this causes that." It's a more poetic reality.

How would God operate through the medium of rock & roll?

It's the principle that unites all the elements: the text and the sound, the rhythm and the attitude. It's an immediate understanding. I've spent years and years trying to put it into words, but the basic understanding comes in an instant.

The fact of it being kind of an epiphany still remains unexplained. I'm not trying to be mystical, but they could be within ourselves. They could be, you know, Jungian things, collective-unconscious archetypes. That kind of rationalizing of it is something I can accept more easily than deities that are out there and separate from us.

I once listened to Chet Baker, in a West Side jazz boîte, and in a certain phrasing of his trumpet, I thought I heard heaven. Have you had a similar epiphany?

[*Laughs*] Yeah. Sometimes I come upon a lyrical phrase, a key to unlock the words to fit a song, and the initial reason for it defies rational analysis. Yet in retrospect it makes perfect sense. Other times, in concert, where all the musicians are playing, and you kind of subsume yourself and become part of the community of musicians. They, in turn, become part of the audience. And everybody senses that. It's not a rational realization. It's a visceral realization that you're part of a larger whole.

In the heat of activity, the vision comes and . . .

That's the whole dilemma about the little sparks that result in creation. It's hard to attribute them. They kind of come from the spaces in between people.

What about the devil?

I have a lot of trouble with that concept. It's so powerful—not the devil, but the concept of evil. It's so powerful, but I haven't been able to come to terms with that. I think I persist in thinking that what we might call evil, or the devil or whatever, is people just not listening to themselves. That might be naive. But I persist in having this optimistic view.

What did you think of the Rolling Stones' "Sympathy for the Devil"?

I took it as kind of raising a question about the potential for becoming disconnected from the energy source or whatever, becoming disconnected from yourself. That potential is in all of us. That's what I thought the song was about, that Mick Jagger and the Stones were saying it's not something *out there*. It's in us and everywhere, so have respect for it.

Hating and falling in love.

Sometimes they're mirror images. They're both obsessive states. They're two sides of the same coin. That's why the lover scorned, or the suspicious lover, can turn into a really vindictive person.

Do you think we learn from daring to go through the obsessive state?

Yeah, yeah. Learning that you can do that is respecting things outside the rational. Respecting things outside of daily living.

Rock & roll is an obsessive state. You dared to enter into that obsessive state. What kind of insights have you gotten from it?

Rock music makes the obsessive okay and turns it into a creative act. Rock deflects that energy and chan-nels it into something creative. Which is odd, because at a certain point you realize that it's not enough to just be obsessive in front of an audience. There's also craft to it. You have to achieve a balance between obsession and craftsmanship. Otherwise, you're just screaming in somebody's ear.

What about the phrase on that Texas-mineral-water bottle at dinner: "Partake, enjoy, proceed."

Elizabethan Africanism! [*Laughs.*]

Yeah, Elizabethan Africanism: that's rock & roll! But if that's rock & roll, how do we partake in joy and proceed through this medium that links you with Elvis and U2 and Linda Ronstadt?

[*Laughs*] Could you ask the question another way?

Okay. Partaking, enjoying and proceeding—is this the gist of rock?

Boy, in three words, it's the whole message of the music.

We clearly enjoy and partake of rock. But proceeding—that seems to be the critical word.

To proceed is to take your own initiative. It's kind of like we've done *our* bit, now translate it into your own terms and go ahead with it.

There's going to be a lot of that in the Nineties, when digital equipment will make it possible for the man in the street to seize the purest sounds from any scene and make his own creation.

It's just amazing what can happen that way. It carries one step further the idea of splicing together different cultures—words, phrases, textures, everything. With a kind of technical perfection, anything can be mixed right in with anything else. You get this massive rhythm going, and it's bigger than any song or musical entity.

What else do you think is going to happen to rock in the 1990s?

Rock's probably going to go two ways. There will be music from many cultures that crosses the generations, that speaks to the greater humanity that we are. That's one kind of thing. And I think we and other musicians are searching for a way to do that. We're certainly not alone. And I think, at the same time, there will always be younger musicians who have a more frantic set of hormones rushing through the body.

What kind of hormones?

A more *frantic* set. They're going to be saying that we're irrelevant. And they'll have something more immediate and more energetic, more of the moment, to contribute. I think that's inevitable. It's about time for that to happen again.

Let's talk about love, about which you can't talk too

much. The late poet Marianne Moore essentially defined it as taking responsibility for somebody else's happiness.

And feeling that it's absolutely linked with your own.

One journalist noted that your songs changed noticeably after you fell in love with your wife.

That assessment seemed too pat to me, too simple. Seems to me there were other factors involved. But it would also be stupid of me to deny that my creative work wasn't affected.

When you're out there wildcatting on the frontier of love, how do you play with sexual fire in your lyrics without getting burned? How do you write about love without getting mawkish?

That's it. It's a real challenge to not bring it down to sentimentality. It took me a long time to feel I could jump into that, because it's dealt with so much in popular songs in a very saccharine way. Often those saccharine sentiments have a strong impact. Nobody's immune to it. But I felt other people were covering that; they had that part covered. I thought I should try to get to some of the other resonances of it—as if ripples were going out from this intense feeling that everybody has, but only certain parts of it have been touched.

How about this line from "The Great Curve," from 'Remain in Light': "The world moves on a woman's hips."

Oh, boy. I'm not talking about one particular woman. I'm not talking about my girlfriend [*laughs*]. You think that's very down and earthy, but I was talking about something metaphysical. That a gesture can resonate outward, like ripples in a pond, causing realms of meaning. An attitude of the body can embody a whole world view [*laughs*].

"This Must Be the Place (Naive Melody)," from 'Speaking in Tongues'?

The most direct love lyrics that I've ever written. But I tried to do it in a way someone once described as a series of non sequiturs.

Like this one: "Sing into my mouth"?

I'd seen a picture of Eskimos singing. They'll sometimes sing into each other's mouths. I thought it was a most beautiful image.

Or "You got a face with a view."

It's romantic in the sense that romantic poets in the nineteenth century would write about a landscape. They'd write a whole poem about standing on the hill and looking out. I'm looking at her face and doing the same thing.

And finally, from that song, "Cover up and say goodnight" and "Hit me on the head."

[*Laughs*] When you fall in love, you feel like a missing piece of a puzzle that's been found. Plus, the epiphany of a love relationship is like being hit on the head, jolted into a different kind of a land.

What does the parenthetical phrase in "This Must Be the Place (Naive Melody)" refer to?

We were deliberately playing instruments we weren't technically good at. Tina was playing guitar, Jerry [Harrison, the band's keyboardist] was playing the bass, and I was playing the keyboards. So our playing was very simple. We couldn't help but be naive.

"Creatures of Love," from 'Little Creatures'?

It came from a daydream, or a dream at night. I can't remember it very well now. But it had something to do with a couple making love. And when they were finished, there were little tiny people all over the bed.

A dream script?

Yes. Most of it's pretty straightforward, but there are a couple of mysterious things, like the "sleep of reason." It's like Rousseau or something.

What about these lines from the same song: "A man can drive a car and a woman can be a boss/I'm a monkey and a flower/I'm everything I want"?

That's where the lyrics of the song kind of jump-cut into something completely different for a while. I think it keeps the song from falling into a rut. It also helps throw the whole thing into a wider context, if you're lucky.

There are Asian as well as African influences in your work, and you contributed music to the soundtrack for Bernardo Bertolucci's film 'The Last Emperor.' Was your wife instrumental in any of this?

She turned me on more to the various theatrical forms over there, but I was pretty much already on my way. Appropriately enough, the big suit for *Stop Making Sense* came from a drawing I did on a napkin in Japan. We were having dinner with a clothing designer, and I was thinking out loud, saying, "We're going to tour again," and wondering what kind of clothing to wear onstage. And he said, "Well, you know what they say about the theater: Onstage everything has to be bigger." I said, "Okay, that's perfect." So, to me, the implied story of that whole show was of this man who frees himself from his demons and finds release and salvation in his big suit. He lives in the uniform of his job. And just like Mr. Jones, he manages to not let that constrain him. He can cut loose in this house made of a business suit.

"Mr. Jones"! Now that song struck me as the mambo revenge of Dylan's Mr. Jones.

Yes, I'm doing it the other way around. He's a

traveling businessman, who's usually depicted in songs by people of my generation as not knowing what's going on. A lot of people would stare at Mr. Jones and declare him the ultimate square. I'm saying, "Okay, now, this guy's breakin' out of that, and he's havin' a good time."

You know, I think the whole generation-gap thing is unique in Western culture. In Japan, the generation gap is there, but it's very small. Here, we often just accept that the generations don't mix as much. Which is a big mistake.

But how would one mount an intergenerational Woodstock?

I don't know. Maybe *that's* what's coming in the Nineties.

There's a song called "The Big Country" on 'More Songs About Buildings and Food,' and you wore a big suit in 'Stop Making Sense.' How about some big questions: What is your big goal?

One thing would be to do stuff that has serious underpinnings but is fun at the same time.

Big dreams?

I don't know. I don't have big, long-range ones.

Big demon?

I suppose that one is kind of outside of myself: dealing with business people and business stuff and that kind of thing, which I pride myself in being able to understand and deal with. I'm proud that I can, you know, that I have some measure of understanding of it, and yet I find that it always seems to be taking too much of my time.

Big regret?

Not that big. I regret that with *True Stories* we didn't put out a record with the cast singing the songs instead of me. They were written with other voices in mind, and to me the other people, like Pop Staples, did it much better than I did. I regret it never worked out to happen that way.

Big idol?

Yeah, but they would change all the time. Every few years there would be someone else. I never felt like one person had all the answers. They may have done some beautiful things, but it's that old Zen proverb: It's easy to mistake the person for the beautiful gifts they bring, or something like that.

Big obsession?

I guess I get obsessed by whatever project I'm doing. In retrospect, one can see a common thread, that maybe there's a common obsession or subject I'm not always aware of at the time.

Big break?

Oh, boy. Well, there's probably quite a few. One would be the first time you write a song and perform it with a musician or collaborate on a song and play it and it really works. I think the first song was "Psycho Killer." So that was a big breakthrough, like, "Yes, we can do this." Another one was when we went from being a four-piece to however many it was—eight or nine. The first gig we played like that was in Toronto. That was something completely new for us. Everybody was energized, of course, and the audience was totally behind us. They could see that we were taking this huge risk, and they supported us in it.

Big love?

I don't know. You put some words together, and you look at it, and it's this new thing, and then it starts speaking back to you.

Of the new songs on 'Naked,' how does "Blind" speak back to you?

It's pure imagination, but it comes out of reading the daily paper. It's a cry of anguish. It's a man crying, rather than a woman. And I think it's directed at the authorities. Someone has been killed, or badly beaten, and someone else is looking out a window. Terrible things are happening, civil strife. It definitely goes beyond just lack of sight. The more it's repeated, the more references are implied and the more it resonates with all the meanings within that word or phrase. And you're asking yourself and the listener to be aware of all that.

"The Democratic Circus"?

We're actually talking about the electoral process. To me, it's not a democracy as we imagined it. It's disillusioning in a way. But part of that might be because it's not what we would have hoped; it's not what we were led to believe it would be. I like the rain coming at the end, washing it all away, like blood [*laughs*]. We referred to the song as being a cha-cha.

"Cool Water"?

It's very dark, that song. It's a pretty bleak view of the end of life, of death. A lot of our stuff has been somewhat positive, but this one is pretty much the other side. Pretty bleak, but I think it would be silly to ignore it and to pretend it doesn't exist.

There's a kind of dirge with flutes. The image of the big cool water is like relief. But you can also drown in it.

"Mommy Daddy You and I"?

I would like to think that it's about all of us being immigrants of one sort or another, that we've all moved from one place to another, even if it's just that we move across town. There's a certain similarity to families that come up from Mexico, or the Okies that went to California, people who've come from Europe. Everybody's transplanted, even if it's just that at some point they have to make a life for themselves, you know? And think what is it they're going to do with it. I'm very happy with the lines, like, "We're wearing our grandfather's clothes." To me, that meant not that you're just wearing old clothes but that you're part of a long line. That you're connected to your family, your ancestors. You're not just in a void. You're kind of a product of your ancestors and something else, but I can't think what.

I don't think it's something personal or autobiographical, but it reminds me of when you're a kid, riding in a car or a bus or train or whatever. And you doze off. And your head goes to the nearest shoulder.

Well, some final words on "(Nothing but) Flowers" and we'll call it a day.

On the surface, it's a pleasant kind of tongue-in-cheek thing of me talking about giving it all up, throwing everything away and going out to live in the forest or the woods or the jungle, whatever. I guess it's a very common wish—but for the moment not all that likely.

33
Roy Orbison

INTERVIEWED BY STEVE POND (1988)

Nobody seemed to miss Roy Orbison's music much until Orbison himself was almost gone. Fortunately, though (and fittingly), he took leave of life on an extraordinary wave of love. By the time of his death on December 6, 1988, at the age of fifty-two, Orbison's great early work was the focus of a renewed and impassioned appreciation, and his second career, as a member of the Traveling Wilburys (a group in which he was joined by such life-long admirers as Bob Dylan and George Harrison), was well under way and lifting him once again toward the top of the charts. 'Mystery Girl,' the solo album he'd recently completed, would have sealed his comeback, had he lived to see its release. At the end of his life, when he granted one last, extensive interview to ROLLING STONE, *he was anything but sorrowful.*

The sweet irony here, of course, is that Orbison's career was built on heartbreak. From 1960 to 1966, Roy Orbison scored twenty-two Top Forty hits. A handful of these were tough, muscular rockers—"Candy Man," "Dream Baby (How Long Must I Dream)," "Mean Woman Blues," the chart-topping Hall of Riffs classic "Oh, Pretty Woman." But the bulk of Orbison's greatest work consisted of ballads—great, big, string-stuffed things athrob with edgy rhythms, anguished lyrics and Orbison's soaring, edge-of-a-sob voice. He took the sort of seemingly depleted pop elements that rock & roll had implicitly trashed only a few years before—cooing chorales, cascading violins and an unabashedly melodramatic vocal delivery—and bent them to the service of an ornate and highly personal pop vision. That none of these songs—"Only the Lonely (Know How I Feel)," "Running Scared," "Crying," "Leah," "Blue Bayou," "It's Over"—sounds trite or dated today, is due in some part to the fact that none of them resembles anything else in the rock & roll canon. They remain as freshly compelling, as emotionally overwhelming—as inimitable—as they were in the time of their creation.

Which may explain why, over the years—from the late Sixties, when his recording career began to fade, through the Seventies and the early Eighties, when it lay largely dormant—Orbison's great oeuvre *came to seem diminished by its lack of reverberation. Where were his acolytes, his inheritors? The Beatles echoed Buddy Holly and the Everly Brothers; the Rolling Stones aped Chuck Berry. Who could have hoped to approach such definitively unapproachable artistry as Orbison's? His music remained magical, but remote, an inscrutable curio of faded youth, locked away in a prestigious, but seldom-visited, back room of pre-Beatles rock.*

This situation began to change in the later Seventies, but subtly and slowly. Orbison's influence gradually became apparent in the phenomenally popular work of Bruce Springsteen. Actual cover versions (or attempts thereat) began to appear: "Blue Bayou," "Crying," Van Halen's 1982 crunch romp through "Oh, Pretty Woman." And then, in 1986, came the David Lynch movie 'Blue Velvet'—one of the most poetically audacious evocations of youthful innocence (and its inevitable, wrenching loss) ever committed to film. And at its center: an otherworldly lip-synch sequence conceived around Roy Orbison's other-worldly 1963 hit "In Dreams."

For all who saw and goggled in wonder at it, 'Blue Velvet' instantly restored Roy Orbison's artistic relevance. The movie illuminated his dark and fearful lyricism, and drew upon it for some of the film's own chilly epiphanies. Suddenly, Roy was reverberating with a vengeance. In 1987, Bruce Springsteen inducted him into the Rock & Roll Hall of Fame, and Cinemax mounted an all-star TV tribute concert featuring Orbison—in terrific voice—immaculately backed by such varied fans as Elvis Costello, Jackson Browne, Tom Waits and Springsteen himself. In 1988 came the Traveling Wilburys and the planned comeback album, and the ROLLING STONE *interview that follows. And then Roy Orbison broke our hearts one final time. He went out, however—as always—on a high note.*

—K. L.

THE MOMENT came early in every concert Roy Orbison gave for the last two decades of his life; in a way, it was as electric a moment as the instant Elvis Presley stepped onto a concert stage and found himself blinded by the glare of a thousand Instamatic flash-bulbs. In Orbison's case, though, that instant of recognition, the tremor that came when audience members were reminded why they'd come, happened not when he ambled on-stage, and not when his backup singers sang, "Dum dum dum dum-bedoo-wah"—the nonsense syllables that began the opening song, "Only the Lonely."

At a Roy Orbison show, the moment of epiphany came when Orbison stepped up to the microphone and sang, "Only the lonely/ Know the way I feel tonight." Every night, in clubs and concert halls and auditoriums and state fairs, you'd hear an audible gasp, a wave of applause. Every night, the audience would be full of people thinking exactly the same thing: "My God, he sounds just like he did in 1960."

And from the early to middle Sixties, when he recorded twenty-two Top Forty hits, to his death of a heart attack on December 6, 1988, he always sounded just like the Roy Orbison of our memories and dreams: the pure, aching melancholy, the bursts of passion that were invariably called "operatic," the overwhelming power of a lonely man in black singing about lost loves and midnight fears. Night after night, he'd take the stage, stand dead still in the spotlight, speak barely a word to the audience and spin out one teenage passion play after another: "Crying," "Running Scared," "Oh, Pretty Woman," "In Dreams." The lyrics told you that love was at stake; the voice could convince you that lives were at stake.

And then he'd walk offstage, and the singer who'd unleashed such tremulous passion became shy, soft-spoken, gentle: If Elvis Presley once called him the best singer in the world, just about everyone else who knew Roy Orbison would add that he was also the sweetest man in rock & roll.

When he had his hits, he toured steadily. When his career faltered after personal tragedies and professional malaise, he kept on touring. And even in 1988, as he worked on one record that would be his first Top Ten LP in decades (*Traveling Wilburys: Volume One*) and another that seemed certain to seal his full-scale comeback (*Mystery Girl*), he still toured, playing the old songs on weekends and working on new ones during the week.

In late October he was a featured attraction at the Arizona State Fair, in Phoenix. While outside Veterans Memorial Coliseum families rode the Ferris wheel and gambled along the midway, inside Roy Orbison sang his hits. "Cover for me on any notes I don't hit," he said to his bass player backstage before the show, and the line got a big laugh; everybody in the room knew he'd hit every note of every song, and he did.

Afterward, he relaxed in the limousine carrying him back to his hotel, looking through the window at the bright neon and flashing lights of the fair. The Phoenix show marked the beginning of a series of ROLLING STONE interviews with Orbison, conversations intended not for an obituary but for a story on the celebrated past and promising future of a rock & roll legend. And as Orbison peered through his thick glasses at the fairground sights, he began to reminisce.

"Ever seen a real medicine show?" he asked. "I played at one when I was ten years old, in Vernon, Texas. They just set up a bunch of benches in the dirt and strung up lights. And they told jokes and did skits and had a talent contest and sold this magic elixir. I was co-winner in the talent contest. Won $7.50, but my buddy went with me and carried my guitar and rooted for me, so he figured he ought to have half." He chuckled softly. "That was my first taste of a manager."

Roy Kelton Orbison was born in Vernon, Texas, on April 23, 1936. When he was six, his parents gave him a guitar; at eight, he showed up so often at auditions for a local radio show that they made him a regular. Orbison loved Lefty Frizzell, Frankie Laine's pop hit "Jezebel," the odd instrumental and, after the family moved to Wink, in West Texas, Mexican music and the rhythm & blues songs that would soon coalesce into rock & roll. In high school, Orbison led a band called the Wink Westerners, later renamed the Teen Kings. A few years later the group recorded "Ooby Dooby," a nonsense rockabilly track written by some of Orbison's college classmates, in a Dallas studio. That version wasn't released, and neither was a version cut in Clovis, New Mexico, with future Buddy Holly producer Norman Petty. But Sun Records head Sam Phillips heard the song and invited the Teen Kings to his history-making studio in Memphis. They cut it one more time, and it became a minor hit.

A handful of rockabilly-style tunes followed; none were hits. All along, Orbison had wanted to sing ballads. He also wanted a better deal on his songwriting royalties, and when Nashville publisher Wesley Rose said he could get the Everly Brothers to record a tune Orbison had written for his college sweetheart and wife-to-be, Claudette, Orbison left Sun and, like Elvis Presley, signed with RCA. Unlike Elvis, he didn't sell many records, and in 1959, after a pair of singles, he moved to producer Fred Foster's label, Monument Records.

This time, everything clicked. Orbison's third Monument single, "Only the Lonely," began a string of lushly arranged, inventively structured pop ballads: "Running Scared," for instance, was a rock & roll bolero that slowly built to a pitch of lover's paranoia before its dramatic, happy ending.

In the early Sixties, the anguished grandeur of those songs was rivaled only by the work of producer Phil Spector and his stable of girl groups. From the Beatles to Bruce Springsteen, young rockers and young dreamers were listening to the sound of Roy Orbison, the heartbreaking balladeer—and, on tunes like "Oh, Pretty Woman" and "Working for the Man," Roy Orbison, the rocker.

But Orbison's momentum faded when he left Monument for a big-money deal with MGM Records in 1965. Subsequent producers, it seems, didn't have the Fred Foster touch. The records were good but not great; a movie for MGM, a Civil War musical titled *The Fastest Guitar Alive*, didn't do well.

In 1966 tragedy struck when Claudette Orbison was killed in a motorcycle accident, with Roy riding just ahead of her when it happened. He found it difficult to write any more songs, but he kept touring. Two years later, a fire destroyed his house in Hendersonville, Tennessee, killing two of his three children. From that point on, he refused to attend funerals.

The albums came sporadically, but the tours were steady. In 1969, Orbison married a young German woman, Barbara Wellhonen, and the couple later had two children. But a 1977 reunion LP with Fred Foster was disappointing; so was a 1979 album on Elektra Asylum Records, which he recorded shortly after he underwent triple-bypass heart surgery.

But pop music never forgot Roy Orbison: Linda Ronstadt, Van Halen and Don McLean had hits with his songs in the late Seventies and early Eighties, and in 1980 Orbison released "That Lovin' You Feelin' Again," a Grammy-winning duet with Emmylou Harris. In 1985 there was *Class of '55*, a reunion LP with Sun Records veterans Johnny Cash, Carl Perkins and Jerry Lee Lewis that con-

tains a standout Orbison performance in the elegiac "Coming Home." That song, like most of the songs he recorded in subsequent years, is suffused with a spiritual glow and full of intimations of mortality; the grandiose ballad "Wild Hearts," from the movie *Insignificance*, is similarly unsettling, while "Life Fades Away," from the *Less Than Zero* soundtrack, is simply a dying man's missive.

At the same time, though, Orbison was preparing his comeback with the aid of fans like director David Lynch (who used "In Dreams" to great effect in his film *Blue Velvet*), Bruce Springsteen (who inducted Orbison into the Rock & Roll Hall of Fame in 1987), T Bone Burnett (who handled the musical direction on the star-studded Cinemax concert *Roy Orbison and Friends: A Black & White Night* and produced the first two tracks for *Mystery Girl*) and Jeff Lynne (who wound up producing much of the album). In the end, a whole crew of admirers lent their support to *Mystery Girl*, which includes songs and productions from the likes of Tom Petty, Mike Campbell, Elvis Costello and Bono.

But at the end of his life, Orbison's best-known collaboration was with Petty, Lynne, George Harrison and Bob Dylan, his partners in the Traveling Wilburys. Recorded quickly and cheaply by musicians who happened to be friends and colleagues, the album was presented, tongues firmly in cheeks, as if it were the work of brothers who had five different mothers but a single footloose father—and in an interview with the Wilburys, the other members were quite vocal about what a thrill it was to hear "Lefty Wilbury" sing. Lefty himself sat quietly as younger colleagues like Petty and Harrison spun outrageous tales of life as a Wilbury; then, just when it seemed the group's elder statesman might be uncomfortable with the elaborate put-on, he softly tossed out a choice remark. "Some people said Daddy was a cad and a bounder," he said, deadpan. "I remember him as a Baptist minister."

With the success of the Wilburys, Roy Orbison seemed on his way to a complete comeback. He finished his own album in mid-November, watching with undisguised pleasure as the Wilburys LP headed for the Top Ten; then he headed to Europe for a couple of television appearances and some promotion. When Roy's chores were finished, Barbara Orbison—who for the past year and a half had been her husband's manager—remained in Germany to visit with her family. Roy returned to the United States, did a few more shows and then went to the house outside Nashville where his mother, Nadine, and his son Wesley live. There, he flew radio-controlled airplanes with his bus driver, all-around aide and friend, Benny Birchfield.

On the evening of December 6, Orbison complained of chest pains. At about 11:00 P.M., he collapsed in the bathroom of his mother's Hendersonville home. Paramedics rushed him to a nearby hospital, but by midnight Orbison had been declared dead of a massive heart attack.

In the three months before his death, the usually private but unfailingly polite Orbison had been generous with his time, inviting ROLLING STONE to his recording and mixing sessions, his concerts, his comfortable, unostentatious house high in the hills overlooking the beach at Malibu. The final session took place over breakfast at a restaurant just down the beach from the pier where he'd once spoken to actor Martin Sheen about playing the lead in the movie version of the autobiography Orbison wanted to write. "I guess I'll give the book a try now," he said, finishing off his meal and smoking from a pack of Camels that he later left behind so that Barbara wouldn't get upset.

And as he sat in the restaurant less than three weeks before his death, flushed with pride at the success of the Wilburys and the completion of what he knew was a strong new album, a happy and productive Roy Orbison said he didn't have a clear picture of where he'd like to be in a year. "That's like predicting the future of rock & roll in 1954 and '55," he said with a laugh. "I have faith that everything will unfold properly."

It seems appropriate to start by talking about your voice. Did you know it was something special from the start?

I was on a flight with Dwight Yoakam to Nashville once, and he told me . . . I don't know if I should repeat this, but he said, "I've always been in love with my voice." And I could relate to that. Once I started singing, it was sort of a wonder. It was a great feeling, and it didn't hurt anybody, and it made me feel good, and some people even said, "Roy, that's nice."

I've always been in love with my voice. It was fascinating, I liked the sound of it, I liked making it sing, making a voice ring, and I just kept doing it. And I think somewhere between the time of "Ooby Dooby" and "Only the Lonely" it kinda turned into a good voice. Though it was always nice to me [*laughs*].

It's remarkable how little it's changed.

Yeah, I sound basically the same. When I was making my older records, I had more control over my vibrato—now, if I don't want to have the vibrato in the studio, I have to do a session earlier in the day, because by the evening it'll be there whether I want it or not.

It's a gift, and a blessing, just to have a voice. And I'm proud that people do appreciate it, you know? It's a long way from being overwhelmed because you don't know whether you're worthy, to realizing that if you have a gift, it should be precious to you and you should look after it and respect it.

What did you think when you were inducted into the Rock & Roll Hall of Fame?

I looked around, looked up in this big room at huge pictures of all the guys who were coming in. And I remember seeing some pictures of guys who weren't there, who couldn't be there because they were gone. And I got into the spirit of the thing. I was really cool until I had to stand on the side of the stage during Bruce's speech. He said so many nice things, I didn't know what in the world to say [*laughs*]. But I took the speech from him. He had it written down, and I said, "Can I take this speech?"

It seems as if that night was the beginning of the resurgence that led to your new record.

I think the renaissance started with Linda Ronstadt

recording "Blue Bayou," which wasn't even the A side in America. It sold 7 to 10 million for her, and I guess I felt validated or something. That was in '77, and then Don McLean did "Crying," and it was a hit. Then Van Halen did "Pretty Woman," and I won a Grammy with Emmylou Harris, for the single "That Lovin' You Feelin' Again." And also, at the same time I started touring in America almost exclusively and realized that you could tour America forever, almost.

Barbara and I felt we had to put everything in order, in my career. We never had the right management, the right agency, the right record company all at once. And then a couple of other things happened. *Blue Velvet* came out with "In Dreams" in it. Then there was the Rock & Roll Hall of Fame, and then Virgin [Orbison's record label for *Mystery Girl*] got in touch. So there has been a concerted effort for the career to make sense for the last three years.

Right now, you're on the verge of trying to reestablish yourself as a viable contemporary recording artist, which is something that very few of your contemporaries have done.

It's a stupendous undertaking [*laughs*]. But great things are stirring, you know? Being someone who was there at the founding of rock & roll, it's good that at the age I am I'm being accepted and recognized. We used to say, "I don't wanna be jumping around and going crazy when I'm thirty," you know? Even Mick Jagger said, "Well, I can't see myself at forty jumping around." Well, here we are, you know?

How did you start playing music?

When I was six years old, Mom and Dad gave me a guitar for my birthday, and Daddy taught me the chords to "You Are My Sunshine." We lived in Fort Worth, Texas, and Mom and Dad were both working in a defense plant during World War II. It was a good place for relatives and everybody to come by and play music. And it was a time of intense emotion in that the boys were going to one front or the other of the war, more than likely to be killed. And so when they were drinking, they'd drink with gusto, and when they were singing, they sang with all their hearts, and I got to stay up with these guys and sing.

I guess that level of intensity made a big impression on me, because it's still there. That sense of "Do it for all it's worth and do it now and do it good." Not to analyze it too much, but I think the verve and gusto that everybody felt and portrayed around me has stayed with me all this time.

How long were you in Fort Worth?

Until the third grade, and then we moved back to Vernon, and when I was ten, we moved to Wink.

If you saw the film *Giant*, it was filmed eighty miles out of Wink. There's nothing. No trees, no lakes, no creeks, a few bushes. Between Wink and Odessa, where I used to drive all the time, one of the towns is called Notrees, Texas. And it has trees. But Wink was an oil-boom town. There was one movie theater, two drugstores, one pool hall and one hardware store, and that was about it. In fact, the Sears, what you did was go to this little office and look at the catalog. It's really hard to describe, but I'll give you a few more things: it was macho guys working in the oil field, and football, and oil and grease and sand and being a stud and being cool.

I got out of there as quick as I could, and I resented having to be there, but it was a great education. It was tough as could be, but no illusions, you know? No mysteries in Wink.

Were you a macho stud or a football player?

I tried till I was a freshman in high school. Just never was big enough. I played football until I was a freshman, and then I just started singing, and that turned out to be okay, too.

I got my group together when I was about thirteen. We had a local radio show, and then we started touring for the principal of the high school—he was in the Lions Club, and so we were the entertainment. We were in this West Texas town once, and a fellow came up and said, "We'd like for you to come and play a dance for us," and I was about to say, "We only know ten songs," when he said, "And we'll give you $400." So we showed up and made $80 apiece for doing what we had been doing for nothing. It was amazing, because I'd worked for the county for two weeks and made $80 shoveling tar. I didn't know what the stumbling blocks were or how likely you were to succeed at singing [*laughs*], but it didn't matter.

But you stayed in school and did other work, too.

Yeah. After high school I still had my band, and we played for dances in the evening. I was working for El Paso Natural Gas in the daytime, cutting up steel and loading it onto trucks and chopping weeds and painting water towers. That's where I came up with the idea for "Working for the Man." Our straw boss was Mr. Rose, and he wouldn't cut me any slack. I worked in the blazing heat, hard, hard labor, and then I'd play at night, come home and some nights be too tired to eat or even to undress. I'd lay down, and I wouldn't even turn over. I'd wake up in the same spot and hit the oil patch again.

Then I went to college for a year. I guess it was an attempt at being legitimate, or not being a free spirit.

336

It was a good year, but it was a lonely year. I think the reason it was really lonely was that I wasn't where I needed to be. But I met a couple of guys at school who had written "Ooby Dooby," and what convinced me that I was in the wrong place at the wrong time was I heard a record by a young fellow on the jukebox called "That's All Right." So I moved to Odessa to junior college, got my band together with different guys and started in doing what I wanted to do.

What was Sun Records like when you got there?

Well, Johnny Cash was on Sun Records—he was making unusual records. And Presley was there, and Carl Perkins. I was really impressed with that little chicken on the Sun label, because it represented something unique. And it was good to work with Sam. He wouldn't accept anything less than all you had, you know? But it wasn't a good studio, and Sam didn't know how to express exactly what he wanted. Elvis and I both were a little bit . . . We didn't think it was really good work, the early stuff, so we didn't play our Sun records onstage for a long time. Until about 1970, I think, when it became instant history, you know? All the information coalesced to the point where everybody thought that was a beginning. And so then I took it more seriously myself, because I had a few years to reflect. And Presley started singing "That's All Right," and I started singing "Ooby Dooby" onstage.

When you started having hits, did you run out and buy a fancy car and all?

Oh, sure [*laughs*]. Yeah. Had to have a Cadillac. A Cadillac and a diamond ring. Then got a little bigger Cadillac and a little bigger diamond ring, and then I said, "That's foolish," and I stopped.

The Cadillac wasn't pink, was it?

No, the first one was white, and the second was turquoise. But we did travel in a pink Cadillac, me and Johnny and Jerry Lee and Carl. It was wonderful.

I've heard that you moved around more onstage in those days.

Yeah, I did. When I had the Teen Kings, we had this number called "The Bug," where we had an imaginary bug we would throw on each other. And when it hit you, you had to shake and stuff. So I shook for a while, but I wasn't very successful at it. That phase of the career didn't last too long.

Guys like Elvis and Jerry Lee Lewis seemed like threats to the public decency, but you weren't quite so dangerous.

Yeah, I was milder. And the Everly Brothers, you know, they were milder, too. But I'm sure that if I'd have had "Pretty Woman" as my first record, I would have been thought of in a different light.

Your image was more of somebody who was mysterious, and maybe a little weird. Bruce Springsteen once said that the first time he saw you, he got the impression that if he reached out to touch you, his hand would go right through you.

That's probably closer to the truth. I wasn't trying to be weird, you know? I didn't have a manager who told me how to dress or how to present myself or anything. But the image developed of a man of mystery and a quiet man in black and somewhat of a recluse, although I never was, really.

You weren't trying to create an image with the clothes?

No, not at all. I thought black was just a smart way to dress. Black was my favorite, from the early days playing cowboys and Indians and being the outlaw and not having a black shirt and then finally getting one. And the dark glasses were a mistake when I left my other pair on a plane in Alabama, and I had to see to get onstage. While I was kinda forced to wear the dark glasses, I didn't mind when it became a thing, you know?

The image of you as a mysterious loner was reinforced by all those songs about being lonely and crying and running scared.

With "Only the Lonely" being the first, I guess they said, "Well, he's a lonely singer." But in "Running Scared" I got the girl, you know?

But at the same time, it's just about the most paranoid love song ever written that has a happy ending.

Yeah, you're right. I was *worried* in that song. But even in "Pretty Woman," it goes through a lot of emotions. I didn't think of this as we were writing the song, but the guy's observing the girl, and he hits on her, real cool and macho, and then he gets worried and gets to pleading, and then he says, "Okay, forget it, I'm still cool," and then at the end she comes back to him, and he turns into the guy he really is. That range of emotion in a short piece of music I think is very important.

Was there so much fear in those early love songs because that's the way you were in real life?

No. When I wrote, let's say, a sad song, a melancholy song, I was feeling good at the time. Because I have to feel good and at peace with myself before I can think creatively. I've heard guys say, "Well, I got my heart ripped out and got wasted for three weeks and wrote this song." I couldn't do that. I'd be crying, I couldn't eat and all that. Of course, I knew what "Only the Lonely" was about when I wrote that. I had been alone and lonely. I wasn't at the time, though.

Why did you leave Monument for MGM?

MGM was a big company, and they painted a rosy picture for me and gave me a lot of money, and I'd had a record on Monument after "Pretty Woman" that didn't sell any. It was called "(Say) You're My Girl," and after doing upwards of 5, 6, 7 million for "Pretty Woman," for the next record not to sell, I couldn't believe it. I was thinking it would probably *accidentally* sell some, you know? I was leaning toward leaving before then, and that convinced me.

And the first few things for MGM were hit records, so I knew that everything wasn't terribly amiss. But the transition wasn't really that smooth. I think the records were okay, maybe, through '68 or so. But I was having to record a lot, plus I'd had some personal problems. My first wife was killed in '66, and then I had the fire in '68, and I'm a bit hazy, but I think the company was sold. So on one hand you had a company that wasn't really viable, and then on the other you had me, with things happening around me and to me. I mean, it was a dark period for me.

It must have been hard to even think about making records after the accident and the fire.

Yeah, that had a definite impact. I remember going on a worldwide tour after . . . after both things happened. Sort of as therapy, but also to keep doing what I had been doing. If you're trying to be true to yourself, and you would normally tour and write and function that way, if something traumatic happens to you, I've never seen the sense in dropping all that. Because it's not necessarily a personal thing, you know? It happens directly to you, but it's not directed *at* you, necessarily. In my case I went ahead and did what I normally did, insofar as I could, and then let love and time and things like that take care of everything. I guess I'm talking about faith, probably. And if you feel really singled out, I think you can make a lot of mistakes. I don't know of anyone who hasn't lost someone. This was something I knew by faith—but until the faith is strong enough, it does affect your work. That's a process that took a while.

You'd hardly have been human if at some point you hadn't thought, "Why me?" or "Why again?"

You have that feeling, but what I was trying to convey is the faith that you have that this has a meaning and is to a purpose. It may be a mystery to you at the time, and is. But if the faith is there, you ask yourself, "What is it all about?" But not every day, every minute.

I feel that that's what went on with me, you know? It was a long, long time ago, but I'm trying to reach back and really give you what went on as opposed to what I would like to have had happen. It was a dev-astating blow, but not debilitating. I wasn't totally incapacitated by events. And I think that's stood me in good stead. You don't come out unscathed, but you don't come out murdered, you know? And of course, I remarried in '69, Barbara and I, and we started our life together. And in fact, we were carrying on a romance long-distance at the time of the fire. I don't know whether she knows this, but she was a source of inspiration and faith, too. So I have to give her credit.

From about 1973 on, you didn't do much recording.

Yeah. In '77 I made a record that I wasn't pleased with, really, for Fred Foster. I didn't write any of the songs, and I only had a few days to do the album. And then I did a record for Elektra, which was like a half-finished project to me. That was less than a year after the surgery.

Triple-bypass heart surgery.

Yes. I had blockage of ninety percent, seventy percent and sixty percent. So they said, "We'll take care of it," and I said, "Well, leave me a nice scar, then." And it came out terrific. And it's still terrific. My doctor here said it's the best work he's ever seen.

Had you just gotten out of shape?

Well, it's the life of rock & roll that takes its toll. Always traveling and playing, and then trying to get rest. And no workouts in between, and eating road food. Like in the Traveling Wilburys song "Dirty World," "I love your quest for junk food" [*laughs*]. So it was that, I think, and probably stress. The doctor said, "I don't care what you do, just don't worry about anything. If there comes an obstacle in your life, either move it or go around it."

Do you feel healthy now?

Yeah, yeah. Having lost a little weight, and my blood pressure's right with the diet. "The diet" not meaning a restricted food intake, but the proper food. And working out here with the trainer from time to time. Everything's terrific. Couldn't be better.

Was it ever frustrating to write new songs but then go onstage and just do the old songs?

No, not until about now. Because I toured in the Sun days with just one hit record. I'd go onstage, and I'd play everybody else's stuff—Chuck Berry's stuff, Little Richard's stuff—then I'd sing my one hit record and get off. And I really did want to have a few to play. And when I got the few, I cared for them enough that I never minded performing them.

But now I feel a phasing going on, from the older songs to the new. And I think I could put maybe any one of these tunes, just drop it into the show, and nobody would know that it wasn't supposed to be in there [*laughs*]. Because I think it *is* supposed to be. So I'm very much looking forward to going into rehearsal with the group and adding about thirty minutes to the show.

In a way, it must have been a pretty daunting task trying to come up with new songs that could stand alongside "Crying" or "Oh, Pretty Woman." Did you feel much pressure making 'Mystery Girl'?

I sure did. When I started, I said, "What kind of song can I write that will equal 'Crying'?" And almost the minute I thought that, I said, "That's idiotic. Just write a different song." But for a while I was looking around for another "Crying" and another "Pretty Woman" or two, and I remember getting in the trap of trying to write for myself as a singer—trying to write for *Roy Orbison,* the rock & roll balladeer, the guy who sings high and low and lonely.

Through writing with various co-writers and being produced by some wonderful people, everything came together, and I relaxed and wrote songs like I knew how to write them. There was some fear involved, because there was a legend in the background haunting me, and no way would I be able to live up to it. And then I realized it didn't matter. What mattered was jumping in with both feet and being committed and working hard and honestly. And like in "Running Scared," it's going to have a happy ending.

But like in "Running Scared," you had some fear along the way?

Yeah. It sort of relates to performing onstage. I used to be more frightened than I should have been. But I pulled in this parking lot at this concert, and the marquee said, Roy Orbison. Sold out. And there were no other names, and it sort of dawned on me that everybody came to see me and that they'd probably heard of me and they might even like me beforehand. So I went on that night, years and years ago, not quite so afraid.

You know, I never dreamed that there were that many people who would dedicate themselves to a project like this. I was working as if I was doing it myself, completely alone, and felt the weight of that whole thing. But then I stopped long enough to be grateful, and I realized that everybody who was doing their thing on this album was doing it with a lot of love and care. It's as if the album had a life of its own. As much as I had to do with this project, I had very little to do with it. That's astounding to me, and it's proven to me, too, that there are no limitations.

It has to do with my being as—some of these things are hard for me to say—as credible and viable today as I was when I just started. When I did start, rock & roll wasn't part of our culture, it wasn't acceptable as an art form. But there again, had I seen any limitations, like "You're only as hot as your latest record" or "What are you gonna do when you're thirty?"—had I listened to any of that, I would have cut the dream short. And I tell people who say, "How do you get started in this business?"—I say just keep carrying on. Go ahead, because you could stop one day short of the good thing that's gonna happen.

Just now you called it "the dream"—that's always been a prevalent image in your songs.

Mm-hmm. Without the word *dream*, or the concept dream, and without the word *blue* and the emotions, I would have been really limited in the things I've written and performed [*laughs*].

Are you ever going to go all the way and write a song called "Blue Dreams"?

I might [*laughs*]. "Lonely Blue Dreams." I might.

When things are written about you in, say, rock & roll reference books, it seems that the one-line take on you is "Sad songs, big voice, dark glasses," and sometimes they'll add, "And he's had a tragic life."

Yeah. The tragic life. . . . That one period of it was tragic. But there were a lot of years before and lot of years after, so that's very far from the truth. In fact, it's totally the other way. But to be in the book is good enough for me right now.

If you wrote your own history, could you sum yourself up in a paragraph?

Hmmm . . . probably not. I might be able to do it in song. I've never done a song to encompass all that, but maybe in pieces of the songs. Parts of "Crying," parts of "Pretty Woman," too, and "Running Scared." . . . Pieces of my songs would tell the story.

34

Keith Richards

INTERVIEWED BY ANTHONY DeCURTIS
(1988)

He never sang, "I hope I die before I get old." But if anyone epitomizes the rock & roll ethic of death before obsolescence, it's Keith Richards. Still, in 1988, at the age of forty-four, Richards found himself making a new start, however reluctantly. After twenty-five years with the Rolling Stones, Richards released his first solo album, 'Talk Is Cheap.'

Honesty and self-knowledge—virtues that come with age, experience and perspective—are themes that Richards returns to again and again in this interview. "I've lived my life in my own way," he says, "and I'm here today because I have taken the trouble to find out who I am." Richards discusses the history of the Rolling Stones and his relationship with Mick Jagger—a partnership as deep as marriage—with remarkable candor. But that is not the only story he has to tell. "I'm not the guys I see on MTV who obviously think they are me," he says. "There are so many people who think that's all there is to it." His life is richer and more complex than his swashbuckling image. He speaks movingly about his marriage to model Patti Hansen and his feelings about his children.

Finally, carrying the music he loves into the future emerges as Richards' main purpose, his "lifelong job." "I mean, what am I gonna do now, go for job retraining and learn to be a welder?" he asks. "I'll do this until I drop. I'm committed to it and that's it. I want to try and make this thing grow up." In his definition of rock & roll as a music of lasting power and dignity, Richards provides a necessary vision for the Nineties.

—A.DeC.

A DRINK in one hand and a cigarette in the other, Keith Richards dances around the New York office of his personal manager, Jane Rose, as *Talk Is Cheap*—his first solo album after a quarter century with the Rolling Stones—blasts out of the stereo. Beyond enjoying the grooves, Keith is also attending to business; he's checking out slides, trying to choose cover art for the record. "Just put it in a brown paper bag," he says jokingly at one point to Steve Jordan, with whom he wrote and produced the album. "I don't give a shit about the goddamn cover."

The emphasis on content is characteristic —and it extends to Richards' collaborators. When Jordan, a hot New York sessionman who used to be the house drummer for *Late Night with David Letterman,* is complimented on the album, he simply says, "It's a real record. We weren't trying to do anything hip." Along with guitarist Waddy Wachtel, keyboardist Ivan Neville and bassist Charley Drayton, Jordan is a member of the core band that plays on *Talk Is Cheap* and will tour with Richards after its release. "In ten days," Richards says, "if you give me the right guys, I'll give you a band that sounds as if they've been together for two or three years. I'll make them sound like a *band.* Mainly because *I* need it, and that communicates itself."

Talk Is Cheap serves up a rich sampling of Richards' musical roots—from the Cajun flavor of "Locked Away" to the funk of "Big Enough," from the Memphis soul of "Make No Mistake" to the rockabilly of "I Could Have Stood You Up." And, of course, "Take It So Hard," "How I Wish" and "Whip It Up" rock with a force reminiscent of his classic work with the Stones.

Another track, however, "You Don't Move Me," evokes the Stones not only in its slashing guitar sound but in its subject: Mick Jagger. The song vents the anger and bitterness Richards felt when Jagger decided to pursue his own solo career in 1986 rather than tour with the Stones after they released *Dirty Work.* Accusing Jagger of greed and selfishness, the song also chides the singer for the commercial failure of his two solo records, *She's the Boss* and *Primitive Cool:* "Now you want to throw the dice/You already crapped out twice."

Later in the week, Richards turns up for his interview at Rose's office sporting red-tinted shades, gray corduroy slacks, a white jacket and the same T-shirt he wore four days earlier: it bears the legend OBERGRUPPEN-FUEHRER ("major general of the troops"). After fixing himself a Rebel Yell and ginger ale and lighting a Marlboro, he drapes his jacket on the back of one of the chrome-and-

leather chairs in the office's conference room and goes to work.

Like everyone in New York this August, Richards complains about the wilting heat, but he seems in an upbeat mood—after the interview he will race down to Madison Square Garden to catch INXS and Ziggy Marley. Now forty-four, Richards describes himself as a family man. In addition to two teenage children from his stormy relationship with Anita Pallenberg, he has two little girls from his marriage to New York model Patti Hansen. He looks weathered but fit, the leathery skin on his arms hugging his well-developed biceps.

Pleased and relieved to have completed *Talk Is Cheap,* Richards nonetheless remembers the frustrations that led him to make the record after years of saying that he had no desire to compete with the Rolling Stones. When he speaks about Jagger—and what he sees as Jagger's betrayal of the Stones—his hurt pride is evident. As he speaks, affection blends with resentment, and a need for reconciliation battles with an equally strong desire to be proven *right* about the integrity of the Stones. Richards' manner at such moments recalls nothing more than one of those exhausting conversations with friends whose lovers have left.

"It's a struggle between love and hate," Richards sings on *Talk Is Cheap.* Amid such ravaging emotional ambivalence, the Stones are talking about regrouping next year for an album and a tour. "Mick's and my battles are fascinating," Richards says. "When you've known somebody that long, there's so much water under the bridge that it's almost impossible to talk about."

And then, for three hours, he talks.

After twenty-five years with the Stones, how does it feel to have completed your first solo record?
It sort of goes like this [*sweeps his hand across his brow*]: Ph-e-e-e-w. It's kind of strange, because it was never in the cards for me. It was not something I

wanted to do. Also, in the back of my mind, doing a solo record meant a slight sense of failure. The only reason I would do a solo album was because I couldn't keep the Stones together.

As far back as 1971, you said that you didn't ever want to be in a situation where you had to decide whether to keep a song for yourself or give it to the Stones.

Yeah, there's all those things. To put yourself into a split situation, to have to decide—it's hard. Fortunately or unfortunately, since the Stones have taken this break or whatever—you know, *weren't working*—I didn't have to worry about that particular problem.

You see, *Dirty Work* I built pretty much on the same idea as *Some Girls,* in that it was made with the absolute idea that it would go on the road. So when we finished the record and then . . . the *powers that be*—let's put it like that [*laughs*]—decided suddenly they *ain't* gonna go on the road behind it, the team was left in the lurch. Because if you didn't follow it up with some roadwork, you'd only done fifty percent of the job.

Do you feel that 'Dirty Work' didn't do well because the Stones didn't support it with a tour?

Well, there was no promotion behind it. As it came out, everyone sort of said, "Well, they've broken up," or "They're not gonna work." So you got a lot of negativity behind it.

It seemed like it was released into a storm of chaos.

It was—mainly, I think, to do with the fact that Stu [Ian Stewart, the pianist with the early Stones and the band's longtime road manager] died at that point. The glue fell out of the whole setup. There's not a lot of people who realize quite what a tower of strength he was and how important he was within the band.

The first rehearsal that was ever called for this band that turned out to be the Rolling Stones, at the top of this pub in Soho, in London, I arrived, and the only guy there is Stu. He was already at the piano, waiting for the rest of this collection of weirdos to arrive. On the surface of it, he was very different from us. He was working—he was a civil servant. The rest of us were, like, just a bunch of layabouts.

Stu was somebody that couldn't tell a lie. I think one of the first things he said to me was, "Oh, so you're the Chuck Berry expert, are you?" At the time, Chuck Berry wasn't in Stu's bag of tricks. His thing was, like, Lionel Hampton and Leroy Carr and Big Joe Williams—you know, swing, boogie freaks. And so Chuck Berry to him was frivolous rock & roll, until I got him to listen to the records and he heard Johnnie Johnson [Berry's longtime pianist]. In fact, one of the

last things Stu said to me before he died was, "Never forget, Keith, Johnnie Johnson is alive and playing in St. Louis." And the funny thing is within a few months I'd found Johnnie, and he's even on this record.

So Stu's death was part of the problem. Then what happened? Was it that Mick didn't want to tour?

In all honesty, it was Mick decided that he could do . . . I don't know whether "he could do better" is the best phrase, but he felt, actually, that the Rolling Stones were like a millstone around his neck. Which is *ludicrous*—and I told him so.

He said that to you?

Yeah. Yeah. He said, "I don't need this bunch of old farts." Little do you know, Sunny Jim.

I spoke to him about it the other week, because now he wants to put the Stones back together—because there's nowhere else to go. And I don't want to knock the cat. Mick's and my battles are not exactly as perceived through the press or other people. They're far more convoluted, because we've known each other for most of our lives—I mean, since we were four or five. So they involve a lot more subtleties and ins and outs than can possibly be explained. But I think that there is on Mick's part a little bit of a Peter Pan complex.

It's a hard job, being the frontman. In order to do it, you've got to think in a way that you're semi-divine. But if it goes a little too far, that feeling, you think you don't need anybody, and Mick kind of lost touch with the fact of how important the Stones were for him. He thought that he could just hire another Rolling Stones, and that way he could control the situation more, rather than battling with me.

My point around *Dirty Work* was this was the time when the Stones could do something. They could mature and grow this music up and prove that you could take it further. That you don't have to go back and play Peter Pan and try and compete with Prince and Michael Jackson or Wham! and Duran Duran. But it's all a matter, I think, of self-perception. He perceived himself as still having to prove it on that level. To me, twenty-five years of integrity went down the *drain* with what he did.

How would you explain that?

Mick is more involved with what's happening at this moment—and fashion. I'm trying to grow the thing up, and I'm saying we don't need the lemon-yellow tights and the cherry picker and the spectacle to make a good Rolling Stones show. There's a more mature way of doing it. And Mick, particularly at that time, two or three years ago, couldn't see a way clear to do anything different. So therefore he had to go backwards and compare himself with who's hitting the Top Ten at that moment.

The last Stones show I saw was at the Fox Theatre, in Atlanta, in 1981, and it was just the band, without the gimmicks.

To me, the interesting thing about Mick is that he could work this *table* better than anybody in the world. And the bigger the stages got, to me it was a feeling that he had to use every inch of space on that stage. He would say that you've got to get to as much of the audience as you can when you're playing stadiums. But the bigger the stage, the more stagy it got. The fact is that Mick didn't appreciate that he had a band that he could rely upon, come hell or high water. I guess he took it for granted eventually and thought that he could hire that. And you can't. You can't hire that kind of thing.

At one point you seemed to feel that Walter Yetnikoff, the president of CBS Records, had encouraged Mick to go solo, that he believed that Mick was the Stones.

I think at the beginning, yes. But it's understandable that somebody just walking in on the Rolling Stones . . . it's an obvious thought. Mick is going to be talking to them. He's the frontman. *Since* then, Walter has certainly changed his mind [*laughs*]. It's understandable that you would think that, oh, if you've got it together with Mick, then you've got the Stones, because the next person to talk to is myself, and I've been a junkie, unreliable—in business people's minds I'm the dodgy artistic freak. I'm not the one that's going to be up in your office talking business at ten in the morning. So it's an understandable attitude to take. But it certainly didn't help keeping the Stones together at the time.

Didn't Yetnikoff hook you back up with Sarah Dash, who sings with you on the album?

She's a friend of Walter's. She happened to be popping by to see him at the time, and I said, "Oh, Sarah, I haven't seen you in donkeys' years." I mean, when I first met Sarah, she was fifteen or sixteen. She'd just started working with Patti LaBelle and the Blue Bells. This was in '65. She had a chaperone with her, you know, nobody could get near her. They used to call her Inch, I think, Sarah. She's still a dinky little thing, but what a girl, what a voice.

So by going to see Walter, I found the chick I wanted to sing on the album. The only other girl singing on it is the now-infamous Patti Scialfa.

Springsteen has managed to tarnish his reputation.

Yeah, it was kind of surprising. In fact, the last overdub that Patti did for this record, she walks in with this guy. "Hi, Patti, how're you doin'?" We're talking. The guy is standing in the doorway, and I turn around, and suddenly I realize it's *Bruce* [*laughs*]. Oh, oh, *naughty, naughty, naughty.*

Had you met him before?

I've met Bruce two or three times. We've had several good chats, usually at some release party or premiere, and we just end up in the corner talking. He's a sweet guy, a nice guy.

Mind you, I think four-hour shows really are *way* over the top. To me, a great rock & roll act does twenty minutes [*laughs*]. I remember the Paramount, where you got the Impressions, Jackie Wilson, Joe Tex, and everybody does just their absolute supreme *best shot!* A lot of the shows you get these days are very self-indulgent. I don't think anybody can be enthralling for four hours onstage playing rock & roll.

You've been recording on your own for years. Had you built up a big backlog of songs?

Not really. All of the songs on this album were written last year. There's also a whole backlog of songs with the Stones that I didn't touch. I wanted it to be completely separate. Of course, certain ways of doing things hung over. For the Stones, I would write for what Mick could sing, what I thought was the best thing that Mick could handle.

On this album, the songs are not *that* much different in structure or in content, even. I managed to do some of the things that with the Stones I'd say, "Nah, can't do that. Too complicated." I realized this writing with Steve Jordan. That was the other great thing: that I found somebody else to work with. To me, teamwork is important. The enthusiasm from the other guys is incredibly important, and these guys gave it to me all the way. They would never let me indulge myself. For instance, with the Stones, if I'm writing something and they're hitting it in the studio and I'd break down because I'm not quite sure how the bridge would go or something, I'd stop playing, and *everybody'd* stop playing, go off for a drink and a phone call and an hour latter come back and try it again. With this lot, if I stopped, they'd just carry on. They'd look at me: "Pick it *up*, pick it *up*, man!" "Why, goddamn! *Nobody's* kicked me up the ass like that." At the same time, I enjoyed it, because they were right. I would just pick it up again and get back in there.

Did you find yourself getting uptight about not wanting a song to sound like a Stones song?

No, I didn't. In fact, it was the other way. My idea was if I allowed myself to think, "I can't do it like that, because it would be just the way I'd do it with the Stones," that would be phony.

My main hang-up, first off, was, "Who the hell am I gonna play with if it ain't Charlie Watts?" If I'm gonna work on my own after twenty-odd years of working with this great drummer, who's going to have, without looking at each other, the same feel, the same contact? The beauty of Steve and myself finding each other at that particular time was that it was a very natural changeover, since Steve and Charlie know each other and respect each other's work very much.

Where are Charlie, Bill Wyman and Ron Wood on all of this? Are you in touch with them?

Well, yeah. In fact, in the last month or so I've been in touch with them. Mick suddenly called up, and the rest of them: "Let's put the Stones back together." I'm thinking, "*Just* as I'm in the middle of an album. Now what are you trying to do, screw me up? Just *now* you want to talk about putting it back together?" But we talked about it. I went to London, and we had a meeting. I think you'll find a new album and a tour next year from the Stones.

Will you be touring with your band?

With this lot, yeah, sure. I need to get on the road, and the only way you're gonna get on the road is to make a record. Since '86, I've slowly been putting the team together. This basic band, you know, Drayton, Steve, Ivan Neville, Waddy.

I don't want to do a big deal, you know, big stadiums and all that. I want to play some good rooms —theaters. We're just starting to talk about it. Basically, I just want to do some class joints, you know, some nice three thousand–, four thousand–seaters.

It's startling to hear "Big Enough," which has such a James Brown feel, as the first track on the album. Was that the first tune you recorded?

It's not exactly the first thing, but it was fairly early on. It was just Steve and myself, just drums and guitar. It was incredibly long, almost a jam. But the groove on it was just so strong and, as you say, the James Brown feel of it was so evident that what happened was, during last winter, James played the Apollo. Steve and I went up there, and we saw Maceo [Parker, James Brown's saxophonist], and we looked at each other, and we went, "Dig it. Maceo." So we got in touch with Maceo to give it that horn thing.

The bass end was another problem, because the fact that we cut it with just guitar and drums, we had the drums tuned very low down. There was an awful lot of bass on the drums. And every time we tried to put a bass on it, it would just get in the way. So we thought

about it, and once again, Steve, who's got a great ear [*snaps his fingers*]: "Ah, it's got to be Bootsy"—who used to play with James. So Bootsy [Collins] drove from Ohio—because he doesn't fly, Bootsy—for one evening and heard it, grinned and did it. So that's how James Brown the track was—it ended up with James' guys on there!

On the other end of the spectrum from "Big Enough," you have "I Could Have Stood You Up."

To me that was "a little stroll through the rock & roll alley." I actually started to cut these tracks a year ago, just about today, at about this *time* [*laughs*]— that's why I'm looking at my watch—up in Montreal. We got about seven tracks in ten days, so I felt already "This thing's going well, this band is cooking."

Who was up there with you?

Charley Drayton, Steve, Ivan, Waddy and myself. Since we'd worked with Johnnie Johnson on the Chuck Berry thing, I really wanted to work with him. My next thought was, "I don't know if I've got anything in that vein for this album." So Steve and I worked on it a bit, and I came up with that one thing. We wanted to do some sessions with Johnnie, so we got it together, and Johnnie—who happens to *love* me, for some reason . . .

Well, your analysis of Chuck Berry's music in 'Hail! Hail! Rock 'n' Roll,' where you point out that it was all based on Johnnie Johnson's piano chords, might have something to do with it.

I would have never thought about it, except I went through that process and saw it. The guy's sixty-eight, sixty-nine years old, and he probably plays more regularly than just about anybody on this planet. He has five or six club gigs a week in St. Louis. He's one of the hidden masters of American music, to me. Also, given the fact that Stu had said what he said . . . [*folds his hands in prayer*].

"I Could Have Stood You Up" is also a reunion of Stones alumni: Mick Taylor, Bobby Keys, Chuck Leavell. Had you played with Mick since he left the Stones?

When he played the Lone Star last year, I popped up for a number or two. I hadn't seen him for quite a few years. It's sort of a mystery to me—and it's also a mystery to Mick Taylor—as to why he left the Stones [*laughs*]. I said, "Why did you *leave* like that?" And he said, "I ask myself that all the time. I don't know why I did that."

But being in the Stones is a weird thing. I guess for Mick, you've been in the Stones for five or six years, and you think you can expand. He wanted to play drums. He wanted to produce and write. Rightly or wrongly—because to me Mick Taylor is just a brilliant guitar player. That's what he is. And still is. But from the inside, you know, you think, "I've done this. I've got this now. Now I can go out on my own. I'm a bit bored with this."

And Mick Jagger made the same decision—and the same mistake. Whether it's a mistake or not, it didn't work out the way he thought it was going to work out. Maybe it's got something to do with the name Mick [*laughs*].

It seems that the Stones developed a very unsentimental attitude over the years about people who were sucked into their vortex and sometimes did great things but sometimes also damaged themselves.

It made them—and maybe even for the better—come face to face eventually with themselves. Maybe sometimes in the worst possible way. Maybe that ultimately is one of the most important things about the Stones—that, for some unknown reason, they strike at a person at a point and in a position that they don't even know exists.

There was always a sense about the Stones and about your own life, certainly, that this is nothing other than what it looks to you to be.

Well, it's certainly for real. The other thing about my life and the Stones' life is that there was nothing phony about it. If anybody was going to take knocks, we were going to take the knocks along with everybody else. It isn't that we were sitting up on some comfortable faraway paradise and putting out this stuff and saying, "Well, fuck yourselves up." We got beat up more than anybody.

I've always just tried to avoid doing anything that would make me cringe. Anything I do, I like to be able to live with. No matter how on the surface—you know, "What a bum, what a junkie"—at least it's real. And I can live with it. If I fuck up, the whole *world* fucks up with me! [*Laughs.*]

You once said that you never wanted anyone to feel that there was anything they could find out by going through your garbage can that they couldn't find out by just asking you.

There's always this thing in show business: you have an "image," and you play it to the hilt, but you're not really like that "*in my private life,*" et cetera. In other words, it's an *act.* And maybe for them that's okay. But for myself, what I do, I'm too intense about it.

Obviously, there are lots of things . . . I mean, I'm a family man. I have little two-year-old and three-year-old girls that beat me up. I'm not the guys I see on MTV, who obviously think they *are* me. There are so many people who think that's all there is to it. It's not *that* easy to be Keith Richards. But it's not *so hard,* either. The main thing is to know yourself.

I was kind of forced into the position of honesty because they *went* through my garbage can and it was all over the front pages. To the point where people think that I'm far more Errol Flynn or notorious than I actually am. But I know what people think: "We'll give them that Keith Richards *look.*" With my friends, the "Keith Richards look" is, like, a great *laugh.* And it's got nothing to do with the moody bit—it's just the way I look if I don't smile. And this [*points to his skull ring*] is to remind me that we're all the same under the skin. The skull—it has nothing to do with bravado and surface bullshit.

To me, the main thing about living on this planet is to know who the hell you are and to be real about it. That's the reason I'm still alive. The chart I was number one on longest was the Next One to Kick the Bucket. I headed *that* chart longer than I ever did Records! [*Laughs.*] But to me, I never had any real doubt, because whatever it was I did, no matter how stupid or flamboyant or irresponsible it may have seemed from the outside—and I can understand it appearing like that—to me it's always been very important to know what I'm made of, and what I'm capable of doing. And making sure that nobody else suffered in the process. And if they did, it would only be from a misconception of *themselves,* not of me.

Obviously a whole mythology has built up around you. You must walk into situations all the time where people expect you to be "Keith Richards." How does that affect you?

I try and disillusion them, because I don't have an "act." It's impossible for me. It's very embarrassing.

Charlie Watts, in fact, is a far more honest man than I am. Charlie Watts to me is the most honest man in the world—to himself, to everybody. He never even wanted to be a pop star. It still makes him cringe. But because he liked the music—and loved playing with me and with Mick and knew that it was a great band—he's willing to go along with it. Chicks screaming at Charlie Watts—to him it's ludicrous. He wanted to be Max Roach or Philly Joe Jones—his idea of himself is that. And to have to live with being some teenybop idol for Charlie is very difficult, because he's not like that at all.

They're such a weird collection of guys—the most unlikely collection of people to be a good rock & roll band. Hell, half of them hate the idea of being a rock & roll star in the first place. It's already embarrassing to them; they want to be serious *artists*. And when you're living and working with people like that, it's very difficult, if you're phony or if you go . . . That's what happened to Brian [Jones]. He really got off on the trip of being a pop star. And it killed him. Suddenly, from being very serious about what he wanted to do, he was willing to take the cheap trip. And it's a very short trip.

Has Mick heard "You Don't Move Me"?

Yeah, he's heard it. I played the whole album to him—what?—last week, two weeks ago.

Here in New York?

Yeah. He talked all the way through it [*laughs*]. But I went to the john and took a pee, and as I was coming out, I saw him dancing in the front room. So then I went back to the john and slammed the door loud and walked out again: he's sitting back like this [*sits straight in his chair and folds his hands in his lap*]. I don't know what he really thinks about it, because it's all tied up with what happened with his solo stuff.

What he put out, to me, is exactly the reason, as we were talking about before, why we didn't go on the road behind *Dirty Work*. He wanted to compete on a different level. The sad thing, to me, about it was that I felt it was totally unnecessary in that he had no grasp of the idea of the integrity of the Stones.

What does it make you feel like since Mick didn't want to tour behind 'Dirty Work' but now he's done a tour of Japan and he's going to do a tour of Australia?

Great. Go to Australia in their midwinter. Go on. I've got other things to do. Go there. Go there with your jerk-off band.

He knows how I feel about it. Whether he'll ever admit it to himself, I don't know. I mean, I'll be totally honest: I *love* Mick. Most of my efforts with Mick go to trying to open his eyes: "You don't need to do this. You have no problem. All you've got to do is just grow up with it." And that's what he should be doing.

I mean, ninety-nine percent of the male population of the Western world—and beyond—would give a *limb* to live the life of Riley, to live the life of Jagger. To be *Mick Jagger*. And he's not happy being Mick Jagger. He's not living a happy life. To me, that's unacceptable. I've *got* to make him happy! [*Laughs*.] To me, I've failed if I can't eventually get my mate to feel good about himself. Even though he's very autocratic and he can be a real asshole. But who can't be an asshole at times?

The siege mentality kind of worries me about Mick. Nobody can get in there, even me, who's known him longer than anybody. What bothers me sometimes about him is not being able to get through to him. He's got his own vision about himself, which is not actually who he is. So he has to play a game; he has to act. He's not about to give you *anything*. He's not about to give *anything* away. He'll be flip.

And I don't mind him reading this shit, because this is part of, as far as I'm concerned, my attempt to help him along. It's a very sad thing to me to have a friend that . . . especially when he's in such a privileged position and should be able to live one of the best lives ever. Everybody, as I say, would give limbs to be Mick Jagger, to be able to live like that. And not to be *happy*? What's so *hard* about being Mick Jagger? What's so tough? It's like Bob Dylan's phrase once: "What's so hard about being one of the Beatles?" Although, you could say that about *Bob,* too, you know. Now I'm *really* gonna get shit, man! [*Laughs*.] I mean, this exaggerated sense of who you are and what you should do and worrying about it so much. Why don't you just get on with it and stop trying to figure all the angles? That to me is a waste of time.

Now you're in the situation where your own solo record is coming out. Do you feel any sense of competition with Mick?

Obviously the situation is there for it to be perceived that way. No, I don't feel any sense of competition with Mick. Whether Mick feels a sense of competition with me—that's another question. Why we didn't go on the road behind *Dirty Work* . . . that might be an answer to that.

You mean he felt that it was more your record or . . .

Or who runs the deal. I think to Mick that's more important than it is to me. You see, I tip my hat to Mick a lot. I admire the guy enormously. In the Seventies, when I was on dope and I would do nothing but put the songs together and turn up and not deal with any of the business of the Stones, Mick took all of that work and weight on his shoulders and did it *all* and covered my ass. And I've always admired him very much for that. I mean, he did exactly what a friend should do.

When I cleaned up and *Emotional Rescue* time came around—"*Hey,* I'm back, I'm clean, I'm ready; I'm back to help and take some of the weight off your shoulders"—immediately I got a sense of resentment. Whereas I felt that he would be happy to unburden himself of some of that shit, he felt that I was horning in and trying to take control. And that's when I first sensed the feeling of discontent, shall we say. It wasn't intended like that from my point of view, but that's when I first got a feeling that he got so used to running the show that there was no way he was going to give it up. That, to him, it was a power struggle.

To turn away from the Stones for a moment, what do you make of the state of rock today? Some have said this is the worst period in the history of rock & roll.

My cheap answer to that would be "Yeah, wait until *my* record comes out!" [*Laughs.*]

I wanted to run the Top Ten singles by you and get your impression of them.

All right, run 'em down.

Number one is "Roll with It," by Steve Winwood.

Steve is great, but the record, eh. He's not pushing anything further. I mean, he's a great musician, but he doesn't seem to me to have a driving desire to really do anything. If he bothers to work, it's fantastic. I think he's one of the best English musicians that we have.

But at the same time, my problem with Stevie—he's gonna fuckin' hate me forever for saying this—is that he's kind of faceless. What's number two, George Michael?

Number two is "Hands to Heaven," by Breathe.

Never heard it. Don't know nothing about it.

Number three is "Make Me Lose Control," by Eric Carmen. He had a hit recently from the 'Dirty Dancing' soundtrack.

A nice PR job.

Number four is "Sign Your Name," by Terence Trent D'Arby.

He's more interested in Terence Trent D'Arby than he is in anything else, as far as I'm concerned. Hey, a nice-looking boy—but hung up on himself. A great voice, but that's not enough.

"1-2-3," by Gloria Estefan and Miami Sound Machine.

A Holiday Inn band, a club band that made it. Very nice. Love the girl. Like *Dirty Dancing*: just to watch, yeah. But it palled really quickly.

"I Don't Wanna Go On with You Like That," by Elton John.

Reg, give me a Rubens, and I'll say something nice. Reg Dwight. Lovely bloke, but posing.

"I Don't Wanna Live Without Your Love," by Chicago.

Chicago? I haven't heard it. Chicago to me was always . . . I mean, you'll get a lot of put-downs this way, guy! [*Laughs.*] You've got to forgive me. I haven't heard that particular record, but I would think "contrived."

"Monkey," by George Michael.

Shave and go home. He's a wimp in disguise.

"Hold On to the Nights," by Richard Marx.

I don't know the particular record, but I have a feeling—why do I say this?—*maybe* there's something interesting in there?

And number ten is "Just Got Paid," by Johnny Kemp.

I wish *I* just got paid! Who the *hell* Johnny Kemp is I don't know.

I also wanted to ask you about the current superstars.

U2 I like. I like Bono very much. When I worked with him, I'd never heard him. I found the guy very interesting and very open. Then, afterwards, I started listening to them. It's human music; it's not push-button music.

To me the disgusting thing about popular music at the moment . . . and especially I'm disappointed with you black guys, just pushing buttons and shit. They are, to me, really fucking up. With the drum machines and the engineers that have never . . . you set up a drum kit and say you're gonna use a live drummer and they go, "What? How do we record a thing like that?"

Music's got to do with people, not pushing buttons. To me, it's kind of weird that George Michael is number one on the black charts. Because, 'ey, 'ey, what happened to Little Milton? What happened to the soul?

You mentioned Bruce Springsteen earlier. What about his music?

Bruce? That's a tough one, because I like the *guy*. But the music . . . I don't know. I'm the toughest taskmaster of all time. I'm going to annoy a lot of people. Bruce? To me, it's pretentious.

What's pretentious about it?

I love his attitude. I love what he *wants* to do. I just think he's gone about it the wrong way. These are just my opinions, and okay, I'll annoy the lot of you. Bruce? Too contrived for me. Too overblown.

I know you haven't liked Prince in the past. Has your opinion of him changed?

Prince, I admire his energy, but he's riding on a wave. To me, Prince is like the Monkees. I don't see anything of any depth in there. I think he's very clever at manipulating the music business and the entertainment business. I think he's more into that than making music. I don't see much substance in anything he does. Too much appealing to . . . a Pee-wee Herman trip. And I like Pee-wee Herman better than Prince. He's appealing to the same audience. To me, it's kid stuff.

What do you think about Guns n' Roses?

Not much. I admire the fact that they've made it despite certain resistance from the radio biz. I admire their guts. But too much posing. Their look—it's like there's one out of this band, one looks like Jimmy, one looks like Ronnie. Too much copycat, too much posing for me. I haven't listened to a whole album to be able to talk about the music.

I'm a very hard taskmaster. I know that everybody's gonna say, "Oh, he's putting everybody down."

Well, tell me what you like.

I don't like much. And I don't want any of these guys to feel like, "Oh, he's an old fart, blah-blah-blah. But we're up there, blah-blah-blah." I'm not interested in that. My main thing is, "What are you trying to do, just be famous? Or have you got something to say?" And if you do, are you forgoing it in order just to be famous?

I've always liked AC/DC, all right? I like U2; I really do. I think Bono, especially, has something special. INXS I'm quite interested in. I like Tracy Chapman. Ziggy Marley I find very interesting because he's not just "the son of." He's avoided being, I hate to say this, Julian. He's taken from his father and built on it, but he's not just "the son of Bob Marley." He's got his own things to say, and he's serious about it.

I wanted to ask you about Chuck Berry. If you take forty-five Chuck Berry songs, fifteen of them will be among the greatest rock songs ever written and thirty will be the most clichéd formulas.

And two or three of them just *trite*. To me, the saddest thing about Chuck Berry is that his biggest-selling record is "My Ding-a-ling." But that's what he deserves, because of his attitude toward what he does. He hasn't sussed out his own worth. He has no *idea* of his impact on popular music. Chuck just wants the bread. And there's nothing *wrong* with that, because it's the only way a guy from his era, from where he came from, could get out.

And also getting ripped off in the past, that's what he learns. But he's carried it around for thirty years.

He's a loner. That's why I could work with Chuck Berry, because he's very much like Mick. It's a siege mentality: "*Nobody's* going to get into *me*." And, "If I give a thing away, I'm a weakling." To me, the truth is the more you give, the stronger you are. The more of a man you are. Who are you scared of? What's so scary that you've got to lock yourself up?

In that scene in 'Hail! Hail! Rock 'n' Roll' where you turn around and give him this look, it looks like you're going to have a fight or something.

A shoot-out? Yeah. Yeah. Yeah. That's pretty true. Yeah, just about. Most of the band, the guys behind me are going, "Keith in this situation is gonna pull out the blade, and just slit the motherfucker's throat."

I'm biting bullets, because I'm trying to show the band that, in order to get this gig together, I am gonna take some shit that I wouldn't take from *anybody*. I'm *not* gonna let Chuck get to me that much. Whereas anybody else, it would be toilet time.

You say the Stones may be getting back together. Given all that's happened, couldn't that be seen as just a case of knowing that this is an opportunity to make $40 million and . . .

A *hundred* [*laughs*].

Well, what do you say to that?

What can I say about it? However much you make, the same percentage goes toward keeping it together. The overhead's tremendous. The amount of money—I find it as mind boggling as anybody out there on the street. You say, "*Yeah, he's a fucking multi-millionaire*, and blah-blah-blah." The one thing you find out when you make a lot of money—and it always sounds *trite* when you say it, but it isn't—is that that's not the important thing. It doesn't add one iota to your happiness in life. It just means you have different problems to deal with. And it brings its own problems. Like, "Who are you going to put on retainer?"

It's much better to be rich than poor, but not for the reasons that you would automatically think. I grew up with no bread at all. In fact, I was talking to Steve Jordan and Charley Drayton—black cats, you know, fairly well-off middle-class cats. I grew up poorer than they did. We just about made the rent. The luxuries were very, very few. I know what it's like down there. I remember it. There wasn't a lot of chances for someone, the way I grew up. My dad worked his butt off in order to just keep the rent paid and food for the family. To me, people are more important than anything else. Rock & roll, anything else, people are more important.

I know you and your father were reconciled a few years ago. Are you still on good terms?

Oh, yeah. Dominoes every Friday night. In fact, I'm late for the game right now!

Does he live in New York?

He lives about forty-five minutes out of town. Oh, yeah, now that we're together, we're very tight.

You described yourself earlier as a "family man." What about your marriage and your kids? Obviously your wife, Patti Hansen, has her own business to do, and you have what you do.

Patti's a mother now. She doesn't do much. She does one job, two jobs a year. I mean, this is my second time around with families. I have a son—Marlon's nineteen. Angela's sixteen, and she's just left school.

I have this new family. I live in a household of women, which sometimes can drive me totally round the bend, which is why I need to work and get on the road. I love 'em all, but it's weird to be living with a load of chicks—it doesn't matter what age they are. For a guy, the only guy in the house, you gotta call up another cat and say, "Hey, come over, or I'll just drop over there!"

And my old lady knows this, bless her heart. I mean, that's why I married her, because I'll only get married once. But Patti and I, we have a good thing going. And it's just kept going. I'm a lucky guy.

With you and Patti, is it the sort of arrangement where somebody is taking care of the kids all the time?

No, I hate that. I'd never have that. It's only Patti and me and the kids. There's other people who clean up the house, but it's not like there's a nanny and she brings the kids down once a day to play with for teatime and then fuck off. No way. You live all together.

I mean, sometimes I wake up in the middle of the night, and there's both my kids in the bed. They've managed to find their way, and we're all in the same bed together [*laughs*]. You get more out of it like that, and so do the kids. Family is a special thing. It's almost . . . you can't really talk about it, except to say that if you get a chance at it, try it out, because it's one of the most special things that you'll ever get on the face of this earth. It gives you that final missing link of what life's about. While they're looking upon you as the most wonderful person in the world because you're "Daddy," they do more for you than you do for them.

How is your health?

You tell me.

You look good. You sound great.

I've lived my life in my own way, and I'm here today because I have taken the trouble to find out who I am.

The problem, however, is people who think they can live like Keith Richards.

That's what I mean. The biggest mistake in the world is to think that you have to emulate somebody else. That is fatal. It's got nothing to do with me. If people want to be like Keith Richards, then they better have the same physical makeup. I come from a very sturdy stock—otherwise I wouldn't be here.

At this point, to what degree is your identity tied into being a Rolling Stone?

Well, I've always been one, from the start of . . . if you want to call it my professional career. And I never wanted to be anything else. For the last couple of years I've had to deal with *not* being one. At first it almost broke my heart.

What I've learned from not being a Rolling Stone for two years probably will help me be, if the Stones come back together, which they will, will help me be . . . what can I say—"a better Rolling Stone"? [*Laughs.*] Or make the Rolling Stones better.

I have a little more confidence in myself, by myself. I found that I can, if I have to, live without the Rolling Stones. And that my only job isn't desperately trying to keep a band together that maybe needed a break.

The last question I want to ask you is about legacy. All the bluesmen you admire—there's a legacy of theirs that you've carried on. Do you have a vision of how you'd like yourself, the Stones, your music, to move forward?

Well, then we get back to the break around *Dirty Work*. My vision of the Rolling Stones was that this was the *perfect* point and opportunity, at our state and our age, to carry on and mature and prove it. I played with Muddy Waters six months before he died, and the cat was just as vital as he was in his youth. And he did it until the day he died. To me, that is the important thing. I mean, what am I gonna do now, go for job retraining and learn to be a welder? I'll do this until I drop. I'm committed to it and that's it.

I want to try and make this thing grow up. Elvis couldn't do it. A lot of them didn't do it. To me, it's important to prove that this isn't just teenage kids' shit and you should feel embarrassed when you're over forty and still doing it. That's not necessary. This is a job. It's a man's job, and it's a lifelong job. And if there's a sucker to ever prove it, I hope to be the sucker.

Contributors' Biographies

TIM CAHILL is a *Rolling Stone* contributing editor, a columnist for *Outside* and the author of three books: *Buried Dreams, Jaguars Ripped My Flesh* and *A Wolverine Is Eating My Leg*.

CHRISTOPHER CONNELLY was an associate editor of *Rolling Stone* and the managing editor of *US*. He is now a senior editor of *Premiere* and the host of the MTV program *The Big Picture*.

MARC COOPER and GREGG GOLDIN have written for *Playboy, The Los Angeles Times* and other publications.

TIMOTHY CROUSE is a *Rolling Stone* contributing editor. He is the author of *The Boys on the Bus*, and he has also written for *The New Yorker, The Atlantic* and *Esquire*.

ANTHONY DeCURTIS is a senior writer at *Rolling Stone*. His work has appeared in *Newsday, The New York Times Book Review, Musician* and many other publications. He holds a Ph.D. in American literature from Indiana University.

BEN FONG-TORRES was a senior editor of *Rolling Stone*. He is now a feature writer and columnist for *The San Francisco Chronicle*. He has also written for *Esquire, GQ, Playboy, Sports Illustrated, Parade, American Film* and *Travel and Leisure*.

DAVID FRICKE is a senior writer at *Rolling Stone*.

WILLIAM E. GEIST is a correspondent for the CBS program *Sunday Morning*. A former columnist for *The New York Times*, he is the author of *The Zucchini Plague and Other Tales of Suburbia*.

MICHAEL GOLDBERG is a senior writer at *Rolling Stone*. His writing has also appeared in *Esquire, California, New Musical Express* and *Boulevard*. He first went to one of Bill Graham's concerts at the Fillmore in 1968 to see Creedence Clearwater Revival.

WILLIAM GREIDER is the national editor of *Rolling Stone*. He is the author of *Secrets of the Temple: How the Federal Reserve Runs the Country*.

JAMES HENKE is the managing editor of *Rolling Stone*. He is the author of *Human Rights Now!*, an account of the Amnesty International World Tour.

LYNN HIRSCHBERG is a *Rolling Stone* contributing editor. She has also written for *Esquire* and *Vanity Fair*.

SID HOLT is a senior editor of *Rolling Stone*.

ELIZABETH KAYE is an *Esquire* contributing editor. She lives in New York City.

KURT LODER is an entertainment-news commentator for MTV and a *Rolling Stone* contributing editor. He is the author, with Tina Turner, of *I, Tina*.

GREIL MARCUS has been a *Rolling Stone* contributing editor since 1969. He is the author of *Mystery Train: Images of America in Rock and Roll* and *Lipstick Traces: A Secret History of the Twentieth Century*.

ROBERT PALMER is a *Rolling Stone* contributing editor. A former columnist for *The New York Times*, he is the author of *Deep Blues*.

STEVE POND is a *Rolling Stone* contributing editor.

Contributors' Biographies

FRED SCHRUERS is a *ROLLING STONE* contributing editor.

ROBERT FARRIS THOMPSON is a professor of African and Afro-American studies at Yale University. He is the author of *The Flash of the Spirit, Rediscovered Masterpieces* and *The Four Moments of the Sun*.

DAVID WILD is the music editor of *ROLLING STONE*.

BILL ZEHME is a *ROLLING STONE* contributing editor. He has also written for *GQ, Playboy, Spy* and *Vanity Fair*.